FAREWELL

the

PEACEFUL
KINGDOM

Also by Joe C.W. Armstrong

From Sea Unto Sea: Art & Discovery Maps of Canada (1982)

Champlain (1987, English)

Samuel de Champlain (1988, French)

Meech Plus: The Charlatan Accord (1992)

FAREWELL *the* PEACEFUL KINGDOM

The Seduction and Rape of Canada, 1963 to 1994

JOE C.W. ARMSTRONG

Published in 1995 by
Stoddart Publishing Co. Limited
34 Lesmill Road
Toronto, Canada
M3B 2T6
Tel. (416) 445-3333
Fax (416) 445-5967

Stoddart Books are available for bulk purchase for
sales promotions, premiums, fundraising, and
seminars. For details, contact the Special Sales
Department at the above address.

Canadian Cataloguing in Publication Data

Armstrong, Joe C. W., 1934–
Farewell the peaceful kingdom : the seduction and rape of
Canada, 1963–1994

Includes index.
ISBN 0-7737-2870-8

1. Canada — Politics and government — 20th century.
I. Title.

FC600.A75 1995   971.064   C95–930054–6
F1034.2.A75 1995

Cover Design: Bill Douglas/The Bang
Typesetting: Tony Gordon Ltd.
Printed and bound in Canada

*Stoddart Publishing gratefully acknowledges the support of the
Canada Council, the Ontario Ministry of Culture, Tourism, and
Recreation, Ontario Arts Council, and Ontario Publishing
Centre in the development of writing and publishing in Canada.*

The material acknowledged on pages 743–746 constitutes a
continuation of this copyright page.

In the past, those societies that have treated persons differently, based upon who they are, rather than what they do, have faltered economically, and opportunity has been foreclosed for almost everyone.

James Dale Davidson and Lord William Rees-Mogg,
The Great Reckoning, 1991

For Jill, Jamie, and Geoffrey, with love.
I pray for a better Canada than the one
my generation bequeathed them.

Contents

ACKNOWLEDGEMENTS *xiii*

INTRODUCTION *1*

Part I The Kingdom and the Foreplay — 1963 to 1982
    1 Lester Bowles Pearson, the Father of
        Bilingualism — 1963 to 1967 *11*
    2 Pierre Trudeau and Robert Stanfield,
        the Two Faces of Dualism — 1968 *27*
    3 "Alas! I Am Turning into a God" — 1968 to 1977 *42*
    4 Joe Clark's Community of
        Communities: Pluralism — 1979 *59*
    5 René Lévesque's Sovereign Association — 1980 *63*
    6 Trudeau's Revolution: Patriation Without
        Representation — 1981 to 1982 *70*

Part II A New Vision for Canada: Existentialism — 1982 to 1990
    7 Martin Brian Mulroney: l'Irlandais, the Irish Kid
        — 1979 to 1983 *87*
    8 John Napier Turner: A Little Interregnum — 1984 *97*
    9 Mulroney's Solemn Commitment to Quebec
        and Patronage Pratfalls — 1984 *105*
    10 The Parties Take Positions on the Promise:
        Quebec — 1985 *111*
    11 Her Majesty's Mafia: Queen's University — 1986 *116*
    12 A Meech Lake Accord and a Free Trade Agreement:
        Farewell to Sovereignty — 1986 to 1987 *128*
    13 Hell Hath No Fury Like Pandora's Box
        — 1988 to 1990 *145*

14 The Power of One Eagle Feather — 1990   *168*

Part III To Each His Own Accord
    15 Deep Thinkers: The Boffins and the Presumptives   *185*
    16 More Deep Thinkers: Lawyers and Law Professors   *205*

Part IV The March Away from Meech Lake — 1990 to 1991
    17 The Leaders Divvy Up the Nation — 1990   *223*
    18 Some Québécois Speak to Some Canucks   *241*
    19 Meech II, the Seamless Web — 1991   *252*

Part V The Fourth Estate: Media Munchkins
    20 The Pulp Prime-Evil: The Four Gospels
        of Central Canada   *277*
    21 Pusillanimous Poltroons and Pecksniffers   *299*

Part VI The March for Meech II — January to May 1992
    22 They're Ba-a-a-ck! More Meech II — January
        to March 1992   *331*
    23 Meech II and the Carry-On Gang — March to
        May 1992   *343*

Part VII A World of Privilege and the Fifth Estate
    24 Power Brokers in the Feudal Kingdom   *367*
    25 The Filtration System, the CBC   *388*

Part VIII The Road to Charlottetown — June to August 1992
    26 The Cat's Breakfast, The Pearson Accord
        — June to July 1992   *405*
    27 Bingo! The Charlottetown Accord — July
        to August 1992   *426*

Part IX The Referendum
    28 On the Way to Judgement Day — September 1992   *453*
    29 A Flirtation With Democracy: The Referendum —
        October 1992   *473*

Part X The Ins and Outs
    30 Some Insiders and Some Outsiders   *497*
    31 Preston Manning, Thy Kingdom Came   *514*

Part XI   Business as Usual — October 26, 1992, to June 25, 1993

    32 Referendum Aftermath — October 26, 1992,
         to February 23, 1993   *537*

    33 The Disarray of the Red Tories — February 24
         to June 25, 1993   *550*

**Part XII   Farewell the Peaceful Kingdom — June 26, 1993, to
December 31, 1994**

    34 Canada on Trial Before the United Nations
         — 1988 to 1993   *573*

    35 Kim Campbell Comes to Bytown, Karl Marx to Ontario
         — June 26 to September 8, 1993   *603*

    36 The Hunt for the Red Tories in October — September 8
         to October 25, 1993   *627*

    37 Jean Chrétien: The Return of Absolutism — October 26,
         1993, to December 31, 1994   *648*

EPILOGUE   *681*

APPENDIX A   The Reform Party Platform   *687*

APPENDIX B   Ontario: A Selection of Laws and Policy
                  Directives   *690*

APPENDIX C   Alliance for the Preservation of English in
                  Canada: A Chronology of History   *695*

APPENDIX D   The Party Platform of the Bloc Québécois   *699*

APPENDIX E   The Parti Québécois Strategic Plan to Gain
                  Sovereignty on Election — 1988 to 1994   *701*

BIBLIOGRAPHY   *703*
INDEX   *725*

Acknowledgements

I N THE LAST EIGHT YEARS there have been many manifestations of this work. Nonetheless, encouraged by my dear wife Barbara to press on, I now complete my task. I am indebted beyond measure to her for her unfailing belief in what I do.

In 1980, during the Quebec referendum on sovereignty, I began accumulating a massive inventory of research material. I had in mind writing something about the visions of Canada. However, I had no idea I would one day have to manage daily some two thousand files and more than forty thousand articles! Over the years many friends, associates, and acquaintances have provided me with books, articles, pamphlets, and a slew of other material that has proven invaluable. I am particularly indebted to Bill Bolt for his many kindnesses. Eric Silver's counsel and hand-holding on the electronic highway have proven invaluable.

It would take a chapter of this work to record all those who have supported it. First and foremost on any list of those who contributed directly is my friend and editor Kathleen Richards, Canada's finest editor. Since 1987, when she completed editing *Champlain*, this enthusiastic companion has fought for high standards on this book. She has worked with me during all the long years of research and on the many, many drafts.

I am indebted to Angel Guerra of Stoddart who joined the cause at the beginning. I also appreciate the support and skilful guidance of his colleague Don Bastian.

There are so many champion helpers. I am deeply indebted to them for their many kindnesses. They include Keith Alcock, Jamie Armstrong, Collin Caswell, Neil and Margaret Currie, Hilary Davidson, Rosa Figliano,

Théodore F. Geraets, Kate Gordon, Sue Gordon, Janette Herman, Wallis King, John Hummenick, Michael Hynchberger, Louise Johnson, Al and Dorianne Lackey, Peter and Sheena Levitt, Miroslava Lhotsky, Kenneth MacDonald, Gord McIntyre, Andrew Mathers, Mark Nowaczynski, Ron Oakley, Lorraine Petzold, David Piper, William Richards, Ron Woodward, Elizabeth Vanstone, and finally Toby — my laptop dog, who saw the project through with an inside view of the whole thing.

Introduction

CANADA IS NO LONGER THE PEACEFUL KINGDOM. In less than half a century, without a military conquest, a civil war, or a natural catastrophe, the northern half of the North American continent has devoured itself in a conflict over values. Only one province in the federation, Quebec, which makes up just less than 25 percent of the whole, demonstrates any national ambition. After thirty years of interminable wrangling, Canada is a nation in name only.

In the decades to come, historians will try to pinpoint the causes for the country's disintegration. As the federation was once a land of promise, they will pass many judgements and attribute considerable blame. Because of the shame, guilt, and betrayal involved, a great deal of the record is buried already. Many people will rationalize the tragedy as inevitable; will say that there was nothing they could have done, anyway. This group is to be simultaneously envied their unearned peace of mind and held in contempt for their arrogance.

Since the Second World War, particularly in the last two decades of this century, the breakdown of nation states has accelerated. While the cultural conflict between the English and the French heritage remains a carbuncle of history that will not heal, this is no longer the main excuse for the dissembling going on now. There are many other more relevant factors in today's interdependent world. Historians now speak with one voice on some of those fundamentals. The Second World War, for example, shattered much of mankind's faith in an afterlife: the promise that personal discipline and good behaviour in this world will be rewarded in the next.

This simple fact underlies any examination of the disintegration of law and order, the destruction of the environment, global insolvency, famine,

1

and the terrible increase of disease and suffering for so many. The remnant empires of the western democracies are particularly under seige. The Judeo-Christian world of our forefathers has passed away. Western man, having turned his attention inward, now worships himself as a superior being. The nation state and even the multinational corporations are proving puny warriors against the pantheistic feudalism of the tribe and the collective. By some terrible twist of fate, western civilization has managed to resurrect the twelfth century, an age of hopeless turmoil and stagnation.

Ours is an anti-intellectual age. We live in a joyless world of shifting peoples and values. If the movement of individuals from place to place was the paradigm of the twentieth century, then massive migration is what nations face for the twenty-first. In the 1990s, nations collapse with such ease that cartographers have to revise their atlases and globes as often as brokers juggle publicly traded securities.

Near the end of the century, in 1993, there were twenty-nine wars on the planet. Almost all of them were civil ones.

This global upheaval is characterized as much by the end of the smallest indicators of civility as it is by terrorism, barbarism, and open warfare. In many societies, particularly in the West, the vulgar has become the ideal. Western man mocks decency as the stuff of sport and ridicule.

The portents of this lesser age surround us. Even the most trivial patterns of daily human behaviour prove dramatically that mankind has learned little from recent history. The world witnesses the passage of the last years of this century without passion or commitment. Sacred monuments are desecrated, not by terrorists, extremists, radicals, and vandals, but by people bored to death. In Britain two eleven-year-old boys methodically bludgeon a baby to death. No one can explain it. No one tries. The importance of the event is as much the fact that the kidnapping was matter-of-factly captured for posterity on a shopping mall's security video tape as it is the heinous crime itself. Swarming, one of the most terrifying phenomena of our age, is now commonplace in the world's major urban centres.

Perhaps the answers are all trite and mundane now because no one poses important questions.

Everyone is rude. Bishop William of Wykeham (1324–1404), educator and founder of two colleges at Oxford, held that "Manners maketh man." Edmund Burke (1729–1797), observing the effects of the French Revolution, wrote in 1790, "The age of chivalry is gone. That of sophisters, economists, and calculators has succeeded and the glory of Europe is extinguished forever" (*Reflections on the Revolution in France*, 1790).

Increasingly it is evident that technocrats will be the only ones with great wealth while the bulk of humankind sinks to a level of slavery previously unknown. In his trenchant work *Technopoly: The Surrender of Culture to Technology*, Neil Postman writes:

> It is to be expected that the winners will encourage the losers to be enthusiastic about computer technology. That is the way of winners. . . . They also tell them that their lives will be conducted more efficiently. But discreetly they neglect to say from whose point of view the efficiency is warranted or what might be its costs. . . .
>
> For one thing, in cultures that have a democratic ethos, relatively weak traditions, and a high receptivity to new technologies, everyone is inclined to be enthusiastic about technological change, believing that its benefits will eventually spread evenly among the entire population. Especially in the United States, where the lust for what is new has no bounds, do we find this childlike conviction most widely held. (p. 11)

The conservative philosopher of America, George F. Will, warned: "Unfortunately, change for the better generally requires the patience of decent politics, the persuasion of a public mind moves more like molasses than mercury. Therefore the rapid acceleration of history is the business of bad men" (*The Morning After*, p. 307).

In such a world Canada is poorly positioned to endure. Initially she survived the French empire in America as a British dominion through abandonment and conquest. Then she survived the counter-revolution to the upheaval in the American colonies. Whereas America has matured, and even declined, as an experiment in civilization, however, Canada has been sliding into a state of decay. She has rigorously retained outmoded colonial institutions at the peril of her future. She has never managed to evolve as a free and democratic society in which her people can peacefully effect meaningful reform.

Where are the principles on which the federation stands? Canadians endure a monstrous canon of slogans and dogma poured over them by an illiterate political class. This group knows nothing of the country's history and still less about individual freedom.

As a result, Canada is not a democracy. It is nearly a totalitarian society, frighteningly close to a dictatorship. The proof is overwhelming. Canadians have no direct say in the constitutional or economic vision of their country. All three of the referendums conducted in Canadian history have been non-binding policy directives only. The two referendums on sovereignty issues, conscription in 1942 and the constitutional Referendum of

1992, have been ignored by the politicians. The citizens continue to be de-democratized by an entrenched autocracy, governments having consistently proved over many years that, regardless of which party is in power, change, however limited, is out of the question. As long as the country had great wealth, the rulers could always salve the sore spots by applying more money to them. This is no longer possible.

Canada's tremendous natural resources enabled her to become one of the most prosperous industrial societies following the post-Second World War years. Now these are significantly depleted, and, more significantly, have become almost irrelevant to her economic and political survival. Except for her invaded titular sovereignty of one-fifth of the world's fresh water, Canada has been stripped of her resources and energy, having either used up, sold, or given away most of her natural inheritance.

Canadian sovereignty no longer exists. In less than half a century it has been squandered, given, or bargained away, all for a two-generation binge of high living. She has never known anything of mankind's greatest tragedies: interminable wars and overpopulation. Yet, because she has savaged her last refuge, her environmental inheritance, she now suffers the deterioration of her cities, forests, and agricultural land, and her other natural resources, including wildlife. Today we witness the end of an era.

Canada's demise is certain. There is so little love of individual freedom among the majority of her citizens that her destruction is unavoidable now. Freedom is never debated here. It is taken as a given. That assumption alone will destroy the country. Canadians lack what Professor Charles Taylor describes as essential to the human condition, a "dialogical character." In this environment, there are no values. In place of ideals Canadians prefer to worship comparisons, according to the doctrine of relativism. Francis Fukuyama, author of *The End of History and the Last Man*, says:

> Relativism — the doctrine that maintains that all values are merely relative and which attacks all "privileged perspectives" — must ultimately end up undermining democratic and tolerant values as well. Relativism is not a weapon that can be aimed selectively at the enemies one chooses. It fires indiscriminately, shooting out the legs of not only the "absolutism," dogmas, and certainties of the Western tradition, but that tradition's emphasis on tolerance, diversity, and freedom of thought as well. (p. 332)

Throughout this historical review, I shall concentrate almost exclusively on this fourth failing, intellectual desuetude. I believe that, more than any other force, it has brought Canada to her knees.

Introduction

For the historian, the failure of the country's citizens to revolt in the face of the obvious is principal. Canada's leaders know this. For the vested interest and the personal gain of a very few, the will of most citizens has been consistently discriminated off the agenda by these leaders.

Without a single challenge from any quarter and in flagrant violation of the law, the politicized public service in all levels of government has played a major role in disenfranchising the population. Many academics in the universities and practitioners in the legal profession have covertly nurtured these conditions. Far too many representations from these two groups are greatly indebted, if not owned, by those with political power who can bestow economic rewards on and guarantee sheer survival to these faithful.

Canadians are on the receiving end of a one-sided conversation from their governments, corporations, media, and educational institutions. While the country may survive superficially into the next century, it cannot recover from this assault on its original values. For anyone who holds personal freedom dear, for the talented and the hardworking, for the risk-taker and the courageous, other societies will prove more and more attractive. Fewer and fewer citizens will settle for slogans as a reason to see their country continue.

For a very long time now, the voice of dissent in Canada has been muted. Citizens face a choice. Through zealous self-censorship, they can keep themselves politically correct — according to the definition of D'Souza, Galbraith, Taylor, Hughes, Limbaugh, Lapham, Bibby, Manning.

People can even choose to consider themselves so-called dissenters.

Or they can remain true outcasts. This, as we shall see, applies even to what have been labelled grassroots movements, such as the Reform Party, which has become fatally infected with self-deception. Silence and cover-up rule every aspect of intellectual and institutional life in the country.

So why this degeneration? The reasons are legion. While a colonial heritage tops the list, an impoverished educational environment runs a close second. In our academic environment the capacity to think is never a consideration. In fact, it is a liability.

Myth and revisionist history can no longer withstand the demand for individual freedom sweeping the rest of the world. Alvin Toffler, who published *Power Shift* in 1990, is right: "Canada hangs together by a thread" (p. 247). There is also the simple, tragic fact that most people in this society have no idea what personal freedom is: that it is a responsibility, not a right; that it demands constant vigilance and struggle; that it is not itself an institution; that it is not found in the corridors of the nation's courts, nor in the writings of prominent men and women, nor in the nation's constitution. It can exist only in the heart and soul of each citizen devoted to preserving it.

Canadians have never been asked what they think of their constitution. In the 1960s those in power ignored them when they began to transform the nation from a federation of provinces to a country based on founding races and founding cultures. Nor were the people consulted about the patriation of their constitution from Britain on November 5, 1981. Nor were they asked what they thought about the radical changes adopted with the passage of the Constitution Act, 1982, on April 17 of that year.

One of these innovations was a Canadian Charter of Rights and Freedoms, which, unlike the American Bill of Rights, served as a legal fiction rather than the paramount law of the land. As it now stands, with its many qualifications, the Charter is little more than a government policy statement. That's all.

Under an archaic provision of law resurrected as an escape hatch or derogation clause — a "notwithstanding" clause, as it came to be known — any provincial legislature in the country can trash the most universal and fundamental human rights, merely by passing a bill. As a sleepy nation was to discover some six years later on December 21, 1988, the Government of Quebec enacted racist legislation restricting the right of free speech, one of the most fundamental rights of any democracy.

The Quebec legislature forged ahead with its blatant affront to international law, while the federal government wholeheartedly endorsed this travesty of human rights — defying their own highest provincial court and their own Charter of Rights.

Between 1980 and 1982 Canadians were never invited to discuss the revolution that swept away their common-law tradition based on individual rights and their parliamentary system as paramount. In their place rose a republic based on a written constitution that strongly emphasized collective rights to be protected by the Supreme Court of the land.

The Referendum of October 1992 was based on no direct consultation with the people about their constitution. It was a policy probe, a poll, a demand from the three national major parties conspiring together that the government be allowed to continue to disenfranchise the people of their right to exercise their democratic will. Of their two houses of Parliament, the Senate, or the Upper House, exists as a refuge for patronage. Senators are appointed at the sole personal discretion of the prime minister. During his term of office from 1984 to 1993, though it was possible to do otherwise, as was demonstrated, Brian Mulroney handpicked all but one of 55 senators appointed. On his retirement, senators in 48 seats of the 104 Senate seats had been appointed by this one man. Canadians have never been asked whether or not they approve of this Byzantine practice.

Under Canada's constitution the prime minister is empowered to appoint all nine justices of the Supreme Court of Canada, the highest legal authority in the land. No one can challenge these appointments or insist on a review of them.

The prime minister appoints all chief justices of all courts. He appoints the Speaker of the Senate and the House of Commons. He appoints all privy councillors, lieutenant-governors, deputy heads of departments, and all senators. He or she selects every single member of the Cabinet, and chooses even the librarians of Parliament. This one person selects the heads of all Crown corporations, Crown boards, and virtually all other power centres concerned with governing the land. As former Prime Minister John G. Diefenbaker wrote:

> The prime minister used to be regarded as a first among equals in the cabinet but since the First World War there are no equals. His powers are so wide and general, there seems little question that a prime minister today in the British parliamentary tradition has greater power than the president of the United States. (*Those Things We Treasure*, p. 51)

Parliament has become a circus of overpaid puffins who believe their prime duty is to their leader and their own self-interest. They do not represent their constituents. Canadians cannot remove any elected official from either of its houses of Parliament or its provincial legislatures, or indeed any lower level of government, let alone the prime minister him- or herself, even for certified insanity. While in public office for whatever prescribed term, the nation's elected and appointed representatives and leaders are immune from recall, their electorate's direct censure, and impeachment by any process. Election to Parliament and legislatures in Canada means a sinecure for whatever time is specified.

Judging from recent constitutional wrangling, Canada's elites boast neither the historical foundation nor the desire to acquire the knowledge necessary to even debate change. The leaders don't have a clue what the problems are. They refuse to hear.

Concentrating on the Canadian constitutional struggle of the last thirty years, I have examined some of these ideals. I have concluded that Canada will break down less because of cultural and ethnic conflicts and a lack of "tolerance," as our leaders would have us believe, than for other, far more serious reasons.

In an essay written in 1921 entitled *The Moral Obligation to Be Intelligent*, the American writer John Erskine (1871–1951) said:

> We make a moral issue of an economic or social question, because it seems ignoble to admit it is simply a question for intelligence. Like the medicine-man, we use oratory and invoke our hereditary divinities, when the patient needs only a little quiet, or permission to get out of bed. We applaud those leaders who warm to their work — who, when they cannot open a door, threaten to kick it in. In the philosopher's words, we curse the obstacles of life as though they were devils. But they are not devils. They are obstacles. (pp. 25–26)

I began this work angry with Canada's politicians and leaders and convinced that Canadian unity was really threatened, that "national unity" by itself was an objective worth monumental effort and dedication. I am no longer convinced of even the relevance of such an objective. After ten years of struggle to document what has happened, I find myself far more disillusioned with the general populace than I am with Canada's leaders. *Farewell the Peaceful Kingdom* shows why my personal focus has so radically changed.

JOE C.W. ARMSTRONG
JANUARY 1995

I

The Kingdom and
the Foreplay

1963 to 1982

1

Lester Bowles Pearson,
the Father of Bilingualism
— 1963 to 1967

THE TIME AND PLACE WERE PERFECT: 1967, the centennial year of Confederation, and in Montreal, one of the oldest cities in North America. Between April 28 and October 27, more than 50 million people came to what was then Canada's only cosmopolitan city. They came to marvel at the extravaganza of "Man and His World," the World's Fair, EXPO '67.

That summer, Montreal hosted a blaze of exhibits from more than seventy countries. At last, Sir Wilfrid Laurier's 1904 prophecy seemed fulfilled: "Let me tell you, my fellow countrymen, that all the signs point this way, that the twentieth century shall be the century of Canada and of Canadian development."

For all the sentiment from then to now, however, historian Donald Creighton's perspective prevails: "Apart from the fact that it showed the world what Canadians could do at the end of their nation's first century, the fair had no connection with the centenary and deliberately excluded all reference to it. English Canadians may have imagined that Expo 67 was a memorial to Confederation; French Canadians saw it as a demonstration of the prowess of French Canada and as a tribute to the glory of Montreal" (*Canada's First Century*, p. 349).

For the first four months the exposition was a celebration, but after July 24, it was downhill — a mirror of the more systemic problems facing

Canada. On that evening in late summer, the most eminent French statesman of his time, General Charles de Gaulle, president of France, had sailed up the St. Lawrence River by way of the great seaway of America, the mighty river Jacques Cartier discovered in 1534, to Quebec City.

Within the labyrinthine government in Ottawa, tension mounted. De Gaulle would be trouble, for certain. He was no diplomat. Whenever anyone of political rank from France paid even the most innocuous visit to Canada, the encounter stirred something in the Canadian soul. Memories of the past glories of New France, and of past defeats, always surfaced.

In *Vive le Québec Libre*, McGill political science professor Dale Thomson writes that the general had confided to his son-in-law, General Alain Boisseau, on July 15 before sailing to Canada: "I am going to strike a strong blow. . . . They are going to hear me over there; it will make some waves" (p. 199). The French president had taken it upon himself to be history's revenge as the "last chance to rectify the cowardice of France."

He dropped the first bombshell in Quebec City at the Château Frontenac. On the evening of July 23, 358 years after the city's founding by Samuel de Champlain, de Gaulle demanded that Quebec "have the right of self-determination in all areas." Quebec and English Canada had to have a partnership, he said, "to save their character and independence from contact with the colossal neighbour to the south." Another author, Jean-François Lisée, writes in *In the Eye of the Eagle* that that evening "de Gaulle . . . invented sovereignty association" (p. 49).

Dramatic as the general's pronouncement was, he held his biggest torpedo in reserve for the next day, July 24. He would wreak the most damage he could in Montreal.

On July 24, even before de Gaulle's visit to the French, Quebec, and Canadian pavilions on the EXPO site, the general chose to greet a huge assembly awaiting him outside City Hall. If you looked carefully at the more than 6,000 people, you could detect a respectable complement of well-dressed anglophone Westmounters mingling with thousands of Québécois below the city centre's balcony. All were eager to hear the resonant voice of France in the first person.

For non-Quebecers and resident anglophones alike, this was a chance to see Churchill's "Cross of Lorraine." For Quebecers it was a chance to see the man dubbed the Liberator of France. A balcony speech! What drama! Everyone waited restlessly. Even de Gaulle was uncertain exactly what he would do.

As always when beginning a public address, he spoke slowly, and then moved swiftly to the core of his message. Noting the waving placards of the little pockets of fifteen or twenty separatist groups below the balcony, he seized the moment. Hijacking the separatist slogan, he declared sonorously, expelling the words powerfully from his large frame, *"Vive le Québec"* — long pause — *"Libre!"*

The following morning, an editorial line in the Washington *Evening Star* summed up the effect: "With the unerring accuracy of a sadistic dentist, Charles de Gaulle has drilled straight to the most sensitive nerve in Canada's anatomy and proceeded to probe it gleefully" (quoted ibid., p. 40).

In his memoirs, René Lévesque, another observer of the period, recalled, "You could see it coming. His landing at L'Anse-au-Foulon, the Port of Quebec, reminded me of his entry into Paris in 1944. Here, too, though in another way, he was coming to wipe out bad memories" (*Memoirs*, p. 205). Lévesque was delighted: "The president of France deserved the triumph Quebeckers prepared for him, and he has a right to expect their admiration and gratitude. . . . Vive de Gaulle!" (*La Presse*, July 31/67).

In a flash, the carnival atmosphere and good will that had radiated across the whole of Canada that summer was lost. One enthusiast in the crowd, a young Robert Bourassa who would later come to hate demonstrations, was thrilled: "He said it! He said it!"

Historian Thomson points out de Gaulle's remarks in Montreal did not end there. As he put it, "On November 27, de Gaulle threw another rock into the pond." In a televised press conference in France he rubbed salt into the wound. He said that while France "took no interest in its abandoned children . . . by . . . a miracle of vitality, energy and fidelity . . . a French nation — part of our people" had survived. "That Quebec should be free, that is indeed what it is all about." General de Gaulle went so far as to call for "a complete change in the current Canadian structure" (*Vive le Québec Libre*, pp. 256–57).

Months later the maestro of mischief shared something more of what he had been thinking at that moment. "I was waiting for the event, the crowd, to judge just what I would say, at what place, at what instant. But I knew I was going to do something" (p. 199).

One of the interesting footnotes in history records that the French government entrusted only one reporter from Canada to cover de Gaulle's evaluation of Quebec — Keith Spicer of the *Globe and Mail*. Did de Gaulle know something of this man's future? Or was he a catalyst?

English-speaking Canada was furious and Canada's Prime Minister Lester Pearson did not help matters. He wavered. He urged Canadians to restrain themselves from acting in any way that would jeopardize relations between Canada and France. He played down the event as "unacceptable to the Canadian people and its government. . . . Canadians do not need to be liberated."

Robert Stanfield, the opposition leader who had replaced John Diefenbaker, supported Pearson fully. He was less offended than most Canadians. Diefenbaker would have chased de Gaulle home in a hurry, wielding a switch. Stanfield meekly observed that Canadians were "mature enough not to allow such an attempt by somebody outside of Canada to affect the relationship among Canadians inside Canada." Tommy Douglas, leader of the New Democratic Party (NDP), sang the same song of moderation.

Stanfield followed the Pearson pattern on cultural matters: orchestrated emotion. And he eventually paid the price for supporting Pearson.

Pearson's pacifying words particularly rankled with English Canada. Those veterans who had fought for France in two world wars and the family members of the thousands who had died liberating France would not honour Pearson's name in the Legion halls of the nation. Annoyed as they were, however, Canadians did not know at this stage about their prime minister's hidden agenda, activated the moment he had won the election in 1963.

René Lévesque interpreted the public outcry otherwise: "The outburst of English Canadian francophobia can be explained by the fact that Quebeckers indisputably greeted this man too well, at a time when many would like him to disappear. . . . Ottawa's attitude toward General de Gaulle seems to me wilfully brutal and almost insulting" (*La Presse*, July 31/67).

No such fanfare greeted another announcement made just nineteen days before the close of Canada's first world fair, on October 8, 1967. That day the Royal Commission on Bilingualism and Biculturalism released their final report. De Gaulle's outburst and the furore it caused made the perfect diversion while the report publicized the Liberal government's real agenda. The de Gaulle incident merely reaffirmed that a "crisis" existed between Canada's English- and French-speaking peoples. Now no one could dispute that the government should engineer some kind of long-term solution to the apparent racial schism. De Gaulle's timely intervention enabled Prime Minister Pearson to accelerate his cultural and language revolution. His plans would change Canada for all time.

In the final volume of *Mike: The Memoirs*, Pearson wrote:

My passionate interest when I was in government, apart from the ultimate question of peace and war, was in the national unity of our country. . . .

I was convinced from the beginning, as I remain convinced now, that a

14

prime element is the recognition of the French language. Nothing could be more important in my mind than an effort to make our French-speaking people feel that their language is an equal language in Canada. . . .

I have mentioned that I took an initial step at that first Cabinet meeting after I became Prime Minister. . . . The French in Canada are a nation in the sense that they are a separate people. . . . But I see no way of holding our country together unless English Canada adopts a new attitude towards the intention of our French-speaking compatriots to maintain their identity, their culture, and their language as a special fact of life within Canada. Those who persist in telling us that we must do away with this idea, that we must insist on talking about our country, race, and nation as one and indivisible — these are the real separatists. (Vol. 3, pp. 236–38)

That was Lester Bowles Pearson's vision of Canada. Throughout his voluminous memoirs and papers, there is no mention of freedom, individual rights, or the importance of citizenship. For him, the collective is what matters. The state and the individual will comfortably co-exist as long as bicultural and bilingual national unity prevails. The Battle of the Plains of Abraham between Wolfe and Montcalm had resumed.

Pearson ran the country as if it were a prefecture of the public service — on a need-to-know basis. For him, debate was unnecessary. This was not a surprising philosophy. In External Affairs, the department from which he had emerged, there was never any debate, only policy, dictated from the top down: "As soon as we were in government, we began the work of setting up the Bilingualism and Biculturalism Commission" (Ibid., p. 240). Then Pearson adds that there wasn't too much difficulty over the terms of reference of the commission — "though we did make one mistake": "We failed to take adequately into account the sensitivities of citizens from other cultural backgrounds and the problems of multi-culturalism, indeed, a problem of almost multi-linguism. We mentioned this, but we gave the impression that there were really only two elements in Canada's development, the English fact, if you like, and the French fact" (pp. 240–41).

He clearly saw a Canada of two founding races and founding cultures. For him, multiculturalism and multilingualism were "problems." For him, there was no ongoing struggle between the state and the individual, the government and the citizen. Pearson talks of his place in opposition as "wrong." He sees a moral significance in not having power, exercising power was the moral imperative. Dissent did not thrive during the Pearson years. To him, it did not exist.

As soon as he took over, he set up a committee of the Privy Council directly under his own authority. This was the Royal Commission on Bilingualism and Biculturalism, established on July 19, 1963. Pearson announced it on July 22, only ninety-nine days after he had won his minority Liberal government of ninety-five seats. Gordon Robertson, whose name would become synonymous with the Pearson regime, became Clerk of the Privy Council. This made him the highest-ranking public servant in Canada — the deputy minister of the deputy ministers.

In a speech on December 17, 1962, when he was opposition leader, Pearson had promised to set up this commission. Seven of the ten commissioners eventually appointed came from Ontario and Quebec, including co-chairs André Laurendeau and Davidson Dunton. The three "outsiders" came from Alberta, Manitoba, and New Brunswick. Four of the ten were francophones. Of the four English-Canadian commissioners, one was a former federal public servant and another a resident of Quebec. No attempt was made to balance the country's regions or even the ethnic composition of Canada.

Commissioner André Laurendeau was, by any standard, a dubious choice for the task of uniting Canada. Formerly editor of *Le Devoir*, the voice of Quebec nationalism, and a former leader of the separatist party the Bloc Populaire, he offered no credentials for championing the constitutional vision of a united country. In a famous editorial entitled "The Nigger-King Hypothesis" in *Le Devoir* on July 4, 1958, he had ridiculed English Canadians. Premier Maurice Duplessis had expelled a reporter from a press conference when no English-language paper in Quebec would report it:

Quebec's Anglophones behave like the British in one of their African colonies.

The British are too wise, politically; they rarely destroy the political institutions of a conquered country. They surround the Negro King, but they let him behave as he pleases. Occasionally he will be permitted to cut off heads as is customary. It would never occur to them to demand of a Negro King that he conform to the high moral and political standards of the British.

The Negro King must collaborate and protect the interests of the British. With this taken care of, the rest counts for little. Does the little king violate the rules of democracy? Well, what could one expect from such a primitive creature?

I do not attribute these attitudes to the English minority of Quebec. But things go on as if some of its leaders believed in the theory and practice of the Negro King. They pardon in M. Duplessis, chief of Quebec's natives, what they would not stand for in their own.[1]

The idea for a Royal Commission on Bilingualism and Biculturalism was Laurendeau's, not Pearson's. In an editorial written for *Le Devoir* early in 1962, on January 20, "A Proposal for an Inquiry into Bilingualism," Laurendeau made a play on the line attributed to the Huguenot king Henry IV (1553–1610) of France. When he rationalized the adoption of Catholicism in 1593 during the Wars of Religion, King Henry had remarked, "Paris is well worth a Mass." As Laurendeau wryly observed in his turn, "Paris, history reminds us, was worth a mass. Perhaps Canada is worth a royal commission."

Pearson dutifully took the hint. The prime minister ensured that the composition of the royal commission favoured central Canada. The terms of reference for the commission, however, revealed the most about its purpose. Given the demographic reality of the country, the commissioners were ordered to define Canada on the basis of the two-nations theory. In fact, this was no commission of inquiry at all. Under the Inquiries Act, the commissioners were simply

> to enquire into and report upon the existing state of bilingualism and biculturalism in Canada and to recommend what steps should be taken to develop the Canadian Confederation on the basis of an equal partnership between the two founding races, taking into account the contribution made by the other ethnic groups to the cultural enrichment of Canada and the measure that should be taken to safeguard that contribution.

As the commissioners perceived Canada, the "Bi-Bi" Commission need never have taken place. They and the Liberal government had already decided exactly what Canada's make-up should be. They began from the principle of an "equal partnership between two founding races," which the commissioners considered the "mainspring of our terms of reference." The course was set. All that was left for them to do was establish the policy and mechanics needed to back up that principle. They saw no need to consult the Canadian people about any of this: "We were not asked to consider merely the recognition of two main languages and cultures which might be granted entirely different rights; we were asked to examine ways in which the Canadian Confederation could develop in accordance with the principle of equal partnership" (*Report*, p. xxxix).

Throughout their final report the bilingual commissioners assumed that Canada was bilingual. They said so. Section 43 begins with, "What makes Canada unique as a bilingual state is that her two official languages are English and French."

The commissioners were not asked to examine Canada's real cultural and language heritage but ordered to assume a false premise and to work from that basis only. Even accepting the false premise, no explanation was offered for excluding Canada's aboriginal peoples as a "founding people."

For the commissioners, the Conquest of Quebec in 1759 was no longer a relevant historical fact. They believed that they had a far greater role to play: saving Canada from breakup. With no debate at all, they adopted the enormous historical fiction in their report: that Canada was based on dualism and that the rest of the country had been historically, physically, and mentally, if not through military force, conquered by the "two founding races." This was revisionist history raised to a new level by Canada's colonial rulers.

All the country needed was a formal implementation plan of what they considered Canadian reality. In the commission's final report in 1965, Commissioner Jaroslav Rudnyckyj from Manitoba wrote, "English and French in Canada have official status" (*Report*, p. 157). In British Columbia? Newfoundland? This was nonsense, of course. The commissioners revealed an appalling lack of knowledge about the country at the time of Confederation and its history since then.

Only one provincial premier spoke against the appointment of the Bi-Bi Commission, Ernest C. Manning of Alberta. In 1981, he wrote: "That was a very, very serious mistake ever setting up that Commission. . . . We happened to be the only province that opposed it at the time. And we opposed it, not on the grounds of anything anti-French or anti-Quebec. . . . If you make [language] a national commission on a local issue, you're going to open a Pandora's box that you'll never get closed" (Sharpe and Braid, *Storming Babylon*, p. 160).

After the commission had been working for a year and a half, it released its Preliminary Report on February 1, 1965. Canadians were shocked. The bombshell in it was the conclusion that "Canada, without being fully conscious of the fact, is passing through the greatest crisis in its history."[2]

Pearson was delighted with the report:

> Those who by choice came to Canada later were expected to fit into one or the other of the two founding groups for language purposes. . . . The first volume of the commission's report presented an important and realistic analysis of Canadian disintegration. Many thought it too pessimistic and much too alarming. I did not. I thought it exactly right. I wanted people to be shocked, and they were. Some Canadians realized for the first time that there were differences serious enough to destroy our country if no remedial action were taken. (*Mike*, Vol. 3, pp. 59–60)

But the question remains: what was this "greatest crisis" in their history that Canadians didn't know about? Historian Hugh Bingham Myers, an Anglo-Catholic, tackled the issue of the "Quiet Revolution" in a controversial book *The Quebec Revolution*, published in 1963: "What do I really mean by the 'revolution'? Essentially, the idea is that in 1958 or 1959 (I call 1958 pre-revolutionary, but won't quibble), a reaction against the Establishment, as the British call it, became too strong to be ignored. For all the separatist noises, this reaction was and is *equally* against the established French Canadian, Quebec order of things" (p. xvii).

Myers also wrote about the events in 1963 that armed the Bi-Bi Commission to present their own dramatic overview of the situation. Various random acts could be judged acts of vandalism and terrorism just as easily as a national crisis:

> Then, on March 8, three of Her Majesty's military establishments in Montreal were the targets of Molotov cocktails. In the weeks that followed, the Wolfe monument on the Plains of Abraham in Quebec City was sent crashing to the ground; a railway track the Prime Minister (Mr. Diefenbaker) was to pass over was dynamited; an R.C.M.P. building was damaged by a bomb; another bomb, exploding behind one of Her Majesty's recruiting centers, killed the night watchman; a Black Watch depot was bombed; an explosion occurred in an oil refinery; five mail boxes blew up in the rich, largely English, Montreal suburb of Westmount; a sergeant-major, about to dismantle a mail box bomb, was nearly killed by it; a bomb exploded in an engineering building; dynamite was found in Quebec City mail boxes. (p. xix)

Still, despite all the confusion and obvious threats that accompanied these incidents, taken together they hardly justified the commissioners' conclusions. One person killed, some bombs and dynamite. Was this really sufficient justification to arbitrarily re-structure the make-up and constitution of a country? This was a revolution? Doubtless many English writers and the English media in Canada felt themselves caught up in the hysteria. Myers, for example, opens chapter six of his book with "By the beginning of 1963, the winds of revolution were not yet at hurricane force."

The English media had a field day fuelling the notion that something cataclysmic was about to happen. Peter Gzowski, associate editor of *Maclean's* magazine, wrote an article in September 1963 for the feature "Conversations with Quebec's Revolutionaries." For this he interviewed a number of leading Quebec separatists, including André Laurendeau, two students, a designer, and a proofreader: "It is now an inescapable fact that we are headed toward separation into two countries. If we are going to stop this momentum, or slow it down so it reshapes Confederation instead of destroying it, we, the English-speaking half of the partnership, are going to have to have something of a revolution of our own" (*Maclean's*, Sept 7/63).

Peter C. Newman was national affairs editor for the magazine at the time. He too was adamant that English Canada had to take major steps. For the February 8, 1964, "Special Issue on Confederation under Fire," he pulled no punches about the seriousness of the threat. After several interviews, he wrote that these and other factors "have convinced me that we now have three . . . and only three choices":

1. to jettison Quebec.
2. to form a latter-day Austro-Hungarian Empire by allowing Quebec and the rest of Canada to split into two virtually independent states.
3. to reform our constitution so thoroughly (and effectively) that it will calm the deepening crisis in which we find ourselves.

Pretty frightening stuff — especially considering the nation was sleeping through it.

What did it all mean? Here was the media going bananas over a crisis, and in the same breath admitting repeatedly that the whole thing didn't amount to a hill of beans. In this same article, for example, Newman wrote that "an independent Quebec remains the dream of marginal conspirators."

A professor of law at the University of Montreal certainly did not think there was any crisis. At age forty-four, the man born as Joseph Philippe Pierre Ives Elliotte Trudeau contributed a piece to this same special issue of *Maclean's*: "Of all the institutional changes which I believe desirable in Canada, I would rank constitutional reform among the least pressing; and consequently I tend to consider much of the present discussion of the BNA Act as a process of alienation or politics of diversion."

He went further. He cited the July 4, 1776, American Declaration of Independence as a warning to those who would disturb the peaceful kingdom: "Prudence, indeed, will dictate that governments long established should not be changed for light and transient causes."

But then he also hinted he was hiding more up his sleeve:

We need a bill of rights, not a new version of the BNA Act. . . . And what is more important in the present context, a constitutionally entrenched bill of rights seems to be the best tool for breaking the ever-recurring deadlock between Quebec and the rest of Canada. . . . If certain language and educational rights were written in the constitution along with other basic liberties . . . French Canadians would cease to feel confined to their Quebec ghetto and the Spirit of Separatism would be laid forever.

The results of the Bi-Bi Commission matched the political agenda perfectly. Both the Preliminary Report of 1965 and the Final Report on October 8, 1967, appeared bursting with political rhetoric and revisionist history. Both incorporated unique word definitions and testimonials from the commissioners themselves about their commission's importance. They happily boasted that they had been fully licensed to perform their task. "So wide are the Commission's terms of reference that it could have legitimately investigated almost every aspect of Canadian society," they smugly acknowledged.

As if to signal that some day history might not be as enamoured of their work as they were, they took some steps to cover themselves. For example, troubled that accusations of racism would attach to their work, they offered a handy little dictionary in a general introduction in the Final Report, "The Key Words of the Terms of Reference." The word *race*, for example, they explained, "is used in an older meaning as referring to a national group, and carries no biological significance."

Of course, there is no such "older meaning." *Race*, a word used in both French and English and especially in connection with founding peoples, can only be taken to refer to an ethnic group in either language. English and French etymological dictionaries are explicit on this point. Both trace the word to the Middle English or Old Norse *ras*, meaning "house, family, tribe, or nation regarded as of common stock; distinct ethnical stock." Even the Latin *radix*, another source, means root.

The problem was obvious. From the start, in 1963, the commissioners were authorized to construct a racist definition of Canada. They could prattle on about "the basically bicultural character of our country" or the "bilingual" character, which simply wasn't the case; yet they also had to add as an afterthought "the subsequent contribution made by the other cultures" to ensure the commission's own credibility.

They dismissed any other rights they trammelled in the process as irrelevant. They dutifully cited the *Universal Declaration of Human Rights* adopted by the United Nations in 1948. They even quoted the wording of Article 2, that rights attach "without distinction of any kind, such as race, colour, sex, language, religion, political or other opinion, national or social origin, property, birth or other status." They carried on in the same vein about the Canadian Bill of Rights, concluding that "these individual human rights are unquestionable, and hold for all Canadians without exception."

Then, in their very next paragraph, they curtly dismissed such matters: "[But] we were not asked by our terms of reference to deal with these fundamental rights."

Agreed. So what then did they think they were doing? What about Commissioner F.R. Scott, that icon of Canada's intelligentsia, the prominent Montrealer, poet laureate of Canada, social philosopher and constitutional expert? Here was the former and most noted dean of the Faculty of Law at McGill, the founder of the League for Social Reconstruction, and a celebrated author with an impeccable record and a reputation for brains, decency, and concern about justice. How did he see his role in this?

There are no answers to these questions. Certainly the clash of visions between Canada as a federation of provinces and as a nation comprised of founding races and cultures was not new. A quarter of a century earlier a Toronto *Telegram* editorial, "Bilingualism in Quebec and Elsewhere in Canada," dealt with bilingualism and its inherent dangers at length, on January 9, 1940. In 1940 the French-speaking population of North America was less than 3 million in an anglophone sea of 140 million. The threat of cultural annihilation was no greater then than it was in Pearson's time or is today. Citing *Le Jour* of Montreal in an editorial about the educational advantages of Italo-Canadians in Montreal who had earlier access to English-language training than francophones, the *Telegram* also noted:

> French-Canadians who are equipped with an adequate knowledge of English are much more numerous than English-Canadians who speak French. This fact has led some English-speaking Canadians to contend that in failing to promote bilingualism throughout Canada we are not doing our part towards national unity. . . . Outside Quebec there are few and limited areas where the ability to speak French would be of the slightest service to English-speaking Canadians. Outside Quebec, as in that province, the teaching of other than the mother tongue in primary schools narrows down to a question of practicability. It is an illusion to regard bilingualism as the shibboleth of national unity.

Fifteen years later Blair Fraser (1909–68), one of Canada's most respected political journalists and CBC broadcasters, verbalized the new world in the making. As the keynote speaker at the Henry Marshall Tory Lecture, delivered at the University of Alberta in Edmonton on October 12, 1965, the star columnist of *Maclean's* magazine painted a very different picture:

You must surely agree that a Canadian ought to be able to move from one part of his own country to another without sacrificing the very essence of nationality, the language and the culture in which he and all his ancestors have spoken and thought, within this their own country, for the past three hundred years. . . .

It is often assumed that anyone who speaks, as I have just been doing, in support of French-Canadian claims for equal rights in language and education, must also be a supporter of Quebec's claims in general for greater autonomy or for special status within Confederation. This is not so. (*"Blair Fraser Reports,"* p. 91)

Canada, unknowing, had entered the revisionist age of relativism where reasoned idealism would always prevail over common sense and history.

The Liberal government under Lester Pearson indulged itself in even more rewriting of history. In their final, October 8, 1967, *Report of the Royal Commission on Bilingualism and Biculturalism*, page after page distorts history. In setting out Canada's foundation, the commissioners repeatedly described not only an "officially bilingual" nation, but one historically rooted in a language crisis. As one small example, here's what they said about Lord Durham's famous *Report of the Affairs of British North America* in 1839: "Lord Durham saw two primary causes for the troubles besetting Canada: the cleavage between the two ethnic groups aggravated by language differences, and the antagonism between the elective and appointive branches of government."

Canada? Really? Not so, worthy commissioners! Lord Durham wrote these words when there was no nation of Canada, just Upper Canada, or Ontario as we now know it, and Lower Canada, or, today, Quebec.[3] In 1839 Durham wrote of *Lower* Canada:

I expected to find a contest between a government and a people: *I found two nations warring in the bosom of a single state*: I found a struggle, not of principles, but of races; and I perceived that it would be idle to attempt any amelioration of laws or institutions until we could first succeed in terminating the deadly animosity that now separates the inhabitants of Lower Canada into the hostile divisions of French and English.

. . . The French majority asserted the most democratic doctrines of the rights of a numerical majority. The English minority availed itself of the protection of the prerogative and allied itself with all those of the colonial institutions which enabled the few to resist the will of the many. [emphasis mine]

Note that the crisis, the upheaval, the racial and language tensions of "two nations warring in the bosom of a single state," apply to Lower Canada — modern-day Quebec *only*.

Durham never discovered any such racial upheaval in what we know as Canada; in the Upper Canada of his time, or in the geographic areas that are the other provinces today. He simply discovered in Quebec what de Tocqueville had feared for America, the tyranny of the majority.

For all their sins of sophistry, revisionist historical manipulation, posturing, and public pandering, the Bi-Bi Commissioners showed they were not completely mad. Aware that the Utopian world they hoped for and noted as an ideal would not materialize, they recommended "that bilingual districts be established throughout Canada and that negotiations between the federal government and the provincial government concerned define the exact limits of each bilingual district."

This could have proved a plausible recommendation. The October 1967 report included a map of Canada showing the "Census Divisions where the Official Language Minority" was "equal to or more than 10 percent of the Population."

Here was the safety valve that could have prevented a national conflagration. Putting such a recommendation into practice wouldn't have been easy, but the commissioners would have found justification enough to experiment, learn, later modify, and even improve. Toronto would not have been designated officially bilingual any more than Quebec City, Vancouver, St. John's, or even Montreal.

As for Pearson's view of the final report of the Bi-Bi Commission, he unequivocally supported the recommendation that an office of the Official Languages Commissioner be created. He wrote nothing else significant about bilingualism in his memoirs.

In the Canada of 1967, few Canadians recognized the interventionist role government was preparing to play in their lives. At the same time, one of the country's very few independent thinkers, Colin M. Brown, had a gnawing premonition of what might lie ahead. That year he founded the National Citizens' Coalition, which claimed to be "Canada's foremost organization for the defence of our basic political and economic freedoms."[4] In the years that followed, the coalition maintained its steady call: "We promote free markets, individual freedom and responsibility under limited government and a strong defence."

LESTER PEARSON ANNOUNCED HIS RETIREMENT from politics at a routine Cabinet meeting on December 14, 1967. The history profes-

24

sor who had graduated to become a mandarin in the Department of External Affairs and then to the highest elected office in the land exited public life as he had come into it — as a high-ranking member of his own secret service. A leadership convention was set for April 4 to 6, 1968.

In his book *The Distemper of Our Times*, one of the country's best-known journalists, the Ottawa editor of the *Toronto Daily Star*, described the end of the era: "The Diefenbaker Years [1957–63] resembled nothing so much as the voyage of the *Titanic* — an inevitable rush to disaster, with the ship of state sinking at the end in a galaxy of fireworks, brass bands playing and the captain shouting hysterical orders to crewmen who had long since jumped overboard" (p. xii).

Yet in his celebrated 557-page tome, Peter C. Newman missed something. He says nothing about Pearson's revolutionary move to change the cultural face of Canada — by establishing the Royal Commission on Bilingualism and Biculturalism. Davidson Dunton appears in only a brief mention, as a former head of the CBC, the president of Carleton University, and a possible candidate to succeed Pearson in the leadership of the party. The name of André Laurendeau, the commission's Quebec co-chair, does not even appear in the book. A new era of politics and of a different kind of political commentary had begun.

Notes

1 This quotation appears in Edmund Wilson's *O Canada: An American's Notes on Canadian Culture* (p. 207). Wilson attributes it as "Translation, slightly revised, from *The Quebec Revolution*, by Hugh Bingham Myers" (p. 5). Another version appears in *Columbo's Canadian Quotations*.

2 In 1978 Dunton wrote an essay entitled "Majority Must Bend to Quebec" for inclusion in a book, *Canada's Third Option* (see Berkowitz and Logan). In it he says: "We did not know whether the crisis would be short or long; we thought the signs of danger were many and serious. We found that French Canadians of Québec were tending to

reject the Confederation of 1867 as it had evolved. We thought that unless there were major changes the situation would worsen with time. . . . The main thrust of our recommendations in language rights and education was to put Francophones living in other provinces on somewhat the same footing as Anglophones in Québec, taking into account relevant circumstances. . . . The commission did not think it had produced a full response to the Canadian crisis. . . . The best prospect and hope is probably for the development of an alternative political approach built around the thinking of men such as Claude Ryan, Claude Castonguay, Léon Dion . . ." (pp. 94–95, 100).

3 Ignorance about Lord Durham's famous remark has taken a firm hold in Canadian history. Preston Manning and Joe Clark are two prime examples. In his credo *The New Canada* (1992), Manning writes: "In his famous report, Lord Durham said he perceived two nations (the English and the French) warring in the bosom of a single state" (p. 301). In Clark's mini memoir *A Nation Too Good to Lose* (1994), he too writes that Lord Durham's report "had described Canada as 'two nations warring in the bosom of a single state' and recommended that French Canadians be assimilated" (p. 108).

The latest "expert" is Jonathan Lemco, author of *Turmoil in the Peaceable Kingdom: The Quebec Sovereignty Movement and Its Implications for Canada and the United States* (1994). His faux pas: "As far back as 1839, Lord Durham could note that Canada was 'two nations warring in the bosom of a single state'" (p. 3).

4 *Colombo's Canadian References* (Oxford University Press, 1976) does not mention the NCC or its founder.

2

Pierre Trudeau and Robert Stanfield,
the Two Faces of Dualism — 1968

THE CLOSING OF EXPO '67 signalled the end of Lester Pearson's career. To succeed him, he chose Jean Marchand, one of the so-called three wise men from Quebec (the other two were Pierre Elliott Trudeau and Gérard Pelletier), who had formed a pact to enter federal politics together.

With Pearson leaving, the three Quebecers saw their chance to breathe new life into a moribund federal system. All three had concluded that government had been corrupted in English Canada's favour. When Pearson approached him, however, Marchand told him he was not interested in the job. In his memoirs, Pearson writes that he "wanted Trudeau to hear from Marchand's lips in my presence that Marchand would, in no circumstances, be a candidate." He added, "I let Mr. Trudeau know that if he were chosen it would meet with my wholehearted approval. . . . I did not, of course, give him any support during the campaign, other than letting a few friends know that I was well-disposed toward him. This seemed to become known" (p. 326).

In due course, Trudeau himself became the anointed one. His entrance into the inner core of the Liberal machinery as justice minister on April 4 was the first move in a careful orchestration of the changing of the guard. As Pearson watched the jockeying of the candidates for position from the safety of the sidelines, he wrote: "Then there was Trudeau, Pierre Elliott Trudeau. From the day in 1965 when he was elected to Parliament, and as a Liberal to many people's surprise, I had pushed him ahead" (p. 325).

Much has been made about Trudeau's apparent disinterest in political power at the time. Publicly he claimed he valued his personal freedom very highly. In an interview with his biographer, George Radwanski, he said: "I never liked to be a leader in anything. I never liked to be responsible — you know, I never sought to be chief of a Boy Scout troop, or if we were a gang off hiking, I never tried to be the first one; I'd sort of rather follow on my own and go off. I didn't want to lead the people along, to be the first in the path and so on. Very often they would thrust me into that position" (p. 86).

When asked directly if he wanted to be prime minister, he answered, "Not very badly. But I can give you another quotation, from Plato — that men who want very badly to head the country shouldn't be trusted" (p. 102).[1]

Radwanski addresses Trudeau's take-it-or-leave-it attitude in his account of the professor's arrival at a Liberal pre-nomination meeting in Montreal. At the time Trudeau was up for scrutiny with the other candidates:

> While Marchand was still working to convince sceptical Liberals that his colleague should be accepted as a candidate, Trudeau almost compounded their misgivings by turning up for a crucial pre-nomination meeting with Liberal organizers dressed in an open-collared sports shirt, a suede jacket, a beat-up old peaked hat, muddy corduroy slacks, and sandals. He was intercepted as he stepped out of his Mercedes SL-300 and sent home to change into more conservative attire before the Liberal organizers could see this further display of unconventionality. (*Trudeau*, p. 90)

In the foreword to *Federalism and the French Canadians*, published in August 1967, three months before Pearson had announced his resignation, Trudeau wrote: "The only constant factor to be found in my thinking over the years has been opposition to accepted opinions. Had I applied this principle to the stock market, I might have made a fortune. I chose to apply it to politics, and it led me to power — a result I had not really desired, or even expected" (p. xix).

His reflections read more like the memoirs of a retired prime minister than a new minister of justice. Mike Pearson assessed his protégé differently. In 1968 he said to *Time* reporter Martin Sullivan, "Trudeau is following along in the tradition of being dragged to the Speaker's chair, as it were, reluctantly but not too reluctantly" (Ibid., p. 85).

In fact, Trudeau wanted and needed power. Such a radical vision as his, its clarity and its proprietorship, demanded that he seek and secure it. What other reason could such a competitive individual have for leaving a successful career in teaching, journalism, and law to come to Ottawa? Lawyers who study and write about power for decades and then exercise the same strategic care in disseminating their own views are ambitious. This was no Abraham Lincoln, who in 1858 campaigned for a Senate seat saying sincerely, "This has been ascribed to me. God knows how sincerely I prayed from the first that this field of ambition might not be opened."

Men like Trudeau do not settle for the back of a classroom. They do not sit waiting for history to call them. They may teach and preach for a long time, but when they sense the right moment they move with dispatch.

Trudeau was elected to Parliament on November 8, 1965. The following year he was appointed Parliamentary Secretary to Pearson. Pearson said: "I had read his pieces for years, and was impressed by them, particularly by his detailed technical knowledge of economics and constitutional law. We're into a period where that's very important, and we'll be dealing a lot with Quebec. Pierre is a Quebecer, and seems to be the kind of qualified person we need" (Ibid., p. 91, citing *Weekend Magazine*, Nov 13/66).

However, the appointment of Pierre Trudeau as justice minister on April 4, 1967, triggered another phenomenon, one that came to be known as Trudeaumania. The force of it rapidly carried him to the throne. Journalist Peter C. Newman's purple prose in the *Toronto Star* demonstrates the mesmerized media's love affair with the rising political star:

> His intelligent, skull-formed face (which might have been carved in alabaster to commemorate some distant war of the crusades) is a pattern of tension, subtlety, unrest and audacity. He is a man who both in his physical presence and intellectual discourse manages to maintain a detached view of his environment, yet at the same time give the impression of being responsive to the play of political forces around him. . . . Trudeau is an agent of ferment, a critic of Canadian society, questioning its collected conventional wisdom. He mistrusts rhetoric, has only disdain for pomposity, and longs for contemporary fulfilment through experience. . . . [He makes] our national future appear very bright indeed. (*Star*, Apr 4/67)

Altogether, Trudeau's meteoric rise to prime minister took less than a year. He announced his candidacy for the Liberal leadership on February 16, 1968, at the National Press Club in Ottawa. The young justice minister had introduced a new divorce bill and an overhaul of the Criminal Code, attracting considerable public attention. For the time being, he kept his real agenda on hold. As law professor Trudeau had written in *Maclean's* in 1964, justice minister Trudeau repeated in June of 1967 that there was no need for constitutional change. "If there were a specific constitutional issue, I would be glad to give it high priority. . . . But this is not the case. In the circumstances, I feel it is much wiser to keep repeating that the constitution must be obeyed . . . that we do not feel it advisable to disrupt the fabric of the country by sitting down now and attempting to redraft it" (*Ottawa Journal*, June 29/67).

He exposed his real agenda in an address to the Canadian Bar Association on September 4, 1967. Clearly, he intended to move quickly. Having said just ten weeks before that constitutional change at that point was unnecessary and unwise, he now announced that, "Politicians and public opinion have had ample opportunity to measure the importance of the problem [of the Constitution] and the difficulties inherent in its solution. The time is ripe. The federal government declares itself ready to discuss any constitutional changes that are proposed."

What an about-face! What had happened to change his mind? The final report of the Bi-Bi Commission, which Trudeau acknowledged in the same speech would have constitutional ramifications, had not yet been published: it would not be available for another month! If Trudeau considered the time ripe, it was only because he himself was ready to move.

He casually informed the assembled lawyers that the necessary changes would be made on the assumption that Canada already had two "official" languages. His assumption of a position uncannily similar to that of the preliminary report of the Bilingualism and Biculturalism commission would typify the way he operated: first declaring a false, unproven, or shaky premise as one set in stone — then following it with the obvious conclusion that debate on the matter was either marginally important or unnecessary:

> While language is the basic instrument for preserving and developing the cultural integrity of a people, the language provisions of the British North America Act are very limited. I believe that we require a broader definition and more extensive guarantees in the matter of recognition of the two official languages. The right to learn and to use either of the two official languages should be recognized. Without this, we cannot assure every Canadian of an equal opportunity to participate in the political, cultural, economic, and social life of this country. I venture to say that, if we are able to reach agreement on this vital aspect of the over-all problem, we will have found a solution to a basic issue facing Canada today. A constitutional change

recognizing broader rights with respect to the two official languages would add a new dimension to Confederation. (*Federalism*, pp. 55–56)

"Two official languages"? The BNA Act provides that French and English are the languages of the Houses of Parliament, in Ottawa and Quebec. But there are no "two official languages" of Canada. Section 133 of the BNA Act of 1867 is explicit about this:

> Either the English or the French language may be used by any Person in the Debates of the Houses of the Parliament of Canada and of the Houses of the Legislature of Quebec; and both those Languages shall be used in the respective Records and Journals of those Houses; and either of those Languages may be used by any Person or in any Pleading or Process in or issuing from any Court of Canada established under this Act, and in or from all or any of the Courts of Quebec.
>
> The Acts of the Parliament of Canada and of the Legislature of Quebec shall be printed and published in both those languages.

In this one speech, Trudeau rewrote Canadian history. The British North America Act does not mention "the two official languages" that Trudeau cites three times in this one part of his speech. In one Brobdingnagian leap, the expert lawyer jumps to an earth-shattering conclusion: that because the BNA Act provided that French and English "may be used" and are the reporting languages in the Commons and Senate in Ottawa, the National Assembly in Quebec, and the courts of those jurisdictions respectively, the nation has "two official languages."

This speech was Trudeau's second testing ground. If this audience, his peers in the legal profession, was undisturbed by his assertions, then the road for him was clear. The Bi-Bi Commissioners had already endorsed the revolutionary vision of Canada that he would implement. Having said, without a shred of evidence, that "Canada, without being fully conscious of the fact, is passing through the greatest crisis in its history," the commissioners had elicited no uproar in the media in 1965. No one had challenged them about the fiction that Canada was already "officially bilingual." The assumptions were sold and the false premise was in place. Trudeau was in fast forward.

What questions did these lawyers ask? How could such a vision make sense for Canada? By any stretch of the imagination, only one province of the four could be described as bilingual at the time of Confederation. Six more provinces and two territories had joined since 1867. In any case, if

Canada were indeed bilingual as these promoters claimed, what then was the pressing need for constitutional language reform?

The answer is obvious. Canada was not "officially bilingual," and neither of the two so-called founding races, let alone the Fathers of Confederation, had intended such dogma to prevail in every province. Our forefathers had more sense.

In his work *Federalism and the French Canadians,* which was not published until February of the year following the Bi-Bi Commission Report, Trudeau set down the extent of the revolution he suddenly deemed necessary to save the federation.[2]

He advocated a complete transformation of every nook and cranny of English-Canadian society along racially engineered lines. In a translation of an essay he wrote in February and March of 1965 while teaching at the Institut de Récherche en Droit Public at the University of Montreal, he laid out the new game plan for Canada:

(a) At the federal level, the two languages must have absolute equality. . . . If a knowledge of English is required in the higher echelons of the civil service, then the same should be true of French. . . .

(b) At the provincial level, similar reciprocal rules must be applied. In principle, the language of the majority will be the only official one. However, when a province contains a French or English minority larger than, say, 15 per cent, or half a million inhabitants, legislative and judicial functions must be exercised in such a way that the two languages are given absolute equality. . . .

Such reforms must certainly be incorporated into constitutional law. It would not be very realistic to rely upon good will or purely political action. . . .

The reforms I am proposing must therefore be written into the constitution itself, and must be irrevocably binding upon both the federal and provincial governments. (*Federalism,* pp. 49–50)

Therefore, he warns, "The Canadian community must invest, for the defence and better appreciation of the French language, as much time, energy, and money as are required to prevent the country from breaking up" (*Federalism,* p. 32).

Finally he states: "If, on the other hand, the essential is not achieved, there is really no point in carrying the discussion any further; for this will mean that Canada will continue to be swept periodically by the storms of ethnic dispute, and will gradually become a spiritually sterile land, from which both peace and greatness have been banished" (pp. 50–51).

Grim. In this one essay, he threatened Canada's breakup or its certain sterility if the country did not embrace the bilingual revolution immediately and absolutely. What was "the essential" that he refers to that made further discussion unnecessary? What was his experience with such matters? More important, what about an open debate across the country about such radical reforms? There was none.

IT HAS BEEN SAID THAT TRUDEAU the pragmatist with a brilliant legal mind was also a philosopher king — a gifted thinker who always took a position based on logic. But is this the case? The American philosopher Charles Sanders Peirce (1839–1914), a founder of the school of pragmatism, greatly influenced William James and John Dewey. He believed that you could decipher the meaning of an idea by examining the consequences to which it would lead. In 1877 he wrote:

> Wherever there is an aristocracy, or a guild, or any association of a class of men whose interests depend, or are supposed to depend on certain propositions [beliefs] . . . cruelties always accompany this system: and when it is consistently carried out, they become atrocities of the most horrible kind in the eyes of the rational man. ("The Fixation of Belief," *Collected Papers of Charles Sanders Peirce*, Cambridge, Mass.: Harvard Univ. Press, 1935)

There has never been any critical debate on the Pearson–Trudeau vision for Canada. Nor has there been any consultation with the Canadian people about this revolutionary concept. Today we are paying for that omission.

By the time Trudeau became prime minister, history, by his own definition, had already passed him by. The anglophone population of Quebec in 1967 had already fallen below one of his "either/or" criteria for "absolute equality": it stood at 13.1 percent in the 1971 census — even less than his specified 15 percent. And what of Quebec? Was he posturing for the benefit of English Canada? Did this Quebecer really intend or expect that Quebec could and would willingly embrace "official bilingualism"?

What of Ontario? With its francophone demographics failing both of his tests, what did Trudeau see as the future for bilingualism in that province? What about the rest of Canada? Aside from New Brunswick and Quebec, every other province and territory in Canada failed his test for "absolute equality."

TODAY TRUDEAU IS STILL REGARDED as the nation's leading political scholar and thinker, a man schooled in the classics and moulded in the philosophy of the eighteenth and nineteenth centuries. Father Jean Bernier taught the young man at the Jesuit Collège Jean de Brébeuf. Of his famous student, he said:

> I taught them French, Greek and Latin literature, and although this was a typical modern French culture, it was open to other streams of thought, like Tagore, the Indian poet, and outside of class we would read and discuss, in English, Hemingway, Faulkner, Henry James, Hawthorne, and Thoreau, particularly what Thoreau said about the wilderness, which was very appealing to Canadians. We could enter easily into the mind of Locke, de Tocqueville, Acton, Jefferson. . . . I insisted not only on facts and dates, but on thoughts: the importance of the democratic spirit and the idea of federalism as a way of having political unity and cultural differences in the same country — a pluralistic society. . . . (*New Yorker* magazine, 1969, cited in Radwanski, p. 56)

Of his own philosophy, Trudeau himself wrote in August 1967: "My political action, or my theory — insomuch as I can be said to have one — can be expressed very simply: create counterweights. As I have explained, it was because of the federal government's weakness that I allowed myself to be catapulted into it" (*Federalism*, p. xxiii).

But what does this mean? A balanced federation? Perhaps. Paralysis when necessary to guard against excess? Could be. Or are these just words tossed out in the full knowledge that they will eventually take their place in history as holy writ?

All that remains for certain today is Trudeau the cultural engineer. He is no liberal thinker in the tradition of Thomas Jefferson, Thomas Paine, John Locke, or the philosopher he tells us he so admired, John Stuart Mill. As we shall see, Trudeau in the crunch does not champion individual rights over those of the state.

Since cultural and racial engineering formed the cornerstones of his thinking, as well as the many constitutional compromises he made throughout his political career, there is little place in his world for dissent and the individual who runs afoul of his centralist dogma. Engineering the balance in society is the moral imperative — the theory of counterweights and balance that Montesquieu set out in his *Spirit of the Laws*. The absolutist Trudeau exposes himself as legalistic and interventionist. In his great credo, Montesquieu, whom Trudeau often cited as one of his greatest influences, wrote, "There are two sorts of tyranny: one real, which arises from oppression; *the other is seated in opinion, as is sure to be left whenever those who govern establish things shocking to the existing ideas of a nation"* [emphasis mine] ("Of Tyranny," *Spirit*, Book XIX, S.3, p. 293).

Trudeau greatly admired professor Harold Laski of the London School of Economics. In 1966 he said Laski was "the most stimulating and powerful influence" he had ever encountered. The renowned socialist professor set out his theory in his most celebrated work, *A Grammar of Politics*:

> The necessarily federal character of society; the incompatibility of the sovereign state with that economic world order so painfully struggling to be born; the antithesis between individual property rights in the essential means of production and the fulfilment of the democratic idea; the thesis that liberty is a concept devoid of real meaning except in the context of equality. . . .
>
> There cannot, in a word, be democracy, unless there is socialism. . . . (quoted in David Somerville, *Trudeau Revealed*, p. 196)

Along with his vision of a bilingual nation, Trudeau's Charter of Rights and Freedoms stands as the great centrepiece of his legacy. Here's what he wrote in 1965:

> The state may resist certain pressures, but not others; it may work to transform the basic situation so that migrations go in one direction and not in another. But the state must take great care not to infringe on the conscience of the individual. I believe that, in the last analysis, a human being in the privacy of his own mind has the exclusive authority to choose his own scale of values and to decide which forces will take precedence over others. A good constitution is one that does not prejudge any of these questions, but leaves citizens free to orient their human destinies as they see fit. (*Federalism*, p. 11)

At first glance, he may appear to embrace the philosophy of John Stuart Mill's *On Liberty*, that the greatest danger lies in *any* kind of interference with individual freedom of thought. But is Trudeau deceiving us about priorities? What is he really saying?

His premise for a free society is that the state must be empowered to "work to transform the basic situation." Only in the "last analysis [does] a human being in the privacy of his own mind [have] exclusive authority." This is Trudeau's refuge. Freedom is strictly confined to this last resort. His vision of freedom allows for all manner of state propaganda and intervention as long as it does not affect a person's conscience.[3]

Yet who is to judge this distinction? In this context, the collective and central authority exists as the dominant force people must endure. The man who wrote these lines is not a liberal thinker. He is one who promotes obedience. This is the discipline of the Jesuit-trained mind. In Trudeau's world, there is no such thing as individual property rights. As Canadians were to discover in the years that followed, property rights would not be included in their constitution.

What's missing in this philosophy reveals the most about Trudeau's theory. The purpose of a constitution is never defined in terms of protecting the individual from the tyranny of the state. Citizens are merely granted rights by the state. They enjoy liberty under which they are "free to orient their destinies" only. "Orient"? Within such a philosophy, individual action is limited. Can such a statement be interpreted to mean that citizens may fashion or pursue their destinies? There is no room in Trudeau's philosophy for individual freedom, beyond the nearly negligible one of non-interference with an individual's conscience. This is not individual freedom; it is tyranny — constitutionalized. And it is certainly not the philosophy of John Stuart Mill.

This is the difficulty we face when dealing with Trudeau the philosopher rather than Trudeau in action. After reading the eventual result of his thinking, the Charter of Rights and Freedoms, we cannot doubt that he sees a strong role for the state, a lesser role for Parliament, and an oligarchy to rule — namely the Supreme Court of Canada.

His call for official bilingualism required that the Canadian psyche be profoundly changed. He understood very well the consequences that could arise from such a radical reform, but pressed on regardless. In 1967, as justice minister, he wrote: "Throughout history all great reformers were sooner or later betrayed by the excessive fidelity of their disciples. When a reform starts to be universally popular, it is more than likely that it has already become reactionary, and free men must then oppose it" (*Federalism*, p. xxii).

Agreed. But how far was Trudeau prepared to go? Revolution? Violence? We can see that he intends that official bilingualism extend far beyond federal institutions and far beyond the recommendations of the Bi-Bi Commission. So, what was the limit? In August 1967, before the final commission report, he wrote that provincial constitutions "would also allow parity between the English and French language in all federal institutions, and the same parity would eventually be negotiated with other provinces." Elsewhere he noted, "The constitution must be so worded that any French-speaking community, anywhere in Canada, can fully enjoy its linguistic rights" (*Federalism*, p. 48). What then of the legislation's bilingual districts?

Today Canadians automatically accept that Trudeau's greatest constitutional contribution has been the Charter of Rights and Freedoms. When he addressed the Canadian Bar Association on September 4, 1967, he reversed his position, calling for immediate action. In fact, he accelerated his agenda:

> We have reached the conclusion that the basis most likely to find a wide degree of acceptance, one that is in itself a matter calling for urgent attention, is a constitutional Bill of Rights — a Bill that would guarantee the fundamental freedoms of the citizen from interference, whether federal or provincial, and that would have a high degree of permanence in that neither Parliament nor the Legislatures would be able to modify its terms by the ordinary legislative process. (*Federalism*, p. 54)

There it all was in one neat package: a Bill of Rights as the premise for repatriation, with a cultural vision of the country. Rather than the agenda of a minister of justice, this was one of a prime minister in waiting, ready to move at a moment's notice.

The essay he wrote in 1965 was translated and published in 1968. The nation slept through it.

After a colourful and suspenseful election at the Liberal convention, Pierre Elliott Trudeau became Canada's fifteenth prime minister just before 8:00 P.M. on Saturday, April 6, 1968. On April 19, he was sworn into office. On April 22, he called a general election for June 25, the day following St. Jean Baptiste Day celebrations in Quebec.

This new prime minister was proving himself a master political choreographer. On election day the headline of the *Toronto Star* declared, "Trudeau Defies Separatists." Frank Jones reported the story in glowing terms:

> Prime Minister Pierre Elliott Trudeau last night stood his ground against raging separatists after almost being hit by a flying bottle in a bloody disturbance that erupted as he reviewed the St. Jean Baptiste Day parade. The violence, described as the worst in Montreal's history since the anti-conscription riots of World War II, saw 43 policemen and 80 civilians injured and 290 persons arrested.

As about 1,200 police fought pitched battles and rioters in the shadows of Lafontaine Park, opposite the reviewing stand, a youth broke out of the crowd and hurled a soft drink bottle filled with oil and gasoline at the Prime Minister. RCMP officers urged Trudeau to leave the stand as other dignitaries had done. Trudeau grabbed up his coat from the floor. Then defiantly he threw it down, swung his arm down in a gesture of supreme disdain and anger, and sat down again. (*Star*, June 25/68)

His showmanship caught the public imagination. Accordingly, Robert Stanfield's Conservatives paid dearly for their wishy-washy campaign. They were slaughtered in the polls. Trudeau won 45.5 percent to the Conservatives' 27.3 percent of the vote. The NDP won a negligible 17 percent. The reign of the philosopher king had truly begun.

But there was much more to the Conservative loss. Robert Lorne Stanfield had been in trouble since the Tory leadership convention in September of 1967. On September 9, Stanfield had taken over the leadership in a bloody battle that would permanently divide the Conservative Party. Dalton Camp, president of the party, performed as giant killer. As head of the "Maritime mafia," he led the attack that toppled the Right Hon. John George Diefenbaker. "Dief the Chief," who had led the Tories to three election victories, was crushed at the convention by Camp's Red Tories.

It was a battle that never should have taken place. The Red Tories were not conservatives. Their radical vision of Canada bore no resemblance whatsoever to the vision of Sir John A. Macdonald, the father of the Conservative Party and the first prime minister of the country. Camp's Conservatives pointedly removed themselves from Canada's history and heritage. They rejected outright the concept of Canada as the Fathers of Confederation had laid it down in the British North America Act of 1867. They believed in a Canada based on two founding races and two founding cultures.

Traditional Conservatives disagreed with this concept, but in August of 1967 at the party's "Thinkers Conference," the new concept gained flesh and foundation. The "Montmorency Resolution" contained this clause:

That Canada is and should be a federal state. That Canada is composed of two founding peoples (deux nations) with historic rights who have been joined by people from many lands. That the constitution should be such as to permit and encourage their full and harmonious growth and development in equality throughout Canada. (quoted in *Stanfield*, p. 185)[4]

The "Montmorency Resolution" proved to be a time-bomb — a dividing line that would plague the Conservative Party and prevent it from ever rising to greatness. Dualism with all its dangers of Quebec separation could not begin to match Pierre Trudeau's vision, flawed as it was by the same hypocrisy. At least Trudeau's vision offered the "honest" concept of a single nation.

Stanfield himself, however, claimed that he never supported the *deux nations* concept: that it was a misunderstanding that grew out of a complex interpretation of one Conservative who attended the Montmorency Falls conference. Marcel Faribault, a financier and close associate of Stanfield, had delivered a barnburner of a speech at the conference in defence of the *deux nations* thesis: "The question of two nations is no longer debatable in the province of Quebec. . . . We might translate it in French 'two nations.' You will translate it 'two founding races, or people,' if you want. We cannot say 'people' because 'people' in our case doesn't mean 'nation,' the same way as 'nation' in English does not mean *nation* [in French]" (*Stanfield*, p. 218).

Stanfield's performance during the campaign was pathetic. He failed miserably to deal with Faribault head on. *Globe* reporter Geoffrey Stevens, who accompanied Stanfield on the hustings, said, "Stanfield did not campaign on a *deux nations* platform in the election of 1968" (Ibid., p. 219).[5] Maybe so, but others disagree with Stevens's perception. In 1983 Hugh Segal, the Tory backroom pundit, wrote a book with Nathan Nurgitz in which he declaimed: "There can be no question, for example, that . . . the Stanfield campaign in 1968 offered a view of Canada based on two founding peoples, and the need for a fundamental duality in the country that would respond to them . . ." (*No Small Measure*, pp. 41–42).

During the election campaign, Stanfield protested that his vision of Canada was unfairly judged: he stated that he never supported Faribault's bravado at Montmorency. In mid-June of 1968 the Liberals took out a full-page ad in Calgary that accused Stanfield and Faribault of supporting the *deux nations* theory. That same night a stung Stanfield fumed in front of a Tory audience of 2,000 in Saskatoon: "I have never advocated two nations. I believe in one Canada. I have never advanced special status. . . . No province should be offered authority that is not offered to all the provinces . . ." (*Stanfield*, p. 220).

Fair enough. But the record is fuzzy. Here's what he said in the House of Commons on October 8, 1971: "I wish to state, Mr. Speaker, that the emphasis we have given to multiculturalism in no way constitutes an attack on the basic duality of our country" (*House of Commons Debates, Hansard,* Oct 8/71).

With the Conservatives in such disarray, all Trudeau had to do was appear prime-ministerial. In 1968 the Red Tories had obligingly made mincemeat of themselves for him. He merely ensured that the duplicity the Conservatives were selling stuck to their leader. No one compared that duplicity to the Liberals' policy of Official Bilingualism, Trudeau's own solution to what ailed the nation. And he had help from strange quarters: former Prime Minister John Diefenbaker was rightly enraged at the Tories' betrayal of their own tradition. He recognized the idea of *deux nations* as a blueprint for the country's eventual demise. In one of history's fine ironies, the Chief almost ended up campaigning for the Liberals.

Notes

1   In Trudeau's book *Memoirs* (1993), he reflected on Pearson's announcement that he would retire: "Let me be very clear that I did not feel at all personally affected by this development. . . . The idea of running for the leadership myself never crossed my mind, not even for a split second" (p. 84).

2   Trudeau recalls his early dedication (fanaticism?) to bilingualism a quarter century later in his book *Memoirs*: "Another subject demanded my attention at the beginning of my mandate, and that was the status of the French language within federal institutions. I had been aware of this problem for a long time. Early on, along with all my contemporaries in Quebec, I had been encouraged during my high school years to campaign for, successively, bilingual postage stamps, bilingual money, bilingual cheques, and other 'table scraps,' to borrow the phrase used by André Laurendeau in an editorial in *Le Devoir*, which shows just how complete was the contempt in which the federal authorities of that period held the language spoken by one-third of the Canadian population" (pp. 118–19).

3   From Trudeau's *Memoirs* (1993): "But thanks to two French thinkers, Jacques Maritain and Emmanuel Mounier, I never came to believe in the doctrine of absolute liberalism. . . . But I deepened my knowledge of their thought during my stay in France

[in 1946]. It was there that I became a follower of personalism, a philosophy that reconciles the individual and society. The person, according to these two teachers, is the individual enriched with a social conscience, integrated into the life of the communities around him and the economic context of his time, both of which must in turn give persons the means to exercise their freedom of choice. It was thus that the fundamental notion of justice came to stand alongside that of freedom in my political thought" (p. 40).

Pragmatic self-interest in an existentialist brew alongside a "fundamental notion of justice"? How so? Surely justice is an ideal above "personalism"? Lazy thinking.

4 In his 1969 book *The Night of the Knives*, Tory MP Robert C. Coates recounts a different version of events. In addition, he names Dalton Camp, the Conservative Party president, as Diefenbaker's "assassin" and co-author of the Montmorency Resolution.

The proposal, developed by a select group of elitists, gained the approval of committees before the delegates defeated it. Diefenbaker had entered the leadership race solely to fight this vision of the country.

5 Aside from the Western Canadian press, the Conservative and Liberal press generally lined up against Diefenbaker with a vengeance. Stevens typified these. He supported the Faribault concept. In his biography of Stanfield, he writes of the Montmorency Resolution: "Was there really anything so terribly frightening about a political party that thought the preamble to a new constitution should recognize the indisputable fact that Canada is composed of 'two founding peoples' (or, in French, *deux nations*) . . ?" (Stanfield, p. 218).

3

"Alas! I Am Turning into a God"[1]
— 1968 to 1977

ON JUNE 27, 1968, only two days after Trudeau's landslide election and eighty-two days after he became prime minister, Official Bilingualism was floundering. The ruckus started in a small way. In the Montreal district of Saint-Léonard, the school board passed a resolution making French the sole language of instruction for all grade one students.

By 1969, riots and violent confrontations broke out over the issue, with the police resorting to tear gas in some demonstrations. The parents of children of Italian descent insisted that their children's right to be taught in English be respected.

Under Bill 63, introduced on October 23, 1969, Quebec denied its English-speaking citizens their English-language rights for the first time. It marked a milestone, the first legislation ever introduced to protect and promote the French language. It established French as the primary language of instruction, but parents were assured they could choose in which of the two languages their children would be taught. The government had respected these rights since the Treaty of Paris of 1763. Bill 63 provided that English-speaking children could be tested to assess whether or not their knowledge of their mother tongue was "sufficient" to justify continued English-language education; however, the minister maintained the discretionary power to "require that a school board reassign pupils on the basis of the results obtained by the pupils in the tests."

Within one week of the bill's passage, the Front du Québec français was formed and a protesting crowd of 20,000 marched on Quebec's National Assembly. A hundred people were arrested and five police officers injured. The Quebec nationalists rejected the legislation on the grounds that the bill gave the English language status equal to that of French. Alarmed by the riots and loud protests from all quarters, and eager to justify their actions, the Quebec government appointed the Gendron Commission to investigate. Its report would not be tabled until 1972.

Historians Robert Bothwell, Ian Drummond, and John English wrote: "The English-speaking Quebeckers reacted with alarm at the threat to rights and institutions they had always enjoyed and for which, as private citizens and as taxpayers, they had paid" (Bothwell et al., *Canada Since 1945*, p. 366).

As far as Quebec nationalists were concerned, the legislation represented a sell-out to anglophones. The result was the virtual destruction of Jean-Jacques Bertrand's Union Nationale government in the 1970 election by the Liberals under Robert Bourassa. In fact, Bourassa rode the wave of anti-anglophone sentiment to power.

Bill 63 offended the English heritage of Quebec. Bertrand's move reversed history. The first British governor of Quebec, James Murray (1722–94), had slammed the English exploitation of Quebec in 1764:

> Little, very little, will content the New Subjects but nothing will satisfy the Licentious Fanatiks Trading here, but the expulsion of the Canadians [the Québécois] who are perhaps the bravest and the best race upon the Globe, a Race, who cou'd they be indulged with a few priveledges which the Laws of England deny to Roman Catholicks at home, wou'd soon get the better of every National Antipathy to their Conquerors and become the most faithful and most useful set of Men in this American Empire. . . .
>
> . . . Certain I am, unless Canadians are admitted on Jurys, and are allowed Judges and Lawyers who understand their Language his Majesty will lose the greatest part of this Valuable people. . . . (*Canadian History in Documents, 1763–1966*, p. 3)

How the tables had turned in nearly two centuries.

Bill 63 was later amended. Armed with the 1971 census statistics, the Gendron Commission noted the demographic deterioration of the franco-phone populations across Canada. Then the government of a young Robert

Bourassa took the step that would shake Canada to its roots. He repealed the 1969 legislation, Bill 63, and eliminated parental choice in Quebec by introducing Bill 22.

Through this bill, the Quebec government declared French the only official language of the province. On behalf of the French-speaking residents of Quebec, Bourassa's government declared war on its English-speaking citizens.

The new legislation flew in the face of the constitutional provisions of the British North America Act. It stipulated that admissions to English-language schools depended entirely on whether or not a child's maternal language was English. The law now divided Quebec education along racial lines.

As expected, more language fireworks erupted. English Canada demanded that the bill be disallowed. The Constitution gave the prime minister and the federal government the authority to overturn such legislation as unconstitutional.

In the crunch, the federal government paused and then waffled. Finally Prime Minister Pierre Trudeau declined to exercise his prerogative. With the highest power in the land behind him, Section 90 of the British North America Act of 1867, Canada's foundation constitutional document, he refused to use it:

> The following Provisions of this Act respecting the Parliament of Canada, namely, — the Provisions relating to Appropriation and Tax Bills, the Recommendation of Money Votes, the Assent to Bills, *the Disallowance of Acts*, and Signification of Pleasure on Bills reserved, — *shall extend and apply to the legislatures of the several Provinces*. . . . [emphasis mine] (S. 90)

Journalists and historians across the country have generally accepted Trudeau's own pretext that he could not disallow legislation that was, as he put it, merely foolish or unjust. This lame excuse represented an even more serious abrogation of responsibility by the fourth estate. The prime minister's dismissal notice would be a costly indulgence for the whole nation — perhaps even a fatal one. His obfuscation on this most fundamental tenet of the federation, the equality of its citizens before the law, triggered a cover-up the media would perpetuate for thirty years.

Quebec nationalism had won a tremendous victory. And they had done it with the complicity of a so-called "federalist" provincial party, Premier Robert Bourassa's Liberals. The new premier recognized in Trudeau a weak leader. Now he knew he was licensed to make further kills. Years later, in

December 1988, the same Robert Bourassa advanced another major step toward an entirely unilingual Quebec under the law, a Quebec of which he could proudly boast, "For the first time since 1759, English then lost its official status in Quebec; and it was me, and my government, who did it" (*Sun*, Feb. 2/92).

While on the provincial level Quebec crafted counter measures to the Pearson–Trudeau vision of bilingualism, Trudeau introduced the *Official Languages Act (Canada), 1968–69* in the House of Commons on October 17, 1968. The legislation received Royal Assent in July of 1969. Author and *Toronto Star* columnist Richard Gwyn hit an accurate chord: "Bilingualism is to Trudeau as the CPR was to John A. Macdonald . . ." (*Northern Magus*, p. 220).

The new act dramatically extended the use of both English and French to all federal government services and to the NCC (National Capital Region). According to Sections 12 to 18, the federal government could proclaim "from time to time . . . one or more federal bilingual districts in a province, and alter the limits of any bilingual districts so established." The law provided for the establishment of a Bilingual Districts Advisory Board (BDAB) as a means to recommend which regions should be designated bilingual. These were supposed to be chosen, again by a law that required that "at least ten percent" of the total population in that district speak the minority language as a mother tongue. The arbitrary criterion "significant demand" and not the more discretionary and political "where numbers warrant" governed the legislation. In the end, it was such a muddle that the politicians could do whatever they wanted.

The first BDAB was established in Ottawa on February 12, 1970. Its report was tabled in the House of Commons in May 1971. Immediately an obvious problem arose. The board based its work on the decennial census figures of 1961; the 1971 census statistics were not available. Planned obsolescence?

Undaunted, the government established the second BDAB on May 25, 1972. Prime Minister Lester Pearson chose the team.

A noted academic and later principal of the University of Toronto's Erindale College was appointed its chairman. Paul Fox had served on the first BDAB, and from 1964 to 1968 on the Advisory Committee of the Bi-Bi Commission.

Though the talents of the board members ranged across the fields of law, linguistics, demography, geography, education, community service, sociology, political science, and public administration, none of the members brought any business or practical credentials to the task.

As with the Bi-Bi Commission, board members were also appointed according to a balance between the two "founding races." Again, too, all the selections strongly favoured Central Canada and the French and English heritage of the country.

More than three and a half years of intense struggle over the ambiguities and unworkable terminology and mandate of the Official Languages Act followed. In a rambling 272-page document brimming with contradictions and frustration, the board managed to publish its first and only BDAB report in October 1975. It reflected how hopelessly at odds its members were with each other and with the most fundamental concepts of Canada:

236. Although the Board was divided in its opinions about the wisdom of recommending bilingual districts in Quebec, notably Montreal, nearly all of the members recognized that the existence of the French language is in jeopardy in Quebec and were loath to augment the pressure upon it.

237. We also believed that it would be completely contrary to the basic intent of the Official Languages Act, which is designed to establish the equal status of French and English, if we were to make recommendations that were disadvantageous to the survival of French in the province which is its essential base. We fully recognized the validity of the argument that in terms of long-run survival it is the French language which needs protection in Quebec rather than English.

238. *Confronted by these facts as well as by the obligation to fulfil its mandate, the Board grappled with the conflicting implications that emerged from applying the Official Languages Act throughout a country as diverse as Canada.* [emphasis mine]

In one stroke, the board members confirmed that Official Bilingualism could not work. They warned that it should not be applied to Quebec. At this point, the government knew the Pearson–Trudeau vision of Canada was a fraud.

Alas, in the end the board elected to play politics. They chose to keep the myth alive and to enforce bilingualism according to the federal government's view of Canada.

In desperation, they did try to define Official Bilingualism. The last paragraph of Chapter 5, "Issues and Rationale," scrapped the policy in Quebec. In its place the board struggled with a vision that would torture the nation for a generation:

For all these reasons a majority of our members, after lengthy discussion and debate in the Board, have arrived at the conclusions which are presented subsequently as recommendations for the provision of federal services to the official language minority in Quebec [English]. In making these recommendations the majority of the Board believes that it has been consistent in applying throughout Canada the criteria which the Board took as its prime concern, namely, the desirability of providing by some means federal services in their own language to all the official language minority groups of reasonable magnitude. (p. 36)

Whatever did this mean in practice?

Board member W. Harry Hickman dissented from the report and exposed the sorry state of affairs. He recommended that metropolitan Montreal be designated as a bilingual district. This made some sense: "It is a bilingual area; indeed to many people it is the very symbol of Canadian bilingualism. The English mother tongue minority group consist of 593,395 persons who comprise 21.7 per cent of the total population" (p. 211).

If the board members could not agree to designate metropolitan Montreal as a bilingual district, what other Canadian city could possibly meet the policy's criteria? The BDAB board proved beyond any doubt that the cornerstone of equity, the law pertaining to bilingual districts, did not meet the Trudeau test of *Realpolitik*. And where was Trudeau as the tragedy unfolded? Silent.

On and on the board struggled. They'd been at it for years. In their report, they wrote they resisted the recommendation of Keith Spicer, Trudeau's first Official Languages Commissioner. He had advised them, as the board phrased it, "that one could rely exclusively or even extensively on Section 9 (2) of the Act to furnish bilingual services."

This section gave the government a free hand to apply bilingualism to any area in Canada where it determined a political need constituted "significant demand." Against the BDAB's recommendations, Spicer won. In a final step, the designation of bilingual districts required under the Official Languages Act of 1969 was scrapped.[2] Very simply and quickly, outside Parliament and the rule of law, Canadians lost any chance to see that Official Bilingualism would be equitably managed — and seen to be so — across the country. In other words, Trudeau's government ignored the bilingual districts entirely, ignored the law.

People's mistrust was justified. By 1976, Toronto, with a deteriorating francophone mother-tongue population of 1.4 percent, was declared a bilingual district. Edmonton, on the other hand, with a francophone population of 3 percent, remained undesignated; so did Quebec City with its 2.5 percent anglophone population.

Many questions remain unanswered to this day about how bilingualism was implemented. Did the government intend that BDAB would fail? Who instructed Keith Spicer to recommend that whole chunks of the law be ignored? Certainly high-profile public servants are not licensed to frolic this way on their own.

In the fall of 1979, Spicer boobed. The wiliest of Canada's media manipulators let it slip out that, as far as he was concerned, Official Bilingualism was a scam. Its real purpose, he admitted, was "to convince the French that we were making serious reforms and to convince the English that we were not making serious reforms" (*Star*, Oct 19/79).

W̲HILE LANGUAGE LAWS were being crafted in Quebec and Canada at the behest of Prime Ministers Pearson and Trudeau and the Bi-Bi Commissioners, another real upheaval was building. Rumblings in Quebec marked the beginning of the FLQ crisis. The structural engineers of this brave new Canada welcomed the news as heaven-sent. So did the media, though for different reasons. Now the country's press corps could imbue the term *crisis* with real meaning and attach it to a specific event, unlike the "Quiet Revolution" of the 1960s. They dubbed the unrest "the October Crisis of 1970."

On October 5, 1970, members of the Front de libération du Québec (FLQ) kidnapped James Cross, the British Trade Commissioner in Montreal. On October 10, they kidnapped a second minister in the Quebec government, the minister of labour, Pierre Laporte, as he played with his children outside his home. The media pounced on this second act of terrorism as proof of a large-scale insurrection in the making. On Friday morning, October 16, at 3:00 A.M., the federal government responded, invoking the War Measures Act, which suspended civil liberties across the country. The police moved in, now empowered to take any measures they deemed appropriate to quell the unrest. They could arrest and detain citizens without notifying them beforehand of the reasons why or the charges against them. On the day after the military declaration, October 17, 1970, the radicals retaliated by assassinating Laporte.

Pandemonium ensued.

Thirty-seven-year-old Robert Bourassa, the young premier of Quebec, turned to the federal government for help. The Canadian army moved in. Truckloads of soldiers rolled down the ominously quiet streets of Montreal.

The city immediately deployed the municipal gendarmerie in full force: "All the police in the Montreal area charged, head down. . . . Given the right to break down any doors and arrest whomsoever they chose, they struck in almost every quarter. . . . It is impossible to give a list of the persons who have been apprehended during the last few hours . . ." (*La Presse*, Oct 16/70, quoted in Lévesque, *Memoirs*, pp. 246-47).

More than two decades later, the question still nags: what really happened? Was there really an "apprehended insurrection" afoot? A military coup in the making? Could the government of the day justify suspending all rights in a democracy, including habeas corpus? What reason could anyone give for arresting artists, writers, union leaders, and any other dissident known to the authorities and keeping so many of them under lock and key for weeks on end?

Federal minister Jean Marchand said, "We know there is an organization that has thousands of rifles and machine guns in their possession, and dynamite enough, about 2,000 pounds, to blow up the heart of the city of Montreal" (Lévesque, *Memoirs*, p. 247). To this day, no one has ever found conclusive proof of any such conspiracy. The whole business adds up to a puzzling and sorry page in Canadian history.

Of the 465 Quebecers arrested, only 62 were ever brought to trial and only 20 were eventually convicted.[3] Cross's captors were never brought to trial. In exchange for the trade commissioner's life, and permission for the terrorists to read their manifesto *Vive La Révolution Québécois*, the government granted them safe conduct out of the country to live in exile. With the federal government's blessings, the murderers headed first to Castro's Cuba and later were given asylum in France. None was ever punished. None was executed.

Polls of the period show most Canadians were delighted with the government's actions. A Gallup poll confirmed that 86 percent of the population supported the Bourassa–Trudeau pact to settle the situation. Journalists and other observers conveniently ignored the fact that the FLQ crisis had proved a dangerous precedent to the government; provoking a fierce minority could pay big political dividends when it wanted to appear tough. Pressed by the media after the crisis, Trudeau was asked how far he would have been willing to go. In a frightening testament to the times, he looked directly into the television camera and said simply, "Just watch me."

The matter did not end with the fall of the Bourassa government on November 15, 1976. When the Parti Québécois came to power under René Lévesque in the spring of 1971, the new government could not find any of the 30,000 files collected on individuals or the 6,000 files on organizations at the CAD (Centre d'archives et de documentation).

Although the FLQ crisis was a black page in Canadian history, by revolutionary standards the crisis itself amounted to a piffle compared to events in the rest of the world. But the years that followed were horrible for many citizens in Quebec who had lost their jobs and reputations. The War Measures Act was a mistake, and it sowed a bitter harvest for national unity.

The issue lives on today. On April 3, 1992, Marc-Andre Bédard, former justice minister in the Lévesque government, hinted that the 30,000 dossiers might not have been shredded as shown in a ceremony on television on March 31, 1977. Asked to confirm these were *the* files, Bédard said they "were returned where they should have been." Asked the direct question by the media, Bédard fudged. He said he must observe a "certain reserve" (*Star*, Apr 4/92).

Documents released on January 30, 1992, under the Access to Information Act revealed that the FLQ crisis was exaggerated and that the RCMP had opposed the passage of the War Measures Act (*Star*/CP, Jan 30/92). In the spring of 1992, more came to light as meeting minutes were released linking the Trudeau Cabinet to more manipulations (*GM*, May 27/92). As the mould of history accumulates, little if anything has surfaced to excuse any or all of the key players for the way they manhandled democracy.

NOT EVERYTHING TRUDEAU'S GOVERNMENT did in the early years was so discoloured by such blatant manipulation of the citizenry. The Victoria Conference of 1971, unsuccessful though it was, stands out as a beacon of what might have been an important step in a positive direction.

The conference of first ministers (FMC) was held in Victoria, British Columbia, in June 1971. All the provincial premiers and the prime minister had agreed to negotiate the conditions for the "patriation" of Canada's constitution, the British North America Act, from Westminster in Britain. The collapse of the conference ended both that dream for the time being as well as a second project, the "Canadian Constitutional Charter, 1971."

But the conference's failure had more far-reaching effects. It ended serious deliberation between the provinces and any prospect of reducing the role of government in Canadian life. The participants had discussed dividing the country anew into five regions, to better represent the population and to better manage the economy.

Initially, then-premier Robert Bourassa agreed to the Victoria Charter. During the ten-day waiting period before the agreement vested, a storm brewed in Quebec. Two close advisors to Bourassa, Claude Morin and Claude Castonguay, threw a monkey wrench into the package. They claimed they were not satisfied that their province had been offered sufficient federal power.[4]

On their advice, Bourassa reversed his position. Without his agreement, the Victoria vision died on June 23, 1971. Its formula would haunt constitutional debate time and again in the years to come. In retrospect, perhaps it is miraculous that the conference accomplished so much before it was scrapped. For the dissenters in Bourassa's court, however, a vital precedent had been established — the notion that some sort of equal status was required between the two founding races.

Trudeau accepted the failure, concluding, "If there isn't agreement, then that's the end of the matter, for now, or for a while, I hope" (Bothwell et al., p. 362). What did he mean by "a while" and "the matter"?

Not much, it seemed. Within four months he had returned to the subject, hammering away at his vision of Canada. On October 8, he introduced multiculturalism into the House of Commons as government policy: "A policy of multiculturalism within a bilingual framework commends itself to the government as the most suitable means of assuring the cultural freedom of Canadians." Thus he proposed to broach another constitutional frontier — a major one, especially in political terms. All the effort to date had been concentrated on the two founding races. There was work to be done to include the other neglected cultures that made up the Canadian mosaic. He proposed more racial and ethnic tampering.

On July 5, 1977, "the Committee of the Privy Council, having had before it a report of the Right Honourable Pierre Elliott Trudeau, the prime minister, concerning Canadian unity," appointed a new commission "to be known as the *Task Force on Canadian Unity*" (*Task Force*, p. 281). The Clerk of the Privy Council orchestrating government activities was Michael Pitfield. The commission was co-chaired by the Hon. Jean-Luc Pépin and the Hon. John Robarts. Aside from the "three chief advisors," among the names of "those who were invited to our private meetings to speak on specific aspects of the Canadian unity debate" were many names that would become media celebrities in the coming years: André Bernard, Robert Bourassa, Edward Broadbent, Alan Cairns, Claude Castonguay, Joseph Clark (opposition leader), Thomas Courchene, Marie-Josée Drouin, Davidson Dunton (Bi-Bi Commissioner), Peter Hogg, Marcel Masse, Gordon Robertson, Claude Ryan, Richard Simeon, Keith Spicer, Paul Tellier, and Max Yalden. Reed Scowen was the executive director of the commission.

The Pépin–Robarts Task Force — aka the Pépin–Robarts Commission — was the strangest of all royal commissions. On September 1, 1977, after their first full meeting, the commissioners issued a communiqué:

The Task Force . . . recognizes that Canada and its present federal system are under great stress. The creation of the Task Force is itself a testimony to this. All regions of Canada are reflecting and expressing this malaise. The most pressing questions are being raised in Quebec and the Task Force intends to give these high priority. Nevertheless, the concerns of the other regions are vitally important and will be given our full attention.

Again the threat of a crisis. But was this a task force to confirm assumptions or was it an open inquiry? While required to "listen, attempting to understand" from a sort of citizens' forum, the commissioners stated, in their terms of reference, the responsibility to:

c) contribute to the knowledge and general awareness of the public of the initiatives and views of the Commissioners concerning Canadian unity.

The commission's final "observations and recommendations" were first published on January 25, 1979, under the title *A Future Together*. The recommendations represented a radical departure from the Pearson–Trudeau vision of a bilingual Canada, whether totally bilingual or only bilingual in English-speaking Canada.

To begin with, the commission retained the provisions of the BNA Act — save and except for Quebec. "Elsewhere," the commissioners recommended "the usual language or languages of work normally used in the province in which the central institution is operating."

They made no mention of bilingual districts. Instead, they made recommendations on the basis of "significant demand, and to the extent that it is feasible to provide such services."

The commission virtually endorsed Quebec's Bill 101. It justified undermining Canada's constitution, the BNA Act. In Quebec, it recommended, "each child of a French-speaking or English-speaking minority is entitled to an education in his or her province, wherever numbers warrant."

In March 1979, the body issued a second publication, *A Time to Speak*, which really should have been the first report. In fact, it was identified as their third report in its text, and so should of course have followed the second report, which turned out to be a glossary entitled *Coming to Terms*. This was the real third report. A veritable paper chase! The strange chronology of the reports was never explained.

In *A Time to Speak*, the commissioners reported on "what the Canadians who appeared before us had to say about their country, its problems and its prospects." Of the 308 pages of the report, 32 were devoted to two chapters on Quebec: "A disaffected province" (chapter 12) and "The sovereignty-association option?" (chapter 13). They loosed a very different vision of Canada from that of Trudeau and Pearson on the country. Trudeau had selected the commissioners, so he knew their backgrounds. Academics Gérald A. Beaudoin and Ronald L. Watts were hardly unknowns. Solange Chaput-Rolland and Jean-Luc Pépin were political brethren.

A FEDERAL ELECTION was long overdue. Trudeau had worn out his welcome. No matter when he called it, the election was going to be a close one, just like the election in 1972, when the Liberals had won by only two seats. Finally, in 1979 the prime minister dropped the writ for May 22.

The Pépin–Robarts report accorded more with the thinking of the winners, the Conservatives and Prime Minister Joe Clark. Meanwhile, in Quebec, the provincial government was busy at work with its own counter-attack on the federal measures, just as they had done in response to the earlier Bi-Bi Cultural Commission report.

Bill 101, which succeeded Bill 22, was introduced by the PQ government of René Lévesque on December 26, 1977. It declared that no municipality with less than a 50-percent anglophone population had to offer English services to the public. It amounted to a declaration that French was the only official language of Quebec. Lévesque's Bill 101 breached Section 133 of the BNA Act, just as Bourassa's Bill 22 had done.

And, for a second time, Trudeau declined to exercise the provision to disallow these laws that offended Canada's constitution. On October 7, 1977, he told his critics, "Frankly, I don't want to give Mr. Lévesque the choice of timing and issues" (Gwyn, *Northern Magus*, p. 248).

Trudeau's failure to disallow Quebec's Bill 22 and Bill 101 would lead to the biggest explosion in Canadian history. The Quebec separatists now controlled the language agenda and, largely, the vision of Canada. From this point on, the policy of Official Bilingualism applied only to English-speaking Canada. The federal government had forfeited any credibility it might have held in the arena of language equality. Where were the media?

In his memoirs (1986), the Quebec premier writes about his motives:

But the Quebec language problem — a terribly localized problem, for it is shared by only a tiny handful of protracted or crypto-colonies and shackled minorities — is absurd. It's the problem of an idiom that is not at home in its own house, like a spineless landlord who lets himself be locked in the basement by noisy, self-confident tenants. And it will only extricate itself the day it stands up, mounts the stairs, and calmly takes over the living room and the kitchen, imposing its own recipes and its own choice of the furniture and curtains. (p. 258)

Among the very few to challenge Trudeau's agenda was his defence minister, James Richardson from Winnipeg. In his letter of resignation of October 13, 1976, he wrote, "It has become increasingly apparent that you and I do not share the same vision of Canada, the land we both love" (quoted in Russell Doern, *The Battle Over Bilingualism*, p. 215). Richardson delivered his parting shot at Trudeau's plans to amend the Constitution on June 27, 1977, before walking across the floor to sit on the other side of the House of Commons as an independent.

> Mr. Speaker, I understand that this afternoon this House will consider a government motion in relation to the Constitution of Canada. In recent days, I have studied and carefully examined the government's proposals as set out in the white paper called "A Time for Action," and in the constitutional amendment bill, Bill C-60, which was given first reading in the House last week.
>
> I am convinced from studying those documents that this government legislation cannot possibly achieve unity in this country. In fact, I find myself in such fundamental disagreement with the government's proposals that I can no longer, in good conscience, sit on the government side of the House.
>
> It is my belief and my conviction, Mr. Speaker, that the government's two-phase plan to amend the Canadian constitution is in fact a blueprint for permanent national division, and for that reason I intend, after this brief statement, to cross the floor of the House and to sit as an independent member of Parliament in opposition to the government. . . . For me, the cause is Canada; for me the ultimate cause is equality and the well-being of all Canadians. (p. 216)

Richardson believed in a bilingual Quebec with English as the common language for all Canadians. He held firmly to the same belief that the founding fathers of the federation had espoused, that Canada was not based on two founding races and cultures but on a federation of provinces. On January 13, 1978, he appeared before the Pépin–Roberts Task Force on Canadian Unity in Winnipeg: "Mr. Chairman, Ladies and Gentlemen: I am appearing today before the Task Force on Canadian Unity because, above all else, I believe in the unity of Canada. I believe that Canada is One Country and that Canadians are One People. I believe that this concept of Canada is shared by millions of Canadians who are today dismayed and confused by the divisive concept being put forward by the federal government."

The government preached unity but practised duality! "This government-appointed task force is itself an unfortunate example of duality. Why does this task force have two chairmen? Having two chairmen symbolizes duality, and duality is not the road to unity" (Doern, p. 218).

Five years after his retirement from politics, Canada's greatest parliamentarian, the former prime minister, the Right Hon. John George Diefenbaker, published his 1972 book *Those Things We Treasure*. Through his chapter "The Twilight of Liberty" he issued a stern warning to the language jugglers:

> Language rights in Canada rest upon constitutional provisions written into the British North America Act. The constitution was bypassed and changed without constitutional amendment, by the extension of language rights by means other than a constitutional amendment. Mr. Justice Thorson, a former Minister in the Mackenzie King [Liberal] government and subsequently President of the Exchequer Court of Canada, after his retirement from the bench, and as a private citizen, attempted to bring an action in the Supreme Court of Canada challenging the Official Languages Act on constitutional grounds. The Supreme Court refused to hear the action. The courts are being denied the right to determine whether what was done was within the powers of Parliament. The Pearson and the Trudeau governments have stored up much trouble for the future in their handling of language rights. . . .
>
> . . . The Pearson Government relied on the instrument of a Royal Commission on Bilingualism and Biculturalism. The harvest of trouble that ensued from that policy is still with us, and it is plainly increasing as the days go by. [Along with only sixteen others,] I voted against the legislation on language rights based on the recommendations of the Bi and Bi commission, and I believe that steps must be taken to rectify the error resulting from a flagrant attempt to evade and bypass the constitution. . . .
>
> What is being done by the Trudeau Government could be summed up in the words of Sukarno as "guided democracy" in which freedom of the individual is diminished and the power of the governing authority is multiplied. (pp. 19, 20, 33)

A year after the publication of Diefenbaker's work, the Hon. Joseph T. Thorson, to whom Diefenbaker had referred, published *his* opposition to the Pearson–Trudeau vision in *Wanted: A Single Canada*.[5]

It is essential that when the time comes for the Canadian people to make their decision [as to the kind of Canada they desire] they should have an accurate knowledge of the facts that have transpired in Quebec in recent years and a clear appreciation of their true import and intent. It is also essential that they should be fully aware of the steps taken by former Prime Minister Pearson and by Prime Minister Trudeau to change the basic character of Canada by making it a dual French-English country and the true purpose and significance of these steps. (p. 12)

Moreover, there is no foundation in fact for the contention that Canada is a bilingual country. On the contrary, the fact is that it is not a bilingual country. According to the 1961 census, only 12.2 per cent of the people of Canada were bilingual in the sense of knowing both French and English. . . . Most of the bilingual persons were French Canadians. . . .

The truth is that Canada never was a bilingual country, it is not a bilingual country now, and it may fairly be predicted that it never will be a bilingual country. The contention that it is a bilingual country is a deliberate "false pretence." But the false pretence continues to be made and acceptance of the contention grows as the false pretence is repeated and it will continue to do so until the Canadian people reject it. They will have the opportunity of doing so when they come to the choice of the kind of country that they wish Canada to be. (pp. 48, 49)

There's the question. Would Canadians ever have that choice, and, if so, when?

Notes

1 Last words of the Roman Emperor Vespasian, AD 79.

2 Official Languages Act (1969):
Section 12   *Federal Bilingual Districts (Power to Create)*

> The Governor in Council [the Cabinet acting with the approval of the Governor General] may from time to time . . . establish one or more federal bilingual districts.

Section 13 (1)

> a) [A district may be established] where both official languages are spoken . . . and;
>
> b) The number of persons in the linguistic minority in the area in respect of an official language spoken as a mother tongue is at least ten percent of the total number of persons residing in the area.

3 There is no consistency in the reports of how many were arrested, convicted, or the number of investigations conducted. In August of 1993, seeking compensation, the Fondation Octobre 70 took action. Canadian Press reported the police arrested 497 people, made 4,600 raids, and conducted 31,700 searches. Of the 26 arrested, CP reports that 21 were convicted (*Star*/CP, Aug 30/93).

4 The collapse of the Victoria Conference echoed the failure of an earlier attempt to patriate the Constitution — the Fulton–Favreau formula of the early 1960s. Initially proposed by E. Davie Fulton, Diefenbaker's minister of justice, the formula was hijacked and altered by Pearson's justice minister, Guy Favreau. Acceptable to all the provinces at first, Fulton's draft bill was released on December 1, 1961. All provincial powers, including language and education, were to be entrenched in the Constitution. One provision allowed for the delegation of provincial powers to the federal government.

If four provinces wanted to legislate in certain areas, the federal government would consent. The Constitution could be amended if there was two-thirds support and 50 percent of the people agreed to it. On December 7, 1961, the Quebec government, the Union Nationale of Premier Jean Lesage, rejected the "Fulton formula" because the provinces had no control over health insurance. Diefenbaker objected as well. He regarded the modified formula as nothing more than sovereignty-association — dualism that would break up Canada.

In his book *Memoirs*, Pierre Trudeau lays most of the blame at the feet of Claude Castonguay: "The Castonguay proposal meant that the federal government would become just an institution to raise taxes, but it would never have any direct relations with the citizens of Quebec" (p. 232).

5   Despite his outstanding credentials, the name Joseph T. Thorson has been virtually stricken from the record by Canadian historians today. From the jacket copy of *Wanted: A Single Canada:* "A former Rhodes Scholar for Manitoba at Oxford, a Barrister-at-Law, and a former Professor of Law, the Hon. Joseph T. Thorson held high offices in Canada and internationally. He served as President of the International Commission of Jurists (1952–1959), was a [Liberal] member of Parliament for Winnipeg South Centre and for Selkirk, was a Cabinet Minister in the portfolio of Minister of National War Services [in the Mackenzie King government], and was President of the Exchequer Court of Canada. Since 1969 he has been President of the Single Canada League [1973]."

Justice Thorson's position on bilingualism and biculturalism is clear. Diefenbaker's is not. Thorson opposed not only the circumvention of Canada's constitution, but the principles of the Pearson–Trudeau vision. In the third volume of his memoirs Diefenbaker reports: "On 29 April 1964 I wrote in reply to a high school student in Montreal: . . . As to bilingualism and biculturalism, these are two necessary and inescapable facets of Canadian nationality. Canada was conceived of by men of two different but equally rich cultures, of two distinct communities. Bilingualism and biculturalism are facets of Canadian life that cannot — and should not — be hidden or avoided. They are important, even vital, to Canada as a nation" (*One Canada*, Vol. III, pp. 250–51).

Diefenbaker's position is fuzzy. After voting against the Official Languages Act in 1969, he was driven to the sticking point at the end. He flinched. The long journey toward the destruction of the Conservative Party of Canada as a populist party had begun.

4

Joe Clark's Community of Communities
Pluralism — 1979

THE MAY 22, 1979, election of the Right Hon. Charles Joseph Clark meant sweet victory for the Conservatives. After so many years out of office, Clark considered it particularly sweet. For the West, the election of an Albertan was even more delicious. The province had suffered more than any other from energy policies that Trudeau's minority government had introduced between 1972 and 1974. Under the BNA Act, revenue from natural resources belongs to the provinces. For this reason most of all, defeating the great interventionist Pierre Trudeau at last was glorious. And to see him whisked to the opposition benches only thirteen days later on June 4, when he resigned, was scrumptious.

Those tired of the arrogance of Ottawa and the centralist approach to Canada welcomed the Albertan chinook. Clark seemed more in tune with provincial needs. He had coined a little slogan that would become an albatross around his neck in future years, that Canada was a "community of communities." Joe Clark was no John Diefenbaker — no prairie populist and no conservative. He was a Red Tory revisionist closer to the centralist camp of Pierre Trudeau than any leader of the Conservative Party had ever been. Intellectually, he was never even a "Westerner."

At the time of Clark's election in 1978, David L. Humphreys had just published his biography of him. He writes in his preface, "I believe today as I did then [in 1976], the country doesn't know the Joe Clark that I know. . . . It is too early in Clark's career for any definitive biography." Fair enough. But was there enough substance to the man for Canadians to judge? Did Clark have a vision of the future? What principles guided this clumsy striver who had been defeated in five Quebec by-elections and was now at the helm of one of the world's advanced industrial societies? Or did it matter?

Clark told his biographer, "I knew they were underestimating me." He was referring to his ambition and his firm belief that he could move onward and upward. "Joe Who?" was dished up by, of all papers, the *Toronto Star*. Even so, who could argue its humour?

At age twenty, Clark had published the following in *Gateway*, a publication of the University of Alberta: "We are a bilingual nation with speakers of both tongues straining their ignorance to remain monolingual. We are a mixing pot of various religions and origins which, on some stubborn point or another, are loath to mix. Any nation great or small is a unity of differences. We in Canada seem persistent, and among large western nations almost unique, in developing the differences, not the unity" (*Gateway*, Jan 5/60, quoted in *Joe Clark*, p. 38).

Not very heady stuff to rely on as insight into a potential prime minister. The young man seemed very negative, and very serious, for his years. The one clear point was that he supported Official Bilingualism. What were his convictions about individual rights and freedoms and the role of the state?

Clark had plodded his way through the Conservative party machinery since his college years. He was known to be worthy and reliable, a dutiful servant who inspired loyalty. By age forty-nine, he had had a career as a journalist, an educator, and a broadcaster. He had not distinguished himself in any of those roles. Did this therefore mean there was nothing there? Many political observers thought so.

Humphreys recounts one interesting anecdote: "Clark, a life-long Roman Catholic, was, at that time [1960], known for a certain irreverence towards another man's religion, that of former Alberta Premier E.C. Manning. Manning, a former colleague of William Aberhart's at Calgary's Prophetic Bible Institute, conducted 'Canada's National Back to the Bible Hour' from the stage of the Paramount Theatre in Edmonton. Clark did an entertaining impersonation of Manning, the preacher" (p. 41).

IN 1960 JOE CLARK TURNED THIRTY. He had graduated from the University of Alberta with a Bachelor of Arts degree and gone to France for four months to study French. Humphreys says he "wrote good letters," adding, "in a way he had made his living by writing speeches, slogans and pamphlets." In one of these letters, from Paris, Clark wrote:

> Trudeau is pictured looking distraught on the front of *L'Express* — and indeed the persistent, if subconscious, preoccupation of any Canadian who knows and fears our national fragility — I was reminded, again, that talk of "deux nations" extends well beyond one electoral campaign, beyond a discussion of the distribution of powers. It is the essence of Canada — that we have that unbridgeable and vital combination of Anglo-Saxon reserve and Latin romance, and that the cross-fertilization has been sufficient that I, from High River [Alberta], can perceive that "doloros" [*sic*] is much deeper than Anglo-Saxon sadness, much more basic, and that a René Lévesque can be so determined to work within the rule of law. (It reminds me also that I don't consider Trudeau a representative Canadian; he is too rationalist to be French, too inflexible to be Anglo-Saxon; when he went to Harvard he followed his true instinct; he belongs in the modern Puritan society, where everything is coded and the code is everything. That is most alarming if one is worried about the various implications of "continentalism" because if earlier prime ministers were continentalists by convenience, Trudeau is by conviction; he prefers the American value system more than that of France or Britain, more than that of Quebec or Ontario. And of course he presumes Alberta not to have one.) (p. 89)

Clark gave his biographer permission to publish this and other insights, so he must have thought they had some value for posterity. As the winner of the Tory leadership over opponents like Brian Mulroney in 1976, he certainly knew when Humphreys's biography came out in 1978 that there was a reasonable chance he might become prime minister.

What, then, were these ramblings supposed to mean? "Unbridgeable and vital combination of Anglo-Saxon reserve and Latin romance"? Clark's definition of *deux nations* was here, but hopelessly garbled. Anglo-Saxon sadness compared with French depression in the same sentence as René Lévesque's determination to work within the rule of law?

As for Trudeau being "too rationalist to be French," where did Clark think René Descartes (1590–1650) and the Cartesian school of rationality came from? What of *"Cogito, ergo sum,"* the light that switched on the French revolution of reason? What of Voltaire, whose work epitomized the Age of Reason?

As for codification, the French love it. They built empires on the basis of bureaucracy. Could Puritans too be codifiers? Perhaps. But what on earth did Clark mean by the "value system" of Quebec or Ontario? Many Tories believed he had the answers. The real question was could this fellow function on all cylinders as a national leader?

Joe Clark's stewardship as PM did not last long. Although he was the first bilingual anglophone to lead a major party, he squandered his opportunity to govern intelligently. He blundered repeatedly. The ill-conceived promise to move the Canadian embassy in Israel from Tel Aviv to Jerusalem, and other pratfalls, such as expressing willingness to negotiate sovereignty-association with Quebec, prepared the media for high sport.

Tory insider wags dubbed him "Jerusalem Joe McTeer." Allan Fotheringham, the wicked pen of English Canada's press, came up with one term referring to Clark that turned him into a national symbol: the "Wimp Factor." Even Trudeau's announced resignation as Liberal leader on November 21 wasn't enough to save Clark's reputation as a bumbler.

The minority Conservative government fell on December 13 on an NDP motion put forward by Bob Rae, an MP studying law at public expense. Clark lost the vote of confidence 139 to 133. He had been warned.

Joe Clark served as prime minister from June 4, 1979, till he became, once again, Leader of the Opposition on March 3, 1980 — 272 days. The Conservatives' hope for a national resurgence was doomed. The way was paved for the resurrection of Pierre Trudeau, the man who had just quit.

Trudeau had informed the nation and the Liberal Party in November that "it's time for a new leader to take up his work." The Clark government was defeated three weeks later. As usual, he wasted no time. A day later, he was forced from his full reverse into retirement into neutral. Carefully he tested the waters. On December 16 the great phoenix held an opinion poll that predicted the Liberals could win again with him as leader. On December 18, he indicated he would fight the next election and that he would stay on as leader. To two other hopefuls, John Turner and Donald MacDonald, the announcement was depressing.

On February 18, 1980, Trudeau slipped back into prime ministerial office after a retirement of several months. The results devastated those who despaired of changing the course he had set for the nation. Not only was the reviled Trudeau unleashed again by rank stupidity on the Tories' part, but he had leaped back to the helm with a majority government: Liberals, 146; Conservatives, 103; NDP, 32.

Same old Tory story. Since 1917, the Tories had never managed to get their act together for any repeat term of office.

5

René Lévesque's
Sovereign Association
— 1980

O N TRUDEAU'S RE-ELECTION, the country breathed a painful sigh
of relief. If he was the devil, at least Canadians knew who he was.
For those with happy memories of Trudeaumania, perhaps it
would all be wonderful again? But this particular universe did not unfold
as it might have. Trudeau had other plans that he had not shared with the
electorate during the 1980 campaign. Before he could act on them, he had
more urgent matters to attend to.

He had assured the country that separatism was dead and then watched
the separatists sweep to victory in 1976. Now he had to deal with René
Lévesque's promise to conduct a referendum on Quebec sovereignty. In
his departure speech as Leader of the Opposition in November of 1979,
Trudeau had already served notice that he would make life difficult for the
separatists. Now in office again, he knew Canadians expected even more of
him. The Parti Québécois premier, René Lévesque, underscored the drama
in his memoirs: "In 1979 we still held to the one great hope that had been
the motivation of our action for the past twelve years. . . . Without further
delay we had to start assiduously to meet our supreme commitment"
(*Memoirs*, p. 296).

The crisis Trudeau foresaw had been coming since November 15, 1976,
when Lévesque's Parti Québécois swept Robert Bourassa's Liberals out of
office. On that evening a happy but wary chain-smoking premier-elect

enjoyed his most glorious moment: "I've never been so proud to be a Québécois. We're not a little people, we're closer to something like a great people!"

Aislin's cartoon in the Montreal *Gazette* said it all. Lévesque, a trademark cigarette dangling from his mouth, stares out at the reader beside his former political comrade and leader, a lean, taller, bespectacled, and defeated Robert Bourassa who had just lost his own riding. Lévesque's advice: "O.K. Everybody take a Valium."

Three years later, the PQ premier decided the time had come for action. He and his party could no longer assume public credibility as they threw themselves into the job of achieving political sovereignty. On December 19, 1979, only a week after the defeat of the Clark government, Lévesque and his cabinet had cloistered themselves in a room he described as having a "wart-shaped vault" and "indirect lighting." The PQ insiders were beavering away at the wording of the referendum question. Everyone in Canada awaited the final utterance, however guarded, with bated breath. English Canada considered itself forewarned and grateful that at least the Quebec government had not chosen to make a "UDI" — unilateral declaration of independence. The question the voters of Quebec would be asked nevertheless shocked the country:

> The Government of Quebec has made public its proposal to negotiate a new agreement with the rest of Canada, based on the equality of nations. . . .
>
> No change in political status resulting from these negotiations will be effected without approval by the people through another referendum; on these terms do you give the Government of Quebec the mandate to negotiate the proposed agreement between Quebec and Canada? (quoted in Lévesque, *Memoirs*, p. 301)

On the one side stood English Canada, with its hands tied, dependent upon Pierre Trudeau, a leader re-elected in desperation over Joe Clark, a bumbler, and on the other side stood René Lévesque, a combatant determined to make two nations out of one.

The scrap would be vigorous and nasty. Lévesque the romantic, the former journalist, war correspondent, and broadcaster, still smarted at the memory of meeting Pierre Trudeau, former publisher of *Cité libre*, in the mid-1950s. Trudeau had asked him, "Very good, but allow me one simple question: Can you write?" (Lévesque, *Memoirs*, p. 150). In his memoirs, Lévesque reflects on the man he so detested:

As for Pierre Elliott Trudeau . . . how can one define the undefinable? He was extremely cultivated, certainly, but almost exclusively only in matters of jurisprudence and politics. I had the impression that, except for show, the additional baggage he had accumulated from studies in the humanities left him supremely indifferent, like seed fallen on rock. Even in conversation his thought constantly took on a dialectical twist, and to have the last word he would stop at neither sarcasm nor the most specious argument. (Ibid.)

In Lévesque's view, Canadian federalism was nothing more than "snares and delusions" and "nothing less than the mirage of a bilingual Canada upon which Messrs. Trudeau and Company so shrewdly built their careers" (p. 221). On April 15, he announced the date for the referendum — May 20 — only thirty-five days away. Lévesque knew that for him to win, many federalists in Quebec had to come on to his side. The campaign had to appeal to their convictions and be based on reason. Emotion alone would not carry the day.

He had been setting this stage for more than a decade. In 1967, after serving in the Bourassa government as minister of natural resources, he quit the Liberal Party to sit as an independent. Early that year he published his manifesto *An Option for Quebec*. It was this call to nationhood that ended the Quiet Revolution. Evoking emotions in precisely the same manner as de Gaulle at EXPO '67, the leader of the new Sovereignty Association Movement capitalized on the French president's performance. As Lévesque was to put it almost ten years later, "General de Gaulle's 'Vive le Québec libre' did more for Quebec's publicity than ten million dollars spent by an ad agency could ever have done" (*Agence France-Presse*, Nov 22/76).

The 1968 manifesto was a stirring call for freedom and liberty. The opening lines of the first chapter stated in full what Lévesque said Quebec had to have:

We are *Québécois*.

What this means first and foremost — and if need be, all that it means — is that we are attached to this one corner of the earth where we can be completely ourselves: this Quebec, the only place where we have the unmistakable feeling that "here we can be really at home."

Being ourselves is essentially a matter of keeping and developing a personality that has survived for three and a half centuries.

At the core of this personality is the fact that we speak French. Everything else depends on this one essential element and follows from it or leads us infallibly back to it. (p. 14)

By the end of 1979, with time running against the PQ before the next provincial election, the agenda was accelerated. As a follow-up to *An Option for Quebec* in the fall of 1979, the PQ circulated their proposal: *Québec-Canada: A New Deal: The Québec government proposal for a new partnership between equals: sovereignty-association.*

Lévesque called for the creation of a new nation, or, as he put it, "A Country That Must Be Made":

> We are children of that society, in which the *habitant*, our father or grandfather, was still the key citizen. We are also heirs to a fantastic adventure — that early America that was almost entirely French. . . . This basic difference we cannot surrender. . . .
>
> For a small people such as we are, our minority position on an Anglo-Saxon continent creates from the very beginning a permanent temptation to self-rejection, which has all the attractions of a gentle downward slope ending in comfortable submersion in the Great Whole. . . .
>
> . . . Quebec must become sovereign as soon as possible. Thus we finally would have within our grasp the security of our collective "being" which is so vital to us, a security which otherwise must remain uncertain and incomplete. (p. 221)

In a lengthy letter of endorsement, "A Call to the Québec People," he described it, too: "[Québécois,] it is time to conclude. For generations and against all odds, we have maintained an identity that sets us apart in North America."

He had taken the gloves off. For 109 pages he invoked the *people* to rise to a new national destiny. One section, "The Need to Negotiate," listed some of the many unwise, foolish, and gratuitous comments federalist spokespeople had made as evidence that the climate in English Canada was neither hostile, intransigent, nor even indifferent to the needs of a sovereign Quebec. Joe Clark's recently deposed and popular minister of health and welfare, David Crombie, for example, was quoted in aid of the PQ cause: "The Federal Government should negotiate sovereignty-association with Québec Premier René Lévesque who is after a deal with honour. . . . I think anyone who refuses to negotiate is silly" (CP, Jan/79).

Prime Minister Clark's widely circulated radio comment, only days before his downfall, was also included: "Yes, or no, I will be there to negotiate" (Radio-Québec, Sept 10/79).[1]

The PQ's typical strategy demonstrated the "be my guest" attitude of the passage lifted from the recent Pépin–Roberts Task Force on Canadian Unity:

> Given a community of the size and character of Québec Society, we believe that the clearly expressed will of the population must prevail, and that it would be both unwise and ethically questionable to deny or thwart it. Practically speaking, this means the renunciation of the use of force to maintain the integrity of the Canadian state and commitment to seek to construct political institutions which reflect the will and aspirations of the citizens concerned. We believe most Canadians and virtually all of the country's leaders would share our view. (*A Future Together*, p. 113)

The battle over sovereignty raged in the press, on radio, television, and in numerous well-publicized events. As the hour of reckoning approached, Trudeau campaigned vigorously in Quebec, giving three rousing speeches. On May 7, he spoke in Quebec City. He saved his blockbuster for May 14. Speaking to the whole province in the Paul Sauvé arena in Montreal, he called on his fellow Quebecers to rally to a united Canada:

> I know that I can make a most solemn commitment that following a "No" vote we will immediately take action to renew the constitution and we will not stop until we have done that.
>
> And I make a solemn declaration to all Canadians in the other provinces: We, the Quebec MPs, are laying ourselves on the line, because we are telling Quebecers to vote "No" and telling you in the other provinces that we will not agree to your interpreting a "No" vote as an indication that everything is fine and can remain as it was before.
>
> We want change and we are willing to lay our seats in the House on the line to have change. (quoted in *The National Deal*, p. 33)

But here's how Lévesque "translates" Trudeau's remarks, as he terms it, "in résumé" in his *Memoirs* in 1986: "We, MPs from Quebec, ask Québécois to vote Non, and at the same time we warn Canadians in other provinces that this Non should not be interpreted as proof that all is well here, or that there are not changes to be made. On the contrary, it is with the aim of getting things changed that we are putting our seats on the line" (quoted on p. 308).

Trudeau's speeches, replete with subtleties and unended thoughts, would be a gold mine for journalists and academics in future. The difficulties in pinning down exactly what he was promising Quebecers if they behaved themselves lasted well beyond the referendum; each year those interpretations gathered greater momentum as succeeding historians misinterpreted his words. Eventually, vested interests from all quarters quickly regurgitated this particular repast to justify all manner of constitutional wranglings. Lévesque's observation about Trudeau's promise to "renew federalism" is the only one that has withstood the test of history: "Change, okay. But what change? That remained a mystery" (*Memoirs*, p. 308).

Trudeau's actual words "renew federalism" rocked Canada for the next decade and more. Professor Pierre Fournier, a Quebec nationalist and one of the Canadian Broadcasting Corporation's favourite commentators during the Meech Lake debate, volunteered that Trudeau's promise that night would be "interpreted as a mandate to change the Constitution, to renew federalism. We want change. We are staking our seats to change." He claimed that Quebecers like Jean Chrétien and Jeanne Sauvé believed these remarks demonstrated Trudeau's support for that province's special status or more powers (*Star*, March 18/89). In 1990, U of T history professor Desmond Morton, principal of Erindale College, remarked: "The trouble is that I was also around back in 1980 when most of Meech's critics, especially the Prime Minister, promised Quebecers that if they voted against the wicked separatists, they could count on getting a new constitution that met their expectations" (*Star*, April 12/90).

Many other academics and journalists indulged in such excess and revisionist history in later years.

MAY 20, 1980, was referendum day for Quebec and for Canada and, by implication, for the United States. Not since December 20, 1860, when the State Legislature of South Carolina declared the American Union dissolved, had an elected body endorsed the legal breakup of a nation through the democratic process.

The results constituted a personal disaster for René Lévesque and a personal vindication for his colleague, the minister of finance, Jacques Parizeau. Lévesque's plan of "*étapisme*" — step by step — to separation was roundly defeated. The No side took 59.5 percent of the vote. Parizeau had believed a referendum was not necessary. The election of the PQ was enough for him; in that case a UDI would do. Lévesque recalled: "As for the idea of a second referendum, it literally brought Jacques Parizeau to a boil, since even the first wasn't easy for him to swallow" (*Memoirs*, p. 300).[2]

One observer, a commentator for CTV on the night of the referendum, happened to be a young Martin Brian Mulroney. Mulroney, contracted as the president of the Iron Ore Company of Canada, had decided not to accept Clark's pressing invitation to run in the 1980 election three months earlier. Following the PQ's election in 1976, he had served as vice-chairman of the Council for Canadian Unity.[3] He had also been involved in the founding of the Pro-Canada Committee. He fully supported Trudeau's actions. Recalling that referendum night years later and only weeks before another referendum was to be held, Mulroney told broadcaster Peter Gzowski: "I want to tell you it is not a pleasant sight to watch a vote on the future of your own country going on" (Goar, *Star*, Sept 1/92).

Lévesque's departure from the stage that night brought little relief to a traumatized nation. Everyone knew his tearful *"À la prochaine fois"* — until next time — was significant. Nothing was solved by the vote. In 1986, Lévesque wrote in his *Memoirs*: "The thing one must guard against above all is the attitude of the victorious frog who speedily deludes himself into thinking he can be as big as an ox. But as will be seen, I scarcely had time, let alone the inclination, to give in to this particular temptation" (p. 321).

Notes

1 The PQ strategy booklet published the Radio-Québec interviewer's exact question to Clark: "So you will not refuse to negotiate with the Québec government if the PQ gets a massive Yes in the referendum?"

2 Every school child in Quebec knows the story of Jacques Parizeau's conversion to separatism in 1968: "When I boarded the train at [Montreal's] Windsor Station, I was a federalist. When I descended in Banff, I was a separatist" (*Star*, Sept 30/94).

3 Founded in 1964, the CCU is a Montreal-based "national, non-profit, non-partisan organization" and claims to have a "wide variety of programs aimed at making Canadians aware of the cultural and linguistic realities of the country."

6

Trudeau's Revolution
Patriation Without
Representation — 1981 to 1982

THE NO FROM QUEBECERS to even *negotiating* sovereignty-association, let alone separation from Canada, marked a tremendous victory for Pierre Elliott Trudeau. He had a hat-trick — a majority federal election victory. He won 74 of the 75 federal seats in Quebec and had dealt a tremendous blow to separatism as well. As far as he was concerned, he could now embark on his mission, to "renew the Constitution." Canadians were soon to find out what that meant.

He set to work on a constitutional revolution beginning with the "patriation" of the British North America Act from Britain. He put the case boldly to his fellow citizens on October 2, 1980, in a television broadcast: "Canadians can no longer afford to have fundamental aspects concerning the nature of our country left unresolved and uncertain, to feed confrontation, division and disunity. We are summoned to a great act of national will: we must take unto ourselves and for our children, the ultimate responsibility for the preservation of our country" (quoted in Bothwell et al., *Canada Since 1945*, p. 391).

The prime minister had given the word. The federal government was prepared to unilaterally patriate the Constitution. Confused and unskilled in such matters, opposition leader Joe Clark could only sputter furiously: "There are times when a government proposes to act against the essential interests of the nation. At such a time, the role of the opposition leader is not to submit to the government but to fight for the larger interests of Canada. The Trudeau government has a majority in Parliament. It will not be stopped unless the people of Canada can be aroused to the abuse — to the potential damage to our country. . . . We will lead the fight in Parliament . . ." (quoted in *The National Deal*, p. 99).

Trudeau swung into action. On June 25, 1980, he met with Britain's Tory Prime Minister Margaret Thatcher and secured her guarded approval of the process. The government moved a constitutional resolution in the House of Commons in Ottawa on October 6 of that year. But the government's plan to secure its quick passage and Royal Proclamation by Canada Day, July 1, 1981, was a pipe dream.

On October 14 the first ministers met in Toronto. Five of them announced they would fight the resolution in the courts; Alberta, British Columbia, Manitoba, Newfoundland, and Quebec all united against Trudeau's plan, though for different reasons. In the House of Commons on October 24, the Liberals applied closure to cut off debate. A Gallup poll released on December 9 highlighted the problem. Fifty-eight percent of Canadians disapproved of the patriation without broader consent.

Momentum against the resolution had grown in Canada by 1981. Sir Anthony Kershaw, who chaired the British parliamentary committee that dealt with the matter, recommended that Westminster reject Trudeau's agenda because it lacked the support of the provincial governments.

By the new year the British had slipped back on to Trudeau's agenda. On January 14, 1982, the British courts rejected aboriginal claims against patriation. The English, eager to rid themselves of this quaint bit of colonial luggage, wanted only to dump the business as fast as they could. After all, the notion of Canada gaining a new constitution beyond its British past was an embarrassment and a reminder of an era long past.

On March 8 the British House of Commons passed its resolution to patriate the BNA Act. Final passage through the House of Lords followed shortly on March 25. On March 29, 1982, the Canada Act received Royal Assent as Canadian law. It was the last time Britain would legislate constitutional matters pertaining to Canada.

Most Canadians sulked when The Constitution Act, 1982, and its accompanying Canadian Charter of Rights and Freedoms were proclaimed at the signing in Ottawa on April 17, 1982.

First, the Constitution Act represented a radical departure from the country's British common-law heritage. Although the new act incorporated the BNA Act and amendments, the addition of a Charter of Rights and Freedoms codified "rights" that had always been inherent for Canadians.

The mere act of defining rights necessarily narrows and reduces them. English-speaking Canada was more affected by Trudeau's machinations than Quebec, which already functioned under its own Civil Code. Singlehandedly, he moved Canada's legal system irrevocably towards the rigidity of the French Civil Code. Over time the loss to Canadians would be immeasurable.

UNKNOWN TO MOST CANADIANS at the time, the new Constitution harboured a critical flaw in its Charter of Rights and Freedoms. A provision within it could potentially destroy the Canadian federation. This was Section 33, a so-called notwithstanding, or *non obstante*, clause, as the lawyers loved to label it. Its full import was not appreciated at the time. The silence of the legal profession was deafening. Lawyers should have marched on Parliament Hill in outrage. In English Canada people only sensed they were witnessing something very dangerous.

Section 33 reads:

(1) Parliament or the legislature of a province may expressly declare in an Act of Parliament or of the legislature, as the case may be, that the Act or a provision thereof shall operate *notwithstanding* a provision included in section 2 or sections 7 to 15 of this Charter. [Emphasis mine]

Although a later provision limited the life of this clause to five years, another provision allowed that "Parliament or a legislature of a province may re-enact a declaration made under subsection (1)."

The implications were incredible. Here was a clause in the country's very constitution that permitted lower levels of government to override the most fundamental rights and freedoms of individual Canadians. The "notwithstanding" clause meant the following fundamental freedoms in Section 2 could be set aside by any province:

(a) freedom of conscience and religion;
(b) freedom of thought, belief, opinion and expression, including freedom of the press and other media of communication;
(c) freedom of peaceful assembly; and
(d) freedom of association.

Sections 7 through 15 of the Charter of Rights and Freedoms could also be set aside. They contained everything else worth preserving in a free society. Section 7, "the right to life, liberty and security of the person and the right not to be deprived thereof," could be overridden. Section 33 threatened other clauses just as much. These included the "right to be secure against unreasonable search or seizure," the right of "habeas corpus,"[1] the "right not to be subjected to any cruel and unusual treatment or punishment" as well as the right "to be presumed innocent."

However, Section 16 is immune from the notwithstanding clause: "English and French are the official languages of Canada and have equality of status and equal rights and privileges as to their use in all institutions of the Parliament and government of Canada." It revolutionized those provisions of the BNA Act dealing with the French and English languages and their use in the parliaments and the courts.

The second reason Canadians distrusted the Trudeau process was even more fundamental. Despite promises to the contrary, they were never directly consulted about any aspect of their constitution. Thirteen years later, in his book *Memoirs*, Trudeau crows about the "enormously improved" draft of the 1980 Charter the Special Joint Committee on the Constitution produced: "We had opened the door to the people to comment on it, and they had rushed through: 914 individuals and 294 groups . . . and as a result we had amended the charter. . . ." From this he concludes that "a national constituency had been created in favour of the charter, and that was as it should be" (p. 322).

Created by whom? The participants were mostly insider academics and special-interest groups. Most Canadians found themselves uninvited and even barred from participating in the one forum that would have entitled everyone to play a role — a national debate and plebiscite. Their own government had used an elitist, restrictive, and undemocratic process to disenfranchise them. A national referendum on the Constitution would have been the only possible option in a truly democratic state.

On that rainy April day in 1982 in Ottawa when Queen Elizabeth and the prime minister signed the final document, 30,000 people gathered to witness the ceremony and get a glimpse of the Queen. For such an august occasion, this was a vastly unimpressive assembly. In fact, the numbers matched those that René Lévesque had mustered in Montreal to demonstrate against what the lone angry premier had colourfully described as being "screwed . . . the Canadian way" (*National Deal*, p. 316). In their discontent with the politicians, Quebecers were not alone, although they have never truly understood this.

In the epilogue of their book, *The National Deal*, Michael Valpy and Robert Sheppard record Trudeau's own measure of his success on November 18, 1981, after the signing of the Constitutional Accord of November 5.

When asked about the whole exercise, he said he was disappointed there would be no referendum, since "the people's will cannot be tested." Then he added, "You're asking me now, if I consider it a success? No, I consider it an abject failure" (p. 322).

And so the fatally flawed Charter of Rights with its numerous clauses, codicils, and *non obstante* provision was foisted on the nation. The new Constitution with its charter was totally foreign to the time-tested tradition of case-by-case fine-tuning that nourished and shaped the previous supremacy of the common law. In effect sovereignty had been transferred in one massive sweep from the people's Parliament to the Supreme Court of Canada.

It took a long time for people to appreciate the full significance of Trudeau's high-wire act. From the beginning, his actions seeded deep resentment in the Canadian psyche. Yet fewer than a handful of politicians spoke up at this most critical point in the country's history.

Years later, long after Quebec had violated international law to crush English language rights in Quebec, Trudeau expressed no remorse for what he had done.[2] In May 1991, at a two-day symposium held at McGill University — which, incidentally, the Canadian media ignored — he rationalized his actions in 1982 before some two dozen North American scholars:

> I think the Charter is fundamentally flawed because of the override clause. I could have got rid of the compromise, of the notwithstanding clause, by getting rid of the Charter. That was quite clear to us in the negotiations imposed on us by the Supreme Court. And I had to ask myself, Well, will it be easier some time in the future to get a full-blown Charter without any compromise clause, any notwithstanding clause, or will it be easier to have a full-blown Charter, flawed with the notwithstanding clause, which pressure of the people — of the electorate on their government — would be able to get rid of some day in the future? And I came to the conclusion that it would be much harder to come back some day with our amending formula to get all provinces to accept the Charter unflawed. That's how the choice was made. (Riggs and Velk, *Federalism in Peril*, p. 14)

"Ask myself"? "I came to the conclusion"? He blamed the Supreme Court of Canada. Why? All the Supreme Court had imposed was a directive stating that the prime minister needed more than two provinces to proceed.

Get rid of the notwithstanding clause? How? If this prime minister with his influence didn't trust the people with a referendum, then by what act of

God would the provision ever be eliminated if the amending formula required unanimous consent?

In fact, the Charter was a ruse. Trudeau wanted to consolidate power in the Supreme Court of Canada and weaken Parliament. In so doing, he altered the legal structure of the country from a constitutional monarchy to an oligarchy in one fell swoop. During this same speech, he said, "If it weren't for the bench and the bar I don't think we'd have the awareness today in Canada of this notion of popular sovereignty, that the people do have rights over and above the power of government."

In 1935 the famous American journalist H. L. Mencken described Canada's British heritage:

> In a few countries, notably England, some of the principal articles in the existing Constitution are not written down at all, but only generally understood. But whether they are written down or not, they have a kind of force that is greatly superior to that of all ordinary law, and changing their terms is looked on as a very grave matter, to be undertaken only on long consideration, and after getting the consent of all the persons, or at least a majority of them, whose rights it is proposed to modify.
>
> In brief, a constitution is a standing limitation upon the power of the government. So far you may go, but no farther. No matter what the excuse or provocation, you may not invade certain rights, or pass certain kinds of laws. The lives and property of the people are at your disposition, but only up to a plainly indicated point. If you go beyond it, you become a public criminal, and may be proceeded against, at least in theory, like any other criminal. The government thus ceases to be sovereign, and becomes a creature of sharply defined and delimited powers. There are things it may not do. (Letter to the *Baltimore Sun*, August 19/35, in *The Impossible H. L. Mencken*, pp. 68–69)

In 1981 more pressing concerns occupied the minds of Quebecers, and these related to hurt feelings and foolish pride. At the top of their list was the "Kitchen Deal," reached behind the scenes early in the morning of November 5, 1981, by the first ministers and their representatives after five days of wheeling and dealing. They had agreed to go ahead with or without Quebec's consent as a province. They rationalized that, after all, the federal Quebec caucus supported the prime minister.

Credit for the actual strategy to implement Trudeau's package has been attributed to Newfoundland's Premier Brian Peckford. The final package was negotiated between Roy Romanow, representing Premier

Alan Blakeney of Saskatchewan; Ontario's Attorney General Roy McMurtry for Bill Davis of Ontario; and Jean Chrétien for Trudeau. In the meantime, Lévesque had slipped away for badly needed sleep, unaware of the plan.

The Kitchen Deal was made in Ottawa's little-used Chateau Laurier pantry, and it sparked a struggle that would become known to Quebecers as the "Night of the Long Knives." The separatists propagandized the business with glee. The officials of four provinces got together, cooked a package, and then sold it to the other provinces and kept the compromise a secret from Quebec. Money matters were muddled with the Charter of Rights and Freedoms, mixed with whether or not to conduct a referendum, and various ideas for a veto. In the end the players conspired to settle for a constitutional mess.

Lévesque was soured. He did not get what Quebec already had for itself alone, the constitutional veto its nationalists always deemed vital to their interests — breaking Canada into *deux nations*. This was the same veto Robert Bourassa had demanded at the Victoria Conference in 1971. In lieu of the veto, Lévesque had taken an earlier shot at securing constitutionally guaranteed funding whenever Quebec chose to opt out of a federal program. Trudeau refused. He promised to deal with such eventualities as a matter of policy after Quebec signed up. The Quebec premier did not accept this. It offered Quebec no more certainty than the duration of any one Parliament.

The two gladiators despised each other. Trudeau the elitist, the philosopher, the lawyer, had no use for Lévesque the populist. Lévesque challenged him to hold a referendum in Quebec. Trudeau refused unless it was on his terms. The rift between them was permanent. Quebec found itself isolated. The notwithstanding clause that Sterling Lyon of Manitoba had initially demanded was, of course, a sort of veto, but it was messy, and once used it could only apply for five years.

As for Jean Chrétien, who one day might take over as Liberal leader or fulfil his lifetime ambition and become prime minister, he had his own agenda. He adamantly opposed conducting a referendum, as he would other democratic frivolities in future. On the matter of conducting referendums, any referendums, he had once scribbled "NEVER" on a piece of paper purloined for posterity.

There were many other problems with Trudeau's Constitution. All Canadians could argue they were shut out just like the Quebecers were. Canada's native peoples could claim the same. Trudeau's treatment of aboriginal peoples laid the foundation for decades of difficulty. His views on aboriginal rights were well known. Authors Sheppard and Valpy put the case:

> The position taken by various Canadian governments on aboriginal rights has been whimsical for more than a century, inviting no confidence from native peoples. Ottawa accepted the notion of aboriginal land claims in the mid-1870s, during part of the early 1900s and since 1973. Otherwise it did not. . . . In 1969, Trudeau delivered the government's edict on native rights: "Our answer is no. We can't recognize aboriginal rights because no society can be built on historical might-have-beens." (p. 165)

In his hour of need, having refused to discuss constitutional matters with the native peoples, Trudeau went further. He had the cheek to meet with native leaders on April 29, 1980, just before the Quebec referendum on sovereignty, to demand their support. He challenged them to join the crusade for a new Canada "in which you and your people have so much at stake" (p. 160).

Trudeau's views on the idea of including aboriginal rights in the new Constitution were also well known. No way, until patriation. Anyway, he would always argue, rights have to be defined. Persuaded otherwise, as a bargaining ploy, he did insert Section 35 into the Constitution Act — Rights of the Aboriginal Peoples of Canada:

> (1) The existing aboriginal and treaty rights of the aboriginal peoples of Canada are hereby recognized and affirmed.

> (2) In this Act, "aboriginal peoples of Canada" includes the Indian, Inuit and Métis peoples of Canada.

The two sections meant nothing. What, in legal terms, was an "Indian"? Did it mean only status Indians on reserves or some other classification? Who and what were the Métis? And exactly what were their rights?

The bigger problem Trudeau planted for Canadians to face was blatant racial discrimination between natives and Caucasians as founding peoples of Canada. Were aboriginal peoples not founding races of Canada just as much as the English and the French? And if so, and if two official languages flowed from this premise, then surely native languages were also "official languages" of Canada. Was the white man's occupation of aboriginal lands any less an injustice or cultural genocide than the English Conquest of the French on the Plains of Abraham in 1759?

What did Trudeau think would happen if the Constitution ignored its native peoples and the country accepted a definition based on founding races and founding cultures? Peace in the kingdom? Surely not. Alas, we don't have the questions from this philosopher, let alone the answers. All we have are his actual moves and his original credo. Sadly, too, the native leadership at this point had not joined together with any common interests and beliefs. Perhaps this was never possible since they are so many different nations, tribes, and groupings. In those days the aboriginal community was just beginning to learn how to marshal the media to bring their case before Canadians.

Trudeau's crime against democracy was monstrous. He took full advantage of the colonial trappings of the country for his own purposes. First, neither he nor any other of the first ministers had any mandate from the electorate to embark on constitutional reform.

Second, neither the Parliament of Canada nor any provincial or territorial legislature has ever been given the right to undertake language reform.

Third, the new Constitution was based on a fraud — two races and cultures, the English and the French.

Fourth, the Constitution Act, 1982, cast in stone Trudeau's anti-democratic Utopia. Under it, the common law and the Parliament were irreparably reduced to government by the Supreme Court of Canada and the various branches of the judiciary. Or, as Lévesque would later put it in his memoirs:

> What he now demanded was nothing less than the hasty repatriation of the constitution, to which he also wished to graft his pet project, a Charter of Rights that had the similar virtue of giving everybody the goose pimples. . . . We knew that it would be an instrument to reduce the powers of Quebec, and so it was on the side of the Anglo-Canadian provinces because this kind of American-style "Bill of Rights" is completely foreign to the unwritten tradition of British institutions. (p. 318)

Not only did Canada's new Constitution signify a shameful international legal landmark, it expressed negative values, and exposed a national neurosis. Even without its infamous notwithstanding clause, the Charter itself read as an arid declaration. While all Canadians shared the "right to life" and "liberty," the Charter assumed no right to "the pursuit of happiness" or any other uplifting ideal but the necessity of a right of "security of the person and the right not to be deprived thereof except in accordance with the principles of fundamental justice." Trudeau was telling Canadians to fear the state.

By the late twentieth century, the notion of including a notwithstanding clause was an archaic concept in law. It enables any province to negate anything of substance in the entire Constitution. Old English statutes and letters patent contained such clauses. *Black's Law Dictionary* (fifth edition, 1979) defines *notwithstanding* as "a power in the crown to dispense with laws in any particular case. This was abolished by the bill of rights in the [English] Revolution [of 1688–89]."

Any first-year law student would recognize the danger to individual freedom embodied in such a constitutional clause. Certainly anyone with a rudimentary knowledge of Canadian and Quebec history could imagine how this clause would be used.

By 1982, Quebec's Bills 63, 22, and 101, discriminatory laws governing language and education rights, had been enacted and were being enforced. Logically, this provision in the Canadian Charter of Rights and Freedoms could lead directly to the breakup of the entire federation for one simple reason: no common principles remained to bind the union.

The use of such an archaic provision in law in Canada was not original. René Lévesque had incorporated a notwithstanding clause (S. 52) in the French Language Charter, Bill 101, of December 26, 1977. The Charter's provision, however, is thought to have come into being solely as a result of Trudeau's National Energy Policy. Everyone knew that the federal government had inserted the clause because of the West's determination never again to lose jurisdiction over their provincial resources to the federal government.

The media, including the CBC, was as unaware as most Canadians of the ugly surprise coming in the years to follow. As his supporters and detractors alike would learn, Trudeau had won his "patriation," and the country would pay a terrible price for it.

T HE LAWYERS AND THE PUBLIC SERVANTS who had sanitized the final document immortalized their struggle in dull, flat, boring prose. Any possible romance and glory were beaten out of it. The Constitution would never win the hearts of the people. What classroom would display it? Who could even understand it?

The last word belongs to René Lévesque. While Trudeau was leading the celebration ceremonies in Ottawa on April 17, the day the Constitution Act became law, severing all ties to Britain, Lévesque was cursing the deal in Montreal. "Le Canada Bill," he said, would lead to incalculable consequences for Canada. As for the Charter of Rights and Freedoms, it was "the most soporific lawyerishness you could find anywhere in the world" (*National Deal*, p. 305). He was right.

Many of the players in these constitutional proceedings through to the date of Royal Assent in 1982 performed a critical function in later years as well. Fifteen years later, the negotiations of the Meech Lake Accord starred first ministers John Buchanan, Richard Hatfield and Brian Peckford, Robert Bourassa, Ed Broadbent, Jean Chrétien, Joe Clark, Bill Davis, Peter Lougheed, Roy Romanow, and Claude Ryan. Senior public servants and other behind-the-scenes players who first took seats at the constitutional table featured Gordon Robertson, Hugh Segal, Norman Spector, and Roger Tassé. Also appearing in significant guest roles were professors Ronald Watts, Edward McWhinney, and Peter Meekison. Bob Rae, who became Ontario's first minister, played his own small part in the constitutional theatrics as well.

The 1981–82 constitutional exercise was a disaster. The nine provinces that signed the accord on November 5, 1981, claimed a majority of Quebec MPs in the federal camp. Quebec's National Assembly, however, overwhelmingly rejected the package in a vote of 111 to 9.

The new constitution would pave a broad path to prosperity for many individual Canadians. Legions of academics, lawyers, journalists, and hungry public servants eagerly prepared to capitalize on the need to interpret the new document. On it, they could climb to recognition and reward, no matter which party governed the country.

No one heeded the ominous words of Robert Stanfield. Before the Kitchen Deal of November 5, 1981, he called Trudeau's work "a constitutional coup d'etat." And afterward, in an interview with journalist Charles Taylor, the elder Tory statesman prophesied: "Mr. Trudeau violated the federal nature of this country. Whatever happens we'll have bitterness and bitchiness for years" (*Radical Tories*, p. 197).

In 1790 Edmund Burke (1729–97), author of *Reflections on the Revolution in France*, observed:

> Men who undertake considerable things, even in a regular way, ought to give us ground to presume ability. But the physician of the state, who, not satisfied with the cure of distempers, undertakes to regenerate constitutions, ought to show uncommon powers. Some very unusual appearances of wisdom ought to display themselves on the face of the designs who appeal to no practice, and who copy after no model.

To ensure the completion of his plan for a bilingual nation, Trudeau had two more tricks up his sleeve: the circumvention of the Official Languages Act (1969) and the legal politicization of the federal public service.

The first, the easiest to accomplish, was already complete by the 1980s. Initially all that was needed was a well-paid high priest, preferably a zealot, to do Trudeau's bidding. Quebec would happily join this conspiracy. In the light of their Bills 22, 63, and 101, and the failure of the federal government to disallow them as constitutionally offensive laws, there was no way that province would ever become bilingual, legally or otherwise. Still Trudeau had to ensure the destruction of sections 12 and 13 of the Official Languages Act (1969) that entrenched Official Bilingualism on a territorial basis (see Chapter 3). Large sections of Quebec, including Montreal, were obvious candidates for this provision to cover. The semblance of the law had to be preserved for public appearances, but in practice it was essential the legislation be ignored until the law could be changed. Keith Spicer, Canada's first Official Languages Commissioner (1970–77), was perfect for the job. Max Yalden, Spicer's heir (1977–84), was equally submissive.

Finally, to complete the transformation of Canadian society into a bilingual state, Trudeau required the support of many fellow travellers who, if paid well enough, would follow orders without question and who, above all, would keep quiet. Control of the federal public service of Canada was absolutely essential.

The Federal Public Service of Canada is governed by two pieces of legislation, the Public Service Employment Act, 1966–67, Ch. 71, S.1, which regulates the Public Service Commission, and the Finance Administration Act, which regulates the Treasury Board. The Pearson administration passed the act governing the PSC and Trudeau amended it in 1974. Section 10 specifies how Canada's federal public servants are chosen. The act's whole purpose is to protect the public interest:

10. Appointments to or from within the Public Service shall be based on selection according to merit, as determined by the commission. . . .

12. (1) The commission has the discretion to prescribe the selection standards as to:

. . . education, knowledge, experience, language, age, residence or any other matters . . . but . . . standards shall not be inconsistent with [those prescribed in the] Finance Administration Act. . . .

Thus, although the PSC determines the standards of the Merit Principle, real power vests in the Treasury Board. As every politician and public servant knows, the Treasury Board is the strongest arm of government. It controls the purse strings.

The Commission was created ostensibly to protect the public interest from raw political power. In fact, the PSC, after its emasculation by competing legislation, ensures the exact opposite. While politically appointed deputy heads (deputy ministers) know they are technically accountable to the Commission on the Merit Principle, the mandarins know the PSC has no power.

It was through a very simple policy directive that Pierre Trudeau, once restored to power, executed the coup de grâce to the Public Service of Canada. On July 31, 1981, the Treasury Board Secretariat and the Public Service Commission jointly announced a revolutionary change. The actual fiat was entitled *Official Languages in the Public Service of Canada: A Statement of Selective Policy Changes*. It came into force on October 1, 1981:

(i) The Public Service Commission is withdrawing the obligation placed on departments and agencies to obtain approval from the commission in each case where imperative staffing is foreseen and is delegating this responsibility to deputy heads [deputy ministers].

(ii) ... the Merit Principle in all bilingual positions has been deferred.

The Imperative Staffing Principle (ISP) regulates which Public Service of Canada positions are arbitrarily designated bilingual. When positions are so designated, the public servants in them are entitled to demand that their work be assessed in the language of their choice. Thus, the ISP ensures over the long term that all senior-level managers throughout Canada will be bilingual.

Trudeau's directive destroyed the last bastion of the Merit Principle in Canada's once proud public service, reducing it to a political puppet show. In plain language *managers without merit* could and would now be appointed to manage employees who had it. This was a blueprint for revolt and corruption. The nation's federal public service died on October 1, 1981, by way of a memo.

This Cabinet directive transfigured the public service into a political army — the personal property of the Prime Minister's Office. The terrified PSC formed to protect the public interest was incapable of resisting the change.

In this final consolidation of power in 1981, completely foreign to the heritage of the country and the rule of law, Trudeau cleared the path to enforce his Official Bilingualism across the nation. As the provisions governing bilingual districts no longer meant anything, the prime minister now held absolute discretion to make all appointments himself, regardless of merit, to any position that *he* or his surrogates deemed bilingual.

Appointed or approved by the government in office, every single deputy minister in Canada of the day participated in the conspiracy. They all marched to Trudeau's tune, fearful of the most powerful public servant of them all, the Clerk of the Privy Council, Michael Pitfield. Known in high circles of government as the Dark Prince, Pitfield, having been out of office under Joe Clark, had been restored to power as the supreme mandarin by Pierre Trudeau on his own reincarnation.

To this day, the cover-up on Official Bilingualism and the politicization of the public service continues no matter what government is in power. The operative directive is well known within the labyrinth of government — KTLO, "Keep The Lid On."

Notes

1 In brief, habeas corpus is defined as "the most celebrated writ in the English law, being the great remedy which that law has provided for the violation of personal liberty.

"The most important species of habeas corpus is that of habeas corpus ad subjiciendum, which is the remedy used for deliverance from illegal confinement. . . ." Any person detained must be brought before a judge (P. Asterley Jones and J.C. Fisher, *Mozley and Whiteley's Law Dictionary*, 6th edition. London: Butterworth & Co., 1950).

2 In *Memoirs*, Trudeau said more: "I would have much preferred not to have included the notwithstanding clause that limited the charter of rights. But I certainly prefer to have a charter with a notwithstanding clause than no charter at all. I regretted the dropping of the referendum provision, and I favoured the Victoria amending formula that would have given Quebec a veto. . . . On the whole, the Constitution Act largely enshrined the values I had been advocating since I wrote my first article in *Cité libre* in 1950" (p. 328).

II

A New Vision
for Canada:
Existentialism

1982 to 1990

7

Martin Brian Mulroney
l'Irlandais, the Irish Kid
— 1979 to 1983

THE FALL OF THE CLARK GOVERNMENT in 1979 devastated the Conservatives. After such a short term in office, such high hopes, and then such bungling, the party recognized the necessity of a leadership review; but Joe Clark, playing the game rather smartly, as he did more often out of office than in, waited. And waited.

Then, a year after Trudeau's reincarnation victory of February 18, 1980, and under seige from within, Clark's chance came. He called for an internal review of his leadership for February 28, 1981. Despite merciless ridicule in the media and carping from the ranks, the results of the review were clear. Clark garnered the support of 66.4 percent of the delegates. He chose to consider the numbers a strong victory. He should have remembered the Diefenbaker years. By failing to declare war on the dissidents at the outset and wiping the floor with them by calling for a leadership convention and settling for a review, he blew it. The successful politician often wins power struggles in the first round with a knock-out blow. Clark chose to behave more like a punching bag than a pugilist. His blunder assumed enormous proportions in a party with a long history of internal backbiting and sabotage.

He had little to fear at the time. The only danger on the horizon was the threat of an ambitious Quebecer, Martin Brian Mulroney. Mulroney had publicly disqualified himself on many occasions. He had, for example, rejected Clark's overture to run in the February 18, 1980, election. At the time, he had still been under contract to the Iron Ore Company of Canada in Schefferville, Quebec, a subsidiary of Hanna Mining of Cleveland.

Joe Clark's decision to lead a crippled, grumbling party for the next two years certified his incapacity for leadership. Had he showed some fire for running the party, he would have earned respect and a clear mandate to get on with consolidating power. Everyone liked him. The country was crying for a winner. A good many admired him for his tenacity and even for his averageness. If only Clark had had courage as well.

Those two years of Conservative disarray in opposition were a boon to Brian Mulroney. Typically, the Tories exposed themselves devouring one another. Despite such mayhem in the ranks, they managed to gain in public popularity under Clark's careful and honest stewardship. Trudeau had long since worn out his welcome as a visionary with a credible blueprint for the future. Clark, on the other hand, sounded like a democrat, a populist. On March 12, 1982, at a PC fundraising dinner in Vancouver, he abruptly shifted the text of his speech from the economy to "another issue" that "has intervened — the basic issue of whether we are a democracy or not":

> The Liberal government, acting without Parliament, has taken a series of measures, some large, some small, which steadily diminish democracy in Canada. They have, for example, authorized the establishment of civilian internment camps in Canada. They have passed an Order-in-Council which gives the Prime Minister, in time of emergency — a condition they have not defined — the power to control information services in the country — that means the media and other services of information. (Official PC Text, Mar 11/82)

Clark soldiered on. Meanwhile, as Mulroney put it on television, "I became a free agent only on June 1, 1981" (quoted in MacDonald, *Mulroney: The Making of the Prime Minister*, p. 123). His forces plied their craft, sniffing whiffs of some distant victory. They connived, plotted, planned any coup they could nurture to build the fortunes of the labour lawyer from Baie Comeau, assiduously covering their tracks as they went. Everyone in the Mulroney camp, including The Boss himself, played the power games to advantage. In the end, the relentless forces of dissent nudged the Tories toward utter chaos.

Clark found himself continually under seige. Finally, when nothing would do but another leadership review, he called it for January 1983. Another stumble. Even at this late date, he could still have called for the leadership convention he should have called in 1981. Although the risks would have been greater, he still had an excellent chance of winning. Whenever he was faced with the choice, Clark avoided risk in favour of rules: leaders in opposition can always win reviews, but not necessarily leadership conventions.

On January 28, 1983, he won his second review as leader. He won 66.9 percent of the vote, ahead of the 66.4 percent he had pulled in in the February 1981 review. His position had improved. Mulroney thought Clark had won and said so: "Well then, Joe's okay. He did better than he did the last time" (MacDonald, *Mulroney*, p. 142). As Ian MacDonald tells it in his biography, *Mulroney: The Making of the Prime Minister*: "Clark had travelled the country, become a stranger to his own daughter, gone up nearly 20 points in the Gallup, but had risen only half a percentage point in his own party. Still, he had gone up" (Ibid.).

Then, Clark did it again. He snatched defeat from the jaws of victory. Unbelievably, he concluded he had lost! And so, predictably, he became another Robert Stanfield, the butt of jokes and cartoons. The pundits snickered; when Clark didn't have the numbers, some said he couldn't count; when he had the numbers, some said he couldn't count.

The opposition leader's assessment of the situation puzzled the professionals, but not those who knew him. He was a strange bird — a pro-francophone Anglo-Catholic from Alberta with enough Protestant leanings to be confused with Prairie puritanism. His voluntary self-defeat paved the way for Brian Mulroney to enter the arena and contest the leadership. This time Mulroney did it openly.

On March 21, 1983, Mulroney began his own earnest, public campaign to win control of the Conservative Party. It would not be easy. His public persona was that of an operator, a deal-cutter who had been less than candid and less than loyal to his leader. He needed a quick-pace strategy. He found one. It was not an original idea.

As Pierre Trudeau had published his tour de force *Federalism and the French Canadians* with Macmillan in 1968, so Brian Mulroney followed suit. He published *Where I Stand* in May 1983, at the invitation of publisher Jack McClelland of McClelland and Stewart. Aware of the impact that Trudeau's work had had on the academics and the media, Mulroney marshalled the best of his public utterances, some twelve speeches, all but one of which had been delivered during the three-year period between 1980 and 1982, and sent them forth to do battle. He knew his audience would not be Trudeau's.

The book hit the stands just a few days before the leadership convention — to Mulroney, a marketing ploy. A good hustler at any time, the ambitious young candidate knew the need for readily available promotional material for the masses. If it worked for Trudeau and one powerful audience, perhaps the strategy would work with an equally powerful constituency, the business community and the beleaguered taxpayers cheated by the Liberals of their dreams of economic freedom.

MULRONEY AND TRUDEAU shared more similarities than differences. In 1976, the Quebec publisher of *Le Devoir*, Claude Ryan, told Mulroney what Trudeau had told him before the Conservative convention that year: "They don't have the brains to elect him," meaning Mulroney (quoted in MacDonald, *Mulroney*, p. 248). Mulroney, an Irish Catholic from Quebec, an *Irlandais* and a Red Tory at heart, belonged in the Liberal Party. As a lad of nineteen, long before Trudeau made his stage entrance, he had written tellingly of his philosophy of Canada's dualism:

> To the French, [Confederation] is a pact between French and English, which guarantees each group an equal right to its own faith, language, laws and customs. . . .
>
> English and French, we climb a double flight of stairs towards the destinies reserved for us on this continent, without knowing one another, without meeting each other, and without even seeing each other except on the landing of politics. (Ibid., p. 49)

Trudeau's repeated invitations to the young man to join his Liberal Cabinet, however, were rebuffed. Mulroney knew that to jump ship for another party was certain suicide for anyone harbouring leadership aspirations. Getting others to do it to satisfy your own purposes as the leader with rewards to hand out was the trick. But such fun would have to wait. At age thirty-seven in 1967, Brian Mulroney lost the leadership to Joe Clark at the Conservative convention. Sixteen years later, the same candidate had mastered the game. Facing the same opponent at another Tory convention on June 11, 1983, Mulroney instinctively knew when to wait and he knew when to move.

His corporate responsibilities were at an end. The shutdown of the Iron Ore plant at Schefferville no longer constituted news of national consequence. Mulroney had stage-managed a public enquiry into the mess brilliantly. L'Irlandais, who spoke French as well as any native from the Gaspésie, was free.

He had an agenda in mind and a published program in the marketplace. All he could do at that point had been done. At the conclusion of *Where I Stand*, he wrote, "The chapters of this book express my thoughts and feelings about Canada and about some of the most pressing problems that face Canadians today" (p. 102). The nation was suffering under an increasingly onerous burden of mounting corporate and individual taxes and a national deficit that could no longer be ignored.

To some extent, Mulroney patterned his modus operandi on that of Trudeau. Trudeau gave speeches on economics and published them. So did Mulroney. Both made speeches and published their views on the Constitution and the place of Quebec in the federation. There were, however, important differences as well. Trudeau, the mystic, Jesuit-trained, diffuse, scholarly, nevertheless expressed his focus clearly. Mulroney, on the other hand, let it all hang out, no matter how exaggerated and bizarre the contradictions and economic constructions sounded.

Mulroney's rhetoric made the better read. Its author knew how to rally the troops. Quickly, deftly, and confidently, he hit all the high spots. After the Liberals had preoccupied themselves with constitutional and cultural matters for so long, Mulroney pretended to seriously address Canada's economic policy. He meant business — big business.

However, *Where I Stand* was not a work any prime minister would want as his monument. The selected speeches are riddled with contradictions over the Constitution and beer foam and emotion over business conditions. Spouting invective, sarcasm, and cheap shots, Mulroney the author burst upon the world with a flippancy far beneath his ability. In his teens he had made himself thoroughly conversant with Mason Wade's masterpiece *The French Canadians*, as well as with other scholarly works on constitutional law, economics, and politics. He knew from personal experience details of the reigns of the tyrannical Maurice Duplessis and company.

All in all, his impoverished credo revealed a great deal about the man: "Woven throughout this book is a vision, my vision of our country, of our greatness, its troubles, its past, and particularly of the future that awaits us if we can only learn from our past the lessons offered to us here" (p. 96).

The use of the word *vision* is interesting. Was it a business plan to get government out of business? More than half of the short work — which at 103 pages is half the size of Trudeau's treatise — concerns economic conditions in Canada. He writes: "Our national economic wizard [Trudeau] has managed the remarkable feat of transforming a $500-million deficit in 1968 into about a $26-billion overrun this year" (pp. 9–10).

Mulroney's bottom line: Trudeau, besides being a Liberal socialist, was a bad money manager. Even Sir Wilfrid Laurier, the Liberal icon of Canadian history who proclaimed that the "the twentieth century shall be the century of Canada and of Canadian development," did not escape blameless. Returning to the real subject of his attack, Mulroney writes: "Our problem is that we believed [Trudeau], literally" (p. 12).

He continues:

> I am a Canadian and want to be free, to the extent reasonably possible, of government intrusion and direction and regimentation and bureaucratic overkill. . . .
>
> There are no fancy-pants heroes anymore with elegant theories and magic wands. There are only overworked and harassed businessmen and labour leaders and ordinary Canadians who get their hands dirty every day dealing with the pedestrian problems of providing jobs, meeting a payroll, and producing a product — only to come home at night to learn on TV that some brave new social artist has invented another government plan that will add to costs, increase paperwork, and lessen competitiveness. (pp. 13–14)

Mulroney's economic ideal was Japan: "what I perceive to be the single most fundamental weakness of our economy [is] our anemic productivity" (p. 11). "Canada," he recommends, "should proceed immediately to the creation of a national, tripartite Productivity Commission, composed of labour, management, and government" (p. 17). Only personal discipline would do it: "The phenomenon of rising expectations can only be broken by unquestioned personal example. The credibility of our elected leaders would be greatly enhanced in the eyes of the ordinary worker if he knew his leaders were bleeding a little bit themselves" (p. 18).

Then there was Mulroney the socialist. He slips from the left to the right and back again with ease. In one instance, Mulroney the labour lawyer and advocate of compromise pleaded that:

> There must be a national commitment to civilizing labour relations in Canada. The adversarial system of labour relations ultimately produces just that — adversaries. It is rooted in a lack of proper two-way communication and results, inevitably, in mutual ignorance, hostility, and mistrust. (p. 19)

> My father was active in his union throughout his working life. I believe strongly in the value of vigorous trade unionism. Unions are indispensable instruments of social progress. The benefits of collective action are there for all to see. (p. 74)

Then there was Mulroney the corporate lawyer and businessman who said:

Canada is not Japan. . . . But Canadian industry must begin, in a thoughtful and progressive manner, to devise programs based on Japan's employment guarantee, industrial lifetime tenure, productivity bonuses, seniority salary differentials, job enrichment or job rotation programs within work teams, ongoing employee retraining programs, and relocation assistance if it is to convince the Canadian workers they have much to gain when productivity rises. (p. 20)

Mulroney's new economic future for Canada was firm on one point. He called for a major commitment to research and development. In an address at Ste-Foy, Quebec, on October 10, 1982, he read the riot act: "As a percentage of its population, Canada employs in research and development one-third as many people as do the Swedes, the Germans, and the Japanese, and one-half as many as the Dutch, the French, and the Americans. Of all the industrialized countries of the Western world, Ireland and Iceland are the only countries that invest less. . ." (p. 39).

His solution, in large measure, was a socialist one: "The National Research Council, which acts as Canada's main research laboratory, needs a funding increase of at least 20 per cent to bring it up to approximately $400 million" (p. 40). And he analyzed the Tories' failure to extract votes:

With few if any exceptions, the Conservative Party has been consigned to the Opposition benches for one reason alone — its failure to win seats in the French-speaking areas of the nation. From northern and eastern Ontario through Quebec and into northern New Brunswick, the electorate has rejected the Conservative Party with a consistency that is at once staggering and overwhelming.

The reasons? Well, take your pick — Louis Riel, conscription, poor organization, Quebec lieutenants, no provincial party, poor policy, unilingual leaders, two-nations theories — take your pick. . . . (p. 90)

"Two-nations theories" not popular in Quebec? Ridiculous. The *deux nations* concept had been at the core of Quebec politics since the Conquest; it was the very essence of all that Quebecers are wed to.

Mulroney had no vision of Canada. For him, the Constitution was merely a by-product of partisan politics, not an ideal. Trudeau won the hearts of many Canadians with a compelling concept of a bilingual and bicultural nation that encompassed justice for all in a pluralistic society. Sir John A. Macdonald, Canada's first prime minister, a Conservative, won the nation with a biblical calling: "He shall have dominion from sea to sea" — building the Pacific Railway to the west coast. Mulroney's concept of Canada could fit any set of circumstances, including *deux nations*. He almost managed to disguise the contradictions: "In any discussion of constitutional reform, I start from the premise of an indivisible Canada. . . . I do not believe in a theory of two nations, five nations, or ten nations. . . . Nor do I believe in any concept that would give any one province an advantage over any other" (p. 59).

In the very next paragraph, he gave himself an out: "Quebec is different, very different. It is not strange or weird, it is just different. And the difference is rooted in language and culture. That is why the preservation and enhancement of these two instruments is so vital. That is why they must be protected and nurtured with a constancy and vigilance that can never be slackened. . . . Quebec will always need a protective device to ensure the survival of the only French-speaking people in North America" (pp. 59, 65).

Trudeau's vision of bilingualism and biculturalism perhaps? Mulroney the street politician knew the pitfalls of such idealistic palaver in a province where the survival of the French language is the essence of daily life. The protective device, of course, was the notwithstanding clause. Years later this would become a central issue as Mulroney tried to revise history to put distance between himself and Trudeau[1]: "The federal government, through a remodelling of the Constitution, has obtained the enshrining of the rights of linguistic minorities outside Quebec, and I can only rejoice in this. However, such a noble and valuable accomplishment should not be tarnished by the possible reduction of Quebec's powers to legislate in the fields which are particularly crucial to this province" (p. 65).

Less than a page later, he offers yet another perspective. He notes the urgent need that he meet with Messrs. Trudeau and Lévesque, who "must now put aside any sense of partisanship . . . and work together toward a clearly superior and more noble goal: that of the welfare of the ordinary citizen": "This meeting is urgent because if Quebec is not in it, what is to become of the famous 'Canadian duality'? Should the word be simply stricken from our vocabulary? What would be done about the deplorable lot reserved for women and native people, for example? Should we now pretend that their fundamental rights as human beings are of secondary importance and will be settled maybe, some day, when we have the time?" (pp. 65–66).

Translation: Brian Mulroney endorsed not only Pierre Trudeau's notwithstanding clause but he took the same position in the same manner as Trudeau. Bill 101, the French Language Charter, should not be tampered with, even though it violates the BNA Act and blatantly contradicts

Trudeau's Charter of Rights and Freedoms. The handwriting was on the wall. Like Trudeau, Mulroney would do nothing to uphold Canada's constitution, historically or currently, to disallow the offensive legislation.

Throughout his credo, Mulroney, like Trudeau, also disguises the language issue. Quebecers understood the code: there would be no federal tampering to upset the superiority of their provincial law. English Canada slumbered on. Mulroney's testament supports Lévesque's French Language Charter for Quebec. If necessary, the province could go so far as to make itself unilingual, while Mulroney simultaneously supported bilingualism and biculturalism throughout Canada.

Mulroney endorsed the very theory he ridiculed — just like Trudeau. Mulroney supported Robert Stanfield's *deux nations* theory just as strongly as Joe Clark's community of communities or Pierre Trudeau's bilingual Canada. But the clever fellow did this while conning his English-speaking audience with the opposite message — just like Trudeau.

As for Canada's aboriginal peoples, he acknowledged serious injustice done to them in the past, but he takes a position no different than Trudeau's. Native people are to be excluded from the "famous duality," kept off the agenda. There was no equality of citizenship in his idea of Canada.

With the convention looming, Mulroney seized the opportunity to share another opinion — this time, on leadership: "The test of great leadership is to harmonize divergent views into an eloquent and thoughtful expression of national purpose. I speak for many when I express the hope that on this sensitive and fundamental issue, Canada's political leadership will not be found wanting" (p. 62).

So leadership was to be defined in terms of a politician's ability to achieve consensus. These are the words of a labour lawyer, not a leader. In the chapter headed "Leadership Today," a speech he gave in St. John's, Newfoundland, in 1980, he ignored the subject till the last moment: "Leadership — that is the question today. If we are led by people who accept sacrifice themselves before inflicting hardship on others; who practise the virtues of thrift, compassion, and humility . . . who tell us the truth even when they think we do not want to hear it — if we have that kind of leadership, and have it we must, Canada may yet fulfil that most splendid promise of her youth" (p. 79).

Word salad. What promise? What vision? What were the ideals worth fighting for?

ON THE EVENING OF JUNE 11, 1983, after defeating Joe Clark on the fourth ballot with 1,584 votes to 1,325, Brian Mulroney conquered the convention and captured the Conservative Party, leaving John Crosbie, David Crombie, Michael Wilson, and three others gasping in his wake.

It had been a long struggle since 1976. At that convention Mulroney was eliminated on the third ballot by Joe Clark and Claude Wagner. Wagner, the runner-up, attracted 1,003 votes to Mulroney's 369. Now Mulroney had only one more dream to fulfil: winning the next federal election.

But if he did, what would he do? No one had the foggiest. Canadians crossed their fingers and hoped for the best.

Notes

1 In his 1988 year-end interview with CBC, Mulroney referred to the 1981–82 Constitution package: "The exclusion of Quebec and the notwithstanding clause were two fundamental flaws that should, in my judgement, have prevented it from going ahead at that time." However, Jeffrey Simpson of the *Globe and Mail* recalls his interview with him over a long lunch at the Mount Royal Club in Montreal. He reports that Mulroney said, "Trudeau faced with a separatist government in Quebec would have no choice but to bring home the Constitution over Quebec's objections" (*GM*, Jan 4/94).

8

John Napier Turner
A Little Interregnum
— 1984

O N THE EVENING OF FEBRUARY 28, 1984, Pierre Trudeau took a walk in the snow behind 24 Sussex Drive, his official residence in Ottawa. Somewhere on the grounds of that ghostly grey edifice he finally decided to quit federal politics. The next day, Leap Year Day, he made the announcement. The theatrics were vintage Trudeau, a grand performance for history's record.

The Liberal Party roared into gear, scheduling the requisite leadership convention for June 13 to 16. Trudeau informed the media he would leave office on June 30.

Meanwhile, two weeks after Trudeau's announcement, his former justice minister, John Turner, was indulging in his own little drama. At the end of the working day of March 15 in Toronto, where he lived and worked in self-imposed exile away from the recognition he craved in Ottawa, he slipped away from his Bay Street law office as a private citizen for the last time. The next day he made his own announcement: he would run for the nation's crown once again.

John Napier Turner had departed Ottawa eight years earlier, on September 10, 1975, after an unhappy one-hour meeting with the prime minister. He had been royally spurned. Since that awful humiliation, he had not been at rest. For years, he had conducted a less than subtle campaign to restore his pilloried reputation.

Since that time, Turner had worked hard. He knew everyone who counted in the finance, business, and legal worlds within central Canada. In Western Canada he had also been working the hustings. Now, in the spring of 1984, opportunity presented itself at last. He could end an era of self-pity and wound-licking. He determined to lick his detractors instead. He knew this might be his last chance to play. "Chick" was ready — well, almost.

If he could win a leadership convention he would become prime minister and quickly, at minimal cost. The last round had been a cheat. The defeat of Joe Clark in December of 1979 had summoned Trudeau back instead of the Liberal leadership convention Turner longed for. When Trudeau decided on November 21, 1979, to call it quits for the first time, after a sound defeat by Clark in the May 22 election that year, he had fired wild speculations. In those days, the handsome John Turner, who looked more like a Blue Tory than a very Pink Liberal, was considered a front-runner and certainly a shoe-in for some high office.

He faced one small problem. He played the game as if he were still at private school, embroiled in a gentlemen's cricket match, keeping himself appropriately aloof — even telling the media after Trudeau's announcement that he wasn't interested in the job.

Jean Chrétien, another obvious contender, said he too had "no commitment with destiny." Donald MacDonald, another Toronto lawyer and former Trudeau Cabinet minister, had replaced Turner as finance minister. He was Trudeau's choice and the only candidate poised to move swiftly into the front ranks. In the end, the choices really narrowed to only two. As Jack Cahill reports in his detailed biography, *John Turner: The Long Run*, "The undeclared race was really between the two Toronto lawyers, both former Finance Ministers, both out of politics for several years and friends who respected each other and had lunched together at Toronto's York Club the day after Trudeau's announcement . . ." (pp. 201–2).

With Trudeau's long-awaited resignation on the table, Turner could move unimpeded. But he underestimated and even ignored the real problem: the magnitude of Trudeau's ruthless commitment to the survival of his vision. Turner's Canada was not Trudeau's. Trudeau was a centralist. Turner was not. Trudeau held strict ideas about Official Bilingualism. John Turner's vision of Canada was vapid, fuzzy. Trudeau knew. Someday Turner would vacillate and perhaps switch gears on just about everything *he* had achieved.

The evidence had been accumulating for many years. During the FLQ crisis in the 1970s, Turner opposed Trudeau's methods and spoke out against the formation of a central body to sift information and co-ordinate all policies pertaining to Quebec.[1] Turner behaved like a courtier who needed parenting or a head prefect who needed a headmaster.

The differences between the two men were more than philosophical. Canadians could feel them. They had nothing in common except the love of physical exercise. Yet even here the differences were glaring. Trudeau swam, canoed, walked, lived alone. Turner socialized. He played squash at clubs. He did lunch. He was one of the boys. Most significantly, Trudeau maintained his silence. Turner talked — too much. Once asked by the media if he would remain neutral in a push for the leadership by his former finance minister, Trudeau expressed his opinion concisely: "Turner — no."

There is one incident that firmed Trudeau's decision against Turner. On December 14, 1979, Prime Minister Joe Clark went to ask Governor General Ed Schreyer to dissolve Parliament. Four days later, on December 18, the same year that Trudeau decided he would change his mind and stay on as leader after all, the prime minister learned of the "Draft Turner" movement. He put a stop to it, pronto. He knew Turner's background from before the leadership struggle of 1968 and much earlier than that. In the 1968 leadership campaign, Turner had mused on the art of politics and being a Liberal: "A liberal, on the other hand, is a reformer; he has the zeal of reform; he is impatient with the imperfections of today and looks forward — eagerly — to a better tomorrow. This being so, the liberal has an openness of mind, a willingness to experiment" (Turner, *Politics of Purpose/Politique d'objectifs*, pp. 1–2). He also wrote, "The art of politics, after all, is the guiding, directing, and controlling of the aspirations of human nature. A political party must be willing to undertake the risk of leadership and thereby the risk of defeat. We must take our chances with the people" (p. 3).

Gooey stuff. Worrisome to his supporters. It was true, though, that Turner was a reformer. He said so many times; Trudeau never made casual remarks about reform. And what did Turner mean by his definition of the art of politics? How long could such a leader survive before he did something unpredictable — even silly?

Candour? Leaders are very sparing with that commodity. Turner's habit of blurting out his innermost thoughts could be traced back to remarks he made in 1963 to the Kiwanis Club in his own riding in Montreal: "The real struggles for power today are not fought on the floor of the House of Commons; they are fought inside the party councils. The caucuses of the government party and of the chief opposition party have become the real battlefields of politics. Democracy has become invisible" (Cahill, *John Turner*, p. 90).

It didn't matter that he captained Trudeau's language revolution. Trudeau could not reward a minion just because he had proved his loyalty, or because of debts owed. Sad for John Turner — he had worked so hard. For months and months, he had crusaded across Canada doing his master's bidding.

I was always in favour of the Official Languages Act, but I always said in cabinet that we had to sell it to the majority of the country and we had to sell it to the public service. You know, one of the difficulties in implementing it was that Trudeau and Pelletier were always coming in saying that it was a matter of right and that the majority had mishandled the minority, and they weren't going to give the public service credit for the efforts they were making to learn French, and that this was a time when people were making immense efforts to try to do something about it. But, you know, the government was hammering them all the time and not once did the Prime Minister or Pelletier ever thank the public service or ever thank the English-speaking majority for their understanding and tolerance and that made it very difficult for me and the English-speaking members in the Ottawa area and across the country.

But I approved the Official Languages Act. . . . I helped draft it, and it was introduced in the House by Gerard Pelletier. (Ibid. pp. 133–34)

Trudeau knew better. Turner openly admitted that Official Bilingualism was lunacy, yet acknowledged he was following orders. This is the stuff of corporals. And the government not thanking people? If he would make such remarks, how much further would he go? At this point support for Official Bilingualism had crumbled, according to the polls. Trudeau wanted a helmsman: someone with sufficient guile for the job. Turner lacked the makings of a prince who could hold onto his state. Machiavelli would never have approved.

In March 1977 at the Canadian Club in Vancouver, Turner delivered a talk on language, the Constitution, and Quebec's place in Confederation:

What direction should negotiations take? First of all, we should recognize that national unity is not a one-dimensional issue. Excessive emphasis has been placed on bilingualism as the sole prerequisite to national unity. This is difficult to swallow, particularly in western Canada where acceptance of two languages means rewriting history, where issues of resource ownership, transportation, and tariff structure are perceived to be equally important.

Bilingualism is not the total answer even to the aspirations of French Canada. . . .

Any reworking of confederation would have to treat all regions of the country equally. It would have to reflect the collective needs of French Canadians as a community or society. It would have to ensure equality of language rights in Quebec and in Canada as a whole. (Ibid., pp. 193–94)

This from one of the authors of the Official Languages Act who had pioneered its execution and who had helped set up the first Office of the Official Languages Commissioner?

John Turner was a first-rate athlete, a very competent scholar full of fun and affection — a thoroughly decent fellow: not bad credentials. Nevertheless, he was not and never could be a trustworthy insider. Old Boys never discuss the inner workings of the system. John Turner had all the makings of a good-hearted fally-go-downy.

His student days anticipated a great deal of the older Turner. He could hit a target so effectively and then fritter away his own accomplishment. A piece from his Honours BA thesis in political science proves his capacity to score points, then defuse their impact with surprising detraction:

What useful purpose does the Senate have today? Neither in its federal nor legislative aspects has the Senate accomplished its purpose. If this is so, there can be no logical impediment to its reform or abolition. The argument, however, is more severe. The waste of talent in the Senate of recent administrations has made that chamber a functionless oddity; but it has been the abuse in the method of appointments which has bankrupted its reputation in the country.

. . . A prime minister once in office is loath to foment any agitation which might result finally in his being deprived of a very convenient source of patronage with which to humour his party followers. . . . (pp. 51–52)

In his sad tale, *Reign of Error*, Greg Weston assesses the man from another angle: "Part of the reason for enduring misgivings about Turner's intellectual depth is a mind that operates like a storeroom full of filing cabinets, each drawer opened and closed as needed to respond to immediate demands. If there is an overall index to it all, or a master blueprint tying all this voluminous data into some conceptual grand design for life and the future of the nation, it is well hidden" (p. 30).

In the spring of 1984 Turner was the most Tory look-alike the Liberals had never elected to lead them. He should have been a Conservative in the tradition of George Drew. But he wasn't. He embraced socialist dogma. Time and again he made this clear, even though the business community never seemed to grasp this essential truth about his character. Only the National Citizens' Coalition screamed about this real live left-winger poised where he wasn't supposed to be — Bay Street.

In an interview with Pierre Berton, Turner once enthused about free education, free housing, free medical services and gave qualified support to a guaranteed annual income, increased inheritance taxes, and a capital gains tax — all at one sitting! He should have scared the hell out of right-wingers hungry to dismantle the socialist empire of Pierre Trudeau. But by 1984 the media world had forgotten what John Turner was all about.

His leadership victory at the convention on January 18, 1984, was sweet if short-lived revenge. He won, fair, square, and handsomely. Jean Chrétien, the runner-up, had collected 1,368 votes to Turner's 1,862. At their highest showing, the five others couldn't muster one-half the votes of either of the two front-runners. The only sour note was the reigning king's ungracious behaviour. Trudeau refused to join in the traditional rallying gesture of raising the winner's hand himself in salute to the crowd. When he was called upon to speak in honour of the prime minister elect he didn't. He couldn't. With this Pyrrhic victory for the Liberal Party, Trudeau found nothing to celebrate. John Turner seemed likely to prove himself the Joe Clark of his party.

Trudeau had a plan to deal with it. Nasty but necessary: he would ensure the hijacking of the federal government for a generation to guarantee the continuation of his vision.

In his remaining weeks in office, Trudeau extracted his price from his party for its folly. He did not see that he had only himself to blame for not finding a better candidate. None of the three front-runners — Chrétien, MacDonald, Turner — met his standards, nor, for that matter, did any of the five other candidates: Donald Johnston, John Roberts, Mark MacGuigan, John Monroe, or Eugene Whelan. There was work to do. The Liberal Party itself no longer mattered to him. With an election due soon, he knew there was a very good chance Brian Mulroney would become prime minister, and, to Trudeau, Mulroney would make a far more desirable choice than any Liberal in the running.

Trudeau planned Turner's interregnum with supreme arrogance. The way he managed it was certainly a bald-faced affront to democracy. As a condition of his leaving Turner in charge of a majority government, Trudeau demanded that the new leader agree to the appointment of seven more MPs to the already bloated patronage list. This would add to the six Trudeau had already appointed since the Liberal convention.

The appointments were negligible compared to Trudeau's greater crime. He cynically and irrevocably corrupted the Federal Public Service. By reducing the Public Service Commission to a rubber stamp of the Prime Minister's Office, by eliminating the Merit Principle in 1981, he now completed his task with his appointment list. He appointed huge numbers of managers to the public service to pay them off for playing along with his vision. A final salute of contempt. The already overloaded management and executive levels of the public service were swiftly doubled with some 2,000 more appointments.

Trudeau's 1984 tidal wave of patronage buried the Merit Principle once and for all. The Clerk of the Privy Council, the deputy minister of the deputy ministers, the policeman and leader of the public service, Gordon Osbaldeston, said nothing, nor did he resign. The press said nothing.

Turner faced a clear choice. He could agree, as Trudeau had demanded in writing, to make the patronage appointments when he judged the timing was right, to hold on to the majority government, or he could tell the outgoing PM to stuff it and take his chances with a minority government and the electorate.

He caved in. He did more than that. To Trudeau's list he added his own names. Between them, they rewarded nineteen followers.[2]

John Napier Turner, the young idealist, had written about political patronage to win his honours degree in political science. When tested in the arena, he assumed proprietorship of Trudeau's conquest of the country.

Canada's seventeenth prime minister was finished the day he took office, June 30, 1984. Having sold out on day one, he had no time to win back credibility from a disillusioned electorate. As the law required them to do no later than early 1985, the Liberals had to issue the writ for a federal election. The party was into its fifth year of office. The fall of 1984 seemed the obvious choice. Only the polls favoured the possible gamble of an early election.

Like Clark before him, Turner stumbled. Without even a graceful flinch, he agreed to all of Trudeau's terms. The whole country winced. He could have consulted with the governor general about whether or not he could have retained power, even with only a minority in the House of Commons. Instead he wasted the power he had on a bad agreement.

Desperate, nine days into office, Turner called the election for September 4.

In its chapter headings alone — "Right Honourable Chaos," "My Kingdom for a Vote," "Bullshit Theatre," "Review: A Dirty Little War," "Shove Comes to Putsch," "The Flying Circus" — Greg Weston's chronicle recounts the story of a man beaten by delusion and circumstance with the aid of his predecessor before he ever started.

Turner's record as prime minister is a non-event in Canadian history. His reign extended Pierre Trudeau's own, bought and paid for by his predecessor. Had Turner told Trudeau, his old mentor, to take a flying leap off the Champlain Bridge and be sure and hit a girder or two on the way down, the nation would have loved it! Big business would have loved it, too.

Instead, John Turner held office from June 30, 1984, till September 17, when prime minister elect Brian Mulroney took over after the election. Turner's tormented reign lasted eighty days. Only Canada's fourth prime minister, Sir Charles Tupper, managed to boast a shorter term in office — just sixty-eight days in 1896.

Notes

1   Turner's opposition to Trudeau's conduct during the FLQ crisis did not come to light until May 22, 1992. Under the Access to Information Act, Cabinet papers revealed that "dirty tricks" had been condoned and even encouraged by the government. Trudeau has been unwilling to comment on the matter.

2   In promoting his book *Memoirs* in November 1993, Trudeau denied that he had forced his successor to accede to the final blast of patronage appointments: "I said 'Well, John, you're the leader now. Do I name these 15 to 20 people now or do you want to do them for me after I've left Parliament?' And he thought about it, and he said, 'Well, I'll do them for you'" (*GM*/CP, Nov 19/93). Turner has not commented officially on Trudeau's little wiggle, but what's the difference?

9

Mulroney's Solemn Commitment to Quebec and Patronage Pratfalls — 1984

B Y DROPPING THE ELECTION WRIT nine days after his own swearing-in ceremony on June 30, 1984, Prime Minister John Turner allowed himself only fifty-seven days to capture the heart of the country. There was no time for strategic planning. Trudeau had made sure of that.

Two issues marked the interval between June and September 4: first, the blunders of both contestants over patronage, and second, the intrigue and the political selling-out of Canada's national interest to win the province of Quebec. Mulroney faltered on patronage and then won by default — thanks to Turner's greater boggle on the same issue. The state of the Quebec issue, a sleeper at first, proved the more important battleground. In less than eight weeks, the campaign was over. Turner lost because the media did a better job of hanging him for appointing separatists to his camp; Mulroney committed the same crime. Throughout the campaign, the politicians wooed and cajoled Quebec. English Canada was relegated to the background, a mere voyeur on the first issue, and uninformed and misled on the second.

Mulroney surged ahead at the beginning of the campaign, buoyed by

Turner's total collapse on Trudeau's patronage pay-offs. To Mulroney, Turner's pratfall must have seemed a gift from heaven. But then he tripped up badly himself.

It happened less than a week following the election call. Mulroney had decided, despite advice to the contrary, to run in his home riding, Manicouagan, Quebec. On July 13, in an opening move in the campaign, Mulroney flew to New Glasgow, Nova Scotia, to say farewell to the pinch-hit constituency that had given him a seat in the House of Commons. The next day he landed at Sept-Îles and before a welcoming crowd of 200 at the airport hammered away at his rival. He concentrated on Turner's agreement with Trudeau to approve the slew of patronage appointments Trudeau had urged on him. The next day the Tory entourage flew to Baie Comeau for a nostalgic meander through the leader's home town. At the end of the day, Mulroney boarded the 727 flight for Montreal. He did not seem aware of the bomb on board — him. On that fateful flight, he did something Turner might have done. He let himself blather with the newsboys in a bull session at the back of the aircraft.

As the story goes (and there are several versions), Mulroney indulged in what he thought was an "off the record" chat. Chided by reporters about the inconsistency of his remarks the previous year about patronage, the candidate, ever anxious to please his audience, repeated some of his earlier remarks. As far as giving a job to a Liberal, he said, "Yes, when there isn't a living breathing Tory left without a job in this country." He did qualify the remarks and the context, but he couldn't leave it alone. He detonated the big one. Trudeau's appointment of Bryce Mackasey to an ambassador-ship was OK, Mulroney explained, something he might accept himself. John Sawatsky provides the details in *Mulroney: The Politics of Ambition*: "'Let's face it,' he quipped, 'there's no whore like an old whore. If I'd been in Bryce's position I'd have been right in there with my nose in the public trough like the rest of them. . . . I hope this is all off the record. I'm taking the high road now'" (p. 533).

Neil Macdonald of the *Ottawa Citizen* published the informal July 14 exchange on Monday, July 16. He was duly reviled for it by many, unjustly. He had provided some badly needed insight into a man seeking the highest office in the nation from a very shallow base of entry.

The Mulroney gaffe levelled the playing field. His quip confirmed what many knew and most already suspected: on patronage, Brian Mulroney positioned himself firmly in John Turner's camp. Mulroney's strategists took two full days to grasp the significance of the widely bruited revelation.

By the time they swung into damage control, Mulroney's studied apology on July 18 in Sault St. Marie, Ontario, rang hollow:

> During the course of an informal conversation with certain members of the media last Saturday night while flying to Montreal from Baie Comeau, certain casual and bantering remarks on the subject of political patronage were attributed to me. I do not deny having made these remarks, but I say simply they were made without any serious intent since they clearly do not represent either my attitudes or my position with respect to this important matter of public policy. I was mistaken to treat so important a matter in a way which might be misunderstood and I very much regret having done so. As I have said since the outset of the campaign, I am committed to the attainment of new standards of quality in making public appointments and that remains my commitment to the people of Canada. (Quoted in Sawatsky, *Mulroney*, p. 535)

Canadians were not convinced. Better no apology than this one. Now voters knew instinctively that there was a serious problem. Mulroney could not bring himself to admit he was wrong. Another arrogant leader, like Trudeau.

The hullabaloo might have cooled at this point, but, ten days later, patronage was on the agenda once again, and on national television. John Turner raised it himself during a public debate with the two other leadership hopefuls, Ed Broadbent of the New Democratic Party and Brian Mulroney.

Turner had just emerged fresh with victory from the considerable feat of besting Mulroney in the July 24 public debate in French. Then, on July 25, during the debate in English, Turner did the unbelievable. He raised the subject of patronage and Mulroney's year-old promise to load the lists with Tories. Martin Brian Mulroney, l'Irlandais, paused for a flicker of a moment and then waded in with his shillelagh. The donnybrook was over in 120 seconds: "I've had the decency, I think, to acknowledge that I was wrong in even kidding about it. I shouldn't have done that and I've said so. You, sir, at least owe the Canadian people a profound apology for doing it" (Sawatsky, *Mulroney*, p. 539).

Turner's lame retort cost him the prize: "I told you and told the Canadian people, Mr. Mulroney, that I had no option."

Mulroney whipped back, "You had an option, sir." Before Turner could gasp, Mulroney winded him again: "This is an avowal of failure. This is a confession of non-leadership and this country needs leadership. You had an option, sir. You could have done better."

Turner limped out of the final TV debate mumbling, "I could not have been granted the opportunity of forming a government" (pp. 539–40). Nonsense. He had never gone to the governor general to test the waters.

Rather than blame the Liberals for their own demise, three Liberal historians at the University of Toronto, Robert Bothwell, Ian Drummond, and John English, formed their own impression of the period: "What stands out at this point is the lost trust. The Conservative campaign in 1984 was deliberately vague, since, as an opposition party, the best tactic is to avoid offending any significant group while letting the government defeat itself. . . . The promises were inherent in the style rather than the substance" (*Canada Since 1945*, p. 438).

They missed the big point. In English Canada Mulroney was more careful if less knowledgeable about the constituency, but he had certainly made no secret in his public speeches and writings of his plans to build an alliance between Quebec and the West if he and the Conservatives were elected. There was nothing vague about his remarks on industrial strategy in *Where I Stand*. At a fundraising dinner at the Westin Hotel in Toronto on May 5, 1982, he shot this bolt across the continent:

> Were it not for the punitive, vexatious, and confiscatory provisions of the National Energy Program [NEP], there is no doubt but that Alsands and Cold Lake [Alberta] — with a $25-billion investment and thousands upon thousands of precious jobs — would be well underway today. Ours is a mixed economy. . . . But the motor of the mixed economy is the private sector. . . . [Alsands] could have worked, but it will only go ahead when there is in Ottawa a government committed to the private-enterprise system. (*Where I Stand*, p. 35)

Mulroney campaigned vociferously on a number of specific issues: dismantling FIRA, the Foreign Investment Review Agency, as well as NEP. Those concerned about the social safety net he soothed. On August 17, 1984, he crooned, "The concept of universality is a sacred trust, not to be tampered with" (*GM*, Feb 25/93).

When it came to the second major issue of the election campaign, however, Quebec's place in Confederation, historians did not underscore the vagueness of his vision. Before the election campaign, Mulroney had no quarrel whatsoever with Pierre Trudeau's constitutional initiative. He accepted the patriation exercise, the notwithstanding clause, and other substantive clauses in the Constitution Act of 1982. He had said so.

In 1981, Mulroney told Jean Pelletier of *Maclean's* magazine that "Trudeau did what had to be done and it serves no purpose to fight him on that." Mulroney's view on the notwithstanding clause was also self-evident. He spelled it out in *Where I Stand*: Quebec would always have to have some "protective device." His silence on other issues spoke volumes. He said nothing against Bourassa's Bill 22, any more than he did against Lévesque's Bill 101.

His speech at Sept-Îles on August 6, 1984, clinched the election for the Tories:

> I know that in the Province [of Quebec] . . . there are wounds to be healed, worries to be calmed, enthusiasm to be rekindled, and bonds of trust to be established. . . . I know that many men and women . . . will not be satisfied with mere words. We will have to make commitments and take concrete steps to reach the objective that I have set for myself and that I repeat here: to convince the National Assembly [Quebec] to give its consent with honour and enthusiasm.

Some have since said that he spoke in code. If this were so, then Quebecers had the key to the cipher, and so did the Quebec press. Elsewhere, were the journalists asleep? Lazy? Inept? Whatever the reason, English-speaking Canada remained in its Rip Van Winkle stupor, oblivious to the magnitude of Mulroney's plan and duplicity. His biographer and former aide, L. Ian MacDonald, makes no direct reference to this particular speech. Yet it signalled a revolution, the alliance of a federal political party with Quebec nationalists. Mulroney had worked hard to forge this union in order to gain his power.

First, he welded a working alliance with his close friend and confidant, Lucien Bouchard, a leading separatist who had aggressively promoted the Yes side in the Quebec vote on sovereignty in 1980. Ian MacDonald described the relationship: "Of all the people Mulroney would meet in the many worlds he would inhabit, none understood him better than Bouchard, a dark-eyed romantic. Of all the people Mulroney had known, Bouchard was the one guy who could look into his soul" (MacDonald, *Mulroney*, p. 68).

Mulroney's speech at Sept-Îles was Bouchard's handiwork. Bouchard drafted the speech, paying particular attention to the opening and closing remarks. Of his own role, he writes, "I handed the speech to Mulroney in a hotel room in Chicoutimi. He read it and seemed satisfied. . . . It was a denunciation of the constitutional ostracism Trudeau had inflicted on Québec with his strong-arm tactics of 1982. . . . The future prime minister proposed changes to the Constitution that would convince Québec to sign it" (Bouchard, *On the Record*, p. 110).

Bouchard based his approach on the work of the prominent Montreal advertising executive, Jacques Bouchard (no relation). This other Bouchard, who, unlike Lucien, makes it clear in his writings that he is a "Canadian," wrote a best-selling book that listed numerous delicate points to consider in dealing with Quebec.

Mulroney's remarks at Sept-Îles remain the most important speech he ever made about Canada. It served as his conduit for dealing with the Parti Québécois. Mulroney's long-time friend Robert Bourassa was not in power at that point. To accommodate Quebec, it was clear to Quebec nationalists, the boy from Baie Comeau would go way beyond Pierre Trudeau in his concessions to René Lévesque.

Too late and toward the end of the campaign, John Turner caught on to what was happening. Suspicious, he made another fatal mistake. He adopted the Mulroney game-plan and nominated separatist sympathizers in three Quebec ridings.

It all came together for "Bones" Mulroney at last. On the evening of September 4, 1984, he became Canada's eighteenth prime minister, winning 211 of 282 seats. The result was not a victory for the citizens of Canada. It was not even a small victory for conservatives in Canada. It was a victory by default for a political instrument that had radicalized itself beyond recognition — the Conservative Party of Canada. Its many years in the political wilderness had transformed it into a ruthless revolutionary movement, easily as remote from the citizenry as the party of Pierre Elliott Trudeau.

10

The Parties Take
Positions on the Promise
Quebec — 1985

OLLOWING THE MULRONEY LANDSLIDE, René Lévesque's separatist government in Quebec moved quickly. The PQ politicians recognized the necessity of Norman caution. They had learned bitter, bitter lessons. Trudeau had betrayed their province before. His patriation pirouettes in 1981, capped by the Kitchen Deal, had put the Constitution Act in place in 1982. And he had followed those sleights of hand since his promise to "renew the Constitution" in the 1980 referendum campaign. As far as Quebecers were concerned, such federal manoeuvres proved that no one was to be trusted.

To many Quebecers, Trudeau's arrogance had meant full speed ahead and damn the torpedoes — eliminating any prospect of a constitutional veto for the province, constitutionally entrenching bilingualism, which simply would not work in that province, and a federal Charter of Rights and Freedoms that would eventually erode the Quebec Civil Code. For Quebec separatists, the Constitution Act, 1982, shifted the federal agenda to fast forward on all manner of intrusions into provincial jurisdictions.

So just what did Mulroney mean in his August 6, 1984, speech at Sept-Îles? Precisely what were the "concrete steps to reach the objective that I have set for myself and that I repeat here: to convince the National Assembly [Quebec legislature] to give its consent with honour and enthusiasm"? Was he cut of the same cloth as Trudeau?

111

By the spring of 1985, the PQ had determined their own position on any new constitutional arrangement. In May they had released a *Draft Agreement on the Constitution: Proposals by the Government of Quebec.* Lévesque's vision was set out after a preamble acknowledging Ottawa's change of the guard:

> Quebec was not a party to the constitutional accord of November 1981, which led to the patriation of the Canadian Constitution and to its amendment in some essential respects. . . .
>
> The present situation is viable neither for Canada nor for Quebec. . . . We must seek an opportunity to remedy this situation.
>
> We believe that this opportunity has been afforded us by the election last September of a new government in Ottawa. It will be recalled that during the election campaign, the now Prime Minister of Canada not only recognized the reality of the problem, but also solemnly committed himself to resolving it. (quoted in Leslie, "Appendix A," *Canada: The State of the Federation, 1985,* p. 61)

In the draft agreement, the Parti Québécois cited Mulroney's Sept-Îles speech. They took it as further federal encouragement to proceed with their own plans, and so published an excerpt from the House of Commons Speech from the Throne of November 5, 1984, just six weeks after Mulroney became prime minister: "my ministers will work to create the conditions that will make possible the achievement of this essential accord" (Ibid.).

That throne speech set the stage for the next eight years. Canada would be governed according to the needs of Quebec. All else would be secondary.

The PQ proposal for the new relationship between Quebec and Canada spelled out the conditions for a nation within a nation. It listed twenty-two requirements — just a teaspoon short of a unilateral declaration of independence (UDI). Quebec would be sovereign, but still exist within another, weaker nation. First and foremost beyond the "Conditions for an Agreement," the deal would "explicitly recognize the existence of a people of Quebec." There would be "Recognition of the Primary Authority of Quebec in the Matter of Rights and Freedoms." As for "Quebec's Responsibility for Language Rights — The distinctiveness of the people of Quebec goes beyond the question of language, but language is at the origin and the heart of that distinctiveness." René Lévesque created the concept of Quebec as a "distinct society." Sovereignty-association was based on that premise.

As ammunition, the PQ government cited the 1977 Pépin–Robarts Royal Commission, the Task Force on Canadian Unity. The separatists seized the opportunity the commissioners provided. They challenged the strong centralist government in Ottawa. They capitalized on Joe Clark's "Community of Communities" proposition and on Robert Stanfield's theory of *deux nations*.

One pernicious argument originating in the draft agreement was the justification of Bill 101, Quebec's French Language Charter. Skilfully the PQ homed in on the weak spots the commission had left: especially the total collapse of the commission on Bill 101. If a royal commission endorsed provincial legislation that offended the nation's constitution, why should Quebec not agree with it wholeheartedly? The Quebec government cited the report:

> We also expect that the rights of the English-speaking minority in the areas of education and social services would continue to be respected. These rights, and this should be stressed, are not now guaranteed by the Canadian constitution. Yet they are recognized under Bill 101, the charter of the French language, a law passed by a Parti-Québécois government. Thus, we already have proof that the rights of the English-speaking community in Quebec can be protected, without any constitutional obligation, and that the governments of Quebec are quite capable of reconciling the interest of the majority with the concerns of the minority. (Ibid., p. 65)

Just desserts for the Pépin–Robarts commissioners' carelessness. Constitutional protection coming from the lesser forum in law, a provincial legislature? It made sense to Quebecers. Neither Bill 22 nor Bill 101 had been disallowed under the BNA Act or tossed to the Supreme Court of Canada by Prime Minister Trudeau for a non-binding opinion. The question now was, what would the new prime minister do? Would Brian Mulroney do anything? After his speech at Sept-Îles, the PQ knew he wouldn't dare pick up the gauntlet they had thrown at his feet. With the draft agreement they were effectively saying, put up or shut up.

The draft agreement is a study in bravado and cheek. It makes for an enjoyable read and remains important for study now as much for the language it employs as for its content. References to the "distinctiveness" of Quebec, for example, appear four times. It is in this report that Quebec is described in a manner that would soon lead to tortuous discussions: "[Quebec] has developed to the point where it has acquired all the characteristics of a distinct society" (Ibid., p. 64).

As long as the separatists were in power, the federal government could expect no direct dealings on constitutional reform. As the leader of Quebec's Liberal Party, Robert Bourassa bided his time in opposition. He was equally aware of Mulroney's promise to give priority to Quebec. His party's policy commission published *Mastering Our Future* in February 1985: "The willingness for redress expressed by the Prime Minister of Canada has given rise to hope on both sides" (Ibid., p. 74).

The Liberals sneered at the PQ government and their strategy. They would be different, they bragged, but only in their style: "This is why the Parti Québécois practice of boycotting federal–provincial meetings is such a futile attitude, detrimental as it is to Quebec interests" (Ibid., p. 75).

The Liberal policy commission established "three main objectives" as a condition for accepting the Canadian Constitution:

i.   an explicit recognition of Quebec as a distinct society, homeland of the francophone element of Canada's duality;

ii. obtain solid guarantees for Quebec's cultural security;

iii. preserve Quebec's existing powers, while restoring its ability to influence the evolution of the Canadian federation.

The sentence that followed encapsulated the main points of the Liberal policy paper:

It is high time that Quebec be given explicit constitutional recognition as a distinct society, with its own language, culture, history, institutions and way of life. Without this recognition, and the accompanying political rights and responsibilities, it will always be difficult to agree on the numerous questions involving Quebec's place in Canada. This recognition should be formally expressed in a preamble of the new Constitution. (Ibid., p. 77)

Now both the Liberals and the Parti Québécois were seeking formal recognition of Quebec as a distinct society. Whether the government of Quebec was a separatist one or Liberal, both parties certainly shared nationalist outlooks and demands. Both claimed the powers of nation states: territorial sovereignty, of course, with unequivocal control over their own affairs. Whether absolute power came by means of a veto within a loose federation, as the Liberals demanded, or by the federal government's relinquishing of all but token federal powers to a newly named nation, as the Parti Québécois demanded, the result would be the same.

"Distinct society"? The phrase would haunt the country. What did it mean for a province to be "distinct"? The term appeared in both the Liberal and PQ position papers without definition. How far were the parties prepared to go? The question hung suspended, unanswered.

On October 3, 1985, following the resignation of René Lévesque earlier that year for health reasons, Pierre Marc Johnson took over as the province's prime minister and leader of the Parti Québécois. He reigned only briefly — just a whisker longer than two months. With Lévesque defeated in the 1980 referendum, the PQ had become a bore. It had lost its sparkle without him at the helm. The new leader was a professional man, a law professor, and a surgeon with none of his predecessor's vision or zeal.

By the end of 1985, the PQ had lost control of their own agenda. Robert Bourassa campaigned on his long-standing relationship with Prime Minister Mulroney and declared he would forge a new constitution with Canada that would protect Quebec's interests. On December 2, 1985, he won easily. The man known as the architect of Bill 22, the 1974 forerunner of Quebec's Language Charter Bill 101, passed by the PQ government in 1977, had his majority government.

The dramatic Liberal victory came six months after the publication of the Parti Québécois's *Draft Agreement on the Constitution* and nine months after the Liberal Party's policy commission released *Mastering Our Future*.

The Trudeau revolution was over. The second revolution in Canada had begun. Before long the game plan and the new players, Brian Mulroney and Robert Bourassa, would become household names to all Canadians.

11

Her Majesty's Mafia
Queen's University — 1986

IN A FREE SOCIETY a nation's educational institutions must maintain their independence of government. Only then can a democracy flourish. This is particularly true of universities. They must always be at the forefront of free thought, experimenting with fresh ideas and encouraging intellectual ferment. The destruction of a liberal society is not far off when the politics of government and the world of academe marry. In 1972 the former prime minister, John Diefenbaker, noted the calamitous conditions that threatened to ruin democracy in Canada: "Law-making has been turned over to a group of self-styled intellectuals who from their ivory towers, cut off from the rest of Canada, and receiving up to $30,000 or $32,000 a year, decide what shall be done" (*Those Things We Treasure*, p. 31). In the Pearson and Trudeau years, Canadians saw that marriage consummated. In the Mulroney era, the same union was exploited and so, as a result, were Canadians.

Just how incestuous the relationship is was proved between 1982 and 1992, between Trudeau's repatriation of the Constitution and Mulroney's Referendum on the Charlottetown Accord. The debate over the Meech Lake Accord exposed all the connections between the players and the events as much as the extent of the damage to the federation.

Many respected educational institutions and their leaders must share the indictment. With the politicians, they are responsible for having disenfranchised their fellow citizens from any meaningful dialogue about the nation's future. And the academics did not act alone. With the press and the broadcast media, many professors and other professionals hastily clambered on board the publicity bandwagon, turning blind eyes to their true duty as educators, to nourish intellectual evolution. No one on any Canadian campus spoke out on behalf of the nation's democratic tradition.

Queen's University has a particularly ample amount to answer for today. Far too many of its faculty members played a role in the mess. Faculty members on other campuses across the country participated, too, on a slightly smaller scale.

Queen's University Professor Peter Leslie won himself a leading role. As director of the university's Institute of Intergovernmental Relations (IIR), he accepted an especially disreputable assignment. During the Mulroney era he is credited with having organized, almost single-handedly, the symposium that set Canada's course for the next eight years. Carol Goar of the *Toronto Star* saw him as a hero: "Peter Leslie was one of the lucky ones. The Queen's University political science professor put the right people in the right place last year, to re-open the stalled constitutional negotiations between Quebec and the rest of the country" (*Star*, Apr 25/87).

The Institute of Intergovernmental Relations at Queen's University in 1965 had been conceived as a "university-based research centre concerned with the problems of Canadian federalism." It was a think-tank for academics and others to research, network, and communicate their ideas between various functionaries of government and politicians in power. Leslie, an anglophone Quebecer from Montreal, had been lecturing in political science at Queen's since 1965. In 1982 he was appointed to the Faculty of Political Studies as a full professor. The following year he was appointed director of the IIR. Bright, articulate, and personable, he was like many academics in Canada who were either duped or saw themselves as political activists rather than independent thinkers. Government funding sealed the bargain between them.

The election of Robert Bourassa on December 2, 1985, coupled with Mulroney's discreet commitment to Quebec were the two ingredients Professor Leslie and his colleagues needed to move. In 1985, as editor of *Canada: The State of the Federation*, a series of IIR publications, he wrote: "After nine months in office the substance of Mr. Mulroney's vision remains ill-defined; the vigour with which he is capable of exercising political will remains unproven. He has been much clearer about process than about most of the choices he will make when consensus is manifestly absent and unachievable" (p. 7).

Leslie pioneered the crucial step that would eventually bring the Mulroney constitutional agenda into the public arena. The Mont Gabriel

Conference in Quebec seemed innocuous enough in the beginning. The gathering at the famous ski resort from May 9 to 11, 1986, would be a little get-together of boffins to play at chewing out the complexities of asymmetric federalism, the most boring subject in Canadian history. The symposium was grandly titled "Rebuilding the Relationship: Quebec and Its Confederation Partners." On the surface, the Queen's IIR, l'École nationale d'administration publique, and the Montreal newspaper *Le Devoir* undertook to arrange the conference jointly. The Government of Canada directly funded the cloistered tête-à-tête, with the support of seven provincial governments. Additional backers included the insurance company Mutual Life of Canada, a corporation deeply involved with the federal government, and the Department of the Secretary of State, through an arrangement set up expressly to channel special donations to it.

In his *Conference Report*, Leslie as chairman offers only a sketchy outline of the proceedings. He infers that the organizers were trying to protect the participants from public disclosure. There were sixty-five of them unaccountable to the public. Even the number of tax dollars given the symposium was never released. Leslie reports that half of the money came from Quebec and half from the rest of Canada.

At the outset, the conference was structured so that it assumed Canada's duality, a balance of French and English. Invitations to the media were strictly controlled: those who came behaved — so it seems — as participants only; they did not attend in order to inform the public about what went on there. Although members of the business community were invited, few of them turned up. The public was conspicuous by its absence.

The Mont Gabriel Conference marks a watershed in Canadian history. It is important not only for what transpired during and after it but for what did not take place. It was at this conference that Pandora's box, Canada's constitution, was brought to the table and torn open. The country would never be the same after this coven of academics, bureaucrats, and select politicians and political advisors indulged themselves in plans to muck about with constitutional complexities. Vibrations from this gathering would ripple across Canada for more than a decade afterwards. Without any public participation, the conference participants gave their blessing to the priorities, the content, and the ground rules for what would become known for the next seven years as "the Quebec round."

In his *Conference Report* of 1986, *Rebuilding The Relationship: Quebec And It's Confederation Partners* [*sic*], Leslie commented on the setting:

Since most of the proceedings were in private, the report — though prepared on the basis of a full record of the discussion, to ensure accuracy — generally avoids identifying individual participants. (p. 4)

- The constitution is a genie in a corked bottle. Before uncorking it, one must be sure the genie will not grow to unpredictable proportions, or become unmanageable. . . . Other parties must be persuaded not to look upon the reopening of the constitutional dossier as an opportunity to air their own grievances or to win approval for whatever amendments they themselves would like to see adopted. If this happens, the agenda will expand uncontrollably, and it will be impossible to negotiate an agreement. All governments must accept — as they subsequently did at Edmonton, during the August [12, 1986] meeting of the premiers — that the items put on the agenda by Quebec will have priority. The justification for this is that the constitutional accord of November 1981 was not acceptable to Quebec, and its moral exclusion from the constitution cannot be allowed to continue.

- Important as it is to reach a new accord, it would be a mistake to start formal negotiations unless there is a strong likelihood of succeeding. Great damage would be done, in terms of Quebec public opinion, if talks began and then failed. Thus a preliminary set of informal discussions must take place behind closed doors, and the outcome of these discussions should determine whether prospects are good enough to move the talks into a public phase. Ultimately there *will be* a public phase, because the 1982 Constitution Act requires that all amendments secure parliamentary and legislative approval . . . by Parliament and all ten provincial legislatures. (pp. 33–34)

The group assembled at Mont Gabriel was not representative of the Canadian population as a whole. However, it probably was a good cross-section of Canadians having an interest in constitutional affairs. . . .

What "kept the juices going" at the conference was the strong and widely-shared conviction that national reconciliation is a national imperative. Quebec, it was recognized, had valid reasons for refusing to give its consent or support to the Constitution Act, 1982. (p. 37)

Much about this historic conference will never be known: what little evidence is available suggests that there were too many reputations at risk for all to be revealed. Even so, at least five conclusions can be deduced from the record.

First, the proceedings were "politicized" long before the conference began. The conference bankers had seen to it that their delegate selection and the format would exclude anyone who disagreed with any fundamental of the prime minister's "vision." Participants had been pre-selected exactly the same way for the Bi-Bi Commission in 1963 and again for the Pépin–Robarts Task Force on Canadian Unity in 1977. This ensured that there would be little or no dissent about the consensus already reached.

Second, critical assumptions had been agreed on about Canada's constitutional climate before the conference, presaging its outcome. For example, even by participating in such a rigged forum, all the participants agreed on the conference's stated priority: to settle Quebec's place in the federation. All other constitutional issues would revolve around this goal — to resolve the Quebec round.

Third, we know that most of the proceedings were held in secret. The actual report admitted that the views of the contributors were "never released."

Fourth, as already noted, the organizers based the conference on Canada's "duality," the premise that Quebec and English Canada are the main and equal partners in Confederation. In 1978 the Hon. James Richardson, who resigned from the Trudeau Cabinet in 1976, complained about precisely this assumption adopted by the Pépin–Robarts Task Force on Canadian Unity.

Finally, perhaps the most important feature of the conference was its selection of the players. These few academics and government apparatchiks unquestioningly adopted the Trudeau methodology. Even today, after the collapse of the Meech Lake and the Charlottetown accords, the proceedings of the Mont Gabriel Conference have never been made public. This despite the fact that taxpayers financed a handsome portion of the expenses through seven provincial governments and the federal Secretary of State. And there's more.

The media, in the form of the CBC, the *Globe and Mail*, and *Le Devoir*, attended the gathering. None of these organs reported anything of substance about what happened there. Those press and broadcast people who went were protected. They were included, Leslie explains in his report, as individual "delegates"; as participants, they did not have to account to their respective organizations or to the public. The public record contains only their names: James Duff, CBC, Montreal; Graham Fraser, *Globe and Mail*; Paul-André Comeau, *rédacteur-en-chef* (editor-in-chief), *Le Devoir*.

Most of those at Mont Gabriel were prominent in the academic world, held high positions in government, or both. Their names would become well known to Canadians in the coming months and years: Gérald Beaudoin, dean of the University of Ottawa law faculty and a former commissioner on the Pépin–Robarts Task Force; Benoît Bouchard, Secretary of State; and Gordon Robertson, former Clerk of the Privy Council during the Pearson–Trudeau era. Norman Spector, Canada's fastest rising senior public servant of the day, represented the government of British Columbia; Roger Tassé had been Prime Minister Trudeau's right-hand man, then deputy solicitor general and constitutional advisor from 1980 to 1982; Professor Ronald Watts came as former principal of Queen's; Dean John Whyte was a member of Queen's law faculty.

Because of this conference and the role so many of its participants played, these Queen's academics became known as "The Queen's Mafia." Six out of sixty-five of the conference participants hailed from Queen's, three times as many as those of any other university. They were David Hawkes and Peter Leslie, John Meisel and Ronald L. Watts, the last two from the Department of Political Studies; and Dan Soberman and John Whyte from the Faculty of Law.

Besides the academics there were twenty-three government representatives, MPs, senators, or public servants. One represented the Prime Minister's Office. As the numbers showed, people from Queen's and the government constituted almost half the conference. In 1988, a new face would join the Queen's Mafia, Thomas J. Courchene, of the École nationale d'administration publique of Montreal. He assumed the position of director of the School of Policy Studies.

The organizers invited some leaders from the business community as well. Leslie does not explain why so few actually attended. However, his *Conference Report* does include the comment of one anonymous Quebec businessperson who did:

> Just when exhaustion [caused by the intense and fruitless political debates of the past few years] is giving way to stability and enthusiasm, you invite me to come and participate in reopening the dossier of our collective insecurity. I'm not interested. Recalling the two solitudes is outdated. The presumed isolation of Quebec is an abstraction. The re-emergence of Quebec is going on, not in the Ministry of Intergovernmental Affairs [Gil Rémillard's portfolio], but in the universities and the factories of the province. . . . The state is giving way to the individual, it is privatising, deregulating, rationalizing, leaving to private enterprise responsibility for wealth

creation. . . . I don't want a new constitutional debate and especially not a new election or a new referendum on the subject. Our job now is to contribute to material well-being. (Conference Report, 1986, p. 10)

This speaker made the most important contribution to the entire conference. He or she alone raised the philosophical questions that should have been the basis of the conference. John Ralston Saul, author of *Voltaire's Bastards: The Dictatorship of Reason in the West*, and Thomas L. Pangle, author of *The Ennobling of Democracy: The Challenge of the Postmodern Age*, may supply some insight into the kind of dialogue one might have expected from such a forum:

There is no great need for answers. Solutions are the cheapest commodity of our day. They are the medicine-show tonic of the rational elites. And the structures which produce them are largely responsible for the inner panic which seems endemic to modern man. (*Voltaire's Bastards*, p. 17)

What is so troubling about our present situation *within* the Western democracies is the philosophic thinness of our answers. . . . (*The Ennobling of Democracy*, p. 2)

No one at Mont Gabriel asked any questions. During the whole Mulroney era no one asked any questions. Everyone else who attended simply accepted the Quebec agenda and its justification. The fact that Trudeau had disenfranchised all Canadians as much as he had Quebecers by his repatriation has never even been suggested. It is impossible to reconcile anything about the Mont Gabriel Conference with the standards Prime Minister Mulroney had set for First Ministers Conferences in *Where I Stand*: "The debate [on the Constitution] would be entirely open to the public at all times. *There would be no sessions behind closed doors*" (pp. 61–62).

Two key players opened and closed the conference: Gil Rémillard for Quebec and Benoît Bouchard, Secretary of State, for Canada. On May 9, 1986, after Leslie's opening remarks, the Hon. Gil Rémillard, Minister of International Affairs and Minister Responsible for Canadian Intergovernmental Affairs for Quebec, mounted the podium. The elegant politician was billed as keynote speaker. It was supposed that he would give his audience the answer they hungered to hear, the answer to the longest standing question in Canadian history: "What does Quebec want?"

He was well known to the august assembly. The year before he entered politics and won an election victory in the Bourassa landslide of December

2, 1986, he had worked as a member of the Faculty of Law at Laval University. Simultaneously he had served as a member of the same Advisory Council of the Queen's IIR that Leslie now directed. By the time of the Mont Gabriel Conference, Premier Bourassa's point man had done his homework. He had spent twelve years studying and teaching law internationally and in Canada.

He had very good connections as well. In 1985, he had advised Prime Minister Mulroney on constitutional matters. During his interlude in Ottawa, he had gained a broader perspective and a very different awareness of Canada than that of the plaintiff seeking redress at the Laurentian resort: "The people of Quebec, holders of sovereignty, have not been consulted with regard to this patriation, nor has anyone else in Canada. It is difficult to understand how a democratic country like Canada has been able to amend substantially its constitution without any kind of formal consultation with its people" (from *Le Fédéralisme Canadien: le repatriement de la constitution*, quoted in Robert Young's *Confederation in Crisis*, p. 15).

Rémillard was destined for centre stage. With his impressive height and aristocratic bearing, he loomed like a modern-day Cardinal Richelieu over modern Canadian constitutional history. Some observers thought him a loose cannon. Even so, he had a lot going for him, including the saving grace of a sense of humour. For example, he owned a horse he called Non Obstante — Notwithstanding.

The demands he enunciated that day amounted to a softened version of Lévesque's "sovereignty-association" credo. He electrified his audience with his seeming conviction that Canada was the rightful home of Quebecers while pressing them to agree Quebec was already a nation all but sovereign, even if Canada were in some way broken in two as a result. He knew his audience. He laid out the ways to heal the wounds Trudeau left behind him, the conditions for Quebec's constitutional reconciliation:

1. explicit recognition of Quebec as a distinct society;
2. guarantee of increased powers in matters of immigration;
3. limitation of federal spending powers;
4. recognition of a right of veto;
5. Quebec's participation in appointing judges to the Supreme Court of Canada.

On Quebec's agenda and Mulroney's covenant to Quebecers at Sept-Îles on August 6, 1984, the nation would now grind slowly on, on the carefully nurtured premise that Quebec had suffered a gross injustice at the hands of the rest of the country.

At dinner that evening, the delegates listened to an address by the Secretary of State of Canada, the Hon. Benoît Bouchard. During the 1980 referendum on sovereignty-association he had actively campaigned with Lucien Bouchard for Lévesque's vision. Benoît Bouchard was one of the many soon to be dubbed "conditional federalists." A lawyer and former history teacher, he was also the perfect mummer. The Secretary of State cited several passages from Mulroney's Sept-Îles speech. Well aware that most people at the conference would know little of the context or substance of Mulroney's remarks, he said:

> For my colleagues and me, it was like a political manifesto, and the orientations it set out touches [*sic*] on almost every point in the concerns being discussed here today. . . .
>
> A lot of water has flowed under the bridge since August 1984, but I still agree wholeheartedly with the vision of Canadian federalism underlying the Sept-Îles speech. (Conference Report, 1986, pp. 49–50)

After declining "to comment upon statements by the Government of Quebec or other participants" who had spoken during the day, he veered off to discuss what he claimed were his own priorities:

> As Secretary of State, I intend to use these improved relations as the basis for a reaffirmation of our official languages policy. This policy is not only the touchstone of our relations with Francophone and Anglophone Canadians, but also the *sine qua non* for real and full participation by Quebec in the life and institutions of our country. (Ibid., p. 51)

> But beyond the bilingualization of the federal government, what concerns me most as Secretary of State is the need to make the whole of Canadian society more open to the country's linguistic duality and to strengthen our official language minority communities so that they may flourish and take full advantage of bilingual services provided by the federal government, the provinces, municipalities and private organizations. (Ibid., p. 54)

Bouchard's speech masterfully concealed his larger role at the conference. He fell back on the old Trudeau ruse of preaching Canadian unity under the Linus blanket of Official Bilingualism. He spoke to his audience as if he were addressing some another conference, referring to Jock Andrew's incendiary book *Bilingual Today, French Tomorrow* (1977) (Ibid., p. 53). Aloud, he also admired the ability of Ontario's premier David Peterson to address the Association canadienne-française de l'Ontario entirely in French.

In fact, Bouchard intended to launch the Quebec round. To do so he played the role of the absent-minded professor, of *le bouffon*. The federal government had done its part, supplying the money the academics needed to set up their conference. Bouchard consciously deflected, obfuscated, bought time from the sidelines, and let others handle the agenda head on. This was Mr. Nice Guy, who would report his success back to Mulroney.

The conference closed with a monumental bargaining blunder by its organizers. Carol Goar unwittingly hinted at it in her *Star* article on April 25, 1987, when she quoted Peter Leslie, the master of ceremonies: "[Rémillard] was supposed to give the keynote speech after the dinner on Saturday, but he wanted to speak on Friday night to get into the Saturday papers. We accommodated him — but not with any great enthusiasm."

She did not explain exactly who "we" were because she did not recognize the deceit. The Quebec delegation did not, either. By winning control of the conference's publicity, they knew they had won an enormous victory. Quebec assumed mastery of the all-important first public impression. Once licensed to take that lead, and armed with prepared statements, Rémillard hijacked the debate for his province. Now it could move into the public arena with confidence. All his mutterings about the premature nature of the conference were garbola. He had been thoroughly groomed for this very moment for more than a decade. English Canada's representatives never knew what hit them. From this point on, the dolts marched resolutely into the losers' circle.

THE FUNCTIONARIES AND ACADEMICS owned by their institutions kept their own peace — partly because of their academic positions and partly because of their own ignorance. To maintain their positions in the loop, such people know they must keep quiet at all costs.

Everyone at Mont Gabriel betrayed Canada. The fact that the organizers failed to establish that all publicity releases would be issued jointly as a condition of participation was a staggering oversight. The media representatives failed in their duty to ensure broad public knowledge of the proceedings.

The academics were easy pickings for the crafty politicians who bought them and set them up. Any bargaining strategy Canada could possibly have maintained was irrevocably compromised from that point on. For all of

Mulroney's mandate, the constitutional agenda was cast in stone as the Quebec round.

Following the conference, Mulroney met with his inner Cabinet. Then he announced that the Constitution would be opened to accommodate Quebec. On July 4, 1986, Senator Lowell Murray, government leader in the Senate and Minister of State for Federal–Provincial Relations, received his orders. He was to mimic Gil Rémillard's role nationally and tour Canada, lobbying support for Quebec's demands from the other provincial premiers.

On July 21 the prime minister wrote to ten of the premiers. He asked that Quebec's five conditions be viewed with an "open mind." He added that the premiers not get bogged down in "paralysing linkages" like their own provincial priorities. The letter was not published (*Star*, Apr 27/87).

On August 12, at the twenty-seventh annual First Ministers Conference (FMC), the eleven agreed to deal with Quebec's constitutional needs as a priority. Their acquiescence became known as the Edmonton Declaration. It comprised two sentences:

> The premiers unanimously agreed their top constitutional priority is to embark immediately upon a federal-provincial process, using Quebec's five proposals as a basis of discussion, to bring about Quebec's full and active participation in the Canadian federation. . . . There was a consensus among the premiers that then they will pursue further constitutional discussion on matters raised by some provinces, which will include, amongst other items, Senate reform, fisheries, property rights, etc. (quoted in Cohen, *A Deal Undone*, p. 83)

As a result of the Mont Gabriel conspiracy, the prime minister's agenda as laid out at Sept-Îles of August 6, 1984, took on life and form. Canada's academics, particularly those from Queen's University, had committed a gaffe of incalculable proportions. Had just one of them screamed bloody murder, the rest of the country would have cheered. Such an outcry was long overdue. The Mont Gabriel Conference locked the nation into a losing proposition, perpetuated the cover-up of Trudeau's mess, and proved Mulroney's intentions to continue along the same lines. All Canadians — including Quebecers — had been carefully left out.

A NOTHER SEEMINGLY UNRELATED EVENT took place in Edmonton two weeks after the Edmonton Declaration. On August 25, in his weekly magazine *Alberta Report*, Ted Byfield, an influential columnist on Western affairs, listed at length Western grievances, concluding simply, "The West needs its own party." Pandora's box now contained at least one fury — Western revolt.

12

A Meech Lake Accord and a Free Trade Agreement
Farewell to Sovereignty
— 1986 to 1987

THE MONT GABRIEL STING WORKED. The Edmonton Conference in August of 1986 boded well for Brian Mulroney. Canada's premiers easily accepted the premise that Quebec was the injured party in the Trudeau constitutional round and her needs had to come first.

Premier Richard Hatfield of New Brunswick was one of the first in line to support Quebec's demands. Ontario Premier David Peterson joined the cheering section, too. He thought the declaration signalled a new dawn for Canada. The support of Newfoundland's Premier Brian Peckford, speaking for a province that depended more than any other on federal largesse, logically followed. Manitoba's Premier Howard Pawley professed scepticism but went along with the rest. Alberta's Don Getty, premier of the province that had spawned more protest parties than any other in Canadian history, also fell into line.

As for British Columbia's Premier William Vander Zalm, he had been in office for only one week at the time of the conference — just long enough to board the constitutional wagon-train, wherever it was headed. Anxious to establish himself as a New Age Founding Father of Canada, he jumped on board without asking a single question.

The Edmonton Declaration assured that the constitutional railroad train, kit and caboodle, would roll on. No one was prepared to stop it. Like it or not, Canadians had no say in the matter. Soon the whole nation would have to accept what Robert Bourassa boasted was "the priority of Quebec."

For the next six months the first ministers and their bureaucratic vassals beavered away at the business of turning generalities into more specific platitudes to sell to the people. Amending Canada's constitution required unanimity from all the provincial legislatures. Even in the best of all possible worlds, gathering it would not be easy.

Lowell Murray, the Conservative House Leader of the Senate and federal Minister of Intergovernmental Affairs, took the lead. Months later, the eternal Tory guru Dalton Camp described Murray's as "one of the hottest offices in Parliament . . . [yet he] never takes off his jacket or tie. . . . No one has ever seen any perspiration on Lowell Murray. Cool is the word, unflappable" (*Star*, Nov 28/89). In the same edition of the same paper, columnist Edison Stewart described the minister as "a fastidious man with close-cropped hair and a penchant for charcoal and navy-blue suits," and Conservative pollster Allan Gregg described him more bluntly: "Just raw grey matter. No one even touches him. Not even close."

Gil Rémillard, the legal scholar cum politician, headed the charge for Quebec, and David Peterson stood ready to act in Ontario. Peterson marshalled the largest army of bureaucrats of any premier in the country to engage in the game of restructuring Canada. He held the keys to the kingdom. His role would be critical.

The Ontario premier fit the Mulroney tag-along role to a T. There was only one thing to know about Peterson: the magnitude of his ambition. The lawyer from London, Ontario, had been waiting outside the throne room for many years. The Peterson family had plans for their handsome son. To prepare him for great office, David had been sent to study at the University of Caen in France, which accounted for his knowledge of the French language.

He was sworn into office as premier of the country's wealthiest province on June 26, 1985. From that moment on, he moved toward only one goal: the bigger stage — Ottawa. Mulroney's constitutional manipulations ensured him a place in the big leagues. His chance came after the Lévesque government released its draft proposals on the Constitution in May 1985 calling for recognition of Quebec as a "distinct society."

His ticket to power in Ottawa had to be language reform in Ontario. He thought this would win him credibility in Quebec and if he stage-managed the business well enough, it would be largely ignored in Ontario.

On November 18, 1986, a little more than a year after being elected, Peterson's Liberal government passed Bill 8, Ontario's French Language Services Act. In exactly the same manner that the federal government had installed bilingualism at the federal level in 1969, and with the help of some federal advisors, Peterson's Liberal government set up bilingual districts across his province according to arbitrarily established needs. His strategy was to introduce measures gradually and maintain a low profile throughout. His government would pass laws and regulations without implementing them until the public saw them as harmless simply because they were not in effect. The Trudeau formula was his blueprint: get the law passed and then discard the districts as unworkable, implementing the changes on a discretionary basis. Peterson estimated three years as a comfortable waiting period.

In the end, there would be two official languages throughout Ontario, in practice if not in law. Queen's Park, the home of the legislature, would set the standard: the government would gradually bring in more and more of its routine and administrative functions in both languages. In one step, Peterson engineered his own version of Trudeau's cultural revolution, without the consent of the voters. Peterson's mentor had laid out the plan to follow in 1965.[1]

It backfired. Bill 8 ran directly counter to the legal and cultural heritage of the province. This revolutionary legislation challenged the legal, historical, and cultural foundation of the province more than any other law in Canada's history. Under Bill 8, Franco-Ontarians were officially fictionalized as a "founding people" of Ontario.

The bald-faced historical revisionism profoundly affected Mulroney's plan to accelerate Trudeau's constitutional vision and create a bilingual nation. After the passage of this bill, Canadians realized one overwhelming truth: if Ontario, with a francophone population of 5 percent, could be so manipulated with historical mythology, then so could any other province. Demographics no longer mattered, nor, obviously, did history.

Ontarians responded to Bill 8 the same way Quebec's anglophones had reacted to Bill 101 a decade earlier. They protested, loudly. This time those English Canadians who opposed the law found themselves treated differently; the press held them up to ridicule and character assassination or completely ignored them. There was no debate whatsoever of Bill 8 in Ontario after its passage. It just happened.

Opponents of the act were on a sound footing. No one could make any case for such an affront to common sense. The 1861 census of British North America just six years before Confederation tabulated a population of only 1.85 percent of Upper Canada's residents being of French descent. At no time in Ontario's history had the French language ever been given official or even token status. Indeed, French explorers had secured a right of passage through the province, but the settlers and colonizers were Loyalists and immigrants from many other lands. Ontario's bicentennial in 1984 commemorated the Loyalist settlements along the St. Lawrence River; there had been no tercentenary in 1913 of the three-hundredth anniversary of Samuel de Champlain's expedition westward on the Ottawa River.

By 1986, the francophone population of Ontario had been shrinking for more than a generation. Even taking into account the blip upward with the exodus of many francophones from Quebec into the neighbouring province after the FLQ crisis of 1970, they remained just 5 percent of Ontario's entire population.

Like Mulroney, Peterson played Trudeau's game: unlike his federal counterpart, Peterson lacked the political savvy to control such a circus. The howler of Bill 8 showed voters that they could not trust their politicians. Ontario's Bill 8 was only one landmine laid in the path of constitutional peace.[2]

A month after the bill's passage in Ontario, the highest court in Quebec, the Court of Appeal, overruled four sections of Quebec's French Language Charter, Bill 101. The December 22, 1986, judgement had been coming for a long time. Clearly and unequivocally, Quebec's highest court ruled that the bill contravened both the Canadian and Quebec charters of Rights and Freedoms. The constitutional battle lines for the soul of Canada were being drawn.

What would Bourassa's government do? Intergovernmental affairs minister Gil Rémillard, who had presented his five demands at Mont Gabriel, had stated that minority francophone rights in English-speaking Canada were Quebec's concern. How, then, could Quebec argue Bill 101?

Bourassa faced an impossible choice: embrace the Trudeau vision of a bilingual Quebec in line with a bilingual Canada, or bite the bullet of duplicity and stand by the position that French would be the only official language of Quebec.

Nobody recognized the real problem. Canada had endured two weak prime ministers. Pierre Trudeau and Brian Mulroney had already made the decision years earlier. Robert Bourassa with his constitutionally offensive Bill 22 and René Lévesque with his equally if not more offensive Bill 101 had successfully defended special status and sovereignty over cultural matters for Quebec. For Trudeau and Mulroney, Section 90 of the BNA Act, the disallowance provision that the Fathers of Confederation had so wisely included, simply didn't exist.

Since Canada lacked national leadership to defend it for more than two decades, the outcome of such wranglings could go only one way.

Two months into the new year, on February 26, 1987, Quebec justice minister Herbert Marx announced that his government would appeal the ruling of Quebec's appellate court against Bill 101 to the Supreme Court of Canada. If Bourassa had his way, Quebec's National Assembly would permit English language rights in that province on sufferance. He rejected bilingualism — for Quebec only.

The question hung out in the open now, plain for all to see, and it had to be answered. If the Supreme Court of Canada struck down Quebec's Bill 101, as seemed most likely, would Quebec use Trudeau's "abject failure," the notwithstanding provision? Would Bourassa act regardless of the decision of the highest court of Canada and defy it? Would he jeopardize "the priority of Quebec" while he was bargaining for special status at the constitutional table?

Under these conditions and with all these characters running around on the national stage, where were the fundamentals for any federation?

With St. Patrick's Day marking the beginning of another spring, the prime minister invited the premiers to an informal luncheon at Willson House on Meech Lake. He proposed April 30, 1987, for their meal together. A two-day First Ministers Conference on Quebec's demands in the first week of March had flopped. On March 27 the first ministers had met again to attempt another impossibility: to resolve the issue of native self-government. This they intended to do before sitting down to the table with Quebec. Nothing came of it.

Mulroney would try a new stratagem. Another meeting was planned, and this time the master negotiator would take control of it himself. This time the trusted insiders and experienced professionals would serve in a different role: they would study all the players. To win the game, both negotiating teams needed detailed profiles showing who would do what, when, and why.

WILLSON HOUSE ON MEECH LAKE would be the perfect backdrop for an Agatha Christie murder mystery. If there were bloody business to be done, this was the place to do it. If there was time to relax, this eerie country home east of the Ottawa River would be ideal for that, too. High above a rocky shoreline, backed by thick coniferous forest hundreds of feet above the long narrow lake in the Gatineau Hills of Quebec, the potential founding fathers of a new Canada could get to know each other. The Connecticut Yankee who came to Quebec in 1821, the Reverend Asa Meech, settled at the southeast end of the lake on 500 acres of land, blissfully ignorant of the infamy his name would draw late in the next century.[3]

Ironically, nothing much happened at this famous meeting. Everyone who attended simply agreed to meet again. Thirty-four days later in Ottawa, on June 3, a meeting took place in the Langevin Block of the Parliament buildings that first gave the gathering at Meech Lake any significance. The conference at Meech Lake was a public relations exercise. One academic, however, Professor Peter Hogg, thought differently. After the Gatineau get-together, he thought the Constitution was in the bag, "a piece of cake" (*A Deal Undone*, p. 101). A curious conclusion considering the turmoil in Quebec within the Liberal Party.

Donald Johnston, the prominent Montreal lawyer and former member of the Trudeau Cabinet, resigned from the Liberal caucus on May 8 after a dispute with Liberal leader John Turner. Johnston called Quebec's demands a "bag of shit" (*Star*, May 9/87). Behind him stood Mulroney's nemesis — Pierre Elliott Trudeau. On May 13 unidentified sources in Montreal reported that the former prime minister had strongly objected to "special status" for Quebec (*Star*, May 14/87). The old warriors were coming out to fight as the battle heated up.

The next day Trudeau put the gloves on and marched into the arena. He scoffed at Mulroney: "What kind of a country will it be?" (*Star*, May 15/87). By May 27, five days before the Meech Lake Accord was reached in Ottawa, Trudeau tossed more Tabasco Sauce into the cauldron. He launched a written attack through the *Toronto Star* and *La Presse* in Montreal:

> Those Canadians who fought for a single Canada, bilingual and multicultural, can say goodbye to their dream: we are henceforth to have two Canadas, each defined in terms of its language. . . . The provincial politicians, whether they sit in Ottawa or in Quebec, are also perpetual losers; they don't have the stature or the vision to dominate the Canadian stage, so they need a Quebec ghetto as their lair. . . . The bunch of snivellers should simply have been sent packing. . . . Alas, only one eventuality hadn't been foreseen: that one day the country would fall into the hands of a weakling.[4] It has now happened. (*GM*, May 28/87; *Star*, May 27/87)

Caught off guard, Mulroney recovered himself quickly. Trudeau, he raged, represented "the old style of federalism, the warring brand of federalism [of] personal abuse and vilification" (*GM*, May 28/87). Robert Bourassa chimed in, "I am in profound disagreement with [Trudeau's] analysis of federalism" (*Star*, May 28/87). The gladiators circled one another warily.

Trudeau's intrusion caught many other observers by surprise, too. At first glance, one of Canada's most celebrated scholars and constitutional authorities thought the Mont Gabriel formula and the undertakings at Meech Lake constituted a worthy endeavour. On April 30, Senator Eugene Forsey had said, "On the whole, it looks to me that the price that would be paid is not an unreasonable one" (*GM*, May 23/87).

After Trudeau's blast, Forsey pulled back and changed sides — not for the first time in his life. In the *Globe and Mail* on June 1, he published an article headed "Vague aspects of the Meech deal pose a big threat." Chewing on the meaning and effect of each section, he went to work as only he could, once given the direction. Through a laundry list of terms and phrases including "distinct society," "national objectives," and the "commitment" to "preserve the fundamental characteristic of Canada," Forsey let fly. Five days earlier he had already hinted at what he might say. Above all, he believed there was the need for a "clarion call to think, and think hard":

> The Constitution Act, 1982 created an extraordinarily rigid Constitution, very hard to amend. The accord would make it still more rigid, make many of its most important provisions totally unchangeable except by unanimous consent . . . which may not truly represent, on these matters, the people. . . .
>
> All these things, and probably more, need to be cleared up. If they are not, we risk landing in a bog we can never escape. (*Star*, May 28/87)

On May 25, the week before the Meech Lake agreement, France's president paid a call to Ottawa. François Mitterand addressed the House of Commons in Ottawa for thirty-eight minutes: "France and Canada are in unison. Vive le Canada, vive la France. . . . I wish to assure you deeply that this bicultural dimension [of Canada's] is something which all of France rejoices in, and which I rejoice in personally" (*Star*, May 26/67).

Shades of de Gaulle? The next day Mitterand moved on to Quebec City where he praised Quebecers for their ongoing success in spreading the French language. Not exactly a neutral stand, nor meddling — just bad taste and timing.

Mulroney's agenda continued on track, but barely. On May 30 another First Ministers Conference had broken up in Ottawa with nothing to show for it.

Meanwhile, out west in Vancouver, the newly formed Reform Association of Canada, under Ernest Preston Manning, was sponsoring a forum from May 29 to 31 billed as "The Western Assembly on Canada's Economic and Political Future." The creator of the conference's slogan, publisher Ted Byfield, had pressed for a new political party two weeks after the Edmonton Declaration in August 1986. Byfield's latest message flashed across the nation: "The West Wants In." There was nothing new about his call to arms. In 1967, the year of Canada's centennial, Ernest C. Manning published his thesis *Political Realignment*. In it he warned the executive-federalists of central Canada to be aware of the serious consequences of their actions. Manning was more specific in a paragraph headed "Consideration of One Remaining Alternative":

> I do not believe that the formation of an entirely new political party is the best way to meet the serious national political needs of the present hour. Nevertheless, having regard to the prevailing mood of the Canadian people, present national party leaders and federal politicians, especially those affiliated with the Progressive Conservative Party of Canada [Stanfield, Clark], should take cognizance of the following fact: if the Canadian political situation continues to degenerate, and if the cause of conservatism continues to suffer and decline, not for lack of merit or a willingness on the part of the Canadian public to support modern conservative principles . . . the idea of establishing a wholly new political party committed to the social conservative position will find an ever increasing number of advocates and supporters among a concerned and aroused Canadian public. (p. 86)

The Western Assembly blossomed into that very party Manning had predicted: the Reform Party of Canada, the first serious challenge to the Pearson–Trudeau–Mulroney centralist vision. Yet its lightning rod for popular support was Trudeau's National Energy Program (NEP).

Trudeau had introduced NEP on October 28, 1980, as part of his first budget on returning to power after Joe Clark's enormous fumble in 1979. Flush with his majority government, the victor extended the raid on Western energy resources that the Liberals had staged since 1972. The NEP of 1980 became the final phase in a rapacious federal grab of Western oil that wiped out the vast profits its producers could have made while world prices were soaring. By fixing prices substantially below the world market and applying punitive new taxes to the producers' gross revenues — not even *net* revenues — Trudeau created all the conditions for a major rift in Confederation. The Reform Party derived its early power from that Western resentment. As Ernest Manning's son Preston later wrote in his book

135

The New Canada: "The effect of the National Energy Program on so many western Canadians led some to question the equity of the whole federal system and the benefits of confederation itself. What type of a system, they asked, would permit a hundred-billion-dollar raid on the resource wealth of one region by the federal government in the name of the national interest?"[5] (*The New Canada*, p. 121).

Central Canada ignored the rumblings. The following month, on June 1, 1987, the first ministers met at the Langevin Block of the Parliament buildings in Ottawa. Their mission was to hammer out the details of the agreement they had reached in principle at Meech Lake on April 30. This "Langevin Agreement" reached in Ottawa would become known as the Meech Lake Accord.

The final agreement left Rémillard's demands at Mont Gabriel a year earlier substantially intact. The veto that Quebec insisted on had expanded to become every province's veto. The Langevin Agreement represented a remarkable cave-in to the prime minister's pressure. The food bill alone to sustain the weary negotiators for three days ran to $6,841.83.

Premiers Pawley and Peterson were the last to sign on around 3:00 A.M. on June 3: one with a qualification, the other with a flourish. Perhaps Manitoba's NDP Premier Howard Pawley knew something of the risks he might have to run.[6] He might even have realized he might have to change sides and follow the will of the people: "There's got to be proper public input or this is going to head for problems. We will be having public hearings in Manitoba, they will not be a rubber stamp, and we may very well be back to this table again" (*GM*, June 1/90).

David Peterson professed himself not very happy with the accord, but he went for it. According to reports from journalist Andrew Cohen, the premier was convinced that to walk out would be calamitous — tantamount to returning to the 1960s.

Peterson was totally under the spell of Pierre Trudeau now. Most Canadians, including Quebecers, would have welcomed a return "to where we were in the 1960s," before the Bi-Bi Commission Report of February 1, 1965, with its propaganda that "Canada, without being fully conscious of the fact, is passing through the greatest crisis in its history."

The Meech Lake Accord had to clear another hurdle to become Canada's constitutional law. The agreement would have to pass through every one of Canada's provincial legislatures, except for the two territories, according to the Constitution Act of 1982. It would also have to pass in the Parliament of Canada. To allow all the jurisdictions the time to make that passage, the ministers approved a three-year deadline. The clock would be deemed to start ticking any time after the first legislature passed a law under this formula of unanimity. The success or failure of the agreement depended absolutely on this proviso.

Some provinces moved quickly, anxious to keep up the momentum. A period of three years contained another potential problem — a big one — the risk of a change of government in any one of the provinces. Foes of the accord across the nation took due note of the legal time frames and began to watch the calendar.

On June 23, 1987, the Quebec National Assembly ratified the Meech Lake Accord. The countdown had begun. From that moment on, the remaining provinces had until June 23, 1990, to ratify the accord in their own governments. On June 29, Ontario and British Columbia followed suit in second and third place. On September 23, Saskatchewan approved it, and then Alberta on December 7, 1987.

The House of Commons voted 242 to 16 in favour of ratification on October 25, on the first reading of the motion. In a break with caucus discipline, eleven Liberals and two New Democrats spoke against it. By year's end the accord had yet to be passed in five legislatures. Trouble was brewing.

Before the end of that first December, the number of unlit firecrackers threatening to explode the accord continued to multiply. Adding to the increasing national acrimony over the passage of Ontario's French Language Services Act, the Quebec government was fanning the flames of unrest in its own way.

The feds were also getting rambunctious. In a move sure to stir the forces of dissent in English-speaking Canada, three weeks after the signing of the accord, justice minister Ramon Hnatyshyn tabled the new Official Languages Act, Bill C-72, in Parliament.

The new bill replaced the Official Languages Act of 1969, the original law that required that Bilingual Districts be set up nationwide. These were to ensure that common rules were enforced nationally as bilingualism was implemented according to a specific percentage of the population. Having abandoned this requirement, the new Official Languages Act would effectively "legalize" the law-breaking of past years.

The government was fully aware of the horrendous legal mess. They pressed even harder for passage of the controversial law. The Official Languages Commissioner was particularly anxious to see the new legislation in place. Under it, bilingual services would be extended not on the basis of population but on the basis of "significant demand."

Bill C-72 broke the back of good will and trust over language legislation in Canada forever. Under the new law, the Official Languages Commissioner would assume draconian powers unprecedented in Canadian law.

The bill would legitimize the transformation of the Commissioner from auditor and ombudsman into judge and jury, police officer and propaganda minister. For example, the Commissioner could initiate complaints and act with complete independence; would no longer be bound by the usual laws of evidence concerning disclosure; would suddenly assume full powers to lay charges; could not be compelled to testify as a witness in any legal action; and would never face criminal or civil proceedings against his or her position.

In short, the Official Languages Commissioner would be immune from actions of libel and slander under Bill C-72. The bill conflicted, flagrantly, with the Constitution Act, 1982, and with Canada's most fundamental legal heritage. The new law shifted the burden of proof onto the accused — whose only remedy was to take action in the Federal Court of Canada.

In one quick swipe, Bill C-72 was to whip language issues away from the public view, away from the courts, and away from Parliament, and into the hands of public servants. It added another major provocation to the Meech Lake obstacle course.

Throughout Canada the politicians were stirring lots of other little pots. The Liberals were not the only party having rows within their own ranks over Meech Lake that first year of the debate. On July 20, 1987, the New Democratic Party leader, Ed Broadbent, one of the first to board the Meech Lake bandwagon, broke his party's own caucus rules and let Yukon by-election candidate Audrey McLaughlin stand by her anti-Meech position. Less than three months later, on October 2, he removed party member Ian Waddell as the party's arts, culture, and communications critic for taking exactly the same position. The media enjoyed more fireworks.

Then, on October 13, less than two weeks after Broadbent's row with Waddell, Richard Hatfield's Conservative government in New Brunswick lost an election. The former government lost every seat in the legislature to one of the most outspoken critics of the accord, Frank McKenna of the Liberals.

As if to follow up on his heated attack against the accord and the prime minister in May, Trudeau pulled out his flamethrower for a second time on August 27. While the first ministers convened an FMC in Saint John, NB, defending their deal, Trudeau spoke in Ottawa before a joint Senate–Commons hearing. He warned that Quebec would be furious if "distinct society" proved to be a mere term without substance (*GM*, Aug 27/87).

On September 21, Liberal MP and former justice minister Robert

Kaplan spoke up. Meech Lake, he said, is "an achievement that can be improved. We reject totally the idea that the accord is a seamless web" (*Star*, Sept 22/87).

Two days before Christmas, the British Columbia Court of Appeal, which serves as the court of appeal for the Yukon and the NWT, ruled that signing the accord did not violate territorial rights. The leaders of the territories, on the other hand, were incensed. The day after the April 30 agreement at Meech Lake, the leader of the Yukon, Tony Penikett, condemned it utterly: "We think this is a good day for Canada but it is a bad day for the Yukon" (*GM*, May 2/87). And: "if this agreement is ratified any one province will have a veto over our constitutional future. One day some 100,000 people in Prince Edward Island will decide if we can join Confederation" (*Star*, May 2/87).

On October 28, in an article in the *Globe and Mail*, Penikett gloomily observed that Meech Lake

> dooms forever our aspirations of provincehood. . . . Northerners are angry that their elected representatives were banned from the Meech Lake meeting that produced the accord.
>
> The Meech Lake Accord changes the amending formula for the creation of new provinces. . . .
>
> Why have the prime minister and the first ministers suddenly decided that the North should no longer have a voice in its own destiny? The fate of the North is now in the hands of provincial leaders who know virtually nothing about life in the Yukon. It is grossly unfair and undemocratic. . . . (*GM*, Oct 28/87)

Northwest Territories leader Nick Sibbeston minced no words either. On October 29, he appeared before the Senate Committee hearings in Yellow-knife, warning of revolt: "Let Canadians be very certain about this. . . . They haven't killed us. . . . They have got our ires up. We shall fight to the bitter end and we shall win" (*GM*/CP, Oct 29/87).

At the First Ministers Conference in Ottawa on November 25 to 27, Denis Patterson, who took over from Sibbeston as leader, added his voice to Penikett's and Sibbeston's: "If we are to be part [of Canada] . . . we do not want to let others decide what is best for us" (*Star*, Nov 28/87).

But "others" deciding "what is best" for Canadians had become a habit for government leaders in Canada. While the Meech Lake Accord occupied the interest of most journalists, the Mulroney government took a far more revolutionary step in the destiny of Canada. It had begun on March 17 and

18, 1985, at Quebec City where Prime Minister Mulroney and U.S. President Ronald Reagan agreed that they "would give the highest priority to finding mutually acceptable means to reduce and eliminate existing barriers to trade in order to facilitate trade and investment flows." Six months later they pledged that their two governments would "negotiate a new trade agreement involving the broadest possible package of mutually beneficial reductions in barriers to trade in goods and services."

The historic Free Trade Agreement was signed on October 4, 1987, and tabled in the House of Commons on December 11. Speaking on the subject in the House of Commons on October 5, Mulroney intoned, "We have set the course for a stronger, more united and more prosperous Canada. It is not a path for the faint of heart but this country wasn't built by timid souls. This is the path for the daring, the innovative, the nation-builders."

What a switch! During his 1983 campaign for the leadership of the Conservative Party, Mulroney had said, "Free trade with the United States is like sleeping with an elephant. . . . It's terrific until the elephant twitches, and if the elephant rolls over, you are a dead man" (quoted in Martin, *Pledge of Allegiance*, p. 43).

In the same campaign, Michael Wilson, later Minister of Trade, made exactly the same noises about the prospects of such an economic revolution: "I think it's not very likely we're going to see that. There's an awful lot of jobs at stake. . . . Clearly there would be a tremendous adjustment process involved in moving to a full free trade agreement. Some smaller companies which are very efficient, very well managed, just would not be able to compete" (*Pledge of Allegiance*, p. 91).

Joe Clark echoed Wilson: "Unrestrained free trade with the United States raises the possibility that thousands of jobs could be lost in such critical industries as textiles, furniture and footwear: Before we jump on the bandwagon of continentalism, we should strengthen our industrial structure so that we are more competitive" (*Maclean's*, June 13/83).

By 1987, corporate Canada was aggressively pushing for free trade. Conrad Black, chairman of Argus Corporation, spoke for big business when he said, "I'm in favour of free trade with the United States. The freer, the better" (*Maclean's*, Oct 19/87).[7]

The noted Canadian author and nationalist Pierre Berton thought differently: "It's dreadful. It is selling the soul of the country. It means we are one step closer to becoming American. Canadians should demand an election. If the Prime Minister thinks it's such a good idea, then he should have the guts to go to the country" (*Maclean's*, Oct 19/87).

Eric Kierans, a former Cabinet minister under Pierre Trudeau, put it even more vehemently: "The underlying crime in all this is that Canadians believe others can create more wealth in Canada than we can create ourselves. The bottom line is that we are asking for a quick fix. What we should be doing is working on our economy. If you can't control your own economy, you have no right to call yourself a nation" (*Maclean's*, Oct 19/87).

In retrospect, the champions of this fast shuffle of Canada's sovereignty would have done well to heed the warning of George Washington's first Secretary of the U.S. Treasury, Alexander Hamilton (1755?–1804). In the "Original Draft" of his farewell address on May 10, 1796, he wrote:

[On external affairs:] Harmony, liberal intercourse, and commerce with all nations are recommended by justice, humanity, and interest. But even our commercial policy should hold an equal hand, neither seeking nor granting exclusive favors or preferences — consulting the natural course of things — *diffusing* and *diversifying* by gentle means the streams of commerce, but forcing nothing — establishing with powers so disposed temporary rules of intercourse, the best that present circumstances and mutual opinion of interest will permit, but temporary, and liable to be abandoned or varied, as time, experience, and future circumstances may dictate — remembering that it is folly in one nation to expect disinterested favor in another, that to accept is to part with a portion of its independence, and that it may find itself in the condition of having given equivalents for nominal favors, and of being reproached with ingratitude in the bargain. (Quoted in Richard B. Morris, ed., *The Basic Ideas of Alexander Hamilton*. New York: Pocket Books, 1957, p. 393)

In 1911 Rudyard Kipling warned Sir Wilfrid Laurier when he and his Liberals fought for free trade. They lost out to Robert Borden who became prime minister. Mulroney's radical Tories did not heed Kipling's message:

It is her soul that Canada risks today. Once that soul is pawned for any consideration, Canada must inevitably conform to the commercial, legal, financial, social and ethical standards which will be imposed upon her by the sheer admitted weight of the United States. Whatever the United States may gain, and I assume the United States' proposals are wholly altruistic, I see nothing for Canada in Reciprocity except a little ready money that she does not need, and very long repentance. (*Victoria Times Colonist*, Sept 19/11)

On the enactment of the Free Trade Agreement on January 1, 1989, Canada lost — badly. Estimates of the jobs lost in manufacturing, not just to restructuring, ran as high as half a million. The country had had warning enough. On October 3, 1987, Clayton Yeutter, head of the U.S. Trade Office, crowed publicly over the agreement: "We've signed a stunning new trade pact with Canada. The Canadians don't understand what they've signed. In twenty years, they will be sucked into the U.S. economy" (*Star*, Oct 6/87).

Despite the warnings from so many quarters, the Free Trade Agreement (FTA) was introduced into the House of Commons on May 24, 1988. There were many side-plays and histrionics on the part of the Canadian bargaining team busy trying to appear tough in the face of the Yankee traders. Eventually, though, the Canada–U.S. Free Trade Agreement was approved by the U.S. Congress and by Canada's Parliament. President Ronald Reagan signed it into law while he was on vacation in Palm Springs on January 2, 1988.

The November 21, 1988, election in Canada was widely considered a referendum on the FTA by the media. It was not. But even so, the percentage of polled Canadian voters opposed to the Mulroney plan, at 57 percent, was a full 5 percent higher than the percentage who opposed free trade in the election of 1891 and in the second round in 1911. The bottom line: Canadians overwhelmingly rejected free trade — but had no real say in the matter.[8]

The year 1987 drew to a close on a melancholy note for some and on a note of hope for others. After nationwide debates about the Meech Lake Accord and the Free Trade Agreement, the nation learned that year of the death of its most colourful contemporary politician, René Lévesque, on November 1. This was also the date of the third and last day of the Founding Assembly of the Reform Party of Canada in Winnipeg. The delegates elected Preston Manning the new party's leader by acclamation. Perhaps the West would save Canada after all.

Notes

1 University of Montreal Professor Pierre Trudeau had laid down the exact specifics in 1965 (see Chapter 2): "In any province where there is a French or English minority exceeding 15 per cent or one-half million inhabitants, no law relating to legislative or judicial functions will be valid if it does not place the English and French languages on a basis of absolute judicial equality" (*Federalism and the French Canadians*, p. 50).

Once elected in 1985, Peterson ensured that high-ranking federal Trudovnic mandarins ousted from office on the election of Brian Mulroney in 1984 found political refuge in his government. The Ontario Ministry of Culture and Communications became Peterson's personal launching pad to ensure the continuing safe passage of Trudeau's dream.

2 On October 27, 1994, David Peterson was awarded France's Legion of Honour.

3 In March 1988, historian Ramsay Cook wrote that the correct spelling of the family name was "Meach." Marion Meech, the great-granddaughter of Asa Meech, responded. She informed *Globe* readers that the correct spelling was indeed "Meech," that old Asa had always written it that way, and that no less a body than the Toponymic Commission of Quebec adopted that spelling in common use.

4 Trudeau used the term "*un pleutre.*" This sent the scribes scurrying to find out what it meant. In the end, linguists and translators, titillated by the etymological challenge, could not decide whether Mulroney had been insulted as a coward or a weakling. According to Loraine Parenteau of the Office de la langue française the two hundred-year-old Flemish term came from "another level of language not used by most ordinary mortals." The word can mean "a contemptible fellow," "a coward," or even "a vile person" (*Star,* May 27/87).

5 Estimates of the wealth transferred to Central and Eastern Canada under the NEP vary, depending on the calculations. One estimate Preston Manning cites was taken from a report compiled by Robert Mansell, an economist at the University of Calgary: approximately $100 billion.

6 No one ever knew what Howard Pawley, one of the weakest provincial leaders in Canada, stood for. He endorsed Meech Lake. And he embraced Official Bilingualism without reservation. Yet he had opposed the Trudeau vision in 1974 when he was Manitoba's attorney-general: "I want you to know that in the province of Manitoba we have more populous groups of people that speak Ukrainian or German than those who speak French. Therefore, you will note that from an administrative point of view it would create a very difficult situation for Manitoba to provide statutes in the French language

without providing for statutes in other languages. I regret I could not be more accommodating to you" (Doern, *Battle Over Bilingualism*, p. 5).

7   In 1993, Edward N. Luttwak, an International Associate at the Institute of Fiscal and Monetary Policy of Japan's Ministry of Finance and Director of Geo-economics at the Center for Strategic and International Studies of Washington, D.C., threw a javelin at the naïvety that characterized the rush to free trade in America: "But free-trade ideology, like all ideologies, has a curious effect: it has a way of creating confusion in the mind of believers between what ought to be and what is. They *know* that the world is far different from Main Street, USA, yet they do not truly accept that reality in their minds. . . . Even when the strongest case is proven, they take refuge in the claim that trade barriers would inevitably end up protecting only sloth and inefficiency. . . . There was certainly no sign of lethargy or corporate self-indulgence in Japan, through decades of protectionism" (*The Endangered American Dream*, p. 26).

8   David Orchard gives extensive background on the FTA and its child, NAFTA, in his book *The Fight for Canada*.

13

Hell Hath No Fury Like Pandora's Box
— 1988 to 1990

BETWEEN JUNE 23, 1987, AND JUNE 22, 1990, Canadians were put through a wringer that mangled the nation from the Atlantic to the Pacific. The Quebec National Assembly had started the ball rolling. It passed the Meech Lake Accord in 1987, which set the constitutional clock ticking off the three years to deadline. According to the Constitution Act, 1982, the remaining provincial legislatures had to secure unanimous passage of major changes affecting the nation within that time. Otherwise, after June 1990, the Meech Lake Accord would die.

The federal and provincial politicians sprang into action. Surrounded by platoons of influence peddlers from the media and the academic world, they enthusiastically dragged the whole nation kicking and screaming through the constitutional quagmire. It took thirty-six months, but in that time the entire Canadian population was transformed into a nation of bickering malcontents. Almost every day the country was convulsed by some argument over its reason for being. Six months after the accord was signed in Ottawa on June 3, 1987, the press and the broadcast media could report little else.

Given the players, the problem was insoluble. Not one leader in the country was personally able to focus on principles and ideals worth preserving. The leaders all seemed to know diddly-squat about Canada's heritage. Caught up in their posturing, the elected and appointed representatives of the people proved themselves incapable of thinking, debating, or intelligently discussing anything controversial. Instead, tongue-tied, fearful of reprisal, and equipped with employee-like minds, most of them clammed up on anything that could disrupt the status quo of the Orwellian world Canada had become.

Intellectual freedom had languished on death row in Canada since the beginning of the Pearson era. At that time it became improper to challenge either bilingualism or multiculturalism. In Mulroney's time it became fashionable and even necessary to avoid those topics completely. No one in Canada in either period ever won the Order of Canada if he or she broke this rule and ventured even a mildly off-beat viewpoint. Canadians invented the attitude in the early 1960s, long before it came into vogue in America in the 1980s. The modernists coined a term for the new censorship: "political correctness."

Many of the experts who maintained the happy front of a brave new world were lawyers with only a rudimentary knowledge of constitutional law. Many were academics who couldn't, didn't, and wouldn't read their nation's history or law. Others were buffoons. Some, like Joe Clark, cheerfully boasted they didn't know anything. Somehow this sort of admission actually added credibility to the speaker.

With little knowledge of the historical or cultural — let alone legal — foundation of the country, Mulroney, like his predecessor, had no difficulty implementing revolutionary change. Since those careless remarks he had made about Bryce Mackasey, he had set the standard for a prime minister of the 1980s and 1990s. Opportunism was the only guiding light; securing and retaining power the only objective.

Mulroney's ascension to power is a classic example of how an ignorant nation can be manipulated. Like Trudeau, he promised one thing and delivered another. Trudeau promised Canadians a "just society" with equality for all, within a pluralistic society with gradations of rights for those he dubbed Canada's founding peoples, the French and the English. He delivered unprecedented division throughout the country and, as a bonus, fiscal insolvency.

Mulroney promised economic and political reform as well as national unity; he delivered economic chaos and brought the country to near ruin. As for the Constitution, he wreaked utter havoc — fracturing the nation into regions that sprouted political parties like noxious weeds.

By the time Mulroney came to power on September 4, 1984, separatism was a spent force in Quebec. That fact meant little in terms of the new prime minister's political goal; he wanted to guarantee the Conservative

Party a power base in perpetuity, and he would have the country pay whatever price necessary to do it. If Trudeau is to be known for the cost of national unity that he imposed, bilingualism, then Mulroney's legacy must be the unholy alliance of the Tories with the destructive forces of Quebec nationalism.

Unlike Pierre Trudeau, Brian Mulroney was in a much bigger hurry to make his mark. Trudeau didn't get rolling on his constitutional agenda until after the suicide of the Clark government in 1979, a full ten years after he was first elected. Mulroney rushed into the constitutional arena like a hungry panther the instant he took power in 1984. Trudeau gradually wove a myth to accomplish his goal — that in order to survive, Canada had to become bilingual, and that it was already bilingual somehow anyway.

Mulroney couldn't have cared less about Canada's history. A man with a coffeetable-book mentality, he saw the Trudeau legacy as sometimes an albatross, most of the time a nuisance, but very much a power base. From its face value, he took what he deemed necessary and pragmatic to consolidate his own power.

It took a long time to expose the personal mythology the two prime ministers touted to secure and hold power, the fiction they promoted that Canada teetered on the verge of collapse if they could not do what they wanted to. Both grossly underestimated the opposition to their private plans for the country. Both barged ahead regardless.

Mulroney's battle for the soul of the country would be fought between the regions. As soon as the starting gun was fired, the Meech Lake Accord ran into trouble in Western Canada. David Elton, the president of the Calgary think-tank organization, the Canada West Foundation, and considered the intellectual godfather of the Triple-E Senate — equal, elected, and effective — fired one of the first cannonballs at Mulroney's efforts. He spoke before the joint Senate–Commons hearings on the Constitution on August 6, 1987:

> [Such a proposal carries with it] the seeds of the ultimate downfall of this nation. Quebec's alienation from the 1982 constitution gave the Canadian body a head cold. But the resolution's [Meech] proposals are the political equivalent of the AIDS virus: an ailment whose symptoms are initially innocuous but build progressively to a debilitating, incurable and inevitably fatal condition. (*London Free Press*/CP, Aug 7/87)

By 1988, the Meech Lake Accord was being criticized in almost every quarter in Canada, including the separatist faction of Quebec. Surprising, for anyone unfamiliar with Quebec politics; it would have seemed logical for the PQ to be ecstatic about such a destructive package that promised the end of a strong central government in Ottawa. Campaigning in Montreal for the leadership of the Parti Québécois, Jacques Parizeau was one of the early birds scrambling for a constituency in the new year. On January 17 he announced that the next time the PQ was elected, it would be with a "mandate to prepare for sovereignty" (*Star*, Jan 18/88).

At the root of every constitutional whim in Canada is language. It is in this context and this context only that the vacillations of Canadian politicians can be understood. On February 25, that issue caught fire again — this time in the West. Upholding the North-West Territories Act of 1886, the Supreme Court of Canada ruled that both Alberta's and Saskatchewan's English-only laws passed since 1905, the year those provinces joined Confederation, were invalid. Though the court suggested the provinces could pass a retroactive English-only law, this only caused another row. Nothing was resolved.

The language furies were loosed. The very day that decision came down, Rupert Baudais, president of the Association culturelle de franco-canadienne de la Saskatchewan, composed of some 25,000 "Fransaskois," led the francophone attack against Premier Grant Devine: "We are extremely disappointed that the main architects of the Meech Lake accord, Premiers Devine and Bourassa, are the first people to destroy the foundations of that accord, the French-English duality across Canada. . . . It means the end for the francophone minorities outside Quebec" (*Star*, Apr 15/88).

Baudais was not without support. Professor Ken McNeil of the Osgoode Hall Law School at York University chipped in: "For 83 years, the province [of Saskatchewan] has acted unlawfully by enacting and printing statutes that are void" (McNeil, "Threatening minority rights," *GM*, Apr 18/90).

In 1988, March came in like a lion and went out like one, too. On the seventh, the FFHQ, la Fédération de francophone hors Québec, the federation that speaks for the one million francophones outside Quebec, reversed its earlier position and opposed Meech Lake. Its executive director Aurèle Thériault condemned Meech Lake as "incomplete and unacceptable." It was not enough to "preserve" Canada's linguistic duality. The duality should and must be "promoted" (*GM*, Mar 8/88).

On March 8, Howard Pawley, Manitoba's founding father on the accord, lost a confidence vote in the legislature, becoming the second major casualty on the Meech Lake roster. Now there were two routed premiers, Pawley and Hatfield. Pawley called an election for April 26.

Ever with his nose to the wind sniffing for political opportunity, newly elected New Brunswick Premier Frank McKenna, the slayer of Hatfield, delivered a slap in the face to his old school chum l'Irlandais, Brian Mulroney, on St. Patrick's Day. He set six conditions whereby New Brunswick would ratify the accord.

The next day, Jacques Parizeau, the fellow who, in 1980, had scoffed at René Lévesque's referendum strategy, was acclaimed party leader. On the day of his victory, the *Toronto Star* reported that rebel Tories had formed a group led by MP Dan McKenzie to stop the "enforced bilingualism of all Canadians."

The language explosion for the month, however, astonished everyone who had only seen the Languages Commissioner promote francophone rights. On March 25, D'Iberville Fortier tabled his 1987 annual report in the House of Commons. He gently chided the Quebec government for Bill 101, saying the Bourassa government's strategy in its treatment of the province's anglophones had been to "humiliate the adversary" and that the survival of French must not "lie in humbling the competition" (*GM*, Mar 25/88; *OFL Report*, 1987). Harmless — one would have thought.

Although it was a first for an Official Languages Commissioner — publicly supporting the anglophone minority in Quebec — no one appreciated Fortier's comments, including Quebec's anglophone community. In the Quebec National Assembly the Parti Québécois censured the Commissioner on a motion. The resolution stated that Quebec must have "linguistic powers in a fully democratic manner so as to assure the survival of the French collectivity and check the threat of anglicization." Bourassa called Fortier's remarks "unrealistic and ill-conceived" (*GM*, Mar 25/88).

Fortier's entrance into the constitutional debate drove a temporary wedge into the heart of the alliance of the Tories and the Quebec nationalists, and so threw a spanner into the prime minister's plans as well. The Quebec Tory caucus, which comprised mostly conditional federalists and outspoken Quebec nationalists, seized its chance to make political hay out of Fortier's remarks. At a Tory policy convention of 700, an overwhelming majority condemned the Commissioner as irresponsible.

Meanwhile, everyone had something to say about the Meech Lake Accord — including Mulroney's favourite nightmare, Pierre Trudeau. Once disturbed from his rest, the former prime minister took up the cause with the fervour of a fanatic. This Merlin the Muddler, who had done so much to seed dissent and distrust with *his* unworkable vision of the country, gathered himself up and sallied forth to Ottawa. As only he could do — with the help of a fawning media — he vigorously stirred the Meech pot. The accord was "the end of the peaceful kingdom" (*Sun*, Mar 31/88). Mild stuff compared to his savage personal attack on Mulroney the year before. Trudeau dared the government to call an election over Meech Lake. There were no takers.

At the end of March, more ill winds blew out of Manitoba. On March 30, before the April election called by ousted Premier Pawley, the newly elected NDP leader Gary Doer declared he would dump the position his predecessor had taken. He demanded substantial changes. The Manitoba NDP and the Liberals opposed Gary Filmon's Conservatives, who supported the accord. The accord, now in as much trouble in Manitoba as in New Brunswick, needed a miracle to survive.

T HE YEAR 1988 will be commemorated in Canadian history as the year of the epidemic of language wars. The prairie grass fires were ignited and several premiers were fanning them fiercely. It all started on April 4, in response to the Supreme Court of Canada's February 25 decision on the rights of the "Fransaskois" in Saskatchewan. Grant Devine's Conservative government passed Bill 2. The premier had taken the Supreme Court's hint that some form of circumvention could be acceptable, so he retroactively legitimized all provincial English-only laws passed since 1905. A furore followed. The francophone community claimed Bill 2 violated the "spirit of Meech Lake" (*GM*, Apr 5/88).

Mulroney's vademecum on the hustings, the laconic Senator Lowell Murray, spoke up the next day. While defending the Devine government for its "small step" in ensuring that Bill 2 enabled some use of French in the courts and the provincial legislature, Murray also expressed disappointment in Manitoba's government. Bottom line — Mulroney's caucus was split.

Ontario's Premier David Peterson lunged at his opportunity. He hastened to the national stage to grab any plaudits he could gather for his ditty bag.[1] Referring to language problems in Alberta and what he described as a "perceived diminution of rights for anglophones in Quebec," he criticized Saskatchewan's Premier Devine: "I don't think this advances the cause at all" (*GM*, Apr 8/88). Statesmanlike stuff. He knew full well there was no solution now.

Then, once more into the breach charged the Official Languages Commissioner. On April 7, he noted the large Liberal majority in Ontario and hinted that more could be done; Premier Peterson had, as he put it, "an aura of influence that is enviable" (*GM*, Apr 8/88).

The prime minister, of course, could not remain silent in the course of such events. As Trudeau's pupil, he too wished to be known as a champion of duality, Official Bilingualism, and minority language rights. On April 8, Mulroney criticized Devine: Saskatchewan's Bill 2 "diminishes existing legal rights" of francophones. The prime minister added there are "ramifications" that go "well beyond the borders of Saskatchewan." The Meech Lake Accord was in jeopardy. If language rights belonged in the provincial arena, then of course Quebec would be justified in taking whatever steps it chose about the anglophone minority within her borders (*Star*, Apr 9/88).

Mulroney offered the big carrot. If Devine would recant, withdraw, rescind, whatever, the federal government would help him. Devine ignored the offer. Language is a provincial matter, he claimed. His province would finance a public relations solution from its own coffers. On April 12 he promised that a French-language institute would be set up and he would muster government millions to improve French-language educational services. He promised better French-language government services, particularly in rural Saskatchewan, as well. On April 25, the Saskatchewan legislature passed Bill 2.

The francophones in Alberta were not convinced. The president of their group, l'Association canadienne-française de l'Alberta (ACFA), Georges Arès, questioned Mulroney's commitment to bilingualism: "We have to question whether he wants a bilingual country from sea to sea . . . or if he is confirming what francophones in Saskatchewan and Alberta have felt for some time, that the only place we can feel at home is Quebec" (*GM*, Apr 6/88).

Day after day in April, the squirming continued. Aware that the Supreme Court of Canada would soon bring down a ruling on Quebec's Bill 101, Bourassa took a tack completely opposite to Mulroney's. On April 13 he rushed to Saskatchewan's aid. He backed Devine's actions by arguing the paramountcy of provincial law over cultural and language matters. The previous week, Mulroney's fear of ramifications that went "beyond the borders of Saskatchewan" had come to life. Canadians watched, fascinated.

Bourassa knew he faced the possibility of imminent and thumping rejection from Canada's highest court in his home territory on Bill 101, so he suddenly discovered that Saskatchewan's Bill 2 was "consistent" with the Meech Lake Accord. The idea was nonsense, of course, but it made for good domestic politics: maintaining the double standard — unilingualism for Quebec and bilingualism for all the other provinces.

Bourassa had other concerns, too. On April 17 in Montreal, 25,000 people marched in support of the supremacy of the French language. This was the largest cultural rally since the FLQ crisis of the 1970s. The crowds shouted a warning to the Bourassa government and to the Supreme Court of Canada in Ottawa — *"Ne touchez pas à la loi 101!"* (*Star*/CP, Apr 18/90).

Election day in Manitoba, April 26, 1988, brought disappointment to Gary Doer, the NDP leader who now opposed Meech Lake. The NDP government went down to defeat. Under Gary Filmon, the Tories won the election, but with a minority government holding only 24 seats. The Liberals, led by Sharon Carstairs, watched their strength grow from a single seat to 20 of the 57 in the legislature, making them the Official Opposition. She too strongly opposed the accord. The NDP now held the balance of power.

Convinced that she owed her party's popularity to her stance on Meech, Carstairs vowed to fight the accord with every breath in her body. The NDP and the Liberals now had the power to turf out the Tories at any time.

At month's end, the action shifted back to Central Canada. On the same day the Meech Lake Accord entered the risk arena after the Manitoba election of a minority government under the Tories, John Turner faced open revolt in the Liberal Party. Twenty-two of thirty-nine MPs signed letters calling for his resignation.

On the twenty-second of June, Alberta followed Saskatchewan's lead. The government overturned rights provided to francophones under the North-West Territories Act of 1886. Both provinces were governed by this law and both took the position that language was a provincial matter, not a federal one.

The federal government seemed oblivious to the storm brewing. On July 7, 1988, pressured by the Official Languages Commissioner and others, the federal government passed Bill C-72, Canada's new and controversial Official Languages Act, which had been introduced in June of the previous year.

Bill C-72, one of the most offensive laws in Canadian history, passed with almost no notice in the media. Many members of Parliament avoided sitting in the House during its passage. All of them knew that speaking out would have cost them dearly. Many took their lead from their press in Ottawa.

Bill Tupper, MP for Nepean–Carleton, was taken to task by Frank Howard, the *Ottawa Citizen*'s staff columnist (Keith Spicer was editor-in-chief). Tupper had said that he knew of dozens of careers that had been destroyed by bilingualism, and the quality of government, he said, had deteriorated as a result. Rather than undertaking investigative reporting, Howard hooted at the idea because those who complained had not revealed their names. Howard wrote: "I find [Tupper's claims] hard to believe. Also I think that unilingualism should be a handicap in Canada. It's unthinkable that anybody should rise to be a director, director-general, assistant deputy minister or deputy minister speaking only French. Why should English-speaking bureaucrats have to struggle with French because of supervisors' linguistic incompetence?" (*Citizen*, Feb 28/88).

Howard's article exemplified the way many columnists wrote about the problem when they knew nothing about it. Howard and those like him published voluminously and authoritatively on the subject.

The way Official Bilingualism was — and is — "enforced" in the Federal Public Service is the best-kept secret in the country. Not a single Canadian journalist in thirty years has had the foggiest idea what the "Imperative Staffing Principle" was or how it works. It was deceptively simple to implement: the manager of any group in government, no matter how small, had to be bilingual once a single position in that group was designated as bilingual.

All management and supervisory positions of any consequence, therefore, gradually became bilingual. All federal public servants suddenly had the legal right to "work in the language of their choice." Under the Imperative Staffing Principle, an anglophone could elect to "become" a francophone for language purposes and force the management issue, or a francophone could elect to "become" an anglophone. Such a policy overwhelmingly favoured the demographic minority. Under this double standard, such a principle also did, and does, a great injustice particularly to English-speaking public servants, most of whom have no practical need to learn the second language.

While it is true that no slave-owner is standing by to ensure such a result with a sjambok in hand, enforcing such racial engineering under these conditions can be accomplished quite easily. Those who wield the tools that crush dissent employ psychology. Within the ranks of the federal public service they conduct the actual war in many subtle and insidious ways. The Annual Performance Review is the primary weapon to intimidate those who dare to raise objections, just as in an environment that condones sexual harassment, fear is the psychological ammunition used. The crux of the problem is a heavy dose of guilt combined with a cultural conflict that legislation can never resolve, let alone a Charter of Rights and Freedoms. In Canada's centennial year the renowned authority on bilingualism Norman Ward (1918–90) stated the problem:

The merit system, whose adoption (from 1908 to 1918) was an event of great significance to Canadian government, itself points up a basic difficulty. To English Canadians, who adapted the system from British sources, merit means ability to do a job in the immediate pragmatic sense regardless of language, though in fact, under the circumstances, English would be *assumed* to be the language in most cases; to French Canadians, though ability to do a job would not be ruled out as irrelevant, merit *includes* bilingualism. (Careless and Brown, *The Canadians*, p. 726)

The result of these conflicting cultural interpretations has been two decades of the abrogation of the Merit Principle in the civil service. Today, what was once one of the greatest public services in the world has been utterly destroyed by this racial manipulation.[2]

Canadians to this day do not know the real cost of Official Bilingualism. They will not find it in the various accounts governments serve up each year to justify their direct expenditures — a sum invariably squeezed under $1 billion.

In 1973, the Hon. Joseph T. Thorson published *Wanted: A Single Canada*, which identified the problem: "The cost of bilingualism includes not only the sums spent by the government in the advancement of its attempts but also the costs imposed on various sectors of the public as the result of the government's policy and the demands of French Canadians, both in and outside Quebec. The cost has risen, and is continuing to rise, at a staggering and alarming rate" (p. 135).

In 1993, Scott Reid, author of *Lament for a Notion: The Life and Death of Canada's Bilingual Dream*, described the dilemma:

As public discourse makes perfectly clear, nobody has a clue how much the federal government's official languages policies cost Canada. The federal government claims the total annual cost of official language spending is less than $700 million. Unofficial estimates range upwards into the multi-billions. . . .

For those who have a genuine curiosity about the real costs, the problem is that neither the supporters nor the critics of Official Bilingualism have ever attempted a systematic costing of each of the many federal government policies that relate to official languages policy. . . .

To say that federal languages spending is expensive is an understatement. In every area of language policy, the federal government has either placed huge burdens on the Canadian economy or it has assumed them directly, thereby placing huge burdens on Canadian taxpayers. (pp. 222, 223, 250)

Even Reid, in his superb survey, does not come close to recognizing the problem. Number-crunching has always been little more than a diversion from the real issue. The country's taxpayers pay a more incalculable price, through the incompetence and mismanagement of public servants promoted according to their ethnic background or language and not on merit. Professionals of ability are actually held back, sideswiped, and sidelined because they cannot be promoted for excellence and according to the needs of the country.

As for Trudeau's fantasy that bilingualism would ensure national unity, Reid sums up his analysis:

Canada's French and English communities have virtually completed the process of polarization or linguistic segregation. French has been confined almost entirely to Quebec and a few neighbouring counties in Ontario and New Brunswick. English has been eliminated from almost all of Quebec except west-end Montreal. The disappearance of Canada's official-language minorities, first predicted in 1967, is nearly complete. . . .

In spite of this trend, the bulk of Canadians still believe there are thriving minority communities right across the country. The federal government, ever mindful of Quebec separatism, does what it can to encourage this misperception among its citizens.

Deception is the only aspect of federal language policy that has actually achieved its goal; none of Ottawa's policies, grants or subsidies to tiny scattered minorities have done anything to slow or stop their assimilation. (pp. 122, 123)

The Charter of Rights and Freedoms constitutionalized the racial classification of citizens. It legitimized the doctrine of founding races and founding cultures. That fury out of Pandora's box has cost the nation its soul. Bill C-72 flowed from that document.

As if Bill C-72 weren't sufficient chili pepper to ignite national discontent, dumped as it was onto the unworkable Official Languages Act of 1969, the government poured more spice into the cultural cauldron the following month. On July 12 the Canadian Multiculturalism Act, Bill C-93, passed unanimously in the House of Commons and the Senate. Mulroney was assiduously carrying on the Trudeau agenda.

The new law provided for the "advancement of multiculturalism throughout Canada in harmony with the national commitment to the Official Languages of Canada." The multiculturalism minister, Gerry Weiner, sent out a letter to Canadians at the time: "This is, after all, the first multiculturalism act anywhere." To the outraged majority of citizens, including many ethnic minorities, multiculturalism was a crock.

So what else was new? Like bilingualism, multiculturalism has never been tested with the Canadian voters. It stands as another example of executive-federalism — the colonial principle governing Canada that, once elected, a government can use its power any way it sees fit, even to pass unconstitutional legislation, and get away with it because the Canadian voter only gets a chance to kick political butt once every half decade. Bill C-93 waved a red flag at Canadians of all cultures, races, and backgrounds who took pride in simply being Canadians.

Many people felt a sense of relief, although little optimism, on October 1, 1988. With the Liberals in complete disarray, the prime minister called an election for November 21. Opposition leader John Turner was toast and everyone knew it. Sure enough, Mulroney's Tories won a majority victory.

The media and the politicians and the apparatchiks nodded sagely and said the election was about the Free Trade Agreement with the United States. How could anyone tell? The *olla podrida* put before Canadians tasted so dreadful and combined so many different ingredients that no one could say for certain just what the election was about. The politics of confusion rather than inclusion ensured a victory for the most corrupt.

The winners really didn't care why the voters had elected them. After the landslide the prime minister could boast that despite his personal unpopularity in taking on the difficult tasks of governing and doing what he thought was right rather than attractive to the public, he had won the only poll that counted. For Martin Brian Mulroney, the boy from Baie Comeau, it did amount to an enormous personal triumph.

In the 1988 election "The Boss" won his double crown — a back-to-back Tory victory — something that had not happened for the Conservatives in the entire twentieth century. Sweet as it was at the time, the victors would have to remember it over the months ahead to comfort themselves. Big trouble was coming. The explosion rumbled out soon enough with the long-awaited decision on Thursday, December 15, 1988, of the Supreme Court of Canada on Quebec's Bill 101, the French Language Charter.

The court ruled that Bill 101 was unconstitutional. It upheld the judgements of Quebec's Superior Court and its Court of Appeal. Altogether, eleven Canadian judges — including eight from Quebec — deemed the prohibition of English on Quebec signs a violation of freedom and one incompatible with a free and democratic society.

Sunday morning, December 18, found the province of Quebec in an uproar, led by the Mouvement Québec français, a coalition of Quebec nationalists, cultural, and labour groups. A mass demonstration in support of Bill 101 paraded through Montreal. They even assured the media of a colourful moment for their various papers, magazines, and news stations, especially when the Canadian flag was torched with lighter fluid.

Emotions were running high. On the same day, Robert Bourassa, who had once called in the federal troops during the FLQ crisis, promised Quebecers a speedy resolution.[3] He meant it this time, too, but not with the use of federal troops. He had a more powerful weapon. The next day he announced that the National Assembly would exercise the notwithstanding clause of the Canadian Constitution. He would override the Supreme Court of Canada's decision. Trudeau's "abject failure" had come home to roost at last.

Addressing the House of Commons on December 19, Prime Minister Brian Mulroney virtually endorsed Bourassa's action:

> I have already communicated with Mr. Bourassa yesterday and told him the position of my Government and of this House on such a matter. I expressed the desire, the wish, that the Government of Quebec could find a formula, as the Supreme Court suggested, whereby the preponderance of French at all times in Quebec would be assured together with the respect of the minorities and their freedom of expression, as the Supreme Court wanted and the Quebec Charter states. . . . I have always thought the notwithstanding clause is inconsistent with a charter of rights. . . . I did not urge Mr. Bourassa or any other Premier to use it. . . . Quebec has no lessons to learn from anyone about how it treats its linguistic minorities. . . . (*Hansard*, Dec 19/88, pp. 296–97)

In a single stroke, Mulroney had assumed that English was no longer an official language throughout Canada. Quebec anglophones were merely a linguistic minority. Bourassa now knew with absolute certainty that Quebec could do whatever it wanted. Mulroney would never exercise Section 90, his constitutional prerogative, to disallow offensive provincial legislation. It was a great day for the separatist cause.

THE NEW BILL 178 would be a constitutionally permitted amendment to Bill 101, Quebec's French Language Charter. Details were immediately released to cool down the nationalists.

Bill 178 became law in Quebec just four days later, on Wednesday, December 22, 1988. It decreed that only French could be used for storefronts, billboards, and other outdoor advertising. As in the case of Bill 101, Bill 178 overrode both the Quebec Charter of Rights and the federal

Charter of Rights and Freedoms. Ironically, Bill 178 legalized the illegal Bill 101.

The notwithstanding clause would remain in force for five years, at which time Bill 178 would have to be reviewed. This would not end the matter. Under the Canadian Constitution the same notwithstanding clause could be used again.

Retaliation was swift. On December 19, Manitoba introduced a resolution in its legislature withdrawing support for Meech Lake. The next day the three "anglo" Quebec members of the National Assembly resigned from Bourassa's cabinet.

The year ended in flames. On December 30, the headquarters of Alliance Quebec, the English-rights organization, was torched by arsonists. Damages amounted to $200,000. A thousand anglophones demonstrated against Bourassa's legislation. In a flood of accusations, Royal Orr, the AQ leader, was maligned in the press, accused of arson. The allegations were preposterous.

By Christmas, Canada had sunk to a state of constitutional anarchy. New Year's Day, 1989, marked roughly the halfway line to the June 23, 1990, deadline.

On April 20, Newfoundland's House of Assembly changed hands, ending seventeen years of Conservative rule. Liberal leader Clyde Wells, an avowed supporter of Trudeau's vision in all save Senate reform, swept to power, gathering 31 of the 52 seats. His predecessor, Tom Rideout, had followed Brian Peckford on March 22, after the latter had stepped down. Rideout had enjoyed the shortest term for any provincial premier — thirty-one days. Being identified in any way with Mulroney's plan was proving very expensive. Premier Brian Peckford had been the third casualty of Meech Lake. Premier Tom Rideout became the fourth.

Once in power, Clyde Wells had the ability to kill the accord. This outspoken critic of the deal had joined the same camp as Frank McKenna of New Brunswick, and both were determined to do it if changes were not made.

Although Newfoundland had been the eighth province to sign the accord on July 27, 1988, Wells had said he would rescind it if he were elected. On April 21, he slammed the deal. Firing a harpoon back at the premier-elect, the binicky federal trade minister, John Crosbie, demanded Wells "play ball," or the Newfoundland economy would pay the price (*Star*, Apr 22/89).

From Ottawa, Mulroney's Delphic oracle spoke again. Senator Lowell Murray said, "As we get closer to the [June 23, 1990] deadline, the question before those provinces and the people of Canada is going to be: Do you want Quebec in, yes or no?" (*Star*, Apr 22/89).

Federal minister Benoît Bouchard, the conditional federalist in Mulroney's Quebec caucus, bullied English Canada, too. According to him, everyone in Quebec would be "outraged" if Meech failed. "If we don't have the guts — I'm sorry — to look at that kind of reality, we will face a year from now the very cruel reality to say that Quebec doesn't have a place in this country" (*Star*, Apr 22/89).

April 25, 1989, marked another major shift in the history of the federation and its British tradition: the separation of church and state. In a revolutionary move, the Roman Catholic church and the Anglicans put church money into the Meech collection plate. Rome spoke first, through a statement issued in Toronto at the twenty-six-member Ontario Conference of Catholic Bishops: The "history and spirit of Confederation indicate that French and English were languages of the founding races and must be given a privileged position as our official languages" (*Star*, Apr 25/89).

On July 19, Anglican Bishop James Maclean of Montreal stated that those who opposed Official Bilingualism within the Anglican church were "the rednecks of the rest of Canada" (*Star*/CP, July 19/89).

Tommyrot. The princes of the church knew absolutely nothing about what was going on or about the sentiments of most Canadians.

At summer's end, Premiers McKenna of New Brunswick and Filmon of Manitoba met in Quebec City and proposed a "parallel" accord. Delighted, the busy boffins in the constitutional industry would chew this idea to death for the next ten months. No one, absolutely no one, had a clue what a parallel accord might be. The smart money bet on the definition of two pathways that travelled side by side, never meeting.

The language fireworks in the fall of 1989 proved that the flames of Meech Lake from 1988 were still burning brightly. On September 6, fifty members of the local chapter of APEC, the Alliance for the Preservation of English in Canada, a non-government-funded activist group in English-speaking Canada, demonstrated at the train station in Brockville. The protesters had gathered to hector Premier David Peterson as he passed through town.

One protester, Gordon LeBlanc, stomped on the Quebec flag. The televised event was fanned across the nation and to the world press. Without checking the facts, the media branded APEC members the culprits. As it turned out, LeBlanc was not with APEC at all but with another group, Alliance Ontario. To this day, APEC, an organization wrongly accused of being anti-French, holds pre-Pearson views of language rights and Canada's Constitution. They have been blamed for all manner of evil. After the "Brockville incident," their organization was slammed as an anti-French group of bigots and WASPs. This was a new low in Canadian journalism. Even the Reform Party — which should know better — still holds fast to the idea that APEC is an "extremist" organization. This although thousands of APEC members helped build the Reform Party.

On September 25, Bourassa won a landslide election victory in Quebec. The Liberals took 92 of 125 seats in the National Assembly. The Equality Party that had just been formed to represent anglophone interests in Quebec won 4 seats.

Through all the chaos, some welcome news did manage to break out in a burp of democracy in the fall. On October 16, Premier Don Getty of Alberta conducted the first "unauthorized" Senate vote in Canadian history. Stan Waters, a member of the new Reform Party of Canada and a retired general, won an unprecedented victory — 42 percent of the vote — the largest ever received by any federal politician sent to Ottawa.

To bring the matter to a speedy close, Don Getty sent the prime minister a list of the candidates who had run. He called Waters "the people's choice." Despite his efforts, it would be a long time before Waters would take his place in Ottawa's Red Chamber.

When it came to Meech Lake, however, the Mulroney government had no intention of experimenting with democracy. Political positions hardened. So, on October 30, another warning came from Premier Clyde Wells. He threatened that the accord would be rescinded in the House of Assembly if there were no changes. He meant business. In the first week of November, he tabled nineteen pages of proposed changes, just in time for the upcoming First Ministers Conference on November 9 and 10.

Wells found himself in good company on the dissent side. The following week, Pierre Trudeau interjected another of his titillating bons mots. Interviewed on CBC's "The Journal," he said, "I think they're all afraid of Quebec. I wasn't" (CBC, Nov 8/89).

On November 8, the eve of another failed FMC, Mulroney turned on Wells, suggesting the Newfoundland premier seek constitutional advice from David Peterson of Ontario. The same day Wells remarked, "You can't have a compromise on [Quebec's] terms. That's not compromise. That's blackmail." Peterson jumped in to accuse him of "poisoning" Meech Lake. Wells's remarks, he said, constituted "a very destructive act" (*Star*, Nov 9/89).

The Maritime premier won the battle for credibility in spite of the media. He referred to the enormity of the propaganda. A week after the failed FMC, he said what most Canadians, muzzled as they were, couldn't say: "It's totally improper for the Prime Minister to now try to lay a guilt trip on Canadians to say that they did something terrible to Quebec in 1982. They did no such thing. . . . Quebec chose not to participate because it couldn't get its own way, because it had a separatist government at the time" (*Star*, Nov 14/89).

While Canadians were kvetching over a constitutional proposal that even its proponents didn't understand, one of the biggest moments in world history was unfolding. On November 9, a huge wave of East Germans breached the Berlin Wall that had divided the East from the West for several decades. The meaning of what they did is monumental. After sixty years, the Second World War had truly ended. The financial ramifications for all the Western democracies would be horrendous.

Back in Canada, business proceeded as usual through more constitutional capers. On December 2, the NDP held a leadership convention in Winnipeg to replace their resigning leader, Ed Broadbent. Audrey McLaughlin won, becoming the first woman leader of a national party in the country's history. In their moment in the spotlights, though, the NDP tergiversated. Under Broadbent, the party had supported Meech Lake; now, during their convention, the NDP adopted a "formula" for compromise and puffed to the world that they wanted changes to the accord either by "direct amendment or another amendment process" (*Star*, Dec 3/89).

Trade minister John Crosbie attacked Premier Clyde Wells for a second time to end off the year. This time he blamed him for his "extreme and absurd" attacks on Meech Lake. Canada's leading punchline politician painted one of his colourful word pictures to catch national headlines: "Is Clyde fiddling constitutionally while Newfoundland burns economically?" (*Star*, Dec 7/89). Canadians badly needed that belly laugh to offset the recent remarks of their head of state's departure speech.

On December 29, the Right Hon. Jeanne Sauvé, governor general and Commander-in-Chief of Canada, dramatically broke with tradition to stride into the political arena. She shot from the hip on national television:

> The profound instinct that we call the feeling of belonging has stirred the two main ethnic families, so much so that we do not blame them for valuing their distinctiveness. And if one of them [Quebec] makes this a condition of continuing as a member of the Canadian Confederation, it is because it is convinced that its contribution is essential to the affirmation and influence of a unique country. . . . The other founding people [English Canada] has bowed to this reasoning and derives pride and profit from it. . . .

> Such testing cannot be undertaken unless we accept, once and for all, the inevitable compromises, and unless the parties ratify their pact. . . . (*Star*, Dec 30/89)

A good many Canadians muttered good riddance to her after that. With a single blow, Trudeau's appointee had wiped out the long-standing tradition of political neutrality the Queen's representative must demonstrate in a parliamentary democracy. Her action didn't surprise those who knew her track record. As Speaker of the House of Commons between 1980 and 1984, she had never taken the trouble to learn either the rules or the members and their constituencies. And the memory of Jeanne Sauvé that burns most in the memories of her fellow citizens remains that of her closing the grounds of Rideau Hall to the public for the remainder of her term in office. Of all the Canadians ever to fill the role, Jeanne Sauvé secured the position of Canada's most despised governor general.

THE YEAR 1989 was annus horribilis for Canada. Maybe 1990 would be better, though there was nothing on the horizon holding out any such promise.

British Columbia kicked off the New Year with its claim that it, like all the other provinces, was a "distinct society." And on January 23 its provincial government introduced a five-point plan to salvage the accord. It demanded a proclamation affirming Senate reform, an amending formula that did not concur with Quebec's five demands and a busload of other provisions on women's rights, native rights, minority and other demands. Federal minister Benoît Bouchard quickly shot down the Vander Zalm plan. Quebec had been a distinct society for 250 years, he said, and "I don't think you can say that for any other province" (*Star*, Jan 24/90). Each had a point but missed what counted: the equality of all citizens.

With the June 23, 1990, deadline looming into view on January 26, Manitoba's Premier Gary Filmon sent a prophetic warning to Ottawa. With only four months to go, he warned of the complexities of Manitoba's requirements for any constitutional amendment. For the province to do its part, the premier said, there had to be agreement no later than March 31. The warning fell on deaf ears. The galumphing behemoths in Ottawa knew better.

By the end of the month, the language revolution that began with the Bi-Bi Commission in the 1960s and became a part of Canada's Constitution in 1982 penetrated Ontario municipal politics. On January 29, Sault Ste. Marie defended itself against Peterson's Bill 8. With a 79.5-percent anglophone population according to the 1981 Census, the "Soo" became the first Ontario municipality to declare itself unilingually English. The Italian population in the northern Ontario city is 8.4 percent and the percentage of francophones is 4.6 percent. Founding races and founding cultures?

This reaction to the intransigence of David Peterson and his personal plans for the province was entirely predictable, another link in a long, ongoing chain reaction. As usual, the people were never consulted. With the passage of Bill 178 in Quebec, Peterson's coffin was nailed firmly shut unless he changed his ways. He didn't. On November 18, 1989, his Bill 8 became law, after the three-year waiting period, massive protests throughout the province, and no electoral say.[4] (See Chapter 12.)

Thunder Bay boldly followed Sault Ste. Marie's example on February 5. Before long, fifty Ontario communities had done the same.

On February 8, Bourassa exhorted Canada to pass the accord: "But if it is not ratified, I can guarantee . . . that there will be [a] superstructure or institution or supranational institution, whatever name we could use, which could reassure the German investors or the foreign investors that Quebec and Canada are safe places to invest" (quoted in IIR, *Canada: The State of the Federation*, 1990, p. 248).

He hinted at more trouble ahead on February 25, too, announcing that he was setting up a committee to study options if Meech Lake should fail: "We are not announcing the formation of a study group because we want to dismantle the country. But . . . we haven't received a mandate to practise federalism on our knees" (Ibid., p. 249).

By March, a crisis was brewing at Oka, Quebec, a boundary dispute over local development plans to build a golf course on native lands. Mohawk warriors set up a blockade in protest.

Mulroney moved on to other matters. He set up a Special House of Commons Committee to study Frank McKenna's — and Gary Filmon's — idea of a "parallel" or "companion" accord. Following Manitoba's example of holding public hearings, the feds called for their own hearings from April 9 to May 4.

Ottawa was becoming desperate. Those who wished to appear before the committee had to submit a one-page summary of what they wanted to say by April 12. The hearings would be chaired by the Hon. Jean Charest. Witnesses would be chosen and rigidly controlled. Ottawa had identified the dissenters across Canada by this time. These were simply left off the agenda: as Charest admitted, "The choices we have made speak for themselves. . . . [Those who were chosen to speak were] mostly from government."

He was even blunter: he told CBC he saw his duty as one of "making sure we heard from the right witnesses" (CBC Newsworld, Apr 30/90).

As the clock ticked on, Clyde Wells introduced a motion to rescind the accord in the Newfoundland House of Assembly on March 22. Charest attacked him on Bill Rowes's open-line radio show, accusing him of "hiding behind the skirts of the people" because he wanted a referendum. Charest's gaffe easily matched anything John Crosbie could ever say. And it revealed a tremendous amount about the chairman and his "public hearings." Political pundits recalled Charest as the minister who had had to resign once from the Mulroney Cabinet after confessing he had phoned a judge during a judicial proceeding.

It was time for more mischief from the Languages Commissioner. On April 2 Fortier announced that in "protest against the current situation, I am going to consider very seriously tendering my resignation unless there are serious improvements." He was referring to the implementation of Bill C-72, the controversial Official Languages Act (quoted in *GM*, May 3/90).

After nearly three years of Canadians airing their dirty laundry, the Deutsche Bank Group of West Germany, Europe's largest bank, recommended investors reduce their holdings in Canadian bonds. In the first week of April the bank stated that "political risks associated with the debate on the Meech Lake Accord and Quebec will probably be destabilizing [to] the Canadian financial market and particularly the Canadian currency" (*FP*, Apr 4/90).

Larry Burns of the Liberal Council of Hemispheric Affairs in Washington commented, too:

> If Canada dismembered, you could be sure there would be calls . . . by legitimate political figures saying that the union of English-speaking Canada with the United States is something that should be really seriously entertained. . . . Canada is looked upon as one endless great lake, one endless forest, one vaultless mountain, and there is a strong naturalist pull on the part of a lot of people. (*GM*, Apr 7/90)

Craig Schoonmaker, chairman of the Expansionist Party of the United States and an office temp. by day, an avowed anti-Israeli "radical centrist" at all times, was overjoyed at the rumblings in America's attic. He envisaged a union of the United States and Canada that would create "the greatest nation in the history of the world." He did stipulate, however, that Quebec nationalists would not enjoy the privilege of exit permits from such a union: "Ours is a perpetual union. We proved it in the civil war. There is no expiration of the Union" (Martin Mittelstaedt, "Continentalist wants the United States to annex Canada," *GM*, Apr 7/90).

On April 5, in an unprecedented act of solidarity, Jacques Parizeau, the PQ leader, and his arch rival, Liberal Premier Robert Bourassa, united. A resolution passed in the Quebec National Assembly to "officially reject, on behalf of all Quebeckers, all constitutional proposals . . . that could constitute an amendment or modification to the Meech Lake accord." The motion passed 105 to 3 (*Star*, Apr 6/90). So much for parallel accords and companion resolutions.

On April 6, Clyde Wells took a second threat from Lucien Bouchard, Mulroney's Quebec lieutenant, who warned that Canada might have to choose between Quebec and Newfoundland. Rémillard, Bourassa's Minister of Intergovernmental Affairs, was even blunter: "Canada can survive very well without Newfoundland" (IIR, 1990, p. 255).

In a refreshing change of pace, Wells came off sounding a bit like John Crosbie. To the chuckleheads who would attack the islanders he retorted, "I don't have horns growing out behind my ears. I am not a devil about to pounce on Canada and do any harm to Canada. I am a patriotic Canadian" (*GM*/CP, Apr 6/90).

Furious that the Charest hearings might lead to an opening up of the Meech Accord, and tired, as he put it, of being called a "frog" by English Canadians, former Quebec cabinet minister Jean Cournoyer told English-speaking Canada to "Go fuck yourself" in the national media on May 4 (*Star*, May 5/90).

For a second time, D'Iberville Fortier threatened to resign as language czar if the federal government didn't move pronto to implement Bill C-72, the controversial new Official Languages Act. Mulroney, too, lost his temper that month. On the fifth, he publicly railed against the "separatists" in the Conservative caucus. Three days later the largest labour federation in Quebec, the Confederation of National Trade Unions (CNTU), which boasted a membership of 244,000, voted to support Quebec independence with or without Meech Lake.

By now, there was just one month before the deadline. All the news about problems with the accord finally prompted Mulroney to take note of the international financial community's reactions. Nervous, the prime minister galvanized his forces to staunch the flood of bad information eroding Canada's credit rating. On May 9 and 10, Messrs. Mulroney, Wilson, and Peterson fanned out to reassure the world that Meech Lake would pass. Finance minister Wilson headed to Wall Street. Premier Peterson headed elsewhere in New York and the prime minister confronted 700 businessmen at the Hilton Hotel in Toronto. In a barnburner of a speech, he commanded that they get out and fight for the accord. Constitutional life in Canada had become a serious matter now — it involved money.

One lighter note broke the tension. On May 11, Canadian Press reported that a paramilitary force had been formed to protect Quebec's sovereignty. Les Forces Québécois, boasting thirty members, claimed that they supported pacifism, and all its troopers declared their loyalty as Canadian citizens first and Québécois second.

In mid-May, Gil Rémillard made mischief during a visit to France. After receiving an honorary degree, he took to the podium to address the international media assembled to hear him. Bourassa's first minister did not disappoint his audience. He speculated on the future of the northern part of North America, opining that Canada would likely be restructured into "superstate structures based on supranational phenomena" (*GM*, May 15/90). Failing that, he said, "the consequences of the Accord's rejection will be serious for the future of the country, and Quebec will have to seek a substantial reorganization of the association that ties it with the Canadian federation, while taking into account its history as a distinct society" (IIR, 1990, p. 258).

News leaked out at 5:00 P.M. on May 15 that the Charest committee had looked at companion agreements and parallel accords and agreed how to resolve Canada's constitutional crisis. The shopping list included twenty-three items. A happy Charest told reporters, "I am satisfied with the contents of the report. I believe the report will help advance this debate. That's what is important to us" (*GM*, May 16/90).

Two sour notes followed. Bourassa made it clear that regardless of the agreement of all three major parties, "there is no question of abandoning the veto right granted us in the Meech Lake accord" (*Star*, May 16/90). "Granted"? By whom?

Once the Charest committee tabled its report in the House of Commons on May 17, a new voice rose above the babble. Georges Erasmus, Grand Chief of the Assembly of First Nations, spoke. He challenged the recommendations: "We wanted to deal with what we believe is absolute nonsense that there are only two founding nations here" (*GM*, May 18/90).

To paraphrase Trudeau, the universe of Martin Brian Mulroney was not unfolding as it should.

Notes

1 Either in or out of office, Peterson could be counted on to lecture Canadians. Within six weeks of his hectoring of Grant Devine, he gave sexual advice to 420 students at Atikokan High School in northern Ontario. After telling the twelve- and thirteen-year-olds that he personally was "the last one" to give advice on abstinence, he preached the necessity to "practice safe sex, and that means . . . condoms must be used" (*GM*, May 21/88).

2 The *Public Service Commission Annual Report 1992* is a revelation about the allocation of power in the federal government. Francophone representation in the Supreme Court of Canada is 58.4 percent; Privy Council Office, 50.2 percent; Finance, 36.2 percent; Treasury Board Secretariat, 39 percent; Secretary of State of Canada, 77.2 percent; Public Service Commission, 59.9 percent; Office of the Governor General's Secretary, 64.8 percent; Office of the Commissioner of Official Languages, 69.4 percent; External Affairs, 31 percent; Federal Court of Canada, 50.0 percent; Law Reform Commission of Canada, 60 percent.

3 During the 1992 Meech II crisis, on the eve of St. Jean Baptiste Day, Guy Laforest, a Laval University political scientist, made an observation about the Quebec Referendum coming in October 1992: "Mr. Bourassa doesn't like to see people in the streets. He's afraid it will be used by the nationalists!" (*Maclean's*, June 22/93).

4 See Chapter 2 on Trudeau's mandatory conditions, which he established in 1965, by which a province must become officially bilingual. He cites a minority population of half a million as the criterion.

14

The Power of One
Eagle Feather
— 1990

DURING THE FIVE WEEKS remaining to the Meech Lake deadline on June 23, the accord died a thousand deaths. Yet it still desperately needed a proper executioner. No one could have expected the coup de grâce at the hand of Mulroney's most trusted friend and supporter, the Hon. Lucien Bouchard, Minister of the Environment and Quebec lieutenant in the Tory caucus. Bouchard, the same fellow who wrote Mulroney's Sept-Îles speech on August 6, 1984, and so cemented the union of the Tories and the Quebec nationalists, would by this incredible act of betrayal even elicit some public sympathy for the most hated prime minister in Canadian history.

Benedict Arnold Bouchard took up the scimitar and moved in for the kill. He entered the Canadian embassy in Paris on May 18 on private business. As a Cabinet minister, he used the embassy to send a supportive telegram to the Parti Québécois National Council meeting held in his own riding of Alma, Quebec.

His back-stabbing was a complete reversal from the position he had revealed in an interview with the *Toronto Star* two years before. Asked about his former allegiance to separatism, Bouchard replied, "Yes, I have set it aside." He was also quoted in the *Globe and Mail*: "I don't like the word 'separatist.' . . . It's a loaded word; you know it's not the reality. . . . I feel that since Quebecers have decided, in a democratic way, that their future was within their federation, it is our duty . . . the duty of francophone Quebecers to make it work" (*GM*, Apr 1/88).

His action triggered another defection: federal MP François Gerin resigned from caucus. In a grand gesture, he departed mimicking General de Gaulle's notorious 1967 outburst *"Vive le Québec! Vive les Québécois et les Québécoises!"* (*Sun*, May 20/90).

Two days later, on May 20, Bouchard's Paris telegram was read out at the PQ convention in Alma, Quebec. A supreme humiliation for Brian Mulroney, for as yet Bouchard had said nothing formally in public.

He had neither resigned nor spoken with the prime minister when he woke the next day at 4:00 A.M., changed the diaper of his newborn son, and fed him his bottle. The honourable minister paused, sat down, and wrote his resignation at the kitchen table. He described the Charest report as a betrayal of Quebec and said that Liberal leader Jean Chrétien's advice had prevailed, not his own. At 7:40 P.M. the five-page resignation letter was delivered to 24 Sussex Drive.

When Gilbert Chartran became the third Tory to abandon the his caucus for the separatists' camp, the barn door was left wide open. The damage prompted Toronto Liberal MP John Nunziata, a rat-pack member,[1] to leap to Mulroney's defence: "Separatists are traitors to Canada. They're no better than the racists and the bigots" (*GM*, Apr 23/90).

The possibility that the government might fall under a flight of deserters from the Mulroney camp sent shivers through the financial community. On May 23 the headlines of the *Financial Post* read, "Markets in turmoil over Meech discord." The Canadian dollar lost almost one cent US. A day later, interest rates shot up and the bank rate hit an eight-year high, 14.05 percent — the highest since 1982. Financial experts blamed the constitutional crisis and the Bouchard desertion.

Once again, Mulroney had to move swiftly. With the Meech Lake deadline five weeks away he had to throw up a lot of dikes, fast. He announced a diversion of private meetings between himself and each of the first ministers at his official residence in Ottawa. "Time is very short and the stakes are enormous . . . overpowering" (*GM*, *Star*, May 25/90).

The one-on-one meetings began on the evening of May 25. At the first news conference that followed, Mulroney's faithful ally Premier John Buchanan of Nova Scotia said, "People are not that interested in the constitutional niceties" (CBC Newsworld, May 25/90). This silly remark typified his disdain for the country. Two months earlier he had won wide press coverage with "What are we going to do? Form our own country? That's absurd. Stay as a fractured part of Canada? A good possibility, but that's all. Or be part of the United States? There's no choice" (*Star*/CP, Apr 19/90).

The next morning went as planned. The "good guys" were on their best behaviour. A three-hour session with Bill Vander Zalm produced the West-coast premier's immediate support. Vander Zalm volunteered to the microphones that he was "impressed with the progress" (*Star*, May 27/90).

After he left, Manitoba Premier Gary Filmon stepped forward, the premier who had given Mulroney so much trouble over procedures in the Manitoba legislature. In fine fettle, with the family poodle by his side, Mulroney graciously greeted the premier. Unlike Vander Zalm, Filmon was not a lap dog: "If we do not see the changes that we believe are absolutely essential, then we will not proceed with Meech Lake in the Manitoba legislature. Quebec will have to accept the fact there are legitimate concerns in other areas of the country" (*Sun*, May 27/90).

Grant Devine of Saskatchewan said despairingly of the mess: "We are very close to seeing us wipe out not only a good part of the past but a whole bunch of the future" (*Sun*, May 27/90). Later, in an evening interview with CBC's Don Newman, he added: "The formula doesn't matter. It's the will of the first ministers that counts" (CBC Newsworld, May 26/90).

As Canada tottered on the verge of a nervous breakdown, Mulroney's former ambassador to the United Nations, the well-known NDPer and socialist Stephen Lewis moaned, "I think Canada is genuinely falling apart" (*Star*, May 26/90). In an interview on the CBC-TV program "Midday," former Newfoundland Premier Brian Peckford echoed Grant Devine's despair. Manitoba's former premier, Howard Pawley, appeared on the same program and said, "The June 23 deadline is very destructive" (May 26/90). Only Sharon Carstairs, the Liberal opposition leader in Manitoba, said anything sensible. She might have been on tranquillizers as was later reported, but no one could quibble with her sanity: "Surely this country is more important than a day on the calendar" (*GM*, May 28/90).

The press columnists were working overtime. The business editor of the *Toronto Sun*, Linda Leatherdale, hit the same note Lewis did with her assessment on May 27: "This is one hell of a mess! The country is falling apart. Investors are fleeing. And you and I are left with strangling interest rates — which are killing our household balance sheets, killing our businesses and putting a knife in our already dead economy."

On and on went the agonizing, and on and on the premiers came and went, to and from 24 Sussex. Mulroney's arch-enemy, Newfoundland's Clyde Wells, came. Frank McKenna, the New Brunswick familiar, arrived to toady. Premier Joe Ghiz, the voice of peace from Prince Edward Island, paid his respects and chatted nicely.

Robert Bourassa visited the prime minister's official residence last, with Gil Rémillard in tow. Mulroney entertained a field corps of their province's advisors and bureaucrats to deal with "the priority of Quebec."

The team descended on Mulroney's doorstep the morning of Monday, May 28. This was the only meeting with the prime minister that was not one-on-one. It lasted two hours. After it was over, Bourassa, like all his provincial counterparts, spoke to the reporters huddled together outside the grey mansion. He repeated much of what he had said many times before: "Why should I be the one to compromise? . . . Three times we have been ready to solve the priority of Quebec" (CBC Newsworld).[2] He was at his polished and elegant best as he entered Mulroney's home. He even threw the reporters a Trudeau-style shrug for good measure.

One interlude in these turbulent times deserves mention in every history of the country: Mikhail Gorbachev, the General Secretary and Supreme Commander of the Soviet Union at the time, was in Ottawa on May 29 doing a walk-about along Sparks Street. When reporters questioned him about the Meech Lake Accord, the celebrated author of *Perestroika* replied, "You're going to break something which is nice . . . [pause] . . . You're going to break something with an axe which is nice" (CBC Newsworld, May 30/90). A lovely remark from the man who had written of his own nation, "My country's progress became possible only thanks to the Revolution" (*Perestroika*, p. 18).

While Gorby did his public relations thingy, another saga unfolded, thanks to Southam News Service: the Peterson government's plan to handle the media. The story hit the press the next day, confessions and cover-up duly followed a day after that, and it was scuzzy stuff. Peterson's chief of staff, Dan Gagnier, took the hit for his superiors. High-ranking public servants know this routine well. If they are afforded the luxury of high office, they must accept the high price and take the abuse — lots of it, well — when their time comes. Regardless of the crime, they will win big Brownie points from their masters, be assured of promotions and guaranteed increases in their incomes for their loyalty.

Once cornered by the newshounds, Gagnier confirmed that the Ontario Ministry of Intergovernmental Affairs was preparing a secret policy paper that called for the manipulation of the media, especially CBC television. With the pro-Meech CBC as the key target, the bureaucrats wanted to corrupt the upcoming and final First Ministers Conference on the Constitution.

The plan had three objectives: to convince the CBC to fuel a sense of crisis; to undermine the credibility of those who opposed the accord, like Premiers Wells and Filmon; and, finally, to ensure that Quebec was never isolated nor blamed in any way for refusing to compromise. Joan Bryden of the *Ottawa Citizen* broke the story on May 30.

Some of the stench from these dirty tricks clung to Peterson's constitutional advisor, Professor Patrick Monahan, director of the York University Centre for Public Law and Public Policy at Osgoode Hall. Monahan worked with the premier and Attorney General Ian Scott.[3]

While Toronto's Queen's Park quaked at publicized misconduct in its high places, the deputy speaker of the House of Commons, Tory MP Denis Pronovost, harpooned Newfoundland on an open-line talk show in Trois-Rivières, Quebec: "This history of Newfies [is of] demagogues for politicians — 44 percent of the Newfoundland population have problems reading and writing. It's a Third World country. . . . This crazy mental case, Clyde Wells, he's not worth much. I've met him. He's a dangerous man" (*GM*/CP, June 1/90, re: radio CHLN).

As the academics, the bureaucrats, and the various political clowns cavorted about making public asses of themselves, the international press took more and more notice of their capers. Robert MacNeil, an expatriate Canadian and co-host of PBS's "The MacNeil/Lehrer Report," observed on air that "ordinary Canadians have become uncivil in the extreme and bitter." Americans were taking notice of the problems and perhaps opportunities for themselves.

On May 31 the *Toronto Star* published the American right-wing perspective of Richard Lesner, the editor of *The Arizona Republic*:

> Canada isn't a real country. It never has been. Not really. Most Canadians don't even think of themselves as Canadians. Why on earth would the U.S. want to absorb 5 million ill-tempered Frenchmen, eh? . . . If Canada the non-country disintegrates, the U.S. should think long and hard before it begins to snap up the leftovers. . . . Statehood should come on our terms, and not before the Canadian brand of socialism was jettisoned. (*Star*, May 31/90)

Canada's financial condition continued to deteriorate, inflating panic in the international money markets. On June 4, the *Financial Post* reported a "crash" in the Canadian bond market at the same time it noted that Canada had fallen to the bottom rating of the G-7 countries. Addressing the Canadian Association of Financial Planners, Stephen Jarislowsky, the renowned financial advisor, predicted a 40-percent chance of currency and asset collapse in the Canadian economy.

And, of course, the Official Languages Commissioner kept up his own brand of pressure on the situation. Regardless of the consequences, he handed down more utterances on the eve of the "final" FMC in Ottawa. On June 2 he warned that once Bill C-72 was implemented, he would immediately begin to prosecute all Crown corporations that did not meet the bilingual standards the law set out.[4] Just what the country needed — a public relations effort from Fortier.

The latest FMC began on Sunday, June 3, 1990. As the first day ended, New Brunswick's McKenna captured the essence of its shenanigans as he addressed the scrum outside: "Meech Lake is the biggest roller-coaster ride in the world; one day you're very up, the next day you're very down" (*Star*, June 5/90). The mesmerized press quoted his words in every medium across Canada the next morning.

What more could be said? This FMC, too, sank beneath undertows of bad-will, mistrust, and mismanagement. As was their habit now, the first ministers met in secret.

The meeting struggled on to the third day, June 5, when the finance department published figures that confirmed that Canada's foreign exchange reserves had lost $1 billion US the previous month (*FP*, June 6/90). Observers cited the Lucien Bouchard affair as a major factor. While the secret meetings carried on in Ottawa, finance minister Michael Wilson tabled the Tories' estimates of the cost of Meech before the House of Commons Finance Committee. This time Newfoundland and Clyde Wells were jointly blamed for the failure to reach a unanimous agreement among the provinces. Wilson said Newfoundlanders will have to pay "a meaningful amount of money over the next 30 years" (*FP*, *GM*, June 6/90).

On the FMC dragged. There were fights over the "Canada clause," the "distinct society" clause, power-sharing, the amending formula, and endless discussions over minority rights.

Day six offered another special moment for history to record about Ontario's premier. At 7:15 P.M., after a particularly exhausting session that no one thought would ever end, Peterson pulled two handwritten sheets of paper out of his pocket. He volunteered to give up 6 of Ontario's 24 Senate seats, while Quebec retained 24, to make the deal work. "Monopoly" in the constitutional boardroom.

According to the Peterson plan, Quebec, the western provinces, and the two territories would emerge the winners. Later, it was disclosed that the idea was in fact Mulroney's, not Peterson's.

The seven-day marathon ended on Saturday, June 9, less than fourteen days before the deadline. Unlike Creation, however, Mulroney's world would not be completed on the seventh day. Canada's croupier had dealt at least one player a phoney deck of cards — and one of his victims found out in the nick of time.

An angry Premier Wells quit the FMC at 1:00 A.M. Saturday morning, furious that his proposed clause to review the "distinct society" provision had "mysteriously disappeared" from the final text (*Star*, June 10/90). At ten o'clock the same morning, he returned to continue the session. Filmon and Wells accused Mulroney of skulduggery (*New York Times*, June 10/90). On instructions from Mulroney, Roger Tassé, an outside advisor with vast experience as a leading government courtier, apologized. He obediently put himself in the line of fire. The old hand at government ploys said he was the one who had decided not to inform Wells there wasn't enough support for the idea (*Star*, June 11/90).

Wells could have walked out then and there and have been fully justified. He didn't. Canadians understood and respected him. He stood his ground, then signed the agreement with an asterisk. The caveat was an irritatingly reticent addition well understood in legal circles.

The media would have a field day misrepresenting his actions after that. The caution was simple enough: the Meech Lake Accord did not have the premier's support until the people of Newfoundland had passed their own final judgement. Wells wanted a mandate that meant something — preferably a referendum.

After a final marathon session of fifteen hours, a conditional agreement was announced. Wells and Filmon did not agree with the other premiers, and it looked like McKenna agreed with Filmon and Wells. No one knew at this point that McKenna was Mulroney's joker in the pack. The prime minister had studied his players well.

One final government foible stands out: an insult to the intelligence of the Canadian people. The whole country knew perfectly well the distinct society clause had to have some legal weight if it were really to work to Quebec's benefit. Why else include it? The government pleaded that the clause was merely an interpretive guideline. Fully aware of the menacing notwithstanding clause, all of Canada knew that the distinct society clause could and would be used to erode the union. A nation exists on inviolate, historical principles above any regional or ethnic interest.

In the face of the obvious, the prime minister pressed on. The pro-Meech participants loudly touted the legal opinion that the distinct society clause had little meaning and did not contradict Trudeau's Charter.

Few people, even Meech supporters, bought this nonsense. If the clause did mean something — which surely was intended — then why was the definition not spelled out so everyone had some idea what the Constitution was all about?

One of the prize comments about the Meech Lake mess came from Nancy Jackman of the Ad Hoc Committee of Women on the Constitution. She called it "a foul-up. . . . It's horsecrap." She noted the failure to define equality of the sexes in the Constitution. Her outburst found a large and appreciative audience (*Star*, June 10/90).

The FMC of June 1990 cost over $1 million. The food bill alone came to $188,000 — with Ontario the biggest spender. To coddle Peterson's handsome coterie, a phalanx of thirty-seven, cost the taxpayers $77,000. For months, complaints about the whole business filled Letters to the Editor pages from St. John's to Vancouver.

On June 11, 1990, Mulroney decided to try something different — momentarily he made the people happy. After delaying for five months he appointed Canada's first "elected" senator, Stan Waters, a founding member of the Reform Party of Canada, to the Senate. Reform's Deborah Grey, who had won her seat in the House of Commons on March 13, 1989, would have company in Ottawa.

Clyde Wells, on the other hand, had to deal with some disturbing news. The day Mulroney reluctantly acknowledged the legitimacy of Stan Waters's election to the Senate, Wells's chief electoral officer advised the premier there wasn't enough time to conduct a referendum on the accord in Newfoundland. For the moment Mulroney looked good — and Wells was in trouble.

The prime minister's good fortune was fleeting. This time he did himself in. Interviewed in Toronto by Susan Delacourt, Graham Fraser, and Jeffrey Simpson of the *Globe and Mail*, he admitted he had manipulated the June FMC: "That's the day we're going to roll the dice" (*GM*, June 12/90). That remark reminded everyone of his careless moment during his 1984 election campaign on the airplane with the reporters. His arrogant statements had neatly guaranteed that his name would live in infamy.

He received two body blows that June 12. As the news flashed across the country that the prime minister considered Canada just a gambling casino, the Manitoba native chiefs met to develop their own nine-point strategy to kill Meech. This second blow came out of the Manitoba legislature. At this point, a totally unknown New Democrat MLA, Elijah Harper, former chief of the Red Sucker Band, leaped onto the national stage in a single bounce. He quietly blocked the required period for debate on the Meech Lake

Accord. After months of signals to the prime minister, Premier Filmon's stern warnings about legislative procedures were coming to pass.

On June 14, Elijah Harper did it again — this time with more far-reaching results. Because of the MLA's brilliant timing, House Speaker Denis Rocan's ruling left no other option than to close off debate until Monday, June 18, or perhaps June 20 if there were any more unforeseen procedural delays. Opposition to the accord had been mounting for months. By this time more than 500 registered individuals and groups were waiting to be heard — with only two to five days of possible hearings left.

On June 15, Premier Filmon served notice that it was "almost impossible" for his province to pass Meech. At the deadline for registering, for example — 6:00 P.M., June 14 — there were now more than 1,500 petitioners lined up for the public hearings, with possibly only three days in which to hear them (*Star*, June 16/90).

Elijah Harper knew he had power. Like Filmon, he too had a threat for the prime minister — to take native concerns seriously and negotiate with the aboriginal peoples. Throughout Canada citizens revelled in their prime minister's discomfiture. It was as good as watching the Canada–Russia hockey series with Mulroney and the Tories in the red uniforms about to be shut out. When Harper hit the stage, a good many of Mulroney's supposed friends cheered the former chief on.

The prime minister could still find some solace, however, in the assurance Clyde Wells offered. Committed to the free vote he had promised on the accord, Wells said, "I can't see us abandoning it unless there is some overwhelming evidence to do so" (*GM*, June 16/90).

Two days later, on June 17, that reassurance dissolved. Wells threw in a new curve with his comment that Newfoundland would "have to consider whether there is any point going through agonizing discussions" if the debate in Manitoba were stalled beyond June 23 (*GM*, June 18/90).

On June 16, Canadians heard about Canadian unity from Deidesheim, Germany. In the presence of Brian Mulroney, German Chancellor Helmut Kohl, "the Cabbage," as he is called in German by his detractors, defended the prime minister:

> Nobody else in the world can understand. . . . This is what I would tell a friend in Canada: it is important to retain one's identity and one's sense of *heimat* and I believe that this is still possible in this time of federalism. . . . In Europe, we have this concept, not because we are any better, but perhaps now we are more reasonable and intelligent after two world wars, after more than 40 million dead. (*GM*, June 17/90)

Elsewhere outside the country other noises were being made. In Mystic, Connecticut, on Monday, June 18, 1990, at the eighteenth annual conference of New England governors and Eastern Canadian premiers, Canada's constitutional crisis dominated the agenda. When he heard Bourassa say that chaos could follow Meech Lake's failure, Massachussetts governor Michael Dukakis, the former presidential candidate, suggested, "All of us would feel a lot better if Canada were stabilized" (CBC Newsworld, June 18/90; *Star*, June 19/90). If the accord failed to pass, the Quebec premier predicted inflation, the fall of the Canadian dollar, and an increased deficit.

The Tory scare tactics were truly impressive. In Ottawa, federal government House Leader Harvie Andre put the House of Commons on crisis alert. Plans to adjourn the House to accommodate the Liberal leadership convention on June 23 were put on hold on June 18. All MPs were put on a twelve-hour alert for recall to Ottawa. "The future of the country is at stake here, and we want to be sure we're ready to respond," Andre grimly told reporters and the country (*GM*, June 19/92). Governor General Ray Hnatyshyn and the MPs prepared themselves for the end of the world.

The next day, Mulroney turned on Filmon. Manitoba, he scolded, had "an obligation to Canada." As for Elijah Harper, who had suggested three days earlier that the prime minister negotiate, Mulroney scoffed that he was merely indulging in a "dilatory tactic" (*Star*, June 20/90).

Filmon was furious at the personal attacks: "They had better accept the fact that they have bungled this and bungled it horribly, and they can't start pointing fingers somewhere else. . . . They chose to roll the dice. . . . They were told time and time again" (*GM*, June 20/90). The next day he added, "We can't do it under our process. And he either doesn't understand the process, or wants to ignore and subvert the process — and that's wrong" (*Star*, June 21/90).

The key point in the drama was revealed the same day that Filmon flung accusations back at the prime minister. Although unanimous consent for debate during the allotted time was no longer necessary, extending the debate did require unanimity. According to the rules, Filmon dutifully tabled the Meech Lake Accord for debate in the legislature and six MLAs spoke on it. By now the list of petitioners who wished to speak had mushroomed from 1,500 to 3,500.

According to the rules of the Manitoba legislature, the last day for debate before the deadline was Friday, June 22: between 10:00 A.M. and 12:30 P.M. Would anyone block a request that the debate be extended? Everyone looked to Elijah Harper.

While Manitoba was enduring its assault from Ottawa, another drama was unfolding in Newfoundland. Addressing the House of Assembly there, Peterson and McKenna — the latter having sold out and signed on to Meech at the last moment in a bargaining ploy — pleaded to the MLAs for passage of the accord.

The Meech Lake proponents faced the task of persuading six of Clyde Wells's Liberals to change sides — an unlikely proposition in view of the tremendous regard the Newfoundland Liberal team had for their leader. David Peterson begged his audience for passage out of "love and respect and accommodation and tolerance," if nothing else.[5]

Then Frank McKenna, latecomer and last-minute side-changer, stepped up to the podium in the House of Assembly. Pounding the lectern to punctuate his points, he warned that Canada was being ridiculed internationally (*Star*, June 21/90). On his return to Saint John, he slobbered that there were "seven million souls [in Quebec] who feel Canada doesn't want them" (*GM*, June 21/90).

Back in Ottawa, Deputy Prime Minister Don Mazankowski poured on the coals. He wanted Filmon to invoke closure to cut off the debate in Manitoba. Request denied. Filmon shot back his best remark during the whole constitutional debate: "What good is a constitution and a democracy if you have to set aside a democracy to achieve it? . . . It doesn't make sense" (*GM*, June 21/90).

Then external affairs minister Joe Clark proudly stalked into the arena. It was June 20. He said the Meech crisis was hurting Canada's international reputation.

On June 21, the prime minister, like Joe Clark, came out of his cocoon. He addressed the House of Assembly in St. John's. For one hour, Mulroney got down on his knees and begged. If Meech failed and a Parti Québécois referendum followed in the future, he rebuked his listeners, "the terms of Meech are going to look very, very reasonable indeed" (*GM*, June 22/90). "Meech wound up carrying baggage for which it was not responsible," he added. Quebecers, he told his Newfoundland audience, "will not accept to be frisked at the door" (*Star*, June 22/90). Sept-Îles all over again.

Gil Rémillard, who had brought forward Quebec's demands in the first place at Mont Gabriel, had his final word too. First he dismissed any prospect of amending the constitutional deadline and then the Quebec intergovernmental affairs minister and justice minister growled, "If on the twenty-third at midnight, less a few seconds, Meech is not accepted, that means that Meech is dead. We have had enough. That will suffice . . . and we will think of something else" (*Star*, June 22/90). But the scare tactics no longer worked.

In Winnipeg the cheers were already going up at the prospect of the accord's defeat. Celebrating Aboriginal Solidarity Day, 3,000 to 4,000 non-natives and aboriginals demonstrated on the lawn of the Manitoba legislature. The juggernaut of native resistance was barrelling along.

Leading the three major parties, Mulroney and the Tories continued to train their weapons on Newfoundland's Liberal premier. Next in line to play the goat was the Conservative MP and chairman of the House of Commons Finance Committee, Don Blenkarn. This time the MP known for his mouth went overboard: "Sometimes, looking at the costs of carrying these parts of the country — Newfoundland, for example — I sometimes feel we could be better off if we towed it out to sea and sank it" (*Star*, June 22/90). Newfoundlanders have a word for the Don Blenkarns of this world: *gommils* — morons.

Meech Lake's death rattle was heard in Ottawa and in St. John's before it finally expired in Winnipeg. Committed to a vote on it in Newfoundland's House of Assembly, Wells welshed on his promise when he saw the accord die in Manitoba. Frankly, he saw no point in continuing.

Just before the vote, Mulroney's high priest of constitutional gamesmanship in Ottawa, Senator Lowell Murray, summoned a press conference. To the amazement of the gathered scribes, he announced that the federal government had completely reversed its previous position. As long as Newfoundland's House of Assembly passed the accord, the legal matter of the deadline — that is, three years from the date of passage of the proposed amendment in a provincial legislature — would be referred to the Supreme Court of Canada. The government would seek an extension, but only for Manitoba. Not for Newfoundland.

Extraordinary! Speaking for Quebec the previous day, minister Gil Rémillard had dismissed any idea of extending the deadline. The Mulroney government had consistently refused point-blank to entertain the thesis first posed by a University of British Columbia law professor, Robert Grant, on January 15, 1989, that the deadline of June 23 was not sacrosanct.

Grant had said, "In my view, the accord is not subject to any deadline at all" (*Star*/CP, Jan 15/89). Others had reached the same conclusion, including Manitoba university law professor Bryan Schwartz and the former Clerk of the Privy Council, Gordon Robertson. In fact, Robertson had published an article in the June 19, 1989, *Globe and Mail*, claiming there was no such deadline.

In the Manitoba legislature on June 22, at 12:26 P.M., Elijah Harper was asked to approve a motion to extend the debate. In a barely audible whisper, firmly holding onto a single grey eagle feather, he answered, "No, Mr. Speaker" (*GM*, June 23/90).

Meech Lake died at that precise moment in that exact place. By withholding the unanimous consent to continue the Meech debate in the Manitoba legislature, the Meech Lake debate exceeded its deadline. Harper's final "No" was his ninth between June 12 and June 22.

Premier Gary Filmon spoke his mind in Winnipeg. He called Senator Murray's proposed referral to the Supreme Court of Canada "another example of the kind of strategic maneuvering . . . the so-called roll of the dice" (*GM*, June 23/90).

In St. John's, Newfoundland, with no contact from Ottawa after four hours of waiting, Clyde Wells learned that Lowell Murray was making his announcement publicly to the people of Canada. The Conservatives had sunk to bad manners and abusive conduct. Following the adjournment of the Manitoba legislature, Wells adjourned the Newfoundland House of Assembly. Like Filmon, he also had words about Murray's last-minute plan and exclusion of Newfoundland from the same privilege accorded Manitoba: "That's the final manipulation. We're not prepared to be manipulated any longer. . . . At the end, when people are trying to be fair and honest and put the interests of the country first, the government of this country is still rolling the dice, still gambling on the future of this country" (*FP*, *GM*, *Star*, *Sun*, June 23/90).

For not going ahead and conducting the vote he had promised in the Newfoundland legislature, Premier Clyde Wells endured a storm of abuse from the Tory politicians and the media. They had decided that he had to be punished. He had not played the executive-federalist game by their rules. As he solemnly pronounced Meech dead, Murray blamed Clyde Wells for breaking a promise that meant "killing the last hope of success of Meech Lake" (*FP*, June 23/90). For his sin, Wells would be sentenced to political purgatory.

Federal trade minister John Crosbie, once a buddy of Wells, also exploded at his fellow Newfoundlander. Mulroney's lead minister in coastal waters permitted himself the luxury of letting loose with Barbara Frum on "The Journal" on June 22: "That's just what his government is responsible for — the failure of the Meech Lake Accord. . . . He's got to be careful when he calls himself an honourable man."

According to Crosbie, Meech Lake was "shot down and mortally wounded by Premier Clyde Wells and nobody else" (*GM*, June 23/90). His remarks were not appreciated by the aboriginal Canadians who were happy to take credit for slamming an agreement that would not recognize them as a founding people of Canada.

Amid all the repercussions, the most vicious abuse flowed from the pen of one of the biggest losers behind the scenes. Peter C. Newman of *Maclean's* magazine skewered, scourged, ridiculed, and blasted Wells for months as the "Evil Knievel" of Confederation. The veteran journalist was simply incapable of understanding what had happened. Canadians would never accept that Meech Lake ever held water as a good deal for Canada. In other words, most Canadians would never accept the concept of Quebec — or any community — as a constitutionally "distinct society."

Notes

1 The rat pack consisted of three members of the Liberal caucus who delighted in abusive parliamentary behaviour: Sheila Copps, Don Boudria, and Nunziata.

2 Noticeable only to those watching their TV screens very closely while Bourassa was addressing the media outside 24 Sussex was a wasp flying persistently around the premier's head. An omen of some sting to come?

3 In *Roll of the Dice*, Deborah Coyne fingers Monahan: "An embarrassed David Peterson immediately disowned it and said that the low-level bureaucrat who prepared it would soon be gone. At the premier's office [that of Clyde Wells, where Coyne was consitutional advisor], all we could do was laugh, since it was obviously accurate and equally obviously not prepared by a low-level bureaucrat. (Later, reliable sources would confirm for me that it was prepared with the knowledge of Patrick Monahan)" (p. 96).

4 Fortier puts great store in his family tradition, and was interviewed about it in England in 1989. Questioned about his first name, he replied, "It was chosen by my godfather because D'Iberville was the name of a great hero of French-speaking Canada who successfully fought on behalf of France against the English and was never defeated. Not many English-speaking Canadians seem aware of this. It may be just as well. . . ." (*Language International*, July/Aug 1989).

5   While the Ontario premier was in Newfoundland promoting the revised accord from the June FMC — including the sacrifice of six of Ontario's Senate seats without notifying the public beforehand — the Ontario legislature went ahead and approved the Meech Lake amendment by a vote of 95 to 10. The media took no interest in what was taking place in the Ontario legislature and reported none of it.

III

To Each
His Own
Accord

15

Deep
Thinkers
The Boffins
and the Presumptives

I T WAS EASY TO BLAME the failure of constitutional initiatives on the politicians. All of them discredited themselves as much for the process as for their own lack of vision. For six years, from 1986 to 1992, from the beginning of the Meech Lake Accord to the Referendum on the Charlottetown Accord, too many of them had lied, bribed, threatened, cheated, corrupted, bullied, and manipulated to win. They had earned Canadians' cynicism.

Yet for all their crimes, the politicians were not alone. The academics and the upper echelons in the public service were used to being, as most of them preferred to be, aloof from the public. The Meech Lake and Charlottetown accords changed all that. There were reputations to be made, and there was big money for those willing to be corrupted into the political process. When the debate was over, the experts emerged in droves from every nook and cranny in Canadian society to explain what was going on. Some fifty of them consistently participated and commented on the content and process for nearly a decade.

When the Meech Lake Accord collapsed on June 22, 1990, Canadians could name any number of opinionated experts with something to say about the Canadian federation. Meech Lake exposed the intelligentsia of the country up for hire. Academics were needed as translators, interpreters for the media, as conference chairs and organizers — for dozens of roles, some visible, most not. The government needed them to lend credibility to the system. The public didn't understand the goings-on, and most of those running the country were completely in the dark. So out came the scholars, professors, and teachers, clucking, in flocks, from the cubbyhole worlds of history, public affairs, law, political science, and philosophy, laying their golden eggs all over the constitutional table.

A very few were serious and knowledgeable scholars. However, most came with more than one motive and, unfortunately for Canada, they offered little deserving the attention it received. All did so at great public expense. The one common denominator for the entire Canadian university environment was the inability to ask questions — any questions.

The boffins infested the public forums like flies. They came from the universities and colleges, and from numerous government and privately funded think-tanks and special-interest groups. At a time when the nation needed the best brains and real thinkers, the country found itself saddled with dozens of dogmatists who knew little of Canada's heritage. Mostly the academics were scared silly — about money, about their next government grants, and about tenure. They were superficial, condescending, and pompously defensive about the issues they knew little about. When the debate ended, the more serious issue on the table was not national unity, but the intellectual degeneration of the country. No knowledge. No debate possible.

Official Bilingualism was one of the noxious ingredients that demanded examination; inter-provincial trade another; economics another; multiculturalism and native rights were others. None of the academics seemed to understand that a nation survives on more than compromise. None offered a national vision or knew that it was paramount that Canada have principles its people all treasured so that it would survive.

The desuetude of the academic institutions was the largest single cause of the breakdown of the national fabric. Not one scholar in any university had ever addressed the cataclysmic change that had nearly dismembered the country, the Pearson–Trudeau revolution. Almost without exception, the academics feared offending their political masters. The state owned their institutions through various forms of funding and so precluded freedom of thought.

Undeterred, the academics spoke on radio and television at every opportunity. They came forth to lecture and influence rather than to listen and learn. While some, the so-called and often quoted senior officials of government, the mandarins, and other high-ranking public servants, were able to retain a degree of anonymity, even these power-brokers soon overcame their shyness and boldly entered the public arena.

At first the experts appeared singly. Then they came in bunches: historians, philosophers, political scientists, law professors, and lawyers, and, last but not least, the economists and the barons of business. In the same way a medical expert would be called upon to explain a breakthrough written up in the *New England Journal of Medicine*, the chosen spokesperson — approved as "politically correct" — was seen as an insider who wouldn't stir the pot too much. Accordingly, he or she would perform for the media.

So there was no public debate. Canada was assumed to be a bilingual country. It was assumed that Canadians embraced multiculturalism. All political parties, except the Reform Party, accepted without question that the country was based on founding races and founding cultures.

For more than six years Canadians had been forced to endure the terrorism of new terminology: bicameral polity, asymmetric federalism, executive federalism, supranational power structures, distinct societies, multiculturalism, pluralistic societies, the collectivity, federalism. The term most frequently used to describe the system of government in Canada, barring oversimplifications like *parliamentary democracy* and *constitutional monarchy*, was *executive federalism*. It simply meant that the nation was governed by the prime minister and the first ministers of the provinces and their appointees to cabinet.

Executive federalism depends on a substructure of non-elected officials who advise, counsel, instruct, and manage all public affairs far removed from public scrutiny and parliamentary accountability. The country's constitutional upheaval unearthed these deeply rooted substructures for public view for the first time. The Meech Lake and Charlottetown accords exposed faultlines and crevasses on an unprecedented scale.

Pierre Trudeau had seized on the vagueness of the Pearson vision and given it form and substance. In order to survive, his vision depended on the false premise of founding races and cultures; the "counterweight" duplicity made it work.

Brian Mulroney had exploited the ruins of that vision to gain his own power. He piloted the vision of its original architects to its logical conclusion — racial pluralism. His sole political objective was preserving power for one political party.

To accomplish such radical change, it was inevitable that Canadians would have to receive some instruction. But change from what to what? This was where the academics came in. A considerable number of them became mini media cult figures. Few had any great moments worth remembering. Most were hopelessly dull and unimaginative.

IN ENGLISH-SPEAKING CANADA, one of the first to speak up was **John William Michael Bliss**, professor of history at the University of Toronto. Early in the debate over Canada's future, he became the state broadcasting corporation's most frequent academic commentator on behalf of English Canada. He radiated an aura of objectivity without professorial arrogance — rare in Canada's academic world. A strong supporter of executive federalism and Trudeau's vision of Canada, he wrote numerous articles for the *Toronto Star*, the *Globe and Mail*, and other publications. He joined Deborah Coyne's anti-Meech group, the Canadian Coalition on the Constitution. Many of his remarks became insiders' slogans during the period. While avoiding core issues of democracy, Bliss soothed his audience rather than address any matter of controversy. He obfuscated. His Andy Warhol moment: "If you are an ordinary Canadian, concerned about the country your children will inherit, you ought to be appalled that our politicians have set up for us a wild constitutional leap in the dark" (*Star*, June 30/87).

After the collapse of the Meech Lake Accord, he burbled at the CBC year-end wrap-up of December 28, 1990:

> We had a bunch of politicians in Ottawa and their highly paid constitutional advisors who said, "Oh yes, we can just open the constitution and then rewrite it and then sell it to the people." . . . The national political elite [failed us] in a massive way. . . . There is in fact a political revolution taking place in Canada now. . . .
>
> I don't think the failure of Meech Lake is going to give us something better. . . . It's going to give us more Meech Lake Accords . . . more revelations of the depth of our disagreement . . . more endless constitutional squabbles and maybe the break-up of the country.

Following the October 1993 federal election, Bliss, in addition to his duties as an historian, became a bi-weekly columnist for the Pulp Primevil, the *Toronto Star*.

Pierre Fortin, professor of economics at l'Université du Québec à Montréal, was another academic given a large public platform. He typified the select few Quebec commentators the CBC offered to English Canada. He played the part of a conditional federalist. He was a separatist. In

1980 he wrote a book to prove that sovereignty-association was viable. He boasted that he had supported the Yes side of Quebec's 1980 referendum on independence. Once the Meech Lake Accord collapsed, he flaunted his views at a symposium at Guelph University on November 9, 1990: "I keep my own opinion for the voting booth. . . . But although I am maintaining the same position as in 1980, there are a lot of people who are going much farther than I am ready to go now; in other words, I was in front of the people in 1980, but now I am in back of many others who are ready to be more radical than I can be" (quoted in Young, *Confederation in Crisis*, p. 59).

Cute. He had been propagandizing one view in English Canada and saying something very different in Quebec. At the Bélanger–Campeau Commission hearings on Quebec's future following the collapse of Meech, he openly favoured sovereignty for Quebec and a unilateral declaration (UDI) to that effect. On November 27, 1990, representing the Groupe de recherche Éthos, he summarized:

> The first hope that we formulate before you is that Quebecers acquire, collectively, bravely and with dignity, all the political levers they need to affirm their right to self-determination and to fully promote their economic, social and cultural development. We feel it is essential for the Québec government to declare the complete political sovereignty of Québec before the rest of Canada and before the international community. . . . We also suggest we grant a particular status to the Amerindians and Inuit who share our territory, by taking their legitimate aspirations into account. (*Journal des débats*, Nov 27/90, p. 761)

Another separatist the CBC promoted was **Pierre Fournier**, professor of political science at the University of Quebec in Montreal. His was the Quebec voice English Canada heard most often. He lectured thousands in English Canada that it was "inevitable" that Quebec would become a sovereign state. The pro-Meech CBC relied heavily on him for their information on attitudes in that province.

On March 7, 1989, he published an article in the *Globe and Mail* entitled "What does Quebec really want?" He held that Trudeau had a "pathological disdain" for nationalism. But this, he argued, was a contradiction. Fournier asserted that Trudeau, having rejected Quebec nationalism, had invented his own brand of it for Canada. Trudeau's "victory over the separatists was, in fact, a devastating, if not fatal blow to the only vision of Canada that could have propelled the country into the twenty-first century without becoming a U.S. state." The former prime minister's error was to ally English-Canadian nationalism with Quebec nationalism, "including many 'separatists.'" His failure was in "crushing" Quebec nationalism rather that "dealing" with it — whatever that meant.

Few Canadians today would agree with this assessment. Whatever one thought of Pierre Elliott Trudeau, no credible academic could justify the accusation that Trudeau was wed to Quebec separatists. This is the one gang Trudeau ridiculed unmercifully. Nonetheless, for the acquiescent CBC, Fournier had the right stuff.

Fournier also accused Trudeau of welshing on his May 14, 1980, promise at Montreal's Paul Sauvé Arena just six days before the referendum on separation: To vote No, Trudeau declared that night, would be "interpreted as a mandate to change the Constitution, to renew federalism. We want change. We are staking our seats to change." Fournier claims that Quebecers like Jean Chrétien and Jeanne Sauvé would take these remarks to signify support for special status or more powers for Quebec (*Star*, March 18/89).

As for the future of francophones outside the province, he concluded accurately that the situation was bleak: "Assimilation will eventually do away with most if not all clusters outside Quebec." He reserved his vitriol for anglophones in Quebec. Here, too, he was on target. He called them generally a lamentable lot unable to "play anything resembling a creative role in the evolving relationship between Canada and Quebec."

Just before Meech collapsed, he again clarified where he stood in the *Globe and Mail* on May 13, 1990: "For me and many young people in my generation, it will be recognition [through Meech] or independence."

A year after the collapse of the accord, however, existentialism overshadowed his philosophy: "The drop in business support for sovereignty started in the spring [1990]. After Meech failed, business leaders were almost all frustrated and angry — like everybody else. But in their hearts, businessmen believe that political independence will endanger the economic security of Quebec. They have to deal with the rest of Canada and they have to be practical" (*Star*/CP, July 2/91).

In his book *A Meech Lake Post-Mortem: Is Quebec Sovereignty Inevitable?* he makes an interesting observation on the so-called success of Trudeau's vision: "The race towards bilingualism in federal institutions was largely artificial and intended mainly to contain the fervour of Quebec nationalism. Too often, we tend to forget that Trudeau won election in English Canada only once, in 1968" (p. 70).

MIXED VOICES were heard from Western Canada. The media's choice of spokesperson from the West reflected their own central Canadian perspective. Political science professor **Alan Cairns** of the University of British Columbia participated at the Mont Gabriel Conference in 1986. A successful author and popular speaker at symposiums and special-interest forums, he offered the following comments in his analysis of the failure of Meech Lake, *Charter Versus Federalism: The Dilemma of Constitutional Reform*:

> The public hearings over Meech Lake displayed a remarkably truculent attitude by individual citizens, interest group leaders, academics and others toward the first ministers and their advisers for their false assumption that the constitution was theirs to amend as they saw fit. It is impossible to read this evidence without concluding that the Charter has, by changing citizens' identities and expectations, eroded the legitimacy of executive federalism, unconstrained by citizen input as a vehicle for formal constitutional change. (p. 116)

Odd. The Charter only proved the problem — that change was all but impossible. What good was a charter if it could be emasculated by a notwithstanding provision? Just as important, Canadians now knew the Constitution was well nigh unamendable and removed from them. Academics failed to recognize the disenfranchisement of all Canadians in 1982, not just Quebecers. That was the problem. Charter-rights activism only indicates the more serious ailment of a lack of democracy. Contrary to the common perception in academic circles, Trudeau's Charter has never been held in high public regard, despite the media's claims and the propaganda of pollsters who have never asked people the real question.

Sometimes academics like Cairns almost caught up with the people and appreciated their lack of ownership of their own constitution:

> A crucial Meech Lake lesson, accordingly, is that a comprehensive constitutional understanding will no longer emerge from studying the élite worlds of executive federalism supplemented by the constrained constitutional discourse of the courtroom. Meech Lake makes clear that the constitution now has a social base. As a consequence, society now has a constitutional existence to a degree that previous generations would not have recognized. . . . Meech Lake continues what threatens to become a tradition of excluding or bypassing those who, it was thought, could be safely ignored.

Its working premise was that extragovernmental opposition to its means and ends could be rendered ineffectual and be overridden if first ministers would simply stick together and employ party discipline to rush the appropriate resolutions through submissive legislatures. . . .

The staggering rebuff of executive federalism in constitutional matters implicit in the failure of Meech Lake is perhaps its most basic lesson. (*Charter*, pp. 99–100, 102)

Another Western voice was the dean of the Faculty of Graduate Studies, historian, and professor, **David Jay Bercuson** of the University of Calgary. As editor of *Canada and the Burden of Unity* (1977), he expressed Western Canadian frustration: "If federalism is to have any meaning as a system in which various states or provinces are united for common goals and purposes, provincial governments must have more limited areas of responsibility and should not be allowed to encroach on areas of truly national jurisdiction. This is why the provincial governments are imperfect guardians of regional interests" (pp. 7–8). This is executive federalism. In the final days of Meech he wrote:

The Meech Lake process is as Canadian as the maple leaf. Virtually every federal-provincial conference dealing with a subject of any real significance to Canada's political leaders has been held in secret. . . .

Canadian political leaders . . . have become drunk on their own supreme authority. And why not? Canadians, after all, have never cared much about political or constitutional principle. (*Star*, June 15/90)

Elsewhere Bercuson concluded that the Liberals were the bad guys and the Tories weren't quite so bad:

One of the worst legacies of the Lester Pearson/Pierre Trudeau years was the Liberal government's assumption that it had a mandate to give Canadians designer government. . . . The Pearson/Trudeau legacy was indebtedness and national disunity. Instead of just wanting to provide good government, they wanted to use the power of government to mould the country into their own image of Canada. (*FP*, Aug 14–16/93)

By 1994, Bercuson and philosophy professor **Barry Cooper** give a somewhat different perspective. In *Derailed: The Betrayal of the National Dream* the two polemicists conclude in the chapter "Bad Government Begins" that it was John Diefenbaker who first betrayed the "pragmatic" Founding

Fathers of Confederation. Diefenbaker is slammed as one of the "idealistic dreamers who had founded the Canada First movement" (p. 78).

In 1993, Bercuson appeared as an expert witness for the Crown in support of Bill C-114, the election "gag law." In an article to the *Globe and Mail* with co-author Barry Cooper, he said, "the way to real free speech is through fair and equitable laws. Bill C-114 is one of those laws" (*GM*, July 5/93). Warren Kinsella acknowledged his assistance in his book *Web of Hate* in 1994.

Perhaps the most vocal Western Canadian academic for the Pearson–Trudeau–Mulroney vision was Professor **Roger Gibbins**. He appeared regularly on CBC. He heads the University of Calgary's political science department where he teaches politics, regionalism, federalism, ideological belief systems, and environmental systems. He edited *Meech Lake and Canada: Perspectives from the West*. He worked with the Canada West Foundation and in 1990 taught a seminar with his colleague, Peter Lougheed, the former premier of Alberta. A political academic more than a scholar, Gibbins, like Lougheed, championed the Meech Lake agenda:

> Undoubtedly Mr. Mulroney deserves particular praise. If constitutional recognition of Quebec as a distinct society was the price to be paid for Quebec's inclusion, I do not feel that the price was too high.
> . . . The Meech Lake Accord went well beyond the inclusion of Quebec to expand significantly the powers of all provincial governments. . . . While it is one thing to recognize Quebec as a distinct society, it is something else entirely to entrench constitutionally a provincialist view of the country for which there is much less sociological, cultural or political support. In short, my quarrel is not with what the Accord says about Quebec, but rather with what it says about Canada. (Gibbins, "A Sense of Unease: The Meech Lake Accord and Constitution-Making in Canada," in *Meech Lake and Canada*, p. 122)

Among the academics much too close to the system was a professor of political science and former principal of Queen's University, **Ronald Watts**, a long-standing member of the "Queen's Mafia." With the departure of Professor Peter Leslie to Ottawa as Mulroney's Assistant Secretary to the Cabinet for Federal–Provincial Relations, Watts assumed the directorship of the Institute of Intergovernmental Relations. He was an old hand at constitutional affairs. As a member of the 1978–79 Pépin–Robarts Task Force on Canadian Unity, he had adopted the stance that Quebec's constitutional demands were "very modest" (*Star*, Feb 26/89). He considered special status for Quebec to be perfectly in order.

In 1977 he wrote that "greater recognition of provincial aspirations across Canada will not by itself hold Confederation together unless we develop a wider sense of destiny for Canada" ("Survival or Disintegration," in Simeon, ed., *Must Canada Fail?* p. 60).

In 1989, with Meech Lake in difficulty, he wrote, "Consequently the failure to ratify the Accord will leave serious scars, even if it does not unravel Confederation, as it well might. The political climate for reconciliation will be poisoned for a considerable period to come" ("An Overview," in IIR, *Canada: The State of the Federation, 1989*, p. 17). He also wrote, "I think there's an enormous responsibility upon those who would deny the approval of the accord. . . . If it is not adopted, I think the long-term effect is that it will be a disaster" (*Star*, Feb 26/89).

Most Canadian scholars held representative democracy in contempt. Professor **Richard Edmond Barrington Simeon**, another of the Queen's Mafia — who, incidentally, did not attend the Mont Gabriel Conference in 1986 — was by no means a rarity. The director of the School of Public Administration was also a member of the organizing committee that wrote the pro-Meech booklet *Meech Lake: Setting the Record Straight*, published by two groups, The Friends of Meech Lake and Canadians for a Unifying Constitution. Simeon, along with law professors Peter Hogg, Robert Prichard, and Katherine Swinton, served as constitutional advisor to David Peterson and was involved in the strategy discussions that took place before the final round of the FMC in Ottawa between June 3 and 9. Simeon remains the classic executive federalist: "It is a fallacy to think that if 'the people' had been able to decide we would have been able to agree on some other vision" (*Competing Constitutional Visions*, Swinton, p. 305). He also said, "My defence of Meech Lake, therefore, is a more pragmatic one. I do not really ask whether it is the best that we could have done but, rather, is it an acceptable, workable compromise or not?" (Behiels, pp. 125–26).

Most academics circumvented the real issues. It was easier and safer to concentrate on the mechanics of structure and the division of powers.

Professor **Paul Barker**, political scientist at the University of Western Ontario, was more diffuse than most. According to his thesis, Canada's constitutional dilemma could be solved by an "equilibrium" vision of nationhood: "The equilibrium vision of Canada leads to a cautious approval of the Meech Lake accord, but stresses that it could be made better. Unlike the vision captured in the dichotomy, this vision requires neither a categorical rejection nor a categorical acceptance of the accord, but instead asks for changes to a largely suitable set of constitutional reforms" (*Star*, June 24/88).

The few voices from outside the raw socialist camp that the media graced with their favour were at least entertaining. **Thomas Michael Hurka**, an associate professor of philosophy at the University of Calgary, sounded like the president of a multinational corporation with a degree in business administration. He frequently contributed articles for the *Globe and Mail*'s "Fifth Column," and turned out historical and legal fiction with such a deft hand that you would miss it if you weren't paying attention:

> Some groups, including Quebeckers, belong to Canada because they've chosen to. That other groups such as natives cannot choose is a harm to them, both collectively and individually. It should be compensated for by special treatment within Canada. . . .
>
> . . . In 1980, Quebeckers exercised their right to national self-determination. In a referendum about negotiating sovereignty-association or remaining in Canada, they chose the latter. It is to Canada's credit that the exercise was respected on all sides. . . .
>
> A group has the right to self-determination when its members can decide collectively whether they will or will not form a sovereign state. They do this by some majority vote. (*GM*, Nov 13/90)

What a crock of historical revisionism. Quebecers belong to Canada because they chose to? Whatever happened to the Conquest?

This great thinker on sovereignty grants Quebec a right it never constitutionally had simply because the province decided to run its own local referendum — the right to self-determination as a separate nation.

This philosopher needs a little training in international law. Sovereignty is determined by international recognition, not by someone's imaginings of rights and history.

> The overriding aim must be results. Was the Meech deal good for Canada? If so, the Meech process was dandy. . . .
>
> . . . There were also complaints about the federal government's pressure tactics and deceit. These were naive. A constitutional conference isn't a tea party. You have an idea what's best for Canada and others have a different idea. You've exchanged arguments, but past a certain point neither side can persuade the other. So you do whatever you can to achieve what you think

is right. You make offers, you apply pressure, and, within limits, you lie. *Lying is essential to all bargaining* [emphasis mine]. (*GM*, July 3/90)

Fine standards for a lover of wisdom.

MANY ACADEMICS were so caught up in promoting government positions that they forfeited all integrity as independent thinkers. Often they managed to cover themselves by suggesting that democracy was good stuff. Then they would suggest that it could be something to practise in the future, once all the deals were done. **Peter Russell**, professor of political science at the University of Toronto, backed Meech Lake and, with Richard Simeon, Ronald Watts, Jeremy Webber, and Wade MacLaughlan, wrote the booklet *Meech Lake: Setting the Record Straight*. The authors ask the question "But can't we make the constitutional reform process more democratic in the future?" Here's their answer:

> Yes, we can. By providing for annual meetings on the constitution, the Accord opens the way for consultation with citizens in advance of discussions among the first ministers. However, the desire for a better future process must not become a ground for rejecting an Accord that, on its merits, represents a rare opportunity to make progress on an important national issue. If Meech Lake is rejected because we believe the process is not ideal, we are unlikely to recapture its substantial benefits. (p. 6)

In other words, the end justifies the means. And so said 190 signatories who joined this crusade, including such prominent figures as Claude Castonguay, Dian Cohen, Thomas Courchene, John Crispo, Thomas d'Aquino, Paul Desmarais, Francis Fox, Peter Hogg, Eric Kierans, Flora MacDonald, Roy McMurtry, Peter Meekison, John Meisel, Geoffrey Pearson, George Pedersen, Brian Peckford, and Anna Porter.

Desmond Dillon Paul Morton, military historian, was another academic incapable of thinking for himself. Because of his avowed beliefs in socialism and his role with the NDP, he became a mini media star in his own right during Meech. The then-president of Erindale College of the University of Toronto made comments that bordered on slapstick. Decades before, when he was in his twenties, the young Morton had submitted a brief to the Royal Commission on Bilingualism and Biculturalism. As a chronicler, he became more polemicist than historian during the debate:

The way we practise democracy in Canada "robs voters of fighting over deeply visceral issues but those same voters should reflect on other societies, from Ulster to Fiji, where race or religion form the basis of politics. Some sacrifices are worth making" (*Star*, June 15/88).

Thus he justifies denying democracy, but as every historian knows it is the smothering of such difficulties instead of airing and resolving them in open, public debate that leads to chaos. During Meech Lake and Charlotte-town Morton churned out regular revisionism in the *Toronto Star*, Canada's leading socialist newspaper. He apparently believed that most people had supported Meech and were heartbroken over its demise: "Those who attacked and destroyed the Meech Lake accord cost Canada its last chance to renew the kind of Confederation that has been pretty good for most of us" (*Star*, June 26/90).

Not all was madness and deceit from the academic world. There were voices, albeit rare ones, of reason and thought. Professor **Michael D. Behiels**, chairman of the Department of History at the University of Ottawa, was one of these. He edited and compiled one of the most important works of the period, *The Meech Lake Primer: Conflicting Views of the 1987 Constitutional Accord*. In the *Globe and Mail*, halfway through the debate, he wrote: "It is imperative that all those who created Meech Lake make an analysis of what went wrong. They must realize what created such widespread disunity in the country rather than the vaunted national recon-ciliation promised by the Prime Minister" (*GM*, Sept 18/89).

He also had words for another Meech supporter, the editor-in-chief of the *Globe*: "Mr. [William] Thorsell's plea for yet another backroom, mid-dle-of-the-night, secret deal between the pro-Meech first ministers and the recalcitrant premiers . . . illustrates his extraordinary elitist mistrust in the democratic wisdom of the people" (*GM*, Jan 18/90).

As for Quebec's Minister of Intergovernmental Affairs, Behiels wrote less than a month before the Meech deadline: "Mr. Remillard's comments simply confirm what many of the Meech Lake accord's critics have been saying since 1987. The accord's inclusion of Quebec's substantially en-hanced five demands is understood by the Quebec government as a consti-tutional entrenchment of the concept of 'two nations'" (*GM*, May 26/90).

Another valuable voice was that of the philosopher **Théodore F. Geraets**. A renowned constitutional scholar, he had appeared on many occasions before various federal and provincial parliamentary committees on Canadian constitutional reform for more than a decade. During the crisis, he was one of the pioneers who established the constitutional information bank, the "Network on the Constitution."

His views as a supporter of the two-nations theory would most certainly displease the majority of Canadians. However, he correctly identified the root of the problem as the fact that, historically, the Constitution has been an elitist matter between governments. Pierre Trudeau's 1982 "people's package," in fact became a "deal," he said, between first ministers. Democracy would solve the constitutional impasse: "Each major part of the Constitution, and each major change to it, ought to be acceptable to a majority of Canadians throughout the country" (*Policy Options*, June/90). He argued that "to preserve the distinctness of the Québécois nation, matters of language and culture have to be attended to with special care. Special incentives and even legislation are appropriate means to this end. We have to recognize that no minority culture can be preserved if it is not promoted" (Ibid., p. 16).

Interesting concept. If this is so, then Canada's anglophone heritage, fast becoming a minority in a pluralistic society, cannot survive.

As for the notwithstanding clause, while pointing out the possible tyranny of the majority if referendums or democracy were carried too far, he said:

> All this, however, should not limit fundamental rights that are enshrined in the Charter of Rights and Freedoms. There ought to be no "notwithstanding" clause, no possibility to invoke such a clause, even for a limited time. (*Policy Options*, June/90)

> My main argument, of course, is that the present system of constitution-making — which is sometimes called "executive federalism" — is really a bad system. (Ontario Legislative Committee on Ontario in Confederation, Mar 22/88, ref. C-791)

> I am really concerned. . . . If we opted for a referendum system . . . in the end minorities would always get hammered in that process . . . the majority of people are not always right. (Ibid.)

> My conclusion is, first, that to leave the process of constitutional reform *only* in the hands of elected politicians, most of which represent provincial interests and who are, most of the time, also interested in extending their own political power, is to court disaster. (Brief to SJC, Feb 17/91)

The agreed king of the insiders' academic world was **Thomas J. Courchene**. In 1992 he held the position as the Jarislowsky–Deutch Professor of Economic and Financial Policy and director of the School of Policy Studies at Queen's. He has written over one hundred articles and books. Although not a member of the Queen's Mafia until later on, he did attend the 1986 Mont Gabriel Conference. In 1991 he was the only outsider Quebec's Bélanger–Campeau Commission chosen to speak. Courchene said later: "After my initial surprise and, I would admit, pleasure in being included among the 'experts' requested to submit papers to *La Commission sur l'avenir politique et constitutionnel du Québec*, the challenge became one of what I could usefully contribute to a process that appears, from my vantage point, to be a societal celebration in full anticipation of a 'birth of a nation'" (*Rearrangements*, p. 72).

No wonder he was picked. He could hardly be described as a Canadian nationalist. He is a number cruncher with no political street sense. His views contributed significantly to the Allaire Report, which recommended that the federal government be virtually stripped of its powers.

Not everyone agrees where Courchene belongs. On the back cover of *Rearrangements: The Courchene Papers*, Peter C. Newman wrote that he is "politically intuitive in his thinking, advocating workable solutions instead of theoretical theses. . . ." In reviewing *Rearrangements*, Professor Ramsay Cook of York University said, "The problem is that he remains, naturally enough given his training, an abstract model builder. His brave, new asymmetrical world has no people in it: no politicians, no political parties, no people except that abstraction, 'the elites'" (*GM*, Jan 9/92).

Courchene's brief before the Bélanger–Campeau Commission on January 15, 1991, was a blockbuster — suggesting a breaking up of the country into what he termed a "Community of the Canadas." Under his formula, there would be Atlantic Canada, Quebec, Ontario, Western Canada, and Aboriginal People (*Star*, Jan 16/91). His suggestions call for abolition of the Senate, the offices of governor general and lieutenant-governor, an asymmetric Charter of Rights and Freedoms, and the territorial application of language rights (*Journal des débats*, Jan 15/91, p. 1759).

Even separatists were shocked. A leading PQ member of the commission, Gérald Larose, who headed Quebec's second largest labour union, the Confederation of National Trade Unions, with a membership of more than 240,000, said: "I am a little surprised by the extent of the surgery you propose. You propose to abolish the Senate and replace it by a federal council. . . ."

Courchene sees Canada as a collection of economic pockets with numerous disjointed societies who need to define themselves. On rejecting Quebec as a "distinct" society, he said:

> Specifically, the failure of Meech Lake will trigger in Quebec a society that is likely to be far more distinct than anything that would arise under a Meech Lake future. . . .
>
> I want to end on a strong note of optimism. Distinct societies are an inevitable part of our future as a nation. Not many years will pass before the west coast will be fully Pacific Rim-peopled. Our next distinct society? . . . The first step on this honourable road is to recognize Quebec as a distinct society.
>
> . . . [There is one] potential cost to the demise of Meech Lake. . . . Institutionalized bilingualism à la Trudeau has probably suffered a major setback. . . . Remember that Bill 178 was enacted *without* Meech. It is precisely this insensitivity to the rest of Canada that we are sanctioning if we don't bring Quebec into the Canadian constitutional family. (*FP*, Nov 14/89)

This is a "note of optimism"? Distinct societies are "inevitable"? Oh my. Professor Courchene is another of those who encourage lots of executive federalism with no direct input from Canadians. Following Meech, at a symposium set up by the Business Council on National Issues on January 16, 1991, he said: "One message that becomes clear is that we cannot make our way to the millennium if all of our challenges are approached via formal constitutional amendments. We must fall back on our tradition of resorting to all manner of creative instruments (tax-point transfers, opting out, altering intergovernmental transfers, ordinary legislation, bilateral agreements)" (with John N. McDougall, in Watts, ed., *Canada's Constitutional Options: Papers and Summaries*).

There can be little doubt that, while not as enthusiastic about the prospects for success as law professor Patrick Monahan, who encourages the use of Section 43, Courchene was enamoured of the idea. Section 43, a fuzzy and controversial provision allows that:

> An amendment to the Constitution of Canada in relation to any provision that allows to one or more, but not all, provinces, including
>
> (a) any alteration to boundaries between provinces, and
>
> (b) any amendment to any provision that relates to the use of the English or the French language within a province,

may be made by proclamation issued by the Governor General. . . .

Whenever constitutional deals are made between the federal government and the provinces without the people, Courchene is there in spirit.

Following the Beaudoin–Dobbie Special Joint Committee's final report and the Federal Renewal Conferences after that, he was commissioned by the federal government to produce a report for public consumption. He proposed the creation of an FNP, a First Nations Province, a novel idea. The new province would encompass all of the 2,231 reserves plus any new territory that resulted from land claims. Non-reserve Indians would retain their status but not be subject to the laws of the new province: "The reserves are run like a province now. The Indian affairs department acts as a provincial government located in Ottawa, administering health and welfare as well as most other provincial jurisdictions. What I am suggesting is that we turn those powers over to the Indians to exercise on their own lands, and those lands in aggregate form Canada's 11th province" (interview with Peter C. Newman, *Maclean's*, Mar 30/92).

His parting words:

> While not in any way downplaying the magnitude of the post-Meech Lake societal challenge, it is equally important not to downplay the way in which the constitutional game has been played in the past nor to underestimate the incredible flexibility of the instruments that are available. There is, in my view, ample scope and flexibility to fashion a renewed federalism that will be first-best economically, politically, and constitutionally for both Quebec *and* ROC [the Rest of Canada]. (*Rearrangements*, p. 225)

So he considers democratic reform unnecessary. As for personal freedom, that's another matter, and one hardly worth mentioning if at all. He takes Joe Clark's "Community of Communities" and turns it into pockets of pockets of collectives of collectives.

CHARLES TAYLOR, PHILOSOPHER and professor of political science at McGill University, is the boffins' boffin. McGill's Anglo-Catholic wunderkind is held in great awe by his peers, especially in Québec. Everyone seems to agree his brain is humungous. Like Hegel, he believes that philosophy is the highest form of knowledge.

Formerly vice-president of the federal New Democratic Party, he has long been credited with inspiring "communitarianism," a doctrine that promotes collective cultural goals through cultural activism. Like Thomas Courchene, he preaches decentralization.

On December 19, 1990, he joined some sixty experts who parleyed with the foregone-conclusion commissioners at the Bélanger–Campeau hearings. Some treats from *Reconciling the Solitudes*:

THE CONSTITUTIONAL PROBLEM

I see four facts. . . .

1   Quebec is a distinct society, the political expression of a nation, and the great majority of this nation lives within its borders.

2   Quebec is the principal home of this nation, but branches of it have settled elsewhere in Canada and North America.

3   Quebec must open itself economically, as must any society that seeks prosperity at the end of the twentieth century.

4   This economic openness must not be bought at the cost of political domination from outside. The danger exists because we share the continent with a superpower. . . . (p. 141)

One last point before I move on to examine the structures of the federation is that it would be good if the new regime could retain the best features of the current one, such as a system of equalization between the regions. (p. 148)

As this philosopher king himself puts it, the purpose of Confederation was, after all, transfer payments — wealth distribution.

As for Trudeau's Charter, "The new patriotism of the Charter has given an impetus to a philosophy of rights and of non-discrimination that is highly suspicious of collective goals. It can only countenance them if they are clearly subordinated to individual rights and to provisions of non-discrimination. . ." (p. 165).

Saints preserve us.

Taylor published an essay in 1992, *Multiculturalism and "The Politics of Recognition,"* an original made-in-Canada socialist thesis justifying multiculturalism, based on his Inaugural Lecture at the opening of the University Centre for Human Values at Princeton. He has been a visiting professor there, at Berkeley in California, and was once, in a past life, the Chichele Professor of Political and Social Theory at Oxford from 1976 to 1981. He opposes what he terms "procedural liberalism," the notion that individual rights prevail over all these. In this essay, which should have been titled "The Polemics of Recognition," he reaches the astounding conclusion that the chief distinction between man and the animals is the fact than man is "dialogical." Man is unique in that he communicates in words with others of his kind. Philosopher Thomas Hurka claims, "Taylor has brought a distinctively Canadian voice to the larger world of political philosophy" (*GM*, Jan 9/93).

Speaking before the Charest Parliamentary Committee between April 9 and May 4, 1990, in defence of Meech, Taylor dismissed concerns about the distinct society clause and the idea that Quebec would gain any additional powers by it. At one point he was held in such high regard for championing Quebec nationalism that Bourassa's Liberal government made him watchdog of Quebec's French-only language law, Bill 101. A dubious honour for an anglophone. But on May 22, 1991, Taylor told the Montreal *Gazette* the language provisions were "utterly ridiculous" and indicated "mass neurosis" (*Star*, May 22/91). Understandably, a huge uproar ensued in the National Assembly. This confused even the Vichy anglais of Quebec and all academics.

Here are some of the grander musings of the ultimate Trudeau groupie:

> Multinational societies can break up, in large part because of a lack of (perceived) recognition of the equal worth of one group by another. This is at present [1992], I believe, the case in Canada — though my diagnosis will certainly be challenged by some. . . .
>
> The main locus of this debate is the world of education in a broad sense. One important focus is university humanities departments, where demands are made to alter, enlarge, or scrap the "canon" of accredited authors on the grounds that the one presently favored consists almost entirely of "dead white males." A greater place ought to be made for women, and for people of non-European races and cultures. (Taylor, *Multiculturalism and "The Politics of Recognition,"* pp. 64–65)

Historians will be hard-pressed to distinguish between René Lévesque's 1968 *An Option for Quebec* — sovereignty-association — and Charles Taylor's solution in *Reconciling the Solitudes*. In the good professor's world, we'll all be happily pronking along the path to rediscover life in a tribal cave.[1]

I N THE INTRODUCTION to *The Ennobling of Democracy: The Challenge of the Postmodern Age*, political science philosopher Thomas L. Pangle asks:

Are individual rights and the competitive free market adequate to sustain the multiparty electoral, federal, and representative politics that so sharply distinguish the "Free World's" interpretation of democracy? Or is the vitality of our citizenship withering — and not by accident, but in accordance with the deepest tendencies of our "liberal democratic" way of life?

What is so troubling about our present situation, *within* the Western democracies, is the philosophical thinness of our answers to these questions. What is so disturbing is the ubiquitous mood of doubt, among our intellectuals, as to the very existence of firm foundations of inquiry into, and judgement of, our gravest political commitments. (p. 2)

The disturbing fact about Canada is that our intellectuals live in a vacuum. They are content and confident the foundations are not only solid, but undeserving of inquiry.

Notes

1 In 1993, Professor Taylor became a member of the Groupe Réflexion-Québec, a so-called brain trust created by the conditional sovereigntist Jean Allaire. Many members of this group would join Allaire's new separatist political force, Parti Action-Québec (PAQ).

16

More Deep Thinkers
Lawyers and Law Professors

THE WORLD'S SECOND OLDEST FEDERATION is a very complex entity. Layers and layers of laws, case histories, customs, and cultural factors underlie it. Few understand these underpinnings. The British North America Act of 1867, Canada's constitution and the linchpin of Confederation, has been so clear and yet so silent on many matters. But it worked. It afforded its citizens breathing space.

For English-speaking Canada, the BNA Act guaranteed the development of non-statutory civil and criminal law based on the Common Law while Quebec, in matters of civil law and property law, was free to develop her Civil Code, based on the Code Napoléon.

The Constitution Act of April 17, 1982, profoundly shifted Canada's legal foundation, by incorporating into the country's structure a body of law foreign to it — particularly to English Canada — a Charter of Rights and Freedoms. Under the Charter, Canada was sharply defined according to the paramountcy of two official languages, as a nation of two founding races and cultures. Unlike the BNA Act, which said nothing about race and culture, the Constitution Act, 1982, hauled the legal system into the cultural field.

The BNA Act spelled out the use of the English and French languages in the parliaments and the courts; the new Constitution enshrined two official languages, enforcing use of the two far beyond the courts, throughout the entire federal government and federal institutions.

The revolution — for that is what it was — was as much one of intellect and culture as it was of law, and it all took place with nary a peep from the legal profession. They had good reason to keep mum. They knew they would benefit tremendously from this shift to a republican legal system. They were also lazy — very, very lazy.

The dramatic change imposed on the country should have incited members of the law profession to take up arms. Instead, without a whimper, the Supreme Court of Canada was handed the ultimate power of determining the most fundamental rights of the country as the Charter outlined them. The loss of freedoms to Canadian society was beyond measure, equivalent only to military conquest.

Trudeau's Constitution Act of 1982 muddied the distinctions between Canada's traditions of common law and the French civil law in Quebec. The Charter paved the way for their eventual eradication as distinct bodies of law. The brilliance of Canada's founding fathers was that they preserved the distinct society of Quebec through the BNA Act while providing the common-law heritage to the other provinces. Through Trudeau's constitution, Quebec lost that protection.

The Constitution Act of 1982 did more than isolate that province. It legally denuded it of its cultural security. In English-speaking Canada, the introduction of a totally foreign legal culture had exactly the same effect. After 1982 no one knew what to do.

For example, what of Section 121, the BNA Act's provision that there be free trade between the provinces? Prime ministers have been consistently weak about this most fundamental requirement. What on earth was the country doing negotiating a free trade agreement with the United States? It had to clean up its own constitutional mess first. Surely it was inevitable that an FTA would mean a loss of sovereignty to the nation. Perhaps Section 121 wasn't clear enough?:

> All Articles of Growth, Produce, or Manufacture of any one of the Provinces shall, from and after the Union, be admitted free into each of the other Provinces. (The British North America Acts, 1867–1975: Consolidation)

According to the Canadian Manufacturers' Association, provincial laws and practices that contravened the Constitution cost the country an estimated $6 billion in annual trade by 1992. What about Section 90, the Constitution's disallowance provision? No prime minister has ever had the courage and sense to use it to preserve the union.

When the time came to deal with Canada's constitutional needs, the members of the legal profession and professors of law did not recognize or address any of these conflicts. The profession certainly spoke and produced volumes about the Constitution and what the clauses meant.

The crisis vomited forth a whole new industry. Aside from the seemingly countless federal and provincial hearings, public debates, and a good many more forums for the insiders, hundreds of books, booklets and pamphlets, magazine articles, and even more briefs and papers were published, almost all for a fee.

Constitutional amendment on this scale meant unanimity was required among the eleven players, all ten provinces represented by their legislatures and the Parliament of Canada. Because of this, Canadians were forced to examine in detail the legal makeup of their country for the first time. They did not like what they saw. Nor did they like the nation's dirty laundry being hung out for the whole world to see.

So the legal experts chewed and jawed away about the complexity of the federation and a new age dawned. Canada's lawyers and law professors were not prepared to trust the people. In the process, to paraphrase Georges Clemenceau's (1841–1929) remark about America, Canada went from infancy to menopause without the grace of youth.[1]

The failure of Meech proved to Quebecers their isolation was both their greatest strength and their greatest weakness. Meech's collapse demonstrated to them that they had the power to force the agenda, but they alone did not hold the mandate to change the course of history.

A S IN THE CASE OF the academics from other disciplines, many law professors, retired justices of the courts, and practising lawyers allowed themselves to be swept up into the process. The Hon. **Thomas Berger**, former politician, eminent legal scholar, and lawyer, was wiser than most. The former Justice of the Supreme Court of British Columbia is best known for his work on royal commissions into the development of the Mackenzie Valley and the welfare of Canada's native peoples. In a critique published in the *Globe and Mail*, he roundly condemned the accord on several fronts, including its abrogation of responsibility to aboriginal Canadians: "The provisions relating to the creation of provinces in the North and to the Supreme Court of Canada reveal the thinking behind Meech Lake: national institutions are thought to be without legitimacy unless the provinces share the power that the national government used to exercise. They represent a diminished federalism, an irresolute idea of Canada" (*GM*, May 20/88).

Aussie-born **Edward McWhinney**, professor of International Law at Simon Fraser University in British Columbia, had no such difficulty with

Meech. A world-renowned expert on constitutional law, he had played a part in the Trudeau constitutional negotiations of 1980 to 1982. In 1978 he served as chief advisor to the Pépin–Robarts Task Force on Canadian Unity — the one that pushed the two-nations theory of Canada. An executive federalist at heart, he suggested the government make a gesture of some sort to the native peoples. On December 2, 1991, after the collapse of the accord, he said on CBC, "In my province, I supported the Meech Lake proposals. . . . I regarded them as a reasonable set of proposals" (Dec 2/91).

Recommending the "give 'em hell" approach when the Meech Lake Accord had only three months to go, a Massachussetts-born professor of law at the University of Ottawa, **Joseph Eliot Magnet**, wasted no words. He published an article in the *Globe and Mail* headed "More ways than one to bail out Meech Lake," on March 29, 1990. He laid the blame squarely on Manitoba and Newfoundland: "Two pipsqueak provinces, representing less than 5% of Canadians going back on their signatures, will ruin Meech Lake and imperil the noble Canadian experiment."

He suggested Ottawa use the "7 & 50" formula, whereby at least seven provinces making up not less than 50 percent of Canada's population would have to vote in favour of a constitutional amendment (Section 38). If necessary, the government should proceed with dispatch to "royal instructions," among other arbitrary steps. This latter is a euphemism for how the Queen dictates that the governor general must act. Then, in a breathtaking reversal, he says, "At the same time as Ottawa implements these reforms, it could establish a rigorous democratic process to overcome the Meech Lake failure" (*GM*, Mar 29/90).

VOICES OF EXPERIENCE tended to speak their quiet common sense rarely and early on in the debate. They were usually ignored. **John Josiah "J. J." Robinette**'s was one such voice. He is recognized as one of Canada's foremost defence attorneys and constitutional legal experts. At age eighty during the debate, he moved swiftly to comment on the Meech Lake Accord: "What is the legal meaning of distinct society? This is a legal document, and to use words so indefinite as distinct society or distinct identity will cause a great deal of difficulty in the future. It places an almost impossible burden on the courts, particularly the Supreme Court of Canada, to define these words in a given situation" (*Star*, June 7/87).

As for the process: "The Prime Minister and the 10 provincial premiers worked all day and all night to settle the wording. This is too short a time and, able and honest as they are, no draughtsman can produce a document under such intense pressure. This underlines the fact that we must have committee hearings in Parliament and in the legislatures in all the provinces to examine the precise wording and to improve the draughtsmanship" (*Star* editorial, June 7/87).

Another academic dramatically out of step with the herd, including the Queen's Mafia, was Dean **John Whyte** of Queen's Faculty of Law. Reflective, thoughtful, and scholarly, the professor posed some important questions:

> Meech Lake is a reflection of the traditional Canadian ethnic tension; it provides an accommodation that is distinctly traditional — the accommodation between French Canada situated in Quebec and the balance of Canada.
>
> The question is whether this tension and this accommodation is appropriate for Canada at the end of the twentieth century. . . .
>
> . . . But Canadians owe to women's rights groups gratitude for causing us to stop and wonder whether the strengthening of the federal structure represents the best possible innovation to our national structure. ("The 1987 Constitutional Accord and Ethnic Accommodation," in Swinton and Rogerson, *Competing Constitutional Visions: The Meech Lake Accord*, pp. 268, 270)

In the dying moments of the accord, he launched a devastating accusation at the first ministers in the *Globe and Mail* of June 15, 1990. Six lawyers signed the letter containing their professional opinions in support of the June 9, 1990, agreement regarding the distinct society clause. They claimed the clause threatened no rights under the Charter of Rights and Freedoms:

> To achieve this goal [ratification of the accord], the values of democracy, directness and a disengaged press all seem to have been discarded. . . . Despite the good reasons for the distinct-society clause, many thoughtful Canadians feel it should not have come at the expense of fundamental human rights. . . . The device of the lawyer's letter is unique in constitutional negotiations. It has confused both the debate and our sense of what counts as authoritative in our legal system. It is yet another shabby innovation in Canadian constitutional politics.

Law professor **Anne Bayefsky** of the University of Ottawa somehow managed to free herself of the web of propaganda and fire off some real zingers. Because she was an affirmative-action supporter of native rights, she was accepted by her colleagues and the media as politically correct. She too published in the *Globe and Mail*. Her piece, published less than three weeks before Meech Lake died, hit the nail on the head, hard: "So, constitutional reform continues to be an elitist activity. The harm to public respect and confidence in our fundamental legal document is profound. Horse-trading with the nation's constitutional heritage is unacceptable" ("It's no time for elitism," *GM*, June 8/90).

The views of the former dean and then professor **Ivan Bernier** of Laval's Faculty of Law exemplified more extremist views in Quebec. He was also executive director of the Quebec Centre for International Relations. Five months after the collapse of the accord, in December of 1990, before the Bélanger–Campeau Commission hearings on Quebec's future, Bernier told the commissioners that "renewed federalism" and "sovereignty-association" were the same thing. He went on to say that a universal declaration of independence from Canada was the only course of action Quebec could endorse.

Deborah Coyne was one of the mini media cult figures the legal profession produced during the debates. A frequent guest on television and radio, and the subject of many magazine articles, she was well known and typified what the media considered one with a gifted mind. Richard Gwyn described her: "Coyne, thirty-five, is elfin, vivacious, voluble, nervy, and as smart as hell: gold medallist at Osgoode Hall, a master's from Oxford. . . . As was grist to conspiratorialists, she and Trudeau are, in her own typically direct phrase, 'good friends'" ("That Was Your Fifteen Minutes, Clyde Wells," *Sat Night*, Jan/Feb 1991).

In 1987 she was a law and public policy professor at the University of Toronto, from which position she co-ordinated the efforts of the anti-Meech group The Canadian Coalition on the Constitution. She wrote numerous briefs and articles on the accord. In 1989, after a brief stint as program director with the Walter Gordon Charitable Foundation, in October she accepted the invitation Newfoundland Premier Clyde Wells had extended to her some time earlier to join him as his constitutional advisor in Newfoundland. She supports Trudeau's vision of Canada un-abashedly, including a veto for Quebec — notwithstanding or otherwise. Like her mentor, she is particularly proud of the Charter despite Bills 101, 178, and others: "The Charter gave the Canadian people rights and freedoms to be asserted against all governments. . ." (*Roll of the Dice*, p. 30).

While the Charter actually reduced the rights that Canadians already held through their common-law heritage, Coyne, like Trudeau, insisted Quebec have it both ways. The double standard should not apply to English Canada: "I consider a veto for Quebec to be a necessary means of enhancing that province's sense of security within the Canadian federation" (Ibid., p. 11).

> If the *people* of Canada want the country to hold together, if the people of Canada believe in a coherent national government and national leadership that will inspire us to pursue our [Canadian] ideal of a bilingual, multicultural nation and a fairer, more compassionate society, then we must let the *people* into the process and allow them to influence constitutional reforms in a meaningful way.
> . . . At the very least, the prevailing vision of a bilingual nation required the *promotion* of such minorities across Canada by all governments, federal *and* provincial. (*Roll of the Dice*, pp. 2–3)

"Pursue our ideal of a bilingual, multicultural nation"? Whose ideal?

The questions about Coyne will always be: Who was she really speaking for? Was that veto she supported Trudeau's notwithstanding clause?

> What has happened to public discourse in Canada? Where are the poets, the F.R. Scotts, of the 1990s? Can our leaders no longer transmit a vision of Canada that captures the essence of our nation and provides us with fundamental principles to guide our collective future? Are we destined to end the twentieth century with a timid whimper, having allowed corporate thinking, corporate frames of reference and the language of materialism to snuff out the intangible, inspirational element of nationhood and all sense of shared purpose and goals? (Coyne, "A Crisis of Leadership," in *Towards a New Liberalism*, p. 21)

The Honourable **Willard Zebedee Estey**, retired Justice of the Supreme Court of Canada, offered some of his thoughts as early as the spring of 1988: "My instinct is that [the accord] is decentralizing, and should therefore be viewed by Canadian citizens with some suspicion. . . . You could ruin Confederation — there is no question about it. That is why it is being nibbled at and attacked. I think we would be better off to stay where we are" (*GM*, Apr 27/88).

On CTV's "Canada AM" the same day, he said, "The Meech Lake Accord is wrong for Canada." As for Official Bilingualism, he wrote after its collapse: "That was a non-starter to begin. It's expensive beyond belief. . . . That was one of Trudeau's very few mistakes" (quoted in Knowlton Nash, *Visions of Canada*, p. 185).

One member of Deborah Coyne's anti-Meech parade saw the Trudeau vision from a different perspective. Early on in the Meech debate, **Timothy Danson**, a prominent Toronto attorney, listed eight complaints about the accord in the *Toronto Star*. The first three tell the story: one, "federal power has been substantially reduced"; two, "in return the provinces gave up nothing"; three, "Quebec has been given such substantial new powers that leave it only a stone's throw away from separation" (*Star*, July 12/87).

With two other members of the Canadian Coalition, **Morris Manning** and **Edward Greenspan**, Danson challenged the *Globe and Mail's* strong support for Meech in their May 10, 1988, editorial "The Meech Lake bargain":

> First, this is not a cocktail party. Supporters of Meech Lake have confused "mutual respect" with equality between the federal and the provincial governments that necessitates the federal government giving up substantial powers. How can we make Canada stronger by weakening the only government that can speak for all Canadians? . . . You [the *Globe*] may be prepared to gamble with Canada's future and hope that at some later date the courts will see it your way just as Mr. Bourassa is prepared to gamble that the courts will see it his way, but most Canadians are not prepared to gamble our future away. . . . You repeatedly argue that the accord does not affect the division of powers between the federal government and the provincial legislatures. Respectfully, this is also false. The federal government is giving up its exclusive powers to select and appoint senators and replacing it with a provincially selected Senate that will have absolute veto power over areas of exclusive federal jurisdiction. (*GM*, June 1/88)

In another article by the same team in the May 1, 1989, *Globe*, Messrs. Danson, Greenspan, and Manning examined the notwithstanding clause itself. These three were among the very few lawyers to put the case against Trudeau's legacy in words that everyone could understand:

> The rights that can be overridden include the right to freedom of religion, conscience, thought, opinion, expression, speech, assembly, press and equality rights, as well as specific legal rights such as the right to fundamental justice, the right to remain silent, the right to counsel and the right to be presumed innocent. . . . The notwithstanding clause has no effect on other

charter provisions such as the right to vote, mobility rights, the entrenchment of English and French as official languages of Canada, or minority-
language education rights.

Canada's future under Meech Lake: "When Canada evolves from a federal
state into a confederacy as a result of Meech Lake, Canadians will learn the
real price they paid for allowing substantial changes to their constitution
without first understanding their true implications" (*GM*, May 1/89).

Professor **Joel Bakan** of the Osgoode Hall Law School of York University
came up with a novel idea. He put it this way in the *Globe and Mail*:
"Increasingly, leading social thinkers advocate blocking off the limited
avenues of participation in politics open to the general public. They argue
that there is a contradiction between 'democracy' and 'governability' — the
idea being that the more people participate and make demands on the
political system, the more difficult it will be for government to exercise its
authority" (*GM*, Aug 18/88).

His suggestion: "Reforming existing democratic institutions to reflect
the ideal of citizen participation in government might be a start. Embracing
flagrantly undemocratic institutions such as the Senate is a dangerous and
possibly self-defeating tactic" (Ibid.).

The voice of constitutional advisor **Colin Irving** was another that cried in
the wilderness. A legal constitutional expert who had acted for the governments of Alberta and Newfoundland in the past, he pointed up the key
problem of Meech Lake in 1987. He compared Bourassa's utterances in
Quebec with those of Richard Hatfield for English Canada, drawing
attention to the double-talk:

> Premier Robert Bourassa has assured the National Assembly that the accord
> gives Quebec a virtual free hand, with no possible interference from the
> courts, over future legislation to preserve and promote the French language
> and culture in Quebec. Do his co-authors agree? Apparently not. Former
> New Brunswick premier Richard Hatfield for one has said that the distinct-
> society clause is nothing more than a rule of interpretation designed to
> assist the courts in cases where the meaning of the Charter, or other parts
> of the Constitution, is in doubt. (*GM*, Dec 29/87)

Like many other Montreal legal beagles, **Eric Maldoff** jumped neatly
from side to side of the fence without missing a beat. The highly paid

constitutional lawyer easily contorted himself into all manner of interesting and contradictory positions related to everything from bilingualism to minority rights.

He founded and became first president of the Quebec English-language rights group Alliance Quebec, which opposed Bill 178 and the infamous notwithstanding clause. During the Meech debate Maldoff's curriculum vitae gained him a key role as he became political advisor to Jean Chrétien. In September 1991 Chrétien boasted of being the only one who supported the notwithstanding clause and its use specifically to implement Quebec's repressive Bill 178. While backing minority rights throughout Canada, Maldoff remained a passionate supporter of special status, or distinct-society status, for Quebec, even while he attacked the legislation that gave Quebec that special status. On May 9, 1986, he had also been a delegate and panellist at the Mont Gabriel Conference that signalled the start of the Quebec round.

At the federal Renewal Conference in Toronto on February 8, 1992, as one of a four-member panel, he made an emotional plea that Quebec be recognized as a distinct society.

He was early off the mark with his critical evaluation of the accord. Here is his assessment from the *Globe and Mail*: "Instead, the 11 first ministers have pursued a process that disregards the ordinary Canadian to a degree verging on contempt" (*GM*, Aug 20/87).

Of the deal, he wrote: "Meech Lake appears to say that henceforth our basic rights may vary or be restricted depending upon the province in which we live, the language we speak or membership in privileged groups" (Ibid.).

But then he whimpered naïvely: "We were told the 'notwithstanding clause' would not be used except in extraordinary situations. Now Meech Lake appears to lend political legitimacy to overriding Charter rights, thereby condoning it" (Ibid.).

However, when it came to Meech II and Quebec as a distinct society, he reversed his position. At the federal Renewal Conference, he suddenly backed the federal proposals, and without any conditions at all supported Quebec as a distinct society. "People [in Quebec] struggle with the question: 'Will we be here for the next generation?' The question then becomes: 'Is Canada part of the solution or is it part of the problem?' For those who care about this country, we must be prepared to open our arms to the challenge of the survival of the French fact in Canada" (*Star*, Feb 9/92).

One lawyer who dealt swiftly with Quebec's language law was **Neil Finkelstein**. A lecturer at York University's Osgoode Hall Law School and at the University of Toronto, he was also with one of Canada's largest law firms, Blake, Cassels & Graydon. Three weeks after the notwithstanding clause had been used to salvage Bill 101, he wrote:

> The suppression by Quebec of English-language rights by legislation should be unacceptable in any free and democratic society. One can imagine the reaction it would arouse in the United States or Britain if comparable legislation were passed making it an offence to include French or Spanish or any other minority language. . . .
>
> . . . Strong measures call for strong counter-measures. Bill C-178 [*sic*] should be disallowed. . . .
>
> . . . Majorities should not be able to preserve themselves by suppressing minorities in Canada. (*GM*, Jan 17/89)

With a colleague from the same law firm, he wrote *The Separation of Quebec and the Constitution of Canada*, a background study sponsored by the York University Constitutional Reform Project. On what Quebec's share of the national debt would be if Canada broke up: "There is no requirement that Québec take responsibility for a share of the national debt upon its departure; creditors are entitled to look to the federal government to repay any specific debt. While Quebec may be required to compensate the federal government for a share of the debt, the method of measuring that debt, and the mechanism of payment, are left to be determined by the two countries" (p. 66).

This line of reasoning prevailed among those Canadians who encouraged Quebec nationalism. Of course there's no "requirement" for how to manage the breakup of a country; there's no law to cover breakup at all. Breakup is not the business of lawyers. It's a political matter. None. Throw the case out of court.

The most disappointing legal contributors hailed from the university campuses and often from the highest platforms. The taxpayers had a right to expect much more from them. Canadians were discovering their institutions of higher learning were in serious trouble. The intellectual property they were supposed to protect and nurture was missing. University presidents were as vulnerable to the infection of nonsense non-speak as any of their colleagues. Two busy administrators whose talents must lie elsewhere, far from the business of provoking thought, were the presidents of two of Ontario's largest universities.

Harry Arthurs, president of Canada's third largest university, York, was also a law professor who served as York's chief executive officer for six years. He was no doubt an excellent administrator and fundraiser. However wanting Arthurs was in his knowledge of constitutional matters, no one could fault him for some homespun honesty. In his speech to the Canadian Club of Toronto on March 4, 1991, entitled "Lies, Damn Lies and the Constitution," he said: "For thirty years we have been listening to a litany of one-sided histories, mutual reproaches, and withering ultimatums, of if-onlys and why-nots and pie-in-the-sky solutions. It used to be said that no one ever died of a broken heart, but Canada may just make medical history. . . ."

But then, oblivious to the dissent he recognized and to the starved intellectual environment, he swung right back to Trudeau and Mulroney revisionism like a faithful homing pigeon: "Canada was, I believe, on the verge of being the very model of [a] civilized modern country: . . . we were just beginning to work out in practical terms how two, and then three, founding nations might live respectfully with each other and creatively with other cultures and communities. . . ."

There it was again — that old shibboleth of founding races and cultures. Who did Arthurs blame for Canada's mess? Not Pearson. Not Trudeau and certainly not Mulroney. Poor old John Diefenbaker, the former prime minister dead and gone, suffered the blow:

> How did it all get started? Innocently enough, as it happens. Thirty years ago, when John Diefenbaker was having one of his northern visions, he woke up one morning with a bill of rights. It wasn't much of a document from a purely technical point of view, but when it was adopted in 1960, and hung on the wall of every school room and government office, we began to scratch an itch which was the first symptom of the disease that now shows signs of being fatal. . . .
>
> . . . We had begun to think of ourselves as citizens, [but then] we scratched the itch again and again, until finally in 1982, Pierre Elliott Trudeau provided blessed relief: the Canadian Charter of Rights and Freedoms.

Dief's idea of translating the ideals of Canada's common-law heritage into a federal bill that was unenforceable and easily overturned was hardly the republican kick-off to Canada's constitutional revolution that Trudeau launched. The Chief's bill provided no new rights. More important, it took no rights away. It was not a revolutionary document. Thousands of Canadians revered Diefenbaker's bill. It hung in the schoolrooms of English-speaking Canada because it was something worth having. At best it gave many a good feeling about the country. At worst it was harmless.

Trudeau's Charter of Rights and Freedoms could not command the same respect. Quebecers ignored it or held it in contempt. Despite the media propaganda, other Canadians regard the Charter with equal suspicion.

So where was Arthurs? He knew there was a problem. He said so. He waffled: "But oddly, ever since the Charter was adopted, we seem to have fallen out of love with each other and with the country itself."

If Harry Arthurs was a bit befuddled by it all, **John Robert Stobo Prichard**, president of the University of Toronto, was truly a goner. The lawyer cum prof cum university administrator participated directly in the debate. He was the thirteenth president of U of T, having taught at Yale and Harvard law schools. He had been educated at Upper Canada College, and had earned an MBA from the University of Chicago. At the prestigious University of Toronto Law School, he became the gold medallist in his final year. On his appointment at age forty-one to the university presidency, he was described as a "whiz kid."

Here was another socialist all gussied up as a Red Tory. In fact, he belonged in the Trudeau camp as a Liberal or in whichever camp was ruling for the day. On the Meech II proposition on the way to the Pearson accord and Charlottetown, he clearly supported the executive-federalist package of twenty-eight treats: "My antennas didn't quiver negative on any of the major points, except for guaranteed property rights which I think is potentially a powder-keg of problems and will attract a lot of concern among legal scholars" (*GM*, Sept 25/91).

Prichard accepted the politically correct doctrine of founding races and founding cultures, and was happy with Quebec as a "distinct society" and the whole extended Trudeau–Mulroney vision. But if you caught him performing in another setting, it was very difficult to make out what was going on in his mind. At a conference of the Institute of Political Involvement on February 6, 1991, and aired on Toronto television on more than one occasion, he spouted rambling observations. On the thesis "The political system is broke and we need to fix it," he went on at length. As a university president, he said, he had to be "both non-partisan and completely uninvolved in politics of any kind, campus or otherwise." So why did he say anything at all? Why was he even there?

In addition, our political leaders fail to understand the type of country multicultural Canada wants to live in. Simply put, multicultural Canada continues to desire a nation where all citizens in all the provinces can have the same freedoms and liberties in all the provinces and have identical authority. Multicultural Canada wants a strong, active central authority.

> ... We are a nation of immigrants. We think of ourselves as multicultural and we, we need not subvert multicultural differences. ...

Gimme a break. If lawyers like this are at the intellectual helm, it must be the end of civilization.

Here's more from the self-censoring university president:

> When one speaks of something being broken [referring to the political system] it suggests that at one time it worked well. ... We've lost something, and what we need is a return, a move backwards, in fact to recapture what we nostalgically remember as a well-working parliamentary system, where democracy was vibrant and vital, and we've lost that. ... We've lost it or it's escaped us and we've lost it, and our job is to repair it and recapture it.
>
> ... I think we may mislead ourselves, mislead ourselves if the ideals of the past are seen to be a guide as to what the challenge is that we face as we go forward.

So much for modern education. One must beg the question, just what kind of society had Canada become?

A PARTING WORD on political correctness from Dinesh D'Souza, author of the superb book *Illiberal Education*, seems called for. In a devastating criticism of America's university heads, he says:

> Many university presidents are not intellectual leaders but bureaucrats and managers; their interest therefore is not in meeting the activist argument but in deflecting it, by making the appropriate adjustments in the interest of stability. When a debate over the canon erupts, university heads typically take refuge in silence or incomprehensibility; thus one Ivy League president responded to Allan Bloom's book [*The Closing of the American Mind*, 1987] by saying that the purpose of liberal education was to "address the need for students to develop both a private self and a public self, and to find a way to have those selves converse with each other." (p. 246)

Notes

1 To Georges Clemenceau (1841–1929), French statesman and prime minister, is attributed the famous observation "America is the only nation in history which miraculously has gone directly from barbarism to degeneration without the usual interval of civilization."

IV

The March Away
from Meech Lake

1990 to 1991

17

The Leaders Divvy up
the Nation
— 1990

QUEBEC PREMIER BOURASSA reacted sharply and as he had promised he would following the Meech Lake failure. One day later, on June 23, he addressed the Quebec National Assembly in the famous red room — the "Salon Rouge": "Henceforth, Quebec withdraws from all constitutional talks and will, in future, negotiate bilaterally with the Canadian government as a Quebec government, legitimately elected and strongly backed by the population" (*Star*, Nov 4/90). He also made the point on national television: "English Canada must clearly understand that whatever is said, whatever is done, Quebec is today and forever a distinct society, capable of insuring its own development and destiny" (*GM*, June 25/90).

June 24, St. Jean Baptiste Day, Fête Nationale, gave Quebec nationalists the chance to show their flag. In Montreal, the police reported, 160,000 people flooded the streets with banners, flags, and slogans: "*Notre vrai pays, c'est le Québec*" (*Star*, June 25/90).

The international press took due notice. "Quebec to set terms for role within Canada," was the leader on the front page of the *Wall Street Journal* of June 25. In London the *Financial Times* led off with "Canada moves to calm markets amid political uncertainty."

Back in Canada, the Business Council on National Issues (BCNI) was taking out some insurance for its own future. Having supported the Meech accord financially and got nothing in return, the group planned to avoid slip-ups the next time. On June 24, while Quebec was celebrating, Thomas d'Aquino, president of English Canada's most prestigious and powerful business lobby group, wrote to the nation's top 150 corporations proposing that $100,000 be spent to review the constitutional options. It was a major signal that despite the collapse, Mulroney's constitutional agenda was alive and well. In a subsequently published conference report, d'Aquino made clear his thoughts at the time: "Having been burned [by Meech], . . . I wanted to get off the mark immediately."

The Meech II process had begun. But it was a whole new ballgame. This time big business would play a much bigger part.

The federal government seemed utterly insensitive or unconcerned about the mood throughout English-speaking Canada. As if to demonstrate this, they moved to mollify Quebec on June 25, just as they had been doing ever since Mulroney took office. The Mulroney government announced it intended to transfer immigration power to Quebec as if Meech Lake had been passed. Canadian nationalists were furious.

At the same time, Lucien Bouchard, who had bolted the Tory benches before the Meech deadline, presented a manifesto of his own to Quebecers. He proposed to create a Bloc Québécois, a federal separatist party to sit in the House of Commons and blatantly promote the breakup of Canada. The next day the BQ was on a roll. Three Quebec Tory MPs and one Quebec Liberal MP quit their caucuses to make seven of them sitting as pro-sovereignty independents.

Forty-eight hours later, Mayor Michel Leger declared that Queen Elizabeth would not be welcome in Hull, Quebec, for the Canada Day celebrations, while she toured the National Capital Region. Likewise, the mayor of Quebec City cancelled the Canada Day celebrations completely, claiming that Canada had slammed the door on Quebec.

Even bigger news came on June 29. Premier Bourassa announced that he had reached an historic agreement with the Parti Québécois. He and leader Jacques Parizeau would form a joint panel to examine Quebec's future.

June ended on two notes that promised further discord. On June 30, news broke that Quebec's largest teachers' union of 160,000 members had voted for independence. "I've been a nationalist for years," the union's president, Lorraine Pagé, boasted. "Now at last I can say it with pride in the name of my union. . . . Schools are a vehicle for education, and when we teach our history, of course we must enlighten students on what Quebec experienced" (*Star*, July 1/90).

The same day, the Quebec Superior Court issued a ruling of its own on another sovereignty issue. It ruled that the Mohawks at Oka were illegally obstructing construction crews building a golf course. The nation was in for a long, hot summer.

Elsewhere in the world there were people not terribly concerned about Canada and its internecine bickering. James Whittaker of the London *Daily Mirror*, more noted for his interest in the Royals and in playing about in Buck House, commented on the old colony disparagingly in the June 28, 1990, *Toronto Star*: "There's always a constitutional crisis in Canada. It's boring."

If he had waited, he might have caught the little morsel of news that splashed the world press in a big way, including a feature story in *Time* magazine, several weeks later. On July 11, one hundred Quebec provincial police assaulted the blockade of the Mohawk Warriors Society at Oka. One officer, Corporal Marcel Lemay, was killed. In sympathy with their brothers at Oka, members of the Mohawk Warriors Society of the Kahnawake Mohawk Reserve barricaded their reserve and the huge Mercier Bridge in Montreal as well.

O N AUGUST 22, the day the Canadian dollar reached a twelve-year high of 88.58 cents US, Commissioners Jean Campeau and Michel Bélanger were named to head what became known as the Bélanger–Campeau Commission, or "B–C." The commission's findings were to be submitted to the federal government no later than March 28 of the coming year.

Life in post-Meech Canada was not without its special moments of reassurance that Quebec would continue to enjoy a special place in the federation. On July 12, the Minister of Industry, Science and Technology, Benoît Bouchard, announced a $400,000 grant for the 1991 World Hot Air Balloon Championship in the province. It seemed fitting.

The next day the Grand Chief of the Cree nation, Matthew Coon-Come, spoke. He claimed 85 percent of Quebec as Cree land. Why not? Stranger things were being claimed all over the country.

Many journalists thought the prime minister was back to drinking and licking his wounds in sorrow, perhaps meditating on the attractions of some other career. But on July 25, l'Irlandais roared back at it, full tilt. He summoned the same old gang of first ministers to an FMC to discuss national unity one more time. The proof was the news that Privy Council Clerk Paul Tellier had prepared a discussion paper on what to do next. It was a backup plan for another go at reforming the Constitution.

The PM's message was clear. There was going to be lots more action. On July 29, he said, "You can take it for granted I will not be waiting for some shopping list from Quebec. . . . This is a country we have here" (*GM*, July 30/90). Nor was Premier David Peterson wallowing in sorrow. On July 30, riding high in the polls at 50 percent, he confidently called a provincial election for September 6.

The insurrection at Oka continued to build sharply. On August 8, in response to Bourassa's request, Mulroney announced that the Canadian Forces would relieve the Quebec police at the barricades at Oka and Chateauguay. The sovereignty implications were obvious and a reminder of the FLQ crisis of 1970 and the same premier's request for federal troops. Especially after having formed his government's cosy, new arrangement with the PQ over the commission, Bourassa hastened to set the record straight: "It is the Quebec government which called for the army and therefore it is the Quebec government, finally, which will give the instructions on the use of the [Canadian] army" (*Star*, Aug 9/90).

On August 14, Chief of Defence Staff General John de Chastelain announced that Quebec had asked for 2,500 troops for the two Mohawk blockades.

Ontario's Peterson was determined to be part of the action. On August 10, he announced the formation of another Ontario committee to study the Constitution: "I am sending a clear message: Ontario will not let its destiny be decided by the actions of others" (*Star*, Aug 11/90). He laid out five principles for future constitutional talks — the same number of bargaining points Gil Rémillard had reeled off three years earlier at Mont Gabriel, kicking off the Quebec round.

Peterson was sending another message, too, to the Ontario electorate. On August 23, he repeated his pledge not to make Ontario bilingual. After Bill 8, the French Language Services Act, few people believed him. Thousands of federal public servants living in Ontario — some of whom had moved to the provincial government — knew only too well the soft-sell lies they had listened to when Official Bilingualism was introduced into the federal public service. If a politician promised not to do something related to language, it was certain he or she intended to do that very thing.

By August 24, Peterson was campaigning hard for the coming election.

He faced grilling on open-line radio shows by fractious callers about political scandals, election opportunism and costs, and the language crisis in Sault Ste. Marie. When interrogated about language and bilingualism, the incumbent premier flubbed: he referred to 300,000 to 400,000 francophones in Metro Toronto. The actual number was less than 50,000.

On August 25 Mulroney assembled his dispirited caucus in Ottawa. He said there would be "two stages of public consultation" with the "entire population of Canada" for the next constitutional round. It was time, he announced, to deal with the "tremendous misunderstandings about language, diversity, regional realities, and the balance between individual and collective rights" (*Star*, Aug 26/90). This two-stage process would include dealing with the "unworkable" amending formula.

The Meech Lake Accord had been dead only nine weeks and already Meech II was publicly committed. In the months ahead it would produce the Charlottetown Accord. Once again the political calendars were pulled out as the politicians and bureaucrats worked back from deadlines. The "senior public servants" were busy orchestrating the federal play to match Quebec's agenda again.

Premier Robert Bourassa tabled Bill 90 establishing the Bélanger–Campeau Commission to study his province's future on September 4. Amazingly, it passed in a vote of 93 to 0, unanimously backed by the PQ and, even more amazingly, by all four members of English Quebec's Equality Party. To secure a non-voting role for himself on the B–C Commission, Equality Party leader Robert Libman agreed to support the legislation. Like so many anglophones in Quebec, he sold out. Another Vichy anglais.

Under Bill 90 all parties agreed that "Quebecers were free to assume their own destiny." And while the English-speaking community and native peoples would have a place in Quebec society, the voting members also agreed that French would be "the language of government and the law as well as the normal and everyday language of work, instruction, communication, commerce and business." As Bourassa soothingly put it, "It's unthinkable that Quebec's economic interests could be achieved with a Quebec currency" (*GM*, Sept 5/90).

In the first months after Meech, the fifth and biggest casualty of the fiasco fell. On September 6, 1990, the Ontario Liberals were routed. Even David Peterson lost in his own riding in London. He resigned bravely and announced the same day that he was quitting politics. No one believed him any more than the Americans had believed Richard Nixon.

The following week, Premier Gary Filmon nearly became the sixth to be "Meeched." On September 11, his Conservatives in Manitoba won only a slim majority government. The person who took the real punishment was the Liberal opposition leader Sharon Carstairs. She had been the real leader in the province's attack on Meech Lake. The Liberal loss of their position as official opposition to Gary Doer's NDP seemed a cruel blow to a woman of tremendous courage.

On September 26, the Oka uprising finally ended. After seventy-seven days of confrontation, soldiers armed with fixed bayonets tackled women and children at the barricades, pulling apart the blockade that magazines around the world had featured in full colour on their front covers. The Mohawks surrendered.

Yet another memorable event brought the first week of October to an end: the "Night of the Kazoos." On the fourth, Mulroney chose to invoke a section of the Constitution never before used, Section 26 of the BNA Act, which requires the Queen's permission, to appoint eight more senators of his own, swelling the upper house from 104 to 112 seats. In another complicated manoeuvre he arranged for a ninth senator to be appointed to replace one who was retiring. The immediate reason he gave for the appointments was simple: he wanted to ensure that the legislation on the hated Goods and Services Tax would pass. The resulting carnival was televised across Canada. While the television cameras rolled, senators shouted, "Dictatorship!" and "Hitler!" One yapped at another, "Crawl under the table because you're a despicable little bugger!" (*GM*, Oct 5/90). The "Red Chamber" of Canada's Parliament exhibited itself as a public disgrace. Mulroney simply endorsed the image.

The Bélanger–Campeau Commission began its hearings on Quebec's future on October 9. As co-chairman, Michel Bélanger stated as he opened the hearings, "If the status quo were acceptable, there would be no Commission." Chairing it with him was Jean Campeau, who described himself and Bélanger for reporters: "We are neither federalists or separatists. We are both good Quebecers." Gil Rémillard, another commissioner, chipped in, "The future of Quebec passes first by Quebecers. . . . So we will decide what we want. . . . It's very difficult, if not impossible, to envisage pure and simple independence. The status quo is unacceptable. So between independence and the status quo there are other possibilities" (*GM*, *Star*, Oct 10/90).

The B–C Commission had firmly committed itself to introspectively examining Quebec's options, at the same time that debate elsewhere in

Quebec zeroed in on more precise arguments: could Quebec survive economically as a sovereign state?

The federalist voice of corporate Quebec, the Conseil du patronat du Québec (CPQ), spoke to the issue. This federation of presidents and CEOs of Quebec's hundred most powerful companies loosely translates as "the bosses' council." To English Canadians it would be Quebec's equivalent to the BCNI. Although Ghislain Dufour, the organization president, has claimed that the CPQ is "at least 75 percent federalist," others describe it as at least one-third separatist (*Star*/CP, July 2/91). Following the collapse of Meech Lake, the Patronat was more pressured than ever to maintain its credibility. CPQ had strongly supported Meech Lake. For that, the separatists ridiculed it, and it was ready for the criticism.

A Montreal economist, André Raynauld, former head of the Economic Council of Canada, was retained to produce an economic study of federalism for CPQ. The report he eventually submitted blandly remarked that Canadian federalism "has been and remains profitable for Quebec." He added that if Quebec had left Canada in 1980 the province would have lost $23 to $27 billion (*Star*, Oct 19/90).

As the leaves began to change colour around the country, several people chose to stir the waters of Meech once again. On October 20, Jeanne Sauvé spoke in Paris at the fortieth anniversary of the Association of France–Canada and forgot her place, yet again. Canada, she told her audience, lacked a leader "who has a clear idea of what Canada is" (*GM*, Oct 21/90).

And, of course, the press dutifully allowed space and time to an old standby to stimulate the feud between English and French Canada. On October 23, reports quoted Languages Commissioner D'Iberville Fortier. He was making good on his promise to prosecute corporations for not playing bilingual ball. He set his sights on Air Canada. The court action cited the Crown corporation for not advertising in French more often.

The impact of his message was interrupted, momentarily, the same day by an announcement from PQ leader Jacques Parizeau that Confederation was costing Quebec $1 billion a year. Fortier didn't miss a beat. Two days later, he was addressing a parliamentary committee — this time to accuse the federal government of "unexplained and unjustified" tactics in delaying implementation of Bill C-72, its draconian new language legislation.

By the end of the month, Mulroney lost any personal control he might ever have had of the agenda. With Charles deBlois leading them, the Quebec Tories revealed their plan for a new arrangement, which they dubbed "confederalism." It was, they explained, a type of sovereignty, a "new formula that would fulfil the needs of the Quebecers" (*Star*, Oct 26/90).

The beleaguered prime minister had been staving off plenty of criticism for his stumbles on the immigration issue nearly four months earlier. Now, on October 25, he announced a delay in federal–provincial power-sharing arrangements like immigration: "It is perhaps a more cautious approach to see what direction Quebec's Commission will take before undertaking discussions . . . with whatever government" (*GM*, Oct 26/90). As with Peterson, no one believed him.

Perhaps Alberta best captured the mood of the month with a small, telling omen. On October 28, the province's Conservative Party voted to eliminate its own constitutional requirement that the provincial party support the federal Tory party.

The separatists gleefully exploited the national confusion. The noted Quebec nationalist Claude Béland was chairman of the Forum de l'Emploi, formed in 1989 to tackle Quebec's chronically high unemployment. He jumped on the bandwagon and swaggered away with the prize for the month. Béland called for immediate sovereignty over unemployment insurance, welfare, and immigration: "We want one ship that knows where it's going" (*GM*, Nov 1/90).

As chairman of Quebec's largest enterprises, the $35-billion Mouvement Desjardins credit union network, Mouvement des caisses Desjardins, he was also given wide coverage in the media. Because he represented the sixth largest financial institution in Canada and sat on the new B–C Commission, he and his views were already well known in Quebec. About the divorce he was sure would follow, the prominent Quebecer had said during the Meech mess: "There are 2 solutions. Either we say we're independent and then we negotiate; it's a divorce and we come back to our wife and say, 'Can we share the house?' Or there's the other model where we divorce little by little, patriating certain powers" (*Star*, Feb 13/90). As if to add insult to injury, he mused that if Meech had been signed, it would have been "too little too late" (*FP*, June 12/90).

E VENTS WERE MOVING so fast now and on so many fronts that most people could barely keep up with them. Mulroney sensed his chance and chose to make his next play at this point. On November 1, he stated that his government would form a new body, the Citizens' Forum on Canada's Future. He was pleased to name as its chairman the former Official Languages Commissioner, Keith Spicer. The new appointee told the media he would hear the views of Canadians with his twelve-member panel and deliver the commission's findings to the government on July 1, 1991: "The assignment is awesome . . . the procedures ill-defined and untested. The outcome is highly dubious and there are prospects of a fiasco" (*Star*, Nov 2/90; Susan Delacourt, *GM*, Nov 1/90).

For the hundreds of thousands of Canadians who had endured the injustices of Official Bilingualism and autocratic dictatorship over the years, Spicer could not have been a more inappropriate choice. Long identified as an anglophone who had sold out, the media czar now headed up the most powerful broadcast organization in Canada, the Canadian Radio-Television and Telecommunications Commission (CRTC). To thousands of anglophone public servants, his record as Commissioner of Official Languages made one long list of grievances. He was well known as a zealot. In 1964 he was a staff researcher seconded to the Royal Commission on Bilingualism and Biculturalism. Thousands in the federal public service had endured the internal manipulations, law-breaking, talk-down-to-the-people rule of this prominent Trudeau courtier, with no legal recourse.

No other move Mulroney made could have offended so many people so quickly. He galvanized his own opposition and absolutely ensured the defeat of his plans for constitutional reconciliation with this single stroke.

Before long Spicer showed his true colours. In anointing Trudeau's language czar, the prime minister was telling English Canadians, especially those in the West, to go to hell. Meech Lake had angered people. The appointment of Keith Spicer to mediate Meech hardened the resolve of many small-c unilingual Conservatives to destroy their own party.

Spicer's avuncular pose on CBC the same day sounded hollow. How could a government run town-hall democracy? For three solid years, nobody in government had listened to the people on constitutional reform. Spicer: "We want to focus on the ideas and aspirations of ordinary Canadians. . . . In this country we've had it all wrong for decades" (CBC Newsworld, Nov 1/90).

"Spicer's Roadshow," as the media quickly dubbed it, was immediately dismissed in a flood of criticism from the media as well as the public. Only the *Toronto Star* and the CBC stoutly backed the chair's appointment. *Toronto Sun* columnist Bob MacDonald characterized the tone of most of the criticism with masterful succinctness in his November 2 column headed, "Fed unity hearings a crock." Even English Canada welcomed the reaction of Quebec minister Gil Rémillard to the Citizens' Forum:

"What is new this time is that we have our own commission [Bélanger–Campeau]. . . . I am not saying it [the Citizens' Forum] won't be useful, but our first reference is our own parliamentary commission" (*GM*, Nov 2/90).

The response from Ontario's new premier, Bob Rae, was better: "What's on most people's minds is not some clause in the Constitution. . . . Most people are really worried . . . [about] how they can survive in economically very difficult times" (*Star*, Nov 2/90).

Whatever credibility Spicer might have had at the beginning he squandered the day after his appointment: "We will create a receptive climate in English Canada for the Bélanger–Campeau commission's recommendations, especially if they are radical" (*GM*, Nov 3/90). The forum would perform as the prime minister's propaganda machine and the vehicle to allow angry anglos to safely blow off steam and cool down before federal negotiations with Quebec got serious.

Like the Bi-Bi Commission before it and the Pépin–Robarts Task Force on Canadian Unity that followed, Spicer's forum would exercise familiar top-down control. One of the forum panellists, Robert Normand, wrote in his editorial in *Le Soleil*: "All Canadians should be conscious of the fact that they, too, will have a price to pay for rejecting Quebec [through Meech]. I will apply myself ardently to demonstrating this" (*Star*, Nov 13/90).

Constitutional lawyer Ronald Leitch, head of APEC, the Alliance for the Preservation of English in Canada, let fly to his 45,000-strong membership: "In his role as official languages commissioner, he continually berated and denounced the English-speaking people" (*Star*/CP, Nov 3/90). Once, Spicer had gone so far as to label anglophones who didn't buy in on Official Bilingualism as "Westmount Rhodesians."

The noted French expert on propaganda, Jacques Ellul, put it brilliantly in his classic work *Propaganda: The Formation of Men's Attitudes* published more than two decades earlier:

> He who acts in obedience to propaganda can never go back. He is now obliged to *believe* in that propaganda because of his past action. He is obliged to receive from it his justification and authority, without which his action will seem to him absurd or unjust, which would be intolerable. He is obliged to continue to advance in the direction indicated by propaganda, for action demands more action. He is what one calls committed. . . .
> (p. 29)

On November 4, Mulroney endorsed his tarnished henchman rather than remove him: "I've given him pretty well carte blanche in terms of how he wants to run it" (*Star*, Nov 5/90).

No one could take the Citizens' Forum seriously after that. Sabotage from within the forum, too, played a part. Commissioner Robert Normand continued to gurgle Quebec's contempt for the whole exercise. The publisher of *Le Soleil* added to his previous confession: "All I can say is that . . . [the forum] doesn't work. The classic commissions don't work. . . . But what do we do? Do we watch [Canada] crumble?" (*Star*/CP, Nov 7/90).

Mulroney's new Quebec lieutenant, Benoît Bouchard, showed himself as equally cynical. A week later, on November 10, he threatened Canadian newspaper readers: "We mustn't be too naive to understand that we must not try a Clyde Wells again" (*Sun*/CP, Nov 11/90), and "We may as well tell you right away that if you're not ready to change [the amending formula of three years] within 6 months or a year, we're going with the other option" (*Star*, Nov 14/90).

Still the prime minister said and did nothing. The only pro-Canada noises that week came from Montreal, from Charles Bronfman, co-chairman of the world's largest distiller, Seagram Co. Ltd. When he was asked on November 12 if he would stay in Quebec if the province separated from Canada, he answered, "Stay? No. I put my country before my province. . . . Seagram's whisky cannot be produced and bottled in another country other than Canada" (*FP*, Nov 12/90).

That same day, news of an even more sobering kind came from the National Cancer Institute in Bethesda, Maryland. Little love as most Canadians had for Robert Bourassa, they could not help but be moved to hear that surgeons had removed a cancerous mole, a melanoma that was affecting the Quebec premier's lower back and groin area. The prognosis was not reassuring. Dr. Steven Rosenberg told reporters that "Mr. Bourassa has tolerated these surgical procedures well and is recovering normally" and "should be able to return to normal activity within a few weeks." His condition seemed to bode ill for Quebec's soft-shoe federalism.[1]

On November 13 and 14 more cracks widened in the national fabric. The prime minister announced in Ottawa that Thérèse Paquet-Sevigny was resigning from the Citizens' Forum: "It appears there were administrative regulations, of which we were unaware, that might preclude [her appointment] and so we will, I suppose, make an appropriate replacement" (*Star*, Nov 14/90). Mighty weird. Why didn't she deliver the news of her resignation herself? This prime minister was never known for being a messenger boy for anyone but big business. Pierre Péladeau, chairman of Quebecor Inc. and publisher of *Le Journal*, Canada's second-largest daily newspaper, followed this up by announcing that he "fully endorses" the Mouvement Desjardins's call for sovereignty: "We're capable of doing it [but] the question now is, do we have the will? . . . Pure and simple secession would create all kinds of problems" (*Star*, Nov 15/90).

At the B–C Commission hearings in Quebec, tempers were fraying. A psychology professor from McGill, Don Donderi, a member of a Montreal group, the Task Force on Canadian Federalism (TFCF), said: "In the long term, the objectives of the Nazis and of the authors of Laws 101 and 178 are the same: to destroy a people and a culture" (*Star*, quote from *La Presse*, Nov 15/90).

By November 16, the media almost expected Keith Spicer's and D'Iberville Fortier's monthly sortie into the news. The Citizens' Forum chair was interviewed after the first forum commissioners' secret meeting, and said that henceforth "I will tell you every time I go to the bathroom" (CBC Newsworld). Three days later he made the gratuitous observation that the Mohawk confrontations with government at Oka were a "moral victory" for native people (*GM*, Nov 20/90).

On November 20, Fortier urged the Commons committee to amend the proposed privatization legislation to ensure that PetroCan would remain bilingual if sold: "To do otherwise would be to set a dangerous precedent that could gradually be applied to other national institutions and little by little restrict the application of the Official Languages Act to a smaller number of institutions" (*GM*, Nov 21/90).

November 1990 was shaping up as more than a month in which highly paid public servants tinkered with the federation. This was the month that a number of Canadians betrayed their country, and did it openly. Appearing before the B–C Commission on Quebec's future, Phil Edmonston, federal MP, the NDP member who had been allowed to endorse separatism by Audrey McLaughlin, his leader, said, "I believe that Quebec can become independent and I am not convinced that it would be a catastrophe" (*Journal des débats*, Nov 20/90, p. 422).

McLaughlin endorsed Edmonston's address to the commission two days later. She insisted that while the NDP "would want Quebec to choose to remain a part of Canada," she fully supported the lone Quebec member in his conviction that Quebec be given "full autonomy." She added almost as an afterthought: "I think Phil has made a very good contribution about a possible new division of powers between Quebec and Canada" (*Star*, Nov 27/90). Those remarks destroyed her political career.

On November 22, seventy-eight days after being named an Officer of the Order of Canada, Phyllis Lambert, a member of Montreal's Bronfman dynasty, delivered a brief of her own to the B–C Commission. Founder of the Canadian Centre for Architecture in Montreal and a sister of Charles Bronfman, she recommended Quebec independence: "I think Quebec should go for sovereignty. I'm not sitting on any damn fence. I'm not going to go against what a majority of Québécois want. . . . My brother can do what he wants . . ." (*GM*, Nov 22/90; *Journal des débats*, Nov 21/90, p. 521).

Pressing for sovereignty and for Quebec to become unilingually French, renowned Quebec author Yves Beauchemin addressed the B-C Commission himself: "If Adolf Hitler had won the war in 1945, Paris would be bilingual: French-German" (*GM*, Nov 21/90). Hmm.

With no evident control over the agenda and the B–C Commission hearings in Quebec going badly, Mulroney tried to regain the upper hand in the final month of the year of Meech Lake. On December 2, he announced the formation of a "Special Joint Committee on the Process for Amending the Constitution of Canada" (SJC) to study ways to amend the Constitution more speedily: "We want a new Canada, a greater Canada, a Canada within which Quebec will exercise its full potential . . . and we will have it" (*Star*, Dec 3/90). Alas, he would not leave the news alone. He also made it absolutely clear the SJC would be a rigged court. To 1,400 Tory supporters in Montreal, he said, "I can assure you the legitimate and reasonable aspirations of Quebec — or any other province — will never again be held hostage to an inadequate and inflexible [amending] process" (*GM*, Dec 3/90).

The move was shot down immediately. In the Quebec National Assembly, Gil Rémillard tore the plan to shreds: "We will negotiate only with the federal government. . . . To be held hostage, so that premiers over three years give their consent, whether it be Mr. Wells, Mr. Filmon, or Mr. McKenna to name those three, is out of the question" (*GM*, Dec 4/90).

On December 4, one lone figure spoke from his balanced position on the Quebec fence. Before the B–C Commission in Quebec City, Claude Ryan, Minister of Security, the boss of Quebec's language commission, offered to his rambunctious compatriots: "I find that we almost never hear about the positive side of the Canadian federal experiment. . . . I am proud to have been a Canadian up until now. I am not ashamed of it. Is that clear?" (*Star*, Dec 5/90).[2]

Who was he trying to fool? How could there be a strong defence of Canada in a rigged court? The ground rules of the B–C Commission kept anglophones off the agenda and members of the Equality Party from voting as commissioners.

Only those invited could testify. The lucky few were screened carefully beforehand to ensure they were favourably disposed toward Quebec's nationalistic aspirations. Professor Thomas Courchene, one of the "Queen's Mafia," earned the dubious honour of becoming the only academic invited to testify from TROC, the Rest of Canada. The commissioners knew that their man would speak as a leading scholar from English Canada, and that he would promote radical asymmetric federalism, different provincial strokes for different provinces and territories.

The hearings had grown hopelessly incestuous. Premier Bob Rae articulated the governing principle of the B-C Commission: "It's my understanding that people from outside Quebec were not invited, that essentially it's there to listen to and collect Quebec opinion" (*Star*, Nov 29/90).

On December 5, Liberal MNA Norman MacMillan joined the chorus of those who despaired: "There is certainly a shortage of people who want to defend Canada. I can only deplore that Canadians are unwilling to appear at a time when the country is being torn apart" (*GM*, Dec 6/90). Nonsense. They were unwelcome and personally denied the right to speak.

That day the Mulroney government pulled another plug. Those who clung to the notion that the CBC was the binder twine holding the regions of Canada together had a rude shock on December 5, 1990. The Tories announced they would cut $46 million from the network's regional stations. In total the cuts to the "Mother Corp." would amount to $108 million. Eleven hundred jobs were put on the chopping block. CBC Newsworld coined the term "Black Wednesday at CBC." (See Chapter 25.)

On December 6, a separatist MP, Gilles Rochelieu, said, on behalf of the Quebec extremists: "We've got the [federal] buildings here in Hull. Those buildings will be part of our assets. . . . We've got specialized [federal] civil servants in Hull who could be used the next day in a sovereign Quebec" (*Sun*, Dec 6/90).

Canadians were treated to another, older vision for Canada on December 10. Jean Chrétien had won the Liberal convention of June 23 in a cake walk, picking up the Beausejour constituency by-election in New Brunswick. The old Trudovnic vowed to fight for a bilingual Canada from "sea to sea to sea" (*Star*, Dec 11/90).

The Citizens' Forum wobbled on. Committee member Jack Webster resigned. He cited "personal reasons and an inability to meet what he believed would prove to be a much more demanding mandate than he expected" (*GM*, Dec 11/90). But according to Allan Fotheringham (who invariably knows about these things), this was not his real reason for stepping down. "Dr. Foth" — or "Froth," if you prefer — writes columns in *Maclean's*, the *Financial Post*, and the *Toronto Sun*. In them he asserted that Order of Canada winner Webster was hoofed off the commission for politically incorrect remarks. He had said what Canadians, including those in Quebec, have admitted for years: "Quebec is impossible."

Unbelievably, Canada was staggering on through its fifth year of constitutional horrors. Two weeks before Christmas, Jacques Parizeau addressed 600 businesspeople at a joint meeting of the Empire and Canadian clubs at the Royal York Hotel in Toronto. That December 11 he told his audience plainly, "I want to discuss economic arrangements as soon as possible."

Typically, he had laid out his terms with appalling timing. There should be a common currency with Canada; he would prefer a "common monetary policy, if [Quebec] could have some say in how it is run." His matter-of-fact presentation earned him a deafeningly ho-hum reception (*FP*, Dec 12/90).

The babble of voices increased in volume. The former leader of the NDP, Ed Broadbent, now resident in Montreal and president of the Montreal-based International Centre for Human Rights and Development, volunteered his thoughts at year end. In Ottawa, he echoed Audrey McLaughlin's perspective: he opined that English Canada had to accept Quebec's right to exercise the notwithstanding clause: "Without agreeing with the details of Bill 101, the Supreme Court affirmed the collective rights of Quebecers to protect their French culture, and in part by denying equality rights to the English speaking minority" (*GM*, Dec 12/90).

As if unwilling to be outdone, Laval law professor Léon Dion made remarks the next day before the B–C Commission that made much more memorable copy: "English Canada will not make concessions . . . and we are not even sure of that . . . unless it has a knife at its throat" (*GM*, Dec 13/90).

Gil Rémillard spoke up in the National Assembly the same day: "What we want is very clear. We want what is ours. We want our taxes that we are paying . . ." (*Star*, Dec 13/90).

The year finally exhausted itself in a flurry of activity. On December 16, the prime minister followed up on the promised parliamentary committee that would start work immediately on ways to break the so-called deadlock over ways to amend the Constitution. The seventeen members of all parties would submit their committee's report on July 1, 1991 — the same date by which the Spicer commission would present theirs (*Star*, Dec 17/91).

Mulroney fleshed out more details about his amending formula committee. He had chosen a long-standing constitutional player, Senator Gérald Beaudoin, an active supporter of Official Bilingualism; and a newcomer, Alberta Tory Jim Edwards, a bilingual former broadcaster who had once been a commissioner on the Alberta Human Rights Commission. The latter was another Trudovnic in the Tory camp. The new parliamentary committee (SJC) would be known as the "Beaudoin–Edwards" committee.

Just two days earlier, federal industry minister Benoît Bouchard, Mulroney's Quebec lieutenant, had made another in a long list of moves that angered English Canada. On December 14, with the law creating the Canadian Space Agency having passed in the House of Commons the previous day, he pledged $289 million to it in financing. A week later, the federal government proclaimed that it would transfer federal immigration powers to Quebec.

The prime minister had now gone back on his earlier promise. And, insulting all Canadians, he did it while Quebec still refused to attend numerous constitutional conferences. Quebec had managed to secure important additional powers for itself with no interprovincial discussion whatever (*GM*, Dec 27/90).

Newfoundland's Clyde Wells was livid and said so with growing national support behind him. Three days before Christmas, he blasted: "If Ottawa is prepared to make that kind of an arrangement for one province it should, I presume, be prepared to make it for all the provinces that want it" (*Star*, Dec 23/90).

Alberta's Premier Don Getty had said a week earlier what the country needed and what his province intended to do: "Alberta is going to have to be a leader. . . . Just look at the face of Canada right now" (*Sun*, Dec 19/90).

By this point, no one seemed to know just what was really going on. For one thing, Canada was sliding into bankruptcy, with Quebec close behind. When the Montreal Urban Community Transit Corporation protested federal government signs because they violated Quebec's Bill 178, the public was not amused. The MUCTC replaced all the signs with French ones, despite the fact that the cash-strapped corporation would lose $800,000 in federal revenues for its non-compliance with the federal laws on bilingualism.

On Christmas Eve another ugly piece of news came out in the press. Jamie Portman exposed it in a special piece to the *Toronto Star*. The culture and communications minister, Marcel Masse, had "derailed the independent process that hands out up to $12 million annually in federal money to museums." Portman also reported that the five-member panel had been shocked to learn two months earlier that the minister's office had arbitrarily removed all Quebec-related applications from the review process, which was supposed to scrutinize all the applications in Canada. A weak prime minister had finally lost all control of the country.

Mulroney appeared on the nation's television sets with year-end messages even more threatening than those of the year before. Four days before Christmas, he grimly stated that the alternative to accepting "substantial changes" to a "fundamentally reformed Canada is probably no Canada" (*Star*, Dec 22/90). His annual address on December 28 reinforced his point: "Canadians will have to make up their minds what kind of a Canada they want, if they want a Canada" (*GM*, Dec 29/90).

The international news compounded the Christmas gloom. In an interview on an American PBS TV program called "American Interests," the disheartened prime minister was introduced as "the man who presides over the dissolution of Canada" (*Star*, Dec 22/90).

That final month of 1990 evoked the utter banality of the Mulroney era. On December 28, Canadians learned that as well as getting raises of $9,000 apiece, MPs would be given exemptions from the Goods and Services Tax for their constituency offices' supplies. Now every Canadian citizen understood the full meaning of the Mulroney era.

The nation was knackered. Canada had become a country of powerless commiserating colonials.

Notes

1 In 1993 it was estimated in Canada that 3,100 people would develop melanoma and that some 540 people would die from it (*GM*, Jan 9/93).

2 In English Canada, Claude Ryan has always been described by the media as a "staunch federalist," a veritable icon. Here's what he wrote in 1978: "One may criticize federalism. But one should admit that it has given Quebec the full use of those

fundamental liberties which are the rockbed of any true democracy. Freedom of speech, freedom of movement, freedom of creed, freedom of congregation: in this respect, what country in the world, besides Canada, can boast of so many advantages, so many positive accomplishments? The acquisition of these freedoms was the fruit of a long and painful evolution. We doubt that the *Indépendantiste* option could offer any improvements from this point of view. The risk is that we might stand to lose" (*A Stable Society*, p. 72).

Wonderful. Indeed the best of Claude Ryan. It's very difficult, if not impossible, however, to reconcile his writing on freedom and liberty with his role as Quebec's public security minister in charge of the infamous "tongue troopers" charged with prosecuting language infractions under Bill 178 (1988).

18

Some Québécois Speak to Some Canucks

THE SAME MALAISE that gripped Canada held other countries equally in its thrall. All of western civilization was finding itself under siege: terrorism, corruption, economic chaos, and struggles over national identity washed over the television screens around the world with thumping regularity. Shamefaced, Canadians watched the reports, painfully aware that their nation lacked an excuse for those same conditions they saw elsewhere.

In 1990, the same isolation Hugh MacLennan had portrayed in his 1945 novel *Two Solitudes*, a classic in English Canada, made it still an unknown work in Quebec. The same applied to English-speaking Canada's knowledge of Quebec. One remark of a Montreal comedian, Yvon Deschamps, struck home throughout Canada, though it was often misquoted: "I don't know why the English think we're inconsistent. All we want is an independent Quebec within a strong and united Canada" (quoted in *Maclean's*, Aug 20/90).

The state promoted the perpetuation of its internal divisions. Over many decades Canadians learned to communicate only in mime. Cultural divisions in Canadian society are very big business. The CBC is only one institution that fosters this insularity.[1]

Because of the abysmal educational system and Canadians' widespread ignorance about their heritage, they were thrown into the constitutional debate prematurely. Without rudimentary schooling, even in the universities, people ended up in a debate that turned into a shouting match in an echo chamber.

Ironically, one bonus of the constitutional debate from 1985 to 1992 is that English-speaking Canadians did learn something about the soul of Quebec. Non-Quebecers were forced to grapple with terms such as "the collective" — the idea that Quebecers banded together along ethnic lines.

Étapisme or "step-by-step" was another term used frequently, wonderfully describing the methodical plodding and pushing the French had employed on this continent since the Conquest in 1759. Claude Morin, the father of Quebec's Quiet Revolution of the 1960s, coined the term in the 1980 referendum campaign.[2]

Robert Bourassa was the prestidigitator of the sidestep and rearguard action; René Lévesque, the implementation artisan of *étapisme*. This Norman approach utterly baffled English Canada. It was Morin's thinking that had won out in the 1980 referendum. The question asked of Quebecers was not, "Do you want to be a part of a sovereign nation?" but rather "Do you authorize the government to negotiate sovereignty?" And even the answer to the "soft" question was "No."

But the bottom line is that for more than thirty years, from 1963 on, there has been no philosophical debate in Canada about either the rationale for the federation nor the magnificent cultural legacy Canadians have shared for 350 years.

PRIME MINISTER LESTER PEARSON set the country on its destructive course by establishing winners and losers. Trudeau defeated English Canada by one of the oldest ruses in history, the guilt trip. There was the original guilt for having won on the Plains of Abraham; guilt because English Canada prospered and Quebec didn't; guilt because English Canada spoke the language of the continental majority; guilt because Quebec was held back by the church; guilt because Quebecers made up a minority in Canada and an even tinier minority on the continent; guilt because the French language was no longer an important world language and English was, and English was growing, gaining, going places; guilt, guilt, guilt. Pearson felt it. Trudeau fanned it. Mulroney dined out on it.

The idea is that, since 1759 and the Plains of Abraham, Quebecers have endured a vast historical injustice that has denied economic opportunities and a triumphant history to them ever since. Accordingly, Quebec has always waved the threat that if the rest of Canada did not recognize these "injustices" and rectify them by denying a conquest ever took place, then there would be no justification for the union.

Official Bilingualism was only one example of Canada's denial of history — what Christian Dufour, the well-known Quebec lawyer, author, and former director of planning and research for the Quebec government in federal–provincial relations, would call an institutional defeat. Implementing it was and is based on this premise that English-speaking Canadians are fully accountable for the "sins" of their fathers.

There had to be a right and a wrong way of thinking about the federation. Those who did not embrace the Pearson–Trudeau–Mulroney vision were outcasts. The depth of the prejudice showed itself in the old-line political parties, and, more surprisingly, in the gestation of new political movements as well, such as the Reform Party.

The moralists, the politically correct, did not argue that their views were the balanced compromise. They *knew* they were right. Only prissy puritan anglophone intellectuals struggled with a jumble of ideologies: the English-speaking view of Canada as a single nation-state of equal parts, or the view of English Canada as an asymmetric federation, a union of unequal parts combined in varying ways according to historical precedence.

While English Canada tortured itself in a navel-gazing debate over form, Quebecers took to the ramparts of another fortress entirely, proclaiming their shared passion and aspirations of living in a racially defined collective. Somehow they believed that they could remain impervious to the demographic changes rapidly reshaping the rest of the globe.

BEST-SELLING AUTHOR YVES BEAUCHEMIN was one of the most outspoken public figures in Quebec. He addressed the Bélanger–Campeau Commission on November 20, 1990, to present his brief "Conditions for developing French in Quebec." He reminded the commissioners of four facts:

(1) French-speaking North Americans account for 2% of the population. In other words, the proverbial mouse and elephant.

(2) The current sociopolitical system has resulted from a military defeat in 1759. . . .

(3) The rights of the English-speaking minority, of Anglo-Quebecers, are privileges conquered by arms.

(4) Canada is not a federation as English-speaking Canadians do not perceive the sharing of powers as a fundamental need. To the contrary, they want a unitary, centralized State which reflects their interests. (*Journal des débats*, Vol. 7, p. 469, Nov 20/90)

An excerpt of his presentation at the B–C hearings was published in the *Toronto Star* on December 24. The reasons he gave for Quebec making itself unilingual were expressed fervently. They represent a view common among Quebec francophones:

> Why French unilingualism? Simply, because two cultures can't both bloom in the same linguistic space. . . . I would compare [bilingualism] to Valium. Taken in small but steady doses, it softens people up, puts them to sleep and finally poisons, dragging the victim into an irreversible coma. . . . Bilingualism makes English the common denominator for immigrants, an all-terrain vehicle which allows people to circulate and get by in all of North America. . . .
>
> . . . As former premier René Lévesque once said, "Every bilingual sign tells immigrants: There are two languages here, French and English. Choose which one you want. It tells anglophones: You don't need to learn French, everything is translated."

Beauchemin also said in his brief,

> Collective bilingualism always suggests that a society has lost something. The inability of a language to impose itself throughout a country is proof that the country's inhabitants are incapable of occupying it politically. (*Journal des débats*, B–C Commission, Nov 20/90, p. 471)

Beauchemin epitomizes the sovereigntist strategy to soften up Canada. He subscribes to the idea that Quebec is strong; it has defined itself as a nation, and all English Canada has to do is recognize how weak *it* is. This means Canada — without Quebec — must define itself, too. Mulroney's minister Marcel Masse promoted this idea constantly, as did most Quebec separatists. In an article in the magazine *Books in Canada*, titled "Quebec: The writers speak" (March 1991), Beauchemin makes a remark that also appeared in the 1991 Rogers Communications Annual Report: "Who is not in favour of national unity? The problem is that Canada is an artificial country made up of two nations. The independence of Quebec will eliminate age-old tensions and a waste of energy, and will allow the new Canada to reinforce its national unity" (*GM*, Apr 28/92).

Perhaps the toughest voice heard from Quebec was that of political scientist and professor **Léon Dion** at Laval University. The noted author of many works, including an ongoing four-part study on Quebec from 1945 to 2000, had a great deal to say. From 1963 to 1971 he acted as special advisor to the Commission on Bilingualism and Biculturalism. Here are his thoughts on a variety of subjects:

> [How far would he himself go?:] I would not hesitate to finally choose the road to independence, if evidence shows that there is no possible constitutional security for French inside the Canadian federation. (*GM*, Dec 26/87)

> [At the prospect of a Meech Lake failure:] Canadians should be aware that, legally and legitimately, Quebec could declare itself out of the constitutional framework, and even say no to a Supreme Court decision. (*GM*, Dec 26/87)

> [Questioned by Gérald Larose about one last try with Canada:] I'm convinced after 30 years of reflection on this question that we are very far from being able to take a final position on the political and constitutional status which would be suitable for Canada. (B–C Commission, *Journal des débats*, Dec 12/90, Vol. 19, p. 1266)

> [On Meech II and the "distinct society" clause:] To me it is not a dangerous expression at all. There are no dangers attached to it. (*Star*, Oct 13/91)

> It's even Meech Lake minus. . . . Distinct society — I could care less! As far as I'm concerned, it's irrelevant. . . . Quebec is a global society! (*GM*, Dec 11/91)

> [On Premier Robert Bourassa:] If I had to follow his ideas from day to day I'd have trouble following him. (*GM*, Dec 13/91)

> [On Quebec separation — just when you think you have him cold!:] [It] would be a tremendous tragedy for the whole of the country, including Quebec. (*GM*, Dec 12/91)

> [On the post-"Pearson accord" — the First Ministers' "Unity Deal":] The strong point in the document is that, over all, it confirms the requests Quebec has made over several decades and corresponds to several federal commissions. The Quebec Liberal Party can only say no with great difficulty to this. Perhaps it can say "You have robbed us" or "We are much better suited than you to implement this." (*GM*, Aug 25/92)

Daniel Latouche was another author who made a significant contribution. During the debate, Professor Latouche taught at the Institut national de la recherche scientific, Université du Québec à Montréal.

During the 1980 Quebec referendum, he was Lévesque's chief strategist. He was the one to develop the separatists' strategy to immediately follow a possible Yes vote, to co-opt the Americans into agreeing with the reasonableness of their requests: "That was, we would play the New England card," and announce Quebec's negotiating points at a conference of the Eastern premiers and New England governors (*In the Eye of the Eagle*, p. 218).

As a twenty-five-year veteran of the independence movement, Latouche turned out a weekly column for *Le Devoir*. In the furore that followed Meech Lake, he was in Belfast, Ireland. Invited to the city of religious torment by Quebec's agent general, Latouche informed the northern Irish that Premier Robert Bourassa was "an intellectual pygmy" (*FP*, Feb 16/92).

During the Meech debate, he and Professor Philip Resnick of the University of British Columbia became literary celebrities. Their wordplay was published in a best-seller, *Letters to a Québécois Friend*.

Here are some gems from Latouche's feud with Resnick: "But when will you English Canadians get it through your thick collective skull that we want to live in a French society, inside and outside, at work and at play, in church and in school. Is this so difficult to understand?" (*Letters*, p. 89).

Latouche's master stroke on the notwithstanding clause hit home: "What kind of a country puts in its constitutional books an escape clause that is only a trap to bring shame on its eventual user?" (Ibid., p. 91).

Like so many Quebec writers and unlike almost all their counterparts elsewhere in Canada, he enjoys a sense of humour: "Our nationalism has been proclaimed dead so many times that we are now convinced it can survive any crisis" (Ibid., p. 101).

Étapisme is the Latouche way. Gentle, inviting, eternally reasonable: "Who would negotiate in good faith with a knife held at their throat anyway?" (*Star*, Dec 12/90).

In a presentation before the Bélanger–Campeau Commission on December 20, 1990, he said:

> Do you believe that English Canada, to which this country also belongs, will forgive us for this emotional blackmail? . . . But there are also costs in not doing anything and, above all, there are costs in not seizing the strategic opportunity when it presents itself. . . . Since . . . we will have to live with Canada, either within or without, everything that is bad for English Canada

is also bad for Québec. . . . English Canada will be our main economic partner. If it were to disappear or fall apart, it will become a sort of Argentina. (*Journal des débats*, B–C Commission, p. 1657)

I do not want to be distinct under any clause. . . . Either I am to be a Canadian just like the others or a Quebecker like all the other Quebeckers. I may not have my day in court and become a free citizen of a new sovereign commonwealth. I can live with that, but they are certainly not going to transform me into a French-ethnic Disney-like character á la Jean Chrétien. . . . I certainly do not need any special constitutional clause allowing me to get married or go bankrupt in French. (*GM*, June 9/92)[3]

Some Quebec writers got away with murder. In 1990 **Jean Larose** was awarded the Governor-General's Award for *La Petite Noirceur*, a work of fiction, and one part of it was widely quoted in the media as proof of the corruption in Canada's honour system: "We must faithfully retain our hatred of Canada. . . . Everything that weakens and humiliates Canada . . . must make us rejoice. It is up to us to see that the word becomes in all countries a synonym for placid stupidity" (*FP*, Nov 26/90).

An infrequent though important guest of the English media was **Pierre Bourgault**, Professor of Communications at the Université du Québec à Montréal. Many people consider him the founder of Quebec's independence movement in the 1960s, Rassemblement pour l'Indépendance nationale (RIN), one of Quebec's earliest separatist parties. After winning only 6 percent of the votes in the 1966 election, the RIN merged with the Parti Québécois in 1968.

Many also regard him as the conscience of Quebec nationalism. He is the author of the best-seller *Now or Never*, published in French in 1990 and in English a year later. For Bourgault, the matter of sovereignty has been very simple since 1962 and 1963. During those two years he and the other purists, André d'Allemagne and Dr. Marcel Chaput, were stumping the countryside demanding that Quebec be a nation. At the same time Chaput, the chemist who once worked for the Defence Research Board, founded his Parti républicain du Québec, the first provincial separatist party.[4]

In the 1990s, his goal remained exactly what it had been in days of yore when he debated with Pierre Trudeau in November 1963 in front of some five hundred University of Montreal students.

Bourgault is a dreamer. He believes a sovereign Quebec must have a treaty with English Canada to protect the French minorities left to flounder in English Canada. After the diaspora he sees all the same institutions in English Canada upholding the Trudeau ramparts of the French fact across Canada, regardless. As for the Bloc Québécois, they have an important role to play. He calls them Quebec's "Trojan horse." America itself is "a society without a soul . . . a doomed society" (*Star*, May 13/91).

But, pushed to the limit, even the founding father of separatism slips. Lo and behold, he unconsciously recommends *étapisme*. Speaking of the new-found self-confidence of the Quebec business world, he warns, "They believe they can conquer the world. It's wonderful to see, but I would urge them to be careful. Capitalism is still very fragile in Quebec. We have to be cautious" (*GM*, May 15/90). He is best when he's full of vinegar, vents his spleen, and speaks in riddles. Here's what he said in English on CBC Newsworld on the first anniversary of the collapse of Meech: "One hundred years ago French was the international language of the world. . . . [Today] there are three international languages in the world, English, French and Spanish" (CBC Newsworld, June 22/91).

Bourgault is a romantic, a reincarnation of Pierre de Ronsard (1525–85), the French poet who once wrote in that cynical age: "Live now, believe me, wait not till tomorrow; gather the roses of life today." His hero is Jacques Parizeau: "Yes, I like the man. And I like his dream: independence for Quebec. It has been mine for 35 years. I know this is probably why you [in English Canada] hate us both" (*GM*, Aug 19/94).

Here's his final word: "If nothing works, there is always that last resort: force. . . . There's no other one. Is this what you [English Canadians] want? If not, you'd better tell Jean Chrétien to change his plan [i.e., negotiate!]." (*GM*, Oct 14/94).

Almost the last words belong to the Hon. **Jules Deschênes**, former Chief Justice of Quebec's Superior Court. On Saturday, May 29, 1993, he addressed the annual Convention of Alliance Quebec at Sainte Adèle:

> Yet there exist gaps between our communities: each one of us must learn to help bridge those gaps. On the French-speaking side, we must learn that ours is not a homogeneous society any more, especially in Montreal: that we must accommodate a multiplicity of ethnic groups who, though oftentimes speaking French, have, however, vastly different backgrounds.
>
> But on the English-speaking side, the challenge may be even stronger. The current francophone generation has found and collected its hitherto unknown strength in numbers, in money and in national pride. It does not

accept any more the result of the 15-minute battle on the Plains of Abraham as conclusive for eternity — "Speak White" is no more tolerated. The "Golden Mile," where French used to be ignored when it was not scorned, does not even exist any more. This is a whole new reality to which English Quebec must adjust.

We assume that, by and large, the loyalty of English Quebecers goes first to Canada, then to Quebec: while the loyalty of French Quebecers goes first to Quebec, and often to Canada not at all. Based on that premise, discussions are, of course, not easy. Add to that deep cultural differences and the intercourse gets most difficult. After centuries of life side by side on the same soil, we do not know each other. (*Gazette*, June 1/93)

Prominent Quebec business executive **Pierre Arbour** is the author of *Québec Inc. and the Temptation of State Capitalism*. His controversial best-seller was published in English in 1993. In the preface he says, "My main motivation for writing this book was to warn the coming generation of the dangers of unchecked state capitalism and to show the consequences of thirty years of state intervention" (p. 16). "The negative perception and publicity generated by the introduction of Quebec's language laws have more than cancelled the efforts made by the province to attract foreign industries" (p. 128). Soberly, he ends his analysis with

I must conclude . . . that Quebec's economic decline relative to Ontario has coincided with the departure of anglophone Quebecers, especially during the years 1976 to 1986. Quebec undoubtedly became poorer with the loss of these people and the relocation of many Montreal head offices to Toronto. In fact, according to my estimates, Quebec has lost more than one billion dollars a year in tax revenues because of the exodus of 150,000 anglophones during these years.

The government of Quebec confirms this hypothesis in a January 1993 document entitled *Living within our means*. According to this official publication, "The proportion of Canadian taxpayers with high revenues residing in Quebec, which was 23.9% in 1976, had fallen sharply and stood at only 18.3% in 1985." (p. 174)

Among Quebec historians, **Réal Bélanger**, professor of history at Laval University, is now considered an authority on Quebec nationalism. In a four-part CBC television series in French in January of 1992, he responded to questions from interviewer Gilles Gougeon about "the meaning of 1867":

From the perspective of French Canadians, 1867 represented a number of different realities. Of course it signified the establishment of the federal structure and the means by which the newly created nation — that is the Canadian nation — could thrive. This nation, as far as French Canadians were concerned, was to be bilingual and bicultural and was to accept the equality of the two founding peoples of Canada. (*A History of Quebec Nationalism*, p. 29)

Another revisionist on the lam from reality — conning the college kids of Quebec. There's nothing equivocal, mysterious, or misleading about Section 133 of the BNA Act, the only provision to deal with these matters in 1867 (see Chapter 2 for the full text of Section 133). Bottom line: the Fathers of Confederation constitutionalized a bilingual/bicultural *Quebec* only — with a bilingual federal parliamentary system and bilingual Federal Court service for the rest of Canada only.

Notes

1 As the unilingual author of *Champlain*, published in English in 1987, I cannot be "invited" to speak through an interpreter on French radio or television in Quebec, even though the book was published in French in 1988 and sold in twenty-six countries. CBC policy does not allow translators, except in political matters like parliamentary debates or major political speeches. Even then, they are allowed only on rare occasions. However, I have been invited to speak in English in France.

2 On May 7, 1992, Lévesque's former cabinet minister, Claude Morin, confirmed a revelation that had hit the press on April 23 — he was a paid informer to the RCMP under the code name "French Minuet." He had been recruited two years after he joined the PQ. In 1992 he claimed he was a double agent and described how he operated: "They posed questions and I answered in my own way, without ever giving away information that they didn't already have." He was allegedly paid $6,000 a month, and admitted to receiving at least $12,000 (*GM*, May 13/92). Daniel Latouche noted the damage Morin's confession did to the PQ's credibility: "It's a strong strike against the sovereigntists. It

creates doubts and suspicions and makes the task of sovereignty more difficult. . . . The target of the revelation was clearly the Bloc Québécois because now the PQ can no longer have confidence in anyone else except those who believe in outright sovereignty" (*Star*, May 9/92).

3 In 1990, Resnick went on about English Canada going "through a moment of collective consciousness-raising with respect to free trade" (*Letters*, p. 47). By 1994 he had come to terms with sovereignty-association as inevitable: "What is required at this point is not a programmatic statement of what English Canada ought to be. . . . If we are to deal with the inevitable institutional restructuring that faces this country, we must, as English-speaking Canadians, begin a dialogue with one another as members of a single national community" (*Thinking English Canada*, p. xii).

4 In 1961 Dr. Marcel Chaput was the president of the RIN. He broke away to form the Parti républicain du Québec. In his book *Pourquois je suis un séparatiste* (1961) he wrote: "The world is made up of Separatists. The man who is master of his home is a Separatist. Each of the hundred nations striving to maintain its national identity is Separatist. France and England are mutually Separatist. . . . And you who long for a real Canadian Constitution, you are a Separatist. The only difference between you and me is that you want Canada to be free in relation to England and the United States, and I want Canada to be free in relation to Canada. . . . Separatism leads on to great things: to independence, liberty, fulfilment of the nation, French dignity in the New World" (quoted in *Quebec States Her Case*, p. 48).

Chaput was a zealot. In the summer of 1963 he went on a hunger strike and refused to eat until supporters contributed $100,000 to his party. It took a month. The first time he fasted, he got the money. Then he became greedy. When he tried Mahatma Gandhi's trick a second time for $50,000, he didn't make it. In the end he found eating more fruitful.

19

Meech II,
the Seamless Web
— 1991

T HE YEAR **1991** started off as badly as 1990 had ended. On January 1, news came out that MPs had given themselves a pay hike — from $61,600 base to $64,400, about 4.4 percent. With bankruptcies and unemployment at record levels, Canadians were deeply offended.

The prime minister worsened matters on January 9 by appointing Laurier LaPierre master of ceremonies for Keith Spicer's Citizens' Forum. This was a government completely out of touch with the people who elected it. Mulroney replaced Jack Webster with a man who would bring an impressive record of bias of his own to the proceedings. Twenty-five years earlier, Spicer's new emcee had opined in the pages of the *Vancouver Sun*: "The will to live together is no longer present. The French who have been brutalized don't have it nor do the English who face this despair and are unwilling to do anything about it but mouth platitudes. French Canada extends from the Maritimes to British Columbia. But you people insist on keeping us in the reserve of Quebec where we can multiply and speak our own language" (Mar 25/66).

LaPierre's credentials for the assignment with the Citizens' Forum should certainly have raised an eyebrow or two in 1991. Yet the Canadian media revealed nothing significant about the man. As one of their own, he was immune. As a journalist and history professor at McGill University, he once wrote in a piece for *Maclean's* during the first year of the Lester

Pearson era, 1964: "The best possible solution [to the conflict between Quebec and the rest of Canada] seems therefore a form of legislative union. This would involve abolishing the present ten provincial governments and turning all legislative, executive and judicial power over to a central government. This new constitutional formula would have to recognize the reality of the Canadian heritage and the equality of its two cultural traditions" (*Maclean's*, Feb 8/64).

The busy academics beavered away in the meantime, steadily churning out more ideas on how to structure the federation. On January 14, Queen's University Professor Thomas Courchene recommended to the B–C Commission in Quebec City the creation of a "community of the Canadas," shocking even the separatist commissioners listening to him.

On January 16, the prime minister declared that Canada was at war with Iraq. On the same day there was news that Quebec provincial police were shopping for tanks in the U.S. to deal with the Oka crisis. Would there be a cost to the beleaguered taxpayers? Of course.

In this same month the federal government continued to pour money into projects in Quebec on a grand scale, infuriating taxpayers across the country. On January 26, the Tories announced the search for an architect to build an $89 million building for the National Archives in Gatineau, Quebec. Ron Leitch, president of APEC, echoed most people when he said, "It's absolutely ridiculous, with the kind of sentiment coming out of Quebec." Liberal historian Michael Bliss disagreed: "The federal government ought to go on with its business. We are one country. I do not think we should be talking as if we were two." Reform Party MP Deborah Grey spoke for Western Canada. She questioned whether such an enterprise was — or indeed would be — a "national archives" for Canadians in the end (*Star*, Jan 26/91).

Claude Castonguay, Quebec nationalist and senior Tory spokesperson, nudged the breakup along at the end of the month as he delivered a speech to the shareholders of the Laurentian Bank of Canada: "What Quebec business people predicted, that is to say a divorce from English Canada, is under way" (*FP*, Jan 28/91).

The full extent of Quebec's orchestrated wrath over Meech blew up on January 29. Bourassa's Liberal Party published the Allaire Report, *A Quebec free to choose*. The sixty-page document — named for its chairman, a well-known extremist in the Liberal ranks — called for a wholesale transfer of almost all federal powers — twenty-two of them — to Quebec.

If the federal government followed the recommendations, it would be left with jurisdiction in only five areas: defence, customs and tariffs, currency, national debt, and equalization payments. The Allaire committee proposed a referendum in Quebec in the late fall of 1992 to ratify the steps the province should take in any agreement with the federal government. If negotiations were not successful by that time, then a referendum on Quebec sovereignty would follow by December 21, 1992.

For the Allaire Report to become the official policy of the Bourassa government, it had to be voted on. Whatever the Quebec government did, their message was clear. The gloves were off. And another message lurked behind the first: the Bourassa government was assuming that the federal government had the sole authority to unilaterally negotiate constitutional matters pertaining to Quebec. This included matters not provided for in the Constitution — the radical restructuring or breakup of the country.

The Vichy anglais of Quebec, the soft-on-Canada anglophones of Quebec, encouraged the Allaire proposals unhesitantly. To the disgust of English Canada, and of most anglophones in Quebec, Robert Keaton, president of the federally funded Alliance Quebec, bent his knee once more[1]: "There have been a few calls from people angry with our policy, but we are going to stay the course. It would be a major mistake for the English-speaking community to dismiss the report out of hand simply because it paints a decentralized view of Canada" (*GM*, Feb 1/91).

On January 30, federal Minister of Culture and Communications Marcel Masse added more fuel to the fire. He announced a grant of $16 million to create a Museum of New France at Quebec. The minister who had identified himself as a leading proponent of Quebec nationalism had waved another red flag at the rest of the country and his government.

The next day, the Mulroney government compounded its mistake. It did something about the report. It secretly assigned the federal public service the obviously political task of saving Canada. Under the direction of the Clerk of the Privy Council, Paul Tellier, and Gordon Smith, the federal–provincial relations secretary, up to forty deputy ministers organized into ten teams of bureaucrats were instructed to come up with what powers Ottawa needed to maintain an economic union.

Snickers rippled across the nation. If this was what everyone had sunk to, then truly all was lost. But the humourless media drudges saw things differently. The press went all rubbery and coy. They covered the whole story with a flurry of articles offering teeny nibbles of information from "unofficial sources," "unidentified officials," or "unnamed officials." Here's a typical revelation from Privy Council Clerk Paul Tellier that was never explained: "This is a big, big exercise. What we're trying to come up with is not less than a concept of Canada that makes sense as we approach the 21st century" (*GM*, Jan 31/91).

Mulroney's chief political strategist and chief of staff, Norman Spector, often served as that "unofficial source" and one of those whom the journalists protected. On February 17, he, Secretary to the Cabinet for Federal–Provincial Relations, slightly illuminated the *L'Etat c'est moi* mentality in Athens-on-the-Rideau, Ottawa. He was captured momentarily in the public eye on CBC Newsworld: "Through the summer the prime minister was of the view he would have to control the debate. . . . It's very clear he's the only person in political life today who can bridge the gap that exists in the country" (*Sun*, Feb 17/91).

The cover-up and masquerade were running into problems for Mulroney. His diversionary tactics weren't working. In February, Keith Spicer was defending his "Roadshow." The master propagandist cum national manipulator was making the news and exploiting every opportunity. On February 5, he answered criticism that his commission was not supporting federalism: "No, absolutely not. No, no, no. Never, never, never. . . . We are not merchants of federalism, we are merchants of lucidity" (*GM*, Feb 6/91). He also said, "I am not sure of the best conclusion. . . . But we will not convince Quebecers [that the forum] is an honest exercise if we start by excluding sovereignty-association. It's an extremely popular option in Quebec at this time" (*Star*, Feb 6/91).

Even he was getting more and more rattled under the intense scrutiny. He was making too many mistakes. A week later, on February 11, he phrased the Trudeau–Mulroney vision of Canada as clearly as anyone has ever stated it: "If we can accept the principle of diversity, of differentness by having Official Bilingualism, then that opens the door to tolerance for a hundred other groups. And I think that the partisans of bilingualism, Official Bilingualism, and multiculturalism should be natural allies" (CFRB, interview with John Stall, 1010 AM radio, Toronto, 9:05 A.M.).

Trouble was, it wasn't what most Canadians had *ever* wanted. Mulroney's address to the Empire Club in Toronto on February 12 was composed of more of the same fibs he had been serving up to the nation since his Sept-Îles speech in 1984:

> We have to be alive to the sense of deep rejection felt in Quebec at the failure to ratify the Meech Lake Accord. A great sadness, followed by anger, overtook those Quebecers who were strongly saying yes to Canada. . . . Divorce is expensive, corrosive, and inevitably leaves bitterness on both

sides. . . . I propose a greater dream: a new Canada, emerging from the darkness of doubt and the dismay of lost opportunity; a new Canada, reconfederated, rebuilt and reborn. . . . Either you have a country or you don't. You can't have it both ways. (*Star*, Feb 13/91)

Mulroney and the Citizens' Forum chairman had learned nothing. Before long, the on-leave-of-absence chairman of the CRTC was making himself the biggest menace Mulroney had to his agenda. Either the prime minister wouldn't or couldn't deal with him.

The media chided Spicer, but none of them really attacked his credentials for his latest job. Having been both architect and implementing field marshal of Trudeau's Official Bilingualism nearly a decade ago, Spicer himself had caused many of the problems that divided the nation. No one dared touch the chairman of the CRTC, the "Telepope" of Canada's electronic media. Even after three months of steady bungling, and Spicer's public admission that the whole rigmarole was a scam, Mulroney's best friend in the media, the *Globe and Mail*, confessed its devotion to the cause: "Even today, some journalists of the so-called serious press — sometimes editors or publishers — are unable to overcome their prejudices about this heretically popular and populist consultation and admit that [the Citizens' Forum] was something beautiful, original and revolutionary" (*GM*, Jan 21/91).

The Citizens' Forum was a joke. Public input was controlled in every way. You only had to phone the 1-800 number to understand how the game was played. If you were an enthusiast, you were quickly tagged for a public role. If you gave the slightest hint that you doubted or dissented from the process, the organizers told you they would "get back to you" and never did. To play on Spicer's team, you had to be squeaky clean on all the basics: bilingualism, multiculturalism, Meech Lake, pluralism. Above all, you couldn't be too bright or be likely to ask embarrassing questions. Political correctness was de rigueur.

The executive federalists running Canada are a very special breed. Marc Ellis, a sociologist who has worked around the world, describes the tragedy of leadership of this century in *Faithfulness in an Age of Holocaust*: "Such a world necessitates special types of people who dwell in abstractions and power, intelligent people who can create and maintain a complex society but who are, in essence, alienated from emotion and compassion" (p. 7).

Spicer exemplified Ellis's definition. In one breath, the chairman would airily toss off the suggestion that an independent review of bilingualism was necessary to "clear the air" — and then make it clear how prejudicial any findings would be. Whether Spicer or Mulroney were at the helm, the strategy was exactly the same one that Trudeau employed: KTLO — "Keep The Lid On." Maintain the cover-up.

Seven months after speaking in January about the necessity for "populist consultation," Spicer identified the danger of the public learning too much about bilingualism: "Otherwise, there is a risk that rising public disaffection and misunderstanding will lead to a rejection of the policy as a whole" (*Star*, Sept 9/91).

For all their clever ploys, there was desperation in Ottawa as power continued to slip away. On February 21, Professor Edward McWhinney, the maverick constitutional expert from British Columbia with centralist Canadian views, the fellow who had had no problem with the Meech Accord, came up with a solution for the crisis. He told the Beaudoin–Edwards SJC on the Process for Amending the Constitution that a "cataclysmic event" of illegal means might be necessary to achieve reform (*GM*, Feb 22/91).

Most others were preaching cave-in to the blackmail. On February 25, an eighty-five-year-old former Liberal Cabinet minister and pro-Meech activist, Jack Pickersgill, informed the Ontario Select Committee on Confederation that the Allaire Report was "federalist from the beginning to the last word" (*Star*, Feb 26/91).[2]

In the first week of March, Spicer's arrogance peaked. Interviewed on "The Journal" on March 4 by Bill Cameron, he once more gave the Trudeau shrug. Asked by his host, "Are you a federalist?" he replied, "I am a Canadian. I don't care what the plumbing is. I am totally indifferent if we have a federal, confederal or sovereignty-association type of regime."

While English Canada was enveloped in the PM's diversionary pretend democracy, Quebec continued to march to its own tune. On March 9, 1991, after seven and a half hours of debate in Montreal, the 2,800 Quebec Liberal delegates adopted the Allaire Report virtually unaltered at their annual convention. Apparently minister Claude Ryan was the lone voice for a Canadian federation. Disappointed in the strong sovereigntist stand his party had taken — the party he had once led — he simply walked out.

But the final acquiescence to breaking up the country came from many quarters in English Canada. Appointed deputy leader of the Liberal Party on January 30, fluently bilingual and a friendly traveller with Quebec nationalists, Sheila Copps — "Nobody's Baby" — jumped into the debate on the Allaire Report. The politician who had composed the line "A Liberal is a Liberal is a Liberal" spoke strongly for the radical Quebec agenda: "Clearly Mr. Bourassa has left the door wide open to federalism. And I believe that a number of the significant amendments do send out a positive signal to the rest of Canada" (*GM*, Mar 11/91).

This was also the politician who supported Meech Lake, "warts and all" (*GM*, Jan 29/90), who had studied at the University of Rouen in France, and who backed whatever side she thought would win. Almost a year earlier she declared on CBC Newsworld that "leadership is about empowering people to define our destiny" (CBC Newsworld, June 3/90). She stood squarely in support of executive something or other but not necessarily federalism and certainly not popular democracy. Her line of reasoning fit Artistotle's (384–22, BC) narrow definition to a T: "What effectively distinguishes the citizen proper from all others is his participation in giving judgement and holding office" (*The Politics*, Book III).

New Democratic Party leader Audrey McLaughlin parroted the Copps line on the radical dispersal of power to the provinces: with the Allaire Report, "Bourassa has left a lot of room to manoeuvre and I think the most encouraging statement that I heard for the rest of Canada in particular is that he remains committed, as his first choice, to a federal structure" (*GM*, Mar 11/91).

Following these astonishing utterances and like statements from Liberal leader Jean Chrétien, Jean Charest, Mulroney's Minister of the Environment, was so encouraged by the disarray of the opposition that he repeated in a CBC interview with Mike Duffy on March 10 what he had said before: Brian Mulroney was "obviously the only leader who can resolve the constitutional crisis." Canadians could only watch and listen slack-jawed.

Senator Lowell Murray, Mulroney's former errand boy and former Minister of Intergovernmental Affairs, played along with Bourassa's conviction about the merits of the Allaire proposal, too: "I think [Bourassa] left himself all kinds of room to manoeuvre and kept his government in shape to do so. . . . There is negotiation somewhere in the future, and it's not on independence or sovereignty-association" (*Star*, Mar 12/91).

Mulroney and his cronies even managed to co-opt the former director of the CIA, U.S. President George Bush, into their camp. On a visit to Ottawa on March 13, Bush told Canadians where America stood in some remarks unprecedented in Canada–U.S. relations: "[We] put a lot of emphasis on how we value a united Canada. . . . We are very happy with a united Canada, a staunch ally" (*GM*, Mar 14/91).

On March 14 Canadians gained another inkling that the academic brethren were still hard at work in their various monasteries. In a rare exposé about the goings-on in Ottawa, CBC National News reported that fourteen academics had joined in private discussions at the Meech Lake site to chew over serious changes to Official Bilingualism.

Amazing! They were actually going to sit down and open the huge can of worms, albeit in secret.

According to the broadcaster, the scholars had prepared their papers at the behest of the Business Council on National Issues. Thomas d'Aquino, its president, had admitted the previous day that the BCNI had been working on a plan for a "re-balanced federation" for some time. There were other signs of behind-the-scenes manoeuvring with big-business interests. On March 12, the *Globe and Mail* reported that d'Aquino had refused an interview by senior reporter Susan Delacourt about those secret meetings the previous week. Audrey McLaughlin raised the point in the House of Commons on March 13 and reprimanded the BCNI and its president: "The recommendations of the Spicer Commission must be taken seriously" (CBC Newsworld).

The idea was that the Meech Lake coven would present their findings to Gordon Smith, Mulroney's Cabinet secretary for federal–provincial relations. But on March 21, the *Star* reported leaks to the press before the meetings finished. Patrick Monahan, York University law professor and former advisor to David Peterson, said: "Let's face it. The Trudeau policy [bilingualism] hasn't worked. It hasn't eased language tensions. It's led to greater demands for sovereignty in Quebec. So if the policy hasn't worked, maybe it's time to re-evaluate that policy" (*Ott Citizen*/CP, Mar 15/91).

The drips became a growing trickle. In yet another surprising disclosure, CBC reported that former Premier Peterson was very much involved in the new strategy. Viewers wondered how this could be. After all, Peterson was the one who had foisted Bill 8 on Ontario against the will of a large majority of its population. He was again reported working with senior federal officials. However, the media almost totally ignored this behind-the-scenes turnabout. Only a flimsy admission was recorded, in the *Ottawa Citizen*:

> One of the main ideas advanced was the feasibility of substantial changes to official bilingualism, a policy instituted in the 1970s by Prime Minister Pierre Trudeau. . . . Unnamed federal officials told the CBC that among the ideas being discussed was a plan to give the provinces control over language and culture. . . . Multiculturalism Minister Gerry Weiner, responsible for bilingualism, told the CBC the policy of two official languages will not be altered without a fight. (Mar 15/91)

There were those "unnamed federal officials" again, so something big had to be going on. The story was quickly hushed. Monahan's own confirmation of the discussions was never backed up in its turn, nor even alluded to in any of the Toronto papers, the *Toronto Star*, the *Toronto Sun*, the *Globe and Mail*, or the *Financial Post*. The real question remained: how could anybody rely on input from David Peterson? But that's not how the issue would be exploited.

Sheila Copps chose that moment to shoot off another cheap shot in the House of Commons on March 15: "This is another example of where the closed-door process of Meech Lake is not going to work." And she loudly let it be known where she and the Liberals stood; there would be no change or review of the assumption that Canada was a bilingual nation. Then she blasted the Mulroney government for wavering so much as to even consider the idea, in secret or otherwise (*GM*, Mar 16/91).

From that point on, the Tories wasted not a moment. For the first time, they had come dangerously close to fully exposing the most divisive issue in the nation's history. It was Joe Clark who galloped in to save the Trudeau–Mulroney vision. This Minister of External Affairs had been avoiding constitutional issues like a man easing his way through a minefield on crutches. Now he launched the volley. "The commitment of this government to official bilingualism is clear, constant and continues" (*GM*, Mar 16/91). It was picked up by every news organ in the country.

The mandarins running the public service were quick to protect their territory. They knew better than anyone their empire of unlit matchsticks would flare and crumble if the true story of bilingualism ever got out. They composed another lie to smother the kerfuffle nicely. Once again they had that anonymous and unnamed senior federal official quietly tell the media, "It's just dead wrong. . . . Somebody mentioned it, yes, but it was one of the academics and I can't even recall who it was" (Susan Delacourt, *GM*, Mar 16/91).

Mulroney mulled over his next move. Besieged by the media, he chose to be coy. The role didn't suit him. At Baie Comeau, he took questions about modifications to Official Bilingualism and replied, "I've always thought that bilingualism was an advantage to any country, so I would have to reflect long on any proposal" (*Star*, Mar 16/91).

Was he acknowledging that there would be a proposal, or that he expected one? Who knew? But he didn't deny it!

Of course, no crisis on bilingualism would have been complete without a sermon from the Official Languages Commissioner. On March 19, as if oblivious to the highly charged atmosphere, D'Iberville Fortier championed greater protection for bilingualism, with "This is a very fundamental part of Canada as we know it" (*Star*, Mar 20/91).

The insiders seemed to know about the explosion the Citizens' Forum chairman was about to drop in its interim report on March 20. It confirmed what Canadians had known since the 1960s and what its leaders had known even better and tried to hide for just as long. Thus far, the Citizens' Forum had cost them $20 million. Among the many observations it produced were three key points:

[First, that] the extent of consensus against official language policy is remarkable. [Official Bilingualism is] almost universally [rejected. Spicer then only recommended an independent review]. (*Sun, GM*, Mar 22/91)[3]

[Next,] people would like Quebec to stay but not at any price.

[Finally,] multiculturalism should be more or less scrapped.

When interviewed, Keith Spicer feigned surprise at what he had heard from Canadians over those long months: "They're talking referenda, impeaching. There is almost an 18th-century French flavour to it all. . . . Canadians are telling us that their leaders must understand and accept their vision of the country — that their leaders must be governed by the wishes of the people, and not the other way around" (*GM*, Mar 21/91).

The interim report meant only one thing. Armed with these findings, Keith Spicer controlled the agenda. The next day Mulroney tried to regain control of a country he had bargained away years ago in his campaign to become prime minister. On March 21 government House Leader Harvie Andre announced yet another national unity panel: "We are going to be looking at some parliamentary structure, to involve all members of parliament, and as much of the Canadian public as possible in this clearly pivotal debate" (*GM*, Mar 22/91).

This time, Mulroney promised, the government would "involve parliamentarians and the people in a broad, all-encompassing dialogue and debate" (*Star*, Mar 22/91). The operative phrase being bandied about came from Iraq's president Saddam Hussein: it would be the "Mother" of all committees.

The latest scramble for power was on. This time, all the players rushed to the fore. It was time for a repeat performance of the man more powerful than Parliament. On March 25, D'Iberville Fortier tabled his 1990 Official Languages Report in the Commons. He stated that Ontario should become officially bilingual: "Language duality remains very much at the heart of our national vision." To alter the course of Official Bilingualism, Fortier warned, was "playing with dynamite" and "hair-raising" (*Star*, Mar 25/91). He was right about hair-raising, but not for the reasons he thought.

March 26 was an historic day in Canadian constitutional history. In a vote of 32 to 2, the Bélanger–Campeau Commission agreed that, failing a deal with the rest of Canada, there had to be a vote on Quebec sovereignty no later than October 26, 1992. The cheekiest words that day came from Gil Rémillard: "You make the offers. We will make no offers. We've been making offers and talking Constitution for 30 years and it hasn't gotten us anywhere. . . . If we receive proposals from the rest of Canada and if we decide to hold a referendum on them, and if Quebeckers say 'Yes,' that means, of course, we will have to postpone the sovereignty referendum. . . . I think it's about time that Quebec received offers from the rest of Canada" (*GM*, Mar 27/91). The operative word was "postponed."

Premier Bourassa continued to play the game with more finesse than anyone else. He kept up the pressure on the centralist forces in Quebec, which were in complete chaos. The B–C Commission recommendations were, in his opinion, "an outstanding achievement" (*GM*, Mar 28/91). He and his minister Rémillard might think they could be flip, but there was no joke issuing out of New York on April Fool's Day. From the business pages of the newspapers, Lansing Lamont, Managing Director of Canadian Affairs at the Americas Society, warned Quebec, "An independent country is an independent country. [Quebec is] going to start from scratch on various treaties" (*FP*, Apr 1/91).

In Western Canada, the Reform Party was moving, not talking. On April 7 at the party's convention, delegates overwhelmingly voted in Saskatoon to expand the party base to all of Canada, except Quebec. Under the party's constitution, the vote would now have to be tested with the party's Western membership. As Preston Manning put it, "I would question anything short of an election in Quebec and Canada as a whole to give either government a real mandate. . . . Our preference would be to have the new Quebec in a new Canada, but we think you have to define the new Canada as such that it is viable with or without Quebec" (*GM*, Apr 8/91).

Buoyed by their rocketing popularity, the Reformers also voted to "support the abolition of the department of multiculturalism" (*Star*, Apr 8/91). The interim report of the Citizens' Forum fit into the Reform Party platform nicely. On April 25, Gallup put the party at 16 percent, ahead of the Conservatives, who had fallen to 14 percent. Both the NDP and the Liberals had surrendered what was traditionally their popular support to Preston Manning's stronger vision.

The wily prime minister took these ill winds from the West into account when he thoroughly shuffled his Cabinet on April 21. He replaced Lowell Murray with Joe Clark from Yellowhead, Alberta, making him Minister Responsible for Constitutional Affairs. Murray, the PM's vademecum, remained Senate Leader. Twenty-three new appointments emphasized greater strength for the West. Don Mazankowski, a prominent Westerner, was appointed Minister of Finance. Joe Clark, it was announced, would head a panel of eighteen Cabinet ministers to examine the Constitution. For the microphones Clark pontificated: "I don't think the challenge is to persuade Canadians anywhere there there's a need to change. I think that's accepted by most Canadians" (*GM*, Apr 22/91).

There were other reasons for shifting Clark from External Affairs. The department was riddled with corruption. The press had kept it quiet for years. If Clark had stayed there too long, some of the mud would have been bound to stick to him, and despite all his foibles, many Canadians held him in high regard. Barbara McDougall, easier to punish, would now take over as minister and brace herself for whatever flak might come.[4]

In recent months Liberal opposition leader Jean Chrétien had been keeping too quiet. With unfortunate timing, he brought out his nine-point program for constitutional reform in Montreal the same day Mulroney announced the muskrat scramble of his crew. The Liberals exceeded themselves in their newly publicized goals, which went way beyond Meech Lake. Under them, Canada would wholeheartedly embrace asymmetric federalism. Quebec would be recognized as a distinct society. Multiculturalism, native self-government, four voting regions in Canada, even a Triple-E Senate were all included in the package. The Liberals had something to please everybody and nobody.

The more confusing federalism became, the more separatist came the sounds from Quebec. On May 16, Gil Rémillard upped Canada's ante: "Quebecers must understand clearly that, first of all, we become sovereign. And then, if others wish it, we have partners with whom we form an association" (*Star*, May 17/91).

A Gallup poll on May 20, 1991, impressed no one in the federal government. It showed, as polls had for years, that bilingualism was going nowhere in the hearts and minds of Canadians. This time 63 percent of Canadians regarded it as a failure.

THE RESULTS of the Reform Party internal referendum on eastward expansion came out on June 5. It was very good news for the fast-growing movement that would soon be cash-starved unless war-chests were built to finance its growing overheads. The party reported that 92 percent of the Western membership had voted to expand nationally. "I am delighted and encouraged by this vote of confidence in Canada," Manning said (*FP*, June 6/91).

Preston Manning was on a roll. Less than a week later in Ottawa on June 11, more than 2,000 paid to hear him tell them, "If the only way to discuss the constitution of Canada is to react to the demands of Quebec . . . then we are in danger of excluding the constitutional needs of the rest of Canada" (*Sun*, June 12/91).

The next day the crowds had swelled to three times that size at the International Centre in Mississauga, Ontario. The leader addressed the 6,000 people who paid $10 each to hear his party's message: "Our aim is to remove racial considerations from the Canadian Constitution altogether, rather than add to such a criteria. . . . Immigrants come here to become Canadians" (*Sun*, June 13/91).

June 14 marked another significant passage; it was D'Iberville Fortier's last day as Official Languages Commissioner, and naturally, the press had to cover the momentous event of his retirement. Speaking of his legacy: "I knew it would be tough. I didn't know it would be quite as tough as it has been" (*Star*/CP, June 17/91).

On June 16, the Canadian constitutional cogitations were interrupted by another international burp, this time from Deidesheim, Germany. Addressing Canada's situation in the same town, same place, and on the same date that he had in 1990, Chancellor Helmut Kohl held forth once again on the prospect of Quebec separation: "Europe is unifying and I don't understand why there should be separation [in Canada]" (*GM*, June 17/91).

It was not a very accurate description of Europe, which seemed to be cell-dividing faster than Kohl realized: Yugoslavia, Czechoslovakia, and the remnants of the Soviet Union. The Maastrich Treaty was also running into considerable difficulty.

Meanwhile, back in Canada, if people thought they might be able to enjoy a bit of a rest from the issue of bilingualism following Fortier's retirement, they were sorely mistaken. The federal government announced Mulroney's chosen replacement five days after Fortier quit the field — Victor Goldbloom, a Montrealer and a provincial cabinet minister during the Bourassa regime of the 1970s.

There was a serious problem with this appointment, and it came to light quickly. In 1974, in Bourassa's cabinet, Goldbloom had supported Bill 22, which stipulated that admission to English-language schools in Quebec depended on a child's maternal language being English. Bill 22 replaced Bill 63. Bourassa's Bill 22 eliminated parental choice. Bill 63, passed in 1969 by the Union Nationale government of Jean-Jacques Bertrand following the recommendations of a provincial Royal Commission, more or less recognized English as an official language of Quebec. Bill 22, on the other hand, dictated that English had no legal status whatsoever in the province. It was Quebec's first clearly restrictive language legislation. Bill 22 was also the very law Bourassa boasted of enacting to crush bilingualism.

The appointment of Goldbloom proved that Brian Mulroney was a strong supporter of Stanfield's *deux nations* theory of Canada. It was a dumb move. Even Keith Spicer, Trudeau's once-anointed bishop of bilingualism, underscored the need for a major review of this most vexatious policy. Mulroney's appointment of Goldbloom as Official Languages Commissioner stands as the most subreptitious in Canadian history.

On June 20, the day after Goldbloom's appointment, another diversion took the heat off the language mess, the report of the Special Joint Committee on the Process for Amending the Constitution — the work of the Beaudoin–Edwards Committee — was released. While the commissioners skilfully wended their way through controversy and behaved pleasantly and accommodated their witnesses, they did go their own way.

The committee recommended that constitutional change require the majority vote of four regions of Canada, with Ontario and Quebec sharing one veto just as the Victoria Conference proposed in 1971. Despite witnesses' vehement endorsements of a constituent assembly, the commissioners rejected the concept completely.

The new constitutional affairs minister had other plans. Joe Clark's political unity team of eighteen Cabinet ministers was now in gear. The government no longer needed Beaudoin–Edwards. So much for that sideshow.

On September 17, the minister began to pave the way for a new secret agenda, the one that would lead to Meech II. He addressed 400 businesspeople at a meeting of the Chambre de Commerce. There was nothing new about Meech II. Nothing learned. Henry Ford was right: "History is bunk":

We are all equal as Canadians. Being equal does not mean the same. And being a "distinct society" does not mean that Quebec is superior to Alberta. (*Star*, Sept 18/91)

Quebec must be able to protect and promote its distinct society. We have to indicate that we are moving toward that. . . . But we also have to do it in a way that also respects, as I've said before, the principle of equality of the provinces. (*GM*, Sept 18/91)

On September 19, Mulroney demonstrated to what desperate lengths his government was reduced: promising to make announcements about announcements. He told the House of Commons he would unveil his latest unity plan on September 26. Newfoundland's Wells reacted sourly: "I am not optimistic now that this process will develop a consensus. . . . I don't see how you can have a parliamentary committee that will travel from province to province, hear the different views, and then declare a position" (*Star*, Sept 20/91).

The new Mulroney vaudeville act was to be a far more raucous affair than the courtly theatre of Messrs. Beaudoin and Edwards. At a fundraising dinner, Mulroney announced that Senator Claude Castonguay and Winnipeg Tory MP Dorothy Dobbie would co-chair a new thirty-member tri-party parliamentary committee. This latest arrival on the committee junket would be mandated as the Special Joint Committee on a Renewed Canada (Castonguay–Dobbie, later Beaudoin–Dobbie). This committee would have one of the most disruptive track records in Canadian history. Castonguay, the equivocator about federalism and the post-Meech champion of separation, let the public know that this was the committee that had the power: "This really is the time when we have to fish or cut bait."

Dorothy Dobbie, a neophyte at the constitutional conference table, obediently mimicked the senator who had sabotaged the Victoria Charter in 1971. She too said that "this is the last committee — I hope — on this constitutional issue" (*GM*, Sept 20/91).

On September 23, Frank McKenna of New Brunswick proved that if you changed sides fast enough and often enough and still managed to play the game with philosophical nonspeak, you might get your wrist slapped but you would not be thrown out of the game. The Mackenzie King of modern-day Liberalism survived a provincial election with 46 of 58 seats. Ironically, in the popular vote his Liberals finished only a squeak ahead of the Conservatives. And a new party in the province rubbed any sheen off the victory. Capturing eight seats, the Confederation of Regions party (CoR) under Arch Pafford moved in as the official opposition. For the first time in Canada, issues of language and race pushed to the forefront of elected office, beyond Official Bilingualism and the Constitution Act of 1982. The CoR Party called for the scrapping of bilingualism. Perhaps the bloom was finally off the rose.

Mordecai Richler, one of Canada's best-known authors, also featured prominently in the news. The famous Jewish curmudgeon of Montreal took his own shot at the country's domestic mess in the September 23 issue of *The New Yorker*. In a thoughtful thirty-one-page article, the literary tiger chided the various governments of his home province, the "disconcertingly tribal society" with a background of anti-semitism. The article elicited yawns in the U.S. North of the border, the Quebec media went ballistic.[5]

The Tory government tabled Meech II with a flourish on September 24. The latest proposal for twenty-eight reforms was grandiosely titled *Shaping Canada's Future Together*. The deal bore no resemblance to what people had been screaming for, either at the Citizens' Forum or any of the committee hearings or in the volumes of Letters to the Editor of newspapers across the country. Official Bilingualism remained intact. Even Spicer's own call for a review was ignored. Quebec was to be defined as a distinct society one more time. Canada's linguistic duality was affirmed yet again.

Meech II differed in what was added: numerous provisions on native rights. Aboriginal self-government, aboriginal participation in constitutional talks, aboriginal representation on the Senate, and a clause defining Canada, though the proposals did not spell out what it would be. The complex package was a lawyers' delight. It would require tons of work, years to define and execute, and a great deal of money.

The hue and cry that greeted it was deafening. The all-party committee players declared themselves all in favour of it; the Canadian public raved against it. The vested interests and minority groups sang the same tunes that they had with Meech Lake.

And the feds still didn't get it. The people did. And so, it seemed, did Governor General Ray Hnatyshyn. After preaching that Canadians must "resist the voices" of division and the language of excess, he acknowledged, "The environment is highly charged" (*Star*, Sept 24/91). Profound.

Treasury Board president Gilles Loiselle defended the bonuses for senior public servants on the same day. His words hardly reassured Canadians that the ship of state was in competent hands. He stated matter-of-factly that it was normal practice to pay up to $84,000 to Crown corporation heads and senior civil servants: "They get that every year . . . to get better productivity" (*Sun*, Sept 26/91). He admitted that 4,000 senior managers received bonuses during the summer.

A sad note interrupted these proceedings on the same day. Canada's first elected senator, Reform Party member Stan Waters, died of a brain tumour. He had been a public figure rare for his love of his country. Many Canadians would miss him.

On September 28, the federal government circulated 15,000 copies of their latest constitutional proposal. Now, and for the first time, it could be examined by anyone. The prime minister made a telling slip in San Francisco on a CNN interview, that "all of the provisions of the Meech Lake accord are there in varying shapes and forms." Those words confirmed Canadians' worst fears. The Tories and their comrades in arms from the Liberal and NDP parties were still behaving as if Meech had never happened.

In an atmosphere of such low expectations, the really big news in October was the reincarnation of Pierre Trudeau. On October 2, the seventy-two-year-old faced a gathering of 300 at an "off the record" meeting of the Young Presidents Organization. On the distinct society provision for Meech II encompassing Quebec as "a French-speaking majority," he said, "It will give the government of this society the power to say: 'Well, let's deport a couple of hundred thousand of non-French-speaking Quebecers. . . . We have a right to expel people, certainly to shut their traps if they think they can speak English in public'" (*Gazette*, Oct 5/91). Good old Trudeau. No one could match Merlin the Muddler when it came to capturing a headline. The anglos of Quebec had been deporting themselves for two decades because of his failure to uphold Canada's constitution.

Co-chairperson Dorothy Dobbie of the new joint parliamentary committee on the Constitution got herself into trouble on the first day of the hearings. She repeated the mistake the government had been making for more than four years — she talked down to people. On the eve of the first day, in Charlottetown, she said, "We're going through an adjustment period while Canadians learn that this is a committee that's going out to them" (CBC, "The Journal," Oct 8/91). Gee willikers. Canadians couldn't have cared less who was on the platform. They were tired of being lectured. They were certainly in no mood for speeches from anyone. Yet two days later she was at it again: "Many Canadians are very unsure of their history and they're very unsure of the facts and what's actually in the proposal. So we have to think now how we're going to help them get better educated . . . so that they can make informed decisions about the proposals" (*GM*, Oct 11/91).

Long before the hearings began, in fact, Dobbie was in trouble. On CBC Newsworld on September 10 she gave her opinion of Canadians: "There is a tendency to dwell on the negative and people who have negative thoughts." On November 16, 1991, the host of CBC Radio's program "The House" exposed what other media types had ignored. Judy Morrison revealed that Dobbie and her husband had left for South America on vacation while owing some $15,000 to various creditors. With a legal caution on its title for the monies owed to the provincial Department of Labour, her house in Manitoba could not be sold. The interview that followed was a deadly one, and a too infrequent example of fine insight from the CBC. Of her role on the committee Dobbie said: "I have a job to do here. I think I can make a contribution. . . . Even when I offered my resignation, I said . . . I will do this [resign] if you believe it is right and if it will solve the problem. If it's right for the country, I am gone in a flash."

There should have been that flash.

AND THE BEAT went on. Few Canadians were spending much time thinking about the International Monetary Fund. No one wading through the domestic mess believed the IMF's prediction on October 11 that Canada would have the strongest economic growth of any of the G–7 countries in 1992. When a Harvard University economist, Michael Porter, released his million-dollar economic study on October 24, a joint federal/BCNI undertaking, it carried far more weight than the IMF news from Bangkok: "The core of Canada's economic success is at risk. . . . The problem is that the old order has left a legacy that literally permeates this economy and that legacy is leaving this economy ill-equipped to respond [to the forces of change]" (*FP*, Oct 25/91).

Meech Lake claimed two more casualties in 1991. On October 17, Michael Harcourt's NDP scored a landslide victory in British Columbia, routing the SoCred Party that Rita Johnston had inherited from Bill Vander Zalm. In quick succession, Roy Romanow's New Democrats won a landslide victory in Saskatchewan on the twenty-first. Grant Devine's Tories had shrunk from 66 to 11 seats.

For two days that month, the Chief of the Assembly of First Nations (AFN), Ovide Mercredi, commanded attention atop the constitutional agenda. On October 20 the AFN began a "parallel" process, conducting the first of seventy-five hearings among aboriginal peoples. The gatherings were jokingly dubbed "The First Nations' Circle on the Constitution." A day later, the AFN leaders said, "A national Indian government is a very viable idea, not in 10 years' time, but within the next few years."

On October 25, the CBC announced it was launching a lawsuit against journalist Michel Vastel, for writing "the message was direct: the [Canadian Broadcasting] corporation had to co-operate with the last-ditch effort to save the Meech Lake Accord" (*Star*, Oct 26/91). Canadians heard what was implied loud and clear.

More frayed nerves and flaring tempers. Those who attended the Guelph University Symposium on October 27 and Ontarians who tuned in to it on TVOntario witnessed an outburst from Professor Pierre Fortin. He picked that moment to lambaste a young English-speaking hockey player, Eric Lindros, who had refused to play for the Quebec Nordiques: "[He's] trying very hard to become an adult. . . . [Instead he thinks of Quebecers] as a bunch of fucking frogs. He should shut up and concentrate on his hockey. . . . Pierre Trudeau should shut up and concentrate on raising his children."

The Castonguay–Dobbie constitutional committee ground on, doomed by its two chairpeople, a Quebec nationalist and a discredited Mulroney crony. Any hopes that they might produce some useful ideas and debate were utterly dashed by the end of the first week of November. On the fifth, at St. Pierre Jolys, Manitoba, public attendance was so small that the TV cameras could not avoid broadcasting shots of the empty room to the nation.

Scenting failure, the Liberal and NDP opposition parties began to close in. They called for the resignation of Dorothy Dobbie, who they blamed for the mess. Undaunted, the co-chair continued to reprimand and repudiate the witnesses for their views. Tory Senator Castonguay, the adenoidal voice of doom from Quebec, intoned grimly, "There will be no more walk-ons." In other words, if the witnesses could not be pre-screened for political correctness, their voices simply would not be heard.

At these particular hearings, "ordinary Canadians" had five minutes to testify. That week Castonguay also announced that controversial plans to use "conflict resolution" experts had been cancelled. No one was surprised when constitutional affairs minister Joe Clark ordered the committee's activities suspended the next day. By that point, both the Liberals and the NDP were refusing to participate.

Not surprisingly, on November 6, an Angus Reid–Southam poll showed that 41 percent of Canadians opposed the Meech II proposals. The politicians and their supporters ignored the news. A news item that did attract some attention was a report the same day in Toronto, that 200 people had attended a conference sponsored by the Canadian Institute of Strategic Studies. The forum examined the prospect of armed conflict should Quebec opt for separation.

By mid-November the Castonguay–Dobbie Committee was hopelessly discredited. Castonguay executed the coup de grâce himself on November 12 when he told the Montreal press the unity committee was a "complete fiasco" (CBC Newsworld). The next day, at 3:30 P.M., he chaired the committee with only Tories present. There was no point continuing without the Liberals and the NDP. He adjourned the hearings. PC committee member Jean-Pierre Blackburn remarked that, as it had been during the "Night of the Long Knives" ten years earlier, on November 5, 1981, "Quebec is isolated" (CBC Newsworld). It was nonsense, of course. Old hands at the constitutional game knew this scenario only too well. Claude Castonguay had pulled off this same stunt in 1971 when he killed the Victoria Charter. Enough was enough.

Still the prime minister's super con man pressed on. Despite the mounting mayhem, on November 13, Joe Clark told the nation that there would be five major "Renewal of Canada Conferences" in major cities across Canada, with possibly a sixth on aboriginal affairs. "The process the government is organizing is too urgent to wait for the parliamentary committee [Castonguay–Dobbie] to get its act together. . . . We hope the committee [if it can] get its act together, will participate" (CBC Newsworld, *GM*, Nov 14/91). In fact, he was orchestrating a damage control exercise while playing Pontius Pilate.

November 13 was not a day of rest for the prime minister. While he was in Baie Comeau, Quebec, announcing a $1-million grant to a local saw-mill — bringing the total federal grants to the region in recent months up to $5 million — foxy Jean Chrétien was in the chicken coop in Ottawa. The Liberal leader's letter to Joe Clark captured the front page: "Your colleagues in the cabinet from Quebec have made no effort to publicly promote your own proposals. Even the Hon. Benoît Bouchard says he will not know before October of 1992 whether he still believes in Canada" (*Ott Citizen*, Nov 25/91).

Castonguay gave up the constitutional ghost on November 25. Citing "exhaustion" and poor health, he quit the Castonguay–Dobbie unity committee. To kill it with the least possible pain required a gentle anaesthetist. Senator Gérald Beaudoin, of Beaudoin–Edwards fame, the quiet team, was called in to assume the task of smoothing things over.

The continuing controversy over government largesse to Quebec flared again on November 28. This time it was Mulroney's Quebec lieutenant Benoît Bouchard who did the honours. He announced that Quebec's share of a $300-million industrial aid package to the whole nation would be $160 million. Bitter exchanges erupted between reporters in Ottawa, between the Quebec press and the newspapers and media from English-speaking Canada.

On December 1, in Montreal, Mulroney, the man without a mandate for most of what he chose to indulge in, dismissed the idea of resorting to arms to stop Quebec's secession as "total idiocy" (*Star*, Dec 3/91). The next day, PQ constitutional critic Jacques Brassard told reporters outside the

National Assembly, "I find it difficult to believe that there is a majority of English Canadians who would follow the direction of civil war or military intervention" (*GM*, Dec 3/91).

Only one Quebec writer, the founding father of separatism, Pierre Bourgault, applied the right turn of phrase. Addressing a rally of 800 in Montreal he noted that, "English Canada assaults us with threats in the hope that we'll lose our heads" (*Star*, Dec 7/91).

Everyone tried shouting different threats at Canadians in December. Imitating Castonguay's earlier threat in Vancouver on December 3, the prime minister said that following the constitutional conferences, "Canadians are going to have to fish or cut bait. . . . Canadians are going to have to decide whether they want to keep a country or whether they want to lose a heritage. This is the question we're all going to have to answer" (*GM*, Dec 5/91).

On December 16, opposition leader Jean Chrétien pulled out his own little battering ram after a long silence in the nation's news. Asked whether a vote of 50 percent plus one vote in a referendum would be sufficient to take Quebec out of Canada, Chrétien casually replied, "Yes — I am a democrat" (*Star*, Dec 17/91).

Another year was ending. On December 20, Canadian taxpayers officially learned of Joe Clark's Renewal of Canada Conferences in the press.

In a year of mind-bending constitutional twists and turns, the year ended with one last one. On the very final day of 1991, the Ontario Conference of (Roman) Catholic Bishops sent a pastoral letter to 3.5 million registered Canadian Catholics asking them to recognize Quebec as a distinct society, a constitutional amendment to guarantee "the right to life from conception until natural death," and to support the adoption of a "Charter of Social Rights and Responsibilities." Archbishop Marcel Gervais warned bluntly, "We don't want a cosmetic admission of Quebec as a distinct society" (*GM*, *Star*, *Sun*).

By now, nearly all of Canada's traditions had been ravaged by most of the country's leaders, political and otherwise. Canadians worked themselves up into a bloodthirsty mood whenever they thought about their politicians, but they couldn't get at them. Yet.

Notes

1 Protesting Keaton's support for the Allaire Report, Peter Blaikie, former chairman of AQ and a former president of the Conservative Party, resigned: "[Allaire] is simply a rape, and there's only one way to deal with rape and that's to fight" (*GM*, Feb 1/91).

2 Some two months earlier, following the collapse of Meech Lake, in a letter to the editor of the *Globe*, professors J.L. Granatstein and Robert Bothwell wrote: "Like the vast majority of our compatriots, we want Quebec to stay in Canada so this country can remain a strong bilingual federation. . . . To keep Quebec a part of Canada we are prepared to go almost any distance and, should it become necessary, to keep a light in the window to welcome Quebec back at any time in the future" (*GM*, Dec 23/90).

3 Laurier LaPierre, professor, historian, and social commentator, contradicts the chairman's words about the forum's findings in *Canada, My Canada: What Happened?* (1992): "On official language policy, they stated what the polls were telling everyone: Canadians want to live in a bilingual country and they consider bilingualism a personal and social asset. . . . 'Why do we have to be bilingual?' was a frequent question. It cost jobs, they claimed; it was expensive, and it 'shoved French down our throats.' This was quite understandable, bilingualism having become an important symbol of what ails Canada" (p. 218). So who should Canadians believe?

4 Canadian Press broke the story on August 14. An External Affairs spokesman, Denis Laliberté, confirmed an RCMP investigation into the department. One hundred and twenty-seven diplomats were "involved at all levels in embassies" in a scam uncovered three years earlier during a routine audit in Paris. Sgt. Parker of the RCMP said, "There are other departments" involved, but no charges were laid.

   The fraud worked worked this way. Senior public servants, including ambassadors, would buy full-fare tickets, cancel them and book cheaper seats for themselves. Then they would submit chits and invoices for the more expensive tickets and pocket the difference. As of August 15, 1991, the public was not told how much the thieves had got away with.

5 The fury over Richler's observations exploded with the publication of his book *Oh Canada! Oh Quebec! Requiem for a Divided Country* in spring 1992. Lise Bissonnette, the pert and pugilistic editor of Quebec's nationalist *Le Devoir*, thumped the anglophone for days for his wicked pen and misbehaviour: "Such defamation propagated across Canada smears all those who are now associated with *Le Devoir*. . . . Here we are people who would have accepted to be linked to a newspaper that was for a time, according to Mr. Richler, the worst Nazi rag" (*GM*, Mar 19/92).

V

The Fourth Estate

Media Munchkins

20

The Pulp Prime-Evil
The Four Gospels of Central Canada

C ENTRAL CANADA'S LARGEST ENGLISH daily newspapers are the *Toronto Star*, the *Globe and Mail*, the *Financial Post*, and the *Toronto Sun*. All four are owned by large corporations, and two are directly related through a common parent corporation. All are immensely wealthy.

Canadians are well aware of the posture and the powerful position of their press. They know that it is concentrated to a degree not in their interest. As Edmund Burke is reported to have once said of the press gallery in the British House of Commons, "Yonder sits the Fourth Estate, more important than them all." Nothing's changed since then.

Three of the above papers operate within huge media conglomerates. The *Globe* is owned by the Thomson Corporation, one of the world's most powerful media empires, which controls a vast network of newspapers across Canada and the United States. Since July 3, 1993, the *Globe* has distributed the *Financial Times* of Canada, which is also controlled by Thomson business interests.

The inter-media links between the large corporations are vast and intricate and in a constant state of flux. *Saturday Night* magazine, which is published by Saturday Night Magazine Inc., is now owned by Conrad Black's Hollinger Inc. The magazine is marketed and distributed by the *Globe and Mail*. The *Toronto Star*, in turn, is owned by Torstar Corp.

However, as of 1985, Torstar and the Southam group exchanged minority share interests between themselves.

The *Financial Post* and the *Toronto Sun* are both part of the Maclean Hunter empire, which owns Canada's largest circulating magazine, *Maclean's*. In 1994 Maclean Hunter had a 62-percent stake in the Toronto Sun Publishing Corporation, which in turn controls the *Financial Post*.

As of August 3, 1992, the four major newspaper companies, Thomson Corp., Southam Inc., and Torstar Corp., along with Vancouver-based Hollinger Inc., own and operate some sixty-nine daily papers across Canada. In the same year, the Canadian Daily Newspaper Association stated that nearly 60 percent of the circulation of Canada's newspapers was controlled by Southam, Thomson, and the Toronto Sun publishing companies.

Disenfranchising Canadians in deference to the interests of large corporations has damaged the democratic spirit in Canada immeasurably. Canadians were strongly forewarned of this in 1961 in the report of the O'Leary Commission on Publications. The Royal Commission on Newspapers, or the Kent Commission, as it is also known, was appointed to examine freedom of the press on December 3, 1980. At that time the situation was considered grave. The commission began from the following terms of reference:

> that there has been a decline in the number of daily newspapers serving major cities and a decline in the number of cities in which competition between daily newspapers exists;
>
> that there has been increased concentration of ownership and control of daily newspapers in Canada; and
>
> that it is desirable that a study be undertaken, without delay, into the extent and causes of the aforesaid situation, and into the implications for the country of that situation. (Order-in-Council, P.C., 1980–2343. Sept 3/80 in Commission Report, Appendix II, p. 259)

The 1980 Royal Commission came into being because of the closing of the Ottawa *Journal* and the Winnipeg *Tribune* in particular. Its report warned the country about the seriousness of the threat such concentrated ownership presented to Canadian civil liberty.

1 The Scope of Concentration

Freedom of the press is not a property right of owners. It is a right of the people. It is part of their right to free expression, inseparable from their right to inform themselves. The Commission believes that the key problem posed by its terms of reference is the limitation of those rights by undue concentration of ownership and control of the Canadian daily newspaper industry. . . . Concentration engulfs daily newspaper publishing. Three chains control nine-tenths of French-daily newspaper circulation. Three other chains control two-thirds of English-language circulation. (Commission Report, Vol. 1, p. 1)

Chains accounted for 77 per cent of all copies of daily newspapers published in Canada in September, 1980, an increase from 58 per cent 10 years earlier. (Vol. 1, p. 9)

13 Conclusions and Suggestions

Newspaper competition, of the kind that used to be, is virtually dead in Canada. The only market where there is anything like the old head-on competition, between two papers published at the same time of day and competing across the community, is French-speaking Montréal. . . .

The death of head-on newspaper competition is one culmination of a long process. This Commission was established because of the events that, in the summer of 1980, followed the purchase of the FP [Financial Post] chain by the Thomson chain. The shape of the newspaper industry in English Canada was then dramatically changed by an agreement — we express no opinion whether or not it was a legal agreement — between the two largest of the remaining newspaper corporations, Thomson and Southam. (Vol. 1, p. 215)

While people now get much of their news and views from the broadcasting media, there are two significant ways in which print retains its primacy.

First, it is the medium of record, which generally gives more detail than the others, which explores issues in more depth, and which stands as the source to which people refer back. Second, the daily newspapers are still the main originators, gatherers and summarizers of news. (Vol. 1, p. 216)

Profitability, however, is the small beer of the newspaper problem. The champagne is power over the minds of Canadian men and women. (Vol. 1, p. 221)

Among the commission's many proposals for "Remedial action by government" were three:

(1) Strengthen competition or anti-combines legislation.
(2) Break up the chains, so that we revert eventually to one newspaper, one owner.
(3) Prevent cross-media ownership. (Vol. 1, p. 227)

The commission's all-inclusive recommendations enlarged on the above. Under Section 14, it was stated of the new proposed legislation that:

(1) It would prohibit significant further concentration of the ownership and control of daily newspapers and of the common ownership of these newspapers and other media.
(2) It would correct the very worst cases of concentration that now exist. (Vol. 1, p. 237)

In their report to the Trudeau government, the commissioners repeatedly stressed the importance of a free press. Various members of the bench in Britain, the United States, and other jurisdictions were quoted as strong evidence of the need for action. Two selections indicate the tone of the report and seriousness of the problem it identified:

Mr. Justice Rand (Alberta), *Boucher* v. *The King*, [1951], S.C.R. 288.

Freedom in thought and speech and disagreement in ideas and beliefs, on every conceivable subject, are of the essence of our life. The clash of critical discussion on political, social and religious subjects has too deeply become the stuff of daily experience to suggest that mere ill-will as a product of controversy can strike down the latter with illegality. . . . Controversial fury is aroused constantly by differences in abstract conceptions: heresy in some fields is again a mortal sin; there can be fanatical puritanism in ideas as well as in morals; but our compact of free society accepts and absorbs these differences and they are exercised at large within the framework of freedom and order on broader and deeper uniformities as bases of social stability. (Vol. 3, p. 6)

In 1947, Robert M. Hutchins chaired a private American commission on the freedom of the press, whose findings were later published as *A Free and Responsible Press* (University of Chicago Press, 1947, pp. 6–11) (cited in the Kent report):

Freedom of the press is essential to political liberty. Where men cannot freely convey their thoughts to one another, no freedom is secure. Where freedom of expression exists, the beginnings of a free society and a means for every extension of liberty are already present. Free expression is therefore unique among liberties: it promotes and protects all the rest. . . .

Civilized society is a working system of ideas. It lives and changes by the consumption of ideas. Therefore it must make sure that as many as possible of the ideas which its members have are available for its examination. . . .

The right of free public expression does include the right to be in error. Liberty is experimental. Debate itself could not exist unless wrong opinions could be rightfully offered by those who suppose them to be right. But the assumption that the man in error is actually trying for truth is of the essence of his claim for freedom. What the moral right does not cover is the right to be deliberately or irresponsibly in error. (quoted in Vol. 3, pp. 7–8)

The Kent Commission of 1980 was by no means the first to note the danger to freedom. In 1970 a Special Senate Committee on Mass Media was headed up by the Hon. Keith Davey. It produced a three-volume report that predicted the problem would likely accelerate:

What matters is the fact that control of the media is passing into fewer and fewer hands, and that the experts agree this trend is likely to continue and perhaps accelerate. . . . This country should no longer tolerate a situation where the public interest in so vital a field as information is dependent on the greed or goodwill of an extremely privileged group of businessmen. (cited in the Commission Report, Vol. 1, p. 17)

To spell out the dangers, the Commission in 1980 quoted two respected authorities:

Words more eloquent than ours have been written on these fundamental principles in many countries and many languages. We limit ourselves, for illustration, to Justice Hugo Black, on behalf of the Supreme Court of the United States, in the case of *Associated Press et al.* v. *United States* (1945) . . . :

Surely a command that the government itself shall not impede the free flow of ideas does not afford non-governmental combinations a refuge if they impose restraints upon that constitutionally guaranteed freedom. Freedom to publish means freedom for all and not for some. . . . Freedom of the press from governmental interference under the First Amendment does not sanction repression of that freedom by private interests.

For Canada, we cannot do better than refer back to the words of an earlier Royal Commission, the O'Leary Commission on Publications (1961):

> There is need to remember that freedom of the press is not an end in itself, but only a function of general intellectual freedom, to remember that no right includes a privilege to injure the society granting it: to understand that a great constitutional doctrine cannot be reduced to a mere business convenience. . . . There must be few left to deny the right — indeed the duty — of the government to act again if faced with demonstrable community necessity.

"We believe," the commissioners concluded, "that our inquiry demonstrates the community necessity." Amen to that.

NOTHING WAS DONE. The 1961 O'Leary Commission was ignored. The recommendations of the 1970 Davey Committee were ignored. The Kent Commission, the Royal Commission on Newspapers of 1980, was ignored.

In the latter case, aware of the potential threat of government intervention in the public interest, the Thomson organization voluntarily disposed of its interest in the *Financial Post*. It was a shrewd move. Opposition silenced, government intervention was pre-empted.

Over a thirty-year period, the concentration of the media in Canada has greatly intensified and become increasingly impervious to reform. During the constitutional debate from 1963 to 1993 the press proved how impoverished and irrelevant it is in defending freedom and democracy in Canada. There were so many examples to prove the case.

As a matter of editorial policy, not one of these four Canadian newspapers permitted open dialogue or dissent in its pages. Not one of them supported real investigative reporting. During the ten years of Canada's constitutional anguish, from 1982 through 1992 and beyond, none of them contributed any true revelations or insights about Canada's constitutional ailments.

All four of central Canada's major papers went much further. They shamelessly manipulated the content of the news for their own purposes, arranged the timing of press reports to suit their corporate objectives, and deliberately ignored particularly important items.

Each journal recognized its social role to mildly admonish government, preach to government, or influence government, but never to challenge any government head on. The papers took no risks. In the end, although they sometimes varied in the way they followed through on this attitude, all four came to very similar conclusions on nearly every major issue. By the time of the October Referendum in 1992, all four, including the last holdout, the *Toronto Sun*, endorsed the principles behind the Meech Lake Accord. And all promoted the Charlottetown Accord aggressively.

The press unabashedly set itself up as a conspirator with the government during these constitutional meanderings. It has played that same role for years now. As a result, it maintains a particularly favoured position, which in turn fuels the government's unwillingness to democratize freedom of the press.

The similarities run deeper than overall editorial policy. A reporter for almost any one of them could be happily employed by any of the others. Dalton Camp, the Red Tory, writes a column for the *Toronto Star*. It was fitting, then, that when he was ill, the socialist historian, Desmond Morton, took his place.

No original "characters" exist in the Canadian media. The country has bred no I.F. Stones, no H.L. Menckens, not even Rush Limbaughs. Individualism has been beaten into the ground by these oligopolical corporate giants. In the 1980s, differences between these four Canadian newspapers practically evaporated.

The *Globe* is the Faculty Club of Canada. It presents itself as more academic than the *Star*, the Pulp Primevil, which sees itself as the champion of legions of underdogs. The *Star* would have a nation of multicultural interests and pluralism with any semblance of Canadian identity lost in a scream of rights activism.

The *Toronto Sun* and its affiliates are now eerily similar to the *Star*. The *Financial Post*, on the other hand, has transformed itself into what the *Globe* used to be.

These centralist papers are all much the same: a mulligatawny stew, each with its so-called left-wing and right-wing reporters. For twenty years, none of them has ever seriously attacked another, exposed another, or even teased another. It simply isn't done.

IN THIS CHAPTER I have selected excerpts from approximately 500 editorials of the big four, specifically those that in some way concern the vision of Canada.

One of the best examples of important news ignored, manipulated, or distorted was the press's deliberate neglect of the Gord McIntyre case, in which the United Nations condemned Canada's inaction and injustice on Quebec's Bill 178 (see Chapter 29). All the editorials on it were sanitized. None could be described as revealing, stimulating, or even thought-provoking.

Under these circumstances, the only valuable communications within Canadian society circulated privately among the thousands of individuals and dissent groups who met in small clusters to talk about the issues. During Meech Lake, between April 1987 and June 22, 1990, the *Star* published some 21,000 articles on the constitutional debates. During Charlottetown, the volume dropped to some 1,300 letters on the same subject.

The Financial Post

In 1988 the Toronto Sun Publishing Corporation, Hollinger Inc., and the Financial Times of London owned the *Post*. Its first daily editions appeared in February 1988. In December 1991, Toronto Sun Publishing owned 60 percent of the paper. From 1988 to 1991, the paper's circulation rose from an average of about 38,000 to 100,000. In 1993, it was variously estimated as anywhere between 150,000 to 170,000. Today the *Post* is shipped daily to all the major cities and markets of Canada. In 1993, Ron Adams of CBC "Business Week" reported that Hollinger Inc., 50.62 percent of which is owned by Conrad Black and Associates, owned 19 percent of the *Post*. Editorial selections:

Don't reject our pride and heritage

"The question for us to ask ourselves is this: Shall we be content to remain separate — shall we be content to maintain a mere provincial existence, when, by combining together, we could become a great nation?"

So said George Etienne-Cartier, a driving force in the creation of the Dominion of Canada during the Confederation debates in 1865. . . .

[The separatists] blithely dismiss the vision of John A. Macdonald. As Prime Minister Brian Mulroney noted in a speech in Toronto yesterday, Macdonald more than a century ago described Canada as a great country, and said it "shall become one of the greatest in the world if we preserve it. We shall sink into insignificance and adversity if we suffer it to be broken." (*FP*, Feb 13/91)

The editor of the *Financial Post* apparently didn't know that Canada had already been a great country and that Canadians only wanted it back.

Meech crisis puts our economic future on the line

The Financial Post has raised serious criticisms of the Meech Lake Accord. We believe the proposal is flawed. . . .

That said, the failure to get Quebec into the Constitution this time around is certain to hurl us into another protracted, divisive and potentially shattering crisis of unity. There is indeed a risk that Canada as we know it will not survive. — Neville J. Nankivell, Publisher & Editor-in-Chief. (*FP*, Mar 24–26, 1990)

Nothing survives "as we know it." Quebec has always been in the Constitution and it *is* in the Constitution today.

Court should still rule on the deadline

It seemed clear, as The Financial Post went to press, that the Meech Lake Accord was doomed. What was also clear was that the government has dangerously mishandled the effort to secure the accord's passage.

. . . What the politicians and their advisers must now do is deal with what has been wrought and see what can be done to salvage the situation. . . .

We have suggested before the deadline should be extended to permit the accord to come to a vote in all provinces. . . . The court may rule against Ottawa and confirm the June 23 date applies. But if the court agrees with the government, at least the accord's fate will be decided up front by votes, not in a wimpish fashion by the expiration of the deadline. (*FP*, June 23/90)

Ho-hum. Same old stuff. The idea was to keep executive federalism alive instead of pushing for democratization of the constitutional process in the first place. Again, here is the press's and big business's push for the accord that most Canadians in every province did not want. A court ruling that there was no deadline would only have prolonged the constitutional agenda as the government's never-ending priority. Bad business advice from a journal that purports to speak for the financial community.

In its June 22 editorial, the *Post* suggested the government should "limit debate and shorten the public hearing process — it would hardly constitute a curtailment of democratic rights" (*FP*, June 22/90).

McKenna's proposal deserves support

This goes a long way toward satisfying Quebec. (*FP*, Mar 22/90)

McKenna's proposal — which was as much the premier's as it was McKenna's — pleased no one. It would have cost the business community zillions just to figure out what it meant. And there was no agreement between the first ministers, anyway. What was meant by native rights, distinct society, the Senate setup, the division of powers, the Canada clause? What was there to support?

The Charter under Meech Lake

Two principles lie at the heart of the Canadian Constitution. . . .
The first is bilingualism, and minority rights. The second is individual liberty, as guaranteed by the Charter of Rights, through which the first may also be secured. (*FP*, Nov 1/89)

Apparently no one at the *Financial Post* realized Canada actually had a history before Pearson and Trudeau and Mulroney came along. Certainly no one on staff had ever read the British North America Act, which does indeed "lie at the heart of the Canadian Constitution." It remains the foundation document of the Constitution today, whatever the papers say. Bilingualism and minority rights do not "lie at the heart of the Canadian Constitution."

Trudeau's 1982 Constitution Act and the Charter, coupled with the notwithstanding clause, guarantee absolutely nothing. So halfway to the Meech deadline the editors of the *Post* rambled on, blithely unaware that this clause renders all the Charter sections on freedom, liberty, and most other fundamental rights hopelessly vulnerable. Yet this editorial came out *after* passage of Quebec's Bill 178! Even then, they didn't get it.

Why we need Senate reform

The Senate, because it is unelected, lacks the legitimacy it needs to act as an effective counterweight to the Commons' bias toward the centre. . . . If it were elected, the present distribution of seats would only make matters worse: It is as centrifugal as the Commons, without even the logic of representation by population to justify its arbitrary allotments of seats to each province. (*FP*, Oct 13/89)

So why not support the Triple-E Senate?

Politics of blame

> Newfoundland Premier Clyde Wells is being blamed for the death of the
> Meech Lake Accord because he didn't have a vote on the accord. That
> interpretation exacerbates Quebec's sense of being rejected by English
> Canada, further weakens the federal government vis-à-vis Quebec, and
> fuels a politics of rejection. . . .
>
> Understandably, there is anger at Wells for not having had a vote after
> giving his undertaking to do so. But his failure to have a vote did not, of
> itself, kill the accord. (*FP*, June 30/90)

What a sappy editorial. Wells was screwed, pure and simple. And most
Canadians and Newfoundlanders were right behind him, whether they
were Tory, Liberal, NDP, Reform, or even National Party.

In an editorial for June 17, 1991, titled "Please, no more reigns of error"
we read: "The Reform Party should run a province for four or five years
before seeking a federal mandate. Alberta or Ontario are the obvious
choices."

A few weeks later, the paper came out with one entitled "Listen to the
bright right" (*FP*, Aug 9/91): "Tories must remember that small 'c' conservatives and no one else put them in power twice. And they will again. But
only if they realize that and make some kind of peace with the Reform
Party — or pre-empt its policies."

Here's the *Post* on the Renewal Conference process as the first of the five
conferences opened in Halifax (*FP*, Jan 21/92): "So what was decided? That
when the experts and the interest groups are counter-balanced by a healthy
dollop of 'ordinary' citizens chosen by lottery, we get a very different
message from when the 11 first ministers meet by themselves, as they did
at Meech."

At least the *Star*, the *Globe*, the *Sun*, and even the CBC referred to the
"extras" on the setting as "so-called ordinary Canadians."

The *Post* fell, hook, line and sinker, for the high-pressure tactics of
Mulroney, the BCNI, and the banks. An editorial entitled "Abandon this
fatal course" came out swinging, in favour of Charlottetown: "The time
has come to stop sleepwalking towards disaster."

"Should we fall apart over recognizing Quebec as a distinct society, when
every fair-minded Canadian knows that in language and culture it is
distinct? Not better, but different" (*FP*, July 1/92).

The signatures under this editorial were those of J. Douglas Creighton,

CEO and Chairman of the Board, Toronto Sun Publishing Corp., which owns 60 percent of the *Post*; Paul V. Godfrey, President and COO, Toronto Sun Publishing Corp.; and Douglas W. Knight, Acting Publisher, The Financial Post. And, as ever, the piece echoed the same message that the other big three blathered to the public: Quebec is a distinct society — or else!

As for the Charlottetown Accord and Section 121 of the Constitution, which deals with interprovincial trade barriers, one would have thought that at least here the *Post* could shine. Even ministers Don Mazankowski and Michael Wilson were tougher than this editorial, "Pact does little to help economy" (*FP*, July 14/92): "The premiers' unity package is seriously flawed because it does little to remove the damaging interprovincial trade barriers afflicting Canada."

"Does little"? Charlottetown did nothing for the economic union; it only raised the price substantially. That was the problem. At least the BNA Act of 1867 got it right.

The Toronto Sun

By 1993 the *Toronto Sun*, which is owned by the Toronto Sun Publishing Corporation, boasted a circulation of some 846,000. On October 8, 1992, President Ron Osborne of Maclean Hunter, publisher of *Maclean's*,[1] *l'Actualité*, the *Financial Post*, and the *Sun*, said publicly that the corporation would be supporting the Yes side in the Referendum over the Charlottetown Accord. He elaborated that they would do so with their own registered committee: "Editorially we will do our damnedest to ensure there is balanced coverage of the debate. But that does not mean Maclean Hunter corporately could not — or should not — come to a view," said President Ron Osborne (*Sun*, Oct 8/92).

It was almost identical to the position the *Sun*, the *Post*, and *Maclean's* magazine had taken on the Meech Lake Accord.

Taboo topic

Yet the three parties display a united front on Meech Lake. Strange, when they can't agree on anything else — from free trade to the environment.... But we can't let this campaign go by without demanding that all three parties listen to most Canadians who ask only that we all get the same deal. (*Sun*, Oct 11/88)

Not bad, but they didn't mean a word of it, as time would tell.

Lake Woebegone

All parties have dirty linen to conceal on this one. . . . Obviously, since the accord must be ratified by all 10 provinces, it's clear it's not going anywhere for a while.

And that's good news because Meech Lake deserves much more tough-minded and honest scrutiny. As we have pointed out before, the accord has a lot of people in this country troubled. Polls show most are opposed. (*Sun*, Nov 28/88)

"Troubled"? This is an editorial?

And what's that business about "dirty linen to conceal"? What dirty linen? Where was the editorial on that? That's the business of investigative reporting — to bring it out and air it. Let the people decide.

A bit Meech

We maintain the country would be fractured by capitulating to Quebec's demands. Quebec is, by its very nature and heritage, a distinct society.

The strength of that distinctness should be tested within the fabric of a country that treats *equally* every region and minority group.

That would be a measure of our shared strengths. Meech Lake is dealing to our weaknesses. (*Sun*, Mar 1/89)

This time they almost got it right.

Deal savers?

We doubt Canadians feel any euphoria over the deal which may yet save the Meech Lake accord.

Rather, the mood will simply be one of relief if the embattled agreement is ratified before June 23. . . .

If the deal does go through, two big winners will have emerged from the week of secret talks in Ottawa.

The first will be Prime Minister Brian Mulroney. While there were many complaints about the secretive process and high-pressure tactics used by the prime minister, the bottom line in politics is success. . . .

> The second winner will be Ontario Premier David Peterson. . . . By offering six of Ontario's Senate seats to alienated regions of the country at a crucial moment in the stalled talks, Peterson may have set a dangerous precedent, but he may also have saved the deal. (*Sun*, June 11/90)

What a gumpy bit of nonsense. David Peterson's fandango was a good idea because it might have saved the deal? Is that all Canada is, a "deal"? What about the precedent set? What about the future? What about the principles involved? Or were there any?

EEEnough!!!

> We're with those who thought the idea should have been killed at birth. . . . Elected is easy, although the wonder is why anyone in this over-governed land would want *another* elected body. . . . But then we would reform the Senate by killing it. (*Sun*, Jan 28/92)

A Central Canadian solution: Kill the sucker! Same solution as the *Globe*, the *Post*, and the *Star*.

A Yes keeps Canada strong

> What will we tell our children if the No vote wins tomorrow? How will we tell them that the majority of our people said No to the Charlottetown Accord, despite studies that tell us that we may well lose the best quality of life in the world?
>
> That we will no longer be second to the United States in income per person. That we cast aside economic stability, which will add, according to research by the Royal Bank, up to 2.5 million new jobs.
>
> What does No mean ultimately?
>
> According to the bank, too few understand what we have at risk if the country comes apart.
>
> Be sure to vote tomorrow.
>
> And be sure to vote Yes for keeping Canada together [signed J. Douglas Creighton, Chairman and CEO; Paul Godfrey, President; Jim Tighe, Publisher]. (*Sun*, Oct 25/92)

Contrary to the opinion some still hold, that the *Sun* is a small-c conservative tabloid, a right-wing paper, it is not and perhaps never was. In *Sunburned: Memoirs of a Newspaperman*, founder Douglas Creighton describes the paper's editorial policy at its beginning: It was "important to be different from the other two papers [*Globe, Star*]. Policy would be of basic 'independence' and ideologically in the centre — more so than either [the] Globe or Star. . . . It would be the mouthpiece of no group — and certainly not the fashionable 'left' elements of our society" (pp. 90, 91).

That might have been the position of the paper in 1971 when it started, but by the 1990s the *Sun* resembled the *Toronto Star* more than any other newspaper in Canada.

The little paper that once roared could never quite come to grips with the fact that Brian Mulroney did not lead a Conservative Party but a radical and reactionary movement that had nothing to do with Canada's traditions, Conservative or Liberal, NDP or Rhinoceros. The *Sun* always treated Mulroney as some sort of wayward child yet still one of the family and to be treated accordingly.

Over the period 1987 to 1993, *Sun* editorials on the Constitution were consistently uninformative, weak, and shallow. The editorials reflected no passion, no anger, no outrage. Canadians are a people "troubled," not enraged or disgusted. The paper's editorials speak of equality among the collectives, not equality and freedom of the individual.

At the end, having supported the Charlottetown Accord, the *Sun* supported all the Trudeau trappings wrapped up in Meech Lake: multiculturalism, bilingualism, affirmative action, the Charter of Rights and Freedoms, and, of course, the notwithstanding clause.

The Globe and Mail

The *Globe and Mail* does not publish its circulation figures, though it is known to have slipped in 1993 to just over 300,000. In December 1991, an article by Tony Van Alphen in the *Toronto Star* referred to circulation having fallen "to 305,000 from 325,000" (*Star*, Dec 22/91). The *Globe* and the *Financial Post* compete for the same business audience. In 1989, Thomson, who owns the *Globe*, bought the *Financial Times*, a junior rival of the *Post*. The *Financial Times*'s circulation is estimated at around 100,000 and is reported as static.

The distinctiveness of Quebec society

. . . but Quebec, with 25 per cent of the country's population, has the numbers to support French-language culture on a mammoth scale and the power to make Quebeckers generally — those who speak English, those who speak a third language — accept the French fact (that power has been rightly tempered, constitutionally and legislatively, by the provision of services to the English-speaking minority in their own language). (*GM*, Nov 7/89)

Even the National Assembly of Quebec goes further than this in recognizing that, like it or not, constitutionally, English is a legal language in Quebec. Indeed, Quebec does live up to the Constitution of Canada as far as parliamentary reporting goes, because the debates are published in both languages. This is typical of the sell-out journalism that infuriated so many Canadians. "That power has been rightly tempered . . . by the provision of services" et cetera. Zonks!

Ratify the accord

Meech Lake remakes our vows of national union with intelligence and care. Its opponents do not serve Canada in their careless obsession with the status quo. (*GM*, Apr 30/88)

Canadians have been screaming for democracy for two generations. Just try it and see what happens. Typical *Globe and Mail*.

If Meech Lake should fail

The likelihood of further negotiation is slim. . . . If Manitoba and Newfoundland cannot accept its negotiated terms without calling for their effective evisceration, they will have denied Canada its best hope for a long while of securing Quebec's support for the 1982 amendments. (*GM*, Apr 2/90)

Missed the point. Most Canadians outside Quebec rejected Trudeau's Constitution Act of 1982.

Saying yes to an accord that keeps options open

The illusion, a comforting one, is that should the accord fail, a new constitutional negotiating process might then begin in which the many concerns voiced by the accord's opponents can be resolved. . . .
  The promise of Meech Lake is the multitude of options it creates for the

first ministers in developing a new vision of Canada in the years to come. . . .
(*GM*, June 22/90)

Problem: the people didn't want first ministers in the business of "developing a new vision of Canada" at all. This member of the press didn't know what Canadians knew — that of course there would be another round. All Canadians want to be is equal before the law in a participatory democracy.

Two options for Quebec

We strongly supported ratification of the Meech Lake accord between 1987 and 1990 in the conviction that it re-established a healthy balance within the federal system, with a place of honour for Quebec. The Charlottetown accord contains most of what Meech Lake did, and adds some further strength to provincial jurisdictions. From the point of view of Quebec alone, Charlottetown is, in our view, more advantageous to Quebec than Meech. . . . But the interests of Quebeckers as Canadians are also very important. (*GM*, Oct 14/92)

Yes to diversity, Yes to the [Charlottetown] accord

What, then, about the relation of groups — our traditional paradigm?

Pierre Trudeau asked in his 1978 paper *Time for Action, Toward the Renewal of the Canadian Federation*, "Why do we tend to complain about the distinctive character of other Canadians, while clinging so fiercely to our own? Why is it often difficult for us to accept that the institutions and symbols of the federation should accept and celebrate the distinctive characteristics of other Canadians, while insisting that ours be respected and celebrated? . . . There can be no doubt that we are different; but we don't quite know to what extent and in what ways. Thus we fear the imaginary harm which the distinctive features of other Canadians might cause us. . . ."

It is our view, expressed in this column in recent weeks, that the Charlottetown accord maintains a rational balance between individual rights "guaranteed" in the Charter, and the recognitions of Quebec and the aboriginal peoples. In the embrace of the Charter as *individuals* we must not lose sight of the rest of the Constitution and the partnership of *groups* that is also fundamental to Canada. We must navigate the waters of two streams, simultaneously. (*GM*, Oct 22/92)

"Partnership of groups": another endorsement of Trudeau's flat-earth policy of tribalism and the protection of "collectives."

Trudeau never grasped that it was simply enough for Canadians to be proud of being Canadians. In the world of the *Globe and Mail*, there are two streams to be navigated simultaneously. What is missing is the knowledge that the principles of navigation are far more important than the physical geography. Trudeau's world and the world of the *Globe and Mail* are the same — apartheid of the mind.

And note: there's that word again, the buzzword of the eighties and nineties, "the paradigm."

> The trouble — no real surprise here — is money. . . . (*GM*, July 26/93)

Right on! But that's not what they meant. The problem is money all right: too much money spent for too little return.

> [At the prospects of the Bloc Québécois attaining real power in the 1993 federal election:] Federalist parties of every stripe must search their souls at the monster they have created in Quebec. By their hopeless corruption, by their endless cynicism, by their matchless misgovernment over the past twenty-five years, they have driven a substantial portion of the population of Quebec into the arms of a party whose sole mission is to destroy the most favoured nation on earth. (*GM*, Oct 9/93)

Yet Canada's self-styled National Newspaper itself was still pandering to Quebec as the injured party with less than three weeks to go before the federal election. Meanwhile, regional parties are clamouring for control of large chunks of Canada's geography.

The Toronto Star

Toronto Star circulation is variously reported as anywhere between 800,000 and one million, making it by far Canada's largest circulating paper. In 1988 its average circulation was 562,232. A survey published in September 1994 placed the newspaper's readership at 1.4 million — larger than the combined total for the *Sun* and the *Globe*. The *Star* is Canada's leading socialist publication, variously known as the "Red Star of Toronto," the "Red Rag of Toronto," or "King Street Pravda." It is decidedly left of centre and consistently champions the government intervening in all aspects of Canadian life.

Time for Ontario to be bilingual

Yesterday, Premier David Peterson expressed his "regret" that Premier Robert Bourassa trampled the Charter of Rights by banning English from signs and billboards in Quebec.

But rather than bemoan Quebec's oppressive action against its large English-speaking minority, he ought to show the same kind of political leadership that he says is needed to protect minority rights everywhere in Canada.

In other words, it's time for Peterson to end the unnecessary delay and declare Ontario an officially bilingual province. (*Star*, Dec 22/88)

Canada Day: Unity in diversity

Our national values are tolerance, understanding, generosity. When we live up to those essential Canadian ideals, our country earns a reputation for decency.

That's why multiculturalism — respect for diversity — has always been an active yeast in our nationhood. . . .

As the Spicer commission says, "Acceptance of diversity is for Canadians a primary value, even if we honor it more than observe it faithfully." (*Star*, July 1/91)

. . . and bilingualism

Judging from what many Canadians told the Spicer commission, bilingualism is not only wasteful, but also intrusive, divisive and despised. And it is still poorly understood among Canadians.

In fact, previous public opinion polls [not identified] — based on representative samples of Canada's 27 million people — show strong majority support for official bilingualism at the federal level. Yet the vast majority of the 400,000 people who called, wrote, or dropped in on the Citizens' Forum complained bitterly about it.

The commission faithfully reported those findings, but it also put them in their proper context. Bilingualism, it concluded, is a "word with many meanings." . . .

Indeed, official bilingualism enables Canadians to remain as unilingual as they want, precisely because it obliges their government to be bilingual.

That being said, the Forum did not dream up all the criticisms — it was bombarded by them. . . .

But as the Citizens' Forum rightly concludes, the principle of official bilingualism "should command universal acceptance." And for the most part, it does. (*Star*, July 1/91)

From day one, the Pulp Primevil never budged from pushing every single platform and policy that has divided and weakened Canada. The list is endless: bilingualism, multiculturalism, affirmative action, minority rights activism, undisciplined immigration — all regardless of cost. Above all, the *Star* is the goliath newspaper for bigger government — state intervention and a steady growth of socialism at the expense of individual freedom. Its editors are certain the state knows what's best for Canadians in all areas. Any historical researcher would go blind before finding a single instance, over many decades, where this newspaper recommended government get out rather than in. Canada's most predictable newspaper.

Beginning with its editor in 1968 — Peter C. Newman — the *Star* that shoved Pierre Trudeau at the Canadian people so many years ago presses on with the same propaganda.

A deal for Canada but at what cost?

Yet Wells cast aside his "grave doubts" to sign the accord, acknowledging indirectly that the debate was not about words but about the very future of the country.

Like many others, we cannot disagree. Canada must come first, again. (*Star*, June 11/90)

At least they asked a question. Rare.

Quebec needs the guarantees

French-Canadians were one of the two nations at the table 125 years ago. It hardly seems excessive, given the compromises Quebecers have made to allow Westerners an equal Senate, to meet them halfway in 1992. (*Star*, Oct 15/92)

"Two nations at the table 125 years ago"? What table? When a national newspaper demonstrates as little knowledge of Canadian history as this, where do you begin?

What two nations? France and England? Quetario and Ontabec? Oh Canada, Oh Quebec? What hope does the next generation have of understanding Canada when a leading newspaper distorts foundation history like this?

'Yes' for Canada

One of the glaring defects of the Meech Lake accord was that it dealt only with Quebec's aspirations, which led many, including the Star, to vigorously oppose it. It lacked a national vision. . . .

After five years of struggle, we feel Canada has done the best it can and arrived at the best compromise, not unlike the Fathers of Confederation did in 1867.

For these reasons, and above all for the love of Canada, we suggest a Yes vote on Oct. 26. (front-page editorial, Oct 17/92)

The collapse is duly noted. In other words, this paper supported Meech Lake after all — distinct societies and all the trappings. This is exactly what this paper should have supported in the first place: the logical extension of the Trudeau vision.

Quebec deserves 25 per cent share

The Charlottetown accord may be inelegant, but no more so than previous arrangements. . . .

Quebec has made unprecedented concessions to accommodate other regions in this round of negotiations. We should reciprocate in the same spirit. (*Star*, Oct 22/92)

What concessions? Quebec's culture and heritage have been so protected and so successful as a result that the province has been able to entertain notions of nationhood at the expense of what enabled it to flourish in the first place. By this point, even the *Star*'s hero, Pierre Trudeau, had to conclude it was time to stop the blackmail. And coming from him, that was a mighty big concession!

Time of decision for nation's future

We have argued in recent weeks for the Yes side. But we would urge people to vote no matter what their position. (*Star*, Oct 25/92)

So it finally all comes down to this: an urge.

A Canadian who hadn't read a single editorial in thirty years would miss nothing avoiding any of these papers. Those who did read them regularly would have difficulty remembering any particular editorials. None of them contains the piss and vinegar that keeps people on their toes and helps keep democracy alive.

On the other hand, the hundreds of published letters to the editors between the four papers during Meech Lake and the Charlottetown debacles were far more stimulating and enlightening. The letter-writers should have been writing the editorials.

The press in Canada needs a very big dose of H.L. Mencken, the great American curmudgeon yet to be surpassed for his daring and his brilliance as well as his excellent factual reporting:

> In all their dealings with the question of free speech the newspapers of the country, and especially the larger and more powerful ones, have been infinitely pusillanimous, groveling, dishonest and indecent. If, as they now pretend so boldly, their editors and proprietors are actually in favour of Article 1 of the Bill of Rights, then their long acquiescence in its violation proves that they are a herd of poltroons. (*Baltimore Evening Sun*, May 2/22)

As Gore Vidal has recently observed, Mencken's column would have been "banned in Canada" today (Vidal, *United States: Essays, 1952–1992*, p. 763).

Notes

1 *Maclean's* magazine has a circulation of 2.1 million, the largest of any magazine in Canada. Largely through its senior contributing editor Peter C. Newman, *Maclean's* vociferously supported both the Meech Lake Accord and the Charlottetown Accord.

21

Pusillanimous Poltroons and Pecksniffers

T HE JOURNALISTS COVERED the news primarily as chroniclers. Some thought they could also think and analyze, which compounded the problems they caused. Amateur "historians" from the media are necessarily trapped within their particular institutions and the way those bodies think and operate, with their press deadlines.

Andrew Cohen, for example, was a columnist and senior editor of the *Financial Post* during the Meech crisis. His book *A Deal Undone: The Making and Breaking of the Meech Lake Accord*, laudable though it is, contains an index of fewer than six pages and a deficient chronology of events. In the rush to print and publish his book, the author recorded only two events for 1989: the election of Clyde Wells and a failed First Ministers' Conference in Ottawa. He ignored the unprecedented political interference of a governor general in the nation's politics, when Jeanne Sauvé recommended passage of the Meech Lake Accord. He also left out the final passage into law of Ontario's French Language Services Act, Bill 8. He omitted the rise of the Reform Party and the appointment of an "elected" Senator from that party to the Upper House, as well as the "Brockville incident" during which the Quebec flag was stomped on.

A strong sense of self-censorship prevails over Canada. So insidiously has it seeped into society that people now accept it as normal and the owners of large newspapers consider its imposition as "in the public interest."

SOME EIGHTY columnists and other journalists produced articles during the constitutional debates. The selections that follow have been made arbitrarily from 32,000 articles, transcripts, and news reports dating from 1986 to 1993. Some columnists, like Jeffrey Simpson of the *Globe and Mail*, wrote very regularly: he turned out more than a hundred pieces between October 1987 and September 1992. Carol Goar, national affairs columnist at the *Toronto Star*, contributed nearly as much over the same period.

Reporting and analyzing events through special reports or columns were many names well known in the Canadian press: David Crane, business editor, *Toronto Star*; Kevin Dougherty, "Inside Montreal" columnist for the *Financial Post*; Graham Fraser, Parliamentary Bureau, Ottawa, for the *Globe and Mail*; Rhéal Séguin and André Picard, Quebec Bureau, *Globe and Mail*; Hyman Solomon, columnist (since deceased), *Financial Post*; Rosemary Speirs, columnist, *Toronto Star*; Geoffrey Stevens and Edison Stewart, columnists, *Toronto Star*; Michael Valpy and Hugh Winsor, columnists, *Globe and Mail*. At the *Toronto Sun*, the Constitution was not featured as often, but many writers — Bob MacDonald, Peter Worthington, Douglas Fisher, and, later on, Michel Gratton — intermittently took swings at it in print.

Some of the eighty I refer to disappeared after the collapse of the Meech Lake Accord, discredited. Others fell by the wayside after the defeat of the Referendum on the Charlottetown Accord. Newcomers quickly replaced them. Like their predecessors, these became national notables in their own rights, such as Kenneth Whyte, Reform Party aficionado, whose column replaced John Dafoe's at the *Globe and Mail*.

Barbara Amiel writes a column for *The Sunday Times* of London and the *Toronto Sun* from London, England, the country of her birth. Periodically she sends in a column for *Maclean's* magazine, too. She lives with her husband Conrad Black, the man who would be king. She is snappy, to the point, and — praise be — a right-winger with zing. Her kookiest ideas — and there are lots of these — are always worth serious reflection. If nothing else, they always stimulate the brain. For those on the right wing of the political spectrum, she rarely misses the mark:

> If Canada had wanted to remain one nation, the use of French would have been a private matter and never an item of national policy. . . .
> I can't blame Quebec separatists for the wanton stupidity of our language policy. They have always said that bilingualism was not their policy: it was the aim of the Trudeau and Chrétien crowd and the whole sycophantic

following of English liberals who tagged along preaching the joys of immersion courses. (*Maclean's*, July 16/90)

Socialism has brought every country that has had it to its economic knees. . . . It means that the very best people try to leave the country for the United States while business simply bypasses the province, or relocates. (*Maclean's*, Apr 20/92)

Daring to speculate on the eventual collapse of Jean Chrétien's Liberals following his humungous federal election victory in the fall of 1993, Amiel did the old Canadian shuffle: "[And if] the old order would finally crash. . . . In my view, what we would need then are the fiscal and social policies of Preston Manning, the constitutional stance of Pierre Trudeau and the foreign policies of Brian Mulroney" (*Maclean's*, Nov 15/93).

Wha'? "The constitutional stance of Pierre Trudeau"? That's what got us into this pickle in the first place.

Under her byline from Montreal and Quebec City, **Lise Bissonnette**, a doctoral graduate of the University of Strasbourg, was a regular guest columnist with the *Globe and Mail* during Meech. With its collapse imminent, she assumed the position of publisher of the Quebec nationalist paper *Le Devoir* on June 11, 1990.

Henri Bourassa (1868–1952), the Quebec nationalist who founded the Bloc Populaire in 1943 and opposed conscription during the Second World War, co-founded *Le Devoir* in 1910 to "unmask fools and exploiters."[1] He committed the paper — whose name translates as "Duty" — to "awaken in the people, especially the people of the ruling classes, the sentiment of public duty in all its forms."

On August 20, 1993, Bissonnette reported *Le Devoir*'s daily circulation at 31,000, save Saturday's, which reached 38,000. In her *Globe* column of August 14, Lysiane Gagnon of *La Presse* stated that one-half of *Le Devoir*'s circulation was made up of "institutional subscriptions." Bissonnette challenged this, claiming only 1,500 copies of each edition sold to companies or institutions. Bissonnette proudly boasted in the August 14, 1993, *Globe* that *Le Devoir* was "the only independent paper in Canada." *Le Devoir*'s principal competitors are *La Presse* (Power Corporation and Hollinger — who also own *Le Soleil*), with a circulation of 200,000 on weekdays and 300,000 on the weekends, and *Le Journal de Montréal*, which has a slightly larger circulation.

For all the paper's protestations to the contrary, *Le Devoir* is not an independent newspaper. For many reasons, it is invariably in financial trouble and behaves accordingly. It has some very powerful friends. It survives on government advertising, very inexpensive loans through a Government of Quebec agency, the Société de développement industrial (SDI), and many other large vested business and labour interests.

Many people, including its arch enemies, agree the paper is needed, viable or not. Following the failure of the Meech Accord, when *Le Devoir* got into trouble, Royal Orr, president of Alliance Quebec, a federalist who opposed *Le Devoir*'s editorial stance, said, "in a nutshell, *Le Devoir* is no longer committed to French Canada [but rather to Quebec sovereignty]." Many other observers said the same thing in Quebec and the rest of Canada. If the paper had to go, he said, Quebec would lose a "dissenting voice and keeper of its flame" (*GM*, Sept 14/90).

During another major financial upheaval in August of 1993, lawyer Julius Grey, another who once worked against *Le Devoir*'s sovereigntist stand, commented, "If Le Devoir were to close permanently, it would be a terrible loss to thinking people in Canada, whether they agree with the paper's editorial positions or not" (*Star*, Aug 8/93).

All of which puts *Le Devoir* in an enviable position. No certain death for this paper. Robert Bourassa's government needed *Le Devoir* for leverage against the federal government. The separatists, of course, have always been delighted to have Thor's hammer subsidized by the taxpayer. As for Quebec's labour movement, the big unions supported *Le Devoir*, even when the paper's actions in August of 1993 amounted to nothing more than an illegal lock-out to win brutal concessions from *Le Devoir*'s employees. No matter what *Le Devoir* does, everybody winks. It is a corporate loser even its enemies love. So Canadian — dissent under state management.

Like many Quebec journalists who speak out, Bissonnette has more heart and spirit than the whole cabal of soporific paper-pushers in English-speaking Canada. She's a fighter, more Canadian than 95 percent of them. She can be fiendish, feisty, friendly, full of prunes and common sense all at once, but never dull. She leads with emotion. Thank God someone does! But beware of the magic. First and foremost, she's a Quebec nationalist. Whatever side she's on, and there are many, Bissonnette can lose an audience in a micro-second.

Her most famous editorial on the Constitution was her succinct rejection of the July 7, 1992, "Pearson accord." On the day that Robert Bourassa made positive noises about the interim consensus, *Le Devoir* printed a one-word editorial in huge block letters across the column space — "NON" (July 9/92). The *Globe and Mail*'s editorial on Canada Day, July 1, in response to this cannonball was not half as good: "NONsense." Bisson-nette says what she means. And she is never at a loss for words. She's a conditional separatist with the occasional hint of a federalist leaning when it proves pragmatic to have one.

[On the "distinct society" concept:] An unpredictable monster. It is a confused and confusing notion, generating some of the silliest discussions this country has ever endured. (*GM*, Nov 4/89)

[On Meech Lake:] Why not a pan-Canadian referendum on the ratification of the Meech Lake constitutional accord? (*GM*, Dec 2/89)

[On herself:] Quebec is my country. There is no doubt about that. I feel a sort of relationship with Canada, but I don't belong. (Nash, *Visions of Canada*, p. 101)

[On the merits of the struggle:] The day Quebec ceases wanting more, when there is no more tension with Canada, will be the day when the peace of the cemetery comes. (*Maclean's*, Oct 5/92, on *Le Devoir*, Oct 2/92)

Peter Brimelow is a senior editor with *Forbes* magazine in New York. He is also the author of a best-selling work on Canadian politics, *The Patriot Game* (1986, 1989). During the Meech debate, the Brit expatriate, writing as a weekly columnist for the *Financial Post*, contributed a number of articles on the Quebec–Canada question. By 1992 he was thoroughly bored with the whole Canadian navel-gazing exercise.

Brimelow is a conservative. He contends that "English Canada and the U.S. are a cultural unity" (FP, Oct 17/89) where "the Quebec issue in Canadian politics may become not whether Quebec will secede — but whether it should be expelled" (*Patriot Game*, 1986, p. 288). "And it is anglophones, not the francophones, who are the colonized group in the Canada devised by Pierre Trudeau," Brimelow writes (*FP*, July 24, 1990).

"The Treauvian [Trudeau] fantasy of Canada as a bilingual, bicultural nation . . . will be seen by history as an attempt to treat the country as a sort of Greater Quebec," he states (*FP*, Aug 15/89).

He dismisses Mulroney as a lightweight grovelling for scraps on the fringes of Quebec politics — a weakling guilty of "unacceptable pandering to French delusions." Accordingly, the ultimate threat to English Canada is not the "sturdy francophones," or even "transitional political trivia like Mulroney, but its own degenerate intellectuals" (*FP*, Aug 15/89).

At the end of 1989, he wrote, "Quebec was emerging as a nation-state on the European model; the rest of Canada is going to draw the appropriate conclusions; the anglophones in Quebec are going to have to fend for themselves" (*FP*, Sept 26/89). During the Meech Lake debate he also pointed out that U.S. politicians have been slow to react to the Canadian reality. This time he was a bit precipitous, I am afraid. But that's Brimelow. Love him: he left you. Brimelow and Conrad Black think alike but use different vocabularies.

Ted Byfield is perhaps the best-known publisher and newspaper man of the West. When the socialist and noted agnostic historian Pierre Berton was commissioned by the Anglican Church of Canada to write *The Comfortable Pew* (1965), Byfield, a Christian teacher, published a fundamentalist diatribe of his own, reflecting the other point of view, *Just Think, Mr. Berton (A Little Harder)* (1965). Byfield is one of the founders of the Reform Party of Canada. He is the author of that famous slogan: "The West Wants In." And he is also founder of the West's most influential magazine — a sort of *Maclean's* magazine in cowboy boots — *Alberta Report* cum *Western Report*. *Western Report* has a circulation list of 250,000. He also wrote the introduction to *Act of Faith*, a big expensive soft-cover magazine book, subtitled *The Illustrated Chronicle of the Reform Party of Canada*. He is not known for pulling his punches:

> Many westerners have reached two definite conclusions on the Constitution, from which Ottawa will have grave difficulty shaking them.
>
> First, the "distinct society." . . . They believe this could be used by Quebec to gain all kinds of exclusive economic privilege. . . . Second, [the most dangerous conclusion is that] westerners will demand the right to vote on any constitutional amendment. (*FP*, Nov 18/91)

> What makes the prospect of referendums so dangerous is the mounting evidence that the people in ROC [Rest of Canada] have concluded the eventual departure of Quebec is not only certain, but probably fair, just and a good thing. They aren't angry about it. They see it as consistent with the principle of self-determination. (*Western Report*, Apr 6/92)

> Remember, apart from this magazine and the few other independent voices, we have no media. Our Toronto-owned newspapers assure us they see things from the "national" viewpoint, meaning always the Toronto–Montreal one. (*Western Report*, Apr 27/92)

Dalton Kingsley Camp, author, political advisor, commentator, and columnist, was the Mulroney government's Senior Advisor to the Cabinet from 1986 to 1988. Long before that, he made a name for himself as the backroom rebel Tory who engineered the political assassination of Prime Minister John Diefenbaker (1957–63). Mulroney's appointment of Camp to the level and pay of an assistant deputy minister made even the *Globe and Mail* puke: "Mr. Mulroney has sanctioned the flagrant politicization of the Canadian civil service" (*GM*, Aug 27/86).

The acknowledged king of the Red Tories published his columns in the *Toronto Star* — where else?

> When the Liberals chose John Turner, I had urged them to pick Chretien. When they next chose Chretien, I had recommended Paul Martin Jr. This time, my choice would be Sheila Copps but I dare say the delegates will settle on someone else. (*Star*, Feb 16/92)

> The idea of Senate reform, for many reformers, is to create a second elected body to diminish the authority and powers of the House of Commons. To do so is, in other words, to shift the burden of responsibility from the Commons, where government governs, to some undefined authority, somehow elected, and uniquely endowed. This is not the way the British have chosen, but it has become the Canadian choice.
>
> It is, so to speak, the way to go for admirers of the American system even while becoming, before our own eyes, less a democracy than a plutocracy, less to be envied than pitied. This may make sense to Premiers Getty and Wells; it makes none to me and John Major. (*Star*, Apr 15/92)

> If the Tories squander their opportunities — such as they are — on the folly of ideological debate, the party will not live out this century. (*Star*, Aug 21/94)

Camp is the great oracle — after the fact. The most amazing fact about him, however, is that he was tolerated in the Conservative camp. Like Trudeau, he studied under the socialist guru Harold Laski at the London School of Economics. Real conservatives don't do the London School of Economics.

During Meech Lake, **Ron Collister** often pinch-hit for regular *Sun* columnists on vacation. The Edmonton journalist and broadcaster became one of the intermittent but steady voices from the West:

The separatist spectre has passed. Instead, surveys show the interests of most Quebecers are the same as they are for most Canadians: Jobs and prosperity. (*Sun*, Apr 13/88)

It is truly an amazing story, from the unity of 1967 and our 100th birthday — to now.

It is a trail of indifference, political opportunism to win elections, and total insensitivity to the principle that all Canadians, inside and outside Quebec, are entitled to shape the community of their choice. (*Sun*, Jan 5/92)

As contributing editor and the assistant editorial page editor of the *Financial Post* during Meech, **Andrew Coyne** (not be confused with Andrew Cohen) wrote frequently about Canada's constitutional upheaval. He is a follower of Pierre Trudeau. Like a passionate puppy, he swallows everything Trudeau fed Canadians with such enthusiasm that he almost makes you believe there's some intelligent thinking going on. He's related to another Trudovnic, Deborah Coyne. After the Meech mess, he joined the editorial board of the *Globe and Mail*. He's been buried there ever since: "If Canada dies, it will be the first nation to perish because it could not think why it should survive" (*FP*, Nov 8/89).

For the July 1989 *Saturday Night*, he posed a thesis on the merits of "connection" as opposed to "identity" as a means of holding a nation together. Four months later he pushed his weird concept a second time: "The fatal weakness of Canadian nationalism lies in its emphasis on identity over connection. American nationalism is more solidly based because in connection it has developed a more appropriate basis of nationhood for a diverse New World country" (*FP*, Nov 8/89).

His solution for Canada appears in an article for the *Post* entitled, "Bilingualism elsewhere would reassure Quebec": "To keep [Trudeau's] promise of a decade ago [of renewed federalism], we need not less, but more" (*FP*, Jan 3/90). If all else fails, he writes, to avoid the breakup of Canada "there must be real barriers — psychological, procedural, economic — to separation. If the prospect is to *deter*, it should be messy. . . . Whatever change comes to Canada will be on Canada's terms" (*FP*, June 28/90).

In May 1991, he joined the academic lemmings attending a symposium at McGill University to worship Pierre Trudeau:

What I want to argue, in contradiction to the latter view of the nation, is that ultimately the individual and humanity at large (the two ends of the spectrum) are the only real valid units of humanity, and only valid because they exist independently of those who make them up. The group, the nation, are simply states of mind. They only exist because we decide they will, but individuals and humanity exist independently of that. Moreover, whatever differences there may be between groups are infinitesimal compared to their filial likeness in the family of man, and whatever similarities there are between members of the group that identify them as a group are infinitesimal, again in comparison to their differences as unique individuals. Yet to read our public debates in the newspapers each day, one would think that the only unit that counts is the group, the ethnic group, the national group, the regional group, or what-have-you. (*Federalism in Peril*, p. 42)

Piffle. Following the collapse of Charlottetown, Coyne shifted from the far left to the centre. By 1994, the media firmly labelled him a conservative thinker.

Susan Delacourt made the mistake of many journalists before her and decided to write history. The reporter who covered so much so well during the debate blows it on the media, misinterprets David Peterson's arrogance, and completely shoots past the point of the Senate. She is overwhelmingly preoccupied with affirmative action. In *United We Fall*, she reveals all — about herself, not the Constitution. Three samples:

The problem [with the Referendum], though, was the media did not have any experience with covering a not-election. (p. 81)

Peterson's real mistake was not in giving up the Senate seats. It was in appearing far too cosy with Brian Mulroney and Robert Bourassa. (p. 115)

And it was the Senate debate that set the stage for Canadians to talk about their dreams of equality. Equality would be a notion that resonated through the referendum later, in the rhetoric of everyone from the women's groups to former prime minister Pierre Trudeau. The new Senate was supposed to embrace and enshrine the new Canadian penchant for equality. (p. 261)

What to make of Susan Delacourt? Beats me.

Alain Dubuc is the editor-in-chief of Montreal's *La Presse*. He was also the other half of that never-ending exchange of viewpoints between himself and the editor of the *Toronto Star*, John Honderich. For months on end during the constitutional debate and periodically thereafter, these two played Tweedle-Dum and Tweedle-Dee, copying the format of the Daniel Latouche–Philip Resnick exchange. What a giggle:

If there is something truly Canadian, and much more important than a flag or an anthem, it's tolerance. . . .

. . . The . . . fact [is] that since Canada could not distinguish itself by language, military or economic achievements, it's probably the only country in the world whose soul lies in government programs — medicare, unemployment insurance and so on. This introduces a lot of rigidity, since countries are built by people, not by bureaucrats or politicians.

So, yes, we can accept the fact that there is a Canadian soul. But it would help a lot if you tried to explain it to us, bring us [Quebecers] to share it. And if you trusted yourself a little more. . . .

In the end, English Canadians and French Quebecers suffer from the same insecurity, which creates a lot of problems. (*Star*, May 18/91)

There was no popular consultation on repatriation of the Constitution, on the Charter or on the 1982 amendments. And nobody complained. People suddenly woke up, not because they disagreed on the process, but because they hated the nature of the deal. (*Star*, Nov 23/91)

Milt Dunnell, the *Star* sportswriter, contributed a more amusing two cents' worth than most: "Sooner or later, [Jacques Parizeau] will have to tell the faithful what new name he has in mind for the Montreal Canadiens, frequently identified in foreign dispatches as the aristocrats of professional hockey. . . . He must have something in mind — like *Le Club de Hockey Parti Quebecois*" (*Star*, May 26/90).

Former MP and Deputy House Leader of the NDP and broadcaster **Douglas Mason Fisher** is a political columnist with the *Toronto Sun* who reported from the Parliamentary Press Gallery in Ottawa. Known for lousy political forecasting, he nevertheless frequently writes something of substance — which is more than can be said of 99 percent of the scribes in the country:

Essentially, although French Canadians didn't win "the battle of the cradle," they've won their vision of Quebec in Canada. The rest of us shouldn't choke on it but soldier on because the segmented whole is still of marvellous worth, particularly over what others elsewhere have. (*Sun*, June 7/87)

The idealists are pushing bilingualism again. . . . And so, be patient with official bilingualism. Bilingualism itself is a long, losing cause. (*Sun*, Feb 21/88)

Well, a month ago it seemed to me the odds against Canada hanging together into the 21st century were 4–1. Now [as a result of Meech II] I would drop the odds to 2–1. (*Sun*, Sept 25/91)

Allan Fotheringham, the weekly columnist for *Maclean's*, is also published in the *Toronto Sun* and the *Financial Post*. "Dr. Foth" is known throughout Canada for his timely quips, devastating word caricatures and occasionally for getting himself into hot water. The man who coined the "wimp factor" phrase for Joe Clark and dubbed Brian Mulroney "the jaw that walks like a man" was described by *Maclean's* in 1989 as a "sit-down comedian." The Foth is an anti-monarchist republican. Like Douglas Fisher of the *Toronto Sun*, he's most amusing when running wild with his wacko predictions about Canada's future:

The standard line on [Premier] Don Getty [of Alberta] . . . is that he played too many football games without his helmet. (*Sun*, Nov 12/89)

Bill Vander Zalm [Premier of B.C.] the Metternich of Lotus-land . . . Vander Zalmian genius is to call every province a distinct society. (*FP*, Jan 25/90)

[Robert Bourassa] was a number cruncher before he became a Napoleon. (*FP*, Apr 26/90)

Meech was a dumb deal from the start . . . done in secret by a prime minister who is not a leader but a labor negotiator — it never was understood or accepted by a suspicious public. (*Sun*, June 18/90)

[Reform Party Leader Preston Manning:] The man who is milking this public frustration of course is Presto! Manning with his instant solutions to all our ills. His Reform Party panacea is ludicrous naturally: his recipe for salvation is to run candidates everywhere but in Quebec, which in effect is to pretend that Quebec does not exist. (*FP*, Nov 19/91)

[Norman Spector:] the secretive and lonesome bachelor who is known as Dr. Death. (*FP*, Dec 16/91)

Midgets? We have got them by the bushel. . . .

A midget who walks in sheep's clothing is our friend Presto!, who has been stealthily trodding [*sic*] the suburban pastures outside Toronto this week, seeking support from people with soft minds who find him the new messiah. (*FP*, Jan 27/92)

The basis [of Canada] is that it was founded on the agreement of two languages and that understanding can't be abandoned now. Thank you, Don Getty, for your help. (*FP*, Feb 13/92)

Canadians are sick and tired, up to the gunnels, with the wrangling and legal nit-picking among the 11 guys, almost every one of them being a lawyer — one of the exceptions, Don Getty, being a quarterback — and lawyers as we know being famous for being able to pick fly droppings out of rice while wearing boxing gloves. . . .

Being sick of the whole mess, the last thing Canadians need is a raucous, bitter referendum battle that can only undo what we thought, as of last week's triumphant cries, was a done deal. (*Sun*, Aug 30/92)

Diane Marie Francis — predictable, lovable — a splendid read. Problem: she is embarrassingly uninformed about Canadian history. She happily spews forth contradictory advice on all the issues with careless abandon. Unwittingly, this conservative often supports Red Tories.

Apart from her career as a columnist and then, as of June 4, 1991, as editor of the *Financial Post*, she spoke on radio and television regularly. At one point, it was reported that she writes fifteen columns a month for the *Post*, the *Toronto Sun*, and *Maclean's*, and makes 300 radio and TV appearances a year — usually on CBC Radio's "Morningside," Toronto's radio station CFRB, or CBC TV's "The Journal." In 1991, her income as a pundit was reported in the range of $400,000.

Commenting on her promotion to the top position at the *Financial Post*, the paper itself announced, "Ms. Francis will no longer look at the 'scam of the week' in her new column . . . but rather she'll write on such issues as national unity and the opportunities that Canada has brought to her and her family. Ms. Francis was born in Illinois and moved to Canada 24 years ago" (*GM*, June 5/91).

Quebec has already separated, but the rest of us haven't quite realized it yet.

This is because French Canadians in Quebec, no matter what their political stripe, regard themselves as a nation-race. And they are. By contrast, Canada's other founding race, British North Americans, have been diluted to a small minority elsewhere in Canada, replaced since the war by immigrants with allegiances to dozens of differing multicultural identities. . . .

In effect, Canadians must realize that Quebec is already a nation within our nation. (*Sun*, June 18/89)

By the way, I'd just like to say I'm in favor of Meech Lake. Not because it is an enlightened policy, but because the most important provinces have signed and Quebec wants it. And if Quebec doesn't get it there's hell to pay and I happen to think the country works just fine as it is. (*Sun*, Apr 22/90)

It upsets me there is not more understanding of the potentially disastrous economic consequences stemming from the Meech Lake Accord. . . .

I believe Meech must be ratified. There is no choice. I believe that without Meech, Canada will become five separate countries. (*FP*, May 7/90)

I happen to think that Brian Mulroney has been a good prime minister. . . . He has nothing to be ashamed of. He must show Canadians that he has the courage of his convictions. . . . (*Maclean's*, Aug 5/91)

English Canada must accept the fact that . . . Quebec has a right to protect its French language and culture. The quid pro quo, however, is that Quebec must back down from its deplorable sign bylaw restriction and otherwise pledge never to trample the linguistic rights of anglophones. (*FP*, Jan 6/92)

So Canada remains an uneasy coalition of two linguistic groups, one secure and another tenuous and threatened with extinction. That's why the suggestion by Alberta Premier Don Getty and by the Reform Party that the act should be scrapped and replaced by "bilingualism by choice, not law" must be rejected. No one is forced to speak either official language and if the coalition is to continue, the public must have access to its federal government in either language. (*FP*, Jan 14/92)

And, in my opinion, there are only two acceptable outcomes to this referendum, in terms of what will be the least damaging economically. First choice is a whopping Yes outcome across the country without exception. Second choice is a resounding No across the country. A mixed result is a disaster.

A Yes means stability, and unity is bullish. A big, fat No by all Canadians means a rejection of the deal itself, not rejection of this or that part of the country. A No should force politicians back to the drawing boards or out of office. (*FP*, Oct 13/92)

The October referendum rejecting the Charlottetown accord finally ended the dangerous drift toward collective rights versus individual rights. . . .

The referendum's outcome was crystal clear and settles things for years. The West, and most of the country, said No to special status for Quebec in the form of guaranteed seats, No to special status for natives, No to Senate reform and No to the rigor mortis which would have resulted from universal vetoes. (*FP*, Jan 2–4/93)

Lysianne Gagnon, political columnist with *La Presse* in Montreal since 1980, took over as the *Globe*'s voice "Inside Quebec" following the departure of Lise Bissonnette in June 1990. Gagnon has more medals than a general for her journalism. By any standard she's a gifted and knowledgeable writer. During the constitutional debate she contributed more than one hundred columns.

The other, more compelling reason for Quebeckers to think of themselves as a distinct people is language. This is the great dividing line. . . .

It is not only a question of language. Even if one is fluently bilingual, the cultural references are different. . . . [Quebec is] a society with a set of distinct institutions, its own literature, its own soaps and stars, a society where Molière is better known than Shakespeare and where kids read *Le Petit Prince* instead of *Alice in Wonderland*. (*GM*, Aug 24/91)

One thing to remember: The ancestors of many French-Canadians were from Normandy and Norman peasants are shrewd and cautious. Whatever the question, they won't answer "yes" or "no," but rather "maybe yes, maybe no." It is, one should note, a typically Canadian attitude. (*GM*, Oct 5/91)

As for Mr. [Marcel] Masse, he is a man used to compromising his principles. In the late '60s, he was a cabinet minister in Quebec's Union Nationale government. . . . I remember covering a small demonstration of *independantiste* activists who were picketing. . . . Mr. Masse stepped down, grinned at the demonstrators and raised his fist like a sports fan encouraging his team: "Keep up the good fight!" he said. Then he went inside to perform his ministerial duties.

The young demonstrators knew he was a "closet sovereigntist." They were sure it was only a question of months before he would join the *independantiste* movement. This was more than 20 years ago. Mr. Masse is still a closet sovereigntist — and still a cabinet minister. What's new? (*GM*, Mar 14/92)

[The Allaire Report is] nothing short of a blueprint for sovereignty-association. (*Maclean's*, Apr 6/92)

If Joe Clark were publisher of a daily newspaper, it would soon become a weekly, then a monthly magazine, before going bankrupt. (*GM*, June 13/92)

The Ottawa Bureau chief of the *Globe and Mail*, **Graham Blair Fraser**, is Mr. Steadfast. A must for balanced insight:

But there is a difference today. The impatience in Quebec does not seem to be coming from the traditional sources of discontent — the labor movement, universities, intellectuals and the left. Instead, it can be found in the business community, entrepreneurs and the aspiring middle class. (*GM*, July 31/89)

In 1969, when Mr. Trudeau was prime minister, the Official Languages Act was introduced, proclaiming equality for English and French in all operations of federal institutions. However, the government did not implement one of the commission's major recommendations, the creation of bilingual districts, instead favouring universal accessibility to service in both languages. (*GM*, June 27/91)

Carol Goar is the national affairs columnist for the *Toronto Star*. From a tonne of opinion came nothing offensive — and nothing very memorable.

No one questions that Canada is a bilingual nation. It is deciding how much power the federal government should have to promote this "linguistic duality" that causes the headaches. (*Star*, May 26/90)

We need not be trapped by an unworkable constitution and an unresponsive government. Democracy was designed to surmount such obstacles. (*Star*, Dec 27/90)

Ottawa — No one acknowledges it, but there is a small club of academics and bureaucrats that sets the constitutional agenda for the rest of Canada.

There are no official entry rules, but Queen's University is the favored training ground. It helps to have been involved in the travails which produced the 1982 Constitution. And preference is given to those who actively promoted the Meech Lake accord. (*Star*, Apr 18/91)

A constituent assembly is, in many ways, a Band-Aid. What Canadians have to decide is whether Band-Aids promote healing or hide festering abrasions. (*Star*, Apr 30/91)

Keith Spicer delivered what he promised: honesty, flashes of poetry and practical advice for a nation in crisis. (*Star*, June 28/91)

The Charlottetown accord is not a blueprint for a happy, prosperous Canada. It is not a safeguard against a new outbreak of separatism in Quebec. It is not even a visionary document. But it allows us to climb out of one of the deepest, most destructive ruts in our history. We just have to say Yes for a change. (*Star*, Oct 18/92)

Philosopher and historian Dr. **John Ferguson Godfrey**, formerly president of King's College in Halifax, became editor of the *Financial Post* in 1987, before Diane Francis. During the Meech debate, he contributed numerous articles. After its collapse in June 1990, he launched "The New Canada Project" on February 13, 1991, a non-government initiative to foster public debate about Canada's constitutional future. On June 4, 1991, Diane Francis replaced him as the *Post*'s editor. Godfrey was one of the delegates selected for the first federal Renewal Conference held in Halifax in January 1992. In the 1993 federal election he was elected as the Liberal member of Parliament for Don Valley West.

So many words, so little heft:

One thing is certain: should the agreement pass, the courts will be tied up for years interpreting what it means. . . . The current agreement will almost certainly guarantee constitutional stasis for some considerable time. . . . Passage of the Meech Lake Accord is probably the preferred solution from the standpoint of national unity. (*FP*, Jan 29/90)

Newfoundland premier Clyde Wells is a constitutional lawyer. He is also a man of stern conviction. The only things he lacks are consistency, common sense and political savvy, unless he is playing a very subtle game indeed by announcing his intention this past week of revoking Newfoundland's ratification of the Meech Lake Accord. . . .

At what point is a deal a deal? . . .

The burden of history rests heavily on his shoulders. (*FP*, Mar 12/90)

Richard John Philip Jermy Gwyn is the international affairs columnist for the *Toronto Star*. His writings on the Constitution followed the collapse of Meech, which, in a February 12, 1992, piece, he's on record for not supporting. Some sermons from the renowned socialist:

To be a Canadian has always been to live risk-free, virtually. Easy affluence, because of our natural resources. Lots of social support programs. No risk of invasion.

Suddenly, all of this has gone. . . . Quebec *is* a "distinct society." Despite Pierre Trudeau, who is being either aridly intellectual or simply old-fashioned, Quebec is not, obviously, a province like the others. It is going to become ever more distinct — or sovereign — whether Meech is passed or not. (*Star*, Apr 6/90)

A society of scarcely 27 million able to produce four of the best novelists in the world [Atwood, Davies, Munro, Richler] — all writing in a distinctively Canadian tone — is a society that has the stuff it takes to survive. (*Star*, July 3/91)

Quebec's ascent to sovereignty in some form or other is sufficiently probable that the rest of Canada must now set out to define its own sovereignty. . . .

To voice such a thought is treasonable to national unity as conventionally defined. But to suppress it is a form of treason to the 20 million or so Canadians outside Quebec. . . . (in Granatstein, *"English Canada" Speaks Out*, p. 374)

Far more important than the rejection of the constitutional changes tomorrow — unless all the polls are scandalously wrong — will be the rejection by Canadians of their governing class and political elite.

It amounts to a revolution, or as close to one as we're ever likely to get within the sedate compass of a society traditionally deferential to authority, from mainstream politicians to officials to lawyers to academics to business leaders to bankers. . . .

We could be on the cusp of chaos. Even those replacing the traditional elites are being rejected. (*Star*, Oct 25/92)

Since we aren't a nation, we have no national identity. We do, though, have a national character: The distinctly Canadian values of civility and tolerance define and regulate much of our public behaviour.

Instead, our distinctive identity is that, in a world where nations are defined increasingly by their ethnicity, we, uniquely, are world citizens. (*Star*, July 14/93)

All Canadians are no longer all Canadians. The one is a black, female, Somali Canadian, say. The other is a white, homosexual, Greek Canadian, say.

Since all Canadians are different, our law has to treat them differently. It has to try to make them all equal by treating them unequally.

In the specific instance of racism, and also of sexual harassment, the law can only do this by transferring the burden of proof. (*Star*, July 18/93)

Michele Landsberg writes for the *Toronto Star*. She is married to the terminally unhappy Stephen Lewis, Mulroney's NDP buddy who was appointed ambassador to the United Nations:

Everything about the Canada of my childhood was prissy, ungenerous, xenophobic, pallid, and conformist. (in Laurier LaPierre, *If You Love This Country*, p. 52)

Somewhere along the path of the past decade or so in the women's movement, it stopped looking normal to me to see 11 men [first ministers at the conference in Ottawa on June 9, 1990] on a platform and not a single woman in sight. . . .

There's surely never been an occasion so soaked in male bonding. (*Star*, June 12/90)

Gary Lautens, the beloved humorist, wrote for the *Toronto Star*. He died on February 1, 1992:

What I wish.

I wish a French-speaking Quebecer would stand up and say he wants to be a Canadian. . . .

If it [Quebec] stays silent, all the Meech Lake accords in this world won't save this nation. (*Star*, Apr 11/92)

But the bottom line is this: Quebec is talking about an open marriage, one that doesn't require fidelity, only help paying the household bills.

Brian says it's all right.

I hate to break the news but Brian's been wrong before. (*Star*, June 1/90)

Maybe it's time to think the unthinkable.

That Quebec should go. . . .

Just don't send Neville (The Big Guy) Peterson to negotiate the divorce. He'll come back shirtless, waving an umbrella, and tell us he's done it — again. (*Star*, June 13/90)

Robert (Bob) MacDonald's column appears in the *Toronto Sun*:

[Memories of school days:] We were lined up outdoors to face the school's flag — the colorful Canadian Ensign, a proud banner under which Canadian troops fought, bled and died in two world wars. We would sing God Save the King (George) and O Canada — and really put our hearts and throats into that blood-racing phrase, "The True North Strong and Free!"

. . . We were healthy, robust children and proud Canadians. To us, our big, free nation was the greatest country in the world. (*Sun*, May 20/90)

When it comes to forced bilingualism and multiculturalism, the emperor wears no clothes.

Both programs were arrogantly imposed in the first place by the most arrogant prime minister Canada ever had — Pierre Elliott Trudeau. (*Sun*, Jan 12/92)

Mulroney now talks tough against Quebec separating. Yet he keeps this peacock spendthrift Masse, despite his longstanding efforts to help Quebec separate — while milking Canada's taxpayers. (*Sun*, Apr 5/92)

There's widespread hostility to the very expensive, hostility-producing, ineffectual official bilingualism program. But — probably because then Liberal PM Pierre Trudeau made Spicer Canada's first language commissioner — the Forum made no recommendation to scrap this foolishness. Instead, it recommended an "independent" review. (*Sun*, June 28/91)

The same Mulroney and his Red Tory cabinet like the vote-buying capabilities of multicultural grants — yep, they even created the department. Also, insiders say there's no way Mulroney would sell the costly, leftist CBC. (*Sun*, Aug 11/91)

Whether the [Charlottetown] referendum passes or fails, Quebec will still be demanding more powers and federal dough in years to come. Quebec will never allow the rest of Canada to separate. Quebecers are not fools and they know a golden goose when they see one. (*Sun*, Sept 9/92)

Robert McKenzie is the *Toronto Star*'s Quebec bureau chief. As a journalist, on-site reporter, and regularly featured columnist during the great constitutional debate over Meech Lake, he provided readers with one of the larger written inventories of the goings-on — more than 200 reports and columns. It is from him that English-speaking readers derived much of their knowledge about the individual players in Quebec.

The real Bourassa stands on expediency, not principle. His horizon is the next poll, not the grand sweep of history. Bourassa-watchers run out of adjectives to describe him: sinuous, oblique, porous, undulating. Or comparisons with the animal world: chameleon, eel, crab (it advances by walking sideways). (*Star*, July 14/92)

Vintage Bourassa. He's for Canada as long as it suits Quebec's needs. He's for federalism as long as sovereignty doesn't become overwhelmingly popular. And he's for this deal for as long as it doesn't become unstuck. (*Star*, Aug 29/92)

Maclean's magazine's senior contributing editor was a latecomer to the constitutional debate on Meech Lake. **Peter Charles Newman**'s interest peaked at the collapse of the accord and the loss of power it represented to his prince of the moment, Brian Mulroney. Newman is a conventional thinker. He holds to no particular philosophy beyond pragmatism. He is the colossus of Canadian political journalism. He happily endorses the winners when they are on the up and up and stomps with relish on those out of favour who do not serve him. His role in the destruction of Canadian nationalism, conservatism, and Canadian tradition is immense and dates back more than three decades. In 1963 he published *Renegade in Power: The Diefenbaker Years*. This polemic did much to terminally infect the Conservative Party with a death wish.[2] He writes of John Diefenbaker:

The philosophy of John Diefenbaker was by no means a consciously contrived creed. It was a cast of mind, lacking coherent and continuing expression even in his own speeches. . . . The philosophy that has to be called "Diefenbakerism" amounted, in essence, to a distrust of the great power groupings in contemporary Canada and the belief that broadly based citizenship participation, speaking through a strong political leader, can reconcile the opposing economic interests of individual citizens. (pp. 179–80)

In Newman's formative years he was one of the key architects of "Trudeaumania": "I thought bilingualism was wonderful for Canada because, first of all, it was a great act of generosity by the rest of Canada to Quebec saying 'Hey, we really want you to stay and we're gonna twist our Scottish tongue around those damned irregular verbs of yours just to make sure you stay'" ("The Originals," City TV, Apr 16/93).

He has always played at the centre of power. He wrote as national affairs editor for *Maclean's* from 1956 to 1964. In 1969 he was appointed editor-in-chief of the *Toronto Star*, the newspaper credited with having brought Trudeau to power. In 1971 he was appointed editor of *Maclean's* magazine. In that revealing interview with Moses Znaimer on "The Originals" aired on City TV on April 16, 1993, he let it all hang out:

I was, and am, always the outsider. . . . And being the outsider means you have certain privileges. The privileges are that you are the passionate observer. . . . I was always being the fellow with the — pressing my nose against the window looking in. It does give you some disadvantages because you're not part of any group. You're outside all those groups that you're writing about, all those groups that you should be part of.

. . . And you take the chance of being ignored, of being left out, being attacked, being ridiculed. So the important thing is first of all to anchor yourself in some institution which is in the mainstream, and I've always done that. I've been with Maclean Hunter now for thirty-three years. I have been — I was with the *Toronto Star* for quite a while and I've, I've always been careful to not temper my attacks but to launch my attacks from a firm platform, and I don't apologize for that.

[On the banks:] The Big Five chartered banks, once run by capable buddhas whom we treated as our fiscal father confessors, turn out to be self-deluded dunderheads who lent money to marginal characters like the Reichmann brothers, without even glancing at their balance sheets. (*Maclean's*, Sept 13/93)

This is not quite the same enthusiasm he mustered when writing about Allan Taylor before he was on the way out as chairman and CEO of the Royal Bank and a captain on the Mulroney constitutional team:

> There's something very Canadian and very solid about this man and his crusade. . . .
> But he knows the details of how economically devastating such a move [Quebec separation] would be. And he's frightened. We should be, too. (*Maclean's*, Jan 27/92)

The real question is: who should Canadians fear the most — the elites or themselves? Here's more Newman on other matters:

> Despite the threats and counterthreats, the Meech Lake accord remains essential to the future of this country, if only because Quebec will never again demand less to remain within Confederation. (*Maclean's*, Oct 9/89)

> [The distinct society clause] is a historically rooted description of one of Canada's founding societies.[3] (*Maclean's*, Feb 12/90)

> Yet, reduced to its fundamentals, the [Meech Lake] accord is a fairly mundane document, merely cleaning up the mess left over from Pierre Trudeau's 1982 constitutional patriation move, which left Quebec out in the cold. (*Maclean's*, Apr 16/90)

> But the real culprit has to be Pierre Trudeau. . . . It was Trudeau who gave his solemn pledge during the 1980 referendum that Quebec would be granted a "renewed federalism," then patriated the Constitution without Quebec's consent or participation.[4] (*Maclean's*, July 9/90)

> The vanity of Pierre Trudeau, the weakness of Jean Chrétien and the malice of Clyde Wells have placed the future of this country in permanent jeopardy. (*Maclean's*, July 16/90)

Insight into the life and times of Peter C. Newman can be found in the September 1982 *Saturday Night* cover story by Elspeth Cameron. The article is entitled "Newman's Progress: How a Czechoslovakian immigrant became Canada's most powerful editor and author." Cameron says Newman seized power "by excelling in a tournament of words": "On the one hand, he seemed to deplore the élitism of the wealthy (he referred to their 'servant-infested mansions'). More often he seemed to approve of the ruthlessness of his subjects" (p. 17).

Comparing 1892 to 1992 in his book *Canada — 1892: Portrait of a Promised Land*, he wrote:

[On Brian Mulroney:] We have a recession, federal-provincial relations are strained, and the Conservative Party is headed by a nincompoop. ("1892 Times Two," *Quill & Quire*, June 1992)

[On the Pearson accord of July 7, 1992:] The greatest puzzle of the current constitutional talks is that the same premiers who seemed to have little trouble granting the aboriginal peoples inherent self-government — which they richly deserve — backed away from bestowing similar status on Quebec. (*Maclean's*, July 27/92)

A "No" vote [in the Referendum on the Charlottetown Accord] would carry precisely the opposite message: that Canadians have become so mesmerized with the petty constitutional expressions of their regional differences, that they would rather lose their country than move a millimetre away from their prejudices, or hold out their hands in a gesture of understanding and goodwill. . . .

The real issue of the [October 26] referendum is deciding whether we have a future — not the shape of what that future will be. . . .

Maybe the 20th century never really did belong to us; but if we don't, as a country, vote "Yes" on Oct. 26, we won't belong to the 21st. (*Maclean's*, Sept 14/92)

The biggest miscalculation by the Charlottetown accord's architects was that the referendum's outcome would swing on the substance of its provisions. (*Maclean's*, Nov 2/92)

The national affairs columnist for the *Globe and Mail* is touted by that paper as a national treasure. For years the Faculty Club billed **Jeffrey Carl Simpson** as one who "helps set the Canadian political agenda." Dubbed the "Pundit Mandarin" by *Frank Magazine*, this member of the Queen's Mafia — a poli-sci graduate — never wavered in his support of the Mulroney government's constitutional position on key issues: the Charest committee report (*GM*, May 18/90), Senate reform (*GM*, June 8/90), and Official Bilingualism (*GM*, Apr 30/89). He also justified the "marriage of Mr. Mulroney to Quebec nationalism" as something that "made political sense as long as that nationalism could be reconciled with modestly changed federalism" (*GM*, Nov 7/90). Following the standard Tory political patter during the Meech Lake debate, he blamed Wells, Carstairs, Filmon, McKenna, and Doer for the accord's failure (*GM*, May 23/90; June 11/90).

He, like Peter C. Newman, was one of the very few journalists who could meander in and out of the corridors of power at will. Mulroney wined and dined him at 24 Sussex. Along with Susan Delacourt and Graham Fraser, Simpson conducted the famous interview with the prime minister on June 11, 1990, that elicited the infamous remark "that's the day I'm going to roll all the dice" (*GM*, June 12 and 20/90):

> Mr. Mulroney was obviously eager that his record be constructively construed when, upon coming to power, he made an arrangement with journalist and author Peter C. Newman to write the inside history of the Mulroney years. In this handing down of reputation nothing is more consequential for a Canadian Prime Minister than how he handled the central dossier of Canadian life: national unity. (*GM*, Aug 12/91)

> Watching some of the coverage of the Conservative convention [and the demonstrations] last week reminded me of David Peterson's last campaign as Premier of Ontario. . . .
> Ontarians were obviously disillusioned with Mr. Peterson, whom they booted out of office and politics. . . .
> But rather than take a suitably ho-hum attitude toward such demonstrations, the media cannot resist the confrontation, colour and fiery rhetoric, and so rush to enlarge the significance of the protests. (*GM*, Aug 13/91)

> In fairness, Mr. Mulroney never favoured Quebec separation. But for a variety of purposes he did favour former separatists with his patronage and support in building the Conservative Party in 1983 and 1984. Those were the days when separatism was flat on its back. . . .
> Brian Mulroney is no Pierre Trudeau. It's just that in talking to Quebeckers, he sounds more like his predecessor every day. (*GM*, Nov 20/91)

> The fundamental incoherence of the No forces guarantees that, if they win, the groups will turn on each other with the venom they now reserve for the accord. (*GM*, Sept 30/92)

By announcing that he would leave if Yes prevailed [in the 1992 Referendum] — since his last political objective would have been achieved [Meech cum Charlottetown] — Mr. Mulroney would give the Yes side an important boost. (*GM*, Oct 12/92)

The dream of a fully bilingual citizenry was always a pipe dream. It was also a nightmare for many, since as a practical matter in North America vast numbers of people do not need two languages, do not live in places where they could use them, and would only get needlessly aggrieved if they tried to learn.

Still, a larger pool of bilingual people would help staff public institutions and perhaps contribute — this may be utterly naive, I concede — to defusing hot buttons of language conflict. . . .

Inevitably, if that demographic drift persists, more voices will be raised questioning the application of existing federal language policy, and perhaps fewer voices of impeding [*sic*] doom will be raised in Quebec about the status of French. (*GM*, Jan 14/93)

In 1993, just before leaving the Faculty Club for a year's sabbatical at Stanford University in California, Simpson published *Faultlines: Struggling for a Canadian Vision.* In this tome of many ponderings, he dismisses Reformers as neither "truly dispossessed" nor "truly voiceless." Manning, he says, leads only a rebellion of the "psychologically dispossessed."

One of the more bizarre offerings the archbishop of the Faculty Club has laid on his altar is his dispensation that "Quebecers are the greatest defenders of the British parliamentary system. . . ."

Really? What of Bill 178? In 1967 Pierre Trudeau wrote: "Historically, French Canadians have not really believed in democracy for themselves; and English Canadians have not really wanted it for others. Such are the foundations upon which our two ethnic groups have absurdly pretended to be building democratic forms of government. . . . French-Canadian lack of concern for the liberties and traditions of Parliament was admirably brought out during the pipeline debate of 1956" (*Federalism and the French Canadians*, pp. 103, 111).

Editor-in-chief of the Faculty Club is **William Thorsell**, Mulroney's number-one apologist and a great admirer of Pierre Trudeau.

The *Globe and Mail* has never been successful because it followed trends. The *Globe and Mail* is successful because it establishes them. (CBC Newsworld, Nov 23/90)

Farewell the Peaceful Kingdom

The Canadian political system offers a chronic seminar in history, law and economics, obliging its leaders to explain differences and defend accommodations. Canada's domestic politics are infamously boring because they are congenitally complex. We are not a nation of geniuses, but our national agenda forces some concentration of the mind on virtually everyone. (*GM*, Aug 22/92)

You cannot herd cats, and Canadians are cats on constitutional matters. (*GM*, Aug 29/92)

Some newspapers assume additional noble missions, such as speaking for the poor or defending certain concepts of national sovereignty. The traditional and more prosaic mission — to inform — does not seem to fill the available sails for many journalists and publishers.

But that *is* the moral mission of a newspaper — to inform in the whole sense of the word, to contribute to understanding. (*GM*, Nov 21/92)

[Mulroney's] retirement would allow his party to look to the Clinton generation for political renewal. The best choice is an intelligent woman from Vancouver, aged 45. If Justice Minister Kim Campbell won the Tory leadership on a U.S.-style ticket with Environment Minister Jean Charest as the woman's French lieutenant, Mr. Mulroney would have bequeathed his party formidable successors. If elected, the Campbell/Charest ticket would express Mr. Mulroney's vision of national reconciliation in flesh and blood, and defend his legacy. And the Conservative Party would keep the keys to the kingdom. (*GM*, Dec 31/92)

Canada was defined in 1791 under British rule as a partnership of two distinct peoples — the French colonists of Quebec, and the United Empire Loyalists who had arrived as refugees from the American Revolution. In the late 20th century, the restless provinces of the Canadian West, newly conscious aboriginals, politicized women and deeply committed partisans for individual rights make the quest for Canadian unity considerably more complex.[5] (*Report on Business Magazine*, *GM*, Jan/93)

Multiculturalism has meaning only if we acknowledge that different groups tend to have different values, strengths and faults. If they do not, or if these differences are only superficial, multiculturalism is a sham. But it is not. (*GM*, July 3/93)

Brian Mulroney picked up Lester Pearson's mantle in 1984. The Meech Lake accord was, in essence, an effort to express in constitutional terms the Pearsonian view of federalism in reference to Quebec. That is why Mr. Trudeau lashed out so bitterly against Meech in 1987 — it excluded the "appeasing" spirit of Lester Pearson. Mr. Mulroney was left to defend Meech against a tide of Trudeau-aided intolerance in English-speaking Canada, in which Preston Manning played a conspicuous part. . . . A big country would understand what equality means in the context of Quebec. Mr. Manning doesn't, as Mr. Trudeau didn't (and Jean Chrétien didn't). Mr. Mulroney and Mr. Pearson were the prime ministers of a big country. We may have to conclude that the little won. (*GM*, Oct 16/93)

Jean Charest speaking for himself offers the only real hope for a revival of the Conservative Party in this decade. . . . **Postscript**: To the immediate question, urgently posed over lunch — "Is there anyone out there who can raise Canadians from their complacency in the face of the threat from separatists in Quebec and defeatists elsewhere before it's too late?" — comes a quick and unexpected answer: "For better or worse, irony of ironies, Pierre Trudeau." Could this be true? (*GM*, May 14/94)

Peter Worthington is a columnist with the *Toronto Sun*. He is also one of the newspaper's founders from the good old days:

The actions of every government since (and including) Lester Pearson's in the '60s have made separation more likely — the policy that one province is more equal than others.

For his part, Pierre Trudeau was obsessed with a written Constitution, which was implemented without Quebec's participation. What sense did that make? What sense did a *written* Constitution make anyway, when an unwritten one had worked fine ever since 1867? . . .

Most of Canada is fed up with Quebec. Resiliency, long a Canadian quality, is exhausted. People no longer care. . . .

Geographically we are a great country, with boundless potential. Our personal misfortune is that we are governed by pygmies — little people, without breadth, vision, scope, courage. Politicians who lead by opinion polls. (*Sun*, May 31/90)

As readers of this space know, with reservations I favored Campbell as Tory leader. (*Sun*, Oct 21/93)

Last, but not least, **Lubor Zink** — now retired — wrote for the *Toronto Sun*. Zippy Zink. Alive — great stuff.

> That's what group rights boil down to: Special treatment and, above all, more power. Unlike individual rights, which foster responsible freedom and egalitarianism, group rights foster inequality by demanding, through its spokesmen, a special status for the group. That requires collectivist mentality (i.e., abdication or suppression of individualism) within the group, and abject subservience to the group's leading demagogues. (*Sun*, May 18/92)

Notes

1 Bourassa was the grandson of the famous Quebec rebel leader Louis-Joseph Papineau (1786–1871), who led the Rebellion in Lower Canada in 1837 and opposed the Act of Union (1841) between Upper and Lower Canada.

2 Canada's greatest philosophical thinker, George Grant, wrote in *Lament for a Nation: The Defeat of Canadian Nationalism*: "Never has such a torrent of abuse been poured on any Canadian figure as that during the years from 1960 to 1965. Never have the wealthy and the clever been so united as they were in their joint attack on Mr. John Diefenbaker. It has made pleasant life for the literate classes to know that they were on the winning side" (p. 1).

3 This is absurd. In Canada's constitution, the BNA Act clearly defines the country as a federation of provinces. Section 133 of the act spells out the use of the French and English languages. The words "distinct" or "distinct society" or "founding races," which is anathema to the British common-law heritage, do not appear anywhere in Canada's constitution. Newman adopts the extended Trudeau fiction and then blames Trudeau for the result.

4 Newman has assassinated almost all of Canada's prime ministers verbally. He did in John Diefenbaker with his cruel diatribe *Renegade in Power* (1963).

5 All kinds of interpretations have been applied to the Constitution Act of 1791. One common misconception is that it provided for two official languages and a partnership between the so-called two founding races.

It did nothing of the sort. Here's the "silent" section so often misrepresented:

> II. And whereas his Majesty has been pleased to signify, by his message to both House of Parliament, his Royal intention to divide his Province of Quebec into two separate Provinces, to be called the Province of Upper Canada [Ontario] and the Province of Lower Canada [Quebec]. . . .

As historian Michael Bliss points out in his assessment of the shortcomings and ambiguities, "These flaws in the Act paved the way for much of the controversy that was to engulf the Canadas" (*Canadian History in Documents*, p. 14).

VI

The March
for Meech II

January to May 1992

22

They're Ba-a-a-ck!
More Meech II
— January to March 1992

WILLIAM THORSELL, THE *Globe and Mail*'s editor-in-chief, sent his fellow citizens the clearest of New Year's messages, that the madness of 1991 would continue into 1992 without let-up: "Brian Mulroney, the most unpopular prime minister in Canadian history, has also become the most needed — the real national story of 1991" (*GM*, Jan 4/92).

Joe Clark, the constitutional affairs minister, sounded the true signal that Canadians were in for another mauling much earlier. During a radio interview on November 14, he said: "Six months ago everyone was demanding all sorts of consultation and public hearings. . . . Then when a process [Castonguay–Dobbie panel] was put in place, even allowing for the weaknesses in organization — and there are some — people are now more weary. . . . We certainly have to find ways in which there is a broad public consultation" (CBC TV, "Midday," *Star*, Nov 15/91).

Canada's most fervent striver set the stage for the New Year — back to the backroom process — another First Ministers Conference: "A way we know [that] works. . . . My view has been for some time that when forced to look at the alternatives the public may well come to the conclusion we have, that a first ministers conference is the best way to proceed" (*GM*, Nov 28/91).

Clark unveiled the plan on December 20. The strategy was the brainchild of Arthur Kroeger, a member of the Ottawa-based Public Policy Forum, a powerful behind-the-scenes lobby group composed of "top executives from government and the private sector" and "dedicated to . . . building excellence in government" (info. booklet, PPF, 1988).

There would be a series of Renewal of Canada Conferences on the Constitution. And this time, Clark said, there would be public participation. This was another ruse. The government announced that it would invite 200 citizens to attend each conference: it ended up being 1,200. However, the application they had to complete carried restrictions: there were only a "few spaces" available for those representing what Clark had called the "knowledgeable public" (*Star*, Dec 22/91).

So the conferences' credibility was destroyed on day one. The process of selecting participants virtually excluded public participation. Of the 200 to 250 people for each conference, only up to 50 "so-called ordinary Canadians" passed the rigorous screening process. The government managed another rather clever ploy, too. This time they arranged for conference sponsors outside government to be co-opted into the exercise. Neat.

When the press formally notified Canadians of the Renewal Conferences on December 20, 1991, readers also learned that the deadline for receipt of the applications was 5:00 P.M., January 3, 1992, in Ottawa. Those interested had to submit a one-page brief, according to strict technical requirements. From these, a random selection would be made on some unspecified basis.

Curiously, of the 13 days allowed for people to respond, 8 fell on either statutory holidays or weekends. Priority Post and the government's fax machine were shut down for another 5 days. And the press made not a peep. By the third conference in Montreal on January 31, 1992, the ordinary-Canadian participation had shrunk to 24 compared with the 42 in Halifax and the 57 in Calgary before it.

The 1992 Renewal Conferences gathered the chosen few together — politicians, academics, various commission members, and some new faces with long records of behind-the-scenes involvement in government games. Ottawa law professor Anne Bayefsky spilled the beans in the *Globe and Mail* on January 10, 1992, claiming the roster of witnesses was rigged.

William Gairdner, author of *The Trouble With Canada*, put the case this way:

> I was a participant at the Calgary Constitutional Conference. . . . To my
> fellow citizens, I say: beware. Like the Halifax conference, Calgary was not

really a "people's conference." . . . The conference seemed dominated by interest groups and *experts*, many of whom argued vehemently that Canada's destiny, as determined by its highest legislative chambers, ought to be determined by legally-mandated groups, whose primary claim to political legitimacy is their sex, color, race, language, ethnicity, religion, physical disability, sexual orientation, or whatever. The permutations are endless. (Letter to the Editor, *Star*, Feb 1/92)

Interestingly, Clark had made numerous public commitments over the years about opening up the government that had been "extraordinarily elitist in Canada, for a very long time" (*GM*, Sept 30/91). The result was vintage executive federalism as it had been practised since the days of Lester Pearson. Less than two months before the announcement about the new process, Clark let it slip: "People do not want so much themselves to come to a committee and be heard, they want to know that the process is open so that people like them — organizations with which they are associated . . . whatever they are . . . have a right to change the proposals" (*Star*, Nov 15/91).

On January 7, 1992, the PMO announced that Mulroney's Chief of Staff, Dr. Norman Spector, would be replaced. Apparently he himself had requested this, so that a more politically on-side player could take over. A long-time Tory backroom boy and former colleague of Dalton Camp, "Hughie" Segal had been chosen.

Segal was an amiable Jewish Montrealer and, more important, the only choice left to the prime minister. The new chief of staff understood the socialist trade-offs the Conservatives had made to rid the party of John Diefenbaker's prairie populism. As a bilingual Quebecer, he also understood the why and wherefore of Mulroney's pact with that province's nationalists.

As a political advisor, however, Segal offered a less-than-dazzling track record. Political junkies and Tory insiders had known for years that he was directly responsible in many ways for the Conservatives' loss of power. He had acted as advisor and key player in the disastrous federal election campaigns of Robert Stanfield. His experience in provincial politics was equally shaky. Many blamed him for the landslide that smothered Bill Davis's Big Blue Machine. At this point in Martin Brian Mulroney's troubled regime, Segal's questionable past made no difference. He was a man who would do what he was told and preserve an alliance that had crumbled with the collapse of Meech. His view of the conditional separatist Marcel Masse is both absurd and naïve: "I've known Marcel Masse for

25 years. I've seen him defend Canada in nationalist circles when no one else would. [Mr. Masse is] a reflective part of the Unioniste-nationalist part of our coalition — which is critical to bringing our country together in the end (*GM*, Apr 1/92).

The lovable Segal had his work cut out for him. On January 9, the lid nearly came off. The most divisive issue in Canada's history, Official Bilingualism, was loudly and publicly added to the roster. Alberta Premier Don Getty said the unthinkable: "I believe the time has come when bilingualism should be removed from the force of law. . . . Multiculturalism should not be a matter imposed by law in Canada. . . . [In that context] there will be no Alberta agreement or constitutional change without the people, whose constitution it is, being asked for their assessment" (*GM*, Jan 10/92).

The next day he elaborated: "The people of Quebec haven't demanded the bilingual law at all. . . . I want to have this issue discussed rationally and calmly. It's a sensitive issue" (*GM*, Jan 11/92).

Pandemonium. The premier was to learn the most awful truth about executive federalism and pay a high price for his ignorance. He found himself maligned, insulted, abused, ridiculed, and mercilessly hounded by the media. Even Reform Party Leader Preston Manning meekly let his fellow Albertan hang. The Westmount-born premier with an honours degree in business administration from the University of Western Ontario's prestigious business school was castigated by cartoonists, lampooned by journalists, academics, and intellectuals.

In Edmonton, the Oblates, the Roman Catholic missionary order, branded him a sinner. The fathers published a news release denouncing his stand: "We deeply regret and wish to dissociate ourselves completely from the unfortunate declaration made by Mr. Getty. . ." (*GM*, Jan 14/92).

He was finally tuned out completely by his fellow first ministers when he reaffirmed his stance on February 6, almost a month after he had first introduced the subject. "I really believe it's sitting there and needs to be discussed and a huge number of people, certainly Albertans, have concerns and want it discussed, not in a negative or vitriolic way as some have responded, but in a thoughtful way" (*Star*, Feb 7/92).

Once again the matter was scuttled under the carpet. The politicians and the media excommunicated the premier. The Pearson–Trudeau–Mulroney vision of Canada rested safe — for the time being. The media saw to it there would be no debate on the subject.

On January 17, 1992, as scheduled, Joe Clark opened the first of the five Renewal Conferences in Halifax, to run for three days. Its sponsor was the

Atlantic Provinces Economic Council. Although "Division of Powers" was the topic, this was not the main item on Clark's agenda. He opened the conference on his favourite subject — the one that had destroyed Meech Lake. "Without question," he intoned, "it would be a grave mistake to believe we could unite the country without changes that allow the distinct society of Quebec to prosper" (*Star*, Jan 18/92).

This was his moment of glory. The Halifax conference was lauded as a great success. Thereafter politicians pushing for a deal of any sort referred wistfully to the "spirit of Halifax." Few people seemed to acknowledge the slight problem that surfaced with the conference, namely, that nothing more concrete than fine and furry feelings was agreed.

Meanwhile, Keith Spicer continued his chirpy parade across the weary nation. He drew some attention away from the Renewal Conference. Speaking in Rimouski, Quebec, on January 20, he came out with: "These high priests of the media-political Canada . . . this tiny group of actors in our political culture manage to impose, on 27 million Canadians, antagonisms and controversies that are often removed from our day-to-day experience" (*GM*, Jan 21/92).

On January 22, 1992, Reform Party Leader Preston Manning received good news. The party's eastward march into Central Canada was steadily swelling party membership and enriching party coffers. When he addressed 4,000 of the faithful and the curious who had paid to hear him speak in Pickering, Ontario, east of Toronto, he announced that national membership had topped the 100,000 mark.

Other political bodies fared less successfully. In government fiscal circles, the Province of Ontario and the federal government faced growing problems. On January 21 on province-wide TV, Bob Rae, the Ontario premier, confessed that the soaring Ontario deficit had reached $14.4 billion and not the $9.7 billion forecast. Two days later Standard & Poor's Corp in New York City had put the province on its credit watch. They grimly added that they intended to monitor the economic situation closely in what had once been Canada's wealthiest province.

Canadian taxpayers absorbed another rude shock with their morning coffee on January 27. At a news conference in Ottawa, finance minister Don Mazankowski announced that the federal government had adopted some crisis measures. From that point on, all of the federal government's discretionary operating expenses would be frozen till fiscal year end, March 31, 1992. The minister predicted a budget shortfall of $1 billion for a total of $31.5 billion. Furthermore, an unspecified shortfall was expected for 1992–93. The Canadian federation was sinking financially.

Farewell the Peaceful Kingdom

On January 30, it was reported that the actual British North America Act, 1867, had arrived in Canada from Britain on a one-year loan to celebrate Canada's 125th anniversary. What price heritage? Reporters discovered it was insured for only $10,000.

The Assembly of First Nations chose this awkward moment to push onstage themselves at the end of the month. Chief Ovide Mercredi spoke: "Whether you like it or not, if we do not address the issues of our people, the First Nations of Canada, it will not be conservative-minded individuals like me who will be leading the people in other directions. I can assure you that while the chiefs want harmony and peace with Canada we do not always control the politics in our society" (*Star*, Jan 30/92).

The government scarcely missed a beat. Renewal Conference #2 was held in Calgary for three days from January 24, on "Institutional Reform," courtesy of the organizational involvement of the Canada West Foundation. Of course, the real topic of interest in the West was Senate reform. There was no agreement.

Just as the first month of the year expired, one more player on the nation's stage had to speak his lines. Languages commissioner Victor Goldbloom picked up where his predecessor had left off. He was feeling the need to defend Official Bilingualism and deemed it time to put Premier Getty formally in his place for daring to question the nation's sacred cow: "There is nothing in it about shoving French down the throats of English-speaking Canadians. . . . It seems to me that the breakup of our country would be far more costly than that, and far more painful than the irritants some Canadians perceive in our official languages system" (*GM*, Jan 31/92).

In such an atmosphere, February could only start badly. The news from the third Renewal Conference on Canada aroused far more concern than its hosts had expected. The conference in Calgary had flopped. The topic for the Montreal conference, sponsored by the C.D. Howe Institute and the Institute for Research on Public Policy, was "Economic Union" — the most important topic of all since it dealt with the very underpinnings of the federation. But in Montreal, the heartland of the economic union of Canada, all the participants rejected the proposed terms of a new economic union.

From Davos, Switzerland, where he was travelling at the time, Premier Robert Bourassa explained why in his succinct way. He let it out that he would not attend the February 10 FMC that the prime minister had called on January 10: "It's an economic union that is functioning quite well" (*Star*, CP, Feb 2/92). This was not the position the Canadian Manufacturers' Association took. They had itemized some 500 interprovincial barriers, which they blamed for the loss of some $6 billion in trade.

The NDP government of Bob Rae had its say on constitutional matters on February 5, 1992. After thirteen months, the Select (all-party) Committee on Ontario in Confederation tabled a $3-million, ninety-one-page final report, the third in the series. They promoted distinct society for Quebec. They urged a veto for Ontario and Quebec. They also soft-pedalled Senate reform and pushed for a Social Charter instead.

NDP Leader Audrey McLaughlin explained why in Ottawa: "Our country is more than just an economic union. Yes, the economy is the engine of the country, but the social aspects of our country are the heart of our country, and you can't have one without the other" (*GM*, Feb 6/92).

Joe Clark played his favourite note again at the opening of the fourth Renewal Conference sponsored by the Niagara Institute in Toronto on February 7. This time the topic fit in with his agenda, "Identity, Rights and Values" — "The distinct society exists. . . . It is time to say yes to Quebec so that it may say yes to Canada" (*Star*, Feb 8/92).

The next day the *Toronto Star* did an amazing thing. It pulled a 180-degree turn. After five years of rejecting incorporation of a distinct society clause for Quebec in the Constitution, the paper suddenly backed it. Most remarkably, its support was unconditional. The paper didn't even demand that Quebec abandon its repressive language law, Bill 178:

> As a matter of principle, we have always opposed violations of basic civil rights, and we still do. . . . A distinct society clause that permits the Quebec government to restrict English would not, *in practice*, give the National Assembly much more power than it already has through recourse to the notwithstanding clause. Thus, in the final analysis, it is a political — almost tactical — judgement call. And after five years of debate, political realities have made it painfully clear that Quebecers — rightly or wrongly — will accept nothing less than a meaningful distinct society clause. (*Star*, Feb 8/92)

Joe Clark was elated. The next day he burbled, "I think we're over the problem of distinct society" (*GM*, Feb 10/92). But if he was seeing progress, three days later David Peterson was not. To an audience in St. Catharines, Ontario, the former Ontario premier noted that only two months remained in which to reach an agreement with Quebec and if it were not reached, "then this country is finished" (*Star*, Feb 12/92).

The smile on Clark's face lasted less than forty-eight hours. On February 11, Ovide Mercredi spoke to the Quebec National Assembly: "Self-determination is not a right of a 'province.' It is the right of all peoples. Are the 'people of Quebec' a 'people' in the international legal sense? The population of Quebec is made up of a wide range of racial and ethnic groups. It cannot be considered to be a single 'people' with the right of self-determination. . ." (*GM*, Feb 13/92).

The chairman of the all-party committee in Quebec, Guy Bélanger responded quickly: "They gave us that damned rubbish but it wasn't a surprise. They rejected Meech; they've objected everywhere" (*Star*, Feb 13/92). Joe Clark was not amused, calling the AFN chief's ideas "dangerous" (*GM*, Feb 13/92).

The federal government bullied successfully. On Friday, February 14, Mercredi backed down on his claim for special status for natives: "You don't take hardline positions forever. . . . The principle is important, that we are founding peoples of Canada, and that we are distinct people with inherent rights. It may be possible to accomplish that in other ways. So we remain open and we will look at possibilities" (*Star*, Feb 15/92).

Most Canadians had either fallen asleep or died of boredom during the six years of constitutional shenanigans. Those who still struggled to retain consciousness allowed themselves to be mildly intrigued by some of the fashionable new political terms the negotiations produced. Indeed, these were the only original things to come out of the multi-million-dollar gab-fest.

Certain people, for example, were designated "raporteurs" or "intervenors." This was a new breed of spin-doctor, specially coached in the fine art of ensuring the public was disinformed about secret proceedings. The "raporteurs" snooped the conference, maintained the party line, kept the real goings-on private, and doled out careful, meaningless sound-bites to the hungry media as necessary.

The result was almost no news at all — particularly when the "intervenor" was in charge. This was usually a conference workshop chairperson, often someone of high profile, experienced in handling the news deftly. Former Alberta Premier Peter Lougheed, an anti-Triple-E Senate supporter, served as intervenor at the dismal Calgary conference.

Experienced intervenors were retained for the more complicated conferences, too. No one in Canada had a clue what was happening among the thirteen government representations or the four native associations. Utter chaos prevailed. At the Calgary conference some seventy-five intervenors milled around, and heaven only knew how many raporteurs.

On CBC AM Radio the morning of the Toronto conference, Anne Bayefsky, professor of law at the University of Ottawa, blasted the Renewal Conferences. Referring to the conduct of former Mulroney aide Peter White in his role as a conference leader she said:

> I heard people come to the microphone, I heard women from Manitoba stand up and say, "We're worried about the effect of the distinct society clause on the Charter's equality rights." I heard workshop leaders presenting reports saying, indicating that some of the people in their groups were concerned about Charter rights. And in one group, for instance, it was the majority of participants. And yet — and I also heard aboriginal leaders stand up and say, "Yes to distinct society, but not as a tool for trampling on our rights."
>
> And then Peter White, the former Mulroney aide, stood up, as really the self-appointed sort of spin-doctor, and said — told the media — not to report any, uh, differences, said, "There's been acceptance of distinct society" — in his words — "without exception, without limitation." So I heard the spin-doctor saying something quite different from what was going on. (Feb 9/92)

The fifth and final Renewal Conference, originally planned for Ottawa, was held in Vancouver from February 14 to 16. The intervenors and raporteurs reported a consensus to the media — though it was never defined. Once again, in spite of the Meech Lake fiasco, there it was: affirmation of Quebec as a distinct society. All the trimmings remained: Official Bilingualism was reaffirmed, along with native self-government, and Senate reform. Yet, despite all the decorations, this was still the Quebec round. Quebec was to have some special powers, though, as usual, these weren't specified. There was to be an economic union of the federation, but no specifics — a Social Charter of some sort, but no specifics. All of this was to be wrapped up in a nice Canada clause, but not one written by lawyers — whatever that meant. Yawn . . .

On February 24, 1992, a Gallup poll placed national support for Brian Mulroney at 11 percent, the lowest rating for any prime minister in the history of Canadian polling. The report out of New York the next day from Patrick Paradiso, vice-president of research for Deutsche Bank in North America, brought grim tidings for the Tories, too. As the bank put it, "the constitutional reform measures were likely to adversely impact the market, particularly Quebec paper [bonds] in the spring." The bank also recommended investors avoid Ontario because of its growing deficit. Two provinces were deemed "safe havens": "Among Canadian economies, B.C. and Alberta are the least likely to be harmed by Quebec separation." Conversely, "Quebec and Ontario are both vulnerable to economic swings caused by constitutional instability since more than half of their trade is done with one another" (*Star*, Feb 26/92; *Western Report*, Mar 16/92).

Canadians were tired of various governments and special-interest groupies crying wolf. Yet the threats continued, stressing the timing and urgency confronting them at the end of February. On Thursday, February 27, faced with feuding between Conservative and Liberal panel members over the contents and release date of the final report of the Beaudoin–Dobbie SJC panel due the next day, Joe Clark insisted the report be unanimous and the deadline met: "I think it would be the worst possible signal for a Parliament that has achieved so much agreement on so many issues to appear unable to keep its deadline. I think that it would be a very major problem to the cause of Canada and to the interest of federalism" (*GM*, Feb 28/92).

On deadline day the Beaudoin–Dobbie SJC on a Renewed Canada reached agreement a scant fifty-four minutes before the clock ran out. The agreement — behind closed doors — the public were notified, was unanimous.

But then there was a kicker. The agreement, everyone was told, was "fragile." This was an agreement on some of the "principles" — whatever that meant. According to news reports, the Liberals and the NDP dissented on some details — whatever these were. Regardless, the published report due by the date specified was unavailable. But everyone, including Clark, talked about "unity" and a "final agreement." More than twenty politicians told the public what it all meant. Their audience couldn't have cared less. Certainly no one believed Joe Clark: "And to suggest that the committee was in a deadlock, or in deep disagreement on fundamental issues is not true, in my judgement. . ." (*GM*, Feb 29/92).

Clark's words on March 4 held little more weight. To an audience of anglophones and business executives in Montreal he said: "[It] is the best offer Quebec has received since Confederation. . . . More of the historic demands of Quebec have been met in this report than at any other time in the history of Canada. . . . [The Beaudoin–Dobbie proposals go] far beyond Meech Lake. . . . You're either in or you're out. . . . Remember that, however it is phrased, the real question is independence, separation, not some other option" (*Star*, Mar 5/92).

The world was watching. In an essay entitled "Canada Might Get Interesting," in *Time* magazine on March 9, 1992, Richard Brookhiser wrote:

There's an even chance that this year or the next, Canada will join the Soviet Union and Yugoslavia on the list of former countries and become two neighbours [with the U.S.]. . . . The main lesson [Americans] . . . should take from their neighbour's troubles is not to import them. Multicultural-ism and bilingualism, once planted, grow like the vine kudzu. America's struggles over its racist problem have lasted 200 years and included a Civil War. It should not add problems that have made even Canada interesting.

Back home, the Mulroney government did not seem to notice. The little red devils in the Tory Party were frantic, hoping to recover their lost reputation in history: that of being anti-francophone and the voice of English Canada. In a truly breathtaking move on March 10, 1992, having arranged beforehand to avoid debate, dispute, and public awareness, con-stitutional affairs minister Joe Clark introduced a controversial resolution in the House of Commons. All three of the executive-federalist parties backed his motion that they recognize the notorious Métis leader Louis Riel (1844–85) as a "founder of Manitoba."

According to revisionist doctrine, Riel, who had shot Thomas Scott, an Irish-Canadian anti-Métis labourer, in 1870, "paid with his life for his leadership in a movement which fought for the maintenance of the rights and freedoms of the Métis people" (*GM*, Mar 11/92). In honouring Riel's memory, the Tories exhibited questionable timing at the least. The Con-servatives have often been blamed for the Métis leader's hanging in 1885.

And Robert Hughes had not yet published his *Culture of Complaint*:

For here we come up against a cardinal rule of the PC [politically correct] attitude to oppression studies. Whatever a white European male historian or witness has to say must be suspect; the utterances of an oppressed person or group deserve instant credence, even if they're the merest asser-tion. Now the claims of the victim do have to be heard, because they may cast new light on history. But they have to pass exactly the same tests as anyone else's, or debate fails and truth suffers. The PC cover for this is the idea that all statements about history are expressions of power: history is only written by the winners and truth is political and unknowable, unless some victim knows it in his or her bones. (p. 146)

Premier Bob Rae captured his own moment when he condemned the Meech II process as too similar to that of Meech Lake: "It's a bit of a sausage factory. You don't cram a Constitution out of a committee. That's not how you make things happen" (*Star*, Feb 29/92).

Or perhaps it was the prime minister's threat on March 6. He informed reporters in a scrum that a few days earlier he had called CTV and offered to sing his version of the national anthem: "I'm an O Canada guy all the way, in English and French, and I've got four kids who can sing it in Serbo-Croatian. I think O Canada should be played all the time. All the time. I love O Canada. I think it's wonderful" (*Gazette*, Mar 7/92).

The season of silliness was truly in full swing.

23

Meech II
and the Carry-On Gang
— March to May 1992

FOLLOWING THE FIFTH AND FINAL Renewal Conference in Toronto on February 16, the provincial and federal governments ground to a halt on the Constitution. The participants could not agree on the legal meaning of Quebec as a "distinct society," the terms of economic union, Senate reform, or the specifics of a formula to amend the Constitution. In short, the conferences were a bust.

As obvious as this outcome was, it never occurred to anybody to just stop. All three parties pressed on, the media obediently regurgitating the pap fed to them.

Every first minister in Canada, all eleven of them, and all the executive-federalist parties committed themselves to the Quebec round — to coming up with a deal and making an "offer" to Quebec, no matter what.

It was time to retreat again, far from the madding crowd. Joe Clark, the fragmentalist, was helpless to call any more shots, so all of them ducked behind the scenery once more.

What followed would be dubbed the "3M" or Multilateral Ministerial Meetings. It was time to cut the charade of public input and arrange a real tête-à-tête between the pols and the apparatchiks. The feds wanted to create a safe forum where the insiders could meet in private, engineer the information to be leaked to the public, and then, if the whole thing failed, allow the whole process to fade while the ministers considered other options. One of these might even be a referendum. Obediently, the bureaucracy employed its favourite means of dealing with internal disagreements. They set to work to paste over the differences with lots of paper.

But it was no longer so simple to turn back the clock. It was gradually dawning on the power brokers just how expensive the Renewal Conferences were proving to be, in every way. They had miscalculated. Having allowed native Canadians to participate, the pols and the mandarins now changed their minds and tried to exclude the four native organizations that had been let through the door at the February conference. After much jostling to and fro, the same organizations initially barred from the closed-door sessions were suddenly permitted to attend.

Chief Ovide Mercredi represented the Assembly of First Nations. The outspoken Ron George spoke for the Native Council of Canada. The Inuit Tapirisat attended in the person of Rosemary Kuptana, and the Métis National Council in Yvon Dumont. The feds supplied the $10 million for native participation. For the first time, Canada's territorial governments were formally included, too.

For the first "3M" meeting held on March 12 — a sort of bastardized FMC — Robert Bourassa maintained his boycott. He did, however, hover on the sidelines through a Quebec delegation of two who allegedly came to observe the proceedings. For some reason, they absented themselves from the meetings the first morning. The sixteen remaining governments and associations went ahead without them.

The politicians scheduled numerous meetings and discussed deadlines. Earlier dates of April 10 and April 15 for the final federal "offer" to Quebec now expanded to ten weeks ending May 31, 1992. The prime minister pressed on relentlessly with his dream of fulfilling his personal promise to Quebec.

Out of those dreary days of mid March, Canadians sick of the propaganda drew one chuckle. The Saturday, March 14, 1992, papers reported the death of the eighty-year-old *Pravda*, the official newspaper of the Communist Party, founded by Lenin in 1912. The paper whose name meant "truth" had run out of funds.

In Canada the day before, March 13, the former Chief Justice of the Supreme Court of Canada waded into the constitutional morass. CBC Newsworld viewers were stunned to hear Brian Dickson, now the interim chairman of the Royal Commission on Aboriginal Peoples, recommend more than mere self-government for aboriginals, including the Métis; he considered it essential that they have a "land base." How many more kingdoms would there be in this community of communities? people wondered.

As if on cue, the New York State Assembly voted 122 to 17 to conduct an independent environmental review of Quebec's Great Whale hydro-electric project for James Bay on March 16. With one stroke, New York dealt Quebec's plans for sovereignty a devastating economic blow. It also threatened Quebec nationalism.[1]

Money matters commanded media attention for the rest of the month. On March 17, the *Financial Post* broke the news that the Canadian dollar had sunk to its lowest level in two years — 83.45 cents US. While Bourassa's dream of economic independence suffered assault from New York, the governor of the Bank of Canada, John Crow, entered the constitutional debate to comment on its impact on Canada's currency: "It can't be a good element. How bad it is is difficult to say. . . . We can't manage constitutions as such" (*GM*, Mar 19/92).

The next day, finance minister Don Mazankowski put it into street language for the Bay Street crowd: "There is volatility in the market place as a result of constitutional uncertainties" (*Star*, Mar 18/92). In fact, he was referring to two rises in the prime lending rate in one month.

Less than a month earlier, on February 25, Germany's Deutsche Bank rumbled another of its far-off warnings about the increased risk of investing in Quebec bonds in the spring money markets. This was a red flag to foreign investors in Canada. As if to compound problems, Canadian Press reported on March 18 that for the first time in history, the deficit for the province had surpassed $4 billion.

Bourassa caught on fast. Twenty-four hours later, the smooth-talking premier addressed the opening of the National Assembly:

> No one can deny that Canada is one of the world's rare and privileged countries in terms of peace, justice, liberty and standard of living. . . . If the rest of Canada wants to force Quebec to make choices without taking into account the events of 1982 and 1990, then it should keep in mind that the Quebec people's pride and dignity are not negotiable. . . . Let's not ·forget that Canada, its institutions, its governments have $260 billion in foreign loans. . . . [Fiscally] the all-providing state has run out of breath here and elsewhere. (*GM*, Mar 20/92)

Translation: for anyone who knew anything about finance and business, the Quebec round was dead. The world investment community had walloped the spoiled children who kept themselves aloof from the country's constitutional table. With the collapse of Great Whale, radical constitutional reform as blackmail became a game of blind man's bluff for Quebec.

Amazingly, the executive federalists, and especially the Tories, couldn't grasp the financial ramifications. They of the big business smarts neither blinked nor budged. None of them realized the loan had even been called. Mulroney, the one-time manager of what was in effect a managed receivership in Schefferville, Quebec, either didn't recognize or simply refused to face the familiar signs.

A report out of New York the next day, March 19, showed how goofy Canada's management of its own affairs had become. The editorial board of the *New York Times* interviewed the prime minister about the state of the nation, and elicited from him the most memorably flip comment on Mordecai Richler's book *Oh Canada! Oh Quebec!*: "Mordecai writes great fiction. Even when he is writing fact it resembles fiction" (*Star*/CP, Mar 20/92).[2]

Another spurt from the international press on March 23 might have prompted the PM to put away childish things. William C. Symonds, a correspondent for *Business Week*, wrote:

> Canada has never been this close to the brink. Even if the Canadians maintain a single nation, there are likely to be permanent shifts in relations between French- and English-speaking Canada. The consequences will resonate throughout the continent. Whether Bourassa or Parizeau prevails, Quebec's future direction is clear. It is only a question of how far, and how fast, it goes.

The many rings of the Canadian circus seemed to pick up the tempo. Bob Rae hardly helped matters. He proclaimed very loudly that Ontario would no longer accept the fiscal arrangements of Confederation. It is, the premier said, "the very raw deal" that cost Ontarians $14 billion: "We don't intend to put up any more with a situation where we are basically . . . forced to pay more and more of the bills and given fewer and fewer resources with which to pay for them" (*FP*, Mar 24/92).

For a third day in a row the international press highlighted economic conditions in Canada. In the *Wall Street Journal*, investment banker Robert Blohm wrote:

> What should make Quebec's nationalist politicians think twice about their drive for sovereignty is the sheer magnitude of the foreign capital Quebec

continues to need of at least $6-billion, made up almost entirely of its huge trade deficit with the outside world. Quebec has the industrial world's worst combination of trade and current-account deficits per capita. (*GM*, Mar 25/92)

On March 25 there was more bad news. Statistics Canada reported "massive foreign disinvestment" amounting to $2.2 billion in the Canadian money market in January — the biggest since May 1990, during the Meech Lake crisis. Still, no one seemed to be paying attention.

Meantime, the Mulroney-in-Wonderland Cabinet carried on goading the taxpayers over Quebec's special treatment. On the twenty-sixth, at Longue-Point, Quebec, defence minister Marcel Masse announced the federal government's $100-million commitment to build a new military warehouse in Montreal — rejecting all the other options his own department recommended. This meant slashing 500 jobs in Moncton, Ottawa, and Downsview (Toronto) while guaranteeing the existing 380 jobs in Quebec and adding 70 more when the plant was due to open in 1994. Confronted about the arrangement, Masse snapped, "When you have the puck on your stick, you shoot and you score" (*GM*, Mar 27/92).

With Masse, Cabinet's leading separatist, grabbing as much as he could lay hold of in funds and jobs for Quebec, Mulroney seemed to have seen the light. He finally reversed the message he had delivered in Baie Comeau in 1984. It was time, he said, to talk turkey to his home province. March 26 marked the first time, in fact, that the PM had spoken up for all of Canada. Every form of media in the country gave the speech wide coverage.

Mulroney preached the debt and doom that would follow separation — or even a referendum. L'Irlandais said bluntly: "Bingo! Beautiful! You win the turkey — and the debt. . . . You ask that question [hold a referendum on sovereignty] and 10 times out of 10, Quebeckers are going to say: 'We want a renewed Canada'" (*GM*, Mar 27/92). A Quebec referendum on sovereignty would have a "disastrous effect" on the economy and the stability of investment in the country.

He was wrong. The last referendum in 1980 had had no such effect. Maybe he'd been taking some talk-tough lessons from Pierre Trudeau.

On March 27, the next economic broadside struck home, sending shudders through Quebec: the New York Power Authority cancelled its $17-billion contract to buy power from Great Whale. Governor Mario Cuomo had recommended the move because the "circumstances have changed dramatically since this contract was originally signed in 1988" (*Star*/CP, Mar 29/92).

347

And there was more. Bilingualism and Senate reform splashed the front pages of the press together on March 28. At Alberta's annual Conservative convention delegates voted against bilingualism in two votes of 125 to 96. Before the gathering of 1,600, Deputy Premier Jim Horsman cautioned Joe Clark: "I'm telling you, you are not going to be re-elected unless you listen to what Albertans are saying. . . . Please, Joe, sell the Triple-E Senate to the rest of Canada" (*Star*, Mar 29/92).

Rather than listen, Clark hit back. On Monday in the House of Commons he reprimanded them: "Mr. Speaker, certainly abolition [of the Senate] is one option if other things do not work" (*GM*, *Star*, Mar 31/92). As for Alberta's stance on bilingualism, "we've seen flexibility from Quebec, we've seen flexibility from aboriginal leaders, we've seen flexibility from the proponents of a social charter. If Canadians, any of them, stick with extreme positions . . . we run the risk of losing this country" (*Star*, Mar 31/92).

Comparatively speaking, April Fool's Day was quiet, if only deceptively so. If the government felt any concern about wasting its resources, they gave no sign. Monthly government cheques went out accompanied by flyers headed a "New Government of Canada Cheque": "With this payment, the Government of Canada is introducing a new look to our cheques. You may have noticed the new multi colour background design." Spend, spend, spend was all they knew.

March turned out to be a bad month for the Parti Québécois, too. On the fourteenth, Jacques Parizeau promised that, should the Liberals fail to do so, "There will be a referendum with a clear question on sovereignty when the BQ is in power" — eight months after their election.

Interestingly, no one thought to work out the actual dates with a calendar. Since Bourassa's mandate didn't run out until October 11, 1994, exactly five years after the date in 1989 on which his government was sworn in, this was actually a dramatic admission. Mulroney told CBC on April 3 that Parizeau had "scored in his own net." Parizeau assumed centre stage with the appearance of the April 13 issue of *Time* magazine on the newsstands. In an interview with Michael S. Serrill, the PQ leader said, "Sovereignty as a word has been a marketing trademark of the Parti Québécois for 20 years because the word independence used to be somewhat frightening. I'm not going to change the logo. Does sovereignty have the same meaning today as independence? Of course it does. [And if Quebec votes No to sovereignty in October,] then obviously I failed, I retire, somebody else takes it up."

Unintended and unrecognized comedy that all this was, the prize of the month did not go to Parizeau in what Mordecai Richler endearingly termed his "tinker-bell suit." It went to PQ president Bernard Landry. Interviewed on April 4 on CBC AM Radio's "The House," Landry went colourful with host Judy Morrison: "If the strategy was to put the knife on the throat of the rest of Canada, why say, 'My knife is a wooden one, and I'm a federalist and don't worry; I just want to comb your hair'?"

The competition was heating up. In the end, the gold medal for being most out of touch with Canadians was won by federal multicultural minister Gerry Weiner during a visit to Toronto. Weiner denounced anyone who criticized multiculturalism for "seeking to divide Canadians for their own ends. . . . Critics of multiculturalism never offer any examples to support their arguments," he complained (*Sun*, Apr 5/92).

Other countries have financed and even cultivated the causes of socialist minorities and affirmative action interests. Canada has seen similar demonstrations of rights activism promoted by its own Liberals, Tories, and NDP. In the United States, the most popular radio talk-show host ever, Rush Limbaugh, sent out a message that was gobbled up enthusiastically by thousands of Canadian listeners anxious to hear some sanity north of the border. Here are some thoughts from the happy right-wing warrior in his 1992 best-selling book *Rush Limbaugh: The Way Things Ought to Be*. Just substitute "Toronto," "Canada," and "Canadian" where appropriate:

> It is my conviction that the people who concocted multiculturalism and are now trying to institute a multicultural curriculum in New York are basically miserable. And rather than look at their own responsibility in this, or try to find solutions that involve a change in attitudes, they simply blame institutions. They blame America. So multiculturalism, which portrays American history and even all of Western civilization as nothing but misery and racist, sexist, capitalist oppression, is the tool of revenge of many who have failed to assimilate and fit into mainstream American life. And the primary targets of their revenge are our children. (pp. 210–11)

B Y THE BEGINNING of April, many people had decided the prime minister had lost all contact with reality. On the other hand, many might have thought perhaps he just didn't give a damn. On April 7 defence minister Marcel Masse handed Quebec another big financial bonus. He announced an untendered $1-billion helicopter contract to Bell Helicopter Textron of Mirabel, a subsidiary of U.S. Textron Inc. Bell Helicopter received the fat package without any competitive bidding. Eurocopters Canada Ltd., which the federal government had lured to Ontario, complained they were "extremely disappointed because it was not fair treatment to receive. . . . We never had a chance." Spokespeople for the firm said they were promised a chance to bid.

Masse defended his decision. As far as he was concerned, it reflected the 1991 defence department policy commitment. Admittedly, there was one problem with this reasoning: that policy specified only 43 helicopters — not the 100 the government promised to buy with this new contract (*GM*, Apr 16/92).

The deal's timing was frightful. On the day Masse was gleefully exhibiting his federal department as a front-runner for Quebec interests, more than 100 journalists, academics, and government officials were in Washington launching a new book, *The Collapse of Canada*. The Brookings Institution, the influential Washington, D.C., think-tank, published it; it was written by three Canadians and one American. One of the authors, a Queen's University professor named Keith Banting, said at the launch, "Agreement on reforms sufficiently dramatic to resolve the constitutional agenda and lay to rest the spectre of Quebec separation seems beyond reach," and any agreement reached would likely be "mushy." If Quebec were to separate, he elaborated, the U.S. might have to "act as an arbiter among the factions; and in the event of a complete collapse the United States might find itself having to respond to applications for statehood from some provinces" (*GM*/CP, Apr 8/92).

The defence minister made things worse. He failed to show up on April 9 at Vimy Ridge and Dieppe in France. He had been scheduled to accompany the prime minister's entourage in honour of the fallen Canadian soldiers. Shades of Lucien Bouchard?

Life went on. Joe Clark continued to struggle to gather the consensus he wanted on the meaning of "distinct society." Mulroney was somewhere over the Atlantic on his way to Paris. Bourassa planned to meet with him later in Montreal.

On the home front, more disruptive news captured the headlines. Hydro-Québec chairman Richard Drouin announced a $16-billion cut in capital spending — 25 percent.

From the safety of his Paris vantage point, the prime minister flicked a small grenade over the water: he and his government might have to follow their own constitutional agenda:

My position is: If the provincial premiers cannot agree on constitutional proposals that could be put to the people, then the federal government, with the other federalist parties in the House of Commons, brings forward proposals and causes these proposals to be put to the people. That means a referendum. That is what we are going to do if we cannot get the kind of agreement we are working so hard to achieve. (*Star*, Apr 9/92)

Not to be so inelegantly yanked off the national stage, the great chameleon transformed himself yet again on April 3. New Brunswick's Frank McKenna proposed another stratagem. To the insiders' group of insiders, the Council for Canadian Unity, he urged "accommodation because the good of the country depends on it." Quebec's constitutional needs have to be the priority, he said; "Whatever works" (*Star*, Apr 4/92). As for consulting Canadians, the premier corked that bottle: "We've had mammoth public consultation. . . . A referendum is a dangerous way to decide the future of Canada."

Joe Clark stepped back onto the stage next. In Halifax on April 9, he danced awkwardly around the issue of native self-government. According to him, agreement had been reached between the various provincial, territorial, and aboriginal counterparts. Sure enough, bristling with pride at his own perception, the constitutional affairs minister returned to his favourite subject a week later: Quebec as a distinct society. He let out the big news on April 13 in an interview with the *Globe and Mail*: "Our most difficult single issue remains distinct society. . . . We have now virtually . . . doubled public acceptance of distinct society in a number of ways. One of them was the definition. One of them was nine months of explaining."

Taxpayers read the news balefully. The April 13 *Toronto Star* reported that estimated costs of federal unity activities now exceeded $100 million, not including provincial government efforts, commissions, conferences, etc.

On April 17, the Montreal law firm of Desjardin Ducharme released a report commissioned by the Quebec National Assembly. In the event of separation, the report recommended the Royal Bank of Canada and the Bank of Montreal could, providing the Bank Act of Canada was amended, retain their head offices in Quebec. The study assumed that a sovereign Quebec would use Canadian currency and that Quebec would and could happily join GATT and FTA and NAFTA at the same time.

On April 18 the newspaper *Le Monde* of Paris published the first part of an earlier interview with Quebec premier Robert Bourassa: "At this moment, I believe there will be offers by the government in Ottawa proposing a renewal of Canadian federalism. The [Quebec] referendum will be on these offers" (*Star*, Apr 19/92). He described them: the federal offers had to contain the substance of Meech Lake, provide for a new division of powers, and they could not reduce Quebec's power.

Why Paris for such an announcement? The excuse given was tight timing under Bill 150, which required that referendum law changes be tabled in the National Assembly by May 15. Same old stuff — lining up friendly fire in case it was needed.

Some eternally optimistic souls dared to believe agreement had been reached. For their benefit a new agreement on native self-government was broadcast in Halifax on April 9. For them, then, the news from Winnipeg on April 21 was a bit confusing.

The Royal Commission on Aboriginal Peoples opened with the Assembly of First Nations presenting a flood of demands, the first for recognition of fifty-three — out of some sixty — aboriginal languages as equal to English and French. They also demanded their own recognition as a distinct society, equivalent to the Meech Lake provision for Quebec. The "First Peoples" sought exemption from the Charter of Rights, and full equality with federal and provincial governments. Begging the question, how much agreement could Clark have been talking about? Fifty-three languages instead of bilingualism? Get a life.

I N THE SPRING of 1992, the sovereigntists in Quebec were busy firming up support for themselves. On April 22, Sylvain Simard, president of Mouvement Québec français, boasted that he had 250,000 signatures on a petition resisting any proposal for renewed federalism. The mouvement had begun collecting signatures in February, and they predicted that they would have one million of them by June.

Puffed up like a penguin, PQ leader Jacques Parizeau addressed his faithful in Quebec City on April 23. An independent Quebec, he said, would have to have its own army: "The national police would be an elite corps, free from political influence, responsible to the state and for assuring the state security. . . . The role of the police will change profoundly from the moment it integrates the duties of the RCMP" (*Star*/CP, Apr 24/92). The Sûreté du Québec would be special: "similar to the American federal police force, the FBI. . . . It would put an end to the schizophrenia with regards to the RCMP" (*GM*, Apr 24/92).

Not to be outdone, Marcel Masse announced yet another little treat for la belle province at the end of the month. Ottawa would spend $108 million upgrading the Valcartier Canadian Forces Base. Mulroney and Masse had finally hit bottom with taxpayers throughout Canada.

A media love-in in Montreal on Sunday, April 26, dramatized just how far apart Canadians and their government leaders stood from each other. The Québec Federation of Professional Journalists sponsored an all-day session of the province's top radio, television, and print journalists. Together they discussed their own handling of the constitutional debate. The editor of the *Financial Post*, Diane Francis, expressed her opinion that Quebec's secession could be "ugly" and "violent." From the *Toronto Star*, editor John Honderich said, "I disagree as fundamentally with Diane Francis as perhaps Lucien Bouchard disagrees with Robert Bourassa" (*Star*, Apr 27/92). A comment from Patricia Poirier of the *Globe and Mail* showed that the trivial now commanded the nation's attention: "Mr. [Lucien] Bouchard said he believes that on the whole journalists are doing 'honest' work. But he did take to task the English media for referring to him and Parti Québécois Leader Jacques Parizeau as 'separatists' — a pejorative word which conjures up images of breaking up Canada — instead of calling them 'sovereigntists'" (*GM*, Apr 27/92).

Helpless, frustrated, and resigned, Canadians awaited the inevitable confrontation. On April 27, Joe Clark informed them that some form or other of referendum legislation was in the works: "But what we want to do is establish for ourselves, for the Parliament of Canada, that basic authority, in the event we choose to use it. There would be no attempt to have a national consultation cancel out or override a decision in Quebec. Moreover, the simple fact of securing authority, creating [such] an instrument does not mean that we would use one. That's something we would determine as events proceed" (*GM*, Apr 28/92).

For weeks, corporate Canada had pressed Mulroney to end the uncertainty about Confederation's future. On March 26, Allan Taylor, president of the Royal Bank, Canada's largest financial institution, had warned the Empire Club that Canada was being turned into "a toothless tiger. . . . After a millennium of turmoil, the Europeans are scrambling to pool some of their hard won sovereignty to join a common cause" (*FP*, Mar 27/92). Two weeks later, on April 8, Ed Neufield, chief economist for the Royal, said, "Until the constitutional issue is resolved, Canada will remain highly vulnerable to sudden adverse shifts in domestic and foreign investor confidence because of uncertainty about prospects for continued Canadian political unity and stability" (*Star*, Apr 9/92). Holding forth from Winnipeg on April 28, Taylor finally blew up: "If Canada breaks up, all of us in every corner of what was once a proud and united country will be hit even harder. . . . Our malaise, I suggest, stems from the flawed way we see ourselves" (*Star*, Apr 29/92).

Custer's last stand. Don't take any prisoners.

That same day, another member of Mulroney's corporate team threw himself into the action. In Montreal to address the annual meeting, the president of Rogers Communications, Ted Rogers, boldly burst forth into the debate: "We're starting here in Montreal because we want Quebec to remain in Canada. Then we're flying to Vancouver because that's as far west as Canada goes. We have to make every effort to reach out and communicate with each other. We can't be afraid to say 'I love Canada'" (*Star*, Apr 29/92).[3]

Raymond Cyr, president of BCE Inc., and Bertin Nadeau, chairman of the food giant Unigesco Inc., hit the hustings in Montreal. Pushing executive federalism to a group of academics, Cyr cautioned, "I believe we should reflect carefully before we throw everything out" (*Star*, Apr 29/92).

This latest concerted effort to retain corporate control of Canada fit the strategy agreed to and co-ordinated by the Business Council on National Issues (BCNI). President Thomas d'Aquino had been on the move himself since the day after the collapse of Meech Lake. He and his colleagues had hurriedly raised $100,000 to mobilize the academic world. The big-business strategy that Canadians were seeing for the first time had been rolling since the new year. As d'Aquino put it in a news piece, "We decided in January that individual members of the BCNI, of whom there are 160, would use every opportunity they could, either from annual general meeting platforms or sometimes in communications with employees, to tell the story of Canadian unity" (*GM*, Apr 28/92).

In this, big business in Quebec agreed. A month before Allan Taylor's latest warning, Claude Beauchamp spoke in Calgary. That March 31, the head of the 12,000-member Regroupment Economie et Constitution, the pro-federalist business group in Quebec, acknowledged, "Of course, there is fear [in Quebec] of separation. The flow of commercial links could be altered tremendously" (*Star*, Apr 1/92). A small warning flare from Boston that day was noticed. A bill was introduced in the state legislature to prohibit the investment of employee pension funds in Hydro-Québec. By this time, six other states had fired similar signals of their own.

Long before the BCNI put together its plan in January, the corporate players had been assembling to do battle for the hearts and minds of their fellow citizens. Matthew W. Barrett of the Bank of Montreal, Canada's third-largest bank, had already marched out as a standard bearer for the praetorians of the banks when the government released its constitutional proposals of September 24, 1991. The chairman and chief executive officer, the man the *Financial Post* described as the "son of a dance-band leader from County Meath, Ireland," behaved as the perfect pawn. He accepted the

Canadian Club of Toronto's invitation to speak at a luncheon on November 18, 1991, on "Year of Decision": "To me the federal proposals have aims that are essentially decent and often even praiseworthy. But I am not asking you to agree with me about any of them. What I *do* want to ask you about every one of them is this: can any of us, in all conscience, believe that rejecting this proposal is worth risking the breakup of our country?"

Neville Chamberlain in a banker's suit.

Months before Barrett sounded off on May 7, 1991, John McNeil, chairman of Sun Life Assurance Co., had outlined corporate Canada's priorities. His firm was once infamous for having moved its head office out of Quebec following the FLQ crisis in the 1970s. "It's vital to the interests of Canada," he said, "that we give the question of Quebec within Canada first place and that other important issues take second place." From start to finish it was the Mulroney line — the Sept-Îles speech spiced with businesslike flavour. McNeil also termed the Constitution Act of 1982 "a mistake" because it excluded Quebec. On top of that, multiculturalism was "unnecessarily entrenched" (*GM*, May 8/91).

April is a very busy month for annual reports and annual meetings. So just as the threats from big business had whistled through the affairs of the nation in the spring of 1991, so the reports emerged in 1992. On April 21, Arden Haynes, chairman and chief executive officer of Imperial Oil Limited, Canada's largest petroleum empire, said at the annual shareholders' meeting, "And so I urge our political leaders and all Canadians of goodwill to seize this opportunity to build a new constitutional consensus" (*FP*, May 1/92). The powers that were were mobilizing a sizeable army of good little soldiers. Company men.

O N APRIL 28 Statistics Canada published the 1991 census figures. The population had reached 27.3 million. Quebec's population, which in the immediate post-war period was nearly 30 percent of the national total, had fallen to just 25.3 percent. The ethnocentric politics of founding races and cultures and multiculturalism was in for a rough ride.

Professor John Richards wrote an interesting essay on federal official languages policies for the C.D. Howe Institute about this time. The Simon Fraser University professor concluded by recommending that language responsibility be transferred away from the federal government to the provinces: "The fraction of non-anglophones in Quebec able to speak English has remained constant at one-third for the past half century. . . . Federal bilingual policies have had only a minute effect on increasing knowledge of French among non-francophones in the rest of Canada; the proportion claiming to speak French rose from 4 to 6 percent between 1971 and 1986" (*GM*, Apr 29/92).

Still the squabbles about language issues went on, disrupting the country and sowing fresh mischief. Montreal was celebrating its 350th anniversary and expected one million visitors for the year. Alliance Quebec chairman Reed Scowen encouraged Quebec businesses to use a small sticker — "F/E" for "French/English" — that the "tongue troopers" had even approved at the Office de la langue française. However, the president of the Société St-Jean-Baptiste, Jean Dorion, was of a different mind. He called the AQ campaign "insulting and provocative" to the French-speaking majority (*GM*, Apr 29/92). One can only wonder if he had ever been outdoors anywhere in North America beyond Montreal?

It was time once again for Mulroney to hold forth. In Hull, Quebec, on April 28, he said:

> It is . . . a reality that 50,000 Quebeckers now work for the federal public service, which makes the Canadian government the largest employer in Quebec after the government of Quebec. . . . Francophones make up 29 per cent of the federal public service — a proportion greater than their demographic weight. And 34 per cent of the deputy ministers and equivalent senior positions in the federal public service are held by francophones. (*GM*, Apr 29/92)

His point about the power of the federal government was a powerful hint, but nothing quite as dramatic as the news story that came out on May 10. Radio-Canada television reporter Normand Lester broke an amazing story in Montreal. Claude Morin, separatist and former Parti Québécois cabinet minister in the Lévesque government, had just admitted that while he was in the Quebec cabinet as a separatist he had also been a paid RCMP informer. The problem was that he was also the architect of "*étapisme*," the step-by-step approach to separation that blew up in the 1980 Quebec referendum. Everyone wanted to know what else lay under the carpet — especially the separatists.

MAY 15 marked the deadline for any changes to Quebec's Referendum legislation, Bill 150. Quebec spoke through its intergovernmental affairs minister, Gil Rémillard:

> There is no obligation for the Quebec government to change Bill 150 if it wants to use the Quebec referendum law to ask the Quebec people to

respond to a constitutional question. . . . The only condition is that we abide by the referendum law, meaning that there would be a 35-hour debate in the National Assembly [by May 15] to determine the question and then the entire process begins. (*GM*, Apr 29/92)

The next day he added, "So if we get something in substance, something like Meech, of course we will go back to the table and discuss the other points we have to discuss for a complete constitutional reform" (*GM*, Apr 30/92).

Intergovernmental affairs critic Jacques Brassard called the government's bluff for the separatists: "You [Bourassa] have no intentions of holding a referendum on sovereignty; you do not have the convictions to hold one and you will not hold one" (*GM*, Apr 29/92). He was right.

Mulroney's bargaining strategy was weak. He had big business on its knees to the separatists, pitching in good money after bad. Unlike the National Citizens' Coalition, the BCNI had missed its chance. Quebec nationalism was stuck in a nose-dive and had been for many months. The province had already returned to the table pleading, but the Mulroney team, under Clark and the woolly thinkers, the Ottawa apparatchiks, imagined they were back in March of 1991 when the Quebec Liberals adopted Jean Allaire's radical proposition to dismantle Canada: "We have made important progress towards the substance of Meech. . . . And I hope it will [be] possible for the government of Quebec to decide to be part of our discussions. . . . We are not structuring our agenda to draw Quebec back" (*Star*, May 1/92).

Three well-meaning English-speaking Tory MPs rose in the House of Commons to attack the media. They blamed them for their extensive coverage of the untendered $1-billion helicopter contract awarded to Quebec. Unfortunately the MPs did not recognize the press doing its job for a change. The Mulroney caucus didn't understand that they themselves were throwing away bargaining chips like so much garbage.

In all this, one may wonder what had happened to the new Official Languages Commissioner. Victor Goldbloom rose to the occasion splendidly. Tabling his first report to Parliament in early May, he said that Official Bilingualism cost $700 million per year.

This was nonsense. More cover-up. He was referring to only some of the operating costs, the directly identified ones. No one could ever have figured out the real cost — trashing the Merit Principle in the public service and replacing it with a system that rewards racial qualifications. Just as his predecessors had, Goldbloom urged:

We cannot preserve the unity of Canada if we set aside the historic premise that we have two official languages. We must strengthen the linguistic security of both language communities. It is of continuing concern that, after more than two centuries of living together, some Canadians should still be questioning why the federal government has a language policy. . . . Dialogue between them is indispensable and it requires a sense of mutual security and trust.

Picking up on the demands of Canada's aboriginal peoples on the royal commission's opening day, he took his great leap forward. There's an "urgent need," he said, to promote and preserve aboriginal languages. The *Toronto Star* emblazoned the story across its front page: "Bilingualism called vital to our future." Goldbloom also let it slip out that annually, Ottawa transferred $264 million to the provinces and territories to advance the French-language promotion and fund training outside Quebec. What he did not let on was that there were some sixty native languages to preserve, depending on the definition you chose.

THIS MONTH the most ironic story in Canadian affairs was tracked down by *Globe and Mail* columnist Stevie Cameron. In her May 4 column, she reported that Pierre Trudeau, the former prime minister, was advising the governments of the Ukraine and Czechoslovakia on how to craft a new constitution. Canadians could only sympathize with their foreign counterparts.

Wednesday, May 13, was not only the final day of a three-day conference of negotiators on the Constitution. It marked the end of a process that had begun with the tabling of the twenty-eight proposals by the federal government on September 24, 1992, *Shaping Canada's Future Together*. Clark declared himself ready to abandon Meech II. He was threatening to call on Parliament to act instead: "We cannot delay much longer dealing with issues that were in the Beaudoin–Dobbie report. . . . We've been able to make quite a bit of progress on some of the issues, for example, relating to the distinct society, in terms of how we express it. But we've always understood that there also had to be some means to give content . . . and that means moving on some of these questions of power" (*Star*, May 14/92).

For a second time in as many months Clark was stringing everybody along on some agreement that Quebec was a "distinct society."

Questioned about what on earth was going on, the prime minister offered CBC a sound-bite: "The principal object of the exercise is to bring

Quebec in [to the Constitution]" (CBC Newsworld, May 13/92). A bit more, but not much, came from him four days later at the official opening of Montreal's 350th anniversary celebrations. He said feelingly: "I cannot stand idly by and allow these people to seek to destroy the greatest country in the world. . . . We're going to have to work hard at the constitutional table to produce attitudes and possibilities to allow us to make an honourable deal for everybody" (*Star*, May 18/92).

As confused as anyone else, Saskatchewan Premier Roy Romanow spoke up about the latest game plan: "I think this is Russian roulette. A referendum on the Constitution has tremendous potential for division within the country, around obviously emotional issues. . . . I think what they're doing here . . . is a method of rounding up the premiers, kind of shepherding them or scaring them into a deal" (*Star*, May 14/92).

Just in time to meet the May 15 deadline for any changes to Bill 150, Bourassa dealt with the Quebec Referendum Act. Now it required that his government reveal the referendum question by August 4, before the Bill 150 deadline for a referendum on or before October 26. Details on the actual question could be delayed to September 12.

On Friday, May 15, despite the previous day's announcement to postpone referendum legislation, House Leader Harvie Andre introduced Bill C-81. The estimated cost of holding the federal plebiscite would be about $100 million. The legislators had given themselves plenty of room. The whole exercise would be fully controlled.

Even the result of the national Referendum would be non-binding on the politicians. No public funding would be available for campaigners and both the Yes and No sides would have equal broadcast time to appeal to the public. Like Quebec, the federal government chose to work out the actual wording of their question later.

All was ready. Canada would hold one referendum in every province and territory but Quebec, and Quebec would hold its own referendum on the same day. This was Mulroney's dualism in practice. To critics, Andre offered, "Trust me. There is nothing sinister here. To those who contend this is an evil, Machiavellian scheme to cook the results, I can only say . . . it would only undermine the results, it would be counter-productive" (*Star*, May 16/92). "Trust me"? Canadians waited eagerly for Referendum day.

THE ENTIRE country seemed to have gone mad. As if to prove it, a Gallup poll released on May 18 showed that, although only 30 percent of the population said residents in Quebec employed by the federal government should be allowed to keep their jobs in the event that Quebec separated, 62 percent of Quebecers favoured such a proposition. Was anybody thinking clearly? Or was it all a dream?

On May 21, Ontario's premier objected to Mulroney's machinations and the federal government's private dealings with Quebec: "I don't like it. If you're there, you're there. If you're not there, you're not there [at the constitutional table]. . . . It's a concern I had and I raised it and a number of other premiers agree with me" (*Sun*/CP, May 22/92).

If Rae was complaining that he had been spun out of the loop and was uninformed about what the big boys were doing, that's not how Mulroney's Quebec lieutenant saw the world unfolding. According to Benoît Bouchard, the federal government and the province of Quebec had agreed to shift major powers to the provinces — culture and job training were confirmed: "It's the first time that I've seen [us] go so far." Bob Rae ate a little crow, and then changed his tune to sound as if he'd been involved all along: "We have an incredible amount of duplication, overlap, misspending, bureaucrats falling over themselves. . . . It's a mess" (*GM*, May 22/92).

At this point no one had the remotest idea what was going on. Then, suddenly, little punishments were meted out. One that leaked out was the trading of insults between finance minister Mazankowski and Bob Rae. In the House of Commons Mulroney violated protocol by reading aloud private letters from Premier Rae on the North American Free Trade negotiations.

Not to worry. The differences were always patched up to keep the people unaware of the trade-offs being made behind their backs. But just when all seemed blackest, after hours and hours and days of ministerial conferences behind closed doors, something happened. Premier Rae pulled a complete turn-around. He told the world all was sweetness and light. On the last day of the multilateral ministerial meetings, May 29, he compared the current proceedings to Meech Lake: "This has been exactly the opposite. . . . Apart from the fact that you're [the press] not in the room . . . [this has been] an incredibly open process. We've had every conceivable form of public and popular consultation" (CBC Newsworld).

News junkies might remember what this same man had already said when the final round began, that the participants and the federal government would paint a pretty face on the business for public consumption no matter what kind of deal came out of it. For now, the premier said mildly, "Whatever the outcome of this final week of negotiations may be, I think it is fair to say that the multilateral process is a success" (*Star*, May 27/92).

In such an atmosphere, no one believed a single word anyone else was saying. Canadians welcomed a little rare common sense on Victoria Day, May 24. The former Parti Québécois premier, Pierre Marc Johnson, observed, "About 80 per cent of Quebec's requirements have already been met within Confederation, and Quebeckers are less passionate about the idea of Quebec independence. An increasing number of Quebeckers are fed up with the debate" (*Star*, May 24/92; *GM*, May 25/92).

To a cynical citizenry, David Peterson's reappearance in the limelight seemed almost inevitable. The former premier waxed eloquent on the innocent way the whole constitutional nation-building business started. Peterson told the Canadian Jewish Congress on May 22 that Quebec "has always had special status — so why they want to start again in the 1990s is beyond me" (*GM*, May 23/92). Most Canadians couldn't imagine why, either. But many wondered why anyone would pose the question if Quebec had always had special status after all. Why was Peterson pushing it so hard himself and for so many years?

Maybe exhaustion had set in with the politicos, too. On the surface, separatism seemed to have died. Two days later in Montreal, answering the call of Parti Québécois leader Jacques Parizeau and Serge Demers, head of Mouvement Québec français, sovereigntists rallied together as a mob in downtown Montreal. Crowd estimates varied, as usual. According to the various media, the crowd ranged from 10,000 to 25,000 in size. Demers himself described it as 40,000 strong. He also now claimed to have 400,000 signatures demanding a clear-cut question on sovereignty for Quebecers. The well-known trade union movement head, Gérald Larose, piped up: "People aren't ready to take to the streets just yet because there's still no date set for the referendum. . . . Besides, this is just the first of many more demonstrations" (*Star*, May 25/92).[4]

Prince Edward Island Premier Joe Ghiz gave a squeak. He always seemed to be missing in action. For the final day of the multilateral ministerial meetings, with political power melting down throughout Canada, he deemed it time to pull a Clark, a Mulroney, a Bourassa, a Castonguay, a Bouchard, a McKenna, a Peterson, a Rae, a Hatfield, and a Rémillard, all at the same time: "Essentially, we have to ask ourselves as Canadians whether we are prepared to see the country dismantled over whether or not one or more of the provinces can get their way on the Senate. To me, that would be a tragedy. Compromise has to be the order of the day" (*GM*, May 29/92).

The 3M circus drew to a close on Saturday, May 31. There had been seven little get-togethers. As usual the differences were snuffed out and the would-be new founding fathers sang in harmony about their wonderful achievements.

The facts pointed to other conclusions. During the weeks from March 12 to May 31, 1992, the behind-the-scenes meetings were conducted in seven different cities. At a cost of millions of dollars, Canadians were once again cheated with their own money. Joe Clark promised that there would be "regular public reporting of progress," yet nothing was made available from the meetings (*GM*, Mar 12/92). For seventy-eight days the executive federalists kept the public in the dark.

The media never complained. By their silence, they endorsed what the governments were doing to the country, and especially what ringleader Joe Clark was doing. Even he, who never in his career believed he might be in trouble, sensed a problem. The day before the series of marathon meetings shut down he said, "We believe we have made an enormous amount of progress . . . and that we should continue this process a little while longer. . . . We shouldn't push people beyond their limits. . . . I think this has been an exercise unparalleled in our constitutional history" (*Star*, May 31/92). And: "We've decided that it would be useful for this process to continue but to take a pause of 10 days [to June 9] so we can consult our governments" (*Sun*, May 31/92).

He was lying outright. There was absolutely nothing resolved on any key issue from Senate reform, aboriginal self-government, the wording of the Canada clause, the amending formula, the distinct society clause, to interprovincial trade barriers, to name only the biggest-ticket items. It was part of the strategy, to carry on no matter what.

The press kept up its own propaganda. Graham Fraser of the *Globe and Mail* offered his perception of things: "The meetings have produced a detailed agreement on aboriginal self-government and agreement in principle on protecting transfer programs from unilateral change, a definition of a Canada clause, recognition of Quebec as a distinct society and an elected Senate. All of these issues raise questions, but the details have not been released. . . . None of the legal texts have been made public" (*GM*, June 8/92).

Heaven knows what he based this on. Yet, Joe Clark was a hero. All you had to do was ask him: "It is strange to compare this with Meech. They didn't have detailed briefings each day on what we are talking about as I have done. This [multilateral] process responds directly to the critique of Meech. The participation is larger. This is a new situation here and we've made important progress partly because it is new" (*Star*, May 31/92).

"They" here obviously referred to the insiders. As for addressing the "critique" of Meech, the message wasn't getting through. Canadians needed to own the process themselves in a democratic state.

Despite the obvious, some allowed themselves to be conned. Manitoba justice and constitutional minister Jim McCrae, for example, bought into it: "I still say Joe Clark is the best person in the whole country to be leading these talks" (*Star*, May 31/92).

Six months to go before the referendum in Quebec with the prospects of a parallel Referendum in Canada. All the consequences that had flowed from Mulroney's speech of supplication at Sept-Îles on August 6, 1984, and the five-point sales pitch Gil Rémillard gave on May 9, 1986, at Mont Gabriel in response were coming home to roost.

And no one said No. Or Non.

Notes

1 In 1989 Hydro-Québec signed a twenty-year, $17-billion contract (presented as anywhere from $12.7-billion and up) to sell electricity to the New York Power Authority. Known as Great Whale or the James Bay II hydro-electric project, the project was to be completed in 1998.

With 36 dams and 579 dykes constructed over an area the size of Lake Erie, Great Whale would generate 3,168 megawatts of electricity — enough for a city of 700,000. The Cree and the Inuit say that the project, which would require the diversion of five rivers and would flood 4,400 square kilometres of land, will destroy their way of life. The Grand Chief of the Cree, Matthew Coon-Come, explains: "People across the world are realizing that our struggle is their struggle — that this is not just denial of industrial development by an isolated group in James Bay. It is part of the global decision to choose between two paths: respect for the environment and the need for sustainable development, or continuation of the rape and pillage of the environment" (*Star*/CP, Aug 7/91; André Picard, *GM*, Aug 10/91).

On September 10, 1991, the Federal Court of Canada ordered a federal review of the project and ruled that Ottawa had ignored its constitutional responsibilities to native peoples.

On September 26, Hydro-Québec failed to appear for a public hearing in New York City on the state's plans to buy power.

2 Mulroney had a point. In his September 23, 1991, article in *The New Yorker*, in *Oh Canada! Oh Quebec!* and in his interview with Barbara Frum on CBC TV's "The Journal" on March 10, 1992; and again at his Elgin Winter Garden Theatre book launch in Toronto on March 11, Richler repeated his own version of Beauchemin's presentation to the B–C Commission: "The obligation to share one's cultural space with a foreign language always expresses a defeat or a state of weakness for someone. If Adolf Hitler had won the war in the 1945, France would be bilingual: French-German" (p. 240).

What Beauchemin actually said was: "Had Hitler won the war in 1945, *Paris* would be bilingual [German and French]. Collective bilingualism always suggests that a society has lost something" [italics mine] (*Journal des débats*, Nov 20/90, p. 471).

3 Rewards for Ted Rogers would come later. On March 8, 1994, Rogers Communications Inc. acquired control of Maclean Hunter Limited. The deal was subject to the approval of the CRTC. Some months later CRTC chairman Keith Spicer "wondered aloud," according to the *Financial Post*, whether or not it was "dangerous for an entire industry to be following the ideas of one man and one company" (*FP*, Sept 24/94). If the deal went through, some 42 percent of what English Canada sees on cable television would come by way of Rogers Communication. To no one's surprise, the CRTC approved the $3.1-billion takeover. The CRTC's blessings came just before Christmas on December 19, 1994, giving Ted Rogers control of numerous influential vehicles including *Maclean's* magazine, the *Financial Post*, and the Toronto Sun Publishing Corporation. The warnings of the O'Leary Commission of 1961, the Special Senate Committee on Mass Media in 1970, and the Kent Commission of 1980 had long since been forgotten (see chapter 20). *Toronto Sun* columnist Peter Worthington, once one of the strongest voices for freedom in Canada, welcomed the new order as an "encouraging start for 1995" (*Sun*, Jan 3/95).

4 Estimating the size of crowds of protesters in Quebec is a sort of game. No one ever really knows what the numbers are. On St. Jean Baptiste Day, June 24, 1991, *Le Devoir* described the crowd as running between 200,000 and 350,000; *La Presse* judged it to be 150,000; and *Le Soleil* came up with 75,000. Taking the uproar into account, a variety of witnesses said they also saw one Quebecer who was high on drugs dive into the festival bonfire and kill himself (*GM*, June 26/91; *Star*/CP, June 30/91).

VII

A World of Privilege
and the Fifth Estate

24

Power Brokers
in the Feudal Kingdom

THE ELECTION OF THE Progressive Conservatives in 1984 sparked a revolution on three fronts.

For one thing, Mulroney's Conservatives were the first federally elected political party in Canadian history who were uncommitted — even unconcerned — about Canadian nationalism. Under the new prime minister, they came together, an odd lot, in a marriage of Red Tories who had abandoned small-c conservatism, the party's traditional roots, and right-wing Quebec separatists. Right from the start, Mulroney's Quebec caucus attracted many political hangers-on dedicated to creating a separate nation of Quebec. This pact with the devil far surpassed Lester Pearson's dalliance with the Bloc Populaire and separatist André Laurendeau that led to the Bi-Bi Cultural Commission in 1963.

The second feature of this new, radical Tory power base would endanger the country even more. This was the union of a federal political party and the interests of big business and multinational corporations and those who consider Canada a commercial component of North America rather than an east–west federation of provinces. Under the Tories, influence-peddling blossomed into a fine art. Democracy became irrelevant.

Hannah Arendt described this environment in her work *On Revolution* (1963): "Corruption and perversion are more pernicious, and at the same time more likely to occur, in an egalitarian republic than in any other form of government. Schematically speaking, they come to pass when private interests invade the public domain . . ." (p. 255).

The list of influence peddlers during the Mulroney years grew and grew and grew. And the country groaned. Topping it were the agents for the major corporations, and the associations that lobbied for them. One of the most notorious was the Ottawa-based **Business Council on National Issues (BCNI)**. According to the organization's literature:

> The Business Council is the senior voice of Canadian business on public policy issues in Canada and abroad. . . . A non-partisan and not-for-profit organization, the Council membership is composed of the chief executive officers of 150 leading Canadian corporations. With 1.5 million employees, member companies administer close to $1 trillion in assets. The Council engages in an active program of research, consultation and advocacy, and its focus nationally is to help build a strong economy, progressive social policies, and healthy political institutions.

The council was formed in 1976. Its president and chief executive officer is **Thomas d'Aquino**. One critic, David Langille, has described it as a "virtual shadow cabinet." Another media observer, Joyce Nelson, who published an essay "Packaging the Populace: Polling in the Age of Image Politics" in 1989, dissected BCNI's cosy, lucrative world in 1982: "[BCNI is] skilled in government relations to the point of determining policy behind the scenes. At the same time, its member corporations jumped on the advocacy ad bandwagon in order to improve image problems revealed in the polls and to promote their own sectoral agendas" (*Best Canadian Essays: 1990*, p. 231).

In both Meech Lake and the Charlottetown Accord, the BCNI strongly supported the final package and all of the interim packages. D'Aquino, described as the "the Council's chief spokesman," appeared frequently on television. He attended various seminars and government committees pressing the corporate agenda as well. The initiative was dubbed "Radically Reconstructed Federalism" (*GM*, Jan. 21/91). Formerly a member of Trudeau's staff, d'Aquino boasts a long record of direct involvement in the corridors of power.

He began, as so many other political creatures do, as a lawyer. During the Meech Lake fracas he joined the Meech Lake support group, Canadians for a Unifying Constitution. When the accord collapsed, d'Aquino bragged that within twenty-four hours he had contacted an academic at Queen's University in Kingston, Ontario, to prepare for the next round. Armed with buckets of money, and himself a member in good standing of the Queen's Mafia, he had cornered $100,000 to guarantee the success of the next round for big-business interests.

For six years, Canadian television viewers were subjected to sermons from d'Aquino, most of them on the CBC. Canadians were fed his ideas on a regular basis. For example, he once allowed that constituent assemblies were not, in and of themselves, a bad idea. He even condescended: "It's a totally respectable idea. Some of the greatest constitutions in the world have had their origins in constituent assemblies" (*Star*, Mar 25/91).

In a move that testified to the "shadow cabinet" mindset, he wrote to Canada's eleven first ministers during the Meech impasse of May 1990 to urge them to ratify the deal. As he put it, he wanted to avert a "crisis of confidence" in the Canadian economy: "[The Meech Lake impasse is adding a] dangerous dimension to our economic problems. . . . We appeal to you to summon those qualities of tolerance, statesmanship and love of country that each of you have demonstrated so often in public life and end this crisis now" (*FP*, May 23/90).

In other words go along — agree.

Two weeks after that, he wrote about the Charest committee report that produced the parallel accord recommendations. He praised its recommendations as "exactly what the country needed" (*GM*, June 11/90).

He met with Premier Robert Bourassa on March 26, 1990, and then claimed to have secured his promise to support federalism. If so, he accomplished more than any prime minister had!

Almost a year after the collapse of Meech Lake, he stepped in to warn the country's leaders: "What this must not become — and is in danger of becoming — is a battle between competing first ministers and their bureaucracies" (Carol Goar, *Star*, Mar 21/91).

Whether it was Meech Lake, Meech II, the Pearson accord, or the Charlottetown Accord, the BCNI concentrated on maintaining a stable investment environment. Democracy was relevant only as long as that state continued.

During the Mulroney years, the BCNI accomplished none of its objectives. The more governments and media pushed and bullied Canadians into accepting what *they* wanted, the more stubbornly Canadians dug their heels in.

Time and again d'Aquino employed the same strategy the politicians did. By the time the Charlottetown Accord reached the table, it was impossible to distinguish between government and big business.

All the people that want to hold this country together will be on the Yes side. . . . Let's look at the advantages of staying together. (CBC Newsworld, Sept 3/92)

If the family doesn't want to live together anymore. That's what it's [the Referendum] going to come down to. (CBC Newsworld, Sept 18/92)

We are not, as the BCNI, going out to raise millions of dollars. . . . The decision will be left to the individual companies. [As for me, I have a responsibility to] tell it like it really is. . . . We believe that a rejection of the Charlottetown agreement could impose incalculable costs on all Canadians. Those costs will be reflected in political strife, social divisions and severe economic consequences. . . . I can't help but think a negative vote is going to have an impact on confidence; it's going to have a negative impact on investors and it's going to have a negative impact on how people outside the country see us. (*Star*, Sept 19/92)

The Charlottetown agreement represents the distillation of a massive exercise in public consultation and intergovernmental negotiation. . . . Trudeau directs a great deal of his fire at the Canada clause — a clause that upon first reading captured, eloquently and imaginatively, I thought, the spirit of the country. . . .

Trudeau condemns the constitutional entrenchment of first ministers' conferences as a step that will undermine existing parliamentary institutions. I see this initiative, on the other hand, as a response to millions of Canadians who thirst for a new era of intergovernmental co-operation. (*Star*, Oct 16/92)

Among the most powerful corporations to ally themselves with government and against the will of the people were the leaders of the banking community. The top five, the Royal Bank, the Canadian Imperial Bank of Commerce, the Bank of Montreal, the Toronto-Dominion Bank, and the Bank of Nova Scotia joined eighteen other corporations in donating more than $100,000 each to the Yes Committee that supported the Charlottetown Accord. The largest single contribution, $214,000, came from the Canadian Pharmaceutical Manufacturers' Association. Of the $7.2 million raised, corporations contributed $7.1 million. Individual Canadians gave a mere $77,000 to support the Yes side.[1]

The merchants of greed came out in full force, waving the spectres of fiscal disruption, Quebec separation, a weakened banking community, and other gloomy scenarios. The largest financial institutions ganged up to peddle the message that Canadians simply had to surrender to the wisdom of the boardroom.

Matthew Barrett, chairman and CEO of the Bank of Montreal, pushed this corporate agenda. The bank reported a record profit of $640 million in the fiscal year ended October 31, 1992, up 7 percent from the previous year. This is the bank that paid its 233 officers some $48.4 million and its 28 directors $940 million during the worst year in the current recession.

Barrett mounted the podium on behalf of the Yes side wherever he could. Like Allan Taylor, he held views contrary to those of the people with whom his institution did business. As far as banking leaders were concerned, Canada's vitality resulted not from individual freedom and its citizens' own aspirations but exclusively from the stability of the investment climate. Anyone who could not understand this, the bankers glowered, was paving the road to certain disaster.

Meech, of course, failed. Two and one-half months after that, Barrett addressed the Vancouver Board of Trade, on September 4, 1990. And he hauled out the threat of western separation. Warning of the nature of public policy issues and separatism, he referred to "a kind of destructive regionalism" infecting the country, adding that there was a "real danger of immobilizing this country if not ripping it apart" (*Star*, Sept 5/90).

He spoke at the Canadian Club of Montreal roughly a year after the Meech Lake demise, on May 6, 1991: "It remains true that for the French language and culture the price of survival is eternal vigilance" (*Star*, May 7/91). Sternly he admonished his listeners: "History has few lessons for us on the results of deliberately breaking up a leading industrial economy. . . . Nobody has yet done it. There is no recipe for turning bouillabaisse back into fish" (*Star*, May 7/91).

On November 18, 1991, almost six months after that speech, Barrett was welcomed to speak at the Canadian Club of Toronto:

> But will we have much to celebrate by the end of 1992? I wonder. So, today I want to speak with candour about our country. Never before have the issues facing Canada been so stark and the stakes so high. . . . We cannot take Canada's strengths and successes for granted. . . . Even without the break-up of the country, the economic challenges are daunting. . . . I didn't consciously come here to depress you, but as I said at the outset, it's hard to give a speech today that isn't serious. For these are dangerous times, and no issue is more critical than the future of our country.

He spoke at the C.D. Howe Institute on October 19, 1992, just six days before the Referendum on the Charlottetown Accord:

I believe the accord taken as a whole represents solid progress on a number of fronts and that this progress substantially outweighs its shortcomings. . . .

At the very minimum, a No vote is a vote for constitutional gridlock . . . [and] a boost for separatist forces in Quebec. Why would we choose an environment of ongoing uncertainty and risk? (*FP*, Oct 20/92)

Like many top executives in Canada who live in the transient vest-pocket world of moveable and multinational head office decision-making, Barrett and Taylor were culturally dysfunctional about Canadian history.

A great number of corporate executives displayed their ignorance during the constitutional debate. Many accepted invitations to speak on the Constitution, particularly in English-speaking Canada. With inflated self-confidence about their positions and their brilliance in the constitutional debates, many scurried up to dizzying heights, imagining themselves responsible leaders in a democratic society. The few smarter ones had the grace to shut up.

Here's one hand-out from the business community, from Kenneth Harrigan, president and chief executive officer of the Ford Motor Company of Canada. A speech he gave in Oakville was repeated in the *Globe and Mail*'s "Report on Business" on April 13, 1990. He expressed himself convinced that failure to sign the Meech Lake Accord "would be more than a tragedy for Canada. In fact it would be a national disgrace" that "would be a clear signal to the rest of the world that economic instability will follow as darkness follows dusk. . . . indeed a dark day for Canada." He expounded his interpretation of Canadian history: "We have come too far during these 124 years of nationhood to lose it now. Created in the 19th century, by two founding races, we became unique. . . ."

O N OCTOBER 7, 1992, just a few days before the Referendum, a poll by the executive search firm Caldwell Partners Amrop International was published. Of Canada's senior executives, 433 believed Canada's next prime minister should be drawn from the business world. Topping the list of twenty essential qualities, 47 percent of them ranked vision as the first priority. Honesty and ethics ranked second, considered most important by only 12 percent.

Gratuitously, the survey participants also offered the Caldwell firm the names of those they thought suitable for the job of prime minister of Canada. In order of priority the choices were Matthew Barrett, Laurent Beaudoin, and Conrad Black. According to Margot Gibb-Clark's article

"Wanted: PM with vision, MBA," in the October 7, 1993, *Globe*, Allan Taylor placed sixth.

Perhaps the nation is safe from Matthew Barrett at least. Months later he disavowed all political aspirations: "None at all — absolutely" (*GM*, Jan 19/93).

Barrett was not the one who attracted the greatest public outrage. That dubious distinction belonged to **Allan Richard Taylor** of the Royal Bank, which in 1991 employed some 55,000 people. Taylor acted as a behind-the-scenes player for the Meech Lake Accord. In the final three weeks of that constitutional pressure cooker, he applied the heat to the "hold-out" premiers, Gary Filmon, Frank McKenna, and Clyde Wells, just before the final FMC from June 3 to 9, 1990. He informed the press of his part: "What I've been doing is talking to them about the specific economic ramifications. The turmoil threatens to bring very negative economic and financial results to the country" (*Star*, June 2/90).

The Meech failure might have slowed him in his crusade but not for long. Soon thereafter he set out on the stump again, for the Charlottetown Accord. Canadians became very familiar with fear-mongering and scare tactics during this period, and his speech at the bank's annual meeting on January 23, 1992, stood out. The *Globe and Mail* reproduced the entire speech the next day under the heading "Do we need to blow Canada apart?" Taylor posed another question to the audience — "Do we really need to destroy Canada?" — no fewer than seven times during the speech.

On September 25, 1992, the Royal Bank published a forty-seven-page study that it mailed out to 800 insiders. For other interested parties, the bank offered a 1-800 number to call and request copies. It attracted 4,500 more orders. The study presents the cost of separation: a mass exodus of 1.25 million people leaving the country — 15-percent interest rates — a 15-percent drop in investment — 720,000, or 15 percent of the population, out of work: "Nothing — nothing — would do more to spur economic recovery than a 'Yes' vote. . . . Nothing would do more to restore confidence in ourselves, or the world's confidence in us. . . . We didn't say anything in our report about the consequences of a No vote. We're not going to speculate on the results of a No vote" (*Star*, Sept 26/92).[2]

Taylor's behaviour was arguably the most irresponsible of any senior corporate official in Canadian history. Canadians were infuriated. In Quebec there were reports of large withdrawals of funds from the bank's branches. It was one of those rare occasions when most Canadians agreed with Jacques Parizeau that Taylor had indulged in "cheap scare tactics": "Mr. Taylor should watch his mouth. The Royal Bank is not exactly a beanery, so the money markets are going to take what he says seriously" (*GM*, Sept 30/92).

Even if Canadians disliked Parizeau's opportunism, the majority did concur with Terence Corcoran of the *Globe and Mail*: "It is illegitimate to suggest, as the Royal Bank and the Prime Minister are claiming, that a No vote means Quebec will separate into a separate country, thereby perpetrating a Canadian economic disaster. That is not the question, that is not the issue, nor is it the alternative. The issue for all Canadians is whether the Charlottetown agreement is the kind of unity Canadians want" (*GM*, Sept 30/92).

Harvard graduate **A.L. (Al) Flood**, chairman and CEO of Corporate Bank, the Canadian Imperial Bank of Commerce (CIBC), was a lower-profile player in corporate intimidation. Speaking in Victoria, British Columbia, he did manage, nevertheless, to stick his neck out for those lined up against the people: "The slightest hint of instability can send global financial markets into disarray" (*Star*, Sept 28/92).

Equivalent to the BCNI as a lobbying institution in Quebec is the **Conseil du patronat du Québec (CPQ)**. Although the organization is federalist in outlook, about one-third of its members supports some form of Quebec sovereignty. Thomas d'Aquino's counterpart, then, is CPQ president **Ghislain Dufour**. In fact, he became the most often quoted spokesperson on behalf of corporate Quebec: on the Meech Lake Accord, he said that it would be wise for the "business world to be prudent" (quoted by Robert Mackenzie, *Star*, Feb 19/90, from *Journal de Montréal*).

In February 1991, on the Bélanger–Campeau Commission's strategy following the Meech collapse, he said: "These guys — my members — are used to dealing with English Canada. They know it takes months and months to negotiate a deal so it's not possible to think renewed federalism in just 18 months" (*GM*, Feb 19/91).

On the Pearson and Charlottetown agreements, he said, "An interesting framework for negotiations as far as Quebec is concerned. The premier should go directly back to the constitutional table and stop negotiating through intermediaries. . . . Everyone sees a turnaround" (*Star*, July 9/92). Again, he stated that "Quebec business clearly says Yes and accepts that gains in autonomy in transportation, manpower and other areas far outweigh any downside" (*FP*, Oct 2/92).

By this time, many mystery players were pushing various buttons in Canada's constitutional debate. Few of them made themselves heard publicly. They tended to keep themselves aloof from the constitutional fray, many of them more concerned about managing their immense wealth, like the Hon. **Paul Desmarais**, for instance, arguably the wealthiest and most powerful industrialist in Canada. A long-standing friend and financial backer of Brian Mulroney, he quietly supported the Meech Lake Accord and the Charlottetown Accord very much in the background.[3] During Meech Lake he served as a member of the joint group Canadians for a Unifying Constitution and The Friends of Meech Lake, which published the bizarre booklet *Setting the Record Straight*. On July 1, 1992, Mulroney appointed Desmarais privy councillor. Besides having accumulated great personal wealth, Desmarais seemed a puzzling choice to Canadians who did not understand the reason for bestowing such an honour on him. There had to be a great deal more behind the story. Certainly, the press would not risk telling most of it, though they happily quoted the most public of his remarks:

[On Meech Lake, under the headline "Meech Row Costs Million in Investment":] I know I have had two big deals where I had interested two groups for several hundred [700 to 800] million dollars. (Kevin Dougherty, reporting on the annual shareholders meeting of Power Corporation, Montreal, May 9/90, reported in *FP*, May 10/90)

I hope [Meech] passes; I think it would be good for the unity of Canada. I think it would be very good for Quebec. It would stabilize things. (*FP*, May 10/90)

When Meech collapsed, he said:

I hope they find a solution that keeps Quebec in Canada. From an economic point of view, this would be the best formula. I think the federal system is best adapted to protect our liberties and continue our economic development. If we find a federal formula which guarantees our culture, our language, and all that Quebec needs to preserve, it would be very good. After all, if we separate what will we become? (*FP*, Dec 13/90, interview with *La Presse*)

Pierre S. Pettigrew was another kingpin of the business world who hailed from Quebec and backed the Mulroney constitutional agenda. The former advisor to Trudeau and member of the Privy Council played his cagey role by default. A selection of comments during the Meech Lake debate reveals his defensiveness about the whole business:

Quebeckers are not aggressive about it, but they are saying we do not need the rest of Canada. We're slowly moving to independence from one another, and fewer and fewer people care. (*GM*, May 25/89)

Ottawa continues to bring into conflict the public and private sectors, and maintains a rhetoric and a policy that are naive. (*GM*, July 31/89)

I don't see aggressivity toward English Canada, just a lack of interest. (*Star*, Aug 15/89)

Another prominent Quebecer and supporter of Meech Lake and the Mulroney agenda was **Bertin Nadeau**, chairman of the corporate giant Unigesco Inc. of Montreal, and a member of the Association in Favour of Meech Lake. He studied commerce at l'Ecole des hautes études commerciales de Montréal, the province's leading graduate business school. He spoke out with particular fervour on behalf of Mulroney's Meech Accord, but his message was so confusing at times that those who actually opposed his views also cited him as a reference. Clyde Wells, for example, quoted Nadeau's February 20, 1990, speech in Montreal:

If Meech fails, do we have to set in motion the process of the separation of Quebec? But to arrive at what? To pass 10 to 15 years negotiating with rancour the new condition of cohabitation and the division of a patrimony, during all the time of which the patrimony is falling apart under the weight of our negligence. In this game, everyone loses. . . . Rather, let us address the problems. (Wells's speech, Rotary Club of Ottawa, Château Laurier, Sept 27/90)

Nadeau's voice was not unlike that of Ghislain Dufour in its call for calm and reason. In his article in the July 25, 1990, *Globe and Mail* following the collapse of Meech, "Better to tackle economic problems than waste energy on secession," he zoomed in on the more pertinent issues facing Canada:

Because I appreciate the advantages of this free, democratic, prosperous country, but also because I believe that Canada, rather than squandering its emotional and intellectual energy on discussing possible terms of

Quebec's secession, must concentrate its vital force on tackling serious economic problems that threaten the whole country — not just Quebec. . . . What concerns me more is the threat of erosion of Canada's competitive ability in the world economy.

Two and a half years later, his reasoning still deserved serious reflection: "Yet, without the Canadian leverage, Quebec's counterbalance to the sheer weight of U.S. culture declines from 26 million to six million. And what does Quebec get in return? An increase in the authority over Quebec's domestic affairs — this, and nothing more. The capacity for self-determination flows from economic strength, from the influence Quebec can exert on the rest of Canada and the world" (*Maclean's*, Jan 6/92).

Raymond Cyr, chairman and CEO of the vast BCE Inc. empire, was another of Quebec's executive federalists. And he seemed to get away with more than most of his fellows in pushing the Mulroney agenda at Canadians. After Meech, he spoke at a Canadian Club luncheon in Montreal: "Today we have the opportunity to redefine a new Canada. . . . Quebecers are organized. English Canada has to wake up . . . to get organized so that a dialogue can begin. . . . It can switch very quickly. What's required now is a demonstration in the rest of Canada that change is possible. If we don't get that, I don't think we can be too optimistic. . . . I think it's too important to leave to the political elite" (*FP*, Feb 12/90).

And then there was **Laurent Beaudoin**, yet another chairman and CEO, this time of Bombardier Inc. He too was a well-known spokesman for Canadian federalism, which surprised no one. Bombardier Inc., the Montreal-based transportation and aerospace empire was bound financially and commercially to every level of government throughout Canada. He cochaired the Régroupement Economie et Constitution (Group for the Economy and the Constitution), a federalist business organization in Quebec organized in September 1991. Initially President **Claude Beauchamp**, publisher of the Montreal daily *La Presse*, headed the Régroupement, which Paul Desmarais chairs. Under Cyr's later co-chairmanship, Régroupement was armed with a budget of $500,000 to sponsor very specific economic studies, to demonstrate the advantages of federalism and set the agenda. Beaudoin found it unnecessary to resort to threats and propaganda:

I do not share the view that the economic, social and cultural development of French-speaking Quebecers has been hampered by Quebec's participation in the Canadian federation. French-speaking Quebecers have never enjoyed more economic influence and power in Canada than they do today. Language issues, tensions between anglophones and franco- phones . . . seem terribly empty, outdated, a throwback to another age. (*Star*/CP, July 2/91)[4]

Aside from Robert Bourassa and Brian Mulroney, **Claude Castonguay** was one of the best-known Quebec voices to the rest of Canada. Under the Tories, he was made a senator and given Canada's highest honour, Com- panion of the Order of Canada, for good constitutional conduct. The father of the Quebec pension plan had spent the previous three decades in Quebec business politics, playing the role of the conditional feder- alist, the Quebec nationalist, and the Péquiste. Always he demanded more for his province, regardless of what satisfying those demands would do to the Canadian federation. Push, push, push was his methodology.

He was about as pro-Canadian as Louis Riel. Pierre Trudeau blamed the provincial Liberal cabinet minister in Bourassa's government for sabotag- ing the Victoria Charter in 1971 after Bourassa had agreed to it. Now, in 1992, he almost succeeded in collapsing the Castonguay–Dobbie Special Joint Committee on a Renewed Canada, too. As Hubert Bauch of the Montreal *Gazette* put it, Castonguay invoked a "transparently diplomatic flu" that necessitated his sudden retirement from the committee. Bauch described the committee as "a total fiasco that surpasses anything that Kafka could have imagined" (Feb 29/92). In the *Globe and Mail* Harvey Enchin reported in September 1990 that "Claude Castonguay, a convert to Quebec separatism after the failure of the Meech Lake accord, parleyed a political career into a successful business strategy. . . . Since then he has advocated that Quebec separate from Canada" (Sept 25/90).

Lots of other Quebecers at least entertained when they did not choose to be particularly informative. Despite the quality of his nasal sermons and lectures, which were a crashing bore, Monsieur Too-Much-of-a-Muchness remained one of CBC's favourite spokespeople on Quebec. The state broadcaster earned itself a lot of resentment by airing so much of his commentary.

According to the Montreal columnist for the *Gazette*, William Johnson, Castonguay's political thinking grew out of the 1960s. It had been inspired by the decolonization theories of Franz Fanon and Jacques Berque, two philosophers who compared Quebec to an African colony. Shades of the Negro King in the Duplessis era (see Chapter 1). Although Castonguay headed up the $11-billion Laurentian Group Corporation, and sits as director of numerous corporations and institutions, his influence in Quebec and across Canada was vastly overestimated during both the Meech and the Charlottetown debates. Robert Sheppard, the *Globe* columnist, called him "a dull actuary who is nonetheless a respected political figure in Quebec" (*GM*, July 14/92). Deborah Coyne's assessment is charitable: "Castonguay is a heavy-set man with an abrasive manner whom I do not consider a truly committed Canadian federalist. My impression of him is that his world revolves around Quebec and especially the business community, which is not surprising, given his provincial government experience" (*Roll of the Dice*, p. 53).

In December 1989 Castonguay founded the Association in Favour of Meech Lake, Quebec's most powerful pro-accord lobby group. Canada was "sleepwalking towards disaster, as he saw it" (*Star*, Feb 21/90):

> Our fellow citizens in the other provinces must understand that, after so many efforts, often humiliating, and after so many years, Quebeckers are fed up. . . .
>
> If the Meech Lake accord is not ratified, it could be disastrous. It would be a failure which Quebeckers would remember for a long time. But it would not stop us. It is obvious to me that the Quebec people will turn to wider and more exciting horizons. (*GM*, Feb 26/90)

After Meech failed, the Quebecer reverted to his traditional role as spoiler and doomsayer. He carried the message into the boardroom. There he grimly presented the Bélanger–Campeau Commission with three options: a highly decentralized federation, a confederal system of sovereign states, or sovereignty-association. On January 25, 1991, the shareholders of the Laurentian Bank of Canada listened to him speak as the company's chairman: "What Quebec business people predicted, that is to say a divorce from English Canada, is under way" (*FP*, Jan 28/91).

After he had slunk away from the Castonguay–Dobbie Special Joint Committee as co-chair, the Senator actually showed up as a witness before the committee — by then Beaudoin–Dobbie — and recommended a return to the two-nations theory of Canada. "I think it's absolutely essential for the federal proposals, instead of being middle of the road, that they correspond closely to the 2 concepts of Canada" (*Star*, Jan 22/92). And the Mulroney government responded in its own inimitable way — by rewarding him.

Castonguay showed no interest in the Pearson agreement of July 7, 1992, which would become the Charlottetown Accord. When the *Financial Post* interviewed him about the agreement on July 14, he told them he wanted to turn back the clock, perhaps to the Meech Lake formula. Or Mulroney, he said, should arbitrate a solution himself to bring before Parliament: "They will say that [Quebec is being favoured], but now we are going to hear from Quebec. . . . [Otherwise] I'm not optimistic. We are headed for a constitutional crisis" (*FP*, July 15/92).

Paul Desmarais might have chosen to remain silent in his support of the Tories and the prime minister; **Conrad Black**, the international media tycoon who had all but left Canada, said far more in public. He measured his remarks carefully, and when he did speak he received star billing, and for good reason. His words could be interpreted in any of a thousand ways. Example — "I am one of those who believes French-Canadians had just grievances about their position in Canada and that English Canadians very conscientiously addressed those grievances" (Empire Club, Nov 2/93). They were once victims and are no longer? Blackmail for the past, but not now? Who knows? Obviously, he found Canada's constitutional crisis simply too inviting a subject to ignore.

Black is a champion of fence-walking and a master of the ethereal nuance. The Protestant-turned-Roman Catholic, Torontonian-turned-Londoner, food-and-tractor tycoon who transformed himself into a transnational media corporation, proved himself one of the few in the corporate world with anything important to say. Spouting observations articulate, amusing, and sometimes outrageous, he could usually convert a mind or two with the wide range of his dismissals of the fools he suffered only for the eventual joy of abusing them.

In 1989 he expressed himself as one "who has spent twenty years toiling in the vineyards of bilingualism, constructive federalism, and mutual respect between the proverbial founding races" (*Sat Night*, June/89). Basically he longs for the good old days when Trudeau reigned: "The only believable rationale for Canada is one based on a bicultural country built not on coercion but on mutual respect" (*FP*, Oct 11/91). Though he would never admit it, he would have been comfortable to have Trudeau in power forever.

In his autobiography *A Life in Progress*, published in the fall of 1993, Black explained:

> I wrote a serious treatise essentially supporting official bilingualism and an amending formula close to the Victoria Charter that emerged in the summer of 1971. (p. 75)

I had known Trudeau casually for some years. . . . His relentless incitements of special-interest groups, multicultural, regional, and sexist organizations, did terrible and perhaps irreparable damage to the social and fiscal structure of the country. He imposed a ruthless economic egalitarianism, especially in such areas as medical care. Yet, withal, I had always supported his championship of federalism, biculturalism, and national unity. (p. 300)

But unlike that former prime minister, Black did support the Meech Lake Accord, however briefly: "Our leaders should aspire to do more than patch up Meech Lake, an arrangement I supported when it appeared to be a settlement and not just another station on a syncopated descent toward what Ernest Manning described 20 years ago as a 'constitutional Munich'" (*FP*, Dec 29/88).

Black let off his big bang on Referendum day, October 26, 1992, in a speech to the Canadian Club. There he put paid to Quebec's infamous Bill 178 in a manner that Canadians had long prayed their prime minister would do:

Quebec in the last 15 years has become of all important Canadian jurisdictions, the most officially hostile to bilingualism. Quebec has chosen to remain a sullen victim and officially oppress its own minorities more thoroughly than French Canadians have been oppressed. . . . If Quebec's version of federalism is to suppress and render invisible the language of 70% of Canadians and 95% [actually 98 percent] of North Americans while expecting English Canadians to continue to pay billions of dollars of real or disguised equalisation transfers to Quebec, it won't work. That version can't work and no one should try to make it work.

Then, one of the most executive federalists of them all held back the most longed-for TKO punch in Canadian history:

I do not question the good faith of the authors of this agreement [the Charlottetown Accord] and I certainly identify with those who vote yes hoping that it will bring an end to the constitutional uncertainties. . . .

Either we will have a Canada, including Quebec, that is durable and functioning, or else we will have a Canada without Quebec that will be able to re-centralize and at last function coherently, or we will have the rest of Canada apart from Quebec achieving an arrangement of closer cooperation with the United States. This last alternative, [for] which I have been widely reviled, most recently by Dalton Camp, of all people, for even considering, would reduce taxes and our cost of living and increase our standard of living. It would be a federal union, not annexation. . . .

A year later he put the boots to Charlottetown in *A Life in Progress*:

In the Canadian constitutional imbroglio of 1992 every conceivable special interest group and jurisdictional appetite was appeased with a terminal devolution that would have emasculated the federal government. . . . For reasons of personal relations, with Mulroney and Bourassa, whose sincerity on this issue I didn't question, only their judgement, I didn't recommend a no vote, though it was obvious I was no great admirer of the proposed deal. (pp. 504–5)

His opinions were as good as anything Allan Fotheringham wrote when he was feeling ornery. Historian Ramsay Cook, for example, he once dubbed a "slanted, supercilious little twit" (*Star*, July 9/89). Bourassa, on the other hand, struck him as big league:

I have known him for 25 years. . . . Always intelligent, always rather gracious, but never a federalist, he is without convictions, a charming chameleon adapting with agility to economic requirements and the arithmetic of the polls. (*FP*, Feb 6/91)

Brian Mulroney and Joe Clark deserve high praise for the federal government's constitutional proposals [post-Meech Lake]. . . .
. . . It is a cautionary fact that the greatest influence on the course of the discussions [on Meech II] will come from the familiar inconstant and psephologically obsessed premier of Quebec.
Robert Bourassa has many virtues, most of them relating to political longevity. He sabotaged the Victoria Charter on the amending formula 20 years ago by flivering [*sic*] and waffling. (*FP*, Oct 11/91)

Many of the corporate players were politicians who had returned to the private sector. People who had survived in politics for any length of time had learned to be much more secretive than the corporation CEOs, who did not know any better. Because of their previous high profiles and their proximity to the limelight, all of them found publicity inescapable.

One of the groups that thought of itself as something along the lines of a constituent assembly and therefore democratic was a Montreal-based organization, **Group 22**. Former premiers, lawyers, business executives, and others rubbed shoulders in common cause, politicians swelling their number. On June 10, 1991, a year after Meech, Group 22 was granted a privileged audience before Prime Minister Mulroney and Premier Bourassa, and invited to table a twenty-eight-page report entitled *Some Practical Suggestions for Canada*.

The group seized the opportunity happily. They recommended a highly decentralized Canada. They wanted federal powers such as energy, pensions, family benefits, and income supplements shifted to the provinces. The only area of constitutional change they considered necessary was in those areas where it was possible to amend the Constitution by avoiding the unanimity provision and employing the "7 & 50" formula. As for the most divisive issue in the country, the group suggested no review and no change:

> We have formed the impression that our language difficulties do not emerge primarily out of bad policy, but more out of inter-community tensions that are being played out at the attitudinal and symbolic level.
>
> **We therefore recommend that no change be made to the legal and constitutional provisions concerning language, recognizing that where new national institutions are created, official languages must be respected.** (*Report*, Recommendation II, p. 18)

Unbelievably obtuse! The report was not nearly as daring and perceptive about bilingualism as the 1978 Pépin–Roberts Task Force on Canadian Unity (see Chapter 3).

Among the influence peddlers in Group 22 were Paul Desmarais, Jr., president of Power Corporation; Hugh Segal, the Red Tory and compadre of Dalton Camp, who had been in his turn former adviser to the prime minister; and the Ontario pinkish Tory, Bill Davis, the former Conservative premier of Ontario. By 1991, Davis was sitting on the boards of fifteen corporations. The premier who once said, "Bland works," changed his mind: "I think we have to become emotional. . . . Surely the essence of what we're discussing is to appeal to the hearts and minds of Canadian people" (*GM*, Dec 6/91).

The two former premiers in Group 22 clung to their executive-federalist ideals. Allan Blakeney and Bill Davis both opposed the idea of a referendum. Blakeney called such a plebiscite "enormously divisive" (*Star*, Dec 9/91). Lawyer "Brampton Billy," as Davis was known, had more to say: "[Sovereignty-association] is the ultimate cop-out: a self-imposed ghetto mentality" (*GM*, Jan 18/92).

As for bilingualism in the Ontario public service, as far back as 1971 he had said:

> I should underline at this point, and I want to be most emphatic about it, that this policy will be implemented in such a way that the careers of those unilingual persons holding these positions will in no way be affected. I am aware of the problems in this regard which have developed at the federal level, and I wish to make my commitment very clear; I repeat, the careers of unilingual persons in the Public Service will in no way be threatened, now or in the future. And I should also add that the future entry or promotion of unilingual persons into the Ontario Public Service will not be affected by our policy on bilingualism. (Ontario Legislature, May 3/71)

He endorsed the idea that Quebec be recognized as a distinct society: "Sure, we're all distinct, but if you're talking about a social structure, the concern about assimilation, the need to preserve a culture and a language, you have to recognize that there is a distinct character about our sister province" (*Star*, Sept 13/91). But what did this mean two decades later, in legal terms?

Harrison McCain, chairman of the board of McCain Foods Limited of New Brunswick, had as good a reason as any. He was confused. In the spring of 1991 he had been one of thirteen prominent Maritimers who formed a pro-centralist-government group, the **Northumberland Group**. It had supported views diametrically opposed to those held by Group 22, of which McCain was also a member. On behalf of all its members, the group said, "We believe that the central government is needed to establish the broad framework, to set the national objectives, national standards, and to provide citizens with a sense of the country. . . . Canada is already highly decentralized" (*Star*, July 22/91).

No history of Canada's constitutional manipulators would be complete without special mention of the Hon. **Peter Edgar Lougheed**, the former premier of Alberta. To the manor born, he is the grandson of Sir James Lougheed, a successful land speculator Sir John A. Macdonald nominated to the Senate. Although he, like Alberta Premier Don Getty, played football for the Edmonton Eskimos, Lougheed made himself an insider. Getty did not, so he was not. For this, Getty was ridiculed. As the province's premier from 1971 to 1985, Lougheed participated in the constitutional patriation process of 1981. After retiring from politics, the aristocratic

Lougheed resumed his law practice and served on the board of directors of many well-known Canadian corporations, including the Royal Bank.

He proved himself the patron saint of executive federalism. A Trudovnic in Conservative clothing and a Red Tory to the core who ran up his province's deficits like there was no tomorrow, he could stickhandle his way through almost anything, until he was confronted with an idea. He admitted it himself: "I am trying to work behind the scenes on a constitutional settlement in a low profile way" (*Maclean's*, Jan 6/92). He has been credited with persuading the federal government to slide the most divisive issue in the nation, bilingualism, off the agenda.

Along with David Elton, he became one of the founding fathers of the **Canada West Foundation**. This is odd because he consistently welshed on the concept of a Triple-E Senate.

Peter C. Newman pushed the Lougheed name, armed with his own numerous connections, at his fellow citizens as the most capable person to head up the formation and leadership of a constituent assembly. The ploy was obvious. Under Lougheed, executive federalism would be as safe as money in a Swiss bank.

This preposterous notion ranked with putting the bilingual language czar and communications emperor Keith Spicer in charge of the Citizens' Forum. A graduate of the Harvard Business School, Lougheed once dared to tackle Trudeau in writing. His October 19, 1992, rebuttal in *Maclean's* of Trudeau's skewering of the Charlottetown Accord perpetuated the illusion that Quebec is not a full partner in Confederation because the province simply refuses to play: "As a westerner, I am pleased that the provisions in the Charlottetown agreement respond to the desire of Quebec to be a full partner in Confederation. Yes, there are many important gains for Quebecers, and that is as it should be" (*Maclean's*, Oct 19/92).

Such meanderings demand answers: Why? Why not gains for all Canadians? Lougheed a Westerner? A Conservative? Under his socialist Tory administration, Alberta's provincial government spending followed Premier Harry Strom's last budget in 1971–72, and that budget called for $1 billion in government spending and a surplus of $300,000. Lougheed's last budget in 1985–86 swelled to $10 billion. The public service ballooned from 11,000 to 43,000. The cabinet posts multiplied from 17 to 30. Lougheed is truly a Central Canada socialist — a Red Tory in the Joe Clark–Dalton Camp tradition. On referenda: "When we're dealing with the Constitution, I believe we have to have a referendum as the ultimate ratification. I believe it is very important . . . that the referendum be, if we believe in the equality of provinces, . . . by province. Not regional. Not national" (*GM*, Sept 30/91).

In other words — no referendum at all. Allow the particular government with power in the provincial legislature to override the people's will.

On constituent assemblies: "The [amending] process, the nature of it, may get us into a position unintentionally where we stumble [off the cliff]. I think there has to be a contingency plan. If the current system can't work . . . then thinking Canadians should be developing a contingency plan that involves citizen involvement" (*GM*, Sept 24/91). Even bolder, he admitted, "I cannot see an agreement reached unless it is behind closed doors" (*GM*, Sept 24/91) and "[a constituent assembly should be tried only] as a last resort, if the traditional methods of constitution-making finally do not work" (*Maclean's*, Jan 6/92). His opinion on the Triple-E Senate: "Looking at it from my background, effective is more important than equal. . . . But for others, perhaps my successor [Getty], equal may be more important than effective" (*Star*/CP, May 4/92).

On Official Bilingualism, he bought the Trudeau myth, holus-bolus. "We put in our Constitution the very essence of Canada, which is official bilingualism. We didn't do it for the popularity basis" (*Star*/CP, May 4/92; *Western Report*, Mar 2/92).

On the reasons for supporting the Yes vote in the Referendum, he said, "when that signature's made, it's over. And in my judgement and my experience, it's over for at least a dozen years. . ." (CBC Newsworld, Sept 24/93).

Could anyone express genuine amazement that *Maclean's*, the pro-Mulroney magazine, picked Peter Lougheed for their Honor Roll in the December 30, 1991, issue?

Notes

1 During the October 1992 Referendum, registered committees spent $393,000 for the No side. On April 8, the *Toronto Star* reported that all but $10,000 came from the Reform Party.

2 The report was quickly pulled and today is extremely difficult to obtain. After the bank promised to circulate it widely, members of the public who called to order a copy within the first week of its release learned that there were no more and no more would be printed.

3 Peter C. Newman writes from his position: "No businessman in Canadian history has ever had a more intimate and more extended influence with Canadian prime ministers than Desmarais. He was a good friend and financial supporter of Lester Pearson . . . ; he was one of the chief backers of Pierre Trudeau's leadership bid and acted as one of his main confidants for his 16 years in office. Desmarais had meanwhile become one of Brian Mulroney's chief mentors, and during the nine Mulroney years, no one outside the prime minister's immediate family had as much influence on the Baie Comeau politician as Paul Desmarais" (*Maclean's*, Nov 1/93).

4 The December 1991 cover story of the *Financial Post Magazine* featured Laurent Beaudoin as its "CEO of the Year."

25

The Filtration System, the CBC

The print and electronic media are in trouble. Profits are declining; audiences are fragmenting. People are more cynical about the media, I suspect, than they've ever been. . . .

Trying to be an informed citizen is hard work. Sometimes it's easier just to tune the media out.

Morris Wolfe, columnist,
Globe and Mail, July 6, 1993

O F ALL THE ORGANIZATIONS THAT betrayed Canada, none performed that role with more consummate arrogance and aplomb than the Canadian Broadcasting Corporation. As the *Globe*'s Jeffrey Simpson put it, "The CBC [is] a behemoth organization full up with journalists, that most gossipy and cantankerous of breeds . . ." (*GM*, Aug 3/93).

The CBC, well known in the media as "Mother Corp.," did not become irrelevant as a national institution because of any one particular episode in the history of broadcasting. The person who tolled the death knell of English Canada's cherished organization for national unity most clearly was Mulroney's Minister of Communications, Marcel Masse. Under Masse, a Quebec nationalist with separatist credentials matching those of Lucien

Bouchard, Mother Corp. was split into English and French sections. Bill C-40, assented to on February 1, 1991, and eventually proclaimed on June 5 of the same year, completed the task of severing English and French Canada into *deux nations*.

The business all came to a head in September 1990, when Masse, with the help of his parliamentary secretary Jim Edwards, an Albertan Red Tory Trudovnic, irrevocably altered CBC's historical mandate. The Conservative Prime Minister R.B. Bennett, who founded it, laid out its mandate unequivocally. Its primary purpose was to "contribute to the development of national unity."

Once at the helm of Mulroney's propaganda machine, Masse dismissed the corporation's historical role as "intolerable propaganda" (*Star*, Mar 21/90). The minister happily boasted of his personal goal to politicize the CBC along the lines of the defeated Meech Lake Accord: "at times there will be a different approach to meet the needs of one society as compared to the approach to meet the needs of the other. . . . If we had carbon copies across the board, it would no longer be possible to speak of distinct society" (*GM*, Sept 21/90). Under the section "Broadcasting Policy for Canada," Bill C-40 spelled out the new direction in its Section 3 (1):

(c) English and French language broadcasting, while sharing common aspects, operate under different conditions and may have different requirements;

(d) The Canadian broadcasting system should

(iii) through its programming and the employment opportunities arising out of its operations, serve the needs and interests, and reflect the circumstances and aspirations, of Canadian men and women and children, including equal rights, the linguistic duality and multicultural and multiracial nature of Canadian society and the special place of aboriginal people within that society. . . .

(m) The programing provided by the Corporation should

(i) be predominantly and distinctively Canadian,

(iv) be in English and in French, reflecting the different needs and circumstances of each official language community, including the particular needs and circumstances of English and French linguistic minorities.

(viii) reflect the multicultural and multiracial nature of Canada. . . .

As the excuse for this *deux nations* policy, Masse sloughed off criticism under the guise of broadcasting freedom; "national unity must be experienced, not inflicted" (*GM*, Sept 21/90).

Bill C-40 endorsed breaking up Canada into a confederation of regions based on ethnicity and multiculturalism.[1] Its passage would legitimize regionalism at the expense of any single national voice speaking to all its listeners as members of a single nation state.

MULRONEY NEEDED political hacks to deflect what was really happening. The most ready, willing and able to champion his cause took form in the person of **John Crispo**, an outspoken acapoohbah and professor at the University of Toronto's Faculty of Management. Crispo had worked overtime in the media and at public hearings to establish his credentials as a loyal devotee of Meech Lake, David Peterson, and Brian Mulroney. A champion of executive federalism, who for some strange reason characterizes himself as a right-wing Tory, he could be counted on to promote big business and big government. Mulroney knew his man as one renowned for his distinctive style of kicking ass. Through Crispo, the prime minister would eviscerate the CBC while the colourful Crispo as gunslinger fired his many random shots. With the professor loaded into the circus cannon, Mulroney was assured no serious discussion about the role of public broadcasting in Canada would surface.

Crispo had made his mark as an enemy of the CBC at a seminar in July 1988. Talking about a broadcaster's coverage of the conservative position in matters of public policy, he blurted out, "That's the kind of rot you get from that lousy, left-wing, liberal, NDP pinko network!" (*GM*, Mar 30/91). He pulled up a seat before the Ontario government's Select Committee on the Constitution on June 14, 1990, and was asked his opinion about David Peterson's offer of Senate seats to Quebec to make Meech work: "To me Canada is worth more than whether Ontario has as many Senators as Quebec. . . . I do not know when I have been more proud of an Ontario Premier" (Ont. brief, *Hansard*). In gratitude Marcel Masse dropped the mouthy one among the propaganda pigeons on March 28, 1991, appointing him to the CBC board of directors for a three-year stint.

Trina McQueen made some revealing comments about Canadian reporting herself. In its February 1992 issue, *Toronto Life* magazine described her as "the country's leading TV news executive and arguably its most powerful and influential journalist." From 1984 to 1989 she was executive producer of CBC TV's "The National." From 1989 to 1991 she was director of TV news and current affairs. For CBC Newsworld's first three years on the air, too, she was overlord.

In the post-Meech era, she published her views on CBC's role in the *Globe and Mail* as "How the CBC Covered Meech Lake"[2]: "Yet, it became obvious in the late spring [1990] that the political consensus no longer included the voters. A strong anti-Meech sentiment was developing in English Canada. It was a deep political sentiment that found almost none of the usual political expression or support available" (July 25/90). Typical, banal CBC, reporting what Canadians already knew perfectly well.

In an amazing revelation of ignorance about how most Canadians think, McQueen said she believed that "a wide range of political leaders usually provides a fair representation of public views." She has never explained how this could relate to the Meech Lake debate when all the leaders were on the same side.

Near the very end of the debate, she did acknowledge that "the politicians and the people were on different tracks." CBC "responded" to this dilemma, she told reporters, by allowing "extra time to anti-Meech leaders."

A surprising remark. The real resistance leaders in hundreds of small protest organizations throughout the country had no time on CBC whatsoever. For thirty years the corporation successfully controlled dissent by airing the politically correct views of selected and well-known establishment members whose form of dissent was approved. This translated into the opinions of a handpicked group of academics, journalists, and politicians. As McQueen interpreted life from her office cocoon, "to a large extent, the public debate is happening on CBC. What we have is people who make the decisions watching other [decision makers] on CBC, reacting to what they see, and then going on CBC to respond to it. That makes us part of the process" (*Star*, June 7/90). She sidestepped the lack of real debate on the most critical issues dividing the nation, Official Bilingualism, immigration policy, crime and punishment. The CBC only spoon-fed the public.

A year after the collapse of Meech, **John Meisel**, professor of political science at Queen's, attacked the CBC. His work-over first appeared in a thirty-page essay titled "Mirror? Searchlight? Interloper? — The Media and Meech." Peter C. Newman gave his complaint good exposure through his column in *Maclean's* on May 6, 1991, "Distorted Images: The CBC on Meech Lake." Later Meisel's piece appeared in another incarnation between the covers of David Smith's *After Meech Lake: Lessons for the Future*. Meisel, incidentally, was one of the Queen's Mafia who attended the Mont

Gabriel Conference in 1986. Later he alleged that the Mother Corp. was biased against the accord from the beginning.

Newman quotes the CBC's political editor and Ottawa bureau chief **Elly Alboim** from Meisel's piece as the key CBC executive who spearheaded the attack on the Meech deal as early as November 1987. At a conference of academics in Calgary, Alboim damned the accord as "a highly political and cynical exercise that had very, very little to do with the reconstitutionalizing of Canada." As for the provincial premiers, he said, they were only on side with Mulroney because they were "determined to capture as much as they could in exchange for their acceptance. . . . This wasn't a nation-building exercise."

Meisel retorted:

> I was aghast and shocked by what struck me as the appallingly arrogant and facile stance of one of the most senior CBC journalists. I find it frightening that anyone could feel so sure of himself in his reading of a government's and prime minister's motives, that he would feel confident enough to plunge the medium for which he is responsible into the political process with the aim of offsetting the perceived cynicism and irresponsibility of the government. . . . My anxiety is all the more acute when the instrument is the public broadcaster. (*Maclean's*, May 6/91)[3]

Fair comment. What also constitutes fair comment is the observation with which Newman weights his own column in favour of Meisel's account, which he considers a "carefully documented study":

> Meisel is quite explicit in his personal support for Meech Lake [as was Newman] and believes that the "delinquent media" helped undermine the accord, a result that "robbed us of the opportunity of Quebec and the rest of Canada thriving within one federal union." [Meisel's] essay ends with an eloquent plea that in the next round . . . the media not abuse their power to influence the process.

It's a thought worth pondering.

The Newman article illuminates far more about the CBC. Alboim defends his position and the way he went about measuring the magnitude of dissent in the country:

> We were focused on the extraordinary story of what appeared to be the collapse of the government with the largest mandate in Canadian his-

tory.[4] ... When confronted with that sort of reality, plus a clear understanding of the fragility of the deal and the rush to text and passage, we began a search for dissent. . . . you look for someone who will question the deal. We went to Chrétien, we went to Romanow. We looked for constitutional experts. I looked around the country, searching for people who were going to say in the first week or two, boy, there's something wrong here. . . . The Trudeau watch started. Every day we sent a reporter down to Trudeau's office. Will he do it today? (*Maclean's*, May 6/91)

That was CBC's problem. The corporation never went to its viewers and listeners. Instead it hurried off, cap in hand, to call on the politicians and the so-called experts about the whole constitutional business. Never did it seriously engage the resistance movement against the deal. Many outspoken opponents of the government's vision of the country addressed audiences ranging from two or three people to standing-room-only crowds in the thousands all over Canada, yet the CBC and the mainstream media turned a blind eye to them, their names, and the events. They never acknowledged them.

Among the dissenters were experienced and knowledgable broadcasters, authors, and pamphleteers. The filtration process spread a thick screen. If an undesirable managed to penetrate it, the mistake was not repeated. Any of them who did squeeze through the censorship screen were soon discovered and ridiculed, and firmly barred from future embarrassment. These people never appeared before the larger public. As long as they were not previously published and therefore approved by the established publishers of books, magazines, or newspapers, they were denied any attention by the state broadcaster and other corporate media.

Another strategy was to permit a dissenting voice to make itself heard and then manage the outcome. The public impression that was left could then be worked to the government's advantage.

Bill Gairdner, author of the best-selling *The Trouble With Canada* (1990), recounts a shocking story in the preface of his second book *The War Against the Family* (1992):

Troubling views or studies that offend the status quo are shunned [in Canada]. Writers like me have been shunned. For example, even though *The Trouble with Canada* had already sold 25,000 copies and had been seven months on the *Globe and Mail* national bestseller list (number one for a week), and despite the fact that 62 radio and television stations across

Canada had already invited me to be a guest on their shows, it took over *10 months* for the CBC to offer an interview on a single national radio show — Peter Gzowski's "Morningside" — and that was only because I had been badgering his staff. With such an iron grip of collectivist stakeholders on the formation of public opinion, it is not surprising that the Canadian public does not relish debate on "sensitive" issues. (p. xi)[5]

As every publisher and author knows, a snub on this scale devastates a book's sales. Gzowski's "Morningside" program on CBC AM influences book sales in Canada more than any other. By 1981 Alain Peyrefitte's comparable indictment of conditions in France, *The Trouble With France* (1976), had sold one million copies in that country alone.

In one of the less polemic comments to be found in her book *Sultans of Sleaze* (1989), **Joyce Nelson** wrote:

But what is new in this century is a powerful system of mass media interlocked with a technological and economic agenda that now threatens the entire planet. The paradox we face is that our lifestyle of luxury and "progress" — promulgated through the media over this century — increasingly reveals itself to be the prescription for planetary suicide. Moreover, that media system — which [Marshall] McLuhan referred to as the externalized nervous system of humanity — does not function to alert us to problems as soon as they are known, but instead is purposely controlled and used to keep us uninformed about their causes and repercussions, and reassured that nothing needs to change. (p. 150)

A respected Canadian think-tank on such matters, the **Mackenzie Institute for the Study of Terrorism, Revolution and Propaganda (MI)** came onto the scene as an authority on such matters in 1986. The Toronto-based institute claims to be "an independent research body." It has a solid reputation for objectivity and researches and comments on issues relating to terrorism, security, revolutionary politics, radical ideologies, propaganda, and conflict. Unlike most other such groups in Canada, MI accepts no government funding.

On the day of the Referendum, October 26, 1992, the Institute published, "For Immediate Release," an information brief entitled *Propaganda and The Referendum Campaigns*. The paper deals with all sides of the Yes and No campaigns, and general propaganda. One excerpt:

Effective propaganda . . . must be organized to insure continuity and to prevent incongruous messages or images from being delivered. *It is imperative that all or nearly all the media of communication are controlled or responsive to the propagandist. . . .*

The multi-party Yes Committee [Tory–Liberal–New Democratic parties] mostly keeps to a simple message — that the Charlottetown Accord is the best that can be done to keep the Country [*sic*] together. . . . Emotions are carefully targeted. . . .

. . . The obvious intent of this government media blitz is the promotion of the "feel good" atmosphere. However, after prolonged exposure to these symbols [woods, fields, mountains, sunlit little towns, etc., with a patriotic song or carefully chosen music as accompaniment], the principal drive of the Yes campaign has been to tell us that Canada is in danger if the Accords fail to pass. . . .

Outside Quebec, the Yes side has the money, experience, skills, organization and networks necessary for success. It should be capable of selling virtually any political package, and began the campaign confident it could do this. After all, it has all the current First Ministers on side and the political elite of the country. The opposition seemed generally insignificant, inexperienced, underfunded and isolated. . . . [emphasis mine]

Long after the collapse of the Charlottetown Accord, March 20, 1993, marked another watershed in disinformation. On a TV special on CBC Newsworld, host Peter Mansbridge held court on "Mulroney & the Media." Such notables as Pamela Wallin, Allan Fotheringham, Dalton Camp, and Michel Gratton all delivered a synchronized performance as conductor Mansbridge held the program's focus on whether or not Mulroney had been fair to the media and whether the media had been fair to the prime minister during his term in office. Mansbridge skilfully managed his guests' remarks so that nothing significant escaped for public consumption.

Only at the very end of this contrived post-mortem, thanks to Allan Fotheringham's welcome grain of honesty, did the players haltingly hint that maybe there was a great deal missing from their delicate coverage of the Mulroney era.

Dalton Camp fired the parting shot that epitomized how the state broadcaster had been co-opted by the government. He called Brian Mulroney "perhaps one of the most competent prime ministers this country ever had."

The CBC allows its listeners and viewers to hear about the dissent side of an issue but never from the actual people who disagree themselves. Between 1963 and 1994 a revolution swept over Canada. Throughout those three decades the public servants at Mother Corp. manipulated the airwaves according to the government's military rubric, communicating information on a strict need-to-know basis only. The CBC arranged Canadians' opinions just as generals manoeuvre their foot soldiers without outlining to them details of the course of the battle. CBC dared not indulge genuine political argument.

Because of this unspoken and well-known policy of self-censorship, Canadians were done a great insult and disservice. For one thing, the corporation feared open dialogue because of the ignorance of its own commentators about Confederation. Where American broadcasters would have pulled together experts of all the possible shades of opinion and backgrounds in debate, CBC avoided controversy with a determination that seemed desperate. So there has been not a glimpse of intelligent dialogue on any constitutional issue for a generation.

U of T Professor **Desmond Morton**, a CBC favourite, got it only half right. He wrote, "A lot of voters are frustrated because all 3 national parties ended up supporting the Meech Lake accord. . . . Have our parties joined a conspiracy of silence on the fine old passions that used to set Canadians at each others' throats? The answer, in all likelihood, is yes. And the further answer is it has always been so" (*Star*, June 15/88).

Of course, in a modern democratic state, that's precisely the problem, as the failure of the Charlottetown Accord subsequently proved. The point is that institutional executive federalists, whether from the academic world or the media, mistrust the electorate. And every dictator in history has used that rationale.

Yet to hear executives of the media cheer their own roles and contributions as guardians of freedom was quite another matter. Explaining the role of a newspaper in a free society, as he saw it, **John Honderich**, editor of the *Toronto Star*, spoke at a media conference during the debate over round one of Meech Lake:

1. Fully inform the populace — that is our primary role; and discuss and foster debate. . . . Media is a participant in the political process and some blame the media for being the problem. . . . The role of the media has become badly understood.

2. Few in Canada would believe they were well served by the media concerning the debate.[6]

The saddest legacy of Canada's constitutional seizure is that no one in the management of CBC affairs thought it important to make sure they themselves knew the implications of what was going on. Certainly none of them believed in assuring freedom of thought and expression on the most difficult questions about the country's make-up. And their verdicts signified the deeper problem of their own ignorance of Canada's history and traditions — a deadly indictment of Canada's educational system.

T HE PUBLIC tuned out the CBC and other media for less idealistic reasons. They were bored. The media did not recognize that healthy debate made for economically valuable public entertainment. American broadcasters have known this and shrewdly capitalized on it for years. This is the real reason for the economic doldrums engulfing the industry. The CBC committed entertainment suicide during Canada's constitutional debate.

Some interesting revelations surfaced, courtesy of Scrum '93, a conference of the Canadian Association of Journalism in March on "How to Increase Trust in the Media." Peter Desbarats, dean of the School of Journalism at the University of Western Ontario, chaired a panel of a half-dozen noted journalists, including **Victor Malarek**, author and co-host of "the fifth estate." Malarek did not confine his reprimand to The Corporation alone, either:

Today we have a news media that overall deals with very few issues. Reporters meander off issues, something that happens, and they tend to be going in more for trite clips. There's no analysis, no depth, there's little illumination; the news media serves to dull the sharp edges. . . . We're drowning in a sea of meaningless chatter. . . .

And most of the time we got [context from] navel-gazers. The media went hog-wild in interviewing itself *and*, what bothers me the most, its chosen gurus! We have a tendency to handpick these gurus and go to them repeatedly, repeatedly, and repeatedly for comments. One big happy family deciding the future of Canada.

But one important element is missing: the public. As far as I'm concerned, . . . the public didn't give a hoot over what the hell the navel-gazers and the gurus were saying, and you know why? The people felt they had no say in the agenda, in the debate, but more importantly, there were more important things happening in this country in their mind. . . . *Because I think they really feel they've truly lost their voice. No one speaks for them any longer, or very few of us speak for them.* . . . I think the public should harbour a healthy distrust of the media [emphasis mine]. (Aug 10/93, Aug 31/93, Part I of "Scrum '93")

On August 13, 1993, **Wayne Skene**, a former CBC manager and author of *Fade to Black: A Requiem for the CBC*, published "Is the Good Ship CBC worth keeping afloat?" in the *Globe and Mail*. He called the CBC "the nation's most important, most troubled and most expensive cultural entity." As if to illustrate part of the problem, he described it as the nation's number-one cultural institution.

Responding to Skene's article, **Tim Kotcheff**, CBC vice-president of English television news, current affairs, and Newsworld, defended CBC. He also warned critics to be careful: "I find it impossible to square my experience of the CBC with the image of resignation and disarray regurgitated in print with such monotonous regularity. . . . Yes, we do have problems. But so does everyone else in the broadcast business, and virtually every other business trying to survive the recession. If the past year here at CBC has taught me nothing else, it is that we are an organization replete with ideas and talent" (*GM*, Sept 2/93).

Undoubtedly he had a point. However, a lot of people were very angry with the CBC. *Sun* columnist Douglas Fisher added his opinion after "a recent, long trip west." He said he "asked almost everyone . . . about news on TV and in the papers. Both Mansbridge and Wallin have their fans but no one likes them together [on 'Prime Time News']. . . . [They] are seen as overbearing in 2-on-one interviews, their bridging chit-chat as banal and witless, the frequent editorializing caveats as sophisticated sermonizing" (*Sun*, Aug 11/93). He took another crack at the corporation during the 1993 federal election campaign:

Should those in a government agency set out to defeat the government? You think not? That this is impossible, un-Canadian. We can't have it here. No . . . well we do! . . .
Since February Campbell has been (and will be for three more weeks)

the chief Tory hope for retaining power. To put her down, to raise doubts about her capacities and truthfulness again and again on network news, is a means of ejecting the government this election. . . .

It's wrong that a Crown company, the largest, costliest news force and interpreter of ourselves to ourselves (though not the most watched) is reality-busting those likely to sustain or increase the company's funding. (*Sun*, Oct 1/93)

CBC's answer came from Tony Burman, executive producer of CBC's "Prime Time News": "Like other media organizations, CBC *Prime Time News* has introduced a *Reality Watch* segment in this campaign to help Canadians distinguish between fact and fiction. Fisher's latest polemic against the CBC is an example of the latter. Report the truth, please" (*Sun*, Oct 6/93).

There it was. The CBC acknowledging itself as propagandist!

T**HE WORLD** of journalism had missed the point completely: the need for good old-fashioned, honest journalism. It's not "context" that was missing as media munchkins believed. It was content — knowledge. (See Chapter 34.)

Douglas Fisher accurately summed up the broadcaster's role in the 1993 election in another column:

By and large the CBC had anti-Tory, anti-Reform tilts, almost matching in the early weeks those of the Toronto *Star* (that prevailed in both its editorial and news phases). The CBC became fairer as the campaign closed, most notably to the Tories. Perhaps the Tim Kotcheffs, Elly Alboims and Peter Mansbridges realized the anti-government bias was too gross. More likely it was because the demise of the [Campbell] government the CBCers hated so much had become certain. (*Sun*, Oct 29/93)

The warning of the world-renowned scholar on propaganda, Jacques Ellul, should have sent shivers through any Canadian who cared:

If I am in favor of democracy, I can only regret that propaganda renders the true exercise of it almost impossible. But I think it would be even worse to entertain any illusions about a co-existence of true democracy and propaganda. Nothing is worse in times of danger than to live in a dream world. To warn a political system of the menace hanging over it does not imply an attack against it, but is the greatest service one can render the system. (*Propaganda*, p. xvi)

Worth pondering, indeed.

Notes

1 In March of 1990, the CBC made a "Submission to the Legislative Committee on Bill C-40." In the introduction, CBC fully endorsed its own politicization: "The CBC supports those aspects of the proposed legislation designed to contemporize the law. . . . As well, those provisions that would have the effect of improving the broadcasting system's reflection of Canada's society, culture and values."

2 Like many media commentators in the constitutional debate, Trina McQueen found herself elevated to stardom because of the debate. She posed as cover girl for the February 1992 edition of *Toronto Life* with the bold heading "Is This the Most Powerful Journalist in Canada? — Meet Trina McQueen, the boss of CBC News. She decides, ultimately, how the news is brought to you."

3 A year later, Meisel, a former head of the CRTC, excused Prime Minister Jean Chrétien for not demanding the resignation of his communications minister Michel Dupuy for influence peddling. The latter had used his position to plump for a constituent. In his ministerial letter to the CRTC, Dupuy also wrote, "I trust that you will keep me abreast of any developments in the matter." Chrétien dismissed the minister's blunder as mere "imprudence . . . a little mistake" (*Star*, Oct 28/94). Coming down from his moral high horse, Meisel was equally dismissive: "It was an oversight" (CBC, Oct 28/94). Problem: the CRTC, a quasi-judicial organization, reports directly to the Minister of Communications.

4 Actually, the largest sweep in Canadian history was the Diefenbaker election victory of 1958, when "the Chief" won 208 seats.

5 During the constitutional uproar over Meech and Charlottetown, Peter Gzowski earned contempt for his blatant left-wing bias. An obvious sore point was his choice of participants for the "Morningside" political panel. The three amigos, Stephen Lewis, Dalton Camp, and Eric Kierans, well-known socialists, were given hundreds of hours

of air time to propagandize some two million listeners weekly. On January 3, 1995, *Calgary Sun* columnist Peter Stockland published Gzowski's teensy-weensy mea culpa. Acknowledging himself as one of Canada's leading "cultural gate keepers," Gzowski allowed: "I think it's true we need to hear from a much wider range of voices." About one of his show's guests, however, the host opined, "Bill Gairdner is just bad radio. He gets so excited and starts babbling on. I told him 'calm down, Bill, you'll have your say.' But he wouldn't listen" (*Sun*, Jan 3/95).

6 After Meech's collapse on February 6, 1991, the Institute for Political Involvement sponsored the conference, chaired by Peter Desbarats, dean of the Graduate School of Journalism at the University of Western Ontario. Honderich's topic was "The Media: Its Influence and Responsibilities."

VIII

The Road to
Charlottetown

June to August 1992

26

The Cat's Breakfast, the Pearson Accord
— June to July 1992

A T THE CLOSING OF THE SEVENTH of the Multilateral Ministerial Meetings in Charlottetown, Prince Edward Island, on May 31, the first ministers again had nothing concrete to report to their fellow Canadians. The press called it the final 3M meeting, which was not the case. At that point, no one really knew where to turn, including the constitutional affairs minister himself.

The only certainty was that the Quebec agenda remained inviolate — and a provincial referendum, according to Bill 150, had to be held on October 26. Even so, Quebec had decided nothing about the wording of its referendum question. So, the 3M process, the biggest mish-mash of all, was postponed. Clark's expressions of enthusiasm about the "enormous amount of progress" that had been made simply didn't wash.

About all that could be said for the hundreds of millions of dollars spent over those last six years was that Canada's native peoples no longer seemed to operate in complete isolation. At least they were now invited to the table, though newspaper readers had to wonder about the way Ovide Mercredi, Chief of the Assembly of First Nations, gushed about native inclusion. He boasted about an "historic breakthrough. . . . Now we have a commitment to honor the spirit and intent of the treaties. We have the beginnings of a process for reconciliation between ourselves and the rest of Canada" (*Sun*, May 31/92).

What "historic breakthrough"? Many Canadians could almost agree with Parti Québécois leader Jacques Parizeau when he said the so-called consensus of the 3M process was nothing more than a "cat's breakfast. . . . That they should have bungled the whole exercise the way they did — I feel sorry for them. . . . It is inconceivable that people who feel their country threatened in its very existence should end up with the kind of result they have produced" (*Star*, May 31/92).

There was certainly no justification for Ontario Premier Bob Rae's assessment: "We've come about 90 per cent of the way in my judgement. The last bit is very important. I don't want to underestimate it for anyone" (*Star*, May 31/92).

Alberta's constitutional minister Jim Horsman disagreed: "I would be far less optimistic" (*Star*, May 31, 1992). Newfoundland's Clyde Wells warned of another constitutional pressure-cooker in the making: "It's very much headed in the same direction. You're cast in the context of having to make decisions that you wouldn't otherwise make within a certain time frame in order to save the country. I think it's shocking to be dealing with the Constitution in that way" (*Star*, May 30/92).

Another voice piped up — the former Newfoundland premier, Brian Peckford: "Today, it would seem that we are headed toward the same high-suspense situations. . . . While I agree that the Meech Lake process could have been more open, I submit that the present process is 'worse' with its open and closed meetings and conferences and a cluttered agenda, which leaves the average citizen in complete confusion" (*GM*, May 30/92).

On May 31 in Hull, Quebec, the 250-member council of the PQ convened to discuss referendum strategy. Parizeau won a unanimous vote of confidence: "We have a very confused situation but, gradually, the impression is that anything that will come out now, in the next few days, will be . . . unacceptable to the Quebec government" (*Star*, June 1/92). As Bloc Québécois leader Lucien Bouchard put it, "Today we have witnessed the clinical death of these bogus negotiations undertaken over the last few months in Joe Clark's circus to make an offer to Quebec" (*GM*, June 1/92).

Quo vadis, Canada? Since May 9, 1986, at Mont Gabriel, there had been nothing to show for all the efforts spent to save a deeply divided nation. The media and the politicians thought the division between Quebec and the rest of Canada was the problem. It was only a red herring. The growing rift sundered the politicians and media from Canadians themselves. The annual comparative Gallup poll released on June 1, 1992, on leadership preferences told the story; Chrétien, 17 percent; McLaughlin, 16 percent; Mulroney, 13 percent; Manning, 9 percent. And on it went.

Just forty-eight hours after the so-called agreement on inherent native self-government, Joe Clark cast doubts on even the success of those publicized discussions. On June 1 he vaguely acknowledged the historical injustices: "I've thought for a long time that the issue that proved more difficult was the issue related to aboriginal self-government. I think there has to be a lot of patient explanation of what we're doing. This is new and a lot of people will naturally be worried about it" (*GM*, June 2/92).

Befuddlement abounded. One bit issued from Phil Fraser, vice-president of the Native Council of Canada, on June 1. He announced that the native groups had reached an agreement privately with the federal government to recognize 500,000 non-status Indians and Métis having rights under federal protection: "We've always felt our people were included in that [1982 Constitution], but the federal government has always taken a very restrictive view of who shall be Indians" (*Star*, June 2/92).

What did this mean? How were they included? Except for warm furry-feeling statements, the Trudeau Constitution Act assigned priority to just two "founding peoples" — the English and French. The negotiators at the table seemed to have forgotten one very big reason for the collapse of Meech Lake.

Oblivious of the contradictions, the executive federalists rolled inexorably on to the next deadline. An exuberant Bob Rae accepted a position as bandleader of the blind-alley mindset: "My preferred route is to go down the route we're going, and I think it's the best one that guarantees success. All the other options are fraught with a high risk of failure, I think" (*GM*, June 2/92).

A lone Robert Bourassa spouted sensibly: "Why should Quebec go back to the table when our friends and Canadian partners can't agree between themselves? . . . So that means there is serious risk of deadlock and, if there is another deadlock, I don't think Canada will benefit from that" (*Star*, June 3/92).

Clyde Wells was more convincing on June 2: It's a "recipe for chaos. . . . Do we create a situation where an aboriginal person walks down Water Street in St. John's and breaches some law and says, 'Uh-uh, your law doesn't apply to me, I'm self-governing'?" (*Star*, June 3/92).

On June 3, they all finally agreed on something besides the cheerful façade they maintained in the public eye. The Liberals, the Conservatives, and five NDP members joined forces to pass the federal referendum legislation, Bill C-81. The vote was 138 to 33 for it. The convoluted pact it produced discriminated heavily in favour of the executive federalists. The new law established punitive limits on spending for some parties while permitting infinite permutations of committees on the matter.

For the rest of June, Joe Clark blathered on about the need for generosity — that this was the Canada round, not the Quebec round — that if great care were not taken, the disputes could "break us into bitter pieces" (*GM*, June 4/93). Before Canadians' weary eyes, he had cloned himself into another David Peterson, preaching without substance.

Don Getty signalled from Alberta just how little the first ministers agreed on. That June 5 he explained, "I am saying we won't be any part of any agreement that doesn't have a Triple-E Senate" (*GM*, June 6/92). The next day, AFN Chief Ovide Mercredi defined what he meant by "native self-government": "There will always be a Quebec territory within which there will be a native territory where a native government will have authority in the same way as provincial governments do" (*GM*/CP, June 7/92). Another Yves Beauchemin.

Clark's comment the following day was absurd: "On all of these issues there is broad agreement on the principles and on the essence of the proposals. . . . In many areas, exact legal text has been agreed word by word, line by line" (*GM*, June 8/92).

Far away in Czechoslovakia, Prime Minister Václav Havel talked about his native land, and the *Globe and Mail* duly recorded his wisdom on June 9: "It is impossible to be half a federal state and half not. Various such confederations and unions have existed for short periods of time, but they were always transitional. . . . This kind of loose federation is strongly held to be without much future."

Every day of the Mulroney era marked the surfacing of another exhibition of ego for posterity to record. If the Official Languages Commissioner wasn't jumping up and down over something, the public could always turn to defence minister Marcel Masse for an impressive performance in favour of regionalism. With the puck still on his stick, as he had phrased it, Quebec's leading forward pressed on. On June 8, the *Globe* reported that the defence department was pressing Cabinet to speed approval of a pending contract of $4.3 billion for the most advanced modern helicopter fleet for Canada — spanking new EH-101s.

Canadians marvelled at the defence minister's professed commitment to the country. They listened blandly to the musings of Saskatchewan Premier Roy Romanow on the Triple-E Senate for the West. On June 9, 1992, though, Romanow managed to shock his own constituents. He had just met with Premier Bourassa in Montreal. Sitting with the Quebec premier, the premier of Saskatchewan let slip a line that sounded suspiciously as if it could have originated in centralist Canada: "I do not close the door on abolishing the Senate" (CBC Newsworld, June 9/92). He added, "The priority for the moment is trying to have reform of the Senate along the lines of the Triple-E. . . . [Abolition] is definitely an option" (*Star*, June 10/92).

Don Getty was sending a message of a very different kind: "I made the point that all the ingredients of the package are there for Quebec, Ontario has got its social charter, the aboriginals will get their inherent rights. Where is this Canada round dealing with Western Canada and Alberta?" (*Star*, June 9/92). Meanwhile, Romanow was selling the West down the St. Lawrence in Montreal by selling out on his 3M commitment to Senate reform.

Even with all the disagreements and doubletalk whirling around, Prime Minister Mulroney could still amaze everyone. The same day that all these meetings were going on behind Canadians' backs, he said he hadn't the "foggiest idea" whether or not those helicopters Masse had committed the Crown to were really needed. Blarney at l'Irlandais's best. Did he care about what happened to Canada or not?

On June 10, federal Information Commissioner John Grace made his own move, his first since accepting his appointment in 1990. He told reporters he was taking the prime minister to court for the secret polls he had conducted on national unity:

> Clearly this is a time when the need is greatest to ensure that informed, democratic discussion is not unreasonably stifled by a government tempted by its good cause to justify excessive secrecy. . . .
>
> The opinion surveys which the government refuses to disclose have been conducted at taxpayer expense. The polls examine public attitudes towards policies, proposals, strategies or ideas in the public domain. . . . The Privy Council Office has stepped outside the bounds of its legal authority . . . dangerous for a democratic society. (*GM*, June 11/92)

Preston Manning had been very quiet for too long, too. On June 10 he offered Joe Clark some advice. The Reform Party leader was touring Ontario at the time, and appearing briefly in Ottawa. There he said to journalists that the 3M arrangement was "a federal proposal behind closed doors that might not carry the judgement of the people back home" (*GM*, June 11/92). The closing of the 3M process, he added, "smacks of Meech

Lake 2." According to him, constitutional talks should be suspended for two years: "Be honest with Quebec — just say we couldn't get a package and the country is in deep trouble in other areas" (*Sun*, June 11/92). In an eerie way, Manning was sounding like Trudeau. Trudeau had recommended the country wait a decade.

June 10 was a big day indeed. Allan Taylor of the Royal Bank was in fine voice in New York. Addressing the Council of the Americas on "Noises In The Attic: Canadian Unity and the New Challenges of North America," he said, "Unfortunately, our constitutional reform process is not complete. And I am still not in a position to state categorically that Canada has met this latest and most serious challenge to its 125-year-old existence" (notes for speech delivered in New York, June 10/92).

The multilateral ministerial meeting process officially died on June 11. As usual, the man quickest off the mark was Joseph Charles Clark. He hastened to reassure the public that the backroom way was the best way, slipping on one of his many brave faces to announce, "There is a new dynamic in this discussion on the Senate" (*FP*, June 12/92).

Nothing stopped the blithering and blathering. What on earth Bob Rae was talking about on June 11, no one could figure out. He surpassed even Clark: "We've set the stage for a successful settlement. . . . We've cleared away a lot of brushwork that will get in the way of a successful settlement. And I think we're almost there. We're terribly, terribly close" (*GM*, June 12/92).

If the squabbling, bafflegab, and busyness of it all weren't so pathetic and expensive, it might have made for good comedy. Bourassa's address in the National Assembly seemed as insane as anything anyone else had said: "So we want to stay together on the economic level by keeping our [Quebec] national identity and a federalism or a neo-federalism or a shared sovereignty *sui generis* [in essence]. . . . Why should Quebec not innovate in order to associate culture and economy as part of the superior interests of the nation?" Which nation?

Parizeau retorted sharply: "Is the Premier trying to tell us that the future is none other than the past?" (*GM*, June 12/92). Exactly.

Joe Clark resumed his comic constitutional role the next day. Speaking to reporters in Toronto, he intoned:

We can't go into July without there being an answer to the question Bourassa put, which is, "What does Canada want?" There's going to be a referendum there. There has to be an answer. . . . I just can't believe that

Canadians would sit back and let their country come apart over a discussion of the Senate. It would be simply absurd. (*Star*, June 13/92)

The fact is that the best country in the world could come apart. . . . As [Nova Scotia] premier Donald Cameron said the other day in our meetings, that's Strike 1 and Strike 2. . . . You know what happens with Strike 3. . . . If it doesn't look like we can get an agreement, we're going to have to consider means by which the federal Parliament can act alone with the three federalist parties that are there. (*GM*, June 13/92)

It was Trudeau and the 1980–82 process all over again. Party deals simmering behind closed doors, the people completely excluded.

On June 13 Bob Rae stepped back in front of the microphone with host Judy Morrison on CBC AM's Saturday morning political program, "The House":

This bird is ready to fly. . . . I mean, these are, these are, enormous, enormous signs of progress. And the ministers, not all of them were in a position to, to, or authorized to make a final agreement, so it's only natural that the next stage will involve the premiers in some way, shape, or form. And that's — that's only natural, it's inevitable, it's healthy — uh, this is all very Canadian and we should all just relax, work hard at it, and be quite confident and serene that we will find a way. Which we will. . . . Quite a mouthful, eh? [chuckling]

Premier Bob's flipness on the airwaves masked something far more ominous developing in the wings. Under Rae's own direction, Mulroney's ex-UN ambassador Stephen Lewis produced a one-man rant on racism for the Ontario government on June 9. In his new position as the Ontario NDP's Advisor on Race Relations, he wrote a thirty-seven-page letter that began with "Dear Bob . . . This letter constitutes my report." What followed were his own opinions about what was wrong in Ontario society in terms of races.

The "Lewis Report" is an extraordinary document (see Appendix B). It exhibits none of the basics a serious report requires to support its conclusions. Its author threw democracy to the wind for an arbitrary jumble of judgements and personal impressions to back up an underlying and deeply troubled bias. He cited no terms of reference for his task. He quoted no statistics, no specific sources for facts or conclusions, no background history, no law, no scholarly or other sources, no charts. Worse, he conducted no public hearings. He simply frolicked on his own at public expense.

Examine his credentials for the task. After his career as UN ambassador from 1984 to 1988 ended, he carried on with his 1986 assignment as Special Advisor to the UN Secretary-General on African Economic Recovery till 1991. He had no qualifications in terms of a university education or other scholarly endeavours. What he apparently could rely on was the political debt owed him. And, unsuccessful in politics or not, he had served as leader of the NDP in the Ontario legislature from 1970 to 1978 and also as former federal leader of the NDP. He was well known, if not held in contempt, for his condescension to his fellow mortals.

Canadians had heard Stephen Lewis preach at them for years, but the young Stephen never mustered the moral authority of his father. He chose the safer route of political correctness.[1]

During the constitutional debate he had said all the things the executive federalists wanted to hear. On Meech Lake he allowed that there was "impatience and hostility in much of English Canada towards Quebec" (*GM*, Jan 6/90).

He also stated, "I have never been as upset about the notwithstanding clause as some" (*GM*, Mar 20/89). On Quebec as a distinct society, he reminded his fellow citizens, "It is terribly important that all of us as Canadians appreciate the affirmation of identity and distinctiveness which Quebec wishes to embrace" (speech to the Canadian Union of Public Employees, fall/89; *Star*, Oct 18/90).

The man who during Meech Lake had lamented that Canada was "genuinely falling apart" (*Star*, May 26/90), concluded of Ontario society in his report:

First, what we are dealing with, at root, and fundamentally, is anti-Black racism. While it is obviously true that every visible minority community experiences the indignities and wounds of systemic discrimination through-out Southern Ontario, it is the Black community which is the focus. It is Blacks who are being shot, it is Black youth that is unemployed in excessive numbers, it is Black students who are being inappropriately streamed in schools, it is Black kids who are disproportionately dropping-out, it is housing communities with concentrations of Black residents where the sense of vulnerability and disadvantage is most acute, it is Black employees, professional and non-professional, on whom the doors of upward equity slam shut. Just as the soothing balm of "multiculturalism" cannot mask racism, so racism cannot mask its primary target. (*Stephen Lewis Report on Race Relations in Ontario*, June/92, p. 2)

Something else was in the wind as well. On June 15 a report prepared by a law student named Donna Young was leaked to the press.[2] The Ontario Human Rights Commissioner, Rosemary Brown, refused to disown it, despite the fact that its recommendations violated the Charter of Rights and Freedoms and Canadian common law. The report, subtitled "The Handling of Race Discrimination Complaints at the Ontario Human Rights Commission," included this surprising observation:

> It appears that the *legal* presumption of innocence has been routinely applied in the investigation stage of race complaints. . . . In the human rights context, once we have established that social and systemic racism is the norm and not the exception, the legal presumption of innocence is inappropriate at the *investigatory* stages of race discrimination complaints. Investigation is not a legal process, and a legal standard must not be applied . . . [because] racism in fact is the norm. (p. 9)

On June 16, fearless Bob Rae told the Ontario legislature he would adopt most of the Lewis Report's recommendations. No details of the report itself came out in the press. Ontarians would only learn what their government was up to a year later. The constitutional training ground had taught the Rae government one very important lesson — Keep as much as you can under wraps for as long as possible and then spring the trap only when you're ready. So much for Rae's diversion on CBC about the bird being "ready to fly." His mind was a million miles away.

But the implementation of the Lewis Report recommendations was a sideshow to his government's plans for employment in Ontario. While the national media frothed over Mulroney's schemes for the constitutional salvation of Quebec, Bob Rae was skimming into the federal arena full steam ahead. On June 25, 1992, Bill 79 passed first reading in the Ontario legislature. *An Act to Provide for Employment Equity for Aboriginal People, People with Disabilities, Members of Racial Minorities and Women* was Ontario's very own Charter of Rights (see Appendix B). No wonder Lewis so readily accepted Quebec's use of the notwithstanding clause. In time, the clause would prove just as useful to his province. As with the Lewis Report, the full measure of Rae's socialist intervention into society would not be known until June of 1993.

The fear of God should have struck Canadians on learning that while Rae was performing his shtick on CBC, former Prime Minister Pierre

413

Trudeau was visiting Premier Clyde Wells's home in St. John's, Newfound-land. What now? Wells later told curious reporters that Trudeau was in town for "a variety of things," including a discussion of the constitutional agenda. Canadians believed him (*GM*, June 18/92).

On June 14, 1992, the *Toronto Star*, via Canadian Press, announced that the Conseil du patronat du Québec (CPQ), Quebec's corporate voice, had completed its own survey. And that blew the final whistle on the separatist game for that year. What it found was sobering. It showed only 13 percent of its 324 member corporations would prefer independence. Money talked. Quebec Inc. was dead.

Joe Clark, on the other hand, must have been smoking the same weed that Bob Rae had on the weekend. Bright-eyed and bushy-tailed, he spoke to the press on Monday. "There's been quite a bit of movement over the weekend. My impression is that the governments are generally quite close together here and I think there is a reasonable chance that we can, with some good will, bring this off" (*GM*, June 16/92). He was soldiering on, eyes firmly fixed on his own yellow-brick road.

Clyde Wells had a handle on the real world. This same day that Clark was sounding off, the Newfoundland premier said he was still as opposed as ever to the Senate reform proposals and most of the other substantive issues Clark assured everyone had been more or less put to rest.

Clark could always fall back on Ontario's premier. Things were peachy keen. On June 15, Rae repeated his morning smile of two weeks earlier: "The package has come a long way, it is 90 per cent there. We should be able to complete this constitutional round successfully within the time available."

The Minister of National Revenue certainly wasn't as optimistic that Monday morning. Otto Jelinek exclaimed, "I can't believe that this country is on the verge of breaking up because of the Senate. Who cares?" (*FP*, June 16/92).

Then the French daily *Le Monde* in Paris chose that same day to publish the second part of an interview they had had with Robert Bourassa two months earlier, in mid-April. Perhaps their timing owed more to mischief than anything else? The issue of separatism was obviously dying: "If there's no offer, there'll be a referendum on another option. The government will prepare a question that takes into account both the failure of constitutional reform and geography. . . . It happens that Quebec is at the centre of Canada's economic space" (*Star*, *GM*, June 16/92).

Many other strange things were happening, too. The newspapers reported that Mulroney's key constitutional player in the public service, Paul Tellier, Clerk of the Privy Council, would be stepping down. If all were really going as well as Clark asserted, this seemed a very odd move for the country's top bureaucrat. Hemmed in by media scrums, surrounded by microphones, lights, and cameras, Tellier faced plenty of questions. No, he would not be leaving immediately, and, yes, he had warm words about "The Boss": "My relationship has been one of the best of any clerk to any Prime Minister. This was important for government and important for the public service. It was an outstanding relationship. . . . On top of this, I'm very pleased that the overall quality of the relationship between the government and the public service has been improving" (*GM*, June 17/92).

To the average Canadian, his move meant nothing. What most Canadians did recognize was that there must have been some kind of reward being given here to the highest-ranking public servant by his satisfied political masters. Public servants always know when to run. And the timing was right.

Tellier would announce shortly that he was taking up the job of chairman of the CN Railway at a salary at least double that paid to a mere Clerk of the Privy Council, who earned $136,000 to $165,000. And there was more. On July 1, he would be appointed to the Privy Council as well, the highest order in the land.[3]

There was another factor of which the public was not aware. With the constitutional game all but lost, the Conservatives had decided to shift their focus. They would tackle a problem they had ignored since they took office in 1984: the unholy mess of the Federal Public Service of Canada. The Tory preoccupation with the Mulroney constitutional agenda had eroded any credibility they boasted as competent managers. Tellier's replacement signalled the change in tack. Glen Scott Shortliffe, known in the labyrinthine caves of the public service as The Dark Prince or The Enforcer, would take over when Tellier took up his new post at CN on October 1. Since the media gave the Shortliffe appointment short shrift, Canadians barely noticed the sea change that had taken place.

People could still see their government floundering in damage control, though. Clark went so far as to visit Clyde Wells at his home in Newfoundland himself on June 17. After months of being threatened, insulted, and abused because he thought differently than members of the three-party mobsters, Wells fought back: "If they're so principled about holding a referendum, why don't they hold a federal referendum in Quebec and determine how the Quebec people feel? What's this picking on Newfoundland to try to pressure Newfoundland into that particular point of view?" (*GM*, June 17/92)

O BSERVERS DEPRESSED by the whole business could turn with a sense of relief and anticipation to Quebec. As ever, the noises coming out of it were more entertaining. The June 22 issue of *Maclean's* repeated Liberal MNA Jean-Guy Lemieux's most recent comments in *Le Journal de Montréal*: "The knife to the throat of English Canada wasn't enough. A little blood will have to start spilling before they realize Quebec is serious."

The mayor of Quebec City loosed another wave of passion of his own on June 19. Jean-Paul L'Allier rejected an invitation from Premier Bourassa to attend a reception for the Russian president, Boris Yeltsin. L'Allier demanded that Quebec first build the appropriate official residence for such dignitaries. A palais de something or other?

Meanwhile, news on the world stage threatened to overwhelm constitutional shenanigans. From Bratislava, Czechoslovakia, filtered stories that after fourteen hours of negotiations, Czech and Slovak leaders had agreed to prepare "for a smooth functioning of 2 sovereign states with international status" by September 30 (*GM*/Reuters, June 20/92). The fruits of Trudeau's constitutional advice?

The masters of Canada's corporations fretted as the Mulroney government bumbled on. On June 23, former U.S. President Richard Nixon spoke to reporters before attending a banquet in Toronto as the guest of Canada's offshore media tycoon Conrad Black. After acknowledging he had met with the prime minister, Nixon admitted their discussions "had something to do with the Constitution and the problems with French Canada." The great discredited American added, "Unlike some who have written [Mulroney] off, I would never underestimate a French-speaking Irish-Canadian" (*Star*, June 24/92).

Richard Brookhiser's remark in the March 9 issue of *Time* magazine was true. Canada was getting interesting.

Some played the blame game. With a forum provided courtesy of Peter C. Newman of *Maclean's* magazine, David Peterson dealt Clyde Wells another belt in the chops:

> Does Wells understand that he is single-handedly responsible for placing the country into its current mess? And if he doesn't, is that through not wanting to understand, or not believing it's true? . . . The abrogation of Meech has similarly realigned Canadian politics, regionalizing the country

and creating such essentially racist movements as the Bloc Québécois and the Reform parties. Our entire political structure has been recast and realigned. (June 29/92)

June 24, 1992: Wednesday. St-Jean Baptiste Day. Parade time in Montreal. This year, the Montreal police refused to try to estimate the crowds. The show that year was a good one, featuring a Train of Confederation — nine dominoes for each province with clowns rolling giant dice. At least somebody was coaxing a laugh out of the whole business.

Not the prime minister. He was doing serious stuff. The message from on high issued from St-Joseph-de-la-Rive, Quebec: Mulroney had called a meeting of all first ministers for Monday, June 29. He also took a risk in not inviting the aboriginal leaders as well. He warned that he intended to recall Parliament on July 15 if the ministers still could not reach agreement on the Constitution on their own by then: "Without an agreement among first ministers — and given that I refuse to leave Bourassa without offers — we will formulate our own offers. . . . In the end, the Parliament of Canada must speak for all Canadians . . . either to confirm an agreement or advance those constitutional amendments most likely to preserve a strong and economically effective Canada, fair to all its people" (*Star*, *GM*, June 25/92).

July 15 would become another deadline chosen by Mulroney for acceptance of the government's "offer." The negotiators had little time left. Under Quebec's Bill 150, the last day for the National Assembly to vote on the details and wording of their Referendum question was September 9.

Bourassa answered quickly. His province's boycott of the talks, he said, would remain in force: "I don't see any reason for the moment to change the government's policy" (*Star*, June 25/92) and "I cannot find justification to be there Monday. Why should I be there Monday? I wasn't there at the last meeting. There are still important issues which are unresolved. I talked to the Prime Minister on Monday and I talked with [Paul] Tellier this morning . . . and I told them that if the situation does not change I will not accept the invitation" (*GM*, June 25/92).

This latest series of negotiations bore predictable fruit. Ovide Mercredi banged at the constitutional front door trying to get himself back in. The AFN Chief still smarted over the snub of being left out after attending all the multilateral conferences up to that point: "It's like you're invited to a feast and you're allowed to have soup but you're not entitled to the full meal" (*Star*, June 26/92).

Meech Lake all over again. The bullying, the sneaky games-playing, the

417

mistrust, and the top-down nonsense. And, of course, as whipping boy Clyde Wells was hauled out again and again onto the carpet. Threats, threats, and more threats.

While Mulroney was holding forth from Quebec and Bourassa was maintaining his "bring me the treats you said we were owed," that old Meech nemesis Clyde Wells was in for even more big-time bullying. In St. John's, Newfoundland, six Tory Cabinet ministers were in the province bad-mouthing the premier about his fight for a Triple-E Senate. The gang included Pierre Cadieux, John Crosbie, and Barbara McDougall. On CBC Crosbie accused Wells of being a "constitutional fanatic." The badgered premier retorted: "I don't anticipate it would be a negotiating session. I just took it as an opportunity [for Mulroney] to advise the premiers of what the federal government intends to do" (*Star*, June 25/92).

By June 26 the rumours and buzz in financial circles were seeping into Canadian newspapers nearly every day. A report out of Toronto from the Dominion Bond Rating Service Ltd. disturbed experienced investors. Canada's largest bank, the Royal, had been put on a rating alert because of its "huge loan portfolio" (*FP*, June 27/92). On the political front, from Calgary, Alberta, there was news that Don Getty was "damn mad" at being labelled a nation-wrecker by Joe Clark over his insistence on a true Triple-E Senate (*Sun*/CP, June 27/92). And in Toronto the Ontario Public Service ran an advertisement that said it all: "Assistant Deputy Minister/Anti-Racism & Ethno-Cultural Equity Division for the Department of Education" (*GM*, June 26/92).

The West was sending more confusing signals too. David Elton, one of the fathers of the Triple-E Senate, was interviewed on CBC's "The Journal" on June 28. Viewers watched him muddle along and then back off: "Senate reform has to do with minority rights, whether it's women, whether it's aboriginals, whether it's the Senate, whether it's Quebec. It's really an attempt to provide a better means, a better set of rules to deal with minority rights right across the country."

Minority rights? Where was the Triple-E in all this?

The FMC on June 29 in Ottawa confirmed the mess. After a four-hour lunch meeting at 24 Sussex, Joe Clark confronted the media with one of his many earnest grimaces for special occasions, saying gamely: "Everybody was here today trying to find a solution for Canada" (CBC Newsworld, June 29/92).

In fact, the only agreement the first ministers had made was to meet again in Toronto on Friday, July 3. In the back of everyone's mind hovered

Mulroney's threat and a unilateral deal after July 15. Formidable — democracy in action.

Prize nominations for silliest observations of the season, though, would have included Saskatchewan's Roy Romanow. Following the FMC he told reporters, "We were a part of the Triple-E [group of supporters]. . . . In a sense we are still a part of the Triple-E" (CBC Newsworld, June 29/92).

What could it possibly mean? What was the photo-op premier trying to say? It was just bubbling enthusiasm. No one was a part of anything and no one had the guts to say so, either. Yet a faint hope glimmered: maybe, just maybe, Bob Rae was coming out of his six-year torpor:

> There was a universal feeling around the room that a question to the people of Quebec which did not put the case for Canada — not some fuzzy wuzzy question about a common market and sovereignty association, but a question about choosing between Canada and an independent Quebec — that's the question that must be put in a Quebec referendum. . . . So for heaven's sake if there's going to be a referendum let's at least make it about something real. Which is about the existence of the country and the country's capacity to reform itself. It's not acceptable to me . . . to have the people of Quebec offered a choice which really isn't a choice, in which case you could have 80 or 85 per cent of people voting for something which really isn't very real. (*Star*, June 30/92)

Bravo, Bob! Was anyone listening? Certainly not the *Toronto Sun*, which was sounding more and more like the *Toronto Star* with each passing edition. The *Sun* actually believed that something serious was happening. They said so in their June 30 editorial: "The constitutional package now being worked out will not be perfect. It will not satisfy everyone in every detail. But it should satisfy all of us in some detail. And that is what really matters — that we are big and bold enough to accept something less to enable something more to endure."

So Canadian. So colonial. Our patriotism sold to us as our capacity to compromise, no matter what the cost. After all, this was only the country's constitution.[4]

None of the papers grappled with the central issue. A constitution should articulate the highest ideals and principles. These are the conditions under which its people consent to be governed. The definition is basic. No nation of significance deliberately sets out to make itself second-rate in its own constitution.

Joe Clark seemed unaware of this. Day after day he poured on the pressure. That day in particular, the same paper diligently reported his latest utterances:

> This country simply cannot survive another failure. And we can't postpone reform any longer. . . . If we can't do that [come to an agreement] in an agreed way with all the provinces, then obviously the Parliament of Canada has an obligation to act on its own. . . . If we don't break the back of this problem, it will break us. We literally cannot afford to fail. (*Star*, July 1/92)

> We know the count, and the count is that Quebeckers regard this as having had two strikes and we're at the plate, and what we do in the next few days will determine if we can score for the country. . . . If we fail there may not be a country at all. (*GM*, July 1/92)

What to do? Nobody knew. Except, of course, Quebec. Gil Rémillard kept on keeping on: "We need the right of veto. For us, the reform of the Senate and the right of veto are directly connected, and we have to find a solution to both issues" (*GM*/CP, July 1/92).

Dan Gagnier knew, too. Remember him? The Deputy Secretary on Communications and Consultation to the Mulroney Cabinet had worked as the former communications chief for David Peterson's Liberal government in Ontario. That was the government that orchestrated the plan to manipulate the CBC during the Meech Lake Accord. Now Gagnier decided it was time to jump ship again. In early July he left the Mulroney government to take up the position of president of the Brewers Association of Canada. The move made a certain kind of sense, mixing politics and beer. Same end product.

Canada Day, July 1, 1992, arrived. This time it disappointed a lot of Canadians. Her Majesty Elizabeth II arrived at noon to spend forty-seven hours at Canada's 125th celebration. *Globe and Mail* readers learned that the cost of the visit to them would come to about $1 million. The Angus Reid–Southam News survey in the *Toronto Star* the previous day had shown that six out of ten Canadians thought the Royal Family made no difference to their lives or that of their country. How much Canada had changed in just a few decades! Despite the political situation, the Queen was greeted by a crowd of 50,000 in Ottawa. To the astonishment of many listeners, Her Majesty's message was pure politics and not one guaranteed to please anyone who disagreed with the premise of founding races and founding cultures:

The two founding linguistic communities of Canada and its aboriginal people have since become a multicultural society enriched by the immigrants from all corners of the globe. . . . Your leaders are attempting to craft a new compromise accommodating the distinctive character of Quebec within Canada, respecting the historic rights of the aboriginal peoples. . . . You have inherited a country uniquely worth preserving. (*GM*, July 2/92)

Queen Elizabeth the Trudovnic! What next?

The last bastion of the honour system in Canada under Mulroney's stewardship would be assaulted. It was obvious that government hacks had composed the Queen's message to promote the rejected distinct society concept. By breaching the remaining ramparts of tradition while pushing patronage on the grandest scale ever, the prime minister named two non-politicians to the Privy Council. Of these, Mark Entwhistle, the prime minister's secretary and the last of the lackies to massage the media, said on his master's behalf, "It's the highest honour in terms of title you can have in Canada" (*GM*, July 2/92). Conrad Black and Paul Desmarais were automatically entitled to use the title "Honourable" before their names. Both supported Mulroney and his cabal.

Two days after its largely irrelevant celebrations of Canada's 125th, the Mulroney government swung hard on Newfoundland. The action wasn't revenge against its premier, only discourtesy. Wells didn't know what was coming until it hit him. On July 3, federal fisheries minister John Crosbie announced the largest lay-off in Canadian history as of that midnight — immediately shutting down the northern cod fishing industry for two years. Some 19,000 inshore fisherman, plant workers, and trawlermen were instantly unemployed. Wells turned the boorish behaviour to the best advantage he could — giving a Triple-E Senate another plug: "Until a few hours ago, we didn't even know what the federal government was going to decide. That's the level of say we had. The reason for it is that we have seven votes out of 300 in the House of Commons. That's where the Triple-E Senate comes in again. If we had an effective say . . . we'd have some means of finding a balance in this country" (*GM*, July 4/92).

Newfoundland writhed over the terrible news. At the FMC in Toronto, going on at the same time, rumours flew behind closed doors that progress was really being made on the stumbling block of Senate reform.

As usual, one had to consider the source of the information. Joe Clark said, "I think it's pretty clear today we've moved beyond that impasse." New Brunswick premier Frank McKenna said, "The logjam, temporarily at least, has been broken." Alberta premier Don Getty contributed his bit:

"This package has the Alberta principles in it." Manitoba premier Gary Filmon gave his opinion: "It's very close to what the Triple-E people put on the table" (*GM*, July 4/92).

Those who could still bear to tune in to the whole business listened incredulously. Premier Roy Romanow's attempts to score political points for the home audience impressed the fewest people of all: "Well, I'm satisfied because of what the meeting accomplished. . . . Oh, I think it'll fly in Saskatchewan all right, because this particular deal has large portions of the Saskatchewan compromise document that we advanced" ("Cover Story," CBC Newsworld, July 3/92).

Wells infuriated his fellow first ministers once more with his deadly accuracy: "I don't think we have a final agreement, or anything like a final agreement, on the Senate" (*Star*/CP, July 4/92).

Mulroney grabbed the last word. En route to the Munich summit of G-7 countries and other conferences that month, he commented from London: "The Canadian population absolutely insists that we turn the page on the constitutional question and solve the problem, and I have the impression that there is clear political will to do this" (*Star*, July 5/92).

On July 6 the first ministers met yet again — this time for twelve hours. This meeting followed up on the July 3 FMC. Twelve days to go before Mulroney's deadline of July 15. Various wisps of information wafted under the closed doors of the meeting rooms. Rumour had it that there was a fragile agreement in the works on native self-government. Transitional arrangements would allow time to pass before a court of law would start handling cases to interpret exactly what self-government meant. This was extended from three years to five. All the first ministers of the provinces agreed that native self-government was to be "one of three orders of government" to be spelled out in the Constitution. As far as natives were concerned, this equalled "provincial status."

The schedule squeezed Clark tighter and tighter as he set the deadline: "Tomorrow will have to be the end of the consultations" (*GM*, July 7/92). "If it is not possible for us to get agreement tomorrow [Tuesday], then the Government of Canada, of course, will have to proceed on our own through Parliament when the House reconvenes on the 15th of July" (*Star*, July 7/92).

On July 7, Canada's first ministers reached a vague agreement. It was prosaically dubbed the Pearson accord, after the Department of External Affairs building in which the meetings were held. The beast itself was an eleven-legged camel that bore little resemblance to anything that had appeared on the table before.[5]

If anyone witnessing this circus could still believe in magic, Clark could count that credulity another personal triumph. He said himself that it was "a historic day. . . . I have good reason to be optimistic" that Quebec will sign (*Star*/CP, July 8/92). It had been an "historic process. I cannot recall another time, literally since Confederation, when there has been so much agreement on such a wide range of issues" (*Maclean's*, Aug 10/92).

That's certainly not the impression Clyde Wells had. The next day, he said what everyone knew: "The whole package hasn't been fully and clearly identified yet. . . . Nobody has seen the final text" (CBC Newsworld, July 8/92).

Would Canadians ever really know what was going on? It sure seemed doubtful. While the final pieces of the Pearson accord were being put into place, Ottawa was hosting other goings-on. Once again Dan Gagnier hit the news. Having just left his job as Deputy Secretary on Communications and Consultations to the Mulroney Cabinet he filed an affidavit before the Federal Court of Canada opposing the application of federal Information Commissioner John Grace. Grace wanted to force the public release of 74 of the government's 690 pages of public-opinion poll research: "The information revealed to provincial negotiators, or indeed others at the negotiating table, by the release of polling results, would thus do injury to the positions of the government of Canada by revealing its internal and tactical deliberations" (*GM*/CP, July 8/92).

So another sorry chapter in the Mulroney era dragged to a close. What would the prime minister do with the mess Clark had agreed to, the Pearson accord? It seemed to give everything to everybody and nothing to anyone. The only certain thing was that Quebec would find nothing in it to accept.

Notes

1 During the Referendum debate in 1992 Lewis was thought to support the Charlotte-town Accord. This was apparently not true as the newspapers had to print a retraction after publishing stories to that effect.

2   Young's credentials and background are unknown. She was paid $9,000 to write the report.

3   A short essay piece published in *Maclean's*, July 22, 1991, issue, "A Degree of Truth," read: "The academic credentials of Canada's senior civil servant, clerk of the Privy Council Paul Tellier, are under scrutiny. Since 1980, both Canadian *Who's Who* and *Who's Who in America* have variously listed Tellier as having a 1963 master's degree or having satisfied most of the requirements for such a degree from the University of Montreal. And until last year, the *Canadian Parliamentary Guide* credited him with a master's in business administration.

But Claude Larouche, registrar at the University of Montreal, says that his records do not show that Tellier ever received any degree there. In an interview with *Maclean's*, Tellier said that he did not actually hold a master's degree from the University of Montreal. Nor, he added, does he have an MBA. But Tellier stressed that he was not aware that errors had crept into his *Who's Who* and *Parliamentary Guide* entries until *The Ottawa Citizen* reported them recently. Said Tellier: 'I'm very unhappy about the whole thing. I feel very much that my integrity here is at stake.'"

Everyone listed in *Canadian Who's Who* receives a proof sheet twice a year showing how his or her name and credentials will be listed. This is the person's opportunity to correct errors. In the lower ranks of the public service, such misrepresentation of one's credentials earns instant dismissal.

After the matter of Tellier's credentials was cleared up in the 1992 *Canadian Who's Who*, the *Financial Post Magazine* of November 1992 ascribed an MA in law to him from the University of Montreal. So the questions continue: Does Paul Tellier really have a master's degree in law from the University of Montreal now? He's not telling.

On January 11, 1993, Governor General Ray Hnatyshyn named him a Companion of the Order of Canada, the highest rank of the insignia.

4   During the Meech Lake Accord I composed a little ditty to describe the Canadian mindset:

> In the search for mediocrity
> We are the second best.
> We much prefer to stay behind
> And follow with the rest.

5   After long hours, the FMC, with Quebec absent, agreed on what to do with the Senate. At the last minute, Ontario's Premier Bob Rae, sporting a new Peace Tower tie, clinched the deal just as his predecessor David Peterson had done at Meech Lake.

The agreement suggested a proportionally elected and equal Senate, but one that was weighted. This Double-E Senate would allow 8 seats for each province, 2 each for the two territories. The House of Commons would expand from 295 to 312. Ontario would gain 10 seats. A simple majority in the Senate could defeat tax legislation on natural resources (NEP).

The Cat's Breakfast, the Pearson Accord

If 60 percent of the Senate opposed a bill, they could vote it down, which would lead to a joint meeting of Commons and Senate. A vote of 70 percent would defeat the bill outright. The double-majority rule applied. To pass changes affecting languages and culture, for example, a majority of the Senate *and* of Quebec senators would have to pass the amendments. At Quebec's request, the distinct society clause would be part of the so-called Canada clause, not of the Charter of Rights and Freedoms.

27

Bingo! The Charlottetown Accord
—July to August 1992

J OE CLARK WAS RIGHT WHEN HE called the Pearson accord of July 7 an "historic" agreement, but not for the reasons he boasted. The so-called consensus he had reached was completely out of kilter with the prime minister's plan. And Mulroney had engineered the whole thing in the first place after all. So loosey-goosey was the accord that the wags were calling it Clark's long-overdue revenge for being swindled out of the Conservative leadership.

Things are always bad when the prime minister communicates with the country only through "senior officials" who fudge the story for the media. When Mulroney returned from the G-7 Conference in Munich on July 8, one unattributed source said, "Mr. Clark persisted. He won the game. We were all going on a different assumption. . . . [Mulroney] was taken aback" (*GM*, July 9/92).

Historian Michael Bliss was invited to comment on CBC about the setting. It was, he said, "Orwellian." About Clyde Wells's comments that there were no final details, he asked simply, "Is there an agreement?" (CBC Newsworld, July 8/92).

From Montreal, Gérald Larose, the union leader (CNTU), dismissed the accord shortly: "It's a farce. Quebecers, please don't even deal with it" (*Sun*, July 12/92). Quebec's premier was in even finer form:

I cannot say today: No deal. I do not think it would be responsible to say to my colleagues who did work for many months to achieve that solution that the government of Quebec is not interested to discuss it. . . . I think, according to the text we have now, we have questions concerning the Senate, and we have questions concerning divisions of powers and aboriginal rights. . . . We must repair the errors of the past. . . . Repair the injustice done to Quebec in 1982: one of the founding nations had imposed on it the fundamental law of the country. . . . (*GM, Star*, July 10/92)

Weird.

And then there are other points — veto, spending powers, Supreme Court, immigration. To all intents and purposes, [the Pearson accord] does not meet the demands of Quebec. . . .

And there's one other thing I'd like to say. Canada is a bicultural country; there's the Official Languages Act, too, French and English, and if we consider all of this we have to realize that with this new Senate, this application of Canadian bilingualism would be rather theoretical, considering the very limited number of francophone senators. . . .

And I'd like to close just by saying that, as you know, my government and my party wish to defend as strongly as possible and as clearly as possible the identity of Quebec. Quebec is a nation, but for us the nation is not an absolute. We are within our own century, and we wish to be able to develop within the Canadian federation, building Quebec without destroying Canada. (CBC Newsworld, July 10/92)

Bourassa did what he does so well: he went into his famous Norman *peut-être* mode. The Quebec premier was sounding like the callow youth Joe Clark. Yet here was the champion of a unilingual Quebec having the right to control all culture, touting Trudeau's line of a bilingual Canada, while caterwauling about "the fundamental law of the country" being imposed on Quebec. Parizeau was dead on: what was new was indeed what was old. Ontario's Bob Rae dubbed Bourassa *"un champion de l'ambiguïté"* (*Le Devoir*, July 10/92).

But did anybody think that just maybe it was time to kick the Constitution into the next century? Not on your nelly. Certainly not the very stubborn Martin Brian Mulroney. Instead he arrived back a day early from Munich to take the reins from his senior official puppets. From this moment on, the deal would be his own: "I didn't understand that it was a package wide open for discussion. Nor did I understand it was a package that couldn't be touched. . . . I have some ideas [for improvements], but I will want to discuss them with my colleagues first" (*GM*, July 10/92).

Mulroney might have thought he could play with the deal the premiers had come to, but Rae didn't think that was what had happened:

> We've made it very clear, and I've certainly made it clear at different points, that I wasn't about to negotiate once and then completely re-open the whole package. (*Star*, July 10/92)

> We have to get on with it. Call a conference. And if [Bourassa] comes, he comes. If he doesn't come, well that sends another message. . . . This is all part of a general agreement. It's quite clear that if one part of the agreement suddenly gets nixed, we don't have an agreement. (*GM*, July 10/92)

Prime Minister Brian Mulroney entered the National Press Theatre on July 10 at 4:00 P.M. The July 15 opening of Parliament would be postponed, he said, because it would be "best if Parliament was asked to address a more final agreement" (CBC Newsworld, July 10/92).

By now the sticking point for his and Quebec's perspective was the inherent right to native self-government. Senator Claude Castonguay did the deed this time. The man who had dumped his own commission, Castonguay–Dobbie, and who had helped blow up the Victoria Charter in 1971, pushed his way into the limelight for a little more messing about. He echoed the sentiments of Benoît Bouchard when he told *La Presse* he was "profoundly disappointed" and that the deal was "unacceptable for Quebec and Canada":

> It is extraordinary that English Canada has agreed to the creation of a third level of government while it refuses to recognize in a significant way the distinctive character of Quebec and its demands of the last 30 years. (*FP*, July 14/92)

> If we isolate the elements of the Meech Lake accord, we can say we are getting close. There has been a certain progress. But if one takes account of the rest, the Senate, the spending power [preserved for the most part], the division of powers [unchanged], the creation of new provinces, in my view we've moved backwards. (*GM*, July 17/92)

Above this rhetoric sounded the voice of the finance minister, Don Mazankowski, "If we're talking about trade and economic activity on a world-wide basis. . . . we certainly have to do the same thing in our own country. . . . What's there doesn't go far enough. There aren't enough broad commitments to eliminate trade barriers" (*Star*, July 14/92).

Mazankowski's parrot, federal Minister of Industry Michael Wilson, squawked: "I have to say that I have some problems as it stands now. . . . The results of the federal-provincial agreement last week are not good enough. We've got to do better" (*GM*, July 15/92) and "It doesn't lead to a stronger Canadian economy and that is really the entire object of the proposals, to improve the functioning of the Canadian economic union" (*FP*, July 15/92).

Bob Rae took over centre stage with a flourish when he announced he would not return to the constitutional bargaining table unless Bourassa did the same:

> I'm simply saying we've done our bit as premiers, and the federal government has been there. We've been working flat out at this for 4½ months and I really think it is now up to the government of Quebec to respond. Why should I? . . . We have not had a clear response yet from the government of Quebec. I think we're entitled to one. I think the people of Canada are entitled to a clear indication from Quebec as to how they feel. . . . The elements of the package are there. (*Star*, July 15/92)

Following a divided Cabinet meeting on July 15, the prime minister lowered the boom. The Pearson accord was simply not up to snuff. He repeated his appraisal of the accord and his ground rules:

> No one has suggested that this arrangement, informally arrived at among nine premiers, is the definitive word. . . . There is no question of my government associating itself with any initiative that could isolate Quebec. If you're going to make an arrangement to be called a Canadian package, then it has to reflect the position of 10 provinces — not nine or seven or four but 10. And we don't have that yet. . . . The only thing we would exclude would be a policy of inaction. (*Star*, July 16/92)

The Boss was back in the saddle.

Then, just when everyone thought Ontario was wising up, Bob Rae retreated into his mouse mode — demanding only to know who was speaking for the federal government: "Mr. Clark, we were told, had a mandate to negotiate. Now we have [international trade minister] Michael Wilson trashing it from one perspective. We have a number of [federal]

Quebec cabinet ministers going at it from another perspective. I think we're entitled to know who speaks for the federal government. What is the federal government's position? Mr. Clark was successful. He gained the trust of everyone in the meetings" (*GM*, July 16/92).

The next day, French presidential aspirant Jacques Chirac was in Montreal. He unveiled a forgettable white granite block eighteen metres high to General Charles de Gaulle, Paris's birthday gift to the city for its 350th birthday, at a cost of approximately $500,000. In his congratulatory speech, Chirac said, "In its symbolic power, it links the past and the future. It's therefore a sign of that which unites, and not that which divides" (*GM*, July 17/92). Canadians recognized the devilment for what it was, and shrugged.

All the previously silent players seemed to be oozing out of the woodwork now. Mulroney's Chief of Staff, Hugh Segal, the most cautious and silent of assistants, said of Joe Clark that he "had a mandate and acted within it . . . and the Prime Minister was aware of what was going on to the extent that anybody not in the room with the premiers could be aware. [Mulroney] was aware of the broad nature of the discussions. . . . There was constant contact" (*Star*, July 17/92).

Mulroney had a problem. He had to put distance between himself and Clark and do it without hurting the minister who had been hailed by the media as Canada's saviour.

No easy task. Segal was sent in to buy time. The government needed it so they could gradually downgrade the minister's achievement without upsetting anyone.

Fortunately for them, Clark always enjoyed defeat. The final "offer" Mulroney would approve to Quebec would bear no relation to the Pearson accord. Ever so slowly, Mulroney would come up with something credible to save face. In propaganda step 1, the vocabulary changed. The Pearson accord became a "discussion" and no longer a consensus on detail.

As the new constitutional affairs minister, in effect, Mulroney repeated his favourite boast on July 17 in Montreal at the inauguration of a city park on the EXPO '67 site: "The unity of Canada has made Canada Number One in the world. When the United Nations tell me that I'm Number One in the world, I don't look for a formula to become Number 13, or Number 15 or Number 42" (*Star*, July 18/92).

He directly challenged Clark's conclusion that the Pearson agreement handed Quebec the essence of Meech Lake. Again he repeated that the deal had to satisfy Quebec.[1] He implied he was taking over: "No one told me that this thing was cast in concrete, here it is take it or leave it. So in the absence of that kind of attitude, I assume flexibility and the desire by all people . . . to try and work to keep Canada together. . ." (*GM*, July 18/92).

Another very different message emanated from Montreal. Citing family reasons, the founder of the Bloc Québécois, Jean Lapierre, resigned from Parliament: "I can't raise [my two children] by telephone any more" (*GM*, July 22/92). Based on a study completed by the National Citizens' Coalition and published in the *Toronto Star* on July 29, Lapierre's estimated parting present for thirteen years' service in the House of Commons was some $4 million in pension benefits. NCC president David Somerville reacted on behalf of many Canadians angry at the news: "Lapierre spent his time on the benches working for the destruction of Canada as we know it. . . . It's sickening" (*GM*/CP, July 29/92).

Petty squabbles marked the next ten days. Ovide Mercredi was furious over some wording that had been changed in one of the drafts without his permission. Clark said Mercredi was so confused that the native chief didn't realize that he had actually chaired the committee overseeing the draft himself.

By this time even the insiders taking instructions didn't know what side they were on, let alone who was conducting the orchestra. It was Meech Lake and Clyde Wells and the missing clauses all over again.

Liberal leader Jean Chrétien delighted in the confusion: "The premiers felt they had an agreement, but Brian Mulroney said no deal. Don't ask me if I agree with a deal that doesn't exist. . . . It's amazing" (*Star*, July 23/92). Joe Clark thought it was time for another FMC. The Tory trouper said he saw some new things cooking: "There's been a sense of exasperation, I think, growing across the country. It's a good thing it's summer. . . . The best way to deal with it is to bring the first ministers together. . . . I don't think [the deal] is unravelling." He said there were some "creative" solutions available, including the designation of certain senatorial seats as francophone.

Chaos. In Toronto, Bob Rae metaphorically folded his arms and said, "I'm only going if [Bourassa's] going [to an FMC]. . . . I don't care whether it's a lunch, a breakfast, a tea, a bridge game, a pyjama party. I'm only going if everyone else is" (*Star*, July 24/92). For the country it was a bit late, but good for Uncle Bobby anyway.

There was a very good reason why no one in the country could figure out what was going on. The only people doing anything were Mulroney and Bourassa. Clark's admission on July 23 that he might have overdone it when he referred to the unsigned Pearson accord as an "historic" achievement struck his fellow Canadians as the first honest statement he had come out with in a very long time.

The month wound up at last. If you were an anglophone, you could take your pick of what and whom to get mad at. On July 24, leaders of the Association canadienne-française de l'Alberta (ACFA) proposed in a letter to Premier Robert Bourassa that 21 francophone seats be provided in a 94-seat Senate. Georges Arès, ACFA director-general, said, "You have to protect the *francophonie* from coast to coast, because if you limit French to Quebec, that will inevitably lead to the separation of Quebec" (*GM*, July 25/92).

Marcel Masse, defence minister, stirred up more trouble. He stressed that Parliament would now be broken up on the bases of founding races and cultures. On Sunday, July 26, 1992, he spoke from Halifax, to announce the award of a $4.4-billion defence contract, the third-largest defence contract in Canadian history. Once again, the major beneficiary was Quebec. The chosen project manager was the Montreal-based American company Paramax Systems Inc. The nationalist minister who had taken over the whole hockey rink by now justified the heavy criticism that rained down on his head: "The [bidding] result just shows that in Montreal you have a large industrial base in electronics and aerospace" (*GM*, July 27/92), and "Montreal is recognized as the centre of Canada's defence industry, so wouldn't it be logical that much of the money would come here?" (*GM*/CP, July 28/92).

No way. The national pie for defence department expenditures was being carved up: Quebec, $947 million; Ontario, $690 million; the West, $698 million; the Atlantic provinces, $496 million; $1.2 billion unallocated — to be spent overseas.

Canadians did a slow burn. The prime minister confirmed their worst suspicions about the depth of the mess on July 28 by calling for an FMC at Harrington Lake for Tuesday, August 4. The negotiators had reverted to their old ways of doing constitutional business together. Native and territorial leaders were excluded again. Yet Mulroney said, "I think it's in the national interest that everybody show up." It was to be a bull session — one could only imagine. Especially after this comment: "The object of the exercise is not to negotiate the modalities of this or that particular clause. I want to make it clear. I am not seeking a meeting to pursue negotiation. . . . I think we have to do something different. We have to try to get the partners to agree on a process that might lead to a favourable conclusion" (*Star*, July 29/92).

Alberta's Don Getty tipped off the game plan. He told Canadian Press,

"I've talked to Premier Bourassa today. He is coming. I am pleased with that" (*GM*/CP, July 29/92). He would not be so pleased soon after that. On July 29, after two years of shunning the negotiations, the Quebec premier made the announcement everyone had been waiting to hear: "I've accepted this invitation [to Harrington Lake] because it has been agreed that the Meech Lake accord will not be challenged. We must conclude that the Meech Lake accord is no longer challenged and that, in this context, I am satisfied in accepting the invitation to examine the evolution of the process. . . . I got total satisfaction on 'distinct society'" (*GM*, July 30/92).

The news was certainly confusing. For example, Bourassa released the wording of the new Canada clause first. Instantly scores of problems sprang up. So much for "process." Everything in the Meech Lake Accord that had offended the people and the provinces outside Quebec had slipped back onto the agenda as if the Meech defeat never happened. Three key clauses read:

> Quebec constitutes within Canada a distinct society which includes a French-speaking majority, a unique culture and a civil law tradition.

> The role of the legislature and government of Quebec to preserve and promote the distinct society of Quebec is affirmed.

> Canadians are committed to the vitality and development of official language minority communities throughout Canada, and the role of their governments to protect the linguistic rights of those communities is affirmed. (*GM*, July 30/92)

Trudeau lived! Meech lived!

PQ constitutional critic Jacques Brassard condemned Bourassa for "betraying the solemn promise he made to Quebeckers" not to return to the table (*GM*, July 30/92). He even wrote a play around the issue. His Mulroney speaks first to Quebec: "Would you kindly put your arm into this wringer I have ready for you here?" Bourassa replies, "Of course, dear friend, if that can give you pleasure" (*Star*, July 30/92).

The Mouvement Québec français (MQF) kept up their own pressure. They released a statement that Quebecers "will not forgive [Bourassa] for going against the opinion of the majority." They also reported they had 640,000 signatures demanding that the question on the referendum ballot be on the sovereignty issue only.

A hot wind blasted in from the cold North. In Whitehorse on July 29, Yukon leader Tony Penikett said, "It looks like the fix is in and the North is going to get shafted again. Mr. Bourassa and Mr. Mulroney made a backroom deal to relegate us to colonial status" (*Star/Ott Citizen*, July 30/92). As for Joe Clark, "We would like him to sell the package that he was part of making. . . . We now see the fix coming. We now see Mulroney and Bourassa getting together to screw us again. And frankly, you say to yourself, what the hell can you do about it? These people just don't give a damn about what happens to the people up here" (*GM*, July 30/92).

On Tuesday, August 4, Bourassa informally returned. He claimed that only "process" and not "issues" were being discussed when the reporters swarmed around him. The closed-door meeting lasted more than six hours. He offered a nearly perfect reprise of the performance he had given on July 9, 1992, endorsing Trudeau's vision: "One of the fundamental characteristics of Canada is to be a bilingual country. That's the essence of the country, Canada being different from the United States, and that it could be very difficult for Quebec to accept a Senate where you will have a handful of francophone senators. I was always saying that" (*GM*, Aug 5/92). On CBC Newsworld, he added, "I would not be exercising my responsibilities if I did not take all possible measures to avoid the breakup of the country" (Aug 4/92).

Mulroney invited the premiers to gather again, even more informally, on Monday, August 10, 1992, to see whether more comprehensive constitutional negotiations should follow. Each premier reacted to Bourassa's reappearance after his self-imposed exile:

Bob Rae: "I'm not prepared to stand idly by and let the country fall apart because people are refusing to talk or because people are being obstreperous or dogmatic about fixed positions" (*Star*, Aug 5/92).

Don Getty: "He presented to us the difficulties he can see from a political reality position. . . . I don't feel any great sense of optimism that [the gaps] can be closed, but we're going to keep working at it" (*Star*, Aug 5/92). As for the July 7 Pearson accord: "It's not for opening up" (*GM*, Aug 5/92).

Roy Romanow: "There will be some tight corners to navigate or some very difficult circles to square, I suspect. But today was encouraging because of the frank discussion" (*GM*, Aug 5/92). The day before, on national television, the Saskatchewan premier had said: "I think the up-side to the day is the fact that there were conversations about process. That is good news. . . . When the next meeting takes place, or presumably sometime afterwards, if there is an agreement on process, there will be some tight corners to navigate or some very difficult circles to square. . . . I am not as pessimistic as Premier Getty was. . . . I am confident, if we can come to an agreement on process next Monday" (CBC Newsworld, Aug 4/92).

Frank McKenna of New Brunswick: "Yes, I'm saying that more compromises have to be made" (*GM*, Aug 5/92).

Gary Filmon of Manitoba: "Premier Bourassa is not looking for a sign of compromise, Premier Bourassa is looking for a sign of surrender. . . . And obviously, I couldn't be true to the Manitoba [constitutional] task force or the people of Manitoba if I were to give in to all of his demands" (*Star*, Aug 8/92).

Clyde Wells quoted Filmon that Quebec was "looking for a sign of surrender," saying, "I can't disagree with him" (*GM*, Aug 10/92).

The FMC at Harrington Lake carried an important footnote, too. AFN Chief Ovide Mercredi had pressed vainly for admission. Bourassa repeated casually what all the first ministers in attendance were saying: that the meeting was about "process" only, implying that he wasn't missing anything. Mercredi wouldn't buy it: "It's just another day of our subordinate role. . . . I will not be going to the meeting I was invited to by the Prime Minister, only to be told what I already know, that I'm not invited to the meeting on Monday [FMC]. Now is the time to take different actions, political demonstrations to show our displeasure from being excluded from being part of the work on the Constitution. . . . The Prime Minister has made it very clear . . . he sides with Quebec before the aboriginal people" (*Star*, Aug 5/92).

The aboriginal leaders arranged their first demonstration for the day of the next FMC, August 10. Tony Penikett from the Yukon turned down the PM's invitation as well. Ron George, president of the Native Council of Canada, which represented non-status Indians, told reporters he would attend: "There's certain things I have to tell the Prime Minister and that I can't do from behind a barricade. I have to do it face to face" (*Star*, Aug 5/92).

In the end, it didn't really matter who met and who didn't. Mulroney could have capitalized on a fragile trust if he had chosen to include the native leaders. Instead, he ignored the historic breakthrough of their earlier participation and irrevocably smashed his own plans for the multilateral talks. To outsiders, all the politicians had become hopeless liars.

Then New Brunswick's McKenna flubbed, too. Mulroney's parallel-accord puppet blurted out the truth in French: "Certain substantive issues were brought up, generally speaking, but at the next meeting we will continue with our conversations dealing with process" (CBC Newsworld, Aug 4/92).

In the meantime, while first ministers jockeyed for position in the excitement of Bourassa's imminent return, the costs of the exercise continued to rise, especially the bills for the government's lobbying of Canadians to tag along with the deal. One large invoice came to public attention on August 4. Ottawa had paid nearly $2 million the previous year in consulting and professional contracts to those who "tailor messages or monitor those who carry them." Canadian Press had obtained the statistics under the Access to Information Act, and unearthed the fact that the feds had paid nearly $400,000 on public opinion polling alone. Direct beneficiaries included academics: Peter Leslie, University of Toronto, $92,700 in expenses and salary; Roger Gibbins, University of Alberta, $85,644; Katherine Swinton, University of Toronto, $62,098. Constitutions are lucrative business for executive-federalist insiders.

Mulroney planned to meet with Canada's native leaders on August 5 to appease them. How much the prime minister's authority had deteriorated! Of the four native leaders and two territorial leaders invited, two prominent faces were conspicuously absent: AFN Chief Ovide Mercredi and Yukon "Premier" Antony Penikett.[2] A day later Mercredi was campaigning in Nemaska, Quebec, preparing cross-Canada protest rallies: "The Prime Minister is stuck with the old ways of dealing with Indian people as inferiors. . . . [Bourassa and Wells] are two so-called enemies coming together for one common purpose: to defeat the Indian people. . . .

"We have tried everything to extend an open hand to this premier [Bourassa], and instead of accepting it, he has rebuffed us. He has ignored every effort of friendship" (*Star*, Aug 7/92).

Whatever was going on, nobody, but nobody, was telling it straight. By that point, they probably couldn't. From Victoria, British Columbia, the provincial constitutional affairs minister, Moe Sihota, said Quebec accepted the Pearson accord of July 7, but, "clearly, there was a miscalculation about public opinion in Quebec toward the package. . . . We have to accommodate a change. I'm making an appeal to the sense of accommodation and compromise that has been so much a part of this country." Sihota said Bourassa tried to sell the package for two days following the July 7 meeting. As Sihota saw it, Quebec agreed to the Pearson accord and "there was sufficient communication between the province of Quebec and the federal government. . . . Quebec was fully informed that was the direction the talks were taking. . . . They never exercised what you might call a veto. They had an opportunity to and did not. At no time in that five-day period [July 7 to 11] did they indicate that was a deal-breaker for Quebec" (*GM*/CP, Aug 7/92).

Bourassa's aide Silvie Godin disputed the BC minister's story: "Even on that very day, July 7, our [Quebec] officials here [in Quebec] had talks with officials in Ottawa, with Rae's officials and the others. On that very morning, we let them know we wouldn't go ahead with that" (*GM*, Aug 7/92).

Mulroney's August 10 FMC made for strange media coverage. The conference participants met the press on a sheltered porch while reporters fired questions from twenty metres away, huddled together in the rain.

The next day, the ministers dressed informally, as Mulroney had specified. They wore short-sleeved shirts, goofy sweaters, and ties. Frank McKenna looked as if he had raided Preston Manning's closet. He glowed in a shiny purple shirt, not unlike the one Manning would make familiar in a feature article in *Maclean's*. It suited the occasion. And it showed just how grassroots these first ministers were at heart. After some seven hours of negotiating, the Pearson accord lay in ribbons. In its place rose a new, even looser consensus that sprouted a dozen and more fresh options.

AFN Chief Ovide Mercredi fulfilled his promise. When the meeting finally broke up, the ministers emerged to find hundreds of native protesters congregated near the house in the miserable weather. Don Getty was one of five premiers to acknowledge the protesters: "We stand behind all parts of that agreement, and we certainly stand behind the aboriginal groups who went through five months with us in trying to reach that agreement. We don't enter into agreements lightly. When we enter into them, we mean them to stick" (*GM*, Aug 11/92).

As with the August 4 FMC, all the ministers at the short-sleeved August 10 meeting described this one as one on "process" only, based on the "framework" or the "plateau agreement" of the July 7 Pearson accord. The mutterings were obviously intended to throw the media and everyone else off the track. As his reason for attending, Bourassa married a platitude to a platitude: "To govern is to choose. Either I choose not to dialogue with my Canadian partners, or I accept to discuss with them" (*GM*, Aug 11/92). And he shrugged.

Getty and Bourassa both confirmed that the Pearson accord had been trashed. Getty took a stab at explaining it before the television cameras: "I am not terribly optimistic, but I do think that there is a sense of open-mindedness, constructive thinking. The fact that the July 7 agreement is the framework for our continued discussions is extremely important, and I am pleased we are moving to the full meeting" (CBC Newsworld, Aug 10/92).

Bourassa's words were even more inane: "I am more confident tonight than I was this morning. . . . There were some attitudes, there were some proposals made today which clearly have as a purpose to take into account the priorities of Quebec" (*GM*, Aug 11/92).

Would it never end? Would the first ministers ever admit they never had a deal from day one? Would Canadians ever be able to keep all the FMCs and various meetings straight? Should they even bother to stay tuned?

Alas, no one was even hinting that the unravelling of the Pearson accord could produce any straight talk. None of the players had the stomach for it.

So the business droned on. Quebec fed the newshounds the big story of the month. The MNA for Westmount, Richard Holden, a former drinking buddy of Mordecai Richler and Brian Mulroney who used to champion anglophone rights as a crusader against Bill 178, made headlines again. He had been ousted from the Equality Party almost a year earlier. Now he told the world he had joined the Parti Québécois: "I haven't given up on Canada. . . . I've decided that Quebec and what is the rest of Canada will be far better off if Quebec becomes a sovereign country and then negotiates a new arrangement, an economic union. Canada was a very wonderful country. I was very pleased to be a Canadian, but it is not the country I once knew. . . . It has become fractious and quarrelsome and bitter" (*GM*, Aug 11/92).

The first ministers might have been oblivious to the damage they were doing, but the international money market understood. On August 10, the Canadian dollar dropped one-third of a cent against the U.S. dollar.

On August 12, at 2:00 P.M. Mulroney called for yet another First Ministers Conference, this time a full and formal one. This FMC would not show shirt-sleeved ministers posing awkwardly in a mob for photo ops in the Gatineaus. No longer would they pretend that only "process" was being discussed. This first complete FMC since the collapse of Meech would boast one important difference. This time all seventeen players involved in the 3M meetings would attend, including the four native representatives and the two territories. The prime minister set the date for August 18.

By this point the Pearson accord had evaporated. Mulroney now dishonoured its memory as well. It was never even mentioned as having taken place as a "discussion," only as a "meeting of minds on a number of important issues." The agreement of the provinces among themselves, flimsy as it was, had lasted for thirty-six days. Again Mulroney reminded everyone who was in charge: "The government of Canada must exercise its responsibility. . . . The federal government is not here as a rubber stamp for the provinces" (*GM*, Aug 13/92) and "I don't know how often you go around the mulberry bush. Everybody knows the problems and it's a question of whether there is the political will to arrive at a solution" (*Star*, Aug 13/92).

The sticking point at the Ottawa news conference this time was not so much the news about the actual FMC in full regalia, but the degree to which Mulroney had publicly overshadowed the constitutional agenda. He announced a new Senate proposal as if it were a fait accompli.

In fact, it had been proposed earlier by Joe Ghiz, the premier of Prince Edward Island. Under it, four provinces with more than 2 million population would get 24 seats apiece — Ontario, Quebec, Alberta, and BC — the rest, 8 seats each. Mulroney tried to get his puppet Frank McKenna to hustle "The Ghiz Proposal" or the "No-Net-Loss" proposal. McKenna refused. After the parallel-accord routine at Meech Lake, he knew better than to play the patsy with no reward for his efforts except Quebec's disfavour. Bourassa's government wanted no Senate at all, let alone a reformed one.

August 12 was a very busy day. It was also an anniversary — six years to the day since the Edmonton Declaration had been announced. That conference had introduced Quebec's five-point agenda to all the first ministers as the priority for Canada. This August 12, like it or not, events outside were moving along on a grander scale. In Washington, D.C., despite tremendous opposition, the North American Free Trade Agreement (NAFTA) was signed in principle between Canada, the U.S., and Mexico.

An Insight Canada poll taken between August 4 and 16 showed that 67 percent of the country would approve a national deal. Computer whiz kid Michael Marzolini, known as the "Pizza Pollster," sized up the people's mood and how they should be approached. "They have to be served hot," he said. "Essentially, the public is not looking at every little clause." His poll dealt with key issues — distinct society, Triple-E Senate, native self-government, the social charter — the Mulroney smorgasbord (*Star*, Aug 31/92).

In a very rare piece for any Canadian newspaper, the TV critic for the *Globe and Mail*, John Haslett Cuff, reprimanded the CBC for its constitutional rhetoric: The media's inability to provide balanced reporting "also raises questions about the media in general and their slavish adherence to the government's agenda. But television, particularly the CBC, has to take the heat because taxpayers spend close to $1 billion on it annually and 'The National' is the most watched news program in the country" (*GM*, Aug 13/92).

Farewell the Peaceful Kingdom

A wind from yesteryear wafted across the country to *Toronto Star* readers on August 13. Former Alberta Premier Ernest Manning, father of the Reform Party leader, wrote: "I would like to make clear that I regard the course Brian Mulroney is now following as dangerous and foredoomed to failure.... The Prime Minister will unilaterally bring in a package designed to enhance the prospect of re-election for himself and Mr. Bourassa" (*Star*, Aug 14/92).

Maybe he knew something. In Ottawa, Quebec's intergovernmental affairs minister met with Mulroney's Joe Clark. They talked for four hours. Rémillard insisted on priorities early: "Power is a major issue we have to discuss at the table next week. . . . What we're saying is, you're going to respect exclusive provincial jurisdiction [in certain fields]." Clark made one of his usual accommodating responses: "The list I agreed to look at is a manageable list" (*Star*, Aug 14/92).

The executive federalists were becoming more agitated as the business whirled around them and the pressure for some kind of final decision mounted in every province and territory. The Prairies were in an uproar over the Triple-E Senate portion of the Pearson accord having been scotched. In Ottawa the Assembly of First Nations was discovering how they too had been betrayed in the new deal shaping up. Ontario officials leaked the information to AFN leaders that Mulroney's latest agenda completely revised the Pearson accord. Native leaders were presented with seven questions about a possible aboriginal package. The Grand Chief of the Quebec Cree, Matthew Coon-Come, spoke bluntly and angrily: "It appears that secret negotiations have been taking place in our absence that profoundly alter the context of the agreement reached on July 7 [the Pearson accord]" (*GM*, Aug 15/92).

Welcome to the club! Betrayed with the rest of the country, the native leaders were in their own quandary about what to do next. Bourassa evinced no such misgivings. On August 16, speaking in St. Jean sur Richelieu, Bourassa set a deadline on the forthcoming FMC: "If there is a chance to get a deal, we should be able to get it in the next ten days. . . . Quebec is a nation. Quebec is a state. Quebecers are a people. The Quebec people is lucid and dynamic" (*Star*, Aug 17/92).

Quebec had set the agenda again, as it had done since 1963 with the Commission on Bilingualism and Biculturalism. Mulroney had his marching orders. Quebec required agreement by month's end. Reform Party leader Preston Manning said what English-speaking Canada was thinking in a CTV interview with Richard Gizbert on "Sunday Edition" on August

16: "The failure of the prime minister to promote federalism in Quebec or anywhere else is a bigger threat than the sovereigntists in Quebec."

Mulroney ignored the warning. He was preoccupied with arranging the stage for whatever deal Quebec wanted. On the eve of the FMC, August 17, Alberta Premier Don Getty expressed his own fears: "I believe that if we fail tomorrow, the Prime Minister does have to do something. I don't think he can just wait until after the referendum and not have done anything" (*GM*, Aug 18/92). For the first time, the notion of a referendum was becoming a probability.

News out of Ottawa on the FMC's first day was ominously concise. Agreement had been reached on Senate Reform after seven hours of debate. The details came out the next day, August 19. The "No-Net-Loss" Senate formula or "The Ghiz Proposal" had been scuttled, producing "The Modified McKenna." Bleary-eyed with it all, Canadians considered the news an insomniac's cure. There had been so many proposals for Senate reform, and none of them had come to anything.

The latest idea was to allow 62 seats, 6 for each province and one for each territory. It was not Triple-E but it was equal. Stripped to the basics, the package operated according to a formula based on the concept that Quebec had to be compensated as one of the "founding" nations of Canada. Now the Red Chamber would house *deux nations*.

The contradictions the package contained raised horrific questions. If natives were now considered a third level of government, what of Senate seats on the basis of racial classification? Aboriginals — so many seats? Francophones — so many? Allophones? The only certainty was that, whatever Canada's demographics, Quebec would have 25 percent of the seats in the House of Commons till the end of time.

As a corollary, the House of Commons would be enlarged by 42 seats, from 295 to 337. The total number of Senate and Commons seats would remain at the current 399. Ontario gained 18 seats, bringing its number up from 99 to 117 — a rise from 33.5 percent to 34.7 percent. Quebec gained 18 seats, from 75 to 93, or a 27.6-percent rise from 25.4-percent. Quebec senators, the papers reported on August 20, would be chosen by a vote in the province's National Assembly.

The politicians reacted in chorus. Clyde Wells thought the proposal "reasonable accommodation" because it protected the two founding linguistic groups, but he did wonder "is it going to be acceptable to Canadians?" (*Star*, Aug 20/92).

Bourassa said there's "one chance out of 100 that we could do it. And now I want to go to Charlottetown" (*Star*, Aug 20/92). So the country's leaders would march down that road.

Don Getty was happy. He called Bourassa "a very good friend and a fine Canadian. . . . I think this is a historic breakthrough" (*Star*, Aug 20/92).

Bob Rae seemed to know what no one else appreciated — and he said it: "We have gained a country, the basis of a country, a unanimous agreement." As the first ministers, most of them lawyers, assumed, Canada was just a contract, after all.

This was one of those rare occasions when even Nova Scotia premier Don Cameron spoke up: "I only appear to be sombre when compared with your overflowing enthusiasm. I think my approach is realistic — I think it's a major step forward, obviously, but it's a change to Parliament, to a central institution — and it requires reflection and prudence, and the premiers, Mr. Clark and I have done that. We'll have to see tomorrow if we're able to transform an interim agreement into a permanent agreement" (*GM*, Aug 20/92).

This time the sleeper was British Columbia. Nobody, apparently, had thought very seriously about the injustice the new package represented to Canada's pacific lotus-land. Premier Michael Harcourt did, just a bit. When he figured it out, there would be a mighty storm: "I said I wanted to sleep on it and reconsider it. We've reconsidered it, and I still think we need to work on it. . . . The issue of representation by population has not been addressed yet. I am going to have to see the whole package before we finish our discussions" (*Sun*, *GM*, Aug 21/92).

The representation problem was serious. Law professor Edward McWhinney knew there was a problem: "It's going to be a very hard sell. [Harcourt] failed significantly to consult his province" (*Star*, Aug 22/92).

He was right. Yet consultation was not the problem. The lack of equitable representation for British Columbia was. Whoever had bargained for BC, probably some unknown "senior official," had goofed — badly. The problem was that, with 12 percent of the population BC would have only 32 seats in the House of Commons, reflecting a population of just 10.8 percent of the whole country. The number of seats for the province should have been 40. With BC the fastest-growing area in Canada, the first ministers should have tried to ensure more equitable treatment. So much for simple arithmetic. Reform's Preston Manning opposed the formula for other reasons: "This double-E Senate — equal and elected — will never fly in Alberta or any other western province. It holds no appeal for the Atlantic provinces whose voice was always weak in federal affairs but is now made even weaker . . . at best no change in the status quo. And at worst, we've traded real say in the House of Commons for equality in a body with minuscule power" (*Star*/CP, Aug 21/92).

Quebec federalists welcomed the window-dressing. The president of Régroupement Economie et Constitution, Claude Beauchamp, allowed that "the agreement on the Senate is entirely acceptable" (*GM*, Aug 21/92). But the obstacle remained: a pretend agreement was no agreement. The number of unsettled conditions far outnumbered the few points of consensus.

Even the weather was strange in the summer of 1992. In Edmonton on August 21, five centimetres of snow fell. The weather map of the world turned topsy-turvy over the erupting Mount Penatubo in the Philippines. But if the elements were misbehaving, a few Canadians might have been momentarily encouraged that some messages were getting through to their politicians when Joe Clark said, "The one thing that is clear about this constitutional debate for the last three or four months is that everybody wants it over, so we can get on to other priorities" (*GM*, Aug 22/92).

Roy Romanow professed himself anxious too: "We should move on a timetable for early ratification if at all possible" (*GM*, Aug 22/92). The most confusing statement of all came from Frank McKenna, who sounded more like Joe Clark with every passing moment: "I'd be a lot further ahead in the lineup and I'd want us to be done quickly. I think it's important for Canadians to have communicated to them the nature of what we've done. . . . Because in isolation, I know it's very possible to rip apart pieces. But the fact is that this country was formed as part of a carefully thought-out Confederation" (*GM*, Aug 22/92).

While mulling over such mysterious utterances, Canadians were subjected to pure soap opera on Saturday, August 22, about the five days of secret meetings. The media rushed off into its own world of rave reviews. Once again Canadians knew by heart the headlines blazing from the newsstands: "IT'S A DEAL," screamed the *Toronto Sun*.

But the most memorable moment was the sight of the prime minister at the end of the day. As he stepped out from the Pearson Block to greet reporters, Graham Fraser of the *Globe* wrote, the prime minister broke down, just as agreement was reached: "Mr. Mulroney's voice cracked, and he wept. 'This is the greatest moment of my life,' he said" (*GM*, Aug 24/92).

The triumph was one for the man himself, not for the country. Such remarks captured in print would later devastate Martin Brian Mulroney. They ranked with his "roll of the dice" speech during the height of the Meech Lake crisis — "I know the enemies of Canada will be out in full force. . . . But they will encounter me and the premiers fighting them off" (*Star*, Aug 23/92).

EVENTS WERE becoming curiouser and curiouser. At a fundraising event in Drummondville, Quebec, just one hour after the tentative agreement had been reached, Mulroney finished off what he called the "historic agreement" with "This is a proud day for Quebec and a proud day for Canada," and then, "Almost all of René Lévesque's demands from 1985 have been met" (*Star*, Aug 23/92).

What an admission! The prime minister confessed publicly that the Meech demands of Premier Robert Bourassa were in fact the same as those set down in the Parti Québécois separatist agenda of 1985. The Meech circle was complete.

Mulroney could not resist bragging further: "All Canadians win. . . . We get to keep Canada — the most magnificent country in the world" (*Star*, Aug 23/92). Canadians listened and wondered. It had never occurred to them to doubt that Canada would survive the politicians' manipulations.

Don Getty emphasized the prime minister's point: "I have a great sense of relief that my country is no longer at risk and that Alberta is going to play a larger and larger role in the future of our country. The Province of Alberta had priorities which we obtained: a united Canada, a united Canada with Quebec in it, and Triple-E senate reform" (*GM*, Aug 24/92). He even gushed, "It's an exceptional arrangement for Canada and an exceptional arrangement for Alberta," and "If you can't sell this in Alberta, then you can't sell anything" (*FP*, Aug 25/92). If the deal failed, Getty was saying, it would mean "probably separation in Canada, a tremendous dashing of expectations of aboriginal people [and] giving up the kind of gains we've got on a Triple-E Senate" (*Star*, Aug 24/92).

Some Triple-E Senate. Neither equal nor effective nor necessarily directly elected. A No-E Senate, actually. Yet the first ministers and Mulroney continued to threaten the breakup of the country if Canadians didn't play along.

Bob Rae crowed loudest at the latest development, swinging into his Archimedes' "Eureka" mode: "I think this is it. I've seen it on many occasions and I recognize it when I see it, and this is it" (*GM*, Aug 24/92).

Frank McKenna joined the Gilbert and Sullivan chorus: "The degree of unanimity we achieved is quite overwhelming" (*GM*, Aug 24/92). People watching remembered that Premier David Peterson had told them Frank McKenna was a statesman, worthy of being the next prime minister.

As for Bourassa — Bou-Bou, as he was often called — he was in fine fighting form: "Do you think I have no arguments for my Péquiste friends? Just watch me" (*GM*, Aug 24/92). Echoes of Trudeau during the FLQ crisis.

Liberal leader Jean Chrétien perched solidly on the fence where he had been waiting and watching and praying for years: "By the time of a referendum we'll look at the question and we'll decide if we advocate approval or not. . . . But probably, if it makes some sense, we'll propose approval because people don't want to talk Constitution for another 10 years" (*Star*, Aug 25/92).

Just when Canadians thought things couldn't sink to any sillier remarks, Audrey McLaughlin added her two cents' worth: "It seems no one in there was pushing for women. Well, I will push now" (*Star*, Aug 24/92). Where had the NDP leader been? Rosemarie Kuptana, Inuit leader, and Nellie Cournoyer, government leader for the Northwest Territories, had both been fighting for constitutional entrenchment of women's rights every inch of the way.

Minister Clark slipped on his best Ernest Manning disguise and went biblical: "The day of judgement is at hand. . . . [It's a time] to discover if we are still large enough in spirit for this large land, to know if the pragmatism that founded this country, that built this country, that has kept us together, is still there" (*Star*, Aug 24/92). A country founded by pragmatism? That was news.

Even the balance-sheet boys breathed a sigh of relief. BCNI president Thomas d'Aquino wriggled a little with joy: "I can't promise a surge [in investment] this week or next, but if it is clear the juggernaut is picking up, that will translate, I promise you, in real terms on the economic front" (*Star*, Aug 25/92). He also volunteered, "This is potentially an enormous achievement. What the Canadian people — certainly the business community — want now is a quick resolution" (*FP*, Aug 25/92).

Claude Ryan, Quebec's language quartermaster, was accommodating. He sounded more like a good old-fashioned, reliable conditional federalist, just as he had in the old days: "It's good for Quebec and good for Canada. . . . In the field of linguistic co-existence, one must choose between suspicion and confidence. We are betting on confidence" (*Star*, Aug 25/92). It was a strange thing for Quebec's language enforcer to say.

Financial Post editor Diane Francis obediently toed the government line: "It is difficult to get excited over this latest 'unity deal' because three years from now some upstart premiers may nix it again, as happened to that other landmark 'unity deal,' Meech Lake. That is why it is absolutely imperative that this deal be ratified immediately, preferably by the end of the year at the latest" (*FP*, Aug 25/92).

Amid the babble of voices, where was Preston Manning? Did he share his father's conviction that the deal was bad for Canada? Was he neutral or perhaps even plugging the deal?: "The federal government can poison this thing by losing their own objectivity. . . . Presenting anybody that's against any aspect of it as an enemy of Canada is just paranoia. That will hurt the package more than help it. . . . Clark should be honest. [The first ministers] didn't get the three Es. But Joe never could count, which is one of the reasons why he's not prime minister" (*GM*, Aug 25/92).

Manning evidently hadn't made up his mind. Or was something else going on in the wings of the Reform Party? This was not what his members expected of him. His party's membership wanted the deal scrapped.

No such problem for Joe Clark. He accepted the challenge on behalf of his government. Addressing a friendly audience, the Canadian Bar Association, in Halifax, he echoed Getty's and Mulroney's threats as if trying them on for size. He told his audience they could expect to hear the "predictable shrill voices of rejection" from "people whose agenda is a cause, not a country" (*Star*, Aug 25/92).

Q UEBEC FIRED off another signal in late August. English Canada didn't recognize it. Léon Dion, the Quebec nationalist who had said nothing would happen unless English Canada had a knife at its throat, sounded almost reasonable: "The strong point in the document is that, over all, it confirms the requests Quebec has made over several decades and corresponds to several federal commissions. The Quebec Liberal Party can only say no with great difficulty to this. Perhaps it can say 'You have robbed us,' or 'We are much better suited than you to implement this'" (*GM*, Aug 25/92).

What a switch. He had abandoned the demand for sovereignty spelled out in the Allaire Report. From this point onward, there was no need for English Canada to beg and give in to blackmail. Any immediate threat of Quebec separation had passed months earlier. It never had been what it was cracked up to be on December 17, 1962, when Pearson first trumpeted cultural intervention in the lives of Canadians. Ghislain Dufour of le Conseil du patronat and Quebec's big business had faced the issue squarely in a speech he delivered a week earlier:

Renewed federalism or not, independence or not, future generations will have to pay heavily for the inertia of today. . . .

The politicians in Ottawa have been talking for years about how they have to raise taxes and cut spending. . . . Yet all this government effort has resulted in almost nothing being accomplished. . . . The political process seems to be plugged with an obsession with the Constitution, the meter is ticking and the national debt is getting larger and larger. (*GM*, Aug 20/92)

Omens appeared on August 26, 1992. To reporters in Ottawa, Clark said, "I think the way to do it is to ask a question nationally, the same [referendum] question, at the same time, of all Canadians, on exactly the same day" (*GM*, Aug 27/92), adding, "Personally, I believe that given the nature of this agreement and the important achievements it represents in our society, it will be substantially supported" (*Star*, Aug 27/92).

Opposition leader Jean Chrétien waved the same flag, sort of. He convened a fifty-minute news conference: "Yes, I'm ready to campaign for people who want Quebec to remain in Canada." Although that was not the case, he claimed the new deal fit in with his April 1991 nine-point party platform: "Generally, this agreement, subject to legal drafting, meets those tests" (*Star*, Aug 27/92).

Canada was so caught up with its own defewpulties that most people expended little energy contemplating a sad event occurring overseas. Word came from Brno, Czechoslovakia, on August 26 that the leaders of the Czech and the Slovak republics had agreed to dissolve the country of Czechoslovakia on January 1, 1993. The people had no say whatever, no referendum in the decision. Canadians faced different circumstances yet, under executive federalism, were fully justified in suspecting theirs might be the same fate.

Charlottetown, August 27, 1992: the big day. The city where Canada's Confederation was born, the city David Peterson had proposed as the triumphant location for the birth of his new Canada, the site of the final conference on the shaky Pearson accord two years after the Meech fiasco. The agreement reached here would form the basis of the nation's "offer" to Quebec. Joe Clark reported on the state of the wrangling: "We are within a few details of concluding the instructions to our legal drafters" (*GM*, Aug 28/92). You had to wonder if he had his fingers crossed behind his back as he said it.

Oodles of unresolved issues remained. Some arose from serious textual differences. For example, while English Canada was described as "committed" to developing minority communities, the French version circulated August 22 used the verb *attacher*. The correct translation of the verb "to commit" should have been *engager*. Bourassa wanted *attachement*; Filmon wanted *engagement*. Dualism indeed. This was pure Trudeau in philosophy, sophistry, and duplicity.

On August 28 the prime minister announced the new agreement to replace the Meech Lake Accord. Anxious to seize that elusive page of history for himself, he dubbed the new proposal the "Charlottetown Accord." What would the great historian Donald Creighton (1902–79) have said? About Meech? About Charlottetown? Here's a hint from his remarks about the three Confederation conferences at Charlottetown, Quebec, and London, England:

> Nobody would have dreamed in 1864 of constituting such a meeting along ethnic or cultural lines. . . . Their purpose was not a bilateral cultural agreement. . . . There was nothing that remotely approached a general declaration of principle that Canada was to be a bilingual or bicultural nation. . . . All the intentions of the Fathers of Confederation concerning language are summed up in section 133 of the British North America Act. . . . The movement to reconstitute Canada in the interest of bilingualism can have only one probable outcome — the creation of a separate, or virtually separate, Quebec. (*Sat Night*, Sept/66)

The Charlottetown Accord assured the breakup of Canada.

THOUGH NOT yet announced, the road to a referendum in Quebec and Canada was laid out and paved by this point, and all the participants knew it. There was no other way out now.

Surely somebody in a high place might have taken to heart the advice Goran Kapetanovic, Yugoslavia's ambassador to Canada, had sombrely offered Canadians on June 30 a year earlier: "Watch what is happening in Yugoslavia and don't repeat it. Stick together and try to continue dialogue and don't impose any deadlines, because deadlines only bring misunderstanding" (*Star*; "Sunday Edition," CTV, July 1/91). Was anyone in Canada listening?

Notes

1 A little-known fact about the Charlottetown Accord was its provision to scrap Section 90 of the BNA Act, the "Federal Power of Disallowance and Reservation." In the "Final Text" of the Charlottetown "Consensus Report on the Constitution," Section 38 read, "This provision of the Constitution should be repealed. Repeal requires unanimity."

Such a move would have freed Quebec, or any province, to do whatever it pleased constitutionally simply by using the notwithstanding clause. No such diminution of federal power was included in the Meech Lake Accord. The media chose to ignore this vital difference between Meech and this latest proposed accord.

Pierre Trudeau, the so-called great defender of federalism, also remained silent. In his well-publicized diatribe "*A mess that deserves a big NO*", there's not one word about it. Through that silence he effectively endorsed separatism.

2 Tony Penikett used the title "Premier" instead of "Leader." His successor John Ostashek rejected the moniker in October 1992. Of it, the latter said, "I think that was arrogance. . . . The Yukon is not a province and we do not have a premier. We have a government leader and that's what I'm going to call myself. I'm not big for titles anyway" (*GM*, Oct 21/92).

IX

The Referendum

28

On the Way to
Judgement Day
— September 1992

T HE CHARLOTTETOWN ACCORD was reached on August 28, 1992. No one had an inkling what had been agreed, least of all the first ministers.

The Mulroney government and the two other executive-federalist parties quickly banded together to set joint priorities. They aimed to avoid a referendum in Quebec on sovereignty at all costs. Back on May 15, 1991, the Bourassa government had introduced its own legislation in the National Assembly to allow for just such a referendum. If the rest of Canada could not agree on what he and Rémillard termed satisfactory "offers" for their province, Bill 150 required that "a referendum on the sovereignty of Quebec" be held by October 22, 1992. "If the results of the referendum are in favour of sovereignty, they [will] constitute a proposal that Quebec acquire the status of a sovereign state one year to the day from the holding of the referendum." The premier had explained how he proposed to word it when he spoke to Laval University students way back in 1979: "Do you want to replace the present constitutional system by the existence of two sovereign states associated in an economic union, responsible to a parliament elected by universal suffrage?" (*Star*, Feb 7/92).

The bill stipulated that any changes to its provisions on any subject other than sovereignty — such as the terms of reference for a referendum — had to be tabled in the National Assembly before May 15, 1992.

453

Nothing had changed since Meech. On May 14, the National Assembly debated amendments to Bill 150. Bourassa's plan enabled him to postpone working out the details of the referendum question till September 12, in effect adding another two weeks to preparation time. So from August 28 on, Quebec began its countdown to approving the question. There were a mere sixty days to the big referendum.[1]

Canadians muttered among themselves, increasingly impatient at the circus they had to watch helplessly. They knew it was moronic to expect them to reach any intelligent conclusion about their nation's constitution when they still had no text to study. The process struck most people as all of a piece with Mulroney's era. For a while, it seemed the politicians might get away with their games-playing, too. Had the lessons of Meech really fallen on ears so deaf?

Meanwhile, a collection of the biggest names in Canadian politics hunkered down behind the latest deal, trying to present a brave and united front to their constituents:

Bob Rae: "I'll go anywhere. We cannot afford another failure. . . . The [federal Referendum question] should be short, sharp, direct, blunt, and unequivocal. . . . But I don't think anyone should underestimate what the consequences of a failure would be" (*Star*, Aug 29/92).

Robert Bourassa: "[Quebec has made] gains [that are] satisfactory [and] encouraging. [This is] a substantial agreement" (*Star*, Aug 29/92).

Brian Mulroney: "This is a very good day for Canada. . . . We have gained a modernized federation, we have gained justice for the aboriginal peoples, we have gained a strengthening of our national institutions. . . . We have gained the strongest affirmation and commitment to national unity that this country has seen in a long time" (*Star*, Aug 29/92).

Audrey McLaughlin: "There was unanimity. . . . Of course there were questions, but those questions were dealt with by our panel. . . . What's been achieved for Canada, in my view, and with the agreement of my party, is not just keeping Canada together. We've made a step toward making Canada a better place" (*GM/Star*, Aug 31/92).

Clyde Wells: "I haven't been happy about anything that has been achieved. I would sooner see a Triple-E Senate. I would sooner see a more specific list on aboriginal powers. But it ended up that we all have to agree to try and get an overall resolution" (*Maclean's*, Aug 31/92).

Preston Manning: "Just don't let it hang out there and be pecked to death in Quebec by people, mainly commentators and politicians, who won't support anything" (*Maclean's*, Aug 3/92).

An observer familiar with the players could have predicted Rae's reaction. And McLaughlin's. Whether she was endorsing separatism, nationalism, provincialism, federalism, or feminism was all the same to her. She asked only that the -isms fit neatly into a socialist, NDP agenda.

As for Bourassa, the Péquistes might have been right all along. He was a conditional Quebec nationalist cum Canadian federalist cum bean-counter. If it served his purpose, he could even agree with his old nemesis, Trudeau, and support Official Bilingualism.

Preston Manning and Clyde Wells leavened the constitutional batter. Against his party's platform and wishes, the western leader sidled into Mulroney's camp, if by default. He simply stopped raging about constituent assemblies, a Triple-E Senate, and the secrecy of the government's process. He stopped cold. He could stall a bit, a few days only, with the excuse that he needed to consult his grassroots. Then he blew it. Until September 10, he said nothing more, nearly two weeks after the Charlottetown agreement and more than two months after its trial run in July, the Pearson accord. Reformers were at a loss to understand what had happened in Calgary, let alone explain it to their members. Had their leader sold out with the rest?

Most Canadians were asking themselves the more obvious question as they anxiously scanned their news channels and newspapers: What on earth had happened to Clyde Wells, the white knight in shining armour? It seemed beyond belief to hear him say, "But it ended up that we all we have to agree to try and get an overall resolution." Everything he had said he loathed about Meech Lake was packed into the Charlottetown Accord and then some. For one thing, it lacked a Triple-E Senate. It reinstated the offensive distinct society provision for Quebec. It gave no details at all on the meaning of "aboriginal self-government."

Had Peter C. Newman finally got to the Newfoundland premier with his regular poisoned-pen attacks in *Maclean's*? Perhaps the Newfoundland warrior was just plumb tuckered out.

He had lots of company. The whole nation was sick of being dragged along behind Brian Mulroney as he galloped off on his personal crusade. After six years and hundreds of millions of dollars spent on this huge ego trip, the entire nation felt ready to accept any solution. As Manitoba Liberal Sharon Carstairs put it, "The present constitution is better than the one envisaged" (CBC Newsworld, Sept 3/92).

The play needed new blood. Judy Rebick, president of the National Action Committee on the Status of Women, volunteered that she had been betrayed in some mysterious way during the secret negotiations. Wallowing happily under the television spotlights, she implied that some of the first ministers had acquiesced to the notion of somehow addressing "gender equality" in the Constitution. As could be expected, Quebec squashed that idea by securing approval from the other first ministers to choose its own senators from the National Assembly.

Rebick dared not complain about Quebec, so she heaped her abuse on English Canada. On the day the accord was signed, CBC viewers across Canada watched the tousle-haired Rebick and a bevy of supporters crooning sarcastically to the staid premier of Newfoundland, "We are gentle women."

Their efforts gained them notoriety and disproportionate attention. But, by some quirk of fate, Rebick did perform a small service to the country. She confirmed absolutely for Canadians that the politicians *were* following some agenda of their own.

It turned out that Ontario's Bob Rae had promised to split his province's Senate seats equally between men and women. (Such generosity was reminiscent of his predecessor David Peterson and his offer of six of Ontario's Senate seats.) Rae's "split-sex Senate" captured the nation's headlines, body-slamming the Merit Principle and delighting special-interest groups. In her September 1 column, Christie Blatchford of the *Toronto Sun* wryly noted that her family referred to the day the Charlottetown Accord was signed as "The Day Democracy Died."

Other premiers besides Ontario's had quietly agreed to a Canada engineered according to sex — Nova Scotia's Donald Cameron, Saskatchewan's Roy Romanow, and New Brunswick's Frank McKenna.

In an all-too-rare revelation, Rosemary Speirs of the *Toronto Star* exposed the lot of them with her story of how the "sex-gender" Senate bit the dust. Her September 6, Labour Day weekend piece said, "At some point behind closed doors last month, the Prime Minister and premiers dropped from the unity package all mention of a voting system that would have put more women in the Senate" (*Star*, Sept 6/92). The politicians clumsily tried to cover what they were up to at Charlottetown, and were caught out. The numerous secret deals being discussed on so-called gender equality could be hushed up no longer. The media completely missed the red flag.

On September 1, Premier Mike Harcourt echoed his NDP colleague Bob Rae in Ontario. He declared that British Columbia would soon present its own legislation to ensure gender equality: "This is a practical way to advance the cause of equality between men and women," he explained (*GM*,

Star/CP, Sept 3/92). BC's Social Credit leader, Jack Weisgerber, disagreed. So did the vast majority of Canadians who were polled. A "split-sex Senate" promised "an unwelcome experiment in social engineering." Three days later, the premier abruptly changed his position. Back-pedalling hard, he protested that he had been expressing only his own "personal preference" (*Star*, Sept 6/92).

Joe Clark went for Rae's sex-equality plan, too. On September 17, on a Vancouver talk show, he defended those provinces who presumed to dabble in efforts to promote a gender-equality Senate.

True to the political form it exhibited during Meech, Quebec moved smartly when it proved advantageous. It moved first to endorse the Charlottetown Accord. Unlike Meech Lake, however, they would not ratify that agreement in the National Assembly first. This time Quebec would sign on only after all the other provinces had agreed to back the deal. For the time being, a political resolution would be the only gesture Quebec made. On August 29, 1992, the following was introduced at the Quebec Liberal Party Convention in Quebec City:

Be it proposed: That the Quebec Liberal Party recognizes that the provisional constitutional agreement . . . while beneath the party's program, represents a genuine progress that is concurrent with Quebec's traditional demands . . . that the National Assembly be called upon to ratify the constitutional agreement once and only if . . . all other provincial legislatures and Parliament have ratified it. (*Star*, Aug 30/92)

One step forward — one step back.

O N SEPTEMBER 2, an Angus Reid–Southam News poll appeared that had been conducted between August 25 and 31. It showed 61 percent of the Canadians outside Quebec supported the new accord. Twenty percent rejected it and 19 percent declared themselves undecided. In Quebec, the numbers differed little: 49 percent for the accord; 38 percent against.

As if drawn by the numbers, droves of politicians descended upon Canada's television and radio shows, newscasts and interviews, exposing themselves in every possible medium once again, to howl the direst of threats if the accord should fail. Bob Rae led the way, aping Mulroney: "Just letting this go would be worse, it would be the death of Canada by one thousand tiny cuts. . . . If the answer is no, we face a major crisis and a major problem. . . . The package is called Canada (for those who only like certain parts). . . . Nothing will be more damaging to the economy at the moment than a failure" (*Star*, *GM*, Sept 1/92).

On September 1, Liberal House Leader Michel Page of the National Assembly announced that on Thursday, Friday, and Tuesday, September 3, 4, and 8, the Quebec House would devote its attention to one debate — how to revise Quebec's Bill 150 and shift the referendum legislation from a vote on sovereignty to one on receiving an "offer" from English-speaking Canada.

Bob Rae briskly put his own case: "I don't think anybody should underestimate the consequences [of rejecting the deal]. It's never been my approach to parade the horrors, in terms of an argument" (*Star*, Sept 2/92). On Saturday, September 5, the *Toronto Star* chimed in: "This time — after two exhausting rounds of negotiations — any changes to an admittedly imperfect deal are out of the question. Last month's agreement happens to be the best possible compromise — or the least damaging deal — at this point in Canadian history."

On September 7, Robert Libman charged in at the head of the pack of Vichy anglais as Canadian Press broke the news: "The English-rights Equality Party has decided to hold its nose, swallow hard and campaign for the constitutional deal in the referendum." The leader outlined his party's position himself: "[Charlottetown] is not a rock-solid guarantee of any kind. We would have liked to see something clearer [but because it could provide minority protection] that potential is one reason why we're willing to hold our noses and support it" (*GM*, Sept 8/92).

While Libman genuflected, the Norman prince of Quebec, Robert Bourassa, fired a rocket at TROC, the Rest of Canada. His remarks should have spooked the Quebec anglophones who supported Libman's posturing: "Nobody can say that Quebec can't make other demands or representations. I mean, you can't freeze the Canadian Constitution for decades" (*Star*, Sept 7/92), and "A Yes vote is not irreversible, because negotiations will continue, because we maintain our right to self-determination" (*GM*, Sept 8/92).

More polls. Environics Research published its latest on September 8 showing that only 51 percent of Canadians now approved the package. Another 25 percent rejected it. And 24 percent gave no opinion. Quebec boasted 43 percent support for the accord and 39 percent against. The results were not particularly good, of course, but to executive federalists convinced of their own immortality, they might be enough.

If both this poll and the Angus Reid–Southam one of August 31 were accurate, then support for the deal had slipped very seriously in just one week.

At long last all three executive-federalist parties had outsmarted themselves. Everyone was committed to the deadline. For themselves, the prime minister and Jean Chrétien, Leader of the Opposition, upped their antes. They uttered threats. Lots of them. Mulroney was primed and ready. In the House of Commons he launched his blitzkrieg a day early, in preparation for the debate the next day, September 9: "Basically, the referendum relates to an appreciation of what it means to be a Canadian. . . . You are either proud to be a Canadian, or you're not. You either love Canada, or you don't. No one can be obliged to do either" (*GM*, Sept 9/92). And he shouted, "If not grasped, [the country] will be lost forever. . . . A Yes to Canada, a Yes to this agreement, a Yes to the common cause" (*Star*, Sept 9/92).

His opponent Jean Chrétien finally climbed off his fence. Although he disliked referendums intensely, he threw himself behind the "Yes" side: "We cannot fail and will not fail. This country is too great to let it go down" (*Star*, Sept 9/92).

Mulroney continued. On the day of the Referendum debate in the House of Commons, he dangled his carrot: "If we can secure ratification of the constitutional proposals before the end of the year, we look forward to holding a first ministers conference on the economy" (*FP*, Sept 10/92).

Citizens disagreed with the priority and the bribe. It was urgent that the nation think about its economy for a change. The world depression was deepening day by day. In Stockholm the government raised its key lending rate from 24 to 75 percent to defend the Swedish krona. The politicos in Canada, however, tuned out such signals. Joe Clark boasted: "Canadians should judge this agreement, not by what others say it says. This is not written in Morse code. . . . This was the Canadian political process at its best" (*GM*, Sept 10/92).

The purported interest in the economy registered only a faint blip on the line. On September 10, Senator Claude Castonguay gave the constitutional ball another shove: "[A failure to vote Yes] would indicate to the rest of the world that Canada can't solve its own internal problems. . . . I don't agree that No means the status quo or more negotiations" (*FP*, Sept 11/92).

The same day he was sounding off, the Referendum bill passed in the House of Commons by an overwhelming 233 to 12. The die was cast.

The players elbowed themselves into position. Nearly two weeks after the Charlottetown Accord of August 28, and still no legal text available. A deadly oversight. Most people distrusted anything the politicians could or would do by now. Joe Clark's dismissal of the point only aggravated matters: "The legal text will be interesting to lawyers, and it will be interesting to some governments. But I think the material that is available now is a very sensible basis for people to judge the agreement" (*GM*, Sept 11/92).

He was up to his old tricks. The *Toronto Star* did some spade work. On September 19, the newspaper notified its readers that it had got hold of a confidential memo outlining discussions among federal officials on September 10: "Heads of delegations reviewed the advantages and disadvantages of releasing legal texts during the referendum campaign." As the *Star* reported it, the prime minister's press secretary Mark Entwhistle explained the delays in producing the text as due to the "long, laborious process" of getting all the parties to agree on the exact wording of it. Rosemary Speirs had performed another good bit of journalism.

"Only one part of the economy will benefit from this deal: the constitutional industry" (*FP*, Sept 11/92), claimed Preston Manning firmly: "It's a national insult that Canadians are being asked to vote on a package so undefined that a legal text has not been produced. . . . All people have to do is read it and ask themselves if this will resolve constitutional conflict or not. . . . This thing will lead to more chaos" (*Star*, Sept 11/92). The only agreement Clark and company had come up with was a cover-up.

Unable to think of a fresh approach, Bob Rae dished out more and bigger threats: "For anybody to think a No vote is going to do anything other than create a huge political crisis in the country is just beyond me," and "Those who are counselling or arguing for a No on any of the bases that I've heard are just out of it, I think, really out of it. Nobody should underestimate the impact of a No vote. A No vote, I think, would be devastating for the Canadian economy. . . . The only Triple-E we'll have to worry about after that [failure] is the collective credit rating of the country because that's what we'll be looking at" (*Star*, Sept 12/92).

After the revelations of secretive deals she had made and the "sex-gender" Senate business, the president of the National Action Committee, Judy Rebick, stated on September 13: "Nothing we asked for is in this accord. . . . This is a bad deal for women." Almost as an afterthought, she added, "We're not going to make any backroom deals. That's not the way we work" (*GM*, *Star*, Sept 14/92). Had she forgotten her own role so soon?

Canadians eagerly snapped up true tales of backroom play in Quebec. On September 15, Diane Wilhelmy, Bourassa's deputy minister of intergovernmental affairs, won a ten-day emergency injunction from Quebec's Superior Court. It prohibited radio stations and other media from broadcasting the tape of a telephone conversation she had had with an unidentified party. To a drooling media she proclaimed melodramatically, "A robbery of my mind has been committed" (*GM*, Sept 19/92).

The transcript the *Globe and Mail* had obtained recorded a civil servant telling her that "[Bourassa] never wanted a referendum on sovereignty. . . . He just caved in. . . . It is a heavy burden to carry, especially on the psychological level, with these people against you. . . . And the Ontarians, they are the worst sons of bitches that you can imagine." Wilhelmy apparently responded, "That is what we said last year, and it hasn't changed" (*Star*, *GM*, Sept 16/92). The revelation led to her swift resignation for "reasons of health" (*GM*, Sept 16/92).

Slips like this unnerved Bob Rae even more. Again, he warned: "I'm here to tell you, if we don't get this thing right on October 26, the economy will be much worse, the level of confidence we feel in ourselves, that our institutions feel . . . will be lower" (*Star*, Sept 16/92).

Maybe Mordecai Richler heard him. In Toronto, the writer said, "The indépendantistes will never accept it. It's a dog's breakfast, an awful mess — but I will vote 'yes' and let's get it over with" (*Star*, Sept 16/92). So much for the intelligentsia and the Vichy anglais.

Coincidentally, Gallup churned out yet another poll on September 16. The trend suggested earlier was gathering momentum. In Quebec and British Columbia the No side surged ahead, from 29 to 48 percent and 31 to 39 percent, respectively. Cross-Canada figures showed the Yes side at 42 percent support and the No, 29 percent.

Joe Clark countered with a beaut on September 17: "And we should recognize that, once, Beirut [Lebanon] was one of the best places in the world to live and it gave in to anger — That could happen here. . . . If we lose this, we lose the country" (*Star*, Sept 17/92).

It was the same day that chief electoral officer Jean-Pierre Kingsley received the proclamation calling the federal Referendum for October 26. The actual question and its accompanying legislation overflowed with new and intricate problems.

First, Albertans and British Columbians would learn the vote results in Eastern and Central Canada before the polls closed in the West. This problem was one of long standing in federal elections.

Several other wacky features were inevitable since the federal Referendum was not truly national. As Graham Haig, one of those disenfranchised from his most important constitutional birthright as a Canadian, put it,

"So I, and the other 20,000 citizens who fell into the legal limbo between the referendum in Quebec, where you needed six months' residency to vote, and the referendum everywhere else, where you needed residency anywhere but in Quebec, didn't vote" (*GM*, Sept 14/93).

The Mulroney government had turned Canada into two nations with no sovereignty referendum at all! Just as in Pearson's 1963 Bi-Bi Commission and Trudeau's 1978 Pépin–Roberts Task Force on Canadian Unity and Mulroney's Meech Lake in 1990, Canada was bisected. For whatever reasons, nobody seemed unduly alarmed. After seeing the Referendum question, they should have been. It read:

> Do you agree that the Constitution of Canada should be renewed on the basis of the agreement reached on August 28, 1992? Yes. No.

> *Acceptez-vous que la Constitution du Canada soit renouvelées sur la base de l'entente conclue le 28 août 1992? Oui. Non.*

Jacques Brassard spoke as the Parti Québécois's constitutional critic. He said the question was loaded three ways: in its choice of words: "renewed," which put a positive connotation on "on the basis of" — which suggested improvement was possible — and the term "agreement" rather than "consensus." "I cannot agree that what was concluded in Charlottetown is truly a renewal of federalism," he concluded darkly (*GM*, Sept 5/92).

Before such united forces promoting the accord, people might have assumed that Preston Manning and his Reform Party were leading the charge against it. Yet that leader's cautious musings before audiences in Ontario baffled, if not insulted, party members who had fought against what the Meech Lake and Charlottetown accords represented: "I think Ontario would be most guided by what Quebec was going to do. If Quebec was going to vote No, then Ontario would be maybe more inclined to vote No, so that the No couldn't be seen as rejecting anybody," Manning said (*Star*, Sept 18/92).

He solidly backed the Yes side for three weeks, despite what the press chose to report, and he did so personally even after that. One of the party's founders, Ted Byfield, explained ten months later in the *Financial Post*: "[Tom] Flanagan [director of policy] militantly opposed the accord. With others at Calgary headquarters he persuaded Manning to authorize a canvass of rank-and-file members that showed them overwhelmingly against it. So Manning went along with this, and became the only national leader to declare for No. . . . Flanagan was bang on. Strangely, however,

Flanagan's influence in the party began to wane. He soon resigned. . . . Other staffers who had urged the No position were fired" (*FP*, Aug 8/93).

There was nothing strange about it. For all his foibles, Flanagan had remained true to Reform Party principles. Manning, on the other hand, had moved the party into the executive-federalist camp.

Later, in the 1993 election, Manning excused his waffling: "There was never any question that the constitutional arrangements proposed by the Charlottetown accord were at variance with the constitutional principles espoused by the Reform Party and me. The question facing us was how to communicate our opposition to the accord in such a way as not to permit the Reform Party to be painted as anti-Quebec or an 'enemy of Canada'" (*Sat Night*, Oct/93).[2]

The September 17 Gallup poll showed the PCs at 21 percent; Liberals, 44 percent; NDP, 18 percent; Reform, 8 percent. The Reform Party faced the biggest loss of all, in Ontario, where it utterly collapsed, mirrored in the poll as a plummet from 10 to 5 percent. In one month, Reform had slid nationally from a high of 11 percent. It was losing ground on the most fundamental plank in its platform, that the country needed major structural change.

Still the Reform Party soft-pedalled its No position. Perhaps it feared the Yes forces might really act on their threats. Certainly lush Tory advertisements blanketed the newspapers, magazines, and airwaves daily, and their cumulative effect was impressive. The Tory House Leader, Harvie Andre, rattled his sabre along with his colleagues:

> It would be horribly disrupting. . . . Once you unleash those forces. . . . Look what's happening in Europe now. . . . If you were looking at making investments in North America . . . and it looked like Canada was going through a protracted period of divvying up national debts and redefining borders. . . . Where would you invest? It's patently obvious we would be on the losing end of such an equation and there would be significant economic consequences. (*Star*, Sept 18/92)

The Minister of State for Finance, John McDermid, was heading up his own brigade: "If, heaven forbid, the Canadian people reject the constitutional proposal, there would be a very strong negative reaction in our money markets" (*Star*, Sept 18/92).

Even Barbara McDougall, Minister of External Affairs, who had studiously avoided saying anything for years, contributed to the doomsaying:

"There will no second chances and there will be no better deals. That is a given" (*Star*, Sept 18/92).

The Business Council on National Issues got into the act, too. On September 18, Newsworld invited Thomas d'Aquino to chat with Don Newman, the CBC's senior parliamentary editor. The BCNI president spoke metaphorically: "If the family doesn't want to live together any more — that's what it's going to come down to" (Sept 18/92). In other media he allowed himself to speak much more dramatically: "We believe that a rejection of the Charlottetown agreement could impose incalculable costs on all Canadians. Those costs will be reflected in political strife, social divisions and severe economic consequences" (*Star*, Sept 19/92).

Bourassa spoke up once more: "If it is No, there will be political instability. . . . The risks are pointless in voting No, whereas a Yes vote is stability and progress" (*GM*, Sept 19/92).

Was he the right oracle? The separatists alternately said the very opposite or plugged for both at the same time.

B ACK HOME IN CALGARY on September 17, Preston Manning tiptoed a bit more aggressively toward the No camp after his pleasant tour of Ontario. He unveiled Reform's slogan for their No campaign — "**Know** More." Weak as its rallying cry was, the Reform congregation had settled on a direction at last: "A No vote is in no way, shape or form to be misinterpreted as a No to Canada or any party thereof" (*GM*, Sept 19/92).

Manning called for "a grass-roots campaign of ordinary people carrying the message one to another, from worker to worker, from neighbour to neighbour, from friend to friend, from relative to relative." A telephone message system was installed in party headquarters: "Thank you for calling. We will advise the Prime Minister that you are a proud citizen of Canada, which includes Quebec, and that you intend to vote No in the constitutional referendum October 26."

A lot of people could have accepted all this. But then Manning surprised them again. He threw in the wimp factor. The party would set up two committees — one using the Reform name and the other to be known as "The New Canada Committee" for those who did not want to be identified with the Reform Party. Was the Reform Party really worth belonging to?

Different observers offered different speculations on why Manning was suddenly wobbling so much on such small-c conservative fundamentals. One columnist alleged that the leader couldn't move because of his ties to Burt Brown, one of the founding fathers of the Triple-E Senate. The *Star*'s

Rosemary Speirs noted in the paper's August 29 edition that Brown had apparently caved in, and she predicted he would support the accord.

Whatever was going on, Manning's slow-motion politics was killing his fledgling party. The No forces forged ahead without him. From August 22 on, as Mulroney wept for joy over what he called his "historic agreement," the agreement he called "the greatest moment in my life," and declared that those who disagreed would be "the enemies of Canada . . . out in full force," Manning dithered.

Newfoundland's premier recovered some lost credibility. Suddenly he rejected the "fear-mongering" the politicians and the intelligentsia were using to hawk the deal. He firmly refused to involve himself in the marketing: "I think those tactics are totally unacceptable, and it is for that reason I'm not joining or participating directly in any co-ordinated, national campaign." As for Mulroney's characterization of voters as "enemies of Canada" and "little Canadians," Wells called it "almost insulting to ask [anyone] to consider it in that light" (*Star*, Sept 19/92). He seemed to be saying No and trying to avoid responsibility for saying it at the same time. This was not the same Clyde Wells accused of — and credited with — routing the Meech Lake rogues.

THE MEDIA kept up frantic pressure for a Yes vote. In the strongest pitch made by the big newspapers, the *Toronto Sun* editorial of September 20 bellowed, "We must say Yes." For the first time in history the *Toronto Sun* and the *Toronto Star* openly shared the same vision of Canada. "We are told this is a culmination, the Canadian political process at its best. . . . You're entitled to be cynical. But our leaders say this is the best they can do now. . . . But to vote No is to slap at Quebec" (*Sun*, Sept 20/92).

Ironically, the *Sun* published a poll at the same time that showed a whopping 83 percent of Canadians lined up against the accord. And 85 percent against was noted by sister papers in Ottawa, Calgary, Edmonton. The *Sun* had forfeited its position as "Toronto's Other Voice" once and for all. It had settled for being just another Toronto voice in the babble, utterly removed from its readership.

Certain themes were emerging. Canadians watched in amazement as events seemed to replay themselves before their very eyes. Exactly as he had done in an earlier debate on another accord, Pierre Trudeau silently waited. He selected his precise moment and . . . KAPOW! On September 28, *Maclean's* magazine featured him and his article on its cover. Inside he said:

Most incredible of all, there are still good souls in English Canada who are ready to take these temper tantrums seriously and urge their compatriots to pay each new ransom for fear of losing each "last chance" to save Canada. Poor things, they have not yet realized that the nationalists' thirst will never be satisfied, and that each new ransom paid to stave off the threat of schism will simply encourage the master blackmailers to renew the threat and double the ransom.

. . . The blackmail will cease only if Canada refuses to dance to that tune. . . .

You cannot *really* believe in Canada and at the same time claim the right of self-determination for Canadian provinces.

Like besotted teenagers, the media pored over the former prime minister's every word, to isolate and interpret every nuance and distil what little gems he might cast before the masses. They found plenty.

And other public figures leaped into the act of lavishly distributing treats. The press caught up to Brian Mulroney in Vancouver the day *Maclean's* hit the streets. His reaction: "I suppose most Canadians would think that it was needless and unhelpful. . . . Mr. Trudeau is unsatisfied with every attempt to clean up the mess of 1981–82 — of which he is the architect himself" (*GM*, Sept 22/92).

Answering the charge that he was an anglo Quebecer, Mulroney retorted, "I am *un Québécois pure laine*. . . . I don't want to make distinctions — we are all Canadians" (*GM*, Sept 22/92). He also said, "On October 26 a No vote would mean, among other things, a No to aboriginal self-government." To really win the Referendum, he warned, the Yes side would have to win "50 plus one" percent in all ten provinces. Clark agreed and was quoted saying so in the *Financial Post*.

The international money markets must have chosen to be ornery out of spite. They agreed with the president of the National Citizens' Coalition. David Somerville said, "This deal is a blueprint for years of more constitutional wrangling" (*Star*, Sept 22/92). The Canadian dollar seemed to back him up, plunging by 1.07 cents US that day in New York — its lowest level in four years.

September 22. Just a little more than a month to go. The Yes side was gaining more than confidence; it was greedily assuming arrogance as the campaign rolled on. On Tuesday, Harry Near, the PC director of operations for the team, scoffed at the No side: "Look, no organization. . . . It's one thing to fight the referendum by popping up and making an announcement. . . . It's another thing to make an announcement and follow that up with organization at the national, provincial and grassroots levels. . . . That's the difference people will see in our campaign. The organization is there" (*GM*, Sept 22/92).

Some grassroots!

On September 23, Mulroney lectured a chamber of commerce meeting in London, Ontario: "The truth is that voting Yes means an end to seemingless endless constitutional wrangling. And while there may be a need for future fine tuning, as has occurred for the last 125 years, a Yes vote will mean the end to the numbing, paralysing constitutional disputes of the past" (*GM*, *Star*, Sept 24/92).

Joe Clark's careful words into the microphones struck closer to home. He admitted he didn't know when the legal text would be finished. It would probably take some time: "The job of the lawyers is not to change it. . . . The job of the lawyers is to put it into legal language, and it would be easier if there were two of them instead of 17" (*FP*, Sept 24/92).

Still Canadians had no idea what the Charlottetown Accord really meant. And Clark was getting desperate. He tipped his hand. He said he never intended to "spread fear"; nonetheless, "a No vote would be viewed as being a vote in favour of something else — a form of sovereignty or separation. If the answer is No, I think the rest of Canada will experience a feeling of rejection just like the one Quebec has experienced in the past. . . . If this fails, my own view is that our chances of keeping the country together are slim" (*Star*, Sept 24/92).

His wife Maureen McTeer quickly agreed with him. Maybe *she* had the text? The *Toronto Star* ran her howler as their Quote of the Day: "With this agreement, I think women would be better served than if there were no country at all" (*Star*, Sept 24/92).

The prime minister chose to shoot his load at Sept-Îles, Quebec, where he had already made so many of his important speeches: "Investors flee political uncertainty. . . . And nothing is more designed to create uncertainty than a No vote in this referendum. . . . To say No to a remarkable package of achievements like the Charlottetown accord would send off a negative signal to international investors. And clearly the consequences would be felt across Canada" (*Star*, Sept 25/92).

He was warming up for the big one: "One thing's sure. If there's a No vote, there will be a climate of constitutional crisis, and crisis is bad for investment. If you have a Yes vote you're opting for political stability. If you vote Yes, you end the constitutional crisis" (*FP*, Sept 25/92).

Unfortunately for him, his outburst competed with another moving plea published in the Toronto newspapers on September 24. The First Nations of Treaty 6 and 7, which were not affiliated with any of the aboriginal organizations approved to join the constitutional consultation, advertised in the *Globe*. "A Message To All Canadians From First Nations of Treaty 6 and 7":

> The First Nations of Treaty 6 of 1876 and Treaty 7 of 1877 and subsequent adhesions, who are a party to this process, are taking this opportunity to give official notification that we do not support nor will participate in ratifying the present constitutional process and the proposed "Unity Package." . . . We are not against "unity." All we are saying is we are not in favour of the process, as it concerns our treaties. (Sept 24/92)

Echoes of Elijah Harper and his single grey eagle feather. Canadians wanted the prime minister who had created the crisis to just go away, to just leave them alone. They only half believed any crisis ever existed in the first place, and if it did, they were quite certain they could not change it anyway.

By September 24, the smooth-running Yes campaign began to reveal cracks that quickly widened into crevasses. In Montreal, Ghyslain Picard, chief of the AFN of Quebec and Labrador, said the aboriginal people under him would boycott the Referendum and run their own: "Quebec can't prevent us from doing things our own way." Grand Chief Matthew Coon-Come, head of the Grand Council of Crees, said, "We have always had our own laws and customs for consultation of the people, and we see little reason to adopt someone else's laws and customs. . . . As for the date, you have to realize that a lot of our people are in the bush hunting, and we can't ask their opinion until they're informed, and that could take some time" (*GM*, Sept 25/92).

In Toronto, Bob Rae was being wagged, as usual, by a much larger animal. A delegation of four from the Association canadienne-française de l'Ontario (ACFO) met with him for fifteen minutes, and even then ACFO would not commit themselves to supporting or opposing Charlottetown. They told the premier they would deliver their answer after another meeting among themselves. Rae looked exasperated at this. The Government of Ontario had supported franco-Ontarians for many years, and with considerable risk, as when they enacted Bill 8: "Frankly, I find it difficult to believe that the francophone community in Ontario does not understand the need for a strong 'Yes' vote to create a more positive atmosphere for Canadian unity" (*GM*, Sept 25/92).

Now that Trudeau had begun to speak his mind, he kept at it: "To view negotiation and the willingness to see the other person's point of view as signs of weakness is a denial of Canada's most generous essence" (*GM*, Sept 25/92). Canadians who fondly remembered David Peterson's "intolerance" now picked up on Trudeau's "generous essence" as a new war cry.

The banking community made its big push on September 25, with the Referendum one month away. Once again Allan Taylor happily took the stage. The Royal Bank chairman released a report entitled *Unity or disunity: An economic analysis of the benefits and the costs*. His own "noise from the attic" had risen to a fearsome howl. The forty-seven-page study laid out the costs of separation: $1.25 million leaving the country; 15-percent interest rates and a 15-percent drop in investment; 720,000 people (15 percent) out of work: "Nothing — nothing — would do more to spur economic recovery than a 'Yes' vote," he stated. "Nothing would do more to restore confidence in ourselves, or the world's confidence in us. . . . We didn't say anything in our report about the consequences of a No vote. We're not going to speculate on the results of a No vote" (*FP/Star*, Sept 26/92).

As a spokesperson from big business and Toronto's Bay Street, Taylor did more than anyone else to sell the No side of the debate.[3] His dire predictions kindled smothered resentment across the country. Clyde Wells spoke for many people: he called his threats "unacceptable" — "I don't intend to have any part of that kind of fearmongering, high pressure tactics" (*Star*, Sept 26/92).

Rosemary Speirs's investigative digging and her article about secret memos detailing exactly what happened on September 10 with the legal text sparked some rare journalistic competition. On September 27, the *Toronto Sun* tried to catch up with the *Star*. It boasted that it too had got hold of a secret memo about what really went on at the September FMCs. The one dated September 15 sent off an illuminating flare on the legal text: "all delegations noted the desire of the principals [the ministers] to approve legal texts as quickly as possible after the referendum."

Mulroney's press secretary, Mark Entwhistle, moved swiftly. He confessed the words "after the referendum" were deleted in the final version, because "these words do not reflect accurately what was discussed."

What it all boiled down to was *there was no agreement*.

The prime minister was showing signs of frustration. By September 28 he had toned down his rhetoric considerably. He was visiting Sherbrooke, Quebec, following an agenda laid down in the twelve-page strategy paper "Towards a Referendum Strategy": "If it's No, it's No. There will be no 'we'll see you later' or 'maybe Yes, maybe No.' It will be interpreted as a

No, pure and simple. And a No will not mean 'business as usual.' It will mean the end of negotiations . . . the beginning of the process of dismantling Canada. That's what really is at stake in this vote" (*GM*, Sept 29/92).[4]

Salacious Crumb had yet to contribute what he thought. Now it was time. He who had played constitutional backroom broker in 1981, Premier Roy Romanow of Saskatchewan, had behaved very well and very quietly for months now. He had admitted little since his exposure as a secret promoter of the "sex-gender" Senate. He said, "I really think that the argument that the text should be out is a bit phoney because the Charlottetown accord consensus itself has a lot of detail to begin with" (*GM*, Sept 29/92).

Addressing judges, lawyers, and other notables in Toronto, he pointed out what he considered the deal's comforting bit — "You don't have to hold your nose in voting for this accord. . . . [it is] the product of Canada's soul" (*GM*, Sept 29/92).

Meanwhile, the international money-market boys in New York and Tokyo passed some judgements of their own, following these up with great sell-offs of the Canadian dollar. Brian Mulroney's and Allan Taylor's speeches were cited as inspirations for the currency collapse. The dollar closed at 80 cents US, down .51 cents on September 29. The next day it tumbled to 79.24 cents US, its lowest point in four and three-quarter years.

Some forecast a sharp rise in loan rates. The director of corporate foreign exchange at the Canadian Imperial Bank of Commerce blamed Mulroney for his hard comments on the dismantling of Canada. The currency slide sparked a further chain of events, which, within one week, toppled the Bank of Canada's reserves from $12 billion US to about $4 billion, according to the *Financial Post*'s interpretation on October 15.

On September 30, 1992, just a few days after these latest threats, the bank's prime lending rate jumped a record 2 percent in one day, from 6.25 to 8.25 percent. It ended fourteen consecutive months of declines in the rate. According to the October 1 papers, mortgage rates and other loans rose too. The Royal Bank might have been losing the constitutional battle, but it wasn't losing on money.

The fiscal instability didn't faze the international trade and industry minister, Michael Wilson. He believed the people in the wrong were those who disliked what the government was doing: "I've been told personally by people involved in investment decisions that they'd just as soon wait until they see how things work out." He said he knew of projects at risk worth "tens of millions of dollars." To a hundred trade commissioners he nonchalantly admitted, "Uncertainty has been created by the recent polls." As for the Charlottetown Accord, "We have a good deal here" (*Star*, Sept 30/92). Mulroney's echo-chamber in a blue suit.

If the polls meant anything, they recorded the slow, natural death of the Yes side by the end of September. To implement the Charlottetown Accord, more than half the population of each province and territory had to vote Yes, and that looked less and less likely. On September 30, Environics let out their poll, too: between September 16 and 29, Yes stood at 41 percent, No at 31 percent. Compared with the poll taken on August 28, the "Nos" had almost doubled their strength, gaining 14 percent.

The executive federalists figuratively huddled together to plot their next big play. Through it all, the Yes side remained optimistic. After all, there were a whole twenty-six days to go.

Notes

1 On September 29, 1994, Canadians learned that Brian Mulroney had orally committed the federal government to pick up the tab for Quebec's independent referendum — as long as the wording and all other conditions of the plebescite were exactly the same as they were for the other nine provinces.

2 See Chapter 31 on the Reform Party's destruction of polling records and other historical materials.

3 On July 7, 1993, the press reported that Taylor had been awarded the Officer level of the Ceramic Snowflake, the Order of Canada, the government's good-conduct medal.

4 On November 16, 1992, after the Referendum, the *Toronto Star* published details of an internal Tory strategy report that the *Ottawa Citizen* had secured. Political watchers felt a discomfiting sense of déjà vu as they recognized in it the tactics of Dan Gagnier and his media manipulation for David Peterson.

This time the government forces were ready to move into immediate damage control. And they wielded the indomitable weapon of fear. With it they demanded humiliation and character assassination.

Their strategy was simple and consistent: 1) threaten Canadians with dire economic consequences; 2) predict a legacy of problems to be passed on to their children; and 3) risk "ripping up" years of effort and compromise. One sentence read, "The evidence is that it is very difficult, if not counterproductive, to try to marshal the case that a No vote means the end of Canada."

The characters topping Canada's most-wanted list, according to this definitive inventory, were Preston Manning and Jacques Parizeau. "Referendum campaigns, bluntly put, are won or lost on the effectiveness or lack thereof of the paid media campaign, particularly in the last few weeks" (*Star*, Nov 16/92). On September 28, when Mulroney threatened the dismantling of Canada, Gagnier had been gone from his post as Deputy Secretary on Communications and Consultation for only three months. Coincidence?

29

A Flirtation With Democracy

The Referendum — October 1992[1]

O N OCTOBER 1, PIERRE ELLIOTT TRUDEAU sprang his attack on the Charlottetown Accord with a book launch for his latest polemic, *Trudeau: "A mess that deserves a big NO"*. The hyped event took place at one of his favourite restaurants, La Maison Eggroll in Montreal. There the fawning members of the media and other fans gathered to listen reverently to the Monsignor many believed had galvanized the successful opposition to Meech Lake.

As with Meech Lake, Charlottetown was already lost by the time Trudeau got into the act. Only the press, the profs, and the politicians could not hear its death rattle. With disapproval swelling particularly in the three weeks before the beginning of October, Trudeau's diatribe was trundled into the nation's bookstores.

What a showman! On cue, its author played his hand to the delight of his many fans and of the pompadours of the academic community especially. For months they had prayed for a reincarnation of the great Himself. For $6.95 a plate the seventy-two-year-old lectured staffers and supporters of the Cité-libre Society, along with other buddies and friends:

When collective rights take precedence over individual liberties, we see, in countries where the ideology forms the collectivity, where race, ethnic origin, language, religion forms the collectivity, we see what can happen to those who pretend to live freely in these societies. When the citizen is not equal to all other citizens in the state, we're in the presence of a dictatorship which sets the citizens in a hierarchy based on their beliefs. (*GM*, Oct 1/92, from partial text translated by Patrick Van de Ville)

And if you vote Yes, the blackmail will continue. . . . The federal government will have thrown overboard all its trump cards. In the future it will present itself stark naked if this goes through (André Picard, *GM*, Oct 2/92)[2]

Merlin the Muddler had spoken again.

Logically, of course, he should have planted himself firmly on the Yes side of both Meech Lake and Charlottetown. This was the great thinker who rigorously trumpeted the collectivities of founding races, founding cultures, collective bilingualism, tribal multiculturalism, and rights activism. Now, when it counted most, he should at least have been hammering his one big regret, the notwithstanding clause, even if he confined his attack only to its use with his precious Charter of Rights and Freedoms.

Ontario's Bob Rae nominated himself to take him on. Like Lougheed and Peterson, when confronted with the former PM Rae was out of his league. The ruffled premier could only manage a personal attack:

He appeals to the least generous, the most mean-spirited, and, in my view, the most destructive forces at work in Canada today. . . . Mr. Trudeau is completely wrong. . . . I profoundly disagree with him intellectually. Politically, I have no respect for what he's doing. I think it's destructive and egotistical. This is, I think, extremely petty of Mr. Trudeau at a personal level and I think that on an intellectual level, it simply lacks any sense of dealing with the realities of a modern federation. (*Star*, Oct 2/92)

While Trudeau was dishing out political what-for to Mulroney in Montreal, constitutional affairs minister Joe Clark was being "Rafed" on a radio talk show in Vancouver. Rafe Mair, the host, challenged him that the only way British Columbia could win change was to "use the only constitutional method known to work — threaten to secede." Little Joe drew a big breath: "For you to suggest the only way to get changes in the future is for a province to threaten to secede is flat wrong. Flat wrong." Mair hit right back: "Flat right. Flat right" (*Star*, Oct 2/92).

Where was Preston Manning? Apparently he had zipped himself up. The press discovered one reason. It seemed that Burt Brown, chairman of the Canadian Committee for a Triple-E Senate and a close colleague of Manning's, had indeed changed his mind — a bit: "I've got major doubts. . . . This thing is being orchestrated and manipulated on a daily basis" (*Star*/CP, Oct 2/92). Such caution!

The politically dead emitted other strange noises. "Jackboots" — Iona Campagnolo, former president of the Liberal party and co-chair of the Yes side's all-party Canada Committee — stressed the importance of keeping people in line: "The issue of a legal text is a red herring. Most people who are demanding to see a legal text haven't even read the instruction manual to their VCR" (*Star*/CP, Oct 2/92). (Who can?)

Justice minister Kim Campbell concurred: "Once you start releasing the text, you will put it in the hands of lawyers who will argue about what it means" (*Gazette*, Oct 2/92). Horrors!

Despite the fear of being discovered without a view on anything, even lifelong Liberal leadership aspirant Paul Martin, Jr., burped a sound bite: "This constitutional accord was not the fruit of blackmail" (*Maclean's*, Oct 5/92). Thanks for comin' out, Paul!

Some people must have felt dreadful about being left out. Nova Scotia premier Don Cameron was on the No side without knowing it: "The people on the No side had nothing better to, to, uh, no better argument than to try to accuse people of fearmongering. You don't have to be very bright to figure out that if it's a No vote, it's the end of the country" (CBC Newsworld, Oct 1/92).

Then came some pretty gutsy stuff from Robert Bourassa: "When [Trudeau] was leader of this country Canadians were more divided than they are now" (*Sun*, Oct 3/92). This from Bou-Bou with his Bill 178, the greatest divider of them all.

Prince Edward Island's Joe Ghiz covered himself: "It's not conceivable that [Trudeau] is right and 10 provincial premiers, two territorial leaders, four aboriginal leaders, the prime minister and the two leaders of opposition in Parliament are wrong" (*Sun*, Oct 3/92).

Mulroney's friends in high places came to his rescue on October 3. Interviewed by Judy Morrison on CBC Radio AM's "The House" about the legal text that was supposed to have been released by October 12, justice minister Kim Campbell sounded as if she wasn't involved:

Well, they are trying very, very hard to get what Joe Clark is calling a "best efforts legal text" into people's hands, particularly in areas that are, are, uh . . . subject to some disagreement — or not to disagreement but to controversy — in the public debate and, and, I mean, I mean, I've some reports of people who claim to have legal texts. It doesn't reflect what's in the agreement — well, that's just rubbish. The legal text will reflect what's in the agreement, because otherwise it won't be accepted by the parties to the agreement.

. . . Nobody's trying to bring in a pig-in-a-poke; nobody's trying to pull the wool over anybody's eyes. (Oct 3/92)

Campbell carried on: "If there is a No vote, I would expend all of my energy to my last breath trying to keep this country together. But if there is a Yes vote, I can spend my energies doing things that are a lot more constructive" (*Star*, Oct 3/92).

No holds were barred now. On October 2, Gordon Cressy, head of Ontario's Yes campaign, advised the media that Thursday, October 19, would be National Unity Day.

Education minister Tony Silipo, architect of Ontario's phoney public hearings on Meech Lake, announced on October 5 that the Ontario government would set aside October 19 as its Constitution Day: "We want students to use their influence in getting the voting members of their families out to vote" (*GM*, Oct 6/92).[3] Big signals. Little signals. Whatever worked. Win at any cost.

Every day Mulroney and his troops whacked away at the No forces as though their very lives depended on it. Speaking at Pointe au Pic, Quebec, on October 4, the PM threw everything but reason at his listeners:

Canadians should consider what common vision for Canada might emerge from a meeting of the No leaders. Can you imagine them sitting around the table . . . Preston Manning, Sharon Carstairs, Jacques Parizeau, Pierre Trudeau, Judy Rebick?

[On the Charlottetown Accord:] Quebec has won 31 important new powers in the Charlottetown accord — but there is even a more important 32nd gain — the preservation and improvement of Canada. (*Star*, Oct 5/92)

The next day he attacked Trudeau, and like Bob Rae he took a personal swipe at him. Radio station CJAD in Montreal interviewed the PM for one hour:

What we have here is a former prime minister who, with very little, if any, cause at all, seeks to undermine all attempts to bring a degree of unity bringing all Canadians together. . . . Trudeau failed with regard to the Notwithstanding clause. . . . Surely English-speaking Montrealers should be the first to understand the enormity of that concession. . . . So for him to say now this is a mess, he's right. We're busy cleaning up on his. (*Star*, Oct 6/92)

There is no concession that I have made that will in any way ever rival the extraordinary concession that he made in 1982 with the notwithstanding clause. He paid the ultimate price, and he still didn't get Quebec's signature on the agreement. (*GM*, Oct 6/92)

Silly boy. In 1982 Mulroney too had absolutely no objection to the entire constitutional package, complete with notwithstanding clause. Trudeau had no choice, Mulroney had said years earlier. So what was his beef?

David Morton, chairman of the volunteers from the three ad agencies who produced the Canada Committee Yes ads, tossed in his bit of insight: "Let's be frank, if another week goes by and if the same stuff continues [the Yes side continues to lose] there ain't much to lose by getting a little stronger in the approach. I don't think we would ever come out saying there would be millions of jobs lost, but there are ways of communicating that" (Hugh Winsor, *GM*, Oct 6/92).

By the end of the first week in October, Clyde Wells was getting riled again. He threatened to cancel his tour of Western Canada on behalf of the Yes side, saying, "I can't in good conscience ask people in Calgary or Vancouver to support the proposal if, when it comes before the Newfoundland legislature, I have to say 'No, the Senate is not good enough, don't support it'" (*Star*, Oct 6/92).

No one knew where Wells stood any more. One minute he was Yes, the next he was No. On October 5 the newscasters reported that he and Clark had reached some kind of secret deal on how the Constitution should be worded, all arranged through an exchange of faxes.

Peter Newman had won a point. Wells had finally proved himself a wimp. He would join the Mulroney team and go west, gung-ho to promote the Yes side deep in the heart of Manning country.

All the walk-on players were spouting their lines on cue. Even as Wells wobbled westward, external affairs minister Barbara McDougall did another line-dance for her master:

If we want to influence international affairs for the betterment of the world and to ensure that our Canadian values, which we think are important and

universal, can be recognized, adopted, shaped to fit other people's requirements, then we must remain strong as a country. . . . I think that the
consensus that has been built is a very significant one. . . . If you can get the
people on the No side like Preston Manning and Judy Rebick to get
together and agree on a new consensus, good for them, but it isn't going to
happen. (*GM*, Oct 6/92)

In the meantime, the country was going to pot financially. Ottawa confirmed on October 6 that the Bank of Canada had spent a record $4.25
billion in U.S. reserves to defend the dollar as it plummeted 3.5 cents on
foreign exchange markets.

Life was becoming more and more insecure on other fronts as well. The
November 16, 1992, *Maclean's* magazine ran a feature about some 6,000 of
Toronto's 7,000-member police force mounting a protest campaign
against Bob Rae's government on October 5. The NDP wanted to require
officers to file reports every time they drew their revolvers from their
holsters. The police feared for their lives as violent crimes in the city were
increasing, yet Rae was promising them more uncertainty, more government bureaucracy, and less protection for citizens.

Canada's great sheep in sheep's clothing, Joe Clark stayed with his fold.
On the sixth he preached to the converted at the BCNI: "This may very
well be Canada's last chance. But I believe it is also our best. . . . The
Charlottetown accord represents the first time in Canadian history that
Canada's leaders have been able to come together — and to agree unani-
mously — on comprehensive constitutional reform" (*Star*, Oct 7/92).

While Clark tried to save Mulroney's hide and his own ego, Rae waxed
maudlin in Sudbury: "We'll be able to go to a new chapter of generosity
and understanding, a chapter of renewal. . . . Canada is a meeting place. Its
Constitution is going to be a meeting place of ideas" (*Star*, Oct 7/92).

By October of 1992, Canada needed comic relief more than it needed
constitutional reform. National Action Committee chairwoman Judy
Rebick and Minister without Fish John Crosbie brought on the entertainment. At a chance airport encounter on October 7, she reamed him for
remarks he allegedly made to her about the "sex-gender" Senate. She told
eager scrums what he had said: "We can't have women representing
themselves or the next thing you'll know we'll have to have the crippleds
and the coloureds. . . ."

Claiming he'd made the remarks in a private conversation, the predictable Crosbie dug a big hole for himself and jumped in: "I was referring to
coloured people as opposed to white people. I was referring, yes, to the

crippled. I've been making donations to associations with respect to crippled children for years" (*GM*, Oct 10/92). So the media rats were off and running on the sideshow.

But wait! In the words of justice minister Kim Campbell, not everyone was "style without substance." Former British Columbia Premier Bill Vander Zalm threw a spitball that earned *him* the *Toronto Star*'s Quote of the Day: "The accord creates three classes of citizens. There will be three types of people if this package is approved: Quebecers, natives, and ordinary Canadians. Their powers will be different" (*Star*, Oct 7/92).

The prime minister's prime pump Hugh Segal squirmed as the evidence poured in to the PMO that not all was going well: "We expected a mid-period of uncertainty with a lot of volatility. . . . I'm not really convinced this referendum is 'pollable.' . . . The Prime Minister's performance was precisely what was needed to energize the team in Quebec and focus the issues" (*Star*, Oct 7/92).

Milton Born With a Tooth, the leader of Alberta's Lone-Fighters' Society, had it about right for those who thought the sum of the parts was greater than the whole: "I'm a Blackfoot. I don't want to be Canadian. No one understands that" (*Star*, Oct 8/92). At least he knew he was something.

If Canadians ever needed a lesson that parliamentary democracy could not be left in the hands of the justices of the Supreme Court they got it on October 8, 1992. Accepting the twenty-sixth annual Royal Bank Award for Canadian Achievement, the former Chief Justice of the Supreme Court of Canada, Mr. Justice Brian Dickson, scolded: "Many Canadians fail to recognize the strength of our great land or the dangers it faces. We are confronted with dangers, serious dangers, to national survival." His legally exalted self then told Canadians that their individual rights were protected under the Charter of Rights and Freedoms (*Star*, Oct 9/92). Sure. By now everyone in the country knew about the notwithstanding clause.

Crosbie the clown. Rebick the rouster. Addressing the Empire Club of Canada, John Crispo, political economics professor at the University of Toronto, joined the circus. The noisy part-time academic had been quiet for some time. He stood firmly behind the Charlottetown agreement and Mulroney: "He gave us leadership on the Meech Lake [and] the Charlottetown Accord. . . . Everything I'm for, the Canadian public's against. It's a real nightmare. . . . I'm fed up with little Canadians. All I run into are little Canadians" (Rogers Cable 10 TV, Oct 8/92). Nice talk.

Disneyland. In Montreal, Major J.P. Sabourin of Canadian Forces Base Valcartier defended plans for a parade of federal army tanks through suburban Quebec City on October 13. The display was merely to "check the operation levels of our vehicles and to show them to the people of Quebec" (*Star*, Oct 10/92). Just the ticket to get people riled up.

For all the clowning, the business over Canada's future was mighty serious. On October 8, the Federal Court of Canada ruled against Graham Haig and another 20,000 citizens. He claimed his voting rights had been quashed when Mulroney gave in to Quebec and allowed the province to exempt itself from a federal referendum. In addition to having lost his residency elsewhere in Canada, he had failed, the judge said, to file a statement of claim under the Charter. Haig would now have to take his landmark case to the Supreme Court of Canada. The news shook those Canadians who had always believed one of the only things Trudeau's constitution left sacrosanct was the right to vote.[4]

Joe Clark kept up the pressure: "If we lose this, we will lose it almost to carelessness. . . . Quite literally, we will lose it to people not caring enough. . . . I tell people there are two dates to worry about this month. One is the 26th, and the second is the morning after, and I think if it's going down we'll all have things to worry about trying to put it together" (*Star*, Oct 10/92).

Lebanon, we were on our way.

S OMETIMES very important news popped up without explanation, and from the strangest places. On October 10, in a downtown hotel in Montreal, the Quebec government released the long-awaited draft legal text. Apparently no one else had it, or was supposed to have it, or could let on they had it. Whatever.

Caught with their pants down, the federal government quickly blustered that the "real" legal text would be released the following Tuesday, October 13. The feds claimed they had a commitment to this date from all parties.

Oh yeah. Sure. So how come Quebec had the text before anyone else? Memories of Gil Rémillard at Mont Gabriel in 1986. The man who played constitutional poker made sure he was armed with a full hand from Mulroney's gang before he joined the game. Here he was again, puffing like an eagle having dined on many rabbits for many months: "The No side says, 'You should have the legal texts. We don't want to sign a blank cheque.' Well now, here's the answer" (*Star*, Oct 11/92).

Not to be outdone by his minister, Bourassa crowed: "With this legal text we have the absolute proof that the current government of Quebec got more in negotiations than any other government in 125 years" (*Sun*, Oct 11/92).

So that's what Confederation was all about!

Meanwhile, the prime minister was taking the high road. He had a vision. He told a Canadian–Polish Congress audience in Steinbach, Manitoba, that a Yes vote would mean that "every Canadian man, woman and child would enjoy the highest standard of living in the entire world by the year 2000." But he qualified his optimism with a more familiar threat: "Don't be surprised if there's a No vote and you start paying the price immediately" (*Star*, Oct 11/92). By 2000, he said, the average income for a family of four would soar to $91,000 (it was then less than $50,000). The number of new jobs would shoot up to 2.5 million. Questioned on his numbers, Mulroney snapped back with authority, "It's all statistically established by StatsCan — read the reports."

On this same Western junket he reached for the heavens in a speech in Winnipeg. Invoking "sacred providence" and hoping to be "blessed," his political eminence promised the government would introduce a bill describing Canada as a country united under God (*Sun*, Oct 11/92).

With the worst recession gripping Canada since the dirty thirties, the country would certainly need the power of the Almighty to make any giant leap in its standard of living. But why was God worth only a bill in Parliament that could be voted out when Mulroney's deal was a constitution that couldn't be budged? Canadians needed more than beatitudes. Whatever juice l'Irlandais was quaffing, it was powerful stuff: "We found a very remarkable shift in attitudes in the last 48 hours in respect of the way that people are looking at the question, simply because they received the Charlottetown accord in the mail. . . . They feel more secure, more confident about the Yes and more concerned about the No" (*Star*, Oct 12/92).

A nation so mad craved therapy. And of course in the welfare state where all things are possible there had to be a doctor in the house. On October 12, Canadian Press reported the findings of a well-known Toronto psychologist who also counselled troubled public servants. Warren Sheppell told the *Star*: "It isn't healthy. What is going on is not healthy." The problem, he explained, was "the R Word" (Oct. 12/92).[5]

On October 12, in a ninety-minute TV debate before an estimated 2.5 million viewers, Robert Bourassa called a No vote a step toward the breakup of the country. PQ leader Jacques Parizeau opined that the No vote was necessary in order to "find a way to save native self-government."

Odd. Aboriginals at the negotiating table were convinced that one of the big features of a Yes vote was that it meant yes to a third level of government — the native self-government that Bourassa abhorred. Even the scripts were getting mixed up now.

Peter Lougheed, the former premier of Alberta, produced another fuddle-muddle on October 13. The self-righteous Red Tory gave this titbit to CBC: "I don't think it's very smart to lose what we've gained. . . . the trade-off to bring this about was a Triple-E Senate" (CBC Newsworld). What gain? What trade-off to bring about what? More important, what Triple-E Senate?

Just two more weeks. Historian Jack Granatstein tantalized constitutional buffs with a bold assertion of his own: "There are a whole lot of things in the legal text that were not in the Charlottetown accord" (CBC Newsworld, Oct 13/92). Maybe so. But the fact that Quebec was only "engaged" to treating its minority communities the same way it did its French majority while English Canada was "committed" to treating its minorities equally was well known.

Mulroney kept on keeping on. His legacy was at stake. Chatting up some 600 students at Holland College in Charlottetown, he pretended calm rationality:

> Here's what would happen with a No. The first thing on television that night, they'd say this is a repudiation of Bourassa. His government is no longer legitimate and we want an early election and a referendum on independence. Even if they didn't get that, there would be 18 months of uncertainty in Quebec leading up to a provincial election. Can you imagine what that 2½ years is going to do to international investors? Do you imagine the impact on interest rates? On investment intentions not only in Quebec, but elsewhere in the country? I don't want to go beyond that. Canada is a strong country. I think we've recovered from things in the past and maybe we will again? . . . We can tell you on the Yes side that if you support the Charlottetown agreement that we're going to turn the page and move on. Matters will be resolved, perhaps imperfectly, but they are going to be resolved. The No side can give you no such guarantee. The only thing we know for sure is we know nothing will have been resolved. (*Star*, Oct 14/92)

The *Sun* quoted Mulroney saying, "The problem in Canada isn't with the leadership, it's with the followship" (Oct 26/92). Amen to that.

BOB RAE still needed his page in history. At a joint meeting of the Canadian Club and the Empire Club, where he somehow earned a standing ovation, the Ontario premier casually lumped Preston Manning and Jacques Parizeau into the same camp: "Anyone in public life who says to you 'I know what will happen if you vote No' is nothing but a peddler of illusion and snake oil. . . . It's not Mr. Mulroney's deal. Mr. Mulroney's name is not on the ballot" (*Star*, Oct 14/92).

All Mulroney's darlin's and high-falutin' mucky-mucks could say what they wanted. The more time passed, the less power they had. Long before the Referendum date finally dawned, the jig was up. For more than a year the focus of sane Canadians concerned about the nation's business — not the bankers — was on the economy and money management, not on Yes or No on the Constitution. Economist Antia Laurie of Saloman Brothers Inc., a New York brokerage house, got it right in a headline story "Canadian dollar gains strength": "The apocalyptic visions of a fragmented Canada — frequently cited as the unavoidable consequence of a rejection of the agreement — are not convincing. Thus the recent selloff in Canadian bond and currency markets appears to be overdone" (*GM*, Oct 14/92).

The day after her article appeared in the *Globe*, the New York bond-rating agency Standard & Poor's posted a very negative rating of Canada's $7.5-billion Canadian government and Crown corporation debt from a Triple-A rating down to a Double-A-Plus. S & P said the cause was the magnitude of Canada's debt rather than its constitution; however, "uncertainties about the future shape of the federation, if they persist, could weaken investor confidence and hamper the conduct of economic policy of the medium term" (*FP*, *Star*, *GM*, Oct 15/92).

In reaction, finance minister Don Mazankowski said, "Clearly the focus is on Canada as we go through this period of constitutional uncertainty. . . . That's really what we've been saying. . . . The consequences of a No vote is that it would perpetuate the uncertainty and who knows just what impact that will have" (*Star*, Oct 15/92).

On October 14, just as the *Toronto Sun* had done earlier, the *Toronto Star* and the *Globe and Mail* came out with editorials swinging in favour of the accord.

The *Star* editorial headline perpetuated the fiction: "Legal text proves true to consensus." Using the term "legal text" five times in the piece, the Pulp Primevil encouraged readers to accept that the "draft text" was the same as the "legal text." At least the editors did acknowledge that even the so-called legal text contained the same duplicity identified earlier: Quebec was only required to be "attached" to its minority communities, like its anglophones, while the rest of Canada was "committed" to the francophone communities outside that province.

True to form, the *Globe* came out on the government's side and in conspiracy with the opposition parties. In their editorial that day, they stated:

We strongly supported ratification of the Meech Lake accord between 1987 and 1990 in the conviction that it re-established a healthy balance within the federal system, with a place of honour for Quebec. The Charlottetown accord contains most of what Meech Lake did, and it adds some further strength to provincial jurisdictions. From the point of view of Quebec alone, Charlottetown is, in our view, more advantageous to Quebec than Meech. . . . But the interests of Quebeckers as Canadians are also very important. (Oct 14/92)

Ordinary Canadians, including Quebecers, could only ask why Quebecers should have any more honoured place in the federation than anyone else?

For the constitutional affairs minister, October 14 was just another day of fearmongering. On the stump in Lethbridge, Alberta, Clark did again what he had done on September 17: he linked the separatist bombings of the 1960s and the Oka crisis of the 1990s and called them a blueprint for what could be expected: "In the real world of Canada, you can't pretend that constitutional issues don't exist. . . . Anyone who thinks that these are false problems, that we can simply take a five-year holiday and that everything will be alright — people like that don't live in the real world. If this agreement fails and frustration grows, one can't predict the consequences" (*Star*, Oct 15/92).

Like Don Mazankowski and Joe Clark, the federal industry minister, Michael Wilson, stepped forward as one willing and able to terrorize fellow citizens to sell the Mulroney message. At Ste. Anne de Bellevue, Quebec, he embraced the warnings of sixty-five economists who were convinced the world was coming to an end: "Common sense tells you there are bound to be negative economic consequences that follow from a No vote. The supporters of a No vote are dreaming at best if they believe such a negative vote won't have important consequences for Quebec and Canada" (*Star*, Oct 15/92).

Whenever Canada gets into real trouble, there's always a saviour. And a bit of humour, too. This time a country singer came to the rescue, "Stompin' Tom" Connors of "Sudbury Saturday Night" fame: "I'm sorry to say that special status for any one group or individual holds no part of my Canadian Dream" (*GM*, Oct 16/92). Hallelujah! Go get 'em, Tom!

The *Toronto Star* never wavered in its support for Mulroney's plan. On October 17 the Pulp-Primevil editors bullied:

One of the glaring defects of the Meech Lake accord was that it dealt only with Quebec's aspirations, which led many, including the Star, to vigorously oppose it. It lacked a national vision. . . . After five years of struggle, we feel Canada has done the best it can and arrived at the best compromise, not unlike the Fathers of Confederation did in 1867. For these reasons, and above all for the love of Canada, we suggest a Yes vote on Oct. 26/92.

The people weren't buying this pitch any more than they had for Meech Lake. The paper's headline that admitted "Support for deal plummeting" backed it up with a Star–CTV News poll by the Environics Research Group of Toronto between October 9 and 15. It showed Yes side support down from 51 to 31 percent. Support for the No side had rocketed from 25 to 41 percent. Even in Ontario, where a landslide Yes had been taken for granted, the race had become too close to call. As the *Star* was reporting on October 17, now 38 percent were saying Yes, 36 percent No. Canadians were not as afraid of their leaders as their leaders had hoped.

As his reign drew to a close, the prime minister and all his henchmen, the leaders of the other political parties and the handmaidens of big business conspiring with them, committed themselves to winning by the same shared methods and agenda, at any price.

The *Toronto Sun* broke its story on October 18, 1992. Peter C. Newman, one of 150 Companions of the Order of Canada, the highest rank in the order, had organized a unity campaign of his own. He mustered as many members of the Order as he could to support an effort described in a two-page spread newspaper advertisement "A Community of Dreams." Hundreds of names of members of the Order filled the space, fully sup-porting the government.

To sway Canadians further, Newman turned to the Council for Cana-dian Unity (CCU), which had been formed in 1964. In 1992 the council, which described itself as "non-partisan," said it had "thousands of volun-teers across Canada."[6] In 1992 it formed the "Friends of Canada," "a mass movement of individual Canadians actively working together to promote Canada and a majority message and a show of strength." Almost one-half of its funding, some $4 million, flowed from that same government.

Newman protested any criticism of his obvious abuse of the nation's honour system: "I stress that it has nothing to do with the referendum. . . . What this is really about is members of the Order of Canada coming out for their country" (*Sun*, Oct 18/92).

In all, the sycophantic medal-holders contributed some $65,000 to the cause. The letters requesting tangible support from the public passed through Canada Post in August, and elicited replies from about half of those who received them, according to the *Sun* on October 18. There was nothing subtle about the original advertisement:

Those of us fortunate enough to have been recognized by our peers and honoured by having received an Order of Canada feel duty-bound to speak out at this perilous moment. Without in any way endorsing the many and shifting positions that are in play, we wish to reaffirm our faith and belief in this great country of ours. . . . We may be a loose federation of wildly diverse regions, but there is a quiver of common intent that has held us together for 125 years — and will continue to do so, if we seize the future that can and will be ours.

The Office of the Governor General of Canada also threw itself into the festivities.[7] As Brooke Jeffrey later confirmed in her book, *Strange Bedfellows, Trying Times*, the ads were accompanied "by a letter on the Governor General's letterhead from his secretary, Judith LaRocque, a former aide to several Conservative Ministers. . . . The idea had been approved by the Order of Canada advisory committee" (p. 126).

Not one of the Order's medal-holders turned in his or her Ceramic Snowflake in protest of such political machinations. Professor Michael Behiels said it all: "This is obscene in the extreme. The campaign is a travesty of democracy. Apparently if you wrap yourself in the flag, anything goes" (*Ott Citizen*, Sept 23/92).

By mid-October the frustration level had reached the boiling point. Day after day Canadians were assaulted by leaders past and present telling them how they should think. On October 18, former NDP leader Ed Broadbent, a bankable panellist for the Yes side, boasted on CBC's "The Journal" that "for once the politicians are ahead of the people."[8]

Broadbent and others were part of a group of prominent Canadians originally called the "Seven Angels." These stalwarts quickly became Mulroney's National Canada Committee, rooting and tooting for the Yes side. Included among the big names that multiplied like rabbits were two Red Tories, Bill Davis and Robert Stanfield. These pumper-uppers from past constitutional disasters rose to rattle their bones at anyone who would listen. By Referendum day, some forty "eminent Canadians" had been dragooned into l'Irlandais's camp under the legion's banner. The list even included that lovable old standby for dualism, regionalism, multiculturalism, and a *deux nations* Canada, none other than Jean-Luc Pépin, of the Pépin–Robarts Task Force of eons past. Of course, as one might have expected, David Peterson's Ontario Attorney General Ian Scott grabbed a piece of the action. His plug for democracy: "No one could be opposed to a constituent assembly, but why does anyone think a constituent assembly would get a different result?"

No matter what Mulroney did, the Tory caucus gave him absolute and unqualified support. Mississauga South federal MP Don Blenkarn led the pack of those defending The Boss: "It's true the guy is not popular in the country but he sure as hell has the support of the caucus. We are not going to force him out of his job. He is doing the job and he has our support" (*Star*, Oct 19/92).

Mulroney must have been inspired by such a blind vote of confidence. The next day, on tour in Toronto, he said, "If you don't have these kinds of arrangements in a Confederation [Meech/Charlottetown], French-Canadians will inevitably become Cajuns. They don't want to become dancers in Louisiana with banjos" (*GM*, Oct 20/92).[9]

Of the five events in Toronto that day featuring Mulroney, only one was public. He visited the Citizenship Court where 231 new Canadians were being sworn in before an audience of 800 family members and friends. Interviewed by the editorial board of the *Toronto Star*, the PM sounded like Burl Ives in *Cat on a Hot Tin Roof*: "We're up against a mountain of mendacity. Every bloody time we go somewhere, there's a new falsehood being propagated about the natives, about the French, about the minorities, the visible minorities. Everybody's got into this, and it's difficult for us to fight. [But as for quitting,] I have no intention of doing that. I have the intention of carrying on, win, lose or draw" (*Star*, Oct 20/92).

Joe Clark's sombre words for the day were a little grimmer than usual but consistent. He spoke to retirees in Victoria, BC: "I'm very pessimistic about our ability to hold this (country) together if we fail this time. . . . I think gradually the country would just come apart. I believe that profoundly. I can be wrong. I'm putting this forward as an observation" (*Star*, Oct 20/92).

A S TIME RAN OUT on the Referendum, the voices of doom and gloom gabbled on:

Editorial comment from *The Catholic Register*: "For the sake of Canada — not any region but our nation — this national weekly, *The Catholic Register*, urges readers to vote Yes" (*Star*, Oct 20/92).

Matthew Barrett, CEO and chairman of the Bank of Montreal: "At the very minimum, a No vote is a vote for constitutional gridlock . . . a boost for separatist forces in Quebec. Why would we choose an environment of ongoing uncertainty and risk?" (*FP*, Oct 20/92).

Ontario premier Bob Rae addressed a business audience in Toronto: "Let's cut the cacophony and cut the rhetoric and cut the antagonism and cut the anger and cut through all those things, and focus on one thing that is in the question: the renewal today of the Canadian Constitution" (*Star*, Oct 20/92).

Canadian novelist and poet Margaret Atwood triviated: "I am still undecided. I feel that I am a representative confused person. . . . If I were the editor, I'd say: 'This needs a rewrite.' Is this a referendum or just a glorified opinion poll?" (*Maclean's*, Oct 19/92).

Pollster Martin Goldfarb: "The Yes side was likely to win next week's referendum on the Charlottetown accord. . . . Our data suggest the No side has peaked, and the Yes side is ready to surge ahead" (*Star*, Oct 19/92).

From New York, Montreal-born Robert MacNeil, co-host of the U.S. Public Broadcasting System's "MacNeil/Lehrer NewsHour": "I sometimes feel that if all the people outside Canada who know and admire Canada were voting, the result would be an overwhelming Yes" (*Maclean's*, Oct 19/92).

On October 21, 1992, blessing the Yes side with the subtlety of a sledge-hammer, the Conference Board of Canada warned that constitutional uncertainty was hurting the retail industry.

Despite all the pressure, political, institutional, and financial, the Gallup poll on October 21 seemed to seal the fate of Mulroney's plans. The No side 50 percent, Yes 40 percent: even safe Ontario was split — 45 percent, Yes and No.

CANADA'S BLATHERSKITE, the great gambler, was unmoved by the numbers. On October 21, with only four days to go, he was in Baie Comeau, back on his knees where he had been since August 6, 1984: "It won't just be No to Charlottetown. It will be saying yes to sovereignty with Jacques Parizeau" (*Star*, Oct 22/92). In his dark brown voice he told the crowd, "He said very, very clearly last night that a No vote will be interpreted by him as a Yes for separation" (*GM*, Oct 22/92).

Shortly thereafter, Mulroney told the *Toronto Sun* editorial board that he hadn't ruled out a second referendum if there was a narrow defeat (*Sun*, Oct 22/92). "The idea of scaremongering, you see — this doesn't bother me at all. This is irrelevant. It's false" (*GM*, Oct 22, 23/92).

On October 22, the *Globe and Mail* reported the governor general would be paying a courtesy call to Premier Gary Filmon to try to bolster the sagging Yes side. The question was never asked whether Ray Hnatyshyn would also attend the Reform Party convention in Winnipeg and whisper sweet nothings into the petal-shaped ears of Preston Manning. Not bloody likely.

Is he in heaven? Or is he in hell? That damned illusive prime pimpernel. Mulroney's warning voice issued from Montreal: "If it's No, it's No. . . . we've lost. If we vote No on Monday, it's all over. . . . we return to the status quo. . . . It's No to aboriginals. It's No to Senate reform. It's No to 31 gains for Quebec and the gains for other provinces. It's No to everything" (*Star*, Oct 23/92).

At least Pierre-F. Côté, chief electoral officer for Quebec, sided with the voters, according to the October 23 *Globe*. He criticized the many business executives who hammered their employees to vote Yes: "With respect to the CEOs, I would say that I find it indecent." Under Quebec's referendum legislation, companies faced fines of up to $10,000 for the offence.

Three days before the Referendum, Ontario's Bob Rae delivered a final word for posterity. On that same Friday, October 23, on a program billed as a "special presentation of the Government of Ontario," the premier described Canadians as wrong-headed. They didn't know their stuff: "Public criticisms are unfair and so off-base." He tried to explain: "What we have [in Canada] is a mosaic of rights" (CFTO TV).

The *Financial Post* printed the only story that mattered that day — foreign investors had dumped a record $4.7 billion of Canadian securities in August.

On October 23, Martin Goldfarb, the pollster, tried to salvage the foolish forecast he had made a scant five days earlier: "With many Canadians still undecided, next Monday's referendum is still too close to call, but the momentum clearly favours the No side" (*Star*, Oct 23/92).

Mulroney's final pleadings to Canadians were humbler than any he had ever made before, urging them "to consider the interests of your children and grandchildren and vote constructively for a Yes. . . . With a Yes, there is an opportunity to turn the page on 35 years of an argument that has often been sterile and time-consuming" (*Star*, Oct 25/92).

On October 25, 1992, the day before Monday's Referendum, the prime minister's October 19 interview with the editorial board of the *Toronto Sun* came out:

If this goes down I don't think there will be a politician brave enough in Quebec to try this again on behalf of Canada. Contrary to all these people who say, "Just vote it down. Nothing is going to happen." Something is going to happen — and it's going to be all bad! A Yes vote gives us a united country. It gives us political serenity and it gives us economic security. A No vote means no vision, no hope, no promise for our kids. Nothing!

Through it all Robert Bourassa was just as manipulative as ever: "Now I'm talking to English Canada. . . . In voting Yes, you are correcting that injustice which was done to Quebec," and "in voting No, you are saying to Quebec we want to keep that 1982 Constitution, we approve of what Trudeau did when he imposed that Constitution on Quebec — and that will not help" (*Star*, Oct 25/92).

As the Liberals had done during the final hours of Meech Lake, with their leadership convention, the Reform Party of Canada was holding its convention in Winnipeg of 1,500 delegates and 100 nominated candidates and their spouses. The couples had been brought in for intensive training, consisting of a forty-eight-hour seminar.

Meanwhile, elsewhere in the West, in Lloydminster, Alberta, Deputy Prime Minister and Minister of Finance Don Mazankowski was hopping mad: "Constitutional uncertainty has been a big drag on our economy. . . . When they call this a 'Mulroney deal,' that is a blatant distortion of the truth. . . . It's not a federal government document. It was not hatched in the bowels of the bureaucracy in Ottawa. . . . One wonders if the likes of Jacques Parizeau, Pierre Trudeau and Judy Rebick and Preston Manning could have come together" (*Star*, Oct 25/92).

Government House Leader Harvie Andre was of a similar mind, but even more livid: "I am surprised at the number of people who are just out-and-out bigoted, saying they hate French and French-Canadians. . . . [There's] more bigotry and hatred than I had thought existed" (*GM*, Oct 26/92).

Premier Robert Bourassa had just one more shot. On Referendum day, October 26, he made a final push and tossed one final threat. "The rupture of the Canadian federation is the parcelling of Canada into three territories. . . . If we say No we return to the Constitution Pierre Trudeau imposed on us" (*Star*, Oct 26/92).

The news on Referendum day was just like any other that Canadians had endured for many long months. Another damning report out of New York from Standard & Poor's. There was a downgrading of the Royal Bank's rating on certificates of deposit and long-term debt. The report cited the deterioration of the bank's credit quality. Nobody on the No side was feeling sorry for Allan Taylor's meddlesome institution by then.

The *Toronto Sun* editorial screamed, "YES! Yes! Yes! Yes! Thank You World Champion Blue Jays" (*Sun*, Oct 26/92). Everyone smiled at the double entendre.

Finance minister Mazankowski filed a report from his home riding of Vegreville, Alberta, that financial experts had been dispatched to ease foreign fears. It wasn't taken very seriously, since the news simply repeated the Meech Lake Accord routine: "We want to make sure the international markets get the right interpretation. . . . Our officials are on the ground to explain the what ifs. . . . If there's fallout, we're going to let people know right away we're in control of the situation and act" (*Star*, Oct 26/92).

Reform Party leader Preston Manning recognized the investment being made: "Canadians will be unleashing a democratic will in Canada that has not been seen in a long time. I think you could liken it to the beginnings of the Quiet Revolution in Quebec . . . where they just one day turned their backs on the traditional leadership. . . . You can no longer assume people are a bunch of sheep who can be herded along with emotional arguments with no content" (*Star*, Oct 26/92)

The results of the national Referendum showed a resounding defeat of executive federalism as interpreted by Mulroney's government and all three of the major political parties. The No vote came in at 54 percent and the Yes vote registered at 45 percent. Altogether, six provinces rejected the Charlottetown Accord. Only one was needed to defeat this radical vision of Canada. All of the West, Quebec, and Nova Scotia piled onto the No side. Even Ontario, where the broadcast media had cut off the voice of dissent, was inconclusive with its 50 percent Yes and 49.9 percent No vote. The Yukon voted No. The Northwest Territories voted Yes. The only strong Yes came from New Brunswick, PEI, and Newfoundland.

Interviewed from Montreal, Premier Bourassa stated firmly, "Quebec is the centre of the Canadian common market. We will always have to have strong relations with our neighbours east and west. We believe that we will be able to build Quebec within Canada. That's the policy of my government" (*Star*, Oct 27/92).

Even in defeat, Brian Mulroney had the last word. To English Canada he said:

The Charlottetown agreement is history. The solutions we thought we had found . . . are now lost. . . . The principal and overriding complex task and obligation before us is to foster strong and durable economic renewal. It is to maintain a high Canadian standard of living in a relentlessly competitive international economy. (*Star*, Oct 27/92)

The solutions which we thought we had found to Canada's political, economic and social problems are now lost; the grievances will remain. . . . In order to deal with Canada's problems, it is essential the spirit of compromise take hold, starting tonight. (CTV News, Toronto, Oct 26/92)

I accept without question the answer which Quebec gave to the referendum question. (Radio-Canada, Montreal, Oct 26/92)

What about the answer Canada gave? For the Tories, there was nowhere to go but down.

Notes

1 There have only been two other national referendums in Canada. The 1898 referendum was on prohibition, and in 1942, during the Second World War, there was one on conscription.

2 There are as many different versions of Trudeau's remarks as there are reporters and publications. The "official" version, published in Trudeau's polemic, varies considerably from the press reports.

3 During Meech, Silipo chaired the Ontario Select Committee hearings on the Constitution. Many witnesses who appeared before the committee were familiar with the way the roster was manipulated, how evidence was squelched, and how arbitrarily the chairman conducted the proceedings, to paper over the public's enormous opposition to Official Bilingualism, Ontario's Bill 8, the French Language Services Act, and the NDP government's promotion of rights activism.

The committee's favourite trick was to severely restrict the time allotment for presentations regardless of the petitioner's expertise. Another stunt was to punch the clock to the second on those who presented ideas the provincial government disliked. Those friendly to the Rae government's views were permitted to carry on beyond their assigned time slot, eating up others' precious time. Whole briefs submitted to the committee were lost. Telephone messages were ignored and letters unanswered.

In 1990 the Law Society of Upper Canada found Silipo guilty of misconduct, for falsifying a mortgage document.

4 On October 22, four days before the Referendum, the Supreme Court of Canada agreed to review Haig's case. However, they ruled they would not hear it until some time in 1993. As with Bill 101, the court followed its own agenda.

5 Sheppell should have known about such things. As a contracted consultant to the Federal Public Service, he peddles his wares throughout the system.

6 On April 2, 1992, the CCU released a poll showing that 71 percent of Canadians supported the direction the Beaudoin–Dobbie Special Joint Committee's report laid out.

7 When he learned he was to be awarded the highest rank of the Order of Canada, the Companion Level, in 1990, Newman flouted protocol. *Maclean's* blabbed the news in their July 9 issue. Government House made the official announcement on September 4, 1990. As a courtesy and a matter of protocol, recipients of the Ceramic Snowflake are asked to allow the governor general to make the announcement first.

8 On his retirement from politics on December 1, 1989, the former NDP leader was handed a handsome post for which he had no credentials whatever. To guarantee the loyalty of the otherwise unemployed politician, Mulroney appointed him head of the federal government-financed International Centre for Human Rights and Democratic Development, based in Montreal (*Star*, Dec 2/89). Just before he left politics, Broadbent the Quebec-born socialist had said, "If the substance of the Meech Lake accord is not put in place by next June, it is not Quebec that will lose out, it is not the federal government of Canada that will lose out, it is all of Canada" (*Star*, Oct 27/89).

9 The United States press noted the prime minister's comments, too. Canadian Press in Washington reported that Barry Ancelet, a member of a Louisiana writers' association, stated, "It is infuriating and disparaging that Mulroney has referred to Cajuns as curiosities who play banjos" (*Star*, Oct 21/92).

X

The Ins and Outs

30

Some Insiders and Some Outsiders

THE COLLAPSE OF THE YES side in the October 1992 Referendum had a variety of interesting and immediate effects. First, it produced strong responses from most politicians, federal and provincial. With power slipping and a bright future melting away before her very eyes, Kim Campbell went berserk before a large audience: "We are not a separate species. We are *of* you. We *are* you!" (Global TV, Oct 26/92). The diminutive federal acolyte and Minister of Justice Campbell summed up the attitude of many of her colleagues in her emotional plea on national television. The outburst stunned her audience.

Perhaps Canadians shouldn't have been scratching their heads after all. For thirty years the ruling class had wrapped themselves in mythological trappings while they postured about Canada's identity. Campbell's gush exposed the politicians' growing panic as tensions rose — and pointed to the rot underlying the system. Many special-interest groups loudly endorsed particular ideals and then turned around and accepted funding from odd sources. In 1992 **Alliance Quebec (AQ)**, for example, the supposedly independent voice of anglophone Quebec, received $1.581 million in federal funds. In the October Referendum on the Charlottetown Accord, the AQ supported the federal government's position — the Yes side.

Against the wishes of Alliance Quebec's own constituency, **Robert Keaton**, its leader, even supported the Allaire Report — the extremist

Quebec nationalist agenda that recommended that Quebec grab almost every federal power save the name "Canada." This departure from its own principles prompted the resignation of many prominent founders and members.

Equally bizarre was the fact that the federal government — and the Quebec government — supplied the **Chateauguay Valley English-Speaking Association (CVESPA)** with more than two-thirds of its funding. According to CVESPA's Annual Report of March 31, 1993, it received a federal operating grant of $95,000, project grants of $20,000 — source unidentified — and a Quebec government grant of $3,634. The latter grant the previous year for the same period was $30,000. The total revenue of CVESPA for 1993 came to only $152,874.

CVESPA spent five years struggling for anglophone and education rights against the federal government and the Quebec government on Bill 178 and the Charter's notwithstanding clause before the United Nations. Simultaneously it happily took taxpayers' money from the very governmental bodies it sought to discredit. Could CVESPA really maintain its credibility without being influenced by its fiscal masters? The Quebec organization even operates out of a federal government building in Huntingdon, Quebec. (For more on the UN case, see Chapter 34.)

Independent dissenters, any organizations that supported themselves entirely and avoided the conflict-of-interest pickle, faced a much greater obstacle. Self-financing groups like the **Alliance for the Preservation of English (APEC)**, headquartered in Toronto, or the **National Citizens' Coalition (NCC)** received no government funding, yet were popularly portrayed in newspapers, magazines, and on television as groups "in the wrong."

By 1992, most Canadians suspected they had lost something very valuable. They had. They were realizing gradually that their most precious privilege — the right to differ from prevailing opinions and be respected for it — was gone. Real debate throughout the country only flourished underground. Anyone who honestly disagreed with the bias of those in power was frustrated by a lack of investigative journalism that legitimized keeping the lid on. So dissent was strangled. Evidence of the decay of real differences of opinion showed in public discussions on national goals and visions.

Few people were permitted to speak their minds in public forums. Their fellow citizens, watching and listening, recognized the familiar platitudes and the "correct" interpretations, yet they also knew they were witnessing careful presentations, plotted and scripted for their consumption. References to the "so-called ordinary Canadian" became a favourite national joke. These were the citizens cherry-picked to express themselves through the media, before the federal and provincial governmental committees, who were screened and selected beforehand.

The widespread ridiculing of the Reform Party proved the point. Although he laid out clearly what his party stood for, **Preston Manning**, always anxious to attain political correctness, was incapable of delivering a knock-out punch when it was called for. His hesitancy fed suspicions. Malicious commentators across the land were quick to exploit his weakness at every opportunity, often portraying him as evil incarnate. An amateur at media relations, Manning never recovered from these earliest impressions.

Of the few independent thinkers in Canada, the most reviled was **Ron Leitch**, QC. The successful lawyer heads APEC, the Alliance for the Preservation of English in Canada. The organization has published a monthly newsletter for nearly two decades. In the early 1990s it boasted a paid membership of more than 40,000. Leitch commanded an army of English-speaking people who agreed with the opinions of a great many other people. What grated on the establishment far more than APEC's historical position was the fact that it sustained itself entirely without public money.

The association envisages Canada as one nation. Like many Canadians, APEC stood firm against the Meech Lake Accord because of its divisive policy of recognizing Quebec as a "distinct" society. Leitch and his team mounted the same battle the following year against the Charlottetown Accord. APEC pushed for a constituent assembly for constitutional reform, Parliamentary reform and a society in which all citizens are equal before the law. Pretty ordinary stuff. It has consistently rejected the Pearson–Trudeau–Mulroney formula. As the association puts it repeatedly in its literature,

> Billions and billions of dollars have been spent on Official Bilingualism since its inception in 1969, much of it concealed in the internal spending of ministries.

> The Official Languages Act is not only racist in concept, it is divisive, destructive and discriminatory in its implementation.

For their work Leitch and his group's members have endured a lot of vitriol over the years. History will show that they represented simply what most

English-speaking Canadians believed and thought before Lester Pearson and Pierre Trudeau bequeathed their peculiar legacies to the country. At all levels and in all forms, Canada's media have treated APEC as harshly as anything George Orwell described in his novel *1984*.

In its two decades of existence, not one columnist, journalist, or academic has challenged a single comma of Ron Leitch's and APEC's work. Instead they concentrate their guns on his character and that of the organization's members.

Kenneth Whyte, a columnist for the *Globe and Mail*, exemplified most journalists' approach to the organization. Two days before the 1993 federal election, he wrote:

> When white-supremacist Wolfgang Droege was discovered to be an Ontario member of Reform and turfed out in 1992, the party's head of policy, Tom Flanagan, did some research on extremist organizations. He found that Ontario, with groups like the Alliance for the Preservation of English in Canada and the Heritage Front, is the hotbed of organized, right-wing racism in Canada. "It was obvious," he says, "that when the Reform Party expanded into Ontario, this element would try to flood in." (*GM*, Oct 23/93)

Whyte tells his readers nothing of his source, Tom Flanagan. The latter had himself been turfed out of the Reform Party for a whole lot of reasons — such as the internecine wars within the Reform family.

In a series of pamphlets circulated widely during the Referendum, "Constitutional Countdown," APEC outlined three distinct periods of Canadian history (Appendix C).

Media character assassination boasts a long and convoluted history in Canada, as it does elsewhere. **George Grant**, the celebrated author of *Lament for a Nation: The Defeat of Canadian Nationalism* (1965), wrote a subsequent work, *Technology and Empire* (1969), in which he recognized the attitudes that cause the problem as he documented the attacks he had endured for his views:

> A couple of years ago I wrote a book about the dissolution of Canadian sovereignty. These days when psychologising is the chief method for neutralizing disagreeable opinions, my psyche was interpreted as harking back in nostalgia to the British empire and old fashioned Canada. This was the explanation of why I did not think that the general tendencies of modern society were liable to produce human excellence. In this era when the

500

homogenising power of technology is almost unlimited, I do regret the disappearance of indigenous traditions, including my own. It is true that no particularism can adequately incarnate the good. But is it not also true that only through some particular roots, however, [*sic*] partial, can human beings first grasp what is good and it is the juice of such roots which for most men sustain their partaking in a more universal good? (p. 68)

Ron Leitch was less fortunate.

The more preferred voices to pontificate on controversial issues were invariably inside experts. Very few of these "authorities" had first-hand knowledge about the protest movements they dismissed as radical and extreme. Luminaries of the left far outnumbered all others in informing Canadians about the state of their nation. One of these was **Murray Dobbin**, a broadcast and print favourite — particularly of the CBC. A Saskatchewan-born writer and journalist, he has studied the grassroots origins of the Co-operative Commonwealth Federation (CCF), the pro-genitor of the New Democratic Party (NDP). In his book *Preston Manning and the Reform Party*, he writes: "Of all the Ontario organizations labelled 'extremist,' the Alliance for the Preservation of English in Canada (APEC) figures most prominently in the fortunes of the Reform Party. The evidence suggests a kind of love-hate relationship between the party and the virulently anti-French, anti-Quebec organization" (p. 109).

Neither Reform nor APEC was presented accurately in this slap-dash appraisal. APEC is neither anti-French nor anti-Quebec. Indeed, as time bore out, far more of that type hung out in Manning's Reform Party than in APEC. Nevertheless, as a left-leaning academic and politically correct journalist, Dobbin enjoyed a broad platform from which to slam anyone of whom he disapproved. He was frequently invited to speak on the CBC. In his quick-and-dirty biography, *The Politics of Kim Campbell* (1993), he dished up this: "Imposing a rigid notion of social cohesion on a country as increasingly diverse as Canada would be extremely difficult. In this determined objective, Campbell is much more akin to Preston Manning and Reform Party guru William Gairdner than she is to Brian Mulroney" (p. 54).

Throughout his writings on what he views as right-wing politicians, Dobbin jumps from one ludicrous judgement to another without missing a beat. **Bill Gairdner**, for example, is not a member of the Reform Party. In fact, he has been persona non grata at party functions since its 1991 convention in Saskatoon. Surely Dobbin should have known that the priests of the Reform Party — such as columnist Kenneth Whyte — openly boasted of how the party had sanitized itself from what Whyte labelled "Author William Gairdner: Anti-Asian and gone" (*Act of Faith*, p. 160). To link the pinkest of the Red Tories, Kim Campbell, with Preston Manning on just about anything, let alone a vision of the country, was worse than silly.

Those who call APEC anti-French and extremist should read a thirty-page booklet presented to the Select Committee on Ontario in Confederation in August 1991. *Constitutions Are For People Not Politicians* never saw the inside of a Canadian bookstore. Ironically, here's a far more popular contribution from *Toronto Star* columnist Richard Gwyn that agrees with APEC very nicely: "Bilingualism, as [Trudeau] saw it, was a basic human right, no different in kind from other human rights like freedom of speech. . . . Part of the problem was that bilingualism, in the end, had to mean, well, *two equal languages;* being a little bit bilingual being as impossible to achieve as being a little bit pregnant. . . . Trudeau knew this all along. He fibbed about it as a necessary means to an end . . ." (*Northern Magus*, pp. 220, 221).

"Fibbed"? Throughout history nations have been destroyed by such deceptions. Canada, too, it seemed, would not escape such a fate.

Mordecai Richler, the prominent Jewish Montreal writer, achieved the status of an icon for two reasons. First, he has raw talent and humour. Second, he is accepted as an ethnically correct dissenter. In the constitutional three-ring circus, he got away with statements as inaccurate as they were daring and commandeered public attention whenever he wanted it. He established himself as a major commentator in the U.S. and Canada on political happenings through essays and a book, *Oh Canada! Oh Quebec!* He wrote for the American magazine *The New Yorker*.

Official Bilingualism divided the insiders and the outsiders. If the country splits, this is the only faultline that historians will discover snaking across the country from one end to the other.

The country's awards system bears this out. Not a single Canadian who opposes the Pearson–Trudeau–Mulroney vision holds any place of honour in the country. Three-quarters of the population are therefore ineligible for public recognition in any form. Trudeau used to assure the citizenry that anyone who disagreed with his vision of a bilingual nation clearly believed in two nations. Mulroney went further. Those who disagreed with *him* were "the enemies of Canada."

On TV screens and in magazines and newspapers, character assassination was fast becoming a bigger national sport than Canada's beloved hockey. Look at the case of the former Alberta premier, **Don Getty**. For a while he played ball with Ottawa. He kept his personal views to himself. For the time being he pushed for a Triple-E Senate and other matters dear to Westerners.

Then he did it. On January 9, 1992, Getty said the unthinkable. Where Preston Manning knuckled under executive-federalist pressure, Getty openly questioned Official Bilingualism. For the effect he had, he might as well have tried to take over APEC. To this day he exists in Coventry for that candour.

Having conspired with Trudeau on bilingualism in 1963, Canada's politicians closed the door on free speech — with one exception. The irony is that Quebec remains the only province where the restrictions on freedom of expression have earned it international condemnation — and yet that same policy, bilingualism, is a legitimate topic for debate there. It is considered bread-and-butter conversation, regardless of the opinions a person holds.

Mel Hurtig presented an interesting anomaly on the scene. Here was an insider from the Trudeau camp, a former book publisher, who, try as he might, never made it as the outsider he yearned to be. He was best known as the founder and spark behind several influential organizations: first the Committee for an Independent Canada and, second, the modern version, The Council of Canadians.

The Council of Canadians gathered together a collection of like-minded economic nationalists — mostly far-left Liberals — who attacked the Conservatives regularly on all fronts, from Free Trade to Meech Lake. Himself inoculated with Trudeaumania, having run for the Liberals in 1968 (and lost when every Liberal of note seemed to have won), Hurtig assumed more shapes than a changeling, which is what the *Star's* Dalton Camp once suggested of him on November 25, 1992. At the height of the Meech Lake crisis, from February to May 1990, Hurtig conjured up noisy roadshows across the country billed "Why Brian Mulroney is the Worst Prime Minister in the History of Canada."

He made good speeches. He entertained appreciative audiences for an hour or two at a time. Like Reform's Preston Manning, he even wrote a book to flesh out and push his ideas to as many people as possible. *The Betrayal of Canada* hit the best-seller lists in 1991. Late the following year he and forty like-minded people announced the formation of a new political party. Predictably, the party attracted and boasted prominent figures from the arts — Margaret Atwood, Farley Mowat, Timothy Findley, and David Suzuki. If the Reform Party was claiming to be a "grassroots" movement of the extreme right, Hurtig's National Party of

503

Canada, without saying so, was donning the obverse label, on behalf of the extreme left. As the new leader put it,

> The Liberal Party of Jean Chrétien has become far too conservative and far too continentalist. Right-wing Liberals now dominate the party and its platform. . . . Meanwhile, Preston Manning's Reform Party (which has a disarming name) seems more and more to be just another extreme right-wing party — more a throwback to the 19th century than true pioneers of modern political and economic change. . . . (*A New and Better Canada*, p. 4)

Of course, Hurtig's wholesale socialism was Trudeau liberalism regurgitated and reconstituted with a good shot of NDP firewater. The National Party adorned itself with the trappings and slogans of the former "philosopher king," right down to a "fair and just society." From the party's genesis, the leader endorsed "bilingual government services so that people from Quebec will feel at home across Canada. . . . We support the Canadian mosaic concept of multiculturalism." And he added, with no apparent awareness of the contradiction in terms, "However, we strongly believe all Canadians should be equal under the law and that this should be the rock-solid basis of any enlightened constitution" (*A New and Better Canada*, p. 37).

Abhorrence of the Free Trade Agreement with the United States ran deep through the Canadian psyche, and the National Party of Canada adopted it as its raison d'être. Just before Meech failed, Hurtig said earnestly, "I really believe there will be no Canada within a few years" (*Star*, May 11/90).

So he hammered away determinedly at the FTA. When it seemed to have merged with Meech Lake, he condemned the hybrid as "a totally deadly combination" (*GM*, Apr 14/90). The year before he founded his party, he set his own agenda: "priority number one: we must get rid of the terrible inept, nation-destroying Mulroney government in the next federal election. Next, as soon as we possibly can, we must abrogate the Free Trade Agreement" (*Star*, Oct 4/91).

One of Hurtig's associates, **Maude Victoria Barlow**, captured a throne for herself — and a magazine cover — as co-founder and head of his brainchild, the Council of Canadians. By 1992 she had become the driving force behind the 21,000-member Ottawa-based organization. After protesting "I hate having my photograph taken," she posed in a hot-pink Holt Renfrew suit for the cover of the June 1992 issue of *Saturday Night* magazine: "The Real Leader of the Opposition: Fed up with politicians, big business, and free trade? Maude Barlow's got all the answers." She once served as Trudeau's social justice adviser on women's issues. To her, David Peterson was a good guy. All the Liberals were good guys, and the NDP were not really all that bad. The Liberals were sort of OK but should really be challenged or merged with the NDP.

With her co-author Bruce Campbell, she wrote *Take Back the Nation*, a simple guide to why Canada needs democracy. The book brushes off the Meech Lake process as deplorable. Plump with platitudes, it offers readers a comfortable kindergarten-level analysis of many of Canada's problems. She happily supports Quebec nationalism — as long as it doesn't break up the country. Unfortunately Barlow does not grasp the cultural, philosophical conflict between the English and the French heritages: "In order to accommodate different versions of equality we will have to seek a fusion of individual and collective rights" (*Sat Night*, June/92).

And she brags, "There is a need for people like me, as part of a democratic nonpartisan movement, to coordinate who coalesces with whom." Since the world is composed of good guys and bad guys, Maudy easily distinguished between the different players for others: Preston Manning was a bad guy. Brian Mulroney with his "corporate agenda" was a traitor who sold out the country. She demanded that Canadians "push the Liberals" to scrap the Free Trade Agreement.

As for the Charlottetown Accord, she was in favour of it — with a possible caveat. She said so to a constitutional conference at York University on September 24, 1992, one month before the Referendum: "What we need is not a bunch of astronauts and hockey stars telling us to go out and love our country. . . . I want the legal text. . . . I want to vote Yes and I mean it sincerely" (*Star*, Sept 25/92).

Like every other group in the country, the arts community copped out en masse and very publicly.

In his musings on the fearful business, **Robertson Davies** demonstrated some of this pussy-footing and play-acting. In the middle of the Meech debate, the internationally respected man of letters wrote an article for *Harper's*, which he grandly titled "Signing away Canada's soul": "A nation of losers, of exiles and refugees. Modern Canada is a prosperous country, but the miseries of its earliest white inhabitants are bred in the bone, and cannot, even now, be rooted out in the flesh" (Jan/89).

The line publicized his own best-selling novel more than it stated any principles. Canadians had to at least welcome his wry humour, which was more than they could attribute to the other anglophones who turned their attention to the subject. On PBS's "MacNeil/Lehrer NewsHour" a month before Meech died, Davies intoned solemnly, "At a time when we needed a Disraeli, we have a Mulroney" (May 25/90).

Humorist **Charlie Farquharson**, alias **Don Harron**, joined the pundits as a refreshing voice of reason: he marched through various booths at a Toronto-area snowmobile show during the federal election in 1993 displaying a placard that read "Vote Refarm Party."

On the whole, arrogance and indifference characterized the writers and artists in English Canada. Rankled by an article by the *Globe and Mail*'s national columnist Jeffrey Simpson ("Silence greets an internal threat," May 16/90), novelist **Timothy Findley** crept out of his precious-pea world to lamely defend intellectual degeneracy, indifference, and bone-laziness:

Mr. Simpson is dead wrong in asserting that the artists and writers of this country are failing to respond to the issues of Meech Lake. He joins most of his media colleagues in apparently believing that Meech Lake is only about Quebec when it is clearly about a great deal more.... Canadian artists and writers are voicing their response to Meech every day in the active role they play in the pursuit of women's rights, native rights, gay and lesbian rights, language rights, the funding of food banks, the war against AIDS, the establishment of public housing, the defeat of government censorship, the preservation of wilderness and other environmental issues. (*GM*, May 29/90)

The little darlings of Canned-Lit could only mewl, unable to muster intellectual champions among their number to win the Canadian soul. Writers have wrung their hands helplessly over many of the great civilizations of history as those societies have steadily declined. So Canada's own behaved true to history. Save for a rare exception like Mordecai Richler, the Canada Council literati, the crew who proudly wore tiny Ceramic Snowflakes for good conduct, knew their places. Their fellow Canadians heard only duck-billed platitudes from most of them.

Among the few activists who did defend something they believed in, even if it was big government, stood **Farley Mowat**. Like most writers, he staunchly supported CBC and other state cultural institutions. The Conservative Policy Conference of August 8, 1991, passed a resolution calling for the privatization of the CBC and then sent out a press release on January 25, 1992, predicting that Manning's Reform Party would dismantle the Mother Corp., given half a chance. Mowat saw his chance. He seized the banner of Mel Hurtig's Council of Canadians to spearhead a fundraising campaign he named "Friends of Canadian Broadcasting" — Friends of

CBC. The powerful lobby group that grew out of this campaign drew celebrity authors and journalists Pierre Berton and Peter C. Newman as well as Deborah Coyne, the constitutional lawyer. In a letter the organization mailed to thousands of Canadians, Mowat blubbered, "The crowning glory and linchpin of our broadcasting system is, of course, the CBC," and he called it "one of the few, *truly* Canadian institutions."

At one point, **Patricia Smart**, an Ottawa writer who had won the Governor General's Award in 1989 for French non-fiction, entered the fray from Carleton University, where she taught French. She launched a feeble offensive against Richler the literary lion. Smart submitted a one-page letter to the media attacking him for daring to say publicly what he thought:

> We respect the rights of artists to be critical of society. . . . [However, Richler's work contains certain statements] that we fear will fuel prejudice and unjustified anger against Quebec in English Canada. . . . Unfortunately, emotional and unreasoned attacks like those of Mordecai Richler can ignite such inter-cultural antagonisms, ones that in the present climate could destroy the possibility that still remains for conciliation between Quebec and English Canada. (*GM*, Apr 3/92)

Of the twenty-five others who affixed their signatures to the letter, some of the most prominent were Stephen Clarkson, co-author of the 1991 best-seller *Grits* and a Governor General's Award winner; New Democrat Pauline Jewett; and James Laxer, Maude Barlow, Judy Rebick, Mel Watkins, and Abraham Rotstein. Even a publisher leavened the mix — James Lorimer. The barb bounced off Richler. Their target merely shrugged and drew another chuckle from his fellow Canadians: "They're the usual rent-a-crowd. They write letters, that's all they're good at" (*Star*, Apr 3/92).

Robert Blohm raised questions about Quebec's plans for independence and general financial stability when he worked as a private investment banker in Montreal and Toronto in 1991. That same year two articles of his were published, one in the *Globe and Mail* — "Financial future: going it alone's a risky business" (*GM*, Jan 14/91) — and another in the *Financial Post* — "Quebec leads way to foreign borrowing: Currency exposure highest in North America" (*FP*, Mar 8/91).

A year and a half later, Blohm had metamorphosed himself into a U.S. investment banker living safely offshore. He could publish whatever he wanted to say about Canada in the *Wall Street Journal*. His critical piece

"Requiem for Quebec Inc." appeared in Canada's prestigious literary journal *The Idler* in September–October 1992. In it, Blohm as Yankee writer opened up:

> Quebec chronically suffers from the industrial world's worst combination of annual external trade and deficits per person. . . .
>
> Quebec, with one-quarter of Canada's population, and with its share of the federal debt, accounts for one-half of Canada's total foreign payments deficit every year, the main reason why the value of the Canadian dollar has sunk below its historical levels and why high Canadian interest rates are needed to bolster the Canadian dollar and service the debt. An independent Quebec would walk away with as much as two-thirds of Canada's total foreign payments deficit, depending on capital flight. . . .
>
> But the Quebec Kremlin planners' dreams [Hydro-Québec] were dealt a death blow when New York state cancelled the pending kingpin export contract last year [1991]. . . .
>
> In the past half-decade, more young people have moved out of Montreal than all other Canadian cities combined. . . . The population is aging more rapidly than any other on either American continent. . . .

Other insiders trapped within the geographical and intellectual confines of Canada wallowed in their own profundities before the enrapt media. As the American-born president of the National Action Committee for the Status of Women, **Judy Rebick** consistently exploited the warm hospitality of the mass media, especially CBC. She could pour generous amounts of abuse on others and be treated and greeted by the media as a respected insider. For all her speechifying and vilification of those she considered enemies because they disagreed with her opinions, she accomplished absolutely nothing. Indeed, she might even have set the women's movement back a century or so.

Mulroney's voluble Minister of Fisheries, formerly a leadership hopeful for the Conservative Party, the Hon. **John Crosbie** sent himself to the doghouse every time he allowed his (in)famous wit out of its box. In a humourless land, he had tried to defend his inability to speak French to reporters on Thursday, May 26, 1983. That stumble cost him the Tory leadership: "I cannot talk to the Chinese people in their own language, either. . . . I can't speak to the German people in their own language" (MacDonald, *Mulroney*, p. 188).

Crosbie never recovered from the storm he kicked up with that flip remark. Forever after the media scorned him as anti-French. This despite his complete capitulation to the revisionist historical concept of Canada in penance. To a Tory gathering, he said, "We have a leader [Mulroney] who is the perfect embodiment of bilingualism in Canada. We have to back him if we want the Canadian people to be comfortable with us. . . . To be accepted as a national party in Canada you have to accept the policies and practices of bilingualism no matter how small the minority" (*GM*, Apr 25/88). A Trudovnic after all.

Meanwhile, the outsiders in Canada multiplied from hundreds into hundreds of thousands, particularly during the Mulroney era. Leaders of dissent, people like **Elmer Knutson**, founder of the Confederation of Regions (CoR) Party, were held up to public scorn. Despite ridicule from every quarter, CoR managed to establish itself as the Official Opposition to the government of New Brunswick. This profoundly shocked Frank McKenna, who had to face an anti-bilingual CoR Party sitting across the floor from him, under the leadership of Arch Pafford.

The triumph of Pafford's provincial party made no difference to Elmer Knutson's public treatment. He continued to be the butt of patronizing and snide articles. Reporters described him as "big" or "beefy." While he was obviously a controversial character, even outrageous, Knutson was also dangerously well informed about political machinations in Western Canada — particularly the inner workings of Ernest C. Manning's Social Credit movement — and armed with a vast inventory of research accumulated over many years. He recognized the terrible threat to Canadian democracy that the mainstream political parties represented, and he talked about it openly. To him, the guilty parties included the Reform Party, which was waffling on its own stated principles and policies by 1992.

An effective promoter, Knutson could rile people in two seconds and make enemies even faster. He liked to seize attention by kicking off any discussion with a zinger. Here's a sampling from Gord McLaughlin's profile of him in the *Financial Post* magazine, "Thunder from the Right" (Nov/91): "It really starts with the fact that we've never confederated." His thesis may be a gross over-simplification in complex Central Canada, but it cannot be dismissed as sheer lunacy. And that, of course, is the appeal of the CoR Party: "If you go back 1,000 years, the British and the French have been continually at war. Why? Language, system of government and their culture. Napoleonic civil code is power from the top – group power. British common law is individual power — power from the bottom. . . . We are gradually being forced into the civil code. Power from the top."

One of the brighter lights in the world of academia, Professor **Philippe Doucet** condescended to pass judgement on the CoR Party's success in

New Brunswick. As far as the Université de Moncton political scientist was concerned, "I don't think [the elected members of the anti-bilingual CoR Party] should be ridiculed. Some of these elected members are not fools. Indeed, they are rather articulate. They're intelligent and educated people and I think we have to come to grips with that and this is serious business. I don't think it will go away by trying to make fun of them" (*Financial Post Mag*, Nov/91).

Such a notion was buried in the avalanche of bafflegab inundating Canadians at that point. Over the years Canada's closed society produced many casualties and unsung heroes. **Jock Andrew** wrote *Bilingual Today, French Tomorrow* to show the great Canadian cultural experiment for what it was. He also wrote *Enough!: (Enough French, Enough Quebec!)* (1988): "Many of you will remember the book *Bilingual Today, French Tomorrow*, which was published in March 1977. That book sold 120,000 copies, even though Trudeau, French Canada and much of the government-subsidized media did everything in their power to stop the book being distributed, and to ridicule both the book and myself" (p. 18).

Andrew has taken more abuse for dissent than any other figure in Canadian political history. Fearful of what he had written, self-appointed censors harassed bookstore managers to return their inventory of the book in its shipping cartons unopened. One of the country's largest chain bookstores, Coles, refused to stock and sell the book and then relented, grudgingly. Turning a blind eye, the company allowed a few copies to be sold at the discretion of store managers. Andrew suffered the same routine with W.H. Smith, though that company did agree to carry some stock at least, thanks to Andrew's great persistence.

> The first printing of *Backdoor Bilingualism* [1979] was stored in a large machine-shop in North Toronto. Within weeks the machine-shop burned to the ground. Not a copy of the book remained. The book was then reprinted, and about ten thousand copies sold. But to my knowledge, *Backdoor Bilingualism* was never mentioned in the whole of the Canadian media, except for one review in the *Toronto Sun*. (p. 18)

In spite of all the attempts to silence this man, the total sales of his three books surpassed 150,000 copies, a publishing record by any standard. As a politically incorrect book, however, no official best-seller list in the country would mention it. To this day, Andrew is a pariah for what he believes and had the courage to write. The former lieutenant-commander in the Canadian Armed Forces has been punished as if he were a criminal.

Andrew's experience is not unique, though his work may be among the more seriously attacked. Through the years of the constitutional debate, a wealth of interesting books and many of the controversial pamphlets that were produced were censored and barred from the mainstream bookstores.

Marjorie Bowker rebelled at a level that was deemed acceptable. She had served with distinction on the bench of the Provincial Court of Alberta's family division for seventeen years. Judge Bowker's "entirely self-financed" book *The Meech Lake Accord: What It Will Mean to You and to Canada* (1990) received wide acclaim from those in power. Her pocket guide allowed that people's desire to debate the premise of founding races and founding cultures was valid but it didn't include the "concerns of minorities, aboriginals, women" (p. 75). On Official Bilingualism, she kept mum. And in due course she was blessed with the Ceramic Snowflake. Naturally, she supported the Charlottetown Accord and voted Yes in the Referendum: "Canada desperately needs a constitutional settlement now to avoid further political instability and a deepening of our economic problems. . . . Whatever misgivings I may have concerning part of the deal, they are not, from my standpoint, sufficient to justify my rejection of the whole. I will be voting Yes" (*Star*, Oct 21/92).

And so it went. So few Canadians would hear any of the voices of their fellow citizens. Sure, some were cranks, extremists, even genuine crazies, and wistful nostalgia buffs living 200 years in the past — or the future, yet they all had ideas and concerns worth discussing.

The infectious Mark Twain humour of **William (Bill) LePoer Trench**, author of another underground publication, *Only You Can Save Canada*, supplied some fun that the country craved. A cartoonist, freelance professional manager, entrepreneur, and philosophical libertarian, "Billy Trench," as he was well known in rebel circles, was a rare bird on the Canadian landscape. Given any opening, he could elevate avuncular corn-shucking to classic art. Here are some Trenchisms that held audiences spellbound from just one session when he spoke:

> More than half of your life you're working for somebody else . . . why does our government need more than 50 per cent when 10 per cent is good enough for God? . . .
>
> I was taught to live within my income. . . . Now I'm being taught to live without it. . . .
>
> It's much better to try and do something and fail then [*sic*] to try and do nothing and succeed. . . .
>
> My message is "do something," even though you're a Canadian. . . .

The only difference between us and the special interest groups is we never speak up and they never shut up. (*Whitby Free Press*, May 12/93)

His trenchant wit conveyed a serious message, too:

The basic problem with our system of education is that it is run by the government. Do you really want the education of your children entrusted to the same type of system that runs Canada Post? The Unemployment Insurance Fund? The Canada Pension Plan? Well, that's who you have doing it, a government bureaucracy. What makes you think they can do a better job at education than they've done at any of their other endeavours? (*Only* You *Can Save Canada*, p. 75; *Consent* #15, a publication of the Freedom Party of Ontario)

Some writers, like Robert Blohm, found their intellectual freedom by leaving the country. The Canadian brain drain.

Insiders and outsiders, executive federalists and thinkers might pause to mull over this reflection from William Greider, the author of *Who will tell the People: The Betrayal of American Democracy* (1992), on "mock democracy":

Governing elites, not surprisingly, tend to their own self-interest but, even when their intentions are broadly public-spirited, the result is generally the same: The people are missing from the processes of self-government and government itself suffers from the loss. Disconnected from larger public purposes, people can neither contribute their thinking to the government's decisions nor take any real responsibility for them. Elite decision makers are unable to advance coherent governing agendas for the nation, however, since they are too isolated from common values and experiences to be persuasive. *The result is an enervating sense of stalemate*. [emphasis mine] (p. 12)

Kenneth McDonald edited the newsletters of the National Citizens' Coalition from its inception in 1976 to 1987. A skilled freelance writer and ex-*Globe and Mail* columnist, he published an excellent paperback that was available mainly *outside* bookstores. In *Keeping Canada Together* he wrote:

What we are witnessing is an extension, over the whole country, of Quebec's way of doing things that has come about through Quebec's effective vote control of the national government. . . .

Clearly, no relief is in sight as long as the present style of government continues. (p. 15)

Victor Forster, an octogenarian, is another underground messenger with guts. In *Conning the Canadians, Book Three: The End of Canada Being One Nation* (1993), he wrote:

Today, Quebec is not a province, but is now the state of Quebec, a nation. . . . When Pierre Trudeau took office as prime minister in 1968, Canada was one nation, there were no distinct people and Quebec was a province of Canada. . . . The time is overdue for Canadians who love their country to face the harsh reality that our Canada of yesteryear is no more. . . . LET QUEBEC GO! (p. 5)

To maintain harmonious relationship [*sic*] between both nations there shall not be dual citizenship. (p. 113)

There's a very important message for Canadians in all this — Legitimize dissent or lose the federation.

31

Preston Manning,
Thy Kingdom Came

FOR CONSERVATIVE CANADIANS, the birth of the Reform Party of Canada in Winnipeg in 1987 seemed a blessing. Preston Manning's "grassroots" movement promised to fulfil that long-awaited dream of participatory democracy and a major shift away from socialism in the country:

> New Canada should be a balanced, democratic federation of provinces, distinguished by the conservation of its magnificent environment, the viability of its economy, the acceptance of its social responsibilities, and recognition of the equality and uniqueness of all its provinces and citizens.

By the spring of 1991, the Reform movement had attracted a paid membership of 100,000 and seemed prepared to storm Parliament. At the very least, its supporters expected it would become the Official Opposition in a minority Conservative or Liberal government. At the April 7 Saskatoon convention, delegates voted to make Reform a national party that would move eastward into Ontario and the Maritimes. A Gallup poll on April 25 showed the party's popularity had shot up to 16 percent of the country's support in one month, almost doubling its previous support. For the first time, too, the young party surged past the Tories, who had 14 percent. From this point on, for more than a year, although the Tories maintained a marginal lead on the Reform Party, Manning could count on a solid range of support — between 12 and 15 percent — a good base from which to build momentum.

His program comprised the most powerful policy platform in Canadian history. Those who bought in on it knew exactly what they were getting. Every year the party turned out a small blue book of *Principles and Policies* that clearly and succinctly outlined where the party stood on every major issue of public concern. Anyone could easily obtain a slick little pamphlet "56 Reasons why you should support the Reform Party of Canada" (Appendix A).

What a program for a country that had become a socialist dictatorship! Manning had a vision. In his New Canada, citizens would be equal before the law, and there would be law and order as well. The Prairie populist offered citizens the most valuable of all political commodities — hope.

In its formative years the Reform Party was powerfully attractive, despite the opposition thrown at it in a flood of media disinformation and dirty tricks. By 1991 and 1992 the sneering press could not disguise the fact that huge numbers of Canadians were joining up.

Even the *Globe and Mail* did a mea culpa. In an editorial on June 14, 1991, entitled "The Reform Party's legitimate voice," they wrote:

> Preston Manning, leader of the Western-based Reform Party, is on a speaking tour of Ontario: Six thousand bought tickets to his Wednesday address at a convention centre near Toronto's Pearson airport. In the process, he has attracted demonstrators who accuse his party of being racist and fascist.[1]
>
> Does the Reform Party deserve the knock? Not from the reports we've heard, or from Mr. Manning's speeches. . . .
>
> His is a defiantly, unapologetically conservative vision, which appeals to many people who are not bigots, who are not xenophobes, but whose vision of Canada is not that of any of the three main parties. One doesn't have to agree with all it says, or even most of what it says, to recognize the legitimacy of its voice.

As Manning himself put it, "Old Canada — the Canada defined as an equal partnership between two founding races, languages and cultures, the English and the French — is dying" (*GM*, Sept 18/93, quoted in Simpson, *Faultlines*).

Eric Kierans is a former member of the Quebec cabinet of Jean Lesage and the federal Cabinet of Pierre Trudeau.[2] He typified the hue and cry at

Manning's call for reform: "This is absurd. When duality dies, Canada dies. . . . We tend to forget that the primary goal of Confederation was to protect two distinct cultures and languages — two nations, not one — from being submerged in the American melting pot, English (British, if you will) distinctiveness as well as French distinctiveness were both at risk" (*GM*, Sept 18/92, quoted in Simpson, *Faultlines*).

But then, in the summer of 1991, for no immediately apparent reason, the Reform Party stalled. As Canadians were to discover over the next two years, there were two Reform Partys of Canada: the one defined in policy and promoted so well by Manning, and the real Reform Party — the party as managed by this same leader.

By 1991, more than four years since its inception, the party was plagued with internal strife. The signs were everywhere. Manning proved himself a lightweight; he pandered to the scribes. Instead of championing the live wires in his movement as the very lifeblood of a populist party, he became paranoid about any hint of unrest or question about his policies. Stung by no-see-ums, he quickly crushed any initiative, concluding his own followers were suspect and not to be trusted. And so the media became more important than the movement he led. If the barons of the press accused his party of being full of racists, extremists, and kooks, he believed it, too. When the media killed him for calling the Charlottetown Accord "Mulroney's deal" during the Referendum campaign, Manning missed the obvious and recanted. Of course it was Mulroney's deal. Mulroney said so.

That same year, he made matters worse. At this turning point in the party's history, he took off for months and months to write *The New Canada*, a Manning family portrait and a history of Reform. In 1992, in the middle of the party's eastern expansion plans into Ontario, where it would win or lose national power, he set off on a book tour to sell his "memoirs." Anyone who tried to approach him, even at what were ostensibly Reform gatherings, was forced to wait while he sat under guard at a desk doing his touring-celebrity thingy. Local organizers were floored that he seemed prepared to devote so much time to playing author.

He never moved in any hurry. As he had said many times, there would be a Reform government some day, sometime before the turn of the century. In the first round, he always said, some forty or fifty Reformers would be elected. Then his small band in second or third place would act as a "body of influence" to persuade government to implement Reform's agenda. Like many Western protest party leaders before him, Manning preferred moral over practical victories.

In the meantime, hundreds of active members were discovering the party operated like a military operation, bristling with rigid procedural manuals, unworkable instructions for constituency executives, and secret bulletins to select party officials. Manning had laid it all out. The executive council in Calgary dispensed an endless stream of written and oral dispositional judgements on correct and incorrect behaviour.

Under seige from within, real and imagined, and from outside, the Reform Party transmogrified itself into a witches' coven. It shifted from a populist movement into a narrow cabal of control freaks mounting a religious crusade. Information was grudgingly released on a need-to-know basis only. Constituency presidents received one level of information; apparatchiks at a lower level in the organization were given less. An ordinary member didn't have a clue what was going on.

The leader on the hustings was the key. Manning himself would come to town, as he had planned to do several months in advance, yet only a handful of the insiders knew he even intended to visit. The promotional backup and the guidance Calgary promised its constituency organizations never materialized. Secrecy prevailed to "protect" the leader. Manning told Reform executives flatly that he would avoid controversy. He repeatedly called it dangerous to "my personal health and well-being" (Kenneth Whyte, *Sat Night*, July–Aug/93).

When disputes arose, ones that might threaten party solidarity, carefully chosen stormtroopers were ordered out from Calgary to douse the potential bushfires. All constituency activities were monitored through regional co-ordinators who instantly fed what they knew back to headquarters. Spokespeople within the party were "tested" and watched for loyalty and purity of motive in joining. From 1991 to 1993, the party in Ontario maintained its own list of people approved to speak on Reform's behalf. Only two people were approved to speak in the Toronto area. Ironically, almost any non-member of the party was permitted to babble about anything he or she chose to Reform members, as long as the subject wasn't racism. The odd time an unacceptable person addressed a party gathering of any sort, Calgary headquarters could plead ignorance of it and hush-hush the matter. Nothing was too trivial to concern what became known as the "Calgary Mafia" — the National Executive Council of the party (NEC).

As a result of its paranoia, the real Reform Party died, smothered from within, long before the 1993 federal election.

How would Manning govern Canada? One had only to look at how the party treated those of the party members Manning judged wayward. Some have estimated that as many as thirty people were ejected from the party before the 1993 election. The problems date back to the very beginning of the movement.

Stan Roberts, Manitoba, 1987–88

The Reform Party acknowledges Stan Roberts as one of its founding members. The Manitoba Liberal MLA of two terms and former president of the Canadian Chamber of Commerce brought an impressive background and outstanding connections to the movement back in 1987.

At the founding convention of the party in Winnipeg, from October 30 to November 1, 1987, however, he quit the leadership race in disgust. In a private letter to his supporters, he complained that the National Executive Council was dominated by "fundamentalists, faith-healers and religious fanatics." In the end the party castigated him as a "two-time loser" (*Western Report*, July 4/88).

Bill Gairdner, Ontario, 1991

The author of the best-selling *The Trouble With Canada* (1990) was a successful "outsider" Canadian with remarkable achievements as an athlete, businessman, and author.

Some 1,200 delegates attended the April 4–7, 1991, annual convention of the party in Saskatoon. Gairdner was guest speaker. As Kenneth Whyte, a party member and columnist, put it, he was welcomed because "so long as he wasn't officially associated with the party, there was no danger of being caught in controversies he might engender." Whyte's description of Gairdner in *Act of Faith*, the big magazine-picture book of the Reform Party put out by B.C. Report Books (1991), was revealing. Under a photo of the author was the caption "Author William Gairdner: Anti-Asian and gone." He added, "reporters began querying Manning about his party's association with William Gairdner. . . . Mr. Gairdner is an extreme libertarian with strong nativist sentiments and an aversion to Asian immigration" (*Act of Faith*, p. 160).

What Gairdner actually wrote was:

Quite understandably, India and China with, between them, massive populations totalling almost a quarter of the world's people, could present more qualified applicants [for immigration to Canada] than most of the other countries put together. So the immigration official asked to use a fair point system could end up allowing vastly more applicants into Canada from

India and China than from any other nation — just because more of them want in. This systemic bias, due not to any discriminatory motive, but to its opposite, will automatically discriminate against less populous nations. . . . Theoretically, in a sufficient number of years they could dominate every profession in Canada. In 250 years Canada could be a Chinese nation. If that's what we want, then let's get on with it. But if it's not, then let's say so and take steps to ensure it doesn't happen. . . .

. . . After all, *surely any nation has the right to defend itself against demographic capture, or, if you prefer, against passive racial or cultural takeover.* (pp. 412-13)

Whyte perverted the facts. Gairdner's points deserved serious consideration. Gairdner had also insisted that the solution be a democratic one. Because of the distasteful inferences, Manning ran. He let Gairdner carry the full weight of every scurrilous attack the left-wing media could make on him. And so Gairdner was branded a racist.

Kenneth Whyte, on the other hand, gained a great deal. He became the Western editor for *Saturday Night* magazine. In 1993, the ambitious reporter became a guest columnist for the *Globe and Mail*. In 1994 he graduated to editor of *Saturday Night*.

Doug Collins, British Columbia, 1988

In British Columbia, Doug Collins, a columnist for Vancouver's *North Shore News*, ran afoul of Manning, too. In 1988 he sought the nomination for Capilano–Howe Sound in the centre of affluent Vancouver. The noisy right-winger, who called himself "Doug Horrible," asked people to think about Canada's immigration policy, which he said was making the country a "Shangri-La for crooks, liars and bums from all over."

There is little doubt that he baited the Reform leader, dismissing him as "wimpish" and someone who "would make a good Sunday school teacher" (*Western Report*, Nov 7/88). But instead of rejecting the prospective candidate on these perfectly legitimate grounds, Manning chose the weaker course. He allowed Collins's personal reputation to be assaulted. Collins was accused of being a racist not for what he said or did but because he refused to submit in writing directly to the party that he was not.

In fact, in spite of his attacks against the leader, the party accepted Collins's candidacy, providing the constituency association would pass a resolution rejecting racial discrimination while Collins was the candidate there. And providing Collins would endorse that in writing.

Collins was cornered. No one mentioned any presumption of innocence.

Once the constituency membership passed a motion condemning Manning's suggestion by a vote of 145 to 13, Collins refused to budge:

> What's [Reform] all about? Political correctness. Manning quakes at the thought of being denounced by the media as a racist. . . .
> He hasn't learned, and probably never will learn, to carry the ball to the enemy — and damn the media.
> He is even fuzzy on official bilingualism. . . . And he can turn political somersaults overnight as he did on the GST, which he [now] supports.
> No other party exercises such iron control over the nomination of candidates though Manning came on the scene yelling about "paramount constituency rule" and similar bilge. His screening process wouldn't shame that of the FBI. (*The North Shore News*, June 2/93)

On Monday, June 7, 1993, a large audience showed up to witness an uproar at North Vancouver's city council meeting. Having been awarded the "Canada 125" commemorative Confederation medal, Collins was attacked by Lionel Kenner, who marshalled a delegation to protest it. "It is appalling," Kenner said, "that a hatemonger like Collins should receive an award from the Governor General. It is my view the Governor General was deceived" (*NSN*, June 9/93).

Preston Manning took the easy way out again. He refused to stand behind this democratically elected candidate of the Reform Party.

Anne Hartmann, Ottawa, 1989–92

Anne Hartmann, a lawyer and former advisor to the Ontario government, was president and founder of the Northern Foundation, an organization described in the *Ottawa Citizen* as "a political umbrella organization for various right-wing groups in Canada" (Nov 4/89). The foundation published the *Northern Voice* newsletter and boasted about 1,000 members across Canada in 1993.

Hartmann, a feisty fighter, brooked no nonsense from people who levelled unfounded accusations in her direction. A Reform Party member in good standing, she was accused of having written a racist article that the party deemed unacceptable.

In fact, the author of the "racist" article was another person who happened to have the same last name. The then director of policy, strategy, and communications for the Reform Party, Thomas E. Flanagan, contacted the Northern Foundation president by phone and confronted her with his own assessment and speculations. She was insulted and furious.

None of the facts in the case as Manning's executive alleged made any sense. Was Stiltz Hartmann, author of the offensive piece, really Anne Hartmann? Could she be judged by Reform on the basis of such flimsy evidence? On March 27, 1992, Flanagan faxed a letter to her demanding:

1. Did you write the attached article?
2. Did you collaborate in writing the article?
3. Do you know who wrote the article?
4. Were you aware of the article before its publication?
5. Might you be closely related to the writer of the article?
6. Is there any other knowledge regarding the article or its author that you could share with us?[3]

A wacky exchange followed between the NEC and Hartmann, during which the accused fired off several somewhat tactless letters to Manning. The party booted her out on November 30, 1992. Like Doug Collins, she had refused to confirm in writing for Calgary her denial of the many allegations. Nor would she deny that she was "Stiltz" Hartmann, although as she said, she was only 5 feet 4 inches tall. The party later retreated and ejected her for "improper" conduct. NEC's judgement was final.

Reform Party executive director Gordon Shaw explained Hartmann's expulsion in a letter dated February 16, 1993, in response to an objection raised by one of her supporters:

. That decision was taken because of a pattern of facts linking the Northern Foundation with persons or organizations that espouse racialist [sic] ideologies. To take an example that is completely within the public domain, the Northern Foundation in April of this year invited Paul Fromm to speak at a conference in Ottawa.[4] Not long afterwards, the Toronto *Sun* revealed the existence of videotape proving that Mr. Fromm had spoken to a rally of the avowedly racist Heritage Front.

As for Hartmann's newsletter, he wrote, "the Northern Voice version [of the circumstances] has been edited to be less overt, but still gets the racist message across."

So she was guilty of association with those who might or might not be racist or appear to be such. Hartmann had even run public forums in which speakers from a wide variety of conservative and right-wing organizations could speak out.

There's a revealing side-play to the Hartmann incident. Geoffrey Wasteneys, a member of the Northern Foundation, wrote to Clifford Fryers, chairman of the NEC, to ask why Hartmann had been expelled from the party. Fryers is a tax lawyer and senior partner with the prestigious law firm Milner & Fenerty in Calgary. For six years he lived in Ottawa and worked in the litigation section of the justice department. Of himself he brags, "I'm the tough side of the party. I drive people to get done what we need to get done to win" (*Star*, Oct 18/93). When he answered Wasteneys's letter on January 4, 1992, he casually dropped another bombshell:

> It is our view that both the Northern Foundation and A.P.E.C. [the Alliance for the Preservation of English in Canada] are special interest groups whose extreme views are in conflict with those of the Reform Party. While we would prefer that our members would understand this conflict and avoid it, we take no action against those members who merely hold a membership in these groups.
>
> However, if a member accepts a senior executive position with such a group and comes into a situation where through their actions or public utterances they adopt a "conduct judged improper, or unbecoming, or likely to adversely affect the interests and reputation of the Party . . . the Party has the right under Section 2(d) (iii) of the Party Constitution to terminate the membership.

What a blooper! Thousands of Reform Party members were APEC members as well. Throughout Canada, prominent Reformers held senior positions in APEC. It was a union as natural as ducks and water. Of course there were differences between them, but they were not all that great. Unless, that is, the Reform Party weren't sincere about language reform along the lines they proposed in their literature. Manning chose to ignore a friendly overture in writing from Ron Leitch, president of APEC.

Gary Cummings, Lloyd Kirkham, Herb Schulz, and George Van Den Bosch and the "Manitoba Question," 1992[5]

The "Manitoba Question" demonstrated just how the Reform Party's leadership functioned by 1992. Manning assessed the problem in a letter sent to all of that province's Reform members on January 8:

Over the last year we have witnessed continuous wrangling over the role of Manitoba Council. Some of our own members and executives have also apparently been involved in circulating confidential party material, and anonymous memos critical of myself and national office, to other Reformers, the media, and our political opponents. Many of these undisciplined actions appear to be rooted in personality conflicts, resentment of the growing numbers and influence of newer people within the party, disputes over who really represents the grass roots in Manitoba (Executive Council members, constituency executives or Manitoba Council) and resentment of anyone from the national office who tries to help. . . .

On the basis of my personal observations, and other Council members and staff people who have attempted to address the dissension in Manitoba, most of this dissension *appears* to centre around the activities of George Van Den Bosch (Winnipeg St. James), Lloyd Kirkham (Winnipeg South Centre), Gary Cummings (Winnipeg South), and Herb Schulz (St. Boniface), although this list is by no means all-inclusive [emphasis mine].

In a party memorandum to all Executive Council Members, which Manning signed on January 8, 1992, he said:

The difference between a traditional party and a democratic populist party like the Reform Party is *the manner in which this internal discipline is exercised*. In a traditional party, internal discipline is exercised almost exclusively "from the top down" by the party leadership, national office, and party whips. In a democratic populist party, internal discipline must be exercised "from the bottom up" by the rank and file membership itself, in consultation and cooperation with the party leadership, caucus, and national office.

As we enter 1992 — a year in which we are most likely to have a federal election — the time has come for our grassroots membership in Manitoba to exercise this internal discipline to deal with several problems which are limiting the development of the party in your province.

In another passage, Manning goes on to say,

While our party constitution is silent on the removal of a member of Council [NEC] for inappropriate behaviour, it does provide for terminating the membership of a member for "just cause." . . .

In my judgement, therefore, the time has come to call upon our Manitoba members to begin to exercise that "bottom-up" internal discipline which must be the hallmark of a democratic populist party.

Some democratic movement! Who's up and who's down?

Manning's call for the removal of several dissident party members went to the Manitoba membership. Enclosed with it was a return card that called for a negative or positive response to having certain members removed according to the leader's January 8 letter. The NEC lied about why they were investigating the Manitoba membership. They promised to "democratize" the party structure to respond better to Reformers in the province.

So some very hard-working Reformers were turfed out of the party — George Van Den Bosch, president of the Winnipeg St. James constituency; a member of the NEC, Lloyd Kirkham, who had served two years as president of the Winnipeg South Centre Constituency: Herb Schulz, the founding president of the constituency of St. Boniface who had also served the Reform Party for two years; and finally Gary Cummings.

The Cummings case is particularly interesting because of a letter Manning sent him on July 22, 1991. Among other things, the leader told him, "Your problem, Gary, is not Gordon Duncan [of whom Cummings had complained in writing]. Your problem is Gary Cummings. If you can make these changes, you may yet be an asset to Reform in Manitoba. If not, I fear (but you would want me to be frank) that you will be a liability and find yourself increasingly isolated."

When it was all over, the Reform Party was flattened in the province. In the 1993 federal election, the Liberals won 13 of 14 seats. In the three ridings where Manning had wielded his sword against the three duly elected senior party officials, the plurality of the winning Liberals skyrocketed from the 1988 election total of 23,303 to 55,836 votes. Six of the 7 seats the Progressive Conservatives held fell to the Liberals. Only one Reformer was elected. Yet Reformers in Manitoba had been active in the movement since before the party decided to move eastward.

Six years of work wasted. Had the party won just three of those Conservative seats, Preston Manning would have become the leader of Her Majesty's Loyal Opposition in the House of Commons in October 1993, instead of the separatist leader of the Bloc Québécois, Lucien Bouchard.

John Gamble, QC, Toronto, 1993

The case of John Gamble reads like H.L. Mencken's description of the famous John Thomas Scopes "Monkey Trial" of 1925 in Rhea County, Tennessee, that pitted Charles Darwin against the Book of Genesis. The problem began when Gamble, a former Tory MP, duly secured the nomination for the Reform Party riding of Don Valley West. Under the direction of the leader, however, the party chose to violate its own constitution and disqualify his nomination *before* he had even been nominated.

A Mr. Wayne Hutchinson visited Toronto from the NEC on March 22, 1993. He asked Gamble to voluntarily remove himself as a candidate in the constituency. Gamble refused. Hutchinson produced a letter dated March 16 that told Gamble bluntly that the NEC had passed a resolution on March 12 and 13 that "the Council will invoke articles 4(c) and 4(d) of the Party Constitution and nullify your nomination."

In terms of the party's own constitution, this was illegal. It does not permit a nomination that has not even taken place to be cancelled. Gamble demanded to know why he would be barred from being nominated. Hutchinson offered him no evidence whatsoever of any complaint against him.

Gamble decided to hang in. Having met all the party's rigorous tests, including the completion of a questionnaire laid out over four newspaper-size pages, he was fairly elected as Reform's Don Valley West candidate on March 31, 1993. The party would have to find concrete reasons to turn him down. There were none.

Manning accused him publicly of being nothing more than a "recycled" politician. Gamble had been elected twice to Parliament, and then twice defeated. Coming from a never-elected politician, the accusation raised serious questions about Manning's motives.

The evidence the NEC eventually presented centred around Manning's interpretation of Gamble's failure to win a Conservative seat in the September 4, 1984, election sweep of Brian Mulroney. Cliff Fryers, chairman of the NEC, wrote to David Andrus, Don Valley West's riding president: "To quote from a Globe and Mail article of Sept. 5/84, 'Upset by his extreme right wing views, there was a revolt within the riding association.'"

Here's what was actually reported in the *Globe* that day in an article by Ross Howard headed, "Conservative tide inundates Metro Toronto area ridings":

The only Conservative loss occurred in York North riding where John Gamble, an arch Conservative and particularly unsuccessful leadership contestant, was defeated by York Region chairman Anthony Roman. Mr. Roman is a well known Conservative but was backed by a massive coalition of defectors from both the John Gamble camp and the Aldo Tollis organization to run as a so-called Independent Candidate. He is expected to support, if not join, the Conservatives [which he subsequently did].

Manning feared the fact that Gamble had once been a leadership candidate. The integrity of the evidence, therefore, was irrelevant. The executive council included the following charge against Gamble:

> In the mid-1980's when Mr. Gamble was head of the Canadian chapter of the World Anti-Communist League, his number two man was Paul Fromm, who for two decades has been publicly perceived as having extreme right wing and fascist views. It is because of his past association with people such as Mr. Fromm, groups and activities in conflict with the principles of the Party, and the perceptions surrounding Mr. Gamble, that we have reluctantly concluded that his candidacy would be injurious to the Party, for it may imply that we in some way accept views of that nature, when in fact we rigorously oppose them.

Every accusation was false. Evidence exploding the allegations included news articles and affidavits and testimony from numerous Reform members, which were shipped off to party headquarters in Calgary. It made no difference. The Star Chamber court hearing in Calgary on May 8 upheld the nullification of Gamble's candidacy.

In fact, in total disregard for due process, even more charges appeared, though without corroborating evidence. *Maclean's* later quoted Fryers calling those who disagreed with the way Calgary handled matters a rump group of "negative and destructive individuals who wanted to wrest control of the party into their own hands. It was a power struggle and they lost" (Oct 4/93). In a news release, the party noted the case against Gamble with exquisite brevity: "Mr. Gamble has a history of constant dissension within the Federal Conservative Party while he was a Member of Parliament" (May 21/93).

In a final send-off "Letter to Candidates and Presidents in Ontario," dated May 21, 1993, and signed by Mike Friese, "Secretary On Behalf of the Leader and Executive Council," even more charges suddenly materialized. Now Gamble was accused of associating with others who had "racist overtones."

Gamble lost his appeal. And three of the four Reformers who flew to Calgary to support him were kicked out of office and out of the party, along with Gamble. The result of their appeal shocked them. David Andrus, Richard van Seters, and John Gamble had worked to build the party in Ontario in spite of the Calgary Mafia.[6] A fourth member of the Reform Party found himself abruptly shown the door, too — Louis Allore, a director of the Ontario constituency.

The Reform Party turned on Gamble savagely after the hearing. Through all its investigations and declarations and summations the NEC failed to mention one very telling fact. Before Gamble and his supporters headed out to Calgary for the hearing, the constituency association had polled its membership about what they thought of Gamble's nomination and the NEC's accusations against him. A full 82 percent of the constituency stood behind both Gamble and their party executive association. The Calgary Mafia never acknowledged the poll Gamble and his supporters presented at the appeal.

Mencken's words about the Scopes Monkey Trial in Tennessee, as he reported on it for the *Baltimore Evening Sun* between July 16 and 20, 1925, ring as true for Gamble as they did for Scopes:

> I do not allege here that there is any disposition to resort to lynch law. On the contrary, I believe that there is every intent to give Scopes [or Gamble] a fair trial, as a fair trial is understood among fundamentalists. All I desire to show is that all the primary assumptions are immovably against him — that it is a sheer impossibility for nine-tenths of those he faces to see any merit whatever in his position. He is not simply one who has committed a misdemeanor against the peace and dignity of the State, he is also the agent of a heresy almost too hellish to be stated by reputable men. (Rodgers, *The Impossible H.L. Mencken*, p. 591)

> Such is the punishment that falls upon a civilized man cast among fundamentalists. As I have said, the worst of it is that even the native intelligentsia help to pull the rope. . . . If they remain, they must be prepared to succumb to the prevailing blather or resign themselves to being more or less infamous. (Ibid., p. 603)

The Reform leader had written a letter to Gamble on June 22, 1990, firing another false accusation at him:

> I should also say that the Party prides itself on its grassroots, democratic nature and will not succumb to "the dictates of the backroom power brokers" you refer to. In this regard I must express a concern. In 1984 you secured a highly disputed P.C. nomination and were subsequently defeated in the general election. Indeed, you were defeated by a fellow-P.C. This is an indication to me of a situation where the process by which you received the nomination clearly thwarted the will of party members. The Reform Party has mechanisms to prevent such situations.

Ross Howard writes in the *Globe and Mail* of September 5, 1984, that Gamble was defeated by an "Independent." The other candidate in York North riding, Anthony Roman, had not joined the Conservative Party at that point. He did so after the election. When confronted with the facts, Preston Manning refused to admit his error. He never corrected a major injustice, but simply went about the business thereafter of inspiring and leading his party on the basis of personal integrity.

Louis Allore, Director, Ontario Constituency, 1993

Louis Allore was forcibly expelled from the party for supporting John Gamble, though the reasons given were the same flimsy ones sent to Gamble himself. He reacted sharply on his own behalf:

> As one who is intimately involved with Reform party matters, I know first hand the extent to which the party will go to silence members and nominated candidates who differ with Calgary's approach including [Wayne] Hutchinson's secret criminal-like investigations, dossiers kept by Manning, officially sanctioned cult-like shunning expulsions and nullification of candidates selected by the grass roots. (*Star*, July 25/93)

Preston Manning proved Niccolò Machiavelli's (1469–1527) famous counsel:

> Here is an infallible rule: a prince who is not himself wise cannot be well advised, unless he happens to put himself in the hands of one individual who looks after all his affairs and is an extremely shrewd man. In this case, he may well be given good advice, but he would not last long because the man who governs for him would soon deprive him of his state. . . . So the conclusion is that good advice, whomever it comes from, depends on the shrewdness of the prince who seeks it, and not the shrewdness of the prince on [the receipt of] good advice. (*The Prince*, trans. G. Bull)

B Y 1992 THE REFORM PARTY no longer bothered anyone. In fact, Manning had made himself very valuable to the three executive-federalist parties. The new boy on the street sought neither power nor even political survival. What many people suspected about him was true: Preston Manning was in politics for some other purpose.

Even as late as mid 1993 he was repeating the same mantra to the faithful time and again — that he sought only thirty to fifty seats in the next election. He wanted to "bring pressure" on the government to adopt Reform ideas, he said. He meant exactly that.

Wild rumours circulate about meetings between Conrad Black and Toronto financier Hal Jackman — before his appointment as Ontario's lieutenant governor — and Manning, beginning with a mysterious luncheon.

The media simply pushed the right buttons — racism, immigration, bilingualism, the social net — and the peripatetic leader learned to spout acceptable platitudes. By 1993, Calgary's Keystone Comedy Company had converted the party into a madhouse. If it hadn't been tragic for the thousands of people who placed their faith in the new messiah, it would have made for great comedy. The NEC's list of the unfaithful grew by leaps and bounds.

Those targeted could expect libel, slander, disinformation, character assassination, and personal abuse for their honesty — in writing. Constituency association presidents were instructed to consult their Green Books, a manual not generally available to members, when faced with questionable behaviour or attitudes in their members. Issued on December 11, 1991, the manual contained policy statements and reference material. Its policies had been so watered down that they differed little from government policy.

On Official Bilingualism, for example, the party caucus statement of 1991 said: "We would support minority language services in response to real public demand. We would use the practical local criteria to assess this, not detailed language formulas developed by federal bureaucrats. Such minority services could be provided in languages other than English or French where appropriate . . ." (Caucus Statement No. 16, Nov 20/91).

This matched, and matches, current government practice by which the whole issue becomes a matter of absolute discretion. The Reform Party was not as advanced in protecting citizens' rights as the 1969 Official Languages Act originally required, since it at least set up Bilingual Districts Advisory Boards with common standards for all of Canada.

Party caucus statements were bursting with nonsense. They lumped language opposition groups together as extremists: "These groups advocate policies to promote the use of English at all levels of society, including opposition to most minority language services (except in Quebec) *and hostility to voluntary personal bilingualism through the educational system*" [emphasis mine] (Ibid.).

Typical disinformation. Not one language protest group in Canada advocates anything so hare-brained as "hostility to personal bilingualism through the educational system."

Official Bilingualism wasn't even included in the 1993 election agenda for the party. The issue that had sucked millions of dollars into the party's coffers and up to easily one-half of its people onto its membership rolls was now treated as a mere matter of numbers and cost-cutting. Instead, a relatively minor and much less expensive issue was pushed into the spotlight — multiculturalism. In the end, once he was elected to Parliament, Manning dropped even his attack on multiculturalism.

As time passed, more and more people caught on to how the party functioned. The Western organization expanded into other regions of Canada motivated only to raise funds to keep the scam going. Ontario was being steadily milked as a cash cow.

Eventually Reform's NEC denied the right of assembly within the party. Its insistence on managing dissent within it killed it as a truly national movement. It was another Western protest party shrinking into its home base. The most talented in the party got the message.

Mark Waters was a party member and the son of Senator Stan Waters, Canada's first elected senator and a Reform member. After serving the NEC for thirty-two months, he submitted his swan song letter to the Lower Mainland Council of the party in New Westminster, British Columbia, on August 18, 1990. In it he described the seige mentality of Manning's movement, and he did it from party headquarters on Reform stationery:

> The executive council [NEC] lacks the confidence and leadership abilities to allow full communications amongst the constituencies. Their activities have become progressively more vague as time has passed. Do not allow their lassitude to infect your activities.
>
> The presidents should continue to meet regularly and exchange information and opinions. If not, you may gradually find yourselves only being allowed to receive one way communications from head office and the executive council.

Toronto Sun columnist Douglas Fisher hit the nail on the head as he mulled over the final days of the 1993 election campaign:

> My hunch is that a silent or unheard majority of Canadians never subscribed to most postulates of that "caring" Canada. It was the consequence of top-down idealism and competitive bidding for the support of well-organized interest groups. . . .
>
> Millions never hankered for bilingualism and multiculturalism, or for a fully unionized and highly paid and nicely pensioned public service, or for a generous immigration program of the "rainbow," or for big scale funding

of cultural endeavors and self-government for aboriginal nations, or for gay and lesbian rights, or for the abolition of capital punishment. Even the establishment of the Charter of Rights and the huge power this delegated to the courts has never been an enthusiasm of most Canadians.

By and large Reform is a lightning rod for a range of discontents. . . . As yet Reform is not an emergence of true believers in right-wing ideology. (*Sun*, Oct 15/93)

Fisher has a point. All too frequently Manning's agenda has been set by the media and others outside the movement.

Warren Kinsella, author of *Web of Hate: Inside Canada's Far Right Network*, pounced on his opportunity. He holds that Reform is a movement that attracts "activists . . . with extreme expressions of bigotry and intolerance" (p. 351). After crediting the Reform leader with getting rid of extremists only at the whim of the media, he accuses Manning himself of failing to address the question that "if his party is not racist, why are so many racists attracted to it?"

It's a slinky shot from a well-connected backroom boy of the Liberal Party.[7] Here's the executive assistant to David Dingwall, Jean Chrétien's Minister of Government Services, posing as an objective authority on a political philosophy diametrically opposed to his own. Why should Manning or any leader account for the political views of each and every one of his or her party members? Kinsella also says that every citizen "must work — and work hard," using the law and the educational system to maintain the "multicultural society that is Canada." What kind of Canada? A Canada for whom? These are key questions he has yet to answer.

In his credo *The New Canada*, Manning writes:

New Canada must be a home for the soft hearts/soft heads, and hard heads/hard hearts who populate the political parties. It must be a home for those who want to preserve the best features of Old Canada and those who want fundamental change. It must be a home for both the dreamers and the pragmatists. (p. 115)

Really? He has yet to demonstrate this. Manning is no populist leader in the tradition of the great parliamentarian John George Diefenbaker.

Notes

1 At one particular rally, for example, forty-five protesters were bused in to represent Queer Nation. There were not as many as 100 protesters as reported. They stood outside the convention centre for a while and then faded. The media, including the CBC and the *Toronto Star*, concentrated on this group. The *Star* reported the wrong location for the rally.

2 Today Kierans is a Halifax economist and an associate of the Institute for Research on Public Policy. He became a member of the pro-Meech group Canadians for a Unifying Constitution. During the Meech Lake crisis he wrote, "Meech Lake represents the true spirit of Confederation. Meech Lake, in some form, is going to be passed sooner or later . . ." (*Star*, Mar 3/90). As for the Referendum two years later, he said, "There is only one reason why I wouldn't vote No, and that is that the people in Quebec would use the vote to say that I didn't like Quebec. . . . We are going to have between two and three million people using food banks by December and we have a constitutional problem" (*GM*, Sept 26/92).

3 This letter and all others quoted in this chapter have been widely circulated by mail and by fax throughout the national Reform movement.

4 The conference to which Flanagan referred, "Reclaiming Canada," was held in Ottawa on April 3, 4, and 5, 1992. Paul Fromm was one of fifteen speakers, including Dr. Marguerite Ritchie, president of the Human Rights Institute of Canada, and Mr. Nicholas J. Patterson, president of the Canadian Development Institute.

5 The term "Manitoba Question" was used in the memorandum from the party chairman of the NEC, dated July 15, 1991. Its text was prefaced with "Confidential To Councillors Only — This is extremely sensitive and may not be discussed outside Council."

6 Following the NEC's final decision, Mr. Les Southwell, a member of the NEC for the Atlantic Region, resigned. In part, his fax transmission to Calgary on May 20, 1993, read: "Tomorrow you will be considering the Gamble issue. I sincerely believe that we have been a little hasty. . . . Since that time, more than sufficient evidence has been submitted to indicate that Mr. Gamble and his constituency should be supported by the reversal of our decision and a note congratulating them for their admirable Reform manner in which they presented their case."

On July 27, 1993, an illegally constituted constituency executive in Don Valley West conducted a "Candidate Nomination Meeting" under Calgary's direction. Dr. Clarke Slemon chaired it, as well as the Candidate Selection Committee. On March 31, the eve of Gamble's election for the constituency, Slemon's name appeared as the third one on the ballot. He won twelve votes, or 12.4 percent of the ballot.

7   On the jacket to his book he is described as "formerly a special assistant to Jean Chrétien, [and] now Executive Assistant to a cabinet minister in the Federal Government."

XI

Business as Usual

October 26, 1992, to June 25, 1993

32

Referendum Aftermath
— October 26, 1992, to
February 23, 1993

DON GETTY KNEW WHAT TO DO after the Referendum — run for the hills: "For me, I'm going hunting with my son and my dog" (*Star*, Oct 28/92). The only leader in the country who had had the guts to tell it as it was had paid a terrible price for his honesty.

Frank McKenna had plans of his own. Despite the Referendum, New Brunswick would be the first province to become constitutionally bilingual, he announced not even twenty-four hours after the people of Canada had spoken.

The premier chose Section 43 of the Constitution Act to bypass the unanimity provision required for any major constitutional amendments that affected the entire country. Like the notwithstanding clause, which was never *supposed* to be used to override the Charter of Rights and Freedoms, Section 43 was, in its drafting, a little-known provision intended to help settle minor boundary disputes. Now it would be used for a purpose its authors never envisioned. McKenna pontificated: "At some point you have to take Yes for an answer. At present, while the province is 'officially bilingual,' it can be changed by the legislature" (*Star*, Oct 28/92). Deborah Coyne snapped back immediately:

Did we not learn anything from the referendum debate? . . . [Instead of the Charter of Rights as the law of paramountcy, protecting individual rights, the McKenna proposal is a] constitutional partition of the province into two communities, each of which has equality of status, and the right to "distinct" institutions. This is linked to special legislative status for the New Brunswick government to "promote" these "distinct" institutions. . . . [The proposal] gives the New Brunswick government and legislature a "role" that no other province has, and affirms the government's power over culture — a matter that is currently not assigned to the provinces in the Constitution. (*Star*, Jan 6/93)

McKenna's actions enraged Dr. Marguerite Ritchie, QC, head of the independent Human Rights Institute of Canada. As the institute's founder–president, an eminent international and legal scholar who had served with the justice department, a legal advisor to conferences at The Hague, the United Nations, and numerous other international legal forums, she charged up Parliament Hill. She barraged all the members of Canada's two Houses of Parliament with a news release dated June 7, 1993:

The Human Rights Institute of Canada today charged the Mulroney Government with deliberately lying to Parliament in order to pass an illegal amendment to the Constitution after the October Referendum.

The Institute released a comparison of the actual wording of the Constitutional provision on which the Mulroney government relied, and the fake version that was put before Parliament. The Government chopped out 43 words from the English version of Section 43 of the Constitution Act, 1982, and chopped out or changed 41 words in the French version.

The Government ended up with a version that claimed that anything in the Constitution can be amended by a simple resolution of the legislative assembly of each Province to which the amendment applies.

The Mulroney Government and the McKenna Government in New Brunswick quoted this butchered version as giving authority to amend the Constitution.

The real question is, who protects the people of Canada against the thieves of the Constitution? The Ministers of Justice have failed us. Where are the leaders we can trust?

Ritchie fingered the prime minister and his entire Cabinet. She nailed Joe Clark, who had seconded the amendment put forward by Bernard Valcourt. She reminded the elected representatives that the justice minister was required by law to "see that the administration of public affairs is in accordance with the law." She demanded to know who had worked with McKenna to put those fraudulent words before the Legislative Assembly of New Brunswick and before the Parliament of Canada.

The Commons slid the bill through on February 1, 1993, at the dinner hour, when the media would not be there. Neither Pierre Blais nor his successor Kim Campbell stopped it. Ritchie stressed that Charest had also voted for it.

In an essay in the *Globe and Mail* on October 27, Thomas Courchene, the Queen's University constitutional scholar, summarized:

> As the No vote gained momentum last night, we Canadians were not merely rejecting the Charlottetown accord. We were asserting in no uncertain terms that the conceptions and traditions governing Canada during the past 125 years were no longer appropriate to the Canada of today and tomorrow. . . . We have seen the passing of the old political order . . . the demise of the two founding nations/elite accommodation approach to governing the federation. (*GM*, Oct 27/92)

Even so, Courchene was off the mark. Canadians were not rejecting their heritage since Confederation. They were kicking ass. They were exploding at more than a generation of manipulation and fraud about their Canada — that it was founded on racial engineering that had been constitutionally entrenched from the beginning.

There was a lot to this latest manoeuvre Canadians would never be told. Courchene identified one likely source: "The most ardent advocate of section 43 as the key to unlocking the constitutional impasse is probably Patrick Monahan of Osgoode Hall Law School. [In reference to Meech Lake as it would have affected Quebec,] Monahan (1990) argues that this section is 'the only realistic prospect for accomplishing constitutional changes'" (*Rearrangements — The Courchene Papers*, p. 224).

BUT WHAT OF CANADA'S ABORIGINAL PEOPLES in this Referendum? After all the media flattery and the millions spent to buy their votes, natives on reserves in every province overwhelmingly turned down Charlottetown as surely as they had rejected Meech Lake. In Alberta, only 110 people out of 7,000 cast a ballot. On the Six Nations Reserve, Brantford, Ontario, 179 people voted out of an eligible 18,000. Before the television cameras and the print journalists, Ovide Mercredi squirmed, rationalizing the worst failure in his career: "I've been too moderate. Many of my people want a more radical approach. The only way we can make progress is to assert our jurisdiction" (*GM*, Oct 28/92). In fact, they rejected the accord more firmly than Canadians did as a whole — by 60 to 70 percent. Their paltry level of participation shocked no one familiar with the native voting record.

Mississauga MP Don Blenkarn, the fellow who had offered a hundred farewells before a retirement that never happened, the man who once opined that Newfoundland should be "towed out to sea and sunk" for not going along with the Meech Lake Accord, couldn't help himself. "Blenkie" thought the people of English Canada should be "intelligent enough to give [Quebec] sovereignty-association" (*Sun*, Oct 29/92): "You can't keep fooling around with the old system, it ain't working."

As for the big kahunas in big business — Allan Taylor of the Royal Bank, Matthew Barrett of the Bank of Montreal, Thomas d'Aquino of BCNI, Senator Claude Castonguay, and their ilk — they had their own way of dealing with rejection: forget it. It never happened. Buckets of money spent with nothing to show for it. Best keep quiet.[1]

On October 27, 1992, the banks had to cut their prime rate to 7.5 percent. The dollar firmed up nearly half a cent — 0.46. The next day, October 28, the stock market blasted off. The TSE 300 index soared 48 points in its third biggest gain of the year. When Armageddon didn't follow thereafter, the predictable did. Interest rates sank lower than they had at any other point in the constitutional debate. On October 29, the Bank of Canada rate toppled to 6.3 percent, down from 7.37 percent. The *Financial Post* called it the largest drop since the stock market crash of October 1987. Tim Reid, a *Toronto Sun* columnist, put into words what a lot of investors and others were thinking: "One wonders, cynically, if the actions of the Bank of Canada, in pushing the bank rate from 4.93 per cent at the end of September to 7.93 per cent just before the referendum, were a ploy by the feds to scare voters into voting Yes. The bank did so in the face of no corresponding increase in U.S. rates and no further weakness in the Canadian dollar in the past four weeks" (*Sun*, Nov 1/92).

In the aftermath of the defeat the media shielded the politicians from the fallout. As co-conspirators with the politicians, they had a vested interest in doing so. The politicians were subjected to no hardball interviews, and no recriminations. Only the odd confession slipped out. On October 28, Joe Clark sighed to the nation, "We have to be much more willing to take account of people's views" (*GM*, Oct 29/92).

Only three days after the plebiscite, Mulroney received a thunderous ovation from the Conservative caucus when he informed them he intended to stay on for a third term. Justice minister Kim Campbell carried the ball: "This was greeted with enthusiastic applause all around the table. . . . I think there was a recognition of the fact that the Prime Minister did an outstanding job in reaching an agreement. It would have been impossible for anybody else to have done that" (*Star*, Oct 30/92). She even went so far as to predict: "By the end of this century, historians will canonize him" (CBC Newsworld).

Canada, a nation gone bonkers. On October 30, Barbara McDougall defended her department against charges of fraud, theft, and incompetence. An update on the 1991 travel scam of high-ranking officers in External Affairs now poured out. They had indulged in wholesale embezzlement, claiming reimbursement for a total of 465 fraudulent travel claims. In August 1991, 127 diplomats had been caught. The number had now risen to 264 public servants skimming a fortune in taxpayers' money. Although $446,000 of it was recovered, the fines levied as a result came to only $4,750. No one was fired. Only 1,332 days of suspensions were doled out, or an average of five days per crook.[2]

Bob Rae's government beavered away. Tony Silipo, chairman of the Ontario Select Committee on Confederation, led the way. In a speech to the Jamaican Canadian Association on October 31, the education minister said that the province might order educational faculties to implement quota programs for Ontario's visible minorities: "We're looking at it aggressively. . . . We can do it without seeming to close the doors on anyone who wants to become a teacher" (*Star*, *Sun*, Nov 1/92).

As far as Victor Goldbloom, Canada's Official Languages Commissioner, was concerned, the Referendum meant nothing at all. Speaking in Regina on November 22, he too demonstrated his peculiar view of history: "Ever since the mid-18th century, there's been an inter-relationship between English-speaking and French-speaking Canadians. . . . We've had a human reality of a two-language co-existence. . . . We have to be able to talk to one another, and talking to one another, because of our diversity, requires us to use two languages. We can't use all the approximately 150 languages that exist in Canada" (*Star*/CP, Nov 23/92).

ELSEWHERE IN CANADA, history was being made. On November 19 in Edmonton, former publisher Mel Hurtig announced the formation of a new but as yet unnamed federal party. It would, he told the press conference, field as many as fifty candidates in the next election.[3] Supporters cited were, not surprisingly, from the arts world: Margaret Atwood,

Farley Mowat, Timothy Findley, David Suzuki. "It is our perception that there is a huge political vacuum out there," said Hurtig, "and although the Liberals are well ahead in the polls their support is a mile wide and one-16th of an inch deep and very, very soft. [The objective is to appeal to] the 96 per cent of Canadians who do not belong to any political party" (*GM*, Nov 20/92).

Late in November, some of the Referendum bills trickled in. On November 24, supplementary estimates were tabled in the House of Commons. The first invoice for the constitutional negotiations since April 1 ran to $86.5 million. Treasury Board said they expected the costs to climb. Every month or so the tally rose. By June 1993, a study by Carleton University put the cost of the constitutional negotiations alone at $288.31 million. The real costs to the nation in loss of productivity and sheer waste would multiply that figure many times over.

On December 5, Bourassa re-emerged to show off one of his famous crab dances on Bill 178, Quebec's repressive language law: "We have to note an evolution among Quebecers that favors some easing of the law. As to how that might be done, what form it would take, it's too soon to say" (*Sun*, Dec 6/92).

The best line on the whole Referendum business, as one might have expected, came from Quebec's Yvon Deschamps on December 5, 1992: "I found the referendum not interesting at all. . . . You know [now] what's the worse. Now they [really] threaten us. . . . don't let them 'focus on the economy'" (CBC, "Midday").

As the worst year in a good many stumbled to its close, more prairie grass fires flared up. In his final election run-off battle for the Alberta premiership with the Red Tory Nancy Betkowski, backed by Joe Clark, her admitted mentor Peter Lougheed, and, coincidentally, the *Globe and Mail*, Ralph Klein seized the crown. Betkowski championed Official Bilingualism and the centralist Ottawa line. Klein, formerly Calgary's mayor, appealed to the "ordinary Joes" of the electorate. Loyal to Don Getty, street-fighter Klein spouted the slogan, "Where vision meets common sense," before wiping the deck clean. Alberta was about to witness a new era in provincial politics. The rest of the country was about to see real fiscal conservatism in action.

Of his rival, Betkowski, Klein offered: "I'm not the status quo candidate. I've only been around for 3½ years. I'm the rookie. Nancy's been there since the beginning of time" (*GM*, Dec 1/92).

In Edmonton, an insecure and petulant Brian Mulroney chastised Albertans for letting him down in the Referendum:

The people of Alberta have said they do not want an elected senator. They do not want an equal Senate and they do not want an effective Senate. And therefore, constitutionally, I have to deal with this pursuant to their judgment. . . . I will be discharging my constitutional obligations. [In answer to a question about Senate reform:] That's right, they turned everything down, including this [an elected Senate]. . . . When the people speak, they can never be wrong. (*GM*, Dec 15/92)

Giving his New Year's sermon on December 29 he sounded eerily like David Peterson: "When am I going to stop blaming my neighbours and my leaders and say I too have a personal responsibility?" and "You can't always blame politicians. You can't always blame your leaders. [It's time] to look yourself in the mirror and say, 'I'm a very privileged person. I'm a Canadian. I've been given the greatest country, the No. 1 country in the world. To keep it together requires generosity by me'" (*Sun*, Dec 31/92).

At this point no one in the country gave a sweet damn what Mulroney had to say — on anything. If only he would just go away.

Two days before Christmas the economy smacked Canadians hard. The Bank Credit Analyst Research Group predicted that Canada would confront "a full-fledged crisis" that would smash the dollar to between 60 and 70 cents US in 1993: "Leadership is weak, directionless, and without vision or principle. . . . Until there is a clean slate of politicians in Ottawa and the provinces with a mandate to change course, you must prepare for the inevitable financial and economic train wreck" (*Star*, Dec 23/92).

At year end, Peter C. Newman announced what everyone already knew: he would be Mulroney's "official biographer." The journalist historian who once boasted he had sifted through ten tons of Hudson's Bay Company material for one of his works bragged he had amassed ten filing cabinets of stuff on Mulroney. John Diefenbaker would have roared with laughter at this assignment. He knew all about Newman, whom he once described as the "Bouncing Czech" (Diefenbaker, *I never say anything provocative*, p. 71).

By this time Canadians couldn't have cared less about a book about the biggest loser in the federation's history. Everyone just wanted to get on with life — preferably within a united Canada — but if not, so be it. The country was so demoralized that many people, Newman among them, thought it could or would fall apart.

Czechoslovakia offered an interesting blueprint. As of December 31, the proud nation that had won the admiration of Canadians at EXPO '67 no longer existed. It had expired from exhaustion and disinterest — fallen apart without a national referendum or any consultation with the people.

Could such a fate overtake Canada? Had it already happened?

On January 4, Mulroney executed a minor Cabinet shuffle. He removed Kim Campbell from her combustible position as Minister of Justice. Mulroney knew the exact details of a potential explosion his government wanted to avoid at all costs (see Chapter 34). If her record could be kept clean and if she could get her act together, Campbell might even prove herself the ideal candidate to take the Tories to a third back-to-back majority victory.

Canada had been spewing out its constitutional innards for all the world to see for years, and by 1993 she was fair game for more than those in think-tanks who pulled off position papers to be quoted in the *Globe and Mail*. Interviewed by *Maclean's*, U.S. consumer advocate Ralph Nader, author of *Canada Firsts*, said:

> But in the last decade in Canada you've had democratic elections to produce a dictatorial government, ramming legislation through with abusive procedures. When the history of the Mulroney government is written, the title can be, "Prime Minister of Canada, on loan from Washington." I have never seen a head of state so contemptuous of preserving the sovereignty of a nation. It is just inconceivable, other than because of a personality failure, that a prime minister would consistently thumb his nose at history, evidence and public opinion. (*Maclean's*, Jan 11/93)

Nader's assessment applies to several decades, not one, and most certainly to more than one prime minister.

On January 13, Preston Manning enthusiastically immersed himself in more hot water. He publicly invited prominent members of the Jewish community to join the crusade and "inoculate" the Reform Party against racism. Former MP David Rotenberg seized the moment: "It has been documented that there have been racists in his party, but he seems awfully defensive about it" (*Star*, Jan 14/93). Ten days earlier, an editorial comment in the *Toronto Sun* had summed up the future of the lone Prairie preacher preoccupied with sanitizing his party's membership: "Reform Party leader Preston Manning now seems destined to become a voice of alienation, not a prime minister" (*Sun*, Jan 3/92).

Poor Joe Clark. Mulroney's underemployed Minister of Constitutional

Affairs couldn't leave well enough alone. At an agricultural convention in Edmonton, he tried once again to sell his old chestnut:

> Community of Communities. . . . I need your advice, your engagement, your commitment. . . . Your perspective on building a new Canadian concept of community, one that includes all Canadians, one that builds unity by accepting difference . . . that we preserve to pass on to our children. . . . It describes what we need for the future. A sense that local strength and national strength can be built together. The proposition that a strong whole is supported, not weakened by strong parts. . . . Much of the conflict in Canada has come from an insistence that one view be adopted to the exclusion of others. Much of the tension in Canada has come from the refusal to accept other people's view of themselves. (*Star*, Jan 15/92)

Richard Gwyn fell for the vacuous remarks, writing in the January 16 *Toronto Star*: "CLARK IS RIGHT. To be Canadian is to accept diversity." Profound.

WILLIAM JEFFERSON CLINTON was sworn in as the forty-second president of the United States on January 20. In a fourteen-minute inaugural quickie, the new president promised "not change for change's sake, but change to preserve America's ideals — life, liberty, the pursuit of happiness. . . . Each generation of Americans must define what it means to be an American." He drew heavily on John F. Kennedy — "It's time to break the bad habit of expecting something for nothing. . . . To renew America, we must revitalize our democracy." To stress his point, he called for "change" and "renewal" nine times.

On January 30, 1993, Canadians watched the state funeral of Jeanne Sauvé on TV. Michel Mandel of the *Toronto Sun* profiled the woman who detested Canada, yet clung to its highest office as if it were her personal property. There was the usual pomp and ceremony in the funeral procession and proceedings — the prime minister attended and so did three former prime ministers, Turner, Trudeau, and Clark, and an Honour Guard of the Governor General's Foot Guards, the Canadian Grenadier Guards, and the Royal 22nd Regiment. Also supplied at taxpayers' expense were a twenty-one-gun salute and a fly-past of two CF-18s: "But unlike other state funerals [world-wide] there was no Canadian flag draped over the mahogany coffin. Instead the family had requested a beautiful spray of pure white roses . . ." (*Sun*, Jan 31/93).

The altar in the ornate cathédrale Marie reine du monde was festooned with white lilies. In fact, no Canadian flags appeared anywhere — the final insult to a patient nation that had put up with milady's tasteless fandangoes for years.

At the beginning of February the prime minister reversed himself on his commitment made in Edmonton forty-eight days earlier. On December 14, he had sworn, "I'm saying that everything [in Charlottetown] was rejected . . . [and] in this business you don't get to cherry-pick" (*GM*, Dec 15/92).

On February 1, the Right Honourable led the House in a supreme gesture of contempt for the Canadian people. On a motion Liberal leader Jean Chrétien put before the House of Commons, the MPs voted by a handsome 219 to 2 to accept a constitutional amendment making New Brunswick bilingual. In the spirit of Frank McKenna, who dismissed the Referendum result, the House used Section 43, voting for legislation to guarantee that Canada's only officially bilingual province would "have equality of status and equal rights and privileges." These included "the right to distinct educational institutions and such distinct cultural institutions as are necessary for the preservation and promotion of those communities." Lucien Bouchard, leader of the separatist BQ, supported the move with the rest. If he were truly a separatist, one has to wonder why he would even have cared.

An independent member, Patrick Nowlan, and the lone Reform Party member Deborah Grey were the only holdouts. The October 26 Referendum had now been effectively shelved by all of Canada's major political parties and all but two of its federal representatives in the Commons. True to form, Reform leader Preston Manning emitted nary a sound. Sure of his role as Canada's supreme statesman, the prime minister addressed the House of Commons on February 1, 1993: "I am honoured to be the Prime Minister of a government that brought this to the Parliament of Canada. . . . It's long overdue, it's justice for a people that have been seeking it for 300 years — and certainly for 125 years of our Confederation — and it constitutes a model of how Canada can and should treat minorities" (*GM*, Feb 2/93).

Ottawa lawyer Deborah Coyne flew off again, publicly pledged to challenge the government before the Federal Court of Canada. She claimed these constitutional amendments gave the rights of groups precedence over individual rights.

Everyone else flew in all directions. After returning from a first exploratory tour of Quebec, Preston Manning told jostling reporters the Reform

Party might run candidates in that province: "It blunts this criticism [that Reform is anti-Quebec]," and "there seems to be a search in Quebec for a third force" (*GM*, Feb 8/93).

Strange stuff from a once-proud Western toughie who repeatedly told his followers that the Reform Party would steer clear until "the Québécois" made up their minds whether or not they wanted to be Canadians first.

On February 16, the C.D. Howe Institute warned of an impending debt crisis. In 1975, the total amount owed by all provincial and federal governments was $50 billion. This figure had by now ballooned to an estimated $665 billion. Put another way, debt had risen from $2,200 for every man, woman, and child to $24,000. There could be no happy ending to this story, and many politicians were preparing to beat lemming-like retreats.

On Saturday, February 21, in his home riding of Yellowhead, Alberta, the constitutional affairs minister made a big announcement. He would retire from politics after the next election. The relentless plodder had had enough.

On Sunday, the Equality Party moved ahead with its plans in Montreal. The rump anglophone movement picked a new leader, Keith Henderson. Unlike his predecessor, this was a Quebec anglophone who would not sell out. He immediately called for the abolition of Bill 101, the French Language Charter: "We'll be there to foil and counter any move to dismantle this country. . . . There will be no accommodation with separatism with us, ever" (*GM*, Feb 22/93).

In Ontario, Premier Bob Rae held as steadfast as his predecessor had to the hope of appeasement. On February 8, Ron Leitch, president of the Alliance for the Preservation of English in Canada (APEC), wrote to Rae to ask a simple question. It deserved a straightforward answer. Why had the Ontario government allowed the Ministry of Colleges and Universities to adopt a logo that gave precedence to French over English? Rae answered on February 24: "The Government of Ontario, through the French Language Services Act [Bill 8], recognizes that all Ontarians should receive provincial government services in either of our country's two founding languages. The act simply ensures that French-speaking Ontarians can get the full range of government services that English-speaking citizens already enjoy" (*APEC Newsletter*, June–July/93).

Even Bill 8 never went that far. It was supposedly based on and restricted to bilingual districts, where French language services would be available in specific jurisdictions. In one breathtaking leap the Ontario premier was stretching Bill 8, exactly the same stunt Trudeau had pulled with the first Official Languages Act, Bill C-69.

According to the 1991 Census figures, only 4.6 percent of the province's population was francophone and only 54,245 Ontarians claimed to speak French only — about one-twentieth of 1 percent. In the same way that Keith Spicer and the Trudeau government had abandoned the "bilingual districts" required by law two decades earlier, the premier abandoned the provisions of Bill 8 that set out twenty-two specific areas where French-language services would be available. Without any legislative approval Ontario had made itself "officially bilingual." And Rae employed exactly the same law-breaking techniques Trudeau had used in the 1970s, when Section 16 of the 1969 Official Languages Act was shuffled under the rug.[4] Thirty years after Lester Pearson had committed the country to the great experiment, Canada was more divided than ever. And now it was bankrupt, too, financially, morally, and intellectually.

For the time being, the question on everyone's mind was more immediate: What would Mulroney do? How long could he hang on?

Notes

1 The *Globe and Mail* summarized Referendum expenditures on June 23, 1993: "Ottawa — the Yes side in last year's constitutional referendum received 13 times more money than the No side, according to Elections Canada figures released yesterday. Even so, Canadians rejected the Charlottetown Accord. The Yes side received $11.8-million, while contributions to the No side totalled $849,465.96. For the Yes side, 340 publicly traded corporations donated $7.1-million, while on the No side, major corporations donated about $9,000. Elections Canada's report, showing financial returns filed by Yes and No committees outside Quebec (which held its own referendum), said 6,411 individuals contributed $383,829.39 to the Yes side, while 8,146 people contributed $137,836.40 to the No side. Yes forces bought $6.2-million worth of advertising, the No side purchased $528,465."

2 News from Argentina: *Time* magazine published a little piece about the introduction at the University of Buenos Aires of an MBA course on corruption. It would be taught by judges, business executives, and high-ranking government officials. "Since

President Carlos Menem took office in 1989, more than 15 government officials have resigned or been fired because of corruption allegations," the article noted (May 10/93). A post-Mulroney-era job for former Tory Cabinet ministers, perhaps?

Ah, but then there was that other problem. In March 1992, McDougall had twice broken finance minister Don Mazankowski's prohibition of flying first class at government expense, which affected Cabinet ministers as well. Caught red-handed, the Red Tory defended herself: "I do not think I am in violation of the guidelines. In the guidelines there is room for exceptions. I wrote a letter to the Treasury Board to clarify the kind of situation I am in — not by exception, but as part of a way of life" (*Star*, Apr 7/92).

3 Hurtig announced the name of the new party on December 4, 1992 — the National Party/le parti Nationale du Canada.

4 The leaders of the Liberal and the PC parties of Ontario were fully informed of the NDP government's actions. Lyn McLeod (Liberal) and Mike Harris (Conservative) were both sent copies of the correspondence. Neither opposition party responded.

33

The Disarray of the Red Tories
— February 24 to June 25, 1993

CANADIANS HAD WAITED nearly a decade for the news they finally heard on Tuesday, February 23. On Shrove Tuesday, Brian Mulroney, Canada's eighteenth prime minister, told his dinner guests at 24 Sussex Drive that he intended to resign after calling for a leadership convention. He had successfully surpassed Pierre Elliott Trudeau's accomplishment as the most reviled politician in the land. Even Trudeau, respected by many, worshipped by a good number, and hated by as many as admired him, knew when to bow off the stage. Mulroney, loathed by a great majority of Canadians, didn't know when to go, or didn't care, or both.

The acolytes at the farewell dinner included finance minister Don Mazankowski; health minister and Quebec lieutenant Benoît Bouchard; Michael Wilson, the trade minister; and Harvie Andre, the House leader. The decision was whispered to a few other trusted souls on the QT. Only a few knew the moment had come. Craig Oliver, CTV's Ottawa bureau chief, was on his toes. He hung around outside 24 Sussex at 11:00 P.M. to catch the scoop. For some reason, Mulroney's most loyal newspaper supporter, William Thorsell, editor-in-chief of the *Globe and Mail*, was left out in left field — in the dark.

The Day of Penitence marked the incorrigible prime minister's resignation, February 24, Ash Wednesday.[1] At 11:05 A.M. he sent his letter to party president Gerry St. Germain.

Canadians reacted either ecstatically, dumbfoundedly, or resignedly. A lot felt cheated. Most wanted the chance to thrash Mulroney at the polls. The Hon. Benoît Bouchard understood the political reality right away: the Tories were toast. On March 4 he announced he would not seek the Tory leadership: "There have been a lot of MPs pressing me to run but it isn't something I have ever wanted" (*Star*, Mar 6/93). Finally, less than two months after Mulroney quit, his Quebec lieutenant revealed he would not even stand for Parliament in the next election: "There is a misunderstanding about Canada by Canadians from coast to coast. . . . I understand the rest of the country much better now. I am the Canadian I was not ten years ago" (*GM*, Apr 20/93).

From abroad came the usual noises. The Brits were diplomatic in their reaction to Mulroney's departure. Prime Minister John Major said, "I shall miss him. He's been a very good friend to the United Kingdom and a great defender of the Commonwealth. So I am sad to hear of his decision today" (*GM*, Feb 25/93). At a private shindig at the Ronald Reagan Presidential Library at Simi Valley, California, the former president paid unique homage to Canada's fallen leader: "[Mulroney] learned not only how to speak the two languages but to unify and lead a whole country" (*Star*, *GM*, Apr 6/93).

Judy Rebick wasn't about to let Mulroney capture all the limelight. On April 20, the Mouth That Roared said she would be stepping down as President of the National Action Committee on the Status of Women on June 7: "I've certainly been a pain in the ass of politicians," as she proudly put it (*Star*, Apr 21/93). No one disagreed with her. In her farewell speech of June 4 at a convention of the NAC at the University of Saskatchewan, she told her audience, "We're standing in front of a tank of neo-conservatism and they want to roll us back" (*Star*, June 5/93).

Before long all the Tory heavies had run for the hills. On March 5, Michael Wilson took the lead, for a change. He said he would not seek the Tory leadership. On June 15, he wrote to Mulroney: "I have just advised Kim Campbell of my decision not to seek re-election in Etobicoke Centre." On June 7, Deputy Prime Minister Don Mazankowski, an elected member since 1968, turned down Mulroney's offer of a Senate post and quit federal politics, too. His wife's opinion had clinched his decision — "She used this piece of advice: a good hockey player knows when to hang up his skates"

(*Sun*, June 8/93). On June 18, Mulroney appointed him to the Privy Council, which entitled him to use the title Right Hon. usually reserved for prime ministers, governors general, and Supreme Court justices. On June 23, the Hon. John Crosbie announced that he too would not be running in the next federal election.

Rallying somewhat after learning they were left out of the loop, the *Globe and Mail* ran the weak editorial leader "It was time to go" (*GM*, Feb 25/93). Canadians asked why the PM hadn't made his announcement as soon as Meech Lake died.

Two days later the prime minister returned home to Baie Comeau. Citizens there had overwhelmingly voted No in the Referendum. Tory organizers tried to muster a crowd to welcome the returning hero, but "only a few dozen townsfolk were at the airport to greet the Mulroney family as the Canadian Forces Challenger jet touched down" (*Star*, Feb 27/93).

Mulroney might have been on the way out, but his appointees to the bench of the Supreme Court of Canada were alive and well. On March 4, the Court brought down a ruling under Section 23 of the Charter of Rights and Freedoms.[2] In a 7-to-0 ruling, the Court ordered Manitoba to give French-speaking parents control over their children's schools. According to the justices, francophones were entitled to a "distinct physical" setting. Chief Justice Antonio Lamer wrote:

> The Manitoba authorities must, without delay, put into place a regime and a system which permit the francophone minority to exercise its rights effectively. . . . The number of potential French-language students (some 3,000) warrants the establishment of an independent French-language school board under the exclusive management and control of the French-language minority. . . . Governments should have the widest possible discretion in selecting the institutional means by which Section 23 obligations are met. (*Star*, Mar 5/93)

On March 9, Quebec's intergovernmental affairs minister Gil Rémillard addressed the National Assembly: "Eventually, we will start another formal process, we need constitutional reform. . . . This constitutional reform must respect the principles which have guided us since we assumed responsibility for the matter [on May 9, 1986, at Mont Gabriel]. The fact remains, furthermore, that constitutional reform is necessary and our objective remains the same. What remains to be determined is in what context it will be situated. But the principle is 'Quebec first' within a Canadian federation that would be as efficient as possible" (*Star*, Mar 10/93).

According to him, Meech Lake and Charlottetown represented not "failures" but "references" (*Star*, Mar 10/93). It was business as usual. Almost.

Bourassa and his martinets shared the same objectives. With the Referendum defeated and Mulroney gone, so too went Quebec's leverage in Ottawa. The province's coffers were empty. Revenue Canada on March 7 signalled part of the problem. While the government's collection arm had secured a judgement for $539,619 against the national all-party Referendum Yes committee, the decision came too late. They couldn't collect the Goods and Services Tax from the Yes committee because the group had checked whether any tax was due beforehand, requested a refund, and had been given all the GST money back, which it then promptly disbursed.

On March 9, Moody's Investors Service Inc. of New York, a leading debt agency rating service, rumbled about a credit crunch coming for the provinces. As had been the case for years, the ship of state blundered up and down high financial troughs without a captain at the helm.

One month after Mulroney's resignation, defence minister Kim Campbell announced what everyone had known for months. She would run for the leadership of the Tory Party. Of her vision, she said:

It's much more the question of political cynicism, the way people feel about the political process as a whole. I think that's a serious crisis. (*GM*, Mar 26/93)

I am certainly not a supporter of separatism and anyone who thinks I am would be woefully disappointed. But I also understand, coming from a province where people feel very strongly about their provincial identity, but are also passionately committed to Canada, I can draw the distinction between being a nationalist and being a separatist. (*GM*, Mar 27/93)

Statistics Canada described a nation wallowing in debt on April 16. The foreign debt had swollen to $300 billion: "All told, Canadians owed $540-billion to foreigners at the end of 1992, but those liabilities were partly offset by $239-billion worth of foreign assets owned by Canadians. The result was a net liability of $301-billion, up from $276-billion at the end of 1991" (*GM*, Apr 16/93).

On April 20, Canadians learned the International Monetary Fund had delivered a severe warning to them *a full two months earlier*, on February 11. The IMF had warned that the Canadian dollar could face tremendous pressure if Ottawa didn't cut its expenditures. At $28.5 billion the current account deficit was becoming a "source of concern" (*GM*, Apr 20/93). Moody's, the IMF, the C.D. Howe Institute and legion upon legion of Canadian taxpayers had been screaming the same message for years.

Interprovincial trade wars fuelled the problem in spring 1993. On April 21, the New Brunswick government served notice that Quebec companies would no longer be eligible to compete for its business unless they were invited to or they had a principal place of business in New Brunswick. New Brunswick would buy no Quebec goods and would employ Quebec workers only as a last resort. First, all the province's own local union members would have to be employed. New Brunswick invited the private sector to follow its example. Federal trade minister Michael Wilson reacted impatiently: "If we get into this sort of tit-for-tat action, it slows down the process of negotiating the removal of these interprovincial trade barriers generally. I don't want to see us slipping backward. . . . [Referring to a planned process to eliminate barriers by June 1994:] We have an opportunity to meet that goal but it's ambitious" (*GM*, Apr 22/93).

For decades Canada's prime ministers had shied away from using the disallowance provision the Constitution gave them to enforce Section 121 of the BNA Act, strictly forbidding interprovincial trade barriers.

On April 25, opposition leader Jean Chrétien won his nomination for the riding of St. Maurice. "Yesterday's Man," as he had been dubbed by his political adversaries, was a seasoned veteran from the Trudeau years. He had served in ten Cabinet positions. He had dreamed of this goal for most of his political life. "It's only a matter of months now. . . . I have no doubt about it — I will become the prime minister of Canada" (*Star*, Apr 26/93).

On May 6 the Bourassa government introduced Bill 86 in the National Assembly. The new sign law, which was to replace Bill 178, would allow some use of English, but was fraught with problems (see Chapter 34). *Globe and Mail* columnist Rhéal Séguin sloughed it off: "Bill 86, as written, contains no restrictions on commercial freedom of expression and complies fully with the Canadian Charter of Rights and Freedoms."

The *Globe*'s editorial the same day put the case with slightly more accuracy but fewer details: "The latest legislative offering is not, however, perfect. Though bilingual commercial signs would be permitted — with French markedly predominant — the law would still ban English from billboards and other signs not on commercial premises, a meanminded restriction sure to be challenged as unconstitutional."

On May 10, writer Yves Beauchemin reprised the presentation he had made to the B–C Commission in 1991, specifically the bit about bilingualism in Quebec being equivalent to Hitler's occupation of France. The federalists, conditional and otherwise, he said, wanted "to impose French–German bilingualism. Bilingualism is always the sign of defeat" (*Star*, May 11/93).

Once again, the man who never knew when to quit made an announcement. On May 12, Joe Clark volunteered that the time had really come for him to do something or other. With Mulroney out of the way, Clark now threw himself into neutral as if to prepare himself to shift into reverse: "My decision [to quit] isn't absolutely final and there's still a possibility, albeit minimal, that I will run," he told *Le Soleil* (*Star*, May 13/93). If the polls showed he was the only one who could lead the Tories to victory, he said, then the question of whether he would run "is open, yes" (*Sun*, May 14/93).

He would encounter other temptations on the way to recapturing the Tory leadership from Brian Mulroney, his old nemesis. Boutros Boutros-Ghali, Secretary General of the United Nations, offered him a part-time job as envoy to Cyprus. Mulroney had set it up.

Kim Campbell started off her campaign for the prize with a stumble. On May 13, in a CBC "Prime Time" leadership debate, the queen of the quips tossed out, "I believe that substance and style are two sides of the same coin." If only Bill Vander Zalm had known! In eons past Campbell had slain the BC premier with her most famous line, "Charisma without substance is a dangerous thing." For some reason the national press glossed over this latest gaffe, but they caught her foursquare and centre when she mimicked her mentor, Brian Mulroney: "The enemies of Canada, of Canadians . . . are those people who are telling Canadians that debt and deficits are not a problem. Those are the people we have to take on in the next federal election. . . . I use that term [enemies] mildly" (*Sun*, May 14/93).

At long last, on May 21, 1993, the greatest survivor of them all quit for real. Without fuss or flurry Joe Clark announced he had accepted Boutros-Ghali's invitation. The job started immediately. On July 12, Canadian Press reported that he would be a Visiting Fellow at the University of California at Berkeley in September. Clark was also committed to teach political science at the University of Calgary. As for Cyprus, "If we're going to get some progress, there has to be some trust in the process of conciliation and an understanding of the motivation of all sides. That's comparable to what we had to do in Canada" (*Star*, May 12/93). Canadians could only pray for Cyprus.

While Ottawa politicos were either running or scrambling for positions, Roy Romanow the socialist gadfly was cutting deep into operating overheads in Saskatchewan out of cold necessity. At the ides of May, the NDP government suddenly announced it would cut 8 provincial seats in the legislature, reducing the number in the house from 66 to 58. The government expected to save $1.4 million or $130,000 for each standing member. Roy Romanow pushing to the right? What next?

In Washington, Ralph Nader, the consumer advocate, warned the United States' northern neighbour against a "global corporation strategy":

> If Canadians do not rouse themselves and each and every one them spend a few hours in the coming weeks informing, mobilizing and opposing the NAFTA trade agreement, the tide will become less and less reversible toward Canada ceasing to be an independent nation. . . . I can envisage in the next few years a movement starting in America which is friendly to Canada, in effect saying if Canada is a colony instead of a country, it might as well be annexed to the United States so that it has 20 Senators in the U.S. Congress and 50 members of the House of Representatives. [As for Mexico] they run a police state. They brutalize and intimidate dissenters. They routinely steal elections. There is no independent judiciary. The rule of law is a farce. (*Star*, May 15/93)

On May 18, a less than flattering article about Kim Campbell by journalist Murray Dobbin appeared in *Vancouver* magazine. By the end of the next week, she was floundering in her bid for the leadership. In his book, *The Politics of Kim Campbell*, Dobbin quoted from a lengthy interview that had taken place some four months earlier between Campbell and Peter C. Newman. (Allan Fotheringham wrote about the interview in the June 21, 1993, *Maclean's*, "Peter C. Newman, with a bottle of good wine over a three-hour lunch, managed to almost unhorse a candidate who had, according to the god Gallup, wrapped up the crown months earlier.") Dobbin quoted Newman quoting the candidate herself:

> The thing that infuriates me is apathy. People who boast about how they've never been involved in a political party. Who do they think is working to keep this society intact so that they can have the luxury of sitting back and being such condescending SOBs? To hell with them.
> . . . I wouldn't want to win the leadership on a kind of technical basis, the way Joe Clark did. . . . He was the least-hated candidate. . . . (*The Politics of Kim Campbell*, pp. 141–42)

The exposé destroyed Campbell's credibility. The damage easily surpassed what Mulroney had brought on himself in 1984 with his smart-aleck remark over Bryce Mackasey and patronage. Portraying Campbell as flip and naïve, Newman had decreed a Campbell reign plagued with troubles for the Tories. Campbell had played into the hands of this particular journalist by permitting him to interview her at all. Her foolish chatter (during her youth, she said, she had become an Anglican "as a way of warding off the papacy") armed her enemies with a heat-seeking missile and made her best friends squirm (*Star*, May 18/93).

Many of her comments could be easily misinterpreted, but no one could miss Newman's most deadly conclusion: "Her French is not as fluent as advertised; most dangerous of all, she has roused expectations that no politician can satisfy" (*GM*, May 20/93).

The question remained: was she set up for her fall? As early as March 10, two weeks before she announced her candidacy, she had been on the defensive about a phoney speech leaked from her office. The business was not explained after that.

But what of the Newman interview itself? His January tête-à-tête was made public on May 18 once it had been tested on a select group of business insiders on March 25, the day Campbell announced she would run. The *Globe and Mail* procured a copy of *The RHA Information Services* newsletter and published it on May 20. What took them so long? Was the timing of its release just coincidence? More important — just how strong was the back-play to push the charming Jean Charest ahead of Campbell? There was more to this story than speculation about the Minister of the Environment, Jean Charest, being invited to enter the race to keep public interest alive. The backroom boys were in full swing.

Campbell's prospects of winning the country diminished daily. It was more than a natural peak in popularity and expectation; her handlers were making major mistakes. For openers, they allowed her to be over-exposed. By the time of the convention, there was nothing left to know about Avril Phaedra (Kim) Campbell. In fact, the candidate enjoyed more media attention in those four scant months than Trudeau had during the entire trance of Trudeaumania, or than Brian Mulroney had in his entire political career. Substance and style without mystery. Fatal for a politician.

Gilbert Lavoie, the publisher of *Le Droit*, sent shivers through Conservative ranks by comparing Campbell's bandwagon to that of John Turner in 1984: "A leadership race whose results are known in advance is bad for ideas. It is even prejudicial to a political party, because it is monotonous and does not attract the voting public" (*GM*, Mar 11/93). Jean-Paul Gagné, editor of the business publication *Les Affaires*, recognized the real need, "[What was required was the] antithesis of Brian Mulroney. He or she will have to be elected as party leader for a vision of the country. . . . Opposite a Jean Chrétien who is better at avoiding the real questions and reciting bromides than at commitments. . . . Meeting this challenge could spare us an Italian-style Parliament" (*GM*, Mar 11/93).

Kim Campbell accelerated what Brian Mulroney had already set in motion — the free fall of support for the Tory Party. She was another Joe Clark — born to lose when it counted. The best of the professionals knew. For them, there was only one chance and one question: Could latecomer Jean Charest catch up?

The real test for Campbell's main rival was his tour of the West. It went well. The only drawback, some said, was that Charest was too young. Others oohed and aahed over him as a winner because he looked like U.S. President Bill Clinton — whatever that meant. On March 8, *Globe and Mail* reporters Miro Cernetig and David Roberts reported that "the 34-year-old protégé of Prime Minister Brian Mulroney is clearly building a base in the West" (*GM*, Mar 8/93). *La Presse* encouragingly dubbed him "the Wayne Gretzky of Canadian politics" (*GM*, Mar 11/93). Charest was on a roll.

The Tories had planned their fallback position earlier in desperation. On March 15, the environment minister had been invited to 24 Sussex. This meant he had Mulroney's endorsement. The next day the Hon. Jean Charest announced his candidacy for the PC leadership in Sherbrooke, Quebec. His entrance into the race immediately absorbed media interest. CBC Newsworld broadcast his entire speech around 8:30 that evening.

With Charest now in the running, Mulroney's personal plan seemed to be clicking along more smoothly. All the would-be threats to his agenda had been washed away, especially the Ontario heavies who had briefly considered running. External Affairs minister Barbara McDougall, trade minister Michael Wilson, and communications minister Perrin Beatty had quit early on, convinced they didn't have a chance. They were right. No one could have produced any evidence in the entire nine-year Tory term that their party had shown any interest in Ontario, home of 40 percent of the population.

Ontario's recession was fast sinking into a depression. The socialist government of Bob Rae applied its solution — more taxes, $2-billion worth. On May 19, the Rae government announced the biggest tax grab in Ontario's history — even bigger than David Peterson had dared in his first budget.[3]

As of July 1, the personal income tax rate was raised 3 percent. John Bulloch, president of the Canadian Federation of Independent Business, reacted angrily: "The $2-billion they're going to take out of the pockets of Ontario citizens is really to pay for their own incompetence" (*FP*, May 20/93). According to Ontario's treasurer Floyd Laughren, "Excluding sovereign countries, Ontario has become the largest borrower in the world. On average we borrow more than $1 billion a month. . . . The recession has ended and the Ontario economy has turned the corner" (Ontario Budget 1993). Apparently Bob Rae had never read Jean-Jacques Rousseau's *Social Contract*:

> In every government in the world, the public person consumes but does not produce anything. Whence does it obtain the substance it consumes? From the labour of its members. It is the surplus of private production which furnishes public subsistence. From this it follows that the civil state can subsist only if men's work yields more than they themselves need. (*The Social Contract*, Bk. III. trans. Maurice Cranston. Penguin Classics, 1968, p. 124)

While "Pink Floyd" robbed Ontario's middle class of $2 billion more, Paul Desmarais, the chairman and CEO of Power Corporation of Canada, announced he was sitting on more than $2 billion in cash and asking serious questions: "Are we going to get out of this recession tomorrow or in three weeks, or are we entering a depression? . . . It's very, very, very hard to say. . . . Everything is timing. . . . There's no use buying anything when everything is going down. . . . You have Europe in recession, you have Japan in recession and Canada in recession and the U.S. say they aren't, but the recovery doesn't look solid" (*FP*, May 20/93).

Quebec fared no better. She too was broke. On May 20, finance minister Gérard Levesque had to perform the unpleasant duty of informing tax-payers of a $1.7 billion in tax hikes. Like the hit on Ontario taxpayers, Quebec's increase set a record in its history: "The day of reckoning is here. We can't go on as before" (*GM*, May 21/93).

On May 28, just two weeks before the Tory convention, the prime minister did an end run on his biographer, Peter Newman. He exposed himself. In a 180-degree turn from his past pronouncements he went berserk before the Confederation Club of Ottawa, revising even his own revisionist history. Canada, he said, was a "time bomb," thanks to the constitutional mess Pierre Trudeau had created. Trudeau's acceptance of the notwithstanding clause stood revealed now as a "stunning surrender of principle." The clause could "be used to override basic human rights . . . thereby eroding confidence in federal institutions" (*Gazette*, May 29/93). As for allegations that Mulroney had allied himself with Quebec nationalists, that was just fiction: "My assumption of office was spawned by a double-barrelled myth by the revisionists: First, that I had won the 1984 election in Quebec as a result of separatist support . . ." (*GM*, May 29/93).

Two days later the self-appointed historian appeared on CNN television's "Larry King Live," where callers attacked him and where King himself accidentally called him Brian Mahoney. A week later, he suffered another dig. On the same program, Ross Perot answered questions and commented on Mulroney's ideas as Larry King put them to him: "Mulroney? What jobs had Mulroney ever created?" (CNN, June 9/93).

On June 4, the prime minister met with Robert Bourassa one final time in Montreal and "clarified" the record:

> Strange to say, a lot of poison has gone out of the system, because the people had an opportunity to consider it and say Yes or No. I find there is a much greater serenity in Quebec and elsewhere regarding the constitutional matter. . . .
>
> . . . One of the problems [in 1982] was the feeling of having been excluded . . . so right away there was a sense of estrangement in Quebec that something unfair had taken place. With the referendum that sentiment is not there any more. No one today in Quebec is saying we were deprived . . . that we made a deal in the middle of the night when the premier of Quebec was not present. (*GM*, June 5/93)

Mulroney's remarks sounded like Davidson Dunton's apologia that there was really no crisis at all prompting the Bi-Bi Cultural Revolution of 1965. But there was a big difference between then and now. Canadians were angry, not asleep.

Even so, the public did not know of the thousands of measures their government had taken to enforce the politically correct vision of the country. A policy directive on Official Languages from the Treasury Board on June 1 typified the enforcement and discrimination the government employed, in its "Grants and Contributions": "It is a government policy that federal institutions providing grants or contributions to voluntary non-governmental organizations for activities, projects or programs involving service to the public composed of members of both official language communities must take the necessary measures to ensure that the recipient of funds respects the spirit and the intent of the *Official Languages Act* when serving the public."

The same old message from the Mulroney camp. The Hon. Monique Landry, newly appointed Secretary of State of Canada, spoke before the Standing Committee on Official Languages: "I am also called upon to advance the equality of status and use of the English and French in Canadian society." She added that "the federal government will be contributing $112-million to the implementation of school management by French-speaking minority communities and the development of post-secondary education in French" (*Hansard*, May 27/93). The minister promised $1.11 billion to renew the Official Languages in Education program.[4] Yet Trudeau and all the prime ministers who followed him had said repeatedly that bilingualism would be confined to federal institutions.

Ironically, while Landry voiced her opinion in Ottawa, another piece of history was being attended to in Montreal. The decapitated statue of Sir John A. Macdonald, Canada's first Father of Confederation, was being moved with heavy construction machinery from its historic location in the Place du Canada on what used to be Dorchester Boulevard.[5] For six months, the monument had stood headless in the middle of downtown. Neither the city nor Victor Goldbloom, Pierre Trudeau, or Brian Mulroney, all residents of Montreal, did a thing. "This is a wrong that had to be righted," said Albert Sévigny, a Montreal foundry employee who raised the $30,000 needed for the repair job. The city said they wanted to wait until the beheading had been completely investigated before proceeding. One of the items found beneath the statue was a newspaper dated May 4, 1895, that had sold for one cent.

On June 5, the *Globe and Mail* reported Mulroney's final splurge of patronage appointments. He broke all previous records: his 241 outstripped Pierre Trudeau's 225 during the latter's final six weeks in office. Since December 17, 1992, Mulroney had made a total of some 665 appointments. The appointment of a brother of Mulroney's backer Paul Desmarais, Dr. Jean Desmarais, a retired radiologist, puzzled everyone, including the appointee himself, who admitted to curious reporters that, although he had once been a member of the Conservative Party, he had never been an active one. He entered the Senate anyway. This confirmed control of the upper house in Tory hands: Conservatives 53, Liberals 41, independents 5. Every political pundit remembered the refrain with which Mulroney had destroyed John Turner in 1984: "You had a choice, sir, you had a choice." Mulroney had chosen, and everyone knew full well he wasn't finished yet.

Not to be outdone by his old rival, Joe Clark chipped in with his idiosyncratic version of history on May 31. Addressing 300 members at the Canadian Club he said:

> While the referendum failed, the negotiations succeeded. As part of the process more Canadians with particular interests began to consider the country as a whole. (*Star*, June 1/93)

> Disaffection with political processes has become pandemic. The sense of gridlock is global. Ask the Italians or the Japanese or John Major or François Mitterand.
>
> It is important to remember that while the referendum failed, the negotiations succeeded. . . . There is still a threat that this country could slip apart, could break along any or several of its fault lines. In my judgement, that remains the real threat to Canada, not the debt or the possibility of a visit by the IMF [International Monetary Fund] or other problems that can be solved by policy. There is a fundamental problem about the will of Canadians to live together in mutual respect. (*GM*, June 1/93)

In other words, while democracy failed, executive federalism succeeded! And going bankrupt was irrelevant.

On June 3, Moody's cut the rating on $98 billion of Hydro-Québec's debt. The provincial Crown corporation had earned its first downgrading in eleven years. Earlier in the week, Canada's deputy finance minister David Dodge confessed to the House of Commons Finance Committee that Canada was "close to the highest" tax jurisdiction of the G-7 countries (*GM*, June 2/93).

Mulroney took another final leave of Baie Comeau. The Santa Claus of the North Shore announced a farewell donation to his home riding of $3 million on June 5. He boasted of all the Tory largesse the community had enjoyed — more than $20 million — during his years. But his parting comment was the one that would be repeated for the last days of his reign: "I realized I could be an effective prime minister of Canada or I could be a popular prime minister of Canada, but I couldn't be both. I chose to be an effective prime minister" (*Sun*, June 6/93).

MULRONEY'S MUSINGS ASIDE, what could Canadians expect in the future? Had anyone learned anything over recent decades? Had the media got the message? If *Financial Post* columnist and author Andrew Cohen were any example, there would be no change. On June 4 the columnist defended Pierre Trudeau from Brian Mulroney's attack: "The Charter of Rights — was shaped in a carnival of participatory democracy. It was forged before a parliamentary committee in 56 days of televised hearings, argued before three provincial courts and debated in Parliament for 14 months" (*FP*, June 4/93).

What "carnival of participatory democracy"? Hearings before the Special Joint Committee on the Constitution? Without a direct vote by the people, this could hardly be considered democratic participation.

CBC hosts Peter Mansbridge and Pamela Wallin of CBC TV's "Prime Time" questioned candidates Campbell and Charest on June 9. One of the interviewees would become prime minister elect within 100 hours, yet neither host asked either candidate what his or her vision of the country was, and none was volunteered.

In a less dramatic sideshow, Information Commissioner John Grace had tabled his report before the House of Commons on June 7: "These yearly reports might as well be put in a space ship to Mars. The Access to Information Act lacks visible champions in Parliament," he admitted (*Star*, June 4/93).

While Grace blew his whistle on MPs' indifference to democratic tradition, Joe Clark stirred himself one more time to predict: "I think Jean Charest will be the best leader for my party and my country" (*Sun*, June 8/93). The editors of the *Globe and Mail* threw in their lot with the Quebec-based candidate two days later, just before the Tory convention kicked off on June 10: "We do not doubt Ms. Campbell's resolve, or her intelligence: but there is about her a brittleness, a nervous insistence on the rightness of her cause that will not wear well with time. She exudes the defensiveness of a political class that considers itself misunderstood and under-appreciated by an unthinking public of which her 'politics of inclusion' is a condescending reflection" (*GM*, June 9/93).

The *Globe* had now fallen into line with the Montreal *Gazette* and *Le Soleil*. The *Toronto Sun* waited until Sunday morning of nomination day, June 13, when its editors joined *Maclean's* magazine and handed the wreath over to Kim Campbell. The pollsters predicted a different story.

On June 12, Gallup forecast that under Kim Campbell the Tories would face "electoral disaster." The percentages predicted that under Jean Charest the party would secure 44 percent of the vote, compared to Jean Chrétien's 37 percent. Put another way, Gallup was stating that Campbell would win only 107 seats compared with Charest's 160.

The front-page news mirrored the slide. Canada's foreign debt at $270 billion US equalled more than half of the U.S.'s foreign debt of $430 billion. Ahead of Canada in economic growth and output ranked Spain, Italy, and Brazil, countries that but a few years before had lagged far behind.

The Tory convention in Ottawa from June 11 to 13 confirmed the disaster. The three front-runners were all Mulroney's mynah birds. None dared to criticize a legacy they had so vigorously and so publicly supported before. The colours the candidates chose for the convention hoopla said more about them than the leadership hopefuls did themselves. Kim Campbell chose hot pink. Jean Charest selected turquoise. Jim Edwards picked yellow.

The convention was the biggest yawn in Canadian political history. Beginning with a $300,000 bash on Friday, June 11, to celebrate the Mulroney years, the affair closed on Sunday on a deeply divided party. After a halting, uninspiring, tedious speech, Kim Campbell won the first ballot. She ran ahead of Jean Charest on the second with 1,817 votes to his impressive showing at 1,664. On the second ballot, third-place runner-up Jim Edwards, the Tory Party whip who never made it to Cabinet minister, attracted only 307 votes. The spoilsport claimed Joe Clark had stolen his fellow Albertan candidates to march under Charest's banner. When it no longer mattered, he worked his way through the mob of excited delegates to Campbell and wheedled himself top place as a public embarrassment. True to his behaviour at the Edwards–Beaudoin hearings, he followed wherever he believed power went. He cited party solidarity and explained, "I made my decision after I saw the results of the first ballot" (*Star*, June 14/93).

To their credit, though it wasn't expensive, the fourth- and fifth-place candidates Patrick Boyer and Garth Turner followed their consciences. Turner stayed neutral and Boyer moved into Charest's camp after the first ballot. That ballot really ended it all when Campbell finally won 1,630 votes to Charest's 1,369. As she phrased it at the podium in a remark deliberately misinterpreted by many observers, "I don't know whether I'm a rabbit or a hare. But, Jean, you are one hell of a tortoise" (*Star*, June 14/93).

The Reds were in utter disarray. Charest, believed for no reason at all to be the more truly conservative of the party, had lost out to the progressive Kim, who represented a Social Credit long past.

Dalton Camp's chickens had come home to roost at last. With Campbell's election the party was split in every conceivable way. Once thought to be a Bay Street Blue conservative, Mike Wilson backed Campbell, not Charest. Red Tory Joe Clark backed the Turquoise Jean Charest. Edwards, whom the media considered a right-wing Tory, cheered on the Campbell team. Hugh Segal, the reddest of the Red Tories, backed the maybe-pink, maybe-blue Charest. At the end of this convention, the Tories were colourless, rudderless and adrift. John Diefenbaker had his long-awaited revenge at last.

Continentalist Conrad Black addressed the Americas Society in New York the next day. As usual, he saved one of his unique punches for the right moment: Charest was "the more appropriate candidate." Campbell the winner was "studiously vague . . . taking her instructions from Marcel Masse, an open and notorious nationalist who has had an ardent flirtation with the independence of Quebec" (*GM*, June 15/93).[6] On June 15, interviewed by Ron Adams on CBC TV's "Business World," he praised Brian Mulroney guardedly for a legacy that was, "on balance, in policy terms, adequately successful," as distinct from Campbell, who was, he repeated, "vague in most policy areas."

Her reign would not be easy. Addressing the National Assembly in Quebec, intergovernmental affairs minister Gil Rémillard again stressed that nothing had changed despite the collapse of the second bout of the Quebec round: "On June 23, 1990, Premier Robert Bourassa said Quebec is a distinct society whatever anyone says or does. That is and will remain the government's position in all matters. We'll seek recognition of Quebec as a distinct society in administrative agreements, not just constitutional texts. We'll pursue both objectives" (*GM*/CP, June 16/93).

On June 17, 1993, the rules in the Quebec National Assembly were suspended to secure the passage of Bill 86, Quebec's new language law, which would replace Bill 178. Jacques Parizeau tried bluffing the province's anglos. The United Nations ruling on Gord McIntyre's case on Quebec's language law, Bill 178, had had "quite an impact" on the new legislation (*GM*/CP, June 18/93). (See Chapter 34.)

The *Globe and Mail* published a curious item about Quebec and language matters the same day. The Quebec nationalist group Mouvement Québec français had retained former U.S. attorney-general Ramsay Clark, a civil-rights activist and expert in international law, to offer his opinion of Quebec's language legislation. Clark said: "I believe the Charter of the French language [Bill 101] is a courageous, affirmative and sensitive effort, respectful of the rights of others, to preserve a precious culture. I believe international law does and ought to protect such legislation because it is necessary to fulfil human rights" (*GM*, June 17/93).

Had Clark read the UN decision on the Gord McIntyre case?

As was his custom, in prose well suited to confuse, the champion of Bill 101, the Quebecer the English media loved to label "a staunch federalist" shrugged off Clark's opinion. Claude Ryan, head of the "tongue troopers," called it "so sketchy that you cannot accord too much importance to it" (*GM*, June 18/93).

The federal government released a mid-June report on its operating deficit for the fiscal year that ended March 31. Its figures brought the nation up short. It showed a jump from $31.6 billion to $34.8 billion — $3.6 billion or 11.4 percent higher than the year before.

In terms of global economic stability, the news from overseas sounded just as grim. On June 18, 1993, to cheers of *Banzai!* from the opposition, the Liberal Democratic Party of Prime Minister Kiichi Miyazawa of Japan lost a no-confidence motion. They had failed to reform a corrupt political system that had kept the LDP in power for thirty-eight years.

The twelve European Community leaders had plenty to discuss when they met in Copenhagen on June 21 about the rapid rise of unemployment — estimated at 17 million.[7] A new word was coined during the conference, too: *Eurosclerosis*, which referred to the slump of the early eighties. The 700-page report out of Geneva the next day from the World Economic Forum and the International Institute of Management Development in Lausanne seemed designed to depress people even further. In just one year, Europe's economic engine, Germany, had slipped from second place to fifth. Canada, as the forum put it, languished in "irons" in eleventh place, the same spot it had held in 1992, compared to its fifth-place position in 1991.

Canada's trade partners in the U.S. were behaving badly, too. This same day Canadians learned that the United States commerce department had sharply increased duties on steel coming into the U.S. from nineteen countries, including its partner to the north. The ruling delivered a double whammy to Canada, exonerating U.S. companies of responsibility for any injury caused by dumping steel over the border. Even Canada's champion of continentalism, trade minister Michael Wilson, professed himself aghast: "The increases in dumping margins for Canadian exporters are shocking" (*GM*, June 23/93).

If corruption in Japan caused the fall of a government, no fallout from it affected Canada or the way Brian Mulroney ran his government. On June 16 the PM awarded former Tory Cabinet minister Robert de Cotret a handsome summer job with promise of a more permanent plum to follow. He named him Canada's representative to the World Bank. And just to make sure his appointee suffered no hardship in the meantime, he handed him another bauble the next day when de Cotret officially quit the Cabinet — a secondment to the finance department paying more than $3,000 a week while he boned up on the job. The tidy sum would carry him over till August 9 when his new salary of $140,000 US tax-free kicked in.

T HE BY-NOW-PREDICTABLE EXPLOSIONS continued into the first week of the summer. On June 22, there was an uproar in the Red Chamber that attracted attention across Canada. The country's most unaccountable lot, its senators, had decided to give themselves a tax-free pay increase of $6,000 apiece — a whopping 60 percent more — on top of the $10,400 tax-free allowance and salaries of $64,000 they received. And it was all on the recommendation of their own internal economic committee. Senator Lowell Murray, the Tory House Leader, told reporters he expected passage and sure enough, despite outraged public reaction and a deafening hue and cry they barged ahead and went for it.

They did feign some restraint. On June 23, the second anniversary of Meech, they voted 26 to 24 for the handsome raise. Of 103 senators, 45 did not show up. More Liberals approved, but more Tories abstained and 24 more Tories stayed away. Even including the cop-outs and the abstainers, more than half the Senate thought the whole idea grand.

While the senators happily gorged themselves at the public trough, Brian Mulroney attended a ceremony that gave Royal Assent to NAFTA, the 4,300-page North American Free Trade Agreement with Mexico and the United States. It would be one of his last acts as prime minister. U.S. President Bill Clinton was in no hurry to agree to it. In fact, the United States would not sign it into law until the side-deals on workers' rights and the environment were worked out.

That same day, Gerry St. Germain, the president of the Conservative Party, made it to the Upper House in another of Mulroney's favourite farewell gestures. The newest senator had been defeated in the 1988 election. With his appointment Mulroney could chalk up fifteen since February 24, the day he resigned. Final scores in the Upper House: Tories 58, Liberals 41, Independents 5.

Three other people reminded Canadians of the state of the nation. Addressing a native community in West Bay, Ontario, AFN Chief Ovide Mercredi said, "It is said by the year 2000 we will be lucky if six [out of 59] native languages survive" (*GM*, June 23/93). In Montreal, after touring a food bank, NDP leader Audrey McLaughlin waxed profound: "I think the people who will vote for the Bloc Québécois are those people who believe Quebec should be separate from Canada" (*Star*/CP, June 23/93). From London, England, came a breach of protocol reminiscent of former

Governor General Jeanne Sauvé. Ontario's Lieutenant Governor Hal Jackman, the federally appointed representative of the Queen, told journalists he supported the NDP's "social contract" in Ontario. Then he excused himself by adding that he was saying so "unofficially and off the record." His Excellency praised Rae for being "fiscally on the conservative side": "In Ontario, without Bob Rae, the New Democratic Party would probably be nothing. I think they realize that themselves" (*Star*, June 23/93).

On Friday, June 25, 1993, the Mulroney era ended. At 10:00 A.M., the prime minister signed the resignation papers and walked away, gone but by no means forgotten.

Notes

1   Shrove Tuesday, or Pancake Day, comes from the English word meaning confession, or shriving — doing penance. Filling up with pancakes the night before Christian Lent is a Roman Catholic and an Anglican tradition, ostensibly to use up all the eggs in the house before the beginning of Lent. The next day, Ash Wednesday, commemorates the eighth-century custom of people marking their foreheads with ash as signs of penitence.

2   Among other things, Section 23, on Minority Language Education Rights, provides that children of the English and French linguistic minority shall have the right to education in their "mother tongue" in primary and secondary school. Section 23 (3a) "applies wherever in the province the number of children of citizens hav[ing] such a right is sufficient to warrant the provision to them out of public funds."

·3   The vibrant scene in the Ontario legislature: treasurer "Pink Floyd" Laughren sported a red carnation in his lapel. Beside Bob Rae sat the health minister, Ruth Grier, in pink. Also in pink sat Liberal leader Lyn McLeod on the other side. But the hottest pink of all appeared on the Conservative deputy leader, Diane Cunningham — right beside Mike Harris, the Red Tory.

4   Following Campbell's "election" to prime minister, Landry's portfolio was enlarged

to encompass Secretary of State, Communications, and Minister Designate of Canadian Heritage.

5   As part of the de-anglicizing of Montreal's history, the name of the street was changed to boulevard René-Lévesque after his death in 1987. For more information, see the National Film Board's 1993 documentary, *The Rise and Fall of English Montreal*, written and directed by William Weintraub (aired on "The Cutting Edge," Vision TV, Toronto, Jan 14/95).

6   On December 21, 1994, Premier Jacques Parizeau anointed Marcel Masse to head one of anywhere from 14 to 16 advisory commissions set up to determine how to build a sovereign Quebec. Even at this late date, the Faculty Club nurtured the Mulroney–Segal myth that Mulroney's former Quebec lieutenant was a federalist. In an article entitled "Parizeau picks two federalists for panels: Selections counter attacks on process," Rhéal Séguin of the Quebec Bureau described Masse as one of two "high-profile federalists" (Dec 22/94). Masse himself made his position clear during Meech Lake: "Like Dante said in Inferno, there is a special place in hell for those who in moments of crisis remain neutral" (*Star*, May 25/90).

7   Various figures have been bandied about. At the G-7 Conference on July 7, 1993, the figure used was 23 million for the G-7 countries alone. For Europe, I have used 33 million.

XII

Farewell the Peaceful Kingdom

June 26 to December 31, 1994

34

Canada on Trial Before the United Nations
— 1988 to 1993

SOUTH OF THE St. Lawrence River in Quebec are a number of regions very distinct from the rest of the province. In the eighteenth century, around the time of the American Revolution, United Empire Loyalists and other English, Irish, and Scottish immigrants seeking freedom and a better way of life came to settle here, in the Garden of Quebec.

The better known of these areas is the Eastern Townships — les Cantons de l'Estrie — which border the states of Vermont and New Hampshire. In Sherbrooke, Knowlton, Lennoxville, Granby, Bromptonville, and many other towns like them, the anglophone population no longer predominates nor makes up the ruling class.

Less well known is the crescent south of Montreal known as the Montérégie. This pie-shaped piece of land is bordered for the most part on the north and west by the St. Lawrence, where Ontario and Quebec touch, and by New York State on the south. Many of the inhabitants of this triangle of pastureland and waterways live by dairy farming and textile manufacturing. The village of Huntingdon, Quebec, squats about twenty kilometres from Malone, New York. The majority of its 3,300 residents speak English.

Gordon McIntyre bought the more-than-a-century-old Kelly's Funeral Home in Huntingdon in 1964. By 1988, Kelly's was one funeral home of the seven in the area that served the English-speaking community.

McIntyre is an unassuming man with a quiet manner and an infectious smile. He hardly looks the part of the man who carried on a five-year battle with the governments of Quebec and Canada over fundamental human rights.

His Quebec roots are as deep as they are rich. Besides a proud Scottish ancestry, McIntyre can claim a francophone lineage back to the days of Jean Talon (1626–94), the Great Intendant who promoted agriculture and industry in the vast empire of New France. Gord's great-grandfather, Louis Gauthier, came from this region.

The battle began in the summer of 1988. In July, the Kelly Funeral Home and its owner received a letter from the *"Gouvernement du Québec Commission de protection de la langue française."* Dated July 8, it ordered him to comply with instructions from Quebec's "tongue troopers," as they had become known. McIntyre read that he had violated the province's language law, Bill 178:

Sir,

The Commission for the Protection of the French language has received a request for an enquiry regarding the display of a sign at your establishment.

A check-up enabled us to ascertain in particular that a double faced sign in the shape of a shield, installed on the grounds of your establishment, carries the following firm name: "KELLY FUNERAL HOME."

This situation constitutes an infraction of article 69 of the Charter of the French Language, which reads as follows:

"Article 69
Subject to the provisions of article 68, only a firm name in the French language may be utilized in Quebec."

Consequently, I request you to let me know in writing, within fifteen days following the reception of the present letter, what measures you will have already taken to correct the situation and prevent the recurrence of a similar incident.

Expecting your cooperation, I remain

Very truly yours,
Pierre Chouinard, Commissioner-Enquirer

The funeral director recalls the moment vividly. He immediately telephoned Alliance Quebec (AQ), the leading anglophone rights group in the province. He reports he had no satisfaction from AQ.[1] By strange coincidence, however, he received a call from Pierre Chouinard, the letter's author, within fifteen minutes of making that phone call. Chouinard asked what he was going to do about the order. McIntyre says he told the tongue trooper, in English, "Those guys [the Quebec government] can pass a law turning me into a sixteen-year-old girl, but I'm not going to start dating guys."

The funeral director laughs, recalling the snappy response he got back: "You're a queer one." The two chuckled, and then the tone changed.

As McIntyre puts it, "They told me to get rid of the words 'funeral home.' . . . I offered to get the words printed up in both English and French, but they told me that was no good. . . . That's when I got mad" (*Maclean's*, May 3/93).

He acted. He enlisted the support of Maurice King, a retired railworker and the head of the Chateauguay Valley English-Speaking Association, a local, much smaller but more effective group than Alliance Quebec. CVESPA was incorporated under Part 3 of the Quebec Companies Act with its "object [being] to represent the English-speaking population of South West Quebec."

The case seemed simple enough. McIntyre had been denied a fundamental freedom, the right to freedom of expression in international law as well as under the Canadian Constitution. Yet he found it almost impossible to find a lawyer in Canada willing to champion his cause.

He gives much of the credit for his moving in the right direction to a retired McGill law professor. Many Quebecers and international jurists know John Humphrey, OC, OQ, BCL, PhD, DScDos, LLD, DCL, Dlitt, as feisty and effective, particularly in the face of injustice. Still roaring at eighty-five, Humphrey showed the Huntingdon funeral director how to proceed.

For a start, he told McIntyre he would have to look beyond Canadian borders for a remedy. Pursuing the case domestically was a waste of time, thanks to the Canadian Constitution itself with its notwithstanding clause that allowed provinces to pass bills that squashed human rights. Humphrey suggested McIntyre bring the weight of international moral authority to bear on the case — not to dishonour Canada, but to clear up the legal knots Trudeau had tied and Mulroney had ignored.

Humphrey offered McIntyre a gold-mine of knowledge. This same year that McIntyre found himself under attack by the Bourassa government, the lawyer won the United Nations Award for outstanding achievement in human rights for previous accomplishments. The wheels were in motion.

After scouring the Quebec legal profession, McIntyre eventually secured the services of another McGill law professor, Julius Grey, a noted civil rights lawyer in Montreal. With CVESPA's support, the team decided to file a complaint under Article 19 of the United Nations International Covenant of Political and Civil Rights. Canada was bound by the international agreement to pay attention; in 1976 she had signed the covenant that established the United Nations Commission on Human Rights.

In the meantime, McIntyre helped organize a demonstration in Ottawa and collected 10,000 signatures for a petition to send to the Secretary General of the United Nations in New York. He and his supporters repeatedly tried to interest the press and the broadcast media in what they were doing. No one responded. McIntyre says he contacted William Johnson, the *Gazette* columnist, but as far as publicity to garner support was concerned, McIntyre was on his own.

The first submissions to the United Nations are dated April 10 and November 21, 1989. Three complainants were recorded — John Ballantyne, Elizabeth Davidson, and Gord McIntyre; a painter, a designer, and an undertaker. For the five long years that followed, the undertaker became the lightning rod for the group challenging Bill 178.

During those years, McIntyre contacted all of Canada's first ministers asking for support. According to the UN final report on the case, a few sympathized with the three Quebecers and even wrote letters back. None of them took any direct action or made a public stand. As Maurice King of CVESPA put it, "On January 15, 1990, we wrote Mr. Yves Fortier, the Canadian Ambassador to the United Nations, requesting the Ambassador lodge a complaint with the United Nations Secretary General over the handling of the communication and asking that he ensure that it was handled. We received no reply" (*The First Step*, p. 19). On Humphrey's advice, McIntyre had written to Pérez de Cuéllar, then Secretary General of the United Nations. De Cuéllar ignored his correspondence of July 11, 1989, as well as the follow-up letter of October 18, 1989. The UN was unmoved by the petition of 10,000 signatures that accompanied the complaint.

The team solicited the help of members of the Canadian Senate. Not a single senator responded. McIntyre wrote to the prime minister's office numerous times. He petitioned members of Parliament. His overtures were all ignored. A few of those contacted wrote back that they regretted the whole business, and that was all. The prime minister himself offered no leadership in the matter, and the Leader of the Opposition, former Prime Minister John Turner, and all of Canada's other political parties did likewise. Audrey McLaughlin of the NDP and Preston Manning of the Reform Party were among these. Through the entire five years, no MP asked a single question in the House of Commons and no member in any provincial legislature raised the issue publicly.[2]

An outsider might well ask how the politicians were able to utterly black out history like this. They did it with the complicity of the media. The press, print and electronic, including the CBC, smothered the case in Canada's biggest cover-up. They missed out on the incident of the missing complaint and the 10,000-signature petition originally filed with the United Nations in New York and then lost. There's the story of how the case made it before the UN at all. There's the story of how the complainants had to travel to Geneva to sneak the case in through the back door; flying so far out of the way was the only way to avoid the Canadian authorities in New York. There's the story that recounts how Canada's justice department somehow filed its response in French only.

A PASSAGE IN Lewis H. Lapham's *The Wish for Kings* captures the arrogance of the media:

> By arranging the ambiguity of events into polite abstractions, the media compose the advertisements for a preferred reality, and their genius consists in the agility of the courtier spirit that allows them to serve, simultaneously, two masters: the demos, whom they astound with marvels and fairy tales, and the oligarchy, whose interests they assiduously promote and defend. (p. 123)

Throughout the entire case, the press offered only the slightest coverage. Irwin Rapoport's report in an October 31, 1990, article in the *Côte St. Luc Suburban* offered more hard information than most: it was mildly informative, confusing — hardly the careful, thorough account one would expect of an international story on the intrigue, corruption, and destruction of civil rights.[3] The national news media ignored Canadian Press's line on what was going on:

> The 18-member UN committee rebuked Canada last Wednesday [October 14, 1990] for allowing its citizens to lose their rights after questioning Canada for two days on its adherence to the International Covenant on Political and Civil Rights.

According [to] the Canadian Press report, Bob Epstein, advisor to the Council of Crees in Quebec is convinced that the UN complaints will send shock waves throughout Quebec because it hits at the heart of the province's language law. (*Suburban*, Oct 31/90)

On December 11, 1990, Rapoport managed a "Special to the Sun" in Toronto: "Que. law goes to UN: March date set for hearing into ban on English signs." His summary slides over the delays and ignores the government games-playing, leaving only a thin and insubstantial account. No reader could possibly deduce from it the full significance of Canada being called up on the carpet before the world. The *Sun* quoted the UN communiqué that noted the "Committee also expressed its intention to decide on the admissibility of [the case] with or without [Canada's] observations, during its 41st session" (*Sun*, Dec 11/90). The *Sun* never followed up.

The *Toronto Star*, the *Globe and Mail*, the *Financial Post*, *Maclean's* magazine, and *Western Report* shared the same silence. News of the UN's first decision on admissibility on April 11, 1991, was available only to those who knew where to find it, from CVESPA, through their small newssheet *Dialogue*, with its circulation of 3,000 or so.

Only because of that April 1991 UN decision, the *Toronto Star* dared a teeny revelation. The paper's management was leery of questioning any development that threatened the sanctity of Official Bilingualism. On June 21, the paper reported one reaction from justice minister Kim Campbell's press secretary, Owen Lippert; he allowed to the media on June 20 that the department was taking the McIntyre case "very seriously." He added that the justice minister had not decided whether to support or oppose him. According to the *Star*, the Crown had been given until December 11, 1991, to respond to the complaint, and they did manage to include some gutsy stuff that Gord McIntyre had said: "I take no pleasure in taking my country before the United Nations. . . . I know that there are some who say that the denial of English on commercial signs is unimportant. But I also know that the appeasement and concessions lead only to ever-increasing denials of rights and are the stuff that racism and intolerance breed on" ("Government preparing case on Quebec sign law for U.N.," *Star*, June 21/91).

The Government of Canada was taking the case seriously, all right. Mulroney, voluntarily aided by the press, had everything to gain by keeping it buried.

Six months later the United Nations exposed some interesting information. In January 1992 the UN Human Rights Committee apologized in an evidently defensive communiqué for there being no mechanism to prevent a state from deliberately stalling the UN's proceedings "for its own political processes." Therefore, "repeat reminders [to the offending State] would continue" (*Southwest Quebec Dialogue*, Jan/92).

Looming over the stalling tactics and secrecy hovered the figure of Kim Campbell, Canada's Minister of Justice.

According to another of Irwin Rapoport's specials to the *Toronto Sun* — this time written with a colleague, Peter Sauve — a more important news item surfaced:

> As a signatory to the covenant and to the UN's Optional Protocol, Canada would have to amend its laws if Bill 178 is deemed to violate the agreement. . . .
>
> The Canadian government told the UN last fall that McIntyre "had not exhausted all domestic (legal) remedies" in fighting Bill 178, which UN bylaws require. . . .
>
> . . . In April [1990], Article 19, a London-based [England] freedom of information and expression watchdog, called Bill 178 "censorship." ("Anglo takes case to UN: Quebec mortician presses sign fight," *Sun*, June 18/91)

The national newspapers totally ignored the fact that the Government of Canada stood firmly against the fundamental rights of a Canadian citizen.[4] And the press barons certainly recognized their own duplicity. When Bill 178 was introduced and passed by the National Assembly in Quebec in December 1988, the media sought and reported Mulroney's reaction: "I neither approve nor do I believe that it meets the tests" as set down by the Supreme Court of Canada (*GM*, Dec 22/88).

T HE *GLOBE AND MAIL* maintained a silence that would have delighted a dictator.

It cannot be argued they knew nothing about it. Canada's self-appointed "National Newspaper" is well staffed in Quebec. The *Globe*'s Quebec bureau in Quebec City covered the Bélanger–Campeau Commission hearings in 1990. As far back as November 14, 1990, the day McIntyre's lawyer Julius Grey appeared before the commission, the *Globe* knew of the remarks chairman Michel Bélanger had made: "On behalf of the Chair, you have referred twice to the United Nations's condemnation of Bill 178. As you are well aware, it was not the United Nations but rather one of the committees of the United Nations" (*Journal des débats*, Nov 14/90).

Even when the case was finally deemed admissible before the UN on

April 11, 1991, the *Globe* remained mum on the sidelines. Yet when it came to collective rights before the UN, the paper changed its tune. On July 9, 1991, the *Globe* published Patricia Poirier's article on the rights of Canada's aboriginals, "UN to grill Canada, group says: Report says rights of natives and non-natives breached."

Not until August 1, 1991 — more than three years after Gord McIntyre received his first written notice from the Quebec language commission — did the *Globe* pussyfoot in to cover the case. Their first piece appeared in the form of a dismissal notice. Through its "Canada In Brief" column, the paper acknowledged in a few curt words: "UN report blasts Quebec."

Wrong. The UN was not blasting Quebec at all. The "State party concerned," as the UN cited it in the complaint documents, was Canada, not Quebec. The *Globe* was more than a little tardy. The decision on admissibility rejecting Canada's claim had come down nearly four months earlier.

One year later, on May 1, 1992, the mainstream media still had not given the story of Canada's position, according to CVESPA's *Dialogue*. The newsletter reported to its members: "On May 1, 1992, we were sent the response of Canada, including one from the Province of Quebec. Canada continued to argue that all domestic remedies had not been exhausted. It developed a history of the Charter of Rights and Freedoms and discussed the notwithstanding clause in detail suggesting it was consistent with the international Covenant on Civil and Political Rights."

Throughout the proceedings the Government of Canada and Kim Campbell's justice department employed all manner of subterfuge. The federal government defended the notwithstanding clause, claiming that there were "extraordinary conditions attached to Section 33 which limit its use" and therefore it was not a bar to justice. Campbell's department pleaded, "Therefore the [UN] Committee's views should be confined to those particular situations and cannot question the existence of Section 33 per se."

B Y THE TIME it ended in the spring of 1993, Gord McIntyre's case against Canada had consumed almost five years, almost the full legal life of Bill 178, while the UN came to its decision. The point at issue remained the same: could McIntyre post a sign for his English-speaking clientele in English in Quebec?

A few weeks before the decision, a small item appeared in the print media. An alert press should have linked it immediately to the McIntyre case. Julius Grey, the lawyer acting for CVESPA and McIntyre, known to the separatists as "The Kiss of Death" or the "Joan of Arc of Bill 101," had apparently changed positions. On February 8, 1993, the *Toronto Star* reported that he had reached a private deal with Professor Josée Legault of the University of Montreal, the extreme Quebec nationalist and the influential author of *L'Invention d'une minorité: Les Anglo-Québécois* (1992). The terms of their agreement involved Grey's own views on Bill 101, the infamous French Language Charter. For Grey to have reached any accommodation with such a radical was astonishing.

Grey's elegy on the French Language Charter had been published in *Le Devoir*. Now he was dancing around in support of Bill 101. Odd. This was the same Julius Grey who had headed up a private initiative called the Task Force on Canadian Federalism during the Meech Lake rumble. He was supposed to be a Trudovnic bilingual federalist! At this point the *Toronto Star* knew that the UN case was proceeding and that Julius Grey was the point man charging against Bill 101 before the UN.[5]

Here's what the lawyer said in the autumn of 1991: "There's tremendous pettiness on the nationalist side. All their nitpicking interpretations of the language laws and going after English-speaking workers hurt only the little guy, but they act as powerful signals. It's been getting worse over the last five years" (*Western Report*, Oct 14/91).

By 1993, he had obviously changed his tune. The compromise he had reached with Professor Legault would allow for a trial period during which other languages could appear on Quebec signs. Tellingly, Grey caved in on the essentials — namely, constitutional protection. There was more, too.

When the UN decision eventually came down in McIntyre's favour, Grey sounded apologetic and almost disappointed in his client's victory: "One must underline that no negative inferences should be drawn about Quebec" (*Dialogue*, Apr 26/93). Whose side was he on? What of Claude Ryan's tongue troopers?

Even Maurice King of CVESPA, McIntyre's partner in the exercise, hastened to protect the Quebec government. When news of the decision broke on CBC on April 8, King said, "The ruling is against Canada instead of Quebec — so the UN supported the argument we made to the Committee" (*Sun*, Apr 9/93).

Fuddle-duddle. Obviously the UN judgement was as much a condemnation of the Bourassa government of Quebec as it was of the Mulroney government in Ottawa.

CVESPA's role is not entirely above suspicion. Even while the organization fought the Government of Canada, it enjoyed 77 percent of its operating funds from that same government; only 13.9 percent came from its members' dues.[6] For all intents and purposes, CVESPA's president and its employees draw government salaries as public servants. The same is true of Alliance Quebec, whose funding sources imply the same controlled dissent.

The public really heard about the McIntyre story nationally for the first time with the release of the United Nations "views," as the UN describes its decisions, on April 8, 1993. Even then, the media was evasive, saying that the actual wording of the judgement had yet to be released. In other words, the Canadian press could confirm that a judgement had been passed but could not tell what the ruling said. They clammed up without explaining what the problem was or why there was a delay.

While the press chose to be cute, the Tories used the time to engineer a diversion. Plans had been in the works as far back as the date Norman Spector departed from the Prime Minister's Office in January 1992. That was when it was announced that Hugh Segal (aka "Bunter"), "a Red Tory who worked for former Conservative Leader Robert Stanfield," would take over as Mulroney's corporal in charge of strategy (*GM*, Jan 8/92).

The McIntyre story broke on the national news on CBC's "Prime Time" on April 8, 1993. It came by way of a report from Paul Carvello of "Le Télèjournal." He devoted only a few seconds to background details and then quoted Gord McIntyre: "It's kinda sad that — that we had to go to the United Nations to get our human rights in, in Canada. I don't know why the Canadian government — why they were always taking the, uh, the part of the nationalists in Quebec. And depriving, depriving the ordinary citizens. . . ." Nothing happened.

And nothing happened, because, by a mighty strange coincidence, a second story hit the country immediately after the McIntyre story should have done. This second story swamped the nation's media: Tory backroom boy Hugh Segal had decided to run for the leadership of the Conservative Party.

On April 6, Hugh Winsor of the *Globe and Mail* wrote in his column that trade minister Michael Wilson supported Segal in his bid. On April 7, Mulroney's chief of staff and number-one apologist told the breathless media mobbing him he would make a final decision in the next few days. He let drop that there was a 50-percent chance he would run against Kim Campbell. The *Globe* dutifully reported that "four senior cabinet ministers are urging Mr. Segal to seek the party leadership and the veteran Conservative organizer seemed to relish the attention as he deliberately kept the speculation alive for a few more days" (Geoffrey York and Ross

Howard, "Tory candidates on tenterhooks as Segal ponders leadership bid," *GM*, Apr 8/93).

Later press reports quoted former Ontario Premier Bill Davis and Tory bagman Eddie Goodman declaring that the party had collected some $750,000 in pledges and they were now only awaiting disbursal instructions. But even accepting that Segal had credentials that "certainly are first rate," Richard Gwyn of the *Toronto Star* noted that his role as Mulroney's principal spin-doctor "more than cancelled that out." As the wily Gwyn asked, after Segal withdrew from the arena he never entered, "What Segal didn't explain is why he almost became a candidate in the first place" ("The sad saga of Hugh Segal and Ontario saps," *Star*, Apr 11/93). Maybe Gwyn didn't ask — or look far enough himself.

On April 9, when the McIntyre story should have grabbed national headlines in every paper, the non-candidacy of Hugh Segal flooded the press. The *Toronto Sun* editorial was headed "So long Hughie." The *Globe and Mail* headline the same day said, "Segal shies at starting gate."

Loaded with easy-to-find fodder, the columnists had a field day. Predictably, Mulroney's acolyte Michel Gratton of the *Sun* jumped in with "A master stroke for Hugh Segal" (*Sun*, Apr 9/93).[7] At the *Globe* Jeffrey Simpson led off with "Now that Hugh Segal has balked, where will his supporters turn?" (*GM*, Apr 9/93). Michel Vastel, columnist for *Le Soleil*, might have been on to something but he offered no details: "In the end, this hoax looks a lot like Segal himself: a great market coup to revive media interest in a race that isn't taking off. After all isn't this the same Segal who emerged from anonymity to say in a 'spontaneous' interview on national English television that his boss had only the return to Parliament, the Speech from the Throne and the next federal election on his mind? Thirty days later, Brian Mulroney announced his resignation, revealing that he had been thinking about it since the summer of 1990!" (Pauline Couture, *GM*, Apr 8/93).

Hughie Segal as prime minister of Canada? One could only imagine.[8] "The Happy Warrior," as Charlotte Gray had dubbed him in the October 1992 *Saturday Night*, no more intended to run for the job than Canada's late beloved John Candy of SCTV did. Segal had been a backroom boy since the age of twelve when he first heard the siren call from John Diefenbaker. He'd lost so many election campaigns for others it would have been masochistic of him to throw in his own hat at the end of his political career. At twenty-three he took his first run at public office and lost. Then he was a principal adviser to Robert Stanfield, who lost. In 1976 he co-chaired Claude Wagner's failed bid for the Tory leadership fight against Joe Clark and Brian Mulroney. In 1983 he backed Joe Clark. Many Blue Tories blame Segal for the collapse of the Tory regime in Ontario under Bill Davis, another Segal-assisted politician. As Robert Fife had understated it in a feature article on Mulroney's latest man: "Obviously Segal isn't a miracle worker" (*Sun*, Mar 22/93).

What he was was a networker, and a good one, but not a team builder, which is the most essential quality of any successful political leader. A pundit, a wit, even at times an accomplished political operator, Segal was nevertheless not one to make things happen. During the grand leadership hoax, a dozen feature articles cropped up, capturing some front-page headlines in the *Globe* and an editorial in the *Sun*. The media buzzed for a whole week on the Segal story. As for Canada's humiliation before the UN, interested readers would have to scratch very hard to find the few passing references.

There was some poetic justice in all this. Having so successfully muffled the McIntyre story for five years, the pecksniffers and the pusillanimous poltroons now found themselves tangled in their own trap. There was also some irony in the discomfort this created for Segal. Here's what he and his co-author, Nathan Nurgitz, wrote of the Liberals in 1983:

> The role of a political party involves more than sustaining the appearance of political unity and single-mindedness. Political parties are instruments not only for self-governance but for society's legitimate aspirations and anxieties. . . . The Liberal party of Canada, worshipping as it does at the altar of superficial administrative competence [or at least its appearance], has never fully understood the salience of the emotional and spiritual element in the politics of a free people. . . . The danger in not embracing our differences is the danger of becoming irrelevant to the process. (*No Small Measure*, p. 11)

At his own expense, Segal had fulfilled his own prophecy.

Some members of the press might have been on the point of waking. Rosemary Speirs of the *Toronto Star* was guarded, yet missed the point: "Hugh Segal's non-candidacy, combined with a couple of the more realistic polls, suggest the Conservative government's resurgence under Kim Campbell may not be a sure bet after all" (*Star*, Apr 10/93). Douglas Fisher, the wise old man at the *Toronto Sun*, sniffed the wind and then wrote about

"Segal's silly little fling" on April 9, 1993. Surely someone in the press corps could have recognized the red herring in the tale of this Red Tory; he had written a letter to the editor of the *Globe and Mail* exactly one month before the McIntyre story broke: "As indicated by me in explicit terms to both the Kingston-Whig Standard and the Ottawa Sun — who were kind enough to ask before rushing into print — it is not my intention to seek the Conservative nomination in the federal riding of Kingston and the Islands. Similarly, seeking elective office at the next election is not in my plans" ("No intention of running," *GM*, Mar 10/93).

There was good reason for deflecting interest away from Canada's humiliation before the United Nations. The star Tory leadership hopeful, Kim Campbell, the justice minister, had had too much to do with the McIntyre case. The ploy worked.

On April 28, 1993, in what is described as a "terse statement" from the Prime Minister's Office, it was announced that Mulroney's chief of staff would quit the government on April 30 to become a Fellow in the School of Policy Studies at Queen's University. Segal would be a welcome new-comer to the Queen's Mafia. There was no explanation for his sudden departure.

Only a few facts about the McIntyre case ever became public knowledge, so Campbell was safe to pursue her ambition. The fact remains, though, that she and the Tories led the fight against McIntyre. She had been in the Mulroney Cabinet since her appointment as the Junior Minister of State for Indian and Northern Affairs on January 30, 1989. When she became justice minister on February 23, 1990, she joined the inner Cabinet of the Mulroney government and served in that portfolio till January 4, 1993. The justice portfolio is one of the most coveted plums in government — often the stepping stone to the prime ministership.

Canadians had every right to know what was going on. Yet though Campbell's department lied to them in 1991, the media sustained the cover-up. In 1991, a junior official fibbed when asked what position the Government of Canada was taking on the case. The previous year External Affairs minister Joe Clark had been questioned, too, by an international human rights group who wanted his reaction to a devastating assessment of Canada by the well-known London human rights group Article 19. Article 19's cross-examination of the federal justice department deserved critical attention, yet, once again, the *Suburban* of Montreal was the only paper that carried the story. On October 31, 1990, it quoted Francis D'Souza, director of Article 19:

"This has allowed the introduction of laws, such as Quebec's sign law which unfairly promotes one language at the expense of others. The Canadian Charter of Rights, which was added to the Constitution in 1982, gives the right to freedom of expression and information but provincial authorities can infringe this right."

The group's statement said, "Article 19 calls on the Canadian government to amend the constitution so that the right to freedom of expression and information is given full protection at all levels of the Canadian legislature."

A reporter asked about the international censure. Clark attacked him instead of dealing with the message: "You would want, as I would, to assure the standing of the group [Article 19]. I am not in a position to comment on that. I just don't know" (*Suburban*, Oct 31/90).

A FTER A TELEPHONE call to UN headquarters in New York on April 8, 1993, McIntyre and the CVESPA team learned that the United Nations Human Rights Committee had handed down their ruling. On April 9, the written text was released. But, even ten days later, the Canadian media were pretending they either didn't have the text or were downplaying the story by referring to it as if readers already knew all the details from earlier, detailed reports. Another favourite stratagem was to avoid the story altogether. For example:

- Although Southam News Service had the full text of the judgement on April 21, the April 22 *Star* simply informed the public that the text had been released and a text was available. It quoted none of the judgement. And they have quoted not a word of it since, either.

- The CBC was worse. Having sputtered a few sound-bites about it on April 8, the network dropped the subject completely.

- The *Globe and Mail* indulged in a variety of little tricks. Referring to the story in the past tense and minimizing its significance were popular ruses. On April 9, the day after the story first hit the media, Rhéal Séguin tossed off the comment that "Pressure was building on the [Quebec] government yesterday over language, the most volatile of the three issues, after reports that a United Nations committee had ruled that Quebec's language law violates individual rights and freedoms."

  The reporter attributed the story to a third party — in a piece entitled "Bourassa's future to be known in May": "Equality member Mr. Libman said yesterday he had received word of the ruling, a response to a case brought before the UN by a businessman from Huntingdon, Que. Mr. Libman said the UN committee ruled that the provisions of the Quebec sign law infringe upon Article 19, Section 2, of the International Covenant on Civil and Political Rights: 'Everyone has the right to freedom of opinion and expression . . . and to seek, receive and impart information and ideas through any media and regardless of frontiers.'"

Libman made a most convenient choice for himself. Apart from supporting both the Meech Lake and the Charlottetown accords, as the *Globe* did, he padded softly all around the issue of Bill 178. Whatever the reason for citing him, Canada's "National Newspaper" cannot be excused for the fact that it actually barred the reader from learning the straight goods. The paper preferred to print hearsay repeated by Libman when they could have used direct evidence.

The *Globe* kept up its pretence, too. On April 16, Séguin turned out "Quebec Liberals propose bilingual signs: Merchants would be required to keep at least two-thirds of space for French." He never mentioned the UN ruling.

In his April 16 column Jeffrey Simpson joined the conspiracy. He noted that "Bilingual signs would not weaken the position of French in Quebec" and ignored the UN ruling as probably nothing more than speculation: "Now according to leaked reports, a United Nations committee is about to criticize the law on unilingual signs."

"Leaked reports"?

Even the CBC had the outline of the story out on April 8. That day, Claude Ryan, Quebec's security minister, acknowledged the judgement and its implications. McIntyre's lawyer Julius Grey had commented on the case in public, and so had many others. Even Bourassa acknowledged a UN report was decidedly unfavourable to his government's position. Memories of the Charlottetown Accord and the "missing" legal text.

An April 20 *Star* article omitted Gord McIntyre's name entirely, referring only to a "businessman from Huntingdon, Quebec."

Using the you-already-know-the-full-details strategy, the *Globe* ran a front-page story on April 21, again under Rhéal Séguin's byline, "UN brief haunts Bourassa: Sign-law defence surfaces as Liberals prepare to meet." The lengthy piece gave no background to the case and quoted nothing from the actual ruling. Similarly, it offered no reaction from Julius Grey, nothing from Maurice King of CVESPA, and nothing from the victim in it all, Gord McIntyre.

For Séguin, the piece marked a dramatic departure from his long-established journalistic habits. His usual practice was to allow the people in a story to supply their own insights. Here, however, Libman alone was allowed to hold forth from centre stage: "Early last year, the Quebec government presented a document to the UN Human Rights Committee in defence of Bill 178, which bans the use of English and other languages on outdoor commercial signs. . . . The government refused yesterday [April 20, 1993] to allow the document to be released, but it was leaked to the media by Equality Party member Robert Libman. Earlier this month, Mr. Libman said the UN had ruled that Bill 178 violates the freedom of opinion and expression" (*GM*, Apr 21/93).

Again, why didn't the media simply quote from the document itself instead of relying on what the soft-on-Quebec sovereignty complainer Robert Libman said about it?

Two days later, the *Globe* confused matters even further. They released a completely different document, dated March 22, "that outlined Quebec's legal arguments presented to the United Nations in support of the law" (*GM*, Apr 23/93). At that point the judgement had been out for more than two weeks.

• At the end, the *Globe* tripped over itself and screwed up proper. On April 22, André Picard wrote the front-page story laid out below its fold-line: "Scrap bilingualism, Tories told: Long shot sparks debate on Quebec language laws." Rather surprisingly, it said nothing at all about the UN decision. Instead, it launched into details about John Long, the dark-horse candidate running for the Tory leadership and his call to scrap bilingualism.

On page 4, however, the same edition of the paper ran the continuation of a story headed "Anglophones rights," marked at the top "From Page A1" — the front page. Problem: there was no beginning of this story on the front page! The short piece on page 4 began,

She said anglophones in Quebec should be considered a minority group. . . .

However, the Committee is categorical about the Quebec language law's violation of freedom of expression. The judgment states that any limitation on an individual's right to freely express his ideas, including commercial advertising, directly violates the international community's principles regarding freedom of speech.

Altogether, the incomplete article quoted only twenty-two words from the UN's ruling: "The committee had no reason to believe that public order is threatened by a language other than French on outdoor commercial signs."

In an awkward attempt to recover their fumble, the *Globe* pretended it had intended to run the piece all along — not cut it out altogether. The next day, April 23, on page A6, Rhéal Séguin wrote an article headed "Quebec considers end to sign restrictions: UN ruling may help government sell reforms on bilingual advertising." Under it ran an apology: "Portions of yesterday's story on the Quebec language law issue that were inadvertently omitted are covered in this report."

Séguin's "replacement" piece was an entirely new article. And it harked back to information never published about the UN ruling in the first place. The article confirms that the "official UN decision was tabled" in the Quebec National Assembly on April 21, and that was it. The mysterious "she" quoted in the incomplete April 22 article — the page 4 "continuation" — was never identified. Nor was Kim Campbell's role ever spelled out. There was just a curious reference to her reticence in discussing Bill 178 in André Picard's article on page 1 on April 21: "But Ms. Campbell, the perceived front-runner, stayed surprisingly mum on Bill 178."

Campbell wasn't about to commit political suicide by proving that, like her mentor, she supported Bill 178.

- Canada's national newspaper, the *Globe*, led the parade of deflection and disinformation. Pauline Couture makes no mention of the UN decision in her column "Quebec Voices," a "weekly media sampling compiled by Pauline Couture, a Montreal writer, broadcaster and consultant" (*GM*, Apr 22/93). The paper also omits any mention of the decision in its summary of major events on the front page, "First Column."

  What of a word from the great whingey, Stephen Lewis, formerly Canada's Ambassador to the United Nations? His uncharacteristic silence on such an important national issue should have intrigued a lot of reporters. Surely he was worth a "no comment"? What about Ed Broadbent, the highly paid head of the Centre for Human Rights and Democratic Development in Montreal? Surely the author of *Possessive Individualism* and the former leader of the New Democratic Party could be inveigled into an unguarded moment?

What, in fact, of all the UN ambassadors? Maybe Professor Charles Taylor of McGill, author of *The Politics of Recognition*, would say something? He didn't. For six years the *Globe* had assaulted its readers with everything Quebecers had to say about the Constitution. Thousands upon thousands of comments from Ghislain Dufour, Gérald Larose, Claude Castonguay, and legions of others consumed thousands of column inches. But now they held their peace.

The Saturday Weekend edition of the *Globe* said not a word about the UN decision on April 24, 1993. On the twenty-sixth, Séguin's byline appeared again under "Bourassa awarded gift of unity: In emotional show of support, Quebec Liberals back language law changes," which muddied the picture even more:

> But with the recent United Nations Human Rights Committee decision that the law is a violation of freedom of expression, the Liberals felt the ruling struck a fatal blow to nationalist objections to softening the law, and that changes were in order.
>
> The party's return toward bilingualism ended years of internal division and brought the Liberals closer to their traditional beliefs. . . .
>
> [Bourassa says] "It is not unlimited freedom of expression which is found in the United Nations report. . . . The policy gives the government a margin of flexibility."

Surely the United Nations judgement deserved media exposure at least as great as that given to the Hugh Segal hoax?

- After its brief feint in the direction of responsible reporting, even the *Toronto Sun* wimped out. The best account came from Bob MacDonald, who quotes Lise Bacon, deputy premier of Quebec. She called the ruling "surprising": "We make our own laws and we can do it ourselves and we are a tolerant and open society — and I don't think we should feel diminished by such a statement." Unfortunately, MacDonald doesn't supply any quotes from the actual ruling in his column, either: "The government of Canada has been sharply criticized by a United Nations body for permitting Quebec's anti-English Bill 178 to go unchallenged" ("Language law draws UN barbs," Apr 9/93).

After that pale glimmer, the *Sun* consistently gave the Segal story precedence and, like the *Globe*, avoided the substance of the judgement.

A sappy editorial followed on April 12. It did acknowledge there was a problem; "Just say oui" to Bill 86, the proposed revision of Bill 178, the *Sun* told its readers:

> Mind you, the recommendation [of Bill 86] is about the only bright spot in the report on a law which even the United Nations says violates fundamental rights.
>
> Still, allowing bilingual signs, even if only for small businesses, would constitute a small step on the way to French-English healing. So what's the big deal?
>
> Anglophone Canadians often complain that Bill 101 [Bill 178 was the amendment], which mandates the supremacy of the French language in Quebec, is difficult to understand. . . .
>
> . . . For the sane majority, in and out of Quebec, this small move [Bill 86] should be hailed as a step, for once, in the right direction.

The editors missed on two counts. While Bill 86 did allow English on commercial signs, many remaining restrictions violated international laws of freedom of expression. If that bill came under attack, the Quebec National Assembly could again invoke the notwithstanding clause and continue to enforce the same tyranny.

Second, a provincial bill provides no constitutional protection of anything. It can be overruled in the Quebec, or any other provincial, legislature at any time.

• The most responsible press in English Canada on the McIntyre case was the *Financial Post*. An editorial on April 29 hit the mark with "Settling Domestic Disputes at Home": "The whole country's international reputation — especially as an outspoken advocate for human rights — was tarnished."

Unfortunately, that's as far as it went. There's no mention, for example, of the fact that the federal government fought on Quebec's side against McIntyre.

The whole point of this national disgrace appears in one letter to the editor from the president of the Alliance for the Preservation of English in Canada (APEC), on May 5, 1993. Ron Leitch wrote: "To its shame the federal government not only opposed McIntyre's application to the UN committee, but stalled as long as possible in putting in their objections in order to delay a decision. . . . It was right and proper that this Canadian aberration be exposed for the whole world to see" (*FP*, May 5/93).

- As might be expected, the *Toronto Star* was the worst of the lot. Canada's largest newspaper, the Pulp Primevil, avoided the issue entirely. On April 8, the day the CBC put the story out across Canada, the paper ran nothing on it. On April 9, when the story hit the press, albeit obliquely, they still kept mum. April 10: still nothing. Canada's largest-circulation paper did not touch the story until April 16, and when they did they covered up.

  They published what amounted to a tiny footnote from Canadian Press, and even it was inaccurate: "The UN Human Rights Committee ruled last week that the law violates the freedom-of-expression provision of the International Covenant on Civil and Political Rights" (Apr 16/93). By April 16, the story was *two* weeks old. In light of one very interesting comment from the Tory leadership hopeful and justice minister, it seems the *Star* had joined forces with Campbell: "As prime minister, I would leave to the province things that are provincial. . . . The worst thing I could do would be to interfere in the debate" (*Star*, Apr 21/93).

  When they finally broke the story on April 22, the editors revealed their own priorities. Six stories appeared on the front page that day in the paper's first edition, including a tidbit about the Gord McIntyre saga: "U.N. rules Quebec law violates free speech." Of these stories, the McIntyre one was printed in the smallest typeface and accorded the smallest column of space. All the other stories reappeared in the second edition; by then the UN story had vanished. In the third edition, all the headlines of the five remaining stories changed; again, the UN story had disappeared.

  Canada's largest newspaper ignored the subject the following week. Then, completely out of the blue, on April 29, they raised it the same way the other newspapers did, writing about it as if they had already dealt with it in great detail before. The editorial "Bad language" does hit the problem harder than any other Canadian paper up to that point, yet the author quoted nothing from the UN judgement itself:

> Quebec has come a long way in its language legislation. But even after being chastised by a United Nations human rights committee, it is still not forthcoming on outdoor signs.
> The U.N. committee ruled that most of the laws limiting the use of English on commercial signs violate the right to free speech. . . .
> With the U.N. judgment in hand, and the Canadian verdict already on record, it's time for Quebec to make a fresh start — by restoring the right to free speech in both official languages, on signs and in schools.

Like every other newspaper and broadcasting outlet in English-speaking Canada, the *Star* did not pick up on the headline story of the *Gazette* of April 23, "Sign law can't stand, Bourassa hints." (Incidentally, the *Gazette* didn't cite a single comma from the UN judgement, either.) In that article Philip Authier reported Bourassa admitted the UN judgement "appears inescapable" — that the sign law clearly violated freedom of speech.

- The Montreal *Gazette*, a Southam paper and Quebec's only major English newspaper, trivialized the story, too. More than any other paper in Canada, it should have led in telling the whole story unfolding in its province.[9]

  Once the UN judgement came down, the paper acknowledged Gord McIntyre's duel with the Quebec and Canadian governments on April 10, 1993, for the first time. Philip Authier of the Quebec bureau wrote "UN ruling could influence language debate: Bourassa" as its second headline on the front page. On this momentous occasion in the history of anglophone rights in Quebec, the paper featured "Panel links city's economic decline to anglo alienation" by Jay Bryan. It discussed the UN ruling as if it were old news. On page A5 appeared a small blurb by Carolyn Adolph that noted "Huntingdon man hails moral victory as UN rules sign law violates rights."

  In his article, Authier excused himself for playing coy: "The impact of the Committee's ruling . . . won't be available in writing for some time yet." When McIntyre was told on April 6 that the written judgement would be available very soon, one has to wonder why the *Gazette* would bother to report anything about the story at all.

The facts differ considerably from what the newspapers tried to convey. The United Nations Human Rights Committee had "adopted its Views" under the Option Protocol on March 31. Authier described the ruling as "made public by decision of the Human Rights Committee." Yet he also described its release as a "restricted distribution" of the full details of the case, which the UN's same April 5 release had already recorded.

There was no secrecy involved here. As is common in international dealings, as a matter of courtesy the UN allowed themselves a short time to ensure all the parties were notified about the details of the decision before releasing it more widely (*International Covenant of Civil and Political Rights*, CCPR/C/47/359/1989 and 385/1989: Forty-Seventh Session).

The question in the McIntyre case will always be: what did the media think they were doing all this time? Professor Stephen Scott of McGill summed up the business: "[The case is] incredibly important in terms of forming public opinion and shoring up the will of the judiciary, if it needs shoring up" (*Gazette*, Apr 10/93).

On April 13, a long-overdue piece appeared in the Montreal *Gazette* by William Johnson, "Quebec's intellectuals continue demonic myth":

> How could such a violation of freedom happen in Canada, and with the complicity, overt or silent, of almost Quebec's entire intellectual class? . . .
>
> The UN body confirms the judgments of Quebec's Superior Court, Court of Appeal and the Supreme Court of Canada. Unanimously, the eleven Canadian judges (8 from Quebec) who sat on the case found that the prohibition of English on signs is not only a violation of freedom, it is a violation of freedom that is incompatible with a free and democratic society.
>
> How, then, could Quebec, through its government, have imposed such a tyrannical law and enforced it for 16 years? [PQ Law 101, 1977; Law 178, 1988]

Was he serious? Johnson, more than anyone else in the Quebec media knew how cover-up operated in Quebec. He had himself virtually ignored the McIntyre case for four years. Another journalist decorated with the Ceramic Snowflake.

Finally on April 22 the *Gazette* sneaked home to its readers. They printed a paltry 113 words from the UN judgement. The editorial assessment of April 23 stands out like a sore thumb:

> The UN ruling is historic. It is not about Gordon McIntyre, the Huntingdon undertaker who petitioned the Committee because he wasn't allowed to keep a sign reading "Kelly Funeral Home." The ruling is about the public place of a non-official language, and as such will apply to many situations around the world. . . . There is something terribly embarrassing for Quebecers in the thought that the UN spent valuable time cataloguing the petty visits and deadlines of the language authorities. Such legalistic harassment is now public knowledge, and will be discussed and written about in the UN's six official languages for some time to come. The Liberal government, and for that matter the Quebecers in general, should consider the UN ruling as a new beginning.

"Something terribly embarrassing for Quebecers"? — English, a "non-official language" in any place in Canada? "Not about Gordon McIntyre"?

On May 11, the paper claimed it had procured a copy of the federal brief defending Bill 178. The story that trumpeted this news carefully avoided any mention of the peripatetic Kim Campbell. The evidence of the justice minister and her department's involvement trickled into another story by Philip Authier, "Canada fought for sign law, brief shows: Notwithstanding clause defended as legitimate 'counterweight'":

> Canada's written legal arguments to the United Nations last year show that the federal government was putting up as strong a defence of Quebec's sign law as the province was.
>
> Canada told the UN in March 1992 that the notwithstanding clause in its constitution is consistent with international human rights standards.

Angered by its own failures, in a vengeful editorial headed "The Choice for Alliance Quebec," on May 8, the *Gazette* finally exposed how it really stood on Quebec anglophones' rights. What had immediately elicited such vitriol was the election of the new candidate to run Alliance Quebec. There were two: Robert Keaton, who supported Bill 178, and Maurice King, who supported Gord McIntyre and helped lead the fight before the United Nations. As the editorial put it, "The two candidates, challenger Maurice King and incumbent Robert Keaton, offer a choice between anger and realism, between fulmination and achievement."

On Maurice King, it went on:

> [He] is certainly good at taking stentorian stands. He talks of "a new vision that confronts the Quebec nationalist vision," and says Alliance Quebec "has been complying . . . all down the line" with the abrogation of English rights. . . .
>
> But there is a huge fundamental flaw in the world view that Mr. King evokes.
>
> The fact is that in its 11 years of existence, Alliance Quebec — *and only Alliance Quebec* — has consistently achieved much of real, practical benefit for English Quebecers.

The piece ended on a flourish about Keaton: "He has handled the task with integrity and dedication."

Yikes! Robert Keaton, also known as "Mr. Compliance Quebec," was a big part of the problem. On January 29, 1991, Robert Keaton and the likes of Robert Libman supported the Allaire Report, which signalled the virtual dismantling of Canada and the complete emasculation of constitutional rights for Quebec's anglophones.

The attacks on CVESPA's Maurice King, on the other hand, were sour grapes. The *Gazette*'s editor didn't have the grace or courage to admit that the reason Bill 178 was headed for the ash-heap of history was inextricably entwined with King's own contribution to the McIntyre case.

Maclean's magazine was as bad as the rest. Its reporting of the case was both late and mean-spirited, if not malicious. In its May 3, 1993, issue, when the media could no longer contain the story, the magazine produced one of its familiar put-down pieces on the underdog who beat the establishment. Photographed beside a couple of coffins, Gord McIntyre appeared for Barry Came's article "A grievance upheld: An undertaker wages war on Quebec's sign laws" on page

26. The page-long piece was slipped quietly into the general news articles. Its existence at all proved that someone on staff had got the message that something was terribly amiss. It was the first time *Maclean's* had touched the case:

> The 18 jurists who studied the issue roundly dismissed Quebec arguments about the need for the sign law.[10] They found that Bill 178 contravened the International Covenant on Civil and Political Rights, which Canada has signed and Quebec has agreed to respect. The 20-page judgment states that any limitation on an individual's right to freely express his ideas, including advertising, violates the principle of freedom of expression. It also argues, contrary to Quebec's position, that francophone rights "are not threatened by the ability of others to advertise in a language other than French."

On May 6, 1993, Bill 86 — the revised Bill 178 — was introduced in the Quebec National Assembly. On May 14, 1993, the most comprehensive article yet on Gord McIntyre's fight appeared in a *New York Times* feature by Clyde H. Farnsworth. It was evident from the piece that Canadians who sought justice in matters of fundamental rights in their own country would probably have to seek authority from international institutions beyond Canada's boundaries for some time in the future as well.

HERE, AT LAST, are some excerpts from the judgement of the United Nations Committee on the International Covenant on Civil and Political Rights. None of this has appeared in Canada's national press or in a book or been aired on television or radio:

The Committee's admissibility decision (April 11, 1991):

> During its forty-first session, the Committee considered the admissibility of the communications [from both parties]. It disagreed with the State party's [Canada's] contention that there were still effective remedies available to the authors in the circumstances of their cases. In this context, it noted that in spite of repeated legislative changes protecting the *visage linguistique* of Quebec, and despite the fact that some of the relevant statutory provisions had been declared unconstitutional successively by the

Superior, Appeal and Supreme Courts, the only effect of this had been the replacement of these provisions by ones that are the same in substance as those they replaced, but reinforced by the "notwithstanding" clause of Section 10 of Bill 178. (para. 7.1)

This unequivocal condemnation by the UN had no effect on the Government of Canada whatsoever. After doing everything they could to frustrate and delay the case, the bureaucrats in the justice department tried another ploy a year later:

The State party's request for a review . . .

In a submission dated 6 March 1992, the Federal Government requests the Committee to review its decision on admissibility. It notes that the number of litigants who contest the validity of Bill 178 has grown, and that hearings before the Court of Quebec on the issue were held on 14 January 1992. The proceedings continue, and lawyers for the provincial government were scheduled to present Quebec's point of view on 23 and 24 March 1992. (*UN Communication*, April 5/93, para. 8.1)

Revelation. In its submission of December 28, 1990, the federal government argued that the complainants, McIntyre et al., had not exhausted all the "domestic" remedies available to them and that they had failed to "seek redress from the Canadian courts or other bodies that may be competent to resolve the issue pursuant to Canadian law" (para. 5.2).

Now Canada was asserting that McIntyre and company had an obvious legal opportunity to do exactly what the Supreme Court of Canada had failed to accomplish when it struck down Bill 101. On January 27, just thirty-eight days before this same federal ministry made Canada's submission on March 6, 1992, finance minister Don Mazankowski announced the cancellation of the Court Challenges Program, also known as the Charter Challenge Program. One of the reasons he gave was its backlog of 88 cases, with 17 other cases under appeal. This same program was the one the federal government had put forward to the UN as one of the legal avenues left open to the complainants in Canada to ease their heavy personal financial burdens in carrying the case. The UN reported this recommended course of action as available to the complainants on December 28, 1990: "The State party [Canada] also points to the availability of the Federal Court Challenges Programme, which alleviates the financial hardship associated with the conduct of such litigation and states that the legal issues raised would be within the scope of the programme . . ." (para. 5.5).

The justice department acted in bad faith, knowing full well opportunity for redress in Canada had been foreclosed deliberately.

In its final judgement the UN Committee commented: "On several occasions, the State party [Canada] requested an extension of time to make its submission, explaining that it needed more time as the issues involved were factually and legally complex and concerned both federal and provincial areas of legislative competence" (para. 5.1).

The Mulroney government tripped all over themselves to defend Quebec's Bill 178. Mulroney never budged from the words he had written in 1983 in *Where I Stand*: "Quebec will always need a protective device . . ." (p. 65). Some of the devious mindset in Ottawa was forcibly exposed to the blinding light of day in the UN report on December 28, 1990: "The State party further submits that Quebec law provides the possibility for the authors to test the constitutional validity or application of Bill No. 178 through the use of an application for a declaratory judgement . . ." (para. 5.4).

The Government of Canada was blowing smoke-rings at the UN committee. Canada was arguing that a provision in the Quebec Code of Civil Procedure allowed a challenge to the notwithstanding clause that Quebec Bill 178 contained. Sure thing.

The Canadian government's strategy came straight from Mulroney and his Sept-Îles speech of August 6, 1984. Quebec could do no wrong. At all costs, that province was to be spared "humiliation."

The final ruling of the United Nations came down on March 31, 1993. By this time, Gord McIntyre was sixty-one. He had endured five years of abuse and a tremendous loss of business. His was a Pyrrhic victory at vast expense with little gain. The media had seen to that.

Consideration of the merits [a selection of quotes]

> The Government of Quebec has asserted that commercial activity such as outdoor advertising does not fall within the ambit of article 19 [of the UN Covenant]. The Committee does not share this opinion. Article 19, paragraph 2, must be interpreted as encompassing every form of subjective ideas and opinions capable of transmission to others, which are compatible with article 20 of news and information, of commercial expression and advertising, of works of art, etc. . . . (para. 11.3)

A State [Canada] may choose one or more official languages, but it may not exclude, outside the spheres of public life, the freedom to express oneself in a certain language. The Committee accordingly concludes that there has been a violation of article 19, paragraph 2. (para. 11.4)

But by 1993, the state institutions had won out over the citizen's fundamental rights. Section 33, Trudeau's infamous notwithstanding clause, has a shelf life of five years. Bill 178 became law on December 21, 1988. By the date of the UN ruling, the case had taken so long that the decision almost didn't matter. Within nine months, Bill 178 would be history. The United Nations, as well as Canada and Quebec, had run out of playtime.

So what kind of role had the UN really played in the case? Why had such a straightforward case taken so long? Could it have had anything to do with the fact that Canada was one of the few member nations that paid its bills? Pressure from the federal government to delay the decision played some part in the process, but it is hard to say just how much and why. In August 1993, some four months after the United Nations released its judgement, the organization sank into the worst financial crisis in its history.

So Canada's press moved on. They eagerly turned their attention to speculating about the forthcoming federal election — particularly about how the vote in Quebec would be split between the Bloc Québécois, the Liberals, and the Tories. After all, there were fewer months left before the federal election hit than there were to the time when Bill 178 would die as a matter of law.

The country's own journalists would never tell the full story of Gord McIntyre's battle for freedom.

Notes

1 Personal interview with Gord McIntyre by the author and his assistant, Sue Gordon, Huntingdon, Quebec, May 23/93.

2 Warren Allmand, Liberal MP for Notre-Dame-de-Grâce, responded to McIntyre and company's overtures. In a letter dated Feb 7, 1990, he wrote that he was "absolutely shocked by the treatment you have received. . . . This very day I am taking action to inquire what happened to your letters and why they weren't properly dealt with" (*The First Step*, p. 19). After this initial interest, he must have dropped the matter.

3 In the 1994 election for the presidency of Alliance Quebec, candidate Irwin Rapoport, identified by Canadian Press as a "school commissioner," was defeated by a lawyer, Michael Hamelin, 119 to 26 (*GM*/CP, May 30/94).

4 Mulroney's office knew about the McIntyre case. The December 1991 issue of *Dialogue*, CVESPA's publication, reported that "there had been no acknowledgement by the office of the Prime Minister to the request of CVESPA to present Mr. Mulroney with the 4000 signature petition requesting that Canada not support Bill 178 before the United Nations Human Rights Committee" (Vol. 5, No. 6, p. 10).

5 After seeing the article in the *Toronto Star*, I wrote to ask CVESPA about it. Maurice King wrote back to tell me that publicity might jeopardize the UN decision. He described CVESPA as satisfied with Grey's role in the case before the UN.

6 According to the CVESPA Annual Report dated March 31, 1993, and tabled at the 10th Annual General Meeting that May 30, $95,000 of their operating revenue of $152,000 is a "Federal operating grant," $20,000 is simply labelled "Project grants," and $3,634 is a "Quebec Government grant." The salaries and fringe benefits were reported to be $84,265.

7 As the Mulroney era ended, Gratton gradually dumped the Mulroney camp, including Segal. Following his slobbery April 9 column, Gratton wrote, "I just don't understand Hugh Segal," on April 14. On August 16, he finally nailed the pretend contender to the floorboards: "I have come to believe that the farcical Hugh Segal leadership three-day saga epitomizes what the Big Blue Machine is really all about. Segal bluffed for two days and folded in two minutes after telling the media he was going to take several days to make up his mind" ("Big, blue and beneath contempt," *Sun*, Aug 16/93).

The Segal scam had been running for some time at this point. On April 6 the "First Column" on the front page of the *Globe* featured a brief come-on, "Tories want Hugh Segal," touting him as "a successful organizer in Ontario provincial politics [with impressive qualifications."

8   The most vomitory article ever written about Mulroney, even surpassing those of the *Toronto Sun*'s Michel Gratton, came from Segal himself after he had taken up his position with the Queen's Mafia as a fellow in the school of policy studies. Spewing praise in "A farewell to Mr. Nice Guy" (*GM*, June 10/93), Segal burbled over his fallen comrade: "When you take an inchoate, bitchy, largely anglophone and fractious group of federal losers like the pre-Mulroney Conservative Party, and shape a bilingual, pan-regional, successful and electorally victorious Conservative Party, you do not do so by stressing where the party is wrong, weak, inept or incompetent. You do the opposite. . . . But whatever the reason, for the nation's being unaware of 'the other Prime Minister' that I worked for, and regardless of who is to blame, Canadians missed knowing more fully one of the most compelling, complex and human Prime Ministers in our nation's history. And that is a genuine shame."

9   The *Gazette* backed the Yes side in the October Referendum of 1992.

10   Not so. Seventeen of the eighteen jurists ruled in McIntyre's favour. Mr. Walid Sadi dissented in favour of the federal government's argument "that a declaratory judgement would not only be an available but also an effective remedy" (p. 18).

35

Kim Campbell Comes to Bytown, Karl Marx to Ontario
— June 26 to September 8, 1993

O NE HOUR AFTER Brian Mulroney returned to private life, at 11:00 in the morning of June 25, Avril Phaedra Douglas Campbell became Canada's nineteenth prime minister. The Clerk of the Privy Council secured permission from Governor General Ramon Hnatyshyn to swear her in: "I, Kim Campbell, do solemnly and sincerely promise and swear that I will truly and faithfully and to the best of my skill and knowledge execute the powers and trusts reposed in me as Prime Minister, so help me God."

Campbell's first prime ministerial act was to reduce the number of federal government departments from 32 to 23. In addition to his role as minister designate of the new industry department, Jean Charest assumed the responsibility of deputy prime minister. He would also oversee the CRTC, Canada's broadcasting police force.

Campbell's appointments surprised observers. She ignored the most powerful and populist province in the country, giving Ontario not a single high-profile portfolio. Tory business as usual. And to protect the Pearson–Trudeau executive-federalist vision of Canada, she created the Department of Canadian Heritage, "being established to support and encourage a strong sense of Canadian identity and heritage based on the fundamental characteristics of Canada — bilingualism and multiculturalism — and our diverse culture and heritage."

In a news release, the PM's Office distributed a "Professional Experience" summary of fifteen members of the "Deputy Minister Community" affected by the change. Some astonishing facts came to light. Six of the fifteen department heads, for example, were francophones. More important, thirteen of them had experience in government only. And of the total 116 career positions ever held, 113 of these were in government. *Translation: the government experience of these 15 appointees totalled 98 percent!*

Between them they shared thirty-three university degrees, excluding those pursuing more education. Only one DM had just one degree — the president of Investment Canada, and he had held seven government positions and boasted no private-sector experience. Campbell had every intention of carrying on in the manner of her predecessors. Practical or private-sector experience swayed her very little in her choices.

As in both the Trudeau and the Mulroney administrations, this massive re-organization was illegal. It was undertaken without the approval of Parliament. As the huge shuffle settled, the Public Service Commission (PSC), which had been created especially to protect the public interest, remained silent. Having endorsed the corruption of the Merit Principle, the PSC had made itself the most irrelevant body in government.

In the Campbell administration, Glen Shortliffe, Clerk of the Privy Council, would virtually run the country. This prime minister handed her chief public servant more power than any of his predecessors had ever had. Called variously "The Enforcer" or "The Dark Prince" within the public service, Shortliffe was known for his quick temper and ruthless behaviour. Even the facts behind his appointment were shrouded in secrecy.

Although Paul Tellier's departure was announced on June 16, 1992, Shortliffe's appointment, like many top appointments within the labyrinth's confines, was "sort of announced" on June 18. When he condescended to address the masses for the first time, Shortliffe had donned the full garb of the politicians' lackey: "What the Prime Minister is doing is belatedly restructuring the government of Canada to better reflect today's society, with all the changes that have taken place in the last decade.[1] The government of Canada of this past year has had the structure and operations of a government built during the 1950s, 1960s and 1970s. . . . It's an orderly reorganization that's been planned for two years and will take three more to complete" (*GM*, July 17/93).

On August 11, Shortliffe ordered all departments to submit their plans for slashing their regional offices, plans to be carried out immediately after the federal election. He assumed the Tories would win. The Enforcer decreed that "service point rationalizations are to be ready for implementation for November." No such directives applied in Ottawa. Shortliffe's slash-and-burn of the ranks would hurt the regions most because 70 percent of the federal public service were deployed there.

The immediate effect was very costly to Canadian taxpayers. Department heads in the regions threw themselves into a frenzy. Within days dozens of draft organization charts, mission statements, deployment plans, integration scenarios, and lengthy work-plans were being reviewed by hundreds of hastily assembled damage-control committees, each vying for power in the radically changed world they believed was coming. Without a law of Parliament, an Order in Council, or even a cabinet directive, Shortliffe triggered the biggest turf war in Canadian public service history.

One person quick to recognize the play was another dark prince from an era long past, Senator Michael Pitfield, Clerk of the Privy Council during the Trudeau era. To the *Globe and Mail* he wrote:

> Ms. Campbell has precious little justification for the exercise that is now tearing the public service apart and costing the treasury millions of dollars. Not only is Ms. Campbell a prime minister without an electoral mandate but her government legally terminates in a few months' time. . . . The simple fact, of course, is that the [re-organization] proposals would have had to be put before Parliament, now conveniently shunted out of the picture, and they would have to be explained, no easy thing to do since lots of what is being done seems to have no other justification than political packaging. (*GM*, July 12/93)

This had to be the pot calling the kettle black. No other Clerk in public-service history had exhibited such contempt for legislative authority as P. Michael Pitfield. Under Trudeau, this most autocratic and feared public servant was known by the mandarinate as "The Black Spider."

Cutting government down to size proved a popular activity outside Canada at this point, too. Speaking in Washington on September 7 from behind a truckload of papers representing mounds of government regulations, President Bill Clinton promised his fellow Americans a leaner government. The September 8 *Financial Post* estimated that by reducing the U.S. government by some 12 percent, eliminating an estimated 252,000 government jobs, the American public service would be reduced below 2 million — its lowest level since 1966. Clinton's words sounded familiar: "We have a government largely organized on a top-down, bureaucratic-industrial model when we are in an industrial age" (*Star*, Sept 8/93).

Campbell's credibility as a power player was brought into question on her first day in office. On Saturday, June 26, U.S. President Bill Clinton authorized an air strike on Iraq's intelligence headquarters. When he had congratulated the new prime minister the previous day, he had not mentioned his immediate intentions. When the press confronted her about the slight, Campbell flubbed. She said she "fully understands" Clinton's omission (Gwyn, *Star*, June 28/93; June 30/93).

Two days later, Lowell Murray, Senate House Leader for the Tories — he who was formerly intergovernmental affairs minister for Mulroney during Meech — announced the senators would be recalled on July 12 to roll back that offensive salary increase they had passed for themselves on June 23. It didn't take a genius to recognize that a cross-Canada call for Senate abolition was in the wind and might just win support — even from Reformers. A Gallup poll the same day showed that 62 percent of Canadians wanted an election right away.

Bob Rae smelled blood and drooled like Dracula. On June 29, when Campbell called for an FMC on the economy in Vancouver for Sunday, July 4, he leapt at the opportunity to say "the idea that we're somehow going to launch some new federal-provincial initiative 4 and three-quarters years [*sic*] into the life of the Conservative government is preposterous" (*Star*, June 30/93). Like him, ministers Perrin Beatty and Jean Charest refused to attend.

The Ontario premier quickly moved in for the kill, raising the subject of the inequity Ontarians had suffered on transfer payments under the Mulroney regime. Under the Canada Assistance Program, the masthead agreement between the federal government and the provinces, it was understood that Ottawa would pick up 50 percent of the costs as it usually did. But under Mulroney this federal commitment had eroded beyond recognition. He had brutally accelerated the imbalance in favour of Quebec. By 1993 the federal government paid Ontario back less than 30 percent of the revenue the province collected — a far smaller share than any other province received. Big trouble waited ahead, especially since Ottawa raised about $10 billion a year more in Ontario than it spent. During her leadership campaign Campbell said nothing on this sore point.

Then a report on immigration appeared from the C.D. Howe Institute and rattled a few cages. It pointed strongly at another problem that could not be sloughed off any longer. In sixteen sharp pages it stressed that as much as 40 percent of current immigration had to be cut, reducing the number from 250,000 annually to 150,000: "Current immigration levels are more than Canada's social infrastructure can bear. . . . For the past 15 years the national interest has been left out of immigration policy. Canada has ceded control of its own immigration program by giving up the right to select immigrants and granting that right to immigrants themselves," wrote author Daniel Stoffman in the *Toronto Star* on June 29. The *Star* itself even financed the report, along with the Atkinson Foundation. Altogether, the Mulroney government had tripled immigration since 1983, when the annual number of newcomers was 83,000. Stoffman blamed the media for the mess. He claimed that Canada's flood of accepted refugees the previous year, a higher percentage than any other country's during very tough economic times worldwide, was insane.

Layer upon layer of Mulroney mud stuck to Kim Campbell in these early days. On June 30, 1993, the federal government announced that the National Capital Commission would pay Mila Mulroney $150,000 for furnishings she and her husband had left behind at 24 Sussex. This was the final straw. As opponents and even Tory friends quickly pointed out, the Tory Party had already been given a tax credit for the donation in the first place. Despite Mulroney's promise on February 24, 1988, that he would end such practices, to dampen even the appearance of conflicts of interest, no such legislation existed by the end of his term. Bill C-114, 1988; Bill C-46, 1989; and Bill C-43 by 1993 had all died on the order table.

When the First Ministers Conference finally convened on July 4, journalists and other premiers alike had snubbed the occasion as just a "photo op" before the coming election. As if the fates were gleefully orchestrating Campbell's lurch to disaster, Clyde Wells missed an interconnecting flight and never did make the conference. The FMC proved a waste of time. The first ministers exchanged pleasantries and expressed concerns about the debt, emerging with the new prime minister's promise not to dump on the provinces. There was nothing else on the agenda.

Campbell and company took another haymaker from Washington on July 6 while attending the G-7 conference in Tokyo. The American president was interviewed on Japanese television, during which he stated casually that "the United States has no more important bilateral relationship than our relationship with Japan." In an internal State Department document titled *State 2000: A New Model for Managing Foreign Affairs*, Canada ranked ninth — coming in after Mexico and Israel. Canada did manage to beat out Iraq, which finished in tenth place.[2]

Two days later Bill Clinton apologized for one of his sins: "I have to admit [Campbell is] absolutely right on, that Canada should have been notified at the time we took action in Iraq" (*GM*, July 10/93). Apology accepted, until a White House aide made matters worse by letting on that a "dozen friends and allies in the region" had been told about the air strike beforehand (*GM*, July 10/93). Campbell handled this latest slight gracefully: "We are each other's best friend and biggest irritant."

Economic news was a mixed blessing. For exporters, conditions were good: on July 6, the central bank's prime lending rate fell to 4.73 percent, its lowest point since 1967.

On a global scale, however, the news was discouraging. A United Nations report out of New York presented a frightening prospect. According to *The State of the World Population, 1993*, "The combination of population pressures and economic imbalances could produce mass migration from poorer to richer countries." At the present rate of population growth, this could mean about one-quarter of a million people leaving their native lands every day. By the year 2000, the demographers predicted, world population would reach 5.57 billion.

TO GRASP the full extent of Confederation's erosion in the 1990s, however, historians will have to study events in the province of Ontario as much as in Quebec.

On July 7, Ontario's New Democratic Party of tinkerers voted in Bill 48 by 66 to 59. According to them, the Social Contract Act would save $2 billion annually by making Ontario public servants take off days without pay, and other measures. The negotiation costs alone had already eaten substantially into the purported savings — most of which were either illusory in the first place or simply unprovable. The point everyone overlooked in all this — the media, the unions, government, and particularly the opposition parties, especially the Conservatives — was that the socialist doctrine of "work-sharing" had been foisted on an unsuspecting public without a squeak from anyone. The litany of Communist failures elsewhere had no detectable effect on Bob Rae and his fellow travellers. Kim Campbell would find herself affected by the premier's grandiose machinations.

On July 14, Ontario Attorney-General Marion Boyd had to save face. She was forced, at least publicly, to reject a report prepared for the Ontario Human Rights Commission (OHRC). The OHRC had kicked off the business nine months earlier, with the Young Report, which stated that it must be assumed that "the legal presumption of innocence is inappropriate at the *investigatory* stages of race discrimination complaints. Investigation is not a legal process, and a legal standard must not be applied . . . [because] racism is in fact the norm" (Young Report, pp. 8–9). This came out three days before the October Referendum. Under severe criticism Boyd tried to recover: "We fundamentally believe in this NDP government that people are innocent until proven guilty" (*GM*, July 15/93).

Attorney-General Boyd's disclaimer rang hollow after her colleague, Ontario education minister Dave Cooke, announced sweeping reforms on July 15 against racism in the Ontario school system. In order to correct "systemic inequities," all 171 of the province's school boards would have to combat racism and "ethnocultural inequities" by September 1995 and *prove* they had complied. The indoctrination techniques would revamp the whole spectrum of education: university hiring, report cards, curricula, policies on harassment, the way history was taught. Whatever Boyd meant to say, the Ontario government considered Ontarians guilty of racism.

The government pressed on. It based their "Mandatory School Board Policies on Antiracism and Ethnocultural Equity" on the Lewis Report. Addressing what the Lewis cum Rae government perceived as "Systemic inequities and barriers for racial and ethnocultural minorities," Dave Cooke, Minister of Education and Training, described the agenda:

[The government would] integrate the principles of anti-racism and ethnocultural equity into all aspects of education programs and board operations. . . . There is a growing recognition that educational structures, policies and programs have been mainly European in perspective and have failed to take into account the viewpoints, experiences and needs of Aboriginal peoples and many racial minorities. . . . Educators therefore need to identify and change institutional policies and procedures and individual behaviour and practices that are racist in their impact, if not intent. (*Star*, July 15/93)

There were eight requirements and policy directives (see Appendix B) in this far-reaching socialist plan born of Stephen Lewis's conviction that Ontario wallowed in racism. Initial funding for the mind-moulding project was set at $1.4 million. The overall cost would mushroom into many, many more millions.

Few of the many Lewis/Rae initiatives would become public knowledge. One of the most insidious of these was a provincial directive loosed on post-secondary institutions on October 7, 1993, by Dave Cooke. Entitled *A Framework Regarding Prevention of Harassment and Discrimination in Ontario Universities*, the paper set out the politically correct way for a university to operate. It omitted both the date it was written and the name of its author or authors. The whole thing went ahead with no legislative foundation. All Ontario universities were ordered to submit their action plans showing their compliance to the Minister of Education and Training by March 1, 1994. Quotes from the "Framework": "The central goal of the policy should be zero tolerance, that is, harassment and discrimination as defined by the policy will not be tolerated by any university in its employment, educational, or business dealings" (p. 3).

The Lewis/Rae government could be certain that evil goblins would be found. The hordes that served the public would do their duty. Under "Definitions" and "Examples" that required "proactive" intervention:

Harassment

Examples include gestures, remarks, jokes, taunting, innuendo, display of offensive materials, graffiti, threats, verbal or physical assault, imposition of academic penalties, hazing, stalking, shunning or exclusion related to the prohibited grounds. (p. 4)

Systemic Harassment/Discrimination

An example is exam schedules that conflict with important religious events. (p. 5)

It was now "illegal" to ignore someone. And that wasn't enough: the directive made it clear that "Institutions are free to go beyond it and to develop other ways of achieving the intent of the policy which best reflects their local environments" (p. 1). It reminded: "Please note that institutions are allowed to seek exemptions from the *Code* [Human Rights Code], to operate special programs designed to benefit disadvantaged groups or individuals."

The press shirked its responsibility again. The first comprehensive article to deal with the directive came out in the *Toronto Star* months later, on February 12, 1994. Rita Daly, education reporter, wrote, "quietly introduced last fall, [the guidelines] were intended to help universities set down a 'zero tolerance' policy and process for dealing with human-rights complaints on campus."

The only reason the government got away with its "quiet introduction" was that the press refused to act. Daly's article did cover the view of Professor John Fekete of Trent University: "This is the most important censorship document ever issued by a Canadian government in recent history with respect to the functioning of universities. It's a threat to student posters, student newspapers, books used in courses, ideas people express in classrooms, and ordinary communication among students off campus" (*Star*, Feb 12/94).

If the Pulp-Primevil was tardy, Toronto's Faculty Club paper was worse. Following the *Star*'s lead, the *Globe* published an article by rights activist and philosophy professor Bill Graham, president of the University of Toronto Faculty Association. Undoubtedly chosen because he had "organized workshops and conferences on sexism and violence against women on university campuses," Professor Graham concluded: "Certainly it is important and urgent to prevent harassment and discrimination anywhere in our society; this requires all citizens, including academics, to be tolerant of diversity and sensitive to others. But there is sometimes a fine line between sensitivity, which enhances freedom, and authoritarianism, which denies it" (*GM*, Feb 14/94).

Would Canada's academics never tell government where to get off? The heart of a university is academic freedom.

Dinesh D'Souza, the celebrated author of *Illiberal Education* (1991), expressed very different views on the quota system in the universities of America:

> By the time these students graduate, very few colleges have met their need for all-round development. Instead, by precept and example, universities have taught them that "all rules are unjust" and "all preferences are principled"; . . . that all knowledge can be reduced to politics and should be pursued not for its own sake but for the political end of power; that convenient myths and benign lies can be reduced to politics and should be pursued not for its own sake but for the political end of power; that convenient myths and benign lies can substitute for truth; that double standards are acceptable as long as they are enforced to the benefit of minority victims; that debates are best conducted not by rational and civil exchange of ideas, but by accusation, intimidation, and official prosecution; that·the university stands for nothing in particular. . . . (p. 229)

While the socialists in Ontario were fighting phantoms in every nook and cranny, Kim Campbell soldiered on. After an uneventful G-7 Conference in Tokyo, she headed out on the campaign trail. In Calgary, she rejected any interim measure toward an elected Senate: "To have the legitimacy that comes with having been elected once, without the accountability of having to stand for re-election, in my view is the worst of all possible worlds" (*GM*/CP, July 13/93). In other words, she would even have opposed the tentative advance her predecessor had made in appointing Canada's first "elected" Senator, Stan Waters. And so she lost the vote of the Triple-E Senate crowd and much of Western Canada.

Even the Senate was getting a better handle on reality than the rookie PM. In a vote of 80 to 1, the Red Chamber fudge-foggies reversed their original vote giving themselves a $6,000 expense allowance. Miracle of miracles. Tory Senate leader Lowell Murray even apologized publicly: "Let us acknowledge that the Senate made a mistake on June 23" (*GM*, July 13/93). In one of her better-timed moments, Audrey McLaughlin called for a fall referendum to abolish the Senate, calling it the "only one sure way to put an end to the abuse — shut down the trough" (*Star*, July 14/93). At this point, even the West would have agreed with her loudly.

Campbell's campaign was suffering, and had been from the beginning, plagued by the ghost of her predecessor. On July 15, following the public uproar over Mila Mulroney's sale of certain personal furnishings at 24 Sussex Drive to the National Capital Commission, "Imelda Muldoon," as *Frank* magazine unaffectionately dubbed her, returned the $150,000. She took her own high road. "After a decade of public service which I performed with pride and pleasure and during which I neither received nor expected to receive remuneration of any kind for any of my activities, I am of course disappointed by the suggestion — even from some partisan sources — that I might have sought to profit from this transaction. . . . I regret this gesture was misconstrued" (*GM*, July 16/93).

On Monday, July 19, Toronto Mayor June Rowlands reported to City Council that Canada's largest city was wobbling on the brink of bankruptcy: "It's absolutely unbelievable and totally unprecedented in the city's history," she exclaimed (*Star*, July 20/93). Taxpayers faced a cash shortfall of $60 million. Two days later the city said it would shut down all municipal services for three days. For the municipal government there would be no social contract.

More rumbling and social tinkering at Queen's Park. On July 20, the Rae government announced that the Caribbean Canadian African (Ontario) Credit Union Ltd. would receive $750,000 to start up and operate its own credit union. This despite the fact that the Ukrainians, Portuguese, and Korean communities had set up and maintained their own credit arrangements and credit unions for years. As municipal affairs minister Ed Philip said, "This credit union will allow members of the black community to invest in themselves, to control their own financial situation." Bob Rae had accomplished a first in Canada — his was the first government to finance the banking requirements of a business community based solely on race.

WITH ALL the nonsense going on, few people really wished to celebrate Canada's heritage or traditions. Alexander Mackenzie, later knighted, had reached Bella Coola Inlet in what is now British Columbia, two hundred years earlier. He and his expedition were the first to cross the continent by land, from Montreal, beating out the famous Lewis and Clark team by twelve whole years. On July 22, 1793, the great explorer recorded his arrival: "I now mixed up some vermilion in melted grease, and inscribed in large characters, on the south-east face of the rock on which we had slept last night, this brief memorial: 'Alexander Mackenzie, from Canada, by land, the twenty-second of July, one-thousand seven hundred and ninety-three.'"

By 1993, Canadians had had the joy of their heritage drummed out of them.

On July 27, an Environics poll commissioned by Ontarians for Responsible Government turned up sobering findings. Forty-nine percent of the province's population would leave Ontario if they could afford it. That same day at the Tsuu T'Ina Reserve in Alberta, Chief Joe Norton of the Kahnawake Nation of Quebec said, "Maybe it's time somebody treated [the Quebec separatists] with boxing gloves. All of the first nations in the province of Quebec have never collectively come together and delivered a strong message to the province, and it's time to do it now. . . . There is no such thing as Quebec sovereignty. There's no such thing as separation. They do not own the land. They do not have the right to separate. If anybody has that right, then it is the first nations in the region that is currently called Quebec" (*GM*, July 28/93). Bully for Chief Joe.

Meanwhile, in a meeting with Bourassa, Campbell negotiated (through an "agreement in principle") a major transfer of power to Quebec — responsibility for job training, despite the country's rejection of the Charlottetown Accord, which would have approved the move. The total federal budget for job training stood at $3.8 billion. During the constitutional uproar the previous year, a Quebec agency, the Société Québécoise de développement de la main-d'oeuvre (SDQM), was created to handle the transfer, all unknown to the general public, and with the approval of the federal government. Campbell's excuse came too easily: "I can't imagine that, in the referendum, that anyone voted against governments working together along with the private sector" (*GM*, Aug 4/93).

613

Reactions to her gamble were strong and predictable. They were also very damaging. The head of the history department at the University of Ottawa, Professor Michael Behiels, termed it "balkanization of the labour market and it's being driven by Quebec nationalist imperatives. Quebec wants to use it as a means of keeping French-Canadian workers in Quebec. But many of these young men and women have to be trained for jobs in other parts of the country. This deal will cut into the mobility of workers." He sneered, "It's simply slicing the baloney, one slice at a time, until you get the whole baloney" (*GM*, Aug 5/93).

The shadows of Charlottetown. Preston Manning said, "For Campbell to unilaterally enter into this agreement with the Bourassa government is a step in the wrong direction at the wrong time. It confirms our view that the federal Conservative administration has still not learned the basic lessons of the constitutional referendum and is bound and determined to pursue its own constitutional agenda regardless of what the Canadian people want or think" (*GM*, Aug 5/93). Richard Le Hir, president of the Quebec Manufacturers' Association, chipped in, "The experience in federal-provincial relations in recent years, notably the infamous Charlottetown accord, teaches us that you can't claim victory before seeing the definitive texts" (*GM*, Aug 3/93).

Once again Quebec succumbed to the temptation to boast to the rest of the nation through André Bourbeau, Quebec's Minister of Manpower: "We have a clear-cut political decision that the federal government wants to transfer to Quebec all responsibilities in the labor force delivery system" (*Maclean's*, Aug 16/93). Bourassa baited Canadians with "for all intents and purposes [Quebec] has control of manpower" (*GM*, Aug 5/93).

When the prime minister insisted that we "will [still] have a direct involvement," no one believed her (*GM*, Aug 5/93).

And the state meddling continued. On August 3, the Ontario Human Rights Commission set a precedent in a case concerning Ontario Blue Cross and York County Hospital in Newmarket, by decreeing that same-sex "spouses" are the equivalent of a family for all the benefits that apply to heterosexual couples. Hospitals were ordered to immediately inform all employees of the available benefits. The next day Blue Cross said it would appeal the decision. The *Financial Post* posted the results of a survey of fourteen major urban centres in North America by the CB Commercial Real Estate Group Canada Inc., Canada's largest real estate broker. Downtown Toronto's taxes showed as the highest in North America. Central Manhattan rates were as much as 30 percent cheaper.

Under these conditions in the country's largest and once wealthiest province and in the rest of Canada, the only certainty that remained was that capital would flee the country. The more immediate question was who would win the forthcoming federal election Campbell had promised for the autumn. If the recent Gallup poll was any indication, Canadians expected a cliffhanger. On July 15, Gallup placed the Liberals at 43 percent, the Tories at 33 percent, the NDP at 8 percent, Reform at 7 percent, and all others at 10 percent.

The Reform Party was no obvious threat and this prompted one of its strongest missionaries, Ted Byfield, to vent his spleen in the *Financial Post*: "The Reform Party of Canada now stands ready to launch a sane, balanced, low-keyed, inoffensive campaign — so sane, balanced and low-keyed the party will be lucky to take a single seat in this fall's election. . . . The Reform party's present course is toward absolutely certain defeat" (*FP*, Aug 8/93).

As Byfield saw it, Manning's acquisition of an Ottawa lobbyist, Rick Anderson, vice-president of the firm of Hill & Knowlton, a "Trudeau Liberal" and a Yes-side supporter in the Referendum, was a definite liability. Tom Flanagan, Anderson's predecessor, had been fired.

A T TIMES CAMPBELL took charge rather well. On August 9, at a Kiwanis Club luncheon, she delivered her first policy speech. She promised Canadians five areas of reform: pensions, Parliament, budget, patronage, and conflict of interest and lobbyist legislation: "At best, for many Canadians, Ottawa is Oz. At worst Ottawa is Canada's forbidden city — a place Canadians are not let into" (*Star*, Aug 10/93). Then she stumbled. She added she would end all patronage appointments — until the election.

Five hours later, she committed suicide once and for all. The PMO confirmed the appointment of Mulroney's immediate former press secretary, Mark Entwhistle, as Ambassador to Mexico. On secondment from the foreign affairs department (formerly External) to the PM's office, Entwhistle had neatly hopscotched several levels within government to this political appointment. He was the Tory tooter who managed the PM's sound-bites during the 1992 Referendum. As Mulroney's public relations filter, Entwhistle was the "senior official" who juggled the news about the wording of the "legal text" of the Charlottetown Accord.

Even at great cost, Campbell remained loyal to her old boss. On the same day she was heralding a new era in government conduct, she defended Mulroney's political pay-off: "It was a routine appointment that's been on the boards for a long time" (*FP*, Aug 11/93). Perrin Beatty's office compounded the blunder. The press secretary to the Minister of Foreign Affairs also defended the appointment as "routine" (*Star*, Aug 10/93). And of course they were all absolutely correct. It was a routine appointment. And routine wouldn't do anymore.

Synchronized with the political unravelling, the Canadian dollar was hammered down four-fifths of a cent by currency speculators the same day in New York. Analysts spoke in low voices about a European-style currency crisis as the dollar plunged to 76.52 cents US, its lowest point since December 28, 1987.

On August 11, the Parti Québécois announced their agenda for a three-day policy convention in Montreal on August 20, 21, and 22. Bernard Landry, the party's vice-president, told reporters that when they came to power, they would scrap Bill 86, legislation to amend the Quebec Language Charter, Bill 101 — the bill that had recently replaced the equally notorious Bill 178. A new law, he said, would "permit us to affirm, in the face of the entire world, that all *genuine* anglophones, including those (of other languages) who have become assimilated, have the right to put up signs in their languages [emphasis mine]" (*Star*, Aug 12/93). Now la belle province would recognize different classes of disenfranchised citizens. Openly!

Time had run out for Kim Campbell. She would have to call an election soon for legal reasons. Some positive signs hinted that she could still pull off a coup. Although the Tories lagged behind the Liberals, her personal popularity was soaring. On August 16, Gallup rated her the most popular prime minister in thirty years. Although she hadn't even called Parliament, or maybe because she hadn't done so, 51 percent of Canadians liked her job performance, while only 22 percent described themselves as dissatisfied. Not since the days of John Diefenbaker in 1959 and Lester Pearson in 1963 had any candidate won such ratings. Campbellmania rivalled even Trudeaumania. Horrors.

Dalton Camp had no doubts. On returning to work as the *Toronto Star's* Tory columnist, following a spat with his employers over their misfeasance, malfeasance, or no feasance at all over the seventy-two-year-old's comparatively short wait for a heart transplant, the greatest of all the Mulroney intonators opined:

> One need not be confirmed as a major oracle to say with gravity and conviction the Prime Minister has convinced most of the country she is the ablest of the party leaders and she is also reviving the electoral prospects of her party, moribund and mired in the ruck of public opprobrium for over four years. . . .

Argument can be made that Canada's Parliament is one of the best in the world, and we have for some time been served by one of the most dedicated and incorruptible cadres of public servants found anywhere. The idea that Canadians will somehow be better governed once the Senate has been abolished, or 50 or 60 senior civil servants have been sacked, or we have made public service, as a parliamentarian, a leaner and meaner thing with more risk attached, is not something we should all take as a given. (*Star*, Aug 15/93)

Campbell waited. She still wasn't sure enough of herself to make the election call. In Kitchener she talked up education:

The basic question is clear: Do we have the right stuff? The answer, unfortunately, is also clear: Not enough. We are not learning well enough for today. We are certainly not learning well enough for tomorrow. . . . Canada is the only country in the developed world that does not have a national department of education. The role of the federal government is not to force but to facilitate co-operation. . . . Canadian governments spend twice what American governments do to train workers, but Canadian corporations spend only one-half as much as American firms, one-third what Japanese firms spend. (*GM*, Aug 28/93)

Her comparison with the U.S. and Japan could have been lifted directly from Brian Mulroney's 1984 campaign notes. He had expounded on the same theme two years before that, on October 10, 1982, to the Conservative Association at Ste-Foy, Quebec.

Campbell's remarks reminded many of her listeners of the shoddy Conservative record in these very fields. Her earmarking some $690 million for education looked like the pittance it was, compared to the Tory commitment of $4.6 billion to build helicopters. Even with the best intentions and the best ideas in the world, she came out with one suggestion that flattened her grand plan to low comedy in one breath. She announced that she would direct all government departments to donate their obsolete computer equipment and computer programs to public schools through-out Canada. Just the ticket to make Canada competitive.

Liberal leader Jean Chrétien tuned his message more effectively. He slammed the greed of the Canadian banks because, as he saw it, they were "strangling" the country. His government, he promised, would launch a $100-million national venture capital fund to be called the Canada Invest-ment Fund: "The banks have done very well in this country. We believe they should give something back to Canada" (*Star*, Aug 18/93). The money would become available over four years. It represented 40 percent of the start-up funding to launch the projects. The balance of the funds would come, in time, from the private sector. High technology would be emphasized. He explained how essential it was to end "the small business credit crunch, boosting research and development and other supports and cutting red tape" (*FP*, Aug 18/93).

O N AUGUST 17, an Ontario legislative committee began hearings on Bill 79, *An Act to Provide for Employment Equity for Aboriginal People, People with Disabilities, Members of Racial Minorities and Women*, Bob Rae's employment equity legislation. This latest intrusion affected every employer in the public sector with more than ten employees, and every employer in the private sector with more than fifty employees. It is the first in North America to promote discrimination against white males directly. Businesses that did not comply faced fines of as much as $50,000. From the beginning of his reign, Rae had constructed solid legal ground for himself. Whereas the Ontario Human Rights Code of 1980 made it illegal to "establish or maintain any employment classification that by its description or operation excludes any person from employment or continued employment," by 1993 times had changed. Now the way to racial discrimination was wide open. The Ontario Human Rights Code, RSO, 1990, ch. 19, contained no such provision any longer (see Appendix B).

On August 18, health minister Ruth Grier announced that seven more health agencies in the province would be designated bilingual under the French Language Services Act, Bill 8. This meant the legislation affected 35 health agencies in Ontario. "These designations ensure accessible health services in French on a permanent basis," the minister said in her news release. Gilles Pouliot, Minister for Francophone Affairs, boasted that "since 1990, 77 agencies have been designated under the Act, bringing the total number of designations to 122" (Govt. of Ont. press release). Although most Ontarians had roundly rejected Bill 8 and had helped bring down the Peterson government because of it, and despite the fact that fewer than 2 percent of the population spoke French only, the Ontario government would push its citizens firmly toward their vision of a bilingual Ontario — all in the name of "national unity."

Rae could always count on the clandestine support of the federal priesthood. On August 19, the Commissioner of Official Languages, Victor Goldbloom, wrote to Ruth Grier, whose ministry absorbs a full third of Ontario's annual budget:

Individuals and organizations within the Franco-Ontarian community have made me aware of their concerns that medical services in French may suffer by virtue of the fact that apart from a small number of students at the University of Ottawa, Ontarians wishing to study medicine in French must indeed apply to institutions in Quebec or even in other countries. They indicate that there are presently some shortages of French-speaking health professionals in certain regions of the province. I am convinced that this is in no way your intention to reduce the availability of health care in French where numbers or concentrations of population require it. I place myself at your entire disposal . . . for any exchange of thoughts you may consider useful.

Of course Goldbloom had no authority for intervening in provincial matters. But who would know? The languages commissioner had a guilt-edged insurance policy. The media favoured the government's agenda. Even at this late date few Canadians were aware that as Minister of the Environment and Municipal Affairs in the Bourassa government in 1974, Goldbloom had voted for Bill 22, making French the only official language in Quebec.[3]

On August 20, Bernard Landry withdrew the PQ's promise of ten days earlier that "genuine" anglophones would be allowed to put signs in English alongside the French ones under a PQ regime.

An August 19 Gallup poll showed the Liberals at 40 percent and the Tories at 36 percent. The summer was nearly over.

Several lighter moments eased the tension in the contest. The Natural Law Party of Canada provided one. On the same day Landry was segregating genuine anglophones from others, the NLP, which embraces the teachings of Maharishi Mahesh Yogi and transcendental meditation, announced it would field candidates in all 295 ridings in the election. As Dr. Neil Patterson, the party leader, put it, the "first initiative will be to create large groups of yogic flyers . . . to bring the support of natural law to the entire nation" (*Star*, Aug 21/93). Why not?

Liberal leader Jean Chrétien expressed some sobering thoughts of his own: "This is the first time, probably since Canada has existed, that there's such a malaise in our society. Today's children are the first generation that will do less well than its parents. We've had three years of no growth at all. We've had a concentration of wealth in the top 5 per cent of the population. It's changing the mentality out there" (*Star*, Aug 23/93).

At the PQ biennial convention in Montreal on Sunday, August 22, Jacques Parizeau hailed his troops with *"Vive le Quebec libre"*, and at the same time slammed party reactionaries who would deny anglophone rights. It was the first time a PQ leader had used General de Gaulle's rallying cry since 1967. The convention closed with a pledge to protect the rights of the English-speakers in the province.

Kim Campbell had been enjoying fairly smooth sailing on her hamburger-and-french-fries pre-election circuit. Two days later the bloom was off the rose. At a meeting in Ottawa with UN Secretary General Boutros Boutros-Ghali she was asked in French about the possibility of setting up a field hospital in Bosnia. Unable to answer coherently in the language, she was caught. In a gallant attempt to save her, Boutros-Ghali whispered a solution — *"hôpital militaire en Bosnie."* Campbell played dumb. The blunder reverberated across the land while her press secretary excused her deficiency by blaming the faulty speaker system (Michel Gratton, *Sun*, Aug 25/93).

Whoops! The *Journal de Montréal* seized the moment: the prime minister's "ability to speak French is going to become an important issue in the coming election campaign." Taking a foolish risk of his own, Jean Chrétien bragged that his rival would have difficulty "because she had to use the Secretary-General of the United Nations on Sunday as her translator. I myself do not have that problem" (*Journal de Montréal/GM*, Aug 26/93).

The Tories held their last caucus meeting before the election writ was dropped on August 25. Eleven of the 14 most powerful ministers in Mulroney's former Cabinet attended, including Joe Clark, John Crosbie, Michael Wilson, and Don Mazankowski. For the 55 MPs retiring from politics, including 14 members of the Cabinet, this would be their final farewell. The prime minister outlined the four themes by which she intended to govern: cutting government bureaucracy, restructuring Parliament, tightening up law and order, increasing jobs and economic development.

Mississauga West MP Bob Horner piped up as the tough guy: members of the Bloc Québécois should be prosecuted under the criminal code for treason. "What do they do with people in India who are trying to separate the Punjab? . . . They should be tried for treason. I think they're treasonous" (*Sun*, Aug 26/93).

At month end the Royal Bank of Canada predicted more economic roadkill. Earl Sweet, the bank's assistant chief economist, opined that "large-scale layoffs will be a feature of this country for the next couple of years" (*FP*, Aug 26/93). Citing the bank's latest study, he estimated that of the 410,000 jobs lost between 1990 and 1992, 40 percent of them, or

165,000 positions, could be attributed to structural change compared to the 9.5 percent lost to similar changes in the 1981–82 recession.

Even Bob Rae was showing dismay at the state of the nation's affairs. At the annual premiers' conference in Baddeck, Nova Scotia, he put on his Preston Manning hat to say, "We can't go on every year borrowing $40-bn to $50-bn more than we are raising in revenues to pay for the ongoing services of government. This is not a sustainable path" (*Star*, Aug 25/93).

No one seemed to have anything good to say about the U.S. or Canada at this point. In Washington, former Republican presidential candidate Patrick Buchanan went off on a rant, calling NAFTA "a leveraged buy-out of American liberty. Sink NAFTA and save the American republic." As for the northern neighbour, he went on, "The welfare state in Canada is even more elaborate than ours and so the jobs have been coming down here rather than going up there" (*GM*/CP, Aug 27/93).

The UN was in worse shape than either country. Not only was it insolvent, it was nearly bankrupt. On his return from Ottawa, the secretary-general confessed, "The organization lives from hand to mouth. There is nothing new about that. But today the situation is unprecedented and it is intolerable" (*GM*/Reuters, Aug 27/93). Only 7 of 184 states had paid their dues in full. Member states owed more than $2 billion for peacekeeping and $848 million in regular dues. The worst offender — the United States — owed $786 million.

The conservative Conseil du patronat of Montreal made similar noises about the state of the Quebec economy. According to a recent study the true unemployment rate of the province hovered near 22.6 percent, with 865,000 people out of work. Richard Le Hir, chairman of Association des manufacturiers, complained of Canada's underground economy, which he blamed on high taxes, yet admitted, "The system is cracking. When we are going bankrupt, there are measures that have to be taken" (*FP*, Aug 27/93).

On August 27 the prime minister did three constructive things. In Toronto, to 1,000 members of the Toronto Rotary Club, she promised to eliminate Canada's annual deficit of $32 billion by 1999. She also said, "Let me state my position clearly: There will be no increase in taxes. There will be no new taxes" (*Sun*, Aug 28/93). Finally, after flying to Vancouver, she officially accepted the Conservative nomination in her home riding with the words "I know Vancouver Centre will be the home of Canada's first elected female prime minister" (*Star*, Aug 28/93). For a fleeting moment she sounded positively prime-ministerial.

The candidates faced many obstacles in their race to win voters' affections, whatever their party affiliation. Even at this late stage, with public anger rising to levels the politicians had never seen before, too many of them, like Frank McKenna and Bob Rae, pretended to carry on as if there had never been a Referendum. Nova Scotia's newly elected premier Dr. John Savage was just such a gambler. At the meeting of provincial premiers and territorial leaders, the host premier behaved as if nothing had ever happened constitutionally, promising he would write to the prime minister as chair of that year's conference to ask the federal government to "define its position on self-government. . . . This [initiative] was a kickstart to negotiations that ended so dismally with the Charlottetown Accord" (*GM*, Aug 28/93). Every first minister agreed with this reincarnation of Charlottetown.

While Bob Rae was in Halifax, his like-minded minions back home continued to chip away at the Merit Principle within the Ontario government. A task force hosted a hearing on recruitment for the Toronto Fire Department. Committee members listened to Diana Green of the United Steelworkers of America, District 6, tell them, "The current practice of ranking the applicants [according to merit] and drawing the number from the top . . . plays into backlash fears of non-minority candidates." Margaret Hageman of the Alliance for Employment Equity demonstrated a more vivid imagination: "The image of what a firefighter is, i.e., big, tall, strong, manly, must change. Aptitude tests should be reviewed for cultural and gender bias" (*Star*, Aug 28/93).

With the usual help from the media, Judy Rebick got her opinion on record: "If employers hired strictly on the basis of merit, and didn't discriminate either systemically or intentionally, we would have 50 per cent women, we believe today, in almost every position of authority. . . ." Merit appointments, she said, are "very subjective." People hire the people they can "relate to best, which is often people of the same gender, people of the same culture. . . . What employment equity does is counter those biases by ensuring that people are hired without discrimination" (*GM*, Aug 31/93).

T HE NIHILISTIC MOOD seemed to be spreading. On August 28, the *Toronto Star* touched another nerve with its editorial "Should we end the monarchy?": "Few Canadians want to abandon the present Queen. She carries out her duties with unquestioned commitment and grace, and represents the finer aspects of our British heritage. But times change, and many Canadians, especially Quebecers and people from non-Commonwealth countries, have little or no identification with the monarchy. . . .

Such an examination may call for a royal commission. But we should also be asking our leaders what they think" (*Star*, Aug 28/93).

Another royal commission? Heaven forfend.

The clowns had taken over the country. At the premiere of the first episode of *Memoirs*, Pierre Trudeau's contrived revelations as told through three ghost writers, two interviewers, and one editor-in-chief and publisher, the former prime minister put on a splendid show. A well-known Montreal spoof artist decided to take on Merlin the Muddler himself. Quebec columnist Pauline Couture described the incident: "Rrrraymond Beaudoin, (in real life, Pierre Brassard) has a habit of attending celebrity events in a wispy-bearded, nerdy disguise and asking outrageous questions." Sporting the fake whiskers, he baited the unshaven dishevelled omnipresence by suggesting the book should have been called "Spitting on Quebecers" or "Taking the dinosaurs out of storage to scare people."

Trudeau turned on Rrrraymond immediately and yanked off his bogus beard. Undaunted, Brassard brags he "picked it up and, faithful to my habit of never letting go no matter who the victim or celebrity is, went after him again.... That's when [Trudeau] decided to give me a slap in the face, which surprised me a little, I must say. . . . But I didn't stop and that's when he gave me a little karate kick in the family jewels" (*Star*/CP/*GM*, Sept 2/93). Just what the country needed — more B-grade acting.

At the end of August everyone in the country was in a bitchy mood. Equating the mass roundups of people suspected as separatists during the FLQ crisis of 1970 to the detention of Japanese Canadians under the War Measures Act, the Fondation Octobre 70 announced it was seeking compensation. "FO 7" claimed that during the October crisis there were 31,700 searches, 497 arrests, 4,600 raids and seizures, 26 people charged and 21 convicted — and they all deserved restitution.

On September 1, Ontario provincial trade minister Frances Lankin threatened to ban Quebec workers from Ontario because Quebec had barred Ontario construction workers and contractors from its sites for years, contrary to Section 121 of the Constitution: "Unfortunately, Quebec has not put anything forward to address our concerns. Now we need to take steps to look at what retaliatory actions we may take," she said. Bob Rae echoed her: "These barriers are prejudicial to Ontario workers and to Ontario" (*Star*, Sept 2/93). Ontario had never restricted Quebec workers before.

By contrast, as another first in interprovincial relations between Ontario and Quebec, Quebec's Minister of Industry, Trade and Technology,

Gérald Tremblay, sounded almost reasonable, if not hypocritical: "The only way we'll find concrete solutions to problems is by negotiating, not by issuing press releases and saying Quebec is the bad guy. We are willing to do things, but we are saying to Ontario, 'Open your books the same way we opened our books.'"

Kim Campbell missed a golden opportunity. She said nothing. Instead, claiming she had now found a way to shave $1 billion off the defence department's plans to buy fifty helicopters, the PM backtracked on one of her most precious stands on September 2. She announced that, under her Tory government, she would chop seven choppers. Depending on which Conservative calculations one chose to accept, the overall costs of the program would now be reduced to $4.8 billion or $3.2 billion. By this time her backpedalling was too little too late. Four months earlier, as defence minister, she had told reporters, "I have no plans to reduce the number of helicopters. . . . That is not a particularly effective way to save costs" (*GM*, Sept 3/93).

She even seemed to relish getting into hot water. In a missive dated September 2 and printed on her official stationery she bombarded every public servant in Canada through the government mails with a personal message: "Will you please take a moment and answer my Questionnaire — then join ranks with me in leading a revitalized, re-energized Progressive Conservative Party to victory in the coming election. . . . Will you please help me build a strong campaign based on the issues important to you by answering the Ten-Point Questionnaire I've enclosed in your name? . . . Will you help me . . . by agreeing to serve as a new Election Year Sustaining Member of the PC Canada Fund. . . ."

No prime minister in Canadian history had ever stooped to this. Snickers and sneers echoed throughout the federal labyrinths.

While Campbell's faux pas rippled through the bureaucracy, another reminder of the Mulroney era emerged into the light of day. On September 3, in a 7–to–2 judgement, the Supreme Court of Canada upheld the Federal Court of Canada ruling against Graham Haig (Chapters 28 and 29). His rights, the Court decided, were not violated because he didn't meet *Quebec's test* on such matters. The High Court ruled the Charter covers elections only, not referendums. So they upheld the objections raised on October 9, 1992, by the Federal Court of Canada. The two-nations theory in practice.

The conclusion had taken the Supreme Court nearly a year to reach, since October 22, 1992. Haig told the media he was furious: "Boy, were you taken in. There was no national referendum. Don't you feel silly now? . . . Parliament never intended to hold a national referendum, and indeed Parliament didn't hold one" (*GM*, Sept 14/93). It had been estimated the ruling affected some ten to twenty thousand voters. Mulroney's hand-picked High Court was indulging in some *deux-nations* building of its own.

On September 5, at Meech Lake, the prime minister confirmed in a taped interview with CBC's "Sunday Report" host Wendy Mesley "the country's worst-kept secret." That coming week she would call the election. As for timing, she warned Wendy with a chuckle, "Yeah, . . . don't go on holidays" (*Star*, Sept 6/93).

Just before the writ was dropped, Mr. Justice René Dussault of the Quebec Court of Appeal and co-chair of the Royal Commission on Aboriginal Peoples spouted some ideas for Canadians to chew on. On September 7 he said what they already knew: the Charlottetown Accord would not have given Canada's natives the right to self-government because they already had it: "The Charlottetown accord would have made that fact explicit, but it would not have created the right; it would only have confirmed it" (*GM*, Sept 7/93).

At 10:00 A.M. on September 8, Kim Campbell asked Governor General Ramon Hnatyshyn to dissolve the Thirty-Fourth Parliament. Under the Great Seal of Canada he issued the royal proclamation and signed the Cabinet minutes that authorized the issuing of 295 individual election writs for all the federal ridings, setting the date for October 25.

For five long years of turmoil Canadians had waited for the rarest opportunity their constitution allowed them: the chance to pass judgement and sentence on their elected representatives. The die was cast.

Notes

1 Mulroney launched his restructuring of the Public Service in December 1989. The 1990 White Paper on Public Service Renewal set out the details. In addition to his regular duties the Clerk is required to inform Parliament annually "on the state of the Public Service" in general, and for the next five years on the implementation of Public

Service 2000 in particular. The stated purpose of PS 2000 was to "reform the classification system" and "to effect better career development and better training . . . to a leaner and more flexible public service." In the first report made on June 30, 1992, Shortliffe stated:

> Future Deputies will be chosen in part because of their capacity to *lead by example* in demonstrating their own personal commitment to the values of Public Service 2000.

> Among the criteria used to identify potential Deputies . . . [are the ability to] demonstrate fairness by example: employment equity. (*Public Service 2000: A Report on Progress*, June 30/92)

In other words, deputies are to be politically correct regardless of the law.

2 The State Department report explained their grading system: "Our larger missions for the most part are also judged to be the most important according to an evaluation of the U.S. interests in mid-1992" (*GM*, July 8/93).

3 The Trudeau government awarded Goldbloom the Ceramic Snowflake in 1983.

36

The Hunt for the Red Tories in October
— September 8 to October 25, 1993

KIM CAMPBELL'S ELECTION KICK-OFF was dull, but not without hope: "I would like to see, certainly by the turn of the century, a country where unemployment is way down and we are paying down our national debt and there is a whole new vision of the future opening up for Canadians" (*GM*, Sept 9/93).

Lucien Bouchard stalked the country with darker thoughts: "We have a structural crisis and there is no way to get out of it. We have to bring substantial and radical change to the situation. . . . The Bloc will try to convince people in English Canada to get ready for the decision [a referendum on sovereignty] that I hope will be made in Quebec two years from now" (*GM*, Sept 9/93).

Preston Manning lectured: "In this election, don't let anyone tell you what the agenda is. This time you tell the old-line politicians what is good for us and what isn't. You tell the old-line politicians what they can do with their political correctness. . ." (*Star*, Sept 9/93). He would often repeat, too: "Ultimately, we would like to see a Reform government in Canada before the end of the century" (*GM*, Sept 9/93). Since Manning had no interest in forming the next government, his message was certain to fall on deaf ears.

Audrey McLaughlin was angry: "Brian Mulroney may be gone, but his economic policies live on, and those policies are ripping the heart and soul out of this country" (*GM*, Apr 9/93). She was living in the past.

Jean Chrétien, the long-suffering warhorse of the Liberal Party, metamorphosed himself with a gimmick — big photographs of himself in "The Shirt," an open-necked denim topper that took years off his age — and he hit home where it counted: "It will be like the good old days. Canadians will be working" (*GM*, Sept 9/93).

Mel Hurtig announced he would seek an injunction to block two scheduled debates between Campbell, Chrétien, Bouchard, McLaughlin, and Manning.

Author **Kenneth McDonald** knew where it was at: "In the run-up to the forthcoming election, it's safe to say that the following topics will be avoided by the three older parties: official bilingualism; official multi-culturalism; immigration; forced membership of and dues payment to labour unions; government funding of single-issue advocacy groups; and the institution of national referendums on major issues of policy" (*GM*, Sept 9/93).

ON **SEPTEMBER 8** there were nineteen political parties registered under the Elections Act. Neither the Liberals nor the Conservatives could claim much success in attracting women candidates. At the outset Kim Campbell's Tories had 52 out of 255 women nominated, 20 percent of the Tory candidates. The Liberals weighed in with 285 nominated candidates and would field 63 women, or 22 percent. The NDP came up with 40 percent of their 89 nominated candidates. In their struggle between managed equality and the Merit Principle, the NDP had hypno-tized itself with gender-specific criteria.

The prime minister looked south of the border for the winning for-mula. Bill Clinton's triumph in the American South did have its attractions and Campbell had nothing to lose. The frantic fawn retained the services of Phil Noble, a noted Dixie Democrat from Charleston, South Carolina. Cornered by reporters curious about his new contract, Noble would say only, "I ain't going to get into what I do and don't do, and what I have and haven't done, and what I am and am not going to do. You know, I just don't talk about my clients or what I do" (*GM*, Sept 11/93).

American media guru Tony Schwartz said it best: "The goal of a media advisor is to tie up the voter and deliver him to the candidate. So it is really the *voter* who is packaged by the media, not the candidate" (quoted in Nelson, "Packaging the Populace: Polling in the Age of Image Politics," in *Best Canadian Essays: 1990*, p. 219).

Sure as shootin', Campbell needed help. While Reform campaign director and former Trudovnic Rick Anderson was making consensual noises, like "We would consider a coalition with the Tories" (*Star*, Sept 13/93), Campbell put people off till after the election: "I have a priority to protect people on low incomes and older people. . . . and also I will ask Canadians to help set priorities. I'll begin a public consultation process right after the election" (*Star*, Sept 13/93).

While the PM was digging herself a very deep grave, Nova Scotia Lieutenant-Governor **Lloyd Crouse** rocked the Maritimes with a throne speech unheard of in Canadian history. "The state of the province's finances makes real the possibility that Nova Scotia could lose the capacity to govern its own affairs" (*FP*, Sept 14/93). For Conservatives in Canada, it was the worst of times, reinforced daily by bad news.

ON SEPTEMBER 13 **Gord McIntyre**, the slayer of Bill 178, climbed back into his armour to do more battle against the Government of Quebec (see Chapter 34). This time his target was Bill 86, Quebec's replacement legislation for Bill 178. He also charged the province with non-compliance regarding the UN's first judgement.[1]

On September 14, Prime Minister Kim Campbell signed the legal texts for the side-deals in the North American Free Trade Agreement (NAFTA). Despite overwhelming opposition to the agreement and its predecessor, she barged ahead. Even Gordon Ritchie, former deputy trade negotiator for the earlier Free Trade Agreement, confessed the labour and environmental agreement NAFTA provided was "pure smoke and mirrors to satisfy a troublesome congress" (*Star*, Sept 15/93).[2]

On this same Tuesday, Premier **Robert Bourassa** announced he was stepping down as party leader. The leadership convention would be held between January 15 and February 15, 1994. He told reporters: "The Quebec Liberal Party is opposed to the breakup of the Canadian federation because Canada with all its problems, with all its tensions, with all its difficulties, remains by far . . . one of the most enviable countries in the world. . . . I cannot see how we can tell Quebeckers that we can attract the investments we need, that we can convince investors to come to Quebec, by initiating the process of dismantling the Canadian federation. . . . Quebec independence is a geopolitical absurdity" (*GM*, Sept 15/93).

The press, especially in English Canada, went berserk at the news.

Financial Post: Canada needs another Robert Bourassa in Quebec to replace the one that will soon leave politics (Sept 15/93).

Globe and Mail: Mr. Bourassa's status as a political phoenix is incontestable. . . . Mr. Bourassa's good intentions and statesmanship are not at issue. . . . His loyalty to the PQ's economic statism, summed up by the phrase "Quebec Inc.," contributed to the wasteful misallocation of resources that has left so much of Quebec's economy in tatters (Sept 15/93).

Lise Bissonnette: English Canada has always seen Mr. Bourassa as an immutable rampart of federalism, able to compensate for all its weaknesses. Perhaps he wanted to shake this false security? (*GM*, Sept 16/93).

Peter C. Newman: It is entirely fitting that Bourassa and Brian Mulroney should leave the scene within months of each other. One of the strangest partnerships in Canadian political history — the technocratically inclined Liberal and the populist-leaning Tory — were good friends and staunch allies (*Maclean's*, Sept 27/93).

Another howler from Newman — Brian Muldoon, the lover of tycoons, was a "populist-leaning Tory."

MORE TO THE point, by September 14, the Canadian dollar had lost .45 cents to settle at 75.64 cents US in New York.

In the next two days Campbell gave her downhill roller-coaster another push. In Calgary she said it was really tough to know where to cut spending — "there is no one consistent set of reporting standards within the federal government. . . . The details of where things will be cut have to be worked out. . . . I don't think I'm being evasive. I'm just saying that I can't come forward with a complete budget" (*GM*, Sept 18/93). The next day in Brandon, Manitoba, she proved that she protested: "I'm telling you I'm absolutely committed, I have a clear vision. . . . I am absolutely determined . . . to show Canadians my strength and my commitment to see things through . . . to show my mettle . . ." (*GM*, Sept 21/93).

And again in Moncton, New Brunswick, she said: "I just don't think we can even begin to quantify what it means to this country — in human terms and economic terms — to live in a country where we don't fear impoverishment from illness. . . . I will not let that be put at risk in this country. I absolutely will not" (*Star*, Sept 20/93).

Lucien Bouchard enjoyed himself. At Lac St. Jean, Quebec, he boldly stated his position on swearing allegiance to the Queen: "I have no problem with that, the Queen is not the real Queen of Canada. She's there as head of state. I will swear allegiance to the state and to my duties as a democratic representative of Quebec" (*GM*/Southam, Sept 20/93). The next day, addressing a joint session of the Empire and Canadian clubs, to which only 160 people turned out, he mouthed the words to "O Canada" and toasted the Queen. Michael Charette of Mel Hurtig's National Party interrupted the luncheon with shouts of *"Vive le Canada libre. . . .* You want to break up my country, mister, you've got to face me!" He was summarily escorted from the room. Bouchard told his retreating figure, "I respect your opinion, sir" (*FP*, Sept 23/93).

Kim Campbell hit her red-letter day as a fally-go-downy on September 23 — just one month before the election. On the Canadian voters at St-Bruno, Quebec, she dumped, "You can't have a debate on such a key issue as the modernization of the social programs in 47 days." Conservatives, she said, were prepared to "completely rethink our system of social security" (*GM*, Sept 24/93). And an election was no time, she said firmly, "to get involved in very, very serious issues" (Newman, *Maclean's*, Oct 25/93).

T HE GALLUP poll of September 25 confirmed the Tories' rush to catastrophe — they watched 6 percent of their popular support trickle away in one month. They held on to 30 percent — down from 36 percent — Liberals 37 percent; Reform 13 percent; NDP 8 percent; Bloc Québécois 10 percent; and the National Party 2 percent.

While Campbell coyly waffled, Cornwall, Ontario, Mayor Ron Martelle emerged from hiding. His Worship had sustained a steady barrage of death threats from local cigarette smugglers. Some 50,000 cartons per day were coming in every which way to tax-evading consumers from the United States, representing $1 billion in lost revenue. The situation had become so dangerous that the RCMP, the Ontario Provincial Police, the Sûreté of Quebec, and the New York State Troopers had set up a joint task force between themselves.

Martelle had come out in public because his fellow citizens could hear gunfire across the St. Lawrence almost any time as smugglers terrorized the area. No longer could Canada gloat over a society based on peace, order, and good government.

In the last week of September the leader of the Public Service Alliance of Canada (PSAC), Daryl Bean, boasted that the federal government's largest union would support the Bloc Québécois candidate Christiane Gagnon against the Tory finance minister, Gilles Loiselle. On-side or not, PSAC members would have to hand over their dues to an organization that backed an avowed separatist who said things like Canadians "are like Greeks or Turks. I am curious to know them as individuals but I don't belong to the same nation" (*Sun*, Sept 26/93).[3]

On September 27, Preston Manning pulled another policy switch. Having seized the ball himself at the Reform convention in 1991 and vowed to fight *for* the GST to fund Canada's humongous debt directly, he reverted to his original sermon, that "others will propose tax relief in other areas or forms. But we propose the removal of the GST because it is the tax most hated by rank-and-file people" (*FP*, Sept 28/93).

Standard & Poor's of New York was unmoved by the shenanigans. The renowned credit-rating agency put Ontario on credit watch, anyway. Deficit predictions for the province were off by nearly $1 billion. S & P read the signs: "This action reflects uncertainty regarding the province's commitment to meeting the deficit reduction plan outlined in its May 1993 budget in the face of revenue slippage" (*FP*, Sept 28/93).

As creditors turned tough with Ontario, so Ontario turned tough with Quebec. The Minister of Economic Development and Trade, Frances Lankin, threw down the gauntlet on the interprovincial trade barriers that were strangling Confederation: "It has become clear to us that Quebec feels little incentive to address our concerns." The new restrictions affected shipments of buses and building materials to Ontario. Quebec contractors would no longer be eligible to bid on Ontario government-funded projects. An estimated 3,500 Ontario construction workers would benefit from the protection (*GM*, Sept 28/93).

Very late in the game, Kim Campbell launched her meat-and-potatoes menu for voters on September 28. In response to the Liberals' famous "Red Book" of promises and happy thoughts for the future, the Conservatives put out *Making Government Work for Canada: A Taxpayer's Agenda*. Too little and too late. The Red Book — *Creating Opportunity: The Liberal Plan for Canada*, a 112-pager — had been circulating across Canada for nearly a month.

Slick, colourful, well-written, replete with charts and subliminal messages about the positive aspects of the Liberal legacy, the Red Book read and felt like the annual report of a corporation on the move. A letter from the Hon. Jean Chrétien graced the opening page: "The key to our success as a nation has been our ability to face change, adapt to it, and prevail. That will be the key to our future."

Compared to it, the Tories' cheesy, thirty-six-page flyer started off with "An Open Letter from Prime Minister Kim Campbell": "It's time to make government work for Canadians again. There are those who will say we can only solve our challenges by turning our backs on the world we live in." She got that right.

On Peter Gzowski's CBC AM radio program "Morningside," Campbell grandly defended the social safety net: "I'll throw myself across the railroad tracks to protect the system." NDP leader Audrey McLaughlin wasted no time picking up on that opening: "We know they [the Tories] destroyed the train system so I think she had better find another analogy" (*GM*, Sept 29/93).

While "conservative" Campbell performed gymnastics to protect the welfare state, Manning marched in the opposite direction. In an interview with the *Globe* he offered his latest musing on the so-called sacred trust the socialists claimed binds all Canadians. Reform would end universal medicare as guaranteed by the federal government: "You can get something that's tailored to your needs. What I prefer is to just have the federal government cut the strings and let the levels of government closest to the public sort this out" (*GM*, Sept 29/93).

For more than four years, he had scoffed at critics who accused him of having a hidden agenda on the social safety net and medicare.

To be exact, the policy the Reform Party convention adopted in Calgary on August 14, 1988, stated, "The sustainability of high-quality social services is as important as the services themselves. Governments must preserve both the availability and sustainability of these services. . . . No citizen should be denied access by reason of financial status or inability to pay" (*Platform and Statement of Principles*, p. 20).

In contrast, the policy adopted at the Reform Party Assembly in Saskatoon, April 4–7, 1991, stated: "The Reform Party recognizes the importance of ensuring that adequate health-care insurance and services are available to every Canadian, and that it is the Provinces which currently possess the legal and constitutional responsibility to provide such services . . ." (*Principles and Policies*, p. 30).

Former Ontario Premier David Peterson led the pack lambasting Reform and the Bloc Québécois: "I think the most destructive thing we can do is institute regionalism in our national Parliament. It's got the capacity to tear this country apart" (*GM*, Oct 1/93); "You're talking to a guy who gave blood to this country, who would do anything to keep this country together, who cares about the economy, knows economic strength has a lot to do with it, who understands the relationship. It's not a question of fear; it's not a question of threat" (*GM*, Oct 1/93).

By the end of September the battle lines in the most boring election campaign in Canadian history were firmly drawn. The Liberals promised to print money. Before an audience of 500 unemployed construction workers in Toronto, Chrétien promised that a Liberal government would devote $6 billion to building and repairing Canada's infrastructure over the next three years. Over a period of two years, municipalities would be expected to match the federal funding with $2 billion each year: "Our priority is not to create jobs in the next century. It's to create jobs right now" (*Star*, Sept 11/93). As Joe Mavrinac, head of the Association of Ontario Municipalities, retorted, "Where the hell are we going to get the money?" (*Sun*, Sept 12/93).

Kim Campbell would have none of such generosity. On September 11, she dismissed the prospect of federal support to build a convention and trade centre at Toronto's Exhibition Place. The Metro Toronto and the Ontario governments had committed $140 million to it. The feds were being asked to put up $40 million. Metro chairman Alan Tonks tried to persuade Ottawa that it would mean $62 million in tax revenue, including 2,300 construction jobs and 1,400 permanent jobs, when it was complete. The provincial government would gain an estimated $24 million in tax revenue. Evidently, cost-benefit payoffs that made sense for both the private sector and the taxpayer didn't count for much in the mind of Kim Campbell.

C AMPBELL'S CAMPAIGN seemed to be bringing out the worst in every-one. AFN Chief Ovide Mercredi said he wouldn't support any political party. Preston Manning's commitment to Canada's heritage was as uninspiring as Lucien Bouchard's performance at the September joint meeting of the Empire Club and the Canadian Club.

Asked two weeks later whether he too would swear an oath of allegiance to the Queen, Preston Manning replied, "Yes, if that's the current oath. We have proposed an amendment to the oath of both the Senate and the House of Commons that they ought to swear allegiance to the people who elect them, and the Queen, in that order" (*Maclean's*, Oct 4/93).

The federal election crept nearer. In apparent anticipation, the *Globe and Mail* made its confession on October 1:

Maybe we just don't get it. Maybe we just don't understand why Canadians are so angry with the political class. Maybe we in the media and universities and political parties are all just policy wonks, strategy wonks and personality wonks, engaged in a political game that few people out there are playing any more. . . . The "real" Canada may be standing up, for better or worse, emerging from decades of paternalistic manipulation, challenging some of the very concepts of Canada laid out by its mainline political parties over the past 30 years. Two founding nations. The equality of provinces. Multiculturalism.

Where was bilingualism? Did the Faculty Club not think the most vexatious issue in Canadian politics deserved a mention?

WHERE, O WHERE, was the Canada of Sir John A. Macdonald, who had forged a railway to bind the nation from coast to coast? In a speech in 1861 the first prime minister said, "Whatever you do, adhere to the Union — we are a great country, and shall become one of the greatest in the universe if we preserve it: we shall sink into insignificance and adversity if we suffer it to be broken."

And where was the Canada of Sir George Étienne Cartier, the realist who rejected the melting pot and knew that fragmenting Canada would destroy the French fact in America?

> Some have regretted that we have a distinction of races, and have expressed the hope that, in time, this diversity will disappear. The idea of a fusion of all races is utopian; it is an impossibility. . . . The objection that we cannot form a great nation because Lower Canada is French and Catholic, Upper Canada English and Protestant, and the Maritime Provinces mixed . . . is futile. . . . In our confederation there will be Catholics and Protestants, English, French, Irish, and Scotch, and each by its efforts and success will add to the prosperity of the Dominion, to the glory of the new confederation. We are of different races, not to quarrel, but to work together for the common welfare. (John Boyd, *Sir George Etienne Cartier, Bart.*, pp. 216–17)

The world of Campbell was not the world of Macdonald and Cartier. Speaking at a railway convention in New Orleans, CN president Paul Tellier reported that by 1995 the railway planned to get rid of one-half of its track: "By 1995, we want to reduce our network in Eastern and Central Canada by roughly 20 per cent. We want to sell another third. This will leave the CN operating a network in the East of about half the current size, fed by a cluster of short lines" (*GM*/CP, Oct 2/93).

October 4 marked one of the most dramatic moments in the campaign, the televised leaders' debate in English. Bouchard took full advantage of the opportunity to knock Campbell nearly out of the race. Fully knowledgeable about the inner workings of government and about when information would be available on Canada's current accounts, Bouchard lunged for his opponent's jugular: "You're hiding the truth, Madame, you're hiding this figure, because it will destroy the credibility of your plan. . . . Answer the question. What is the real deficit of last year? It's a simple question. Yes or no. . . . What is the figure?" (*Star*, Oct 5/93). And because she wouldn't or couldn't answer, she stood naked before the one candidate she had to prove she could handle like Play-Doh.

At this point, David Peterson just had to get into the act. On "Fourth Reading," an interview program on TVOntario, he waded in: "If we want to build a whole political structure on resentment and envy — some people take advantage of that — Bouchard's building his whole campaign on the basis of Quebec's humiliation. I mean, I'll tell you another parallel of that, I mean Hitler built the whole Nazi movement on the basis of the humiliation of Germany after the First World War and built it into a political movement" (*GM*, Oct 9/93).

Three days later he did it again. Questioned about his odd analogy, he triumphantly justified himself: "You are talking to a guy that gave blood for Meech Lake. . . . You're talking to a guy who cares passionately about this country and who understands the differences" (*GM*, Oct 9/93). More blood.

Lucien Bouchard was much better at making mischief. The leader of the Bloc credited Bourassa with helping the BQ win a by-election in August 1990. According to Bouchard, two other Liberals went "to get [Bourassa's] blessing, his stamp of approval" (*GM*, Oct 9/93). According to a Canadian Press report on Saturday, October 9, Bouchard said, "I really spoke to Mr. Bourassa when I quit [Mulroney's Cabinet]. He helped the creation of the Bloc."

Bourassa the Crab didn't deny it.

PRESTON **M**ANNING fired his parting arrow in the campaign on October 11 in Cambridge, Ontario: "Reform is committed to making itself the fiscal conscience and the democratic conscience of the 35th Parliament, whether you give us 10 seats or 100 seats. . . . Thanks largely to the NDP, the Canadian Parliament now has a social conscience that permeates every party and Parliament itself. That's why medicare, pensions, UIC are safe as long as we can figure out how to refinance them" (*FP*, Oct 13/93). What was he saying? Just two weeks earlier universal medicare was on Manning's chopping block.

The next day, in time-honoured tradition, the Tories were killing each other in public. At a Conservative rally in Red Deer, Alberta, Kim Campbell floundered while a clutch of oil-patch heavies from the party — the Honourables Joe Clark, Yellowhead; Don Mazankowski, Vegreville; and Harvie Andre, Calgary Centre — busied themselves elsewhere. It was a flashback to the Diefenbaker years, with no help from Dalton Camp this time.

Life on Manning's campaign trail was no bowl of cherries, either. On October 13 at York University in Toronto, students confronted the Reform leader. They alleged that John Beck, the party's candidate for York Centre, had been making racist remarks. The university student newspaper *Excalibur* quoted him: "You have a $150,000 guy there coming to buy a citizenship to Canada to create a job, fine, he's bringing something [to Canada]. But what is he bringing? Death and destruction to the people." In another interview with the *Financial Post*, Beck sounded off big-time: "I feel the time has come for white Anglo-Saxons to get involved" in politics (*Star*, Oct 14/93).

Of course, the Reform Party dropped him like a hot potato as a candidate and booted him out of the party. During Manning's presentation the protesting rowdies vigorously waved signs around with slogans like "Blame the Poor, Vote Reform" and "Support Racism, Vote Reform" (*GM*, Oct 14/93).

Beck 'fessed up to the media, the Canadian Press and the *Toronto Star*: "They think I'm nuts, but I've had no [mental] breakdown. They asked me to resign, so I resigned" (CP), and "I feel we have lost control of our country here. . . . It seems to be predominantly Jewish people who are running this country. . . . If I was to say some bad things about other cultures, I guess it's racism" (*Star*, Oct 15/93).

Manning had to deal with the press, too. He called the expulsion an "embarrassment. . . . Well, I wouldn't exaggerate the problems we've had with our candidates. . . . We've had one so far out of 207 [who has resigned], which is pretty good. . . . This [Beck's riding] was one of these weaker ridings that was desperate to get a candidate because we were pressing them so hard. And it looks like they did a whole bunch of short-circuits of our screening process" (*GM*, Oct 15/93).

Unfortunately for his party and the Reform movement, though, Manning could never seem to deal up front when it came to the crunch: "Those ones [candidates] that were in the WCC [Western Canada Concept] because they were mad [at the federal system] but will say, 'No, no, we're federalists,' we have no problems with them. . . . The ones that bother me the worst are these ones that have these racist views and disguise them or hide them until they get some position where they can speak on a public platform. Those are the ones that worry me the most" (*GM*, Oct 15/93).

In other words, you could be a Reformer in good standing if you were a separatist but not if you were a racist. Even while Beck was leaping from the frying pan into the fire, the Reform candidate in Oakville, Richard Malboeuf, an aboriginal Canadian, was making Manning's life miserable in other ways. He said that Reform had to change one of its basic platform policies if it was to succeed in Quebec. It had to recognize the two-founding-nations theory of Canada. Manning swallowed the bad medicine in silence.

Liberal leader Jean Chrétien, of course, ignored the whole fuss. Instead he turned his most powerful ammunition on Manning to discredit him where it counted — fiscal management: "To go to zero deficit in three years or five years [as the Reform Party proposes], you know it's not reality. It could be done. . . . You might have 25-percent unemployment, too. And when you have 25-percent unemployment, don't worry about the deficit any more. It's a revolution. Nobody in Yugoslavia is talking about the problem of the deficit there today" (*GM*, Oct 14/93).

O N OCTOBER 14, the Tory campaign hit rock bottom. For many years journalists, photographers, cartoonists, and others had made fun of Jean Chrétien's facial disfigurement from Bell's palsy when he was a child. It had permanently affected his speech. With Campbell on the ropes, her witless campaign strategists decided to exploit the Liberal leader's disability in a national television campaign. Running across the screen underneath the most unflattering picture of Chrétien to be found were the words "Is this a Prime Minister? . . . I would personally be very embarrassed if he would become Prime Minister of Canada." As if this wasn't bad enough, John Tory, chairman of the Tory party, defended dirty tricks: "I think all the ads do is call into question — and it's a very legitimate question — Mr. Chrétien's competence, particularly on the economy but also in general terms." The three photos of Chrétien, Tory pomped, "are no different than the picture that appears on the front cover of *Maclean's* magazine this very day." He was right on only his last point. The *Maclean's* cover shot employed the same tactic for the October 18 issue.

Campbell clinched the election for the Liberals with a graceless retraction: "I would apologize to Mr. Chretien and anyone who found them offensive. It certainly was not my intention to be offensive. The intention was to deliver a very important message in this campaign about Mr.

Chretien's competence as a leader. I will continue to deliver that message but I will do it in a way that will not cause offence" (*Star*, Oct 16/93). She pulled the ads.

John Tory stuck to his guns: "It's a tough question [whether or not this strategy should have been used]. It's an important question. It's a legitimate question in an election campaign" (*GM*, Oct 16/93).

Tory MP Patrick Boyer of Etobicoke–Lakeshore raged, quite rightly, "Whoever is responsible should be given their walking papers today" (*Star*, Oct 16/93). Tory MP Don Blenkarn was also fast off the mark. He faxed a message to party headquarters in Ottawa: "Things are tough enough without the campaign attacking handicapped people. Your Chretien ad is a national disgrace. I denounce it and those who produced it" (*Star*, Oct 16/93).

Yet, for all their foibles, the Tories remained a united bunch. In fact, their togetherness actually grew daily as they continued their steady march toward the cliff. In an interview with *La Presse*, Campbell remained fixed on her pathway to destruction. On Mulroney: "I believe that during the last eight years, we have done things in a way that did not work, that sapped the credibility of the political process. . . . I was not there from 1984 to 1988, a lot of things were done in a way that I would not have done them." On her fellow Tory opponent, Jean Charest, while referring to the end of the leadership campaign: "You know, Jean Charest was saying 'less deficit, more jobs,' but with no fleshed-out vision explaining how to achieve it . . ." (*GM*, Oct 18/93). At the end of the interview she surrendered all semblance of political savvy. In spite of it all, she said, she was "proud of Brian Mulroney" (*Sun*, Oct 18/93).

Snubbed in the West, she was thrown by her handlers to drooling hyenas in Quebec. Tory transport minister Jean Corbeil led the party dissidents with a letter: "Your smearing of certain members as a way of justifying the derailment of the campaign . . . which you [Campbell] conceived and directed . . . is far from the politics of inclusion which you so ardently promote."

Though marked "In Strict Confidence" and sent to Campbell on Saturday, the letter was released to the media at the same time, according to the *Globe* on October 18. Corbeil neither retracted it nor apologized for sending it. The arrow hit home. The prime minister refused to attend her own final campaign rally in Montreal. Corbeil was one of the two senior Quebec ministers in the Campbell Cabinet who supported Charest. Yet Campbell fired neither him nor John Tory. Instead she contacted Charest to plead with him to cut short his campaigning in Toronto and join her in Montreal. He agreed but was supposedly overruled by party strategists.

By October 18 every Conservative riding in Canada had been flooded with news flyers that read "A Warning To All Canadian Taxpayers. On October 25th you can take a chance. Before you do, you should know that you have two out of three chances of paying *a lot more in taxes* by next year. It's time to think twice." Surely three out of three would have been more convincing?

Flattened by her opponents inside and outside the party, Campbell could no longer get up with her fists flying every time she was knocked down. Asked whether the Tories would ever consider an alliance with the Reform Party, she went defensive instead of whipping out a sabre and slicing all around her: "I am seeking to win a mandate, not to, by some kind of legal technicality, stay on in office" (*GM*, Oct 19/93).

The *Toronto Star* had already twisted its knife with a perverted headline, "Campbell may back a Liberal minority." The editors knew full well they could destroy her who was once their darling with a single remark from her own lips: "The survival of our country is the most important thing for me. I will do whatever is necessary to ensure it" (*Star*, Oct 18/93).

A rather gallant Michael Wilson stood steadfast by her side as the Conservative ship gurgled further into the deep: "Without a strong, truly national voice in Parliament, the debate could become nasty and divisive for the country. . . . I say this as a retiring politician who can be objective, drawing on past experience of enduring pressures of regional policies. . . . Bloc and Reform" (*GM*, Oct 19/93).

A T THIS LATE date, knowing who was with the leader and who was against her had become truly difficult. The feminist Red Tory MP from Rosedale, Isabel Bassett, took her turn at command. Furious at the party's bungling over the Chrétien ads, Isabelita drafted a stiff reprimand to the prime minister — *and* made *her* letter public: "I think it time, in these last days of the election campaign, that you put aside the contrived strategies and speak frankly to Canadians. Your personal message carries much strength and your hope and vision is stronger than any well-planned, theoretical political strategy. . . . It appears though that the interest of the political elite have caused this vision to be over shadowed [*sic*]. This action has resulted in petty political infighting in the party over whose strategy is more correct and whose vision of Canada is more saleable."

Some Tories admitted defeat early. Senator Pierre-Claude Nolin, chief organizer in Quebec, issued a clipped message: "I think the Liberals are going to form a minority government" (*Star*, Oct 19/93). Campbell more or less agreed. With less than a week to go, she drifted into Etobicoke just west of Toronto to deliver what amounted to a swan song. The country, she warned, can't afford "an Italian Parliament — to be strong, Canada must have a strong national voice." In light of the polls, she was clearly implying that the Tories should push for a Liberal majority. Revenue minister Garth Turner on tour with her was more explicit: "Liberal or Conservative, a majority is better because it is more stable . . . and there is no question that in the economic times that we're at, with a great deal of debt, that right now we need to send out a message of stability" (Stewart, *Star*, Oct 20/93). Losers.

While Campbell ruminated on the rout to come, Pierre Trudeau emerged from his usual hiding to vote. On the day after his seventy-fourth birthday, he swept to the ballot box attired in trademark beret, cape, and red rose. He paused, surveying the kingdom that had always been his, before casting some pearls before the media multitudes scrambling to film and tape him and ask questions: "[Liberals] would be the best government against the forces of disintegration. . . . Listen, a vote for the Bloc is a vote for a party that wants to break up Canada, so let's not have any pretence about that. (If Reform gains power) we would inevitably have uniquely French Quebec and a uniquely English Canada. That was the formula of René Lévesque. . . . [Reform will also] contribute to the forces of disintegration" (*Gazette*, Oct 20/93).

He could have said nothing and have been safe. On October 22, Gallup predicted the Liberals at 44 percent; Reform, 19 percent; PC, 16 percent; Bloc, 12 percent; NDP, 7 percent. Since the previous poll the Liberals had sprung ahead 7 percent. Reform, on the other hand, had slipped 6 percent; the Undecided vote had jumped from 19 to 28 percent — results taken October 17 through 20. An earthquake was rumbling beneath Canada's political surface.

Campbell gave up the ghost in a speech in Kitchener on October 20. She conceded that her rival Jean Chrétien had run "a wonderful campaign . . . [but] I'm not prepared to give him control over the agenda of this country for the 1990s" (*Star*, Oct 21/93). Laughable. Almost.

JUST AS HIS predecessors had done before him in times of difficulty — Spicer, Yalden, and Fortier — the Official Languages Commissioner stuck his oar in. Victor Goldbloom cheered his troops on with a reminder that they were right to be enraged by any threat to Official Bilingualism. Goldbloom had good reason to worry. For the first time in more than a generation, the bankruptcy of Official Bilingualism was being discussed openly. The languages commissioner scorned his critics: "The law is not an ass. . . . The law is reasonable. The law makes sense. Its only purpose is to ensure appropriate, understandable (and hopefully courteous and efficient) services to Canadian citizens. That surely is their fundamental, incontrovertible right" (*GM*, Oct 21/93). At this point only the media cared, and, within that small group, the Pulp Primevil in particular.

At midnight on October 22, a far more serious event passed relatively quietly. Section 322.1 of the Canada Elections Act came into effect. Bill C-114, now known as the infamous "Gag Law," would prohibit the press and broadcasters from publishing any scientific poll results within three days of a federal election. The unholy trinity of Canada's federalist parties, the Tories, the Liberals, and the NDP, had endorsed this latest denial of a basic freedom. Yet while the legislation forbade professional polling, it was not all-inclusive: kooks, crystal ball-gazers, and bookies could still ply their crafts with impunity.

By Saturday, October 23, it was obvious the Liberals were headed for a majority. Preston Manning groaned: "I really feel we are down to just three more days of democracy. If the public gives somebody a blank-cheque majority, then real democracy — where politicians have to seek people's opinion and seek their advice — is gone for five years. [A majority government] does not have to listen on constitutional issues, it doesn't have to listen on taxation. The last nineteen years of majority governments have demonstrated that" (*Sun*, Oct 24/93).

Financial markets begged to differ. At the close of business the previous day, the Canadian dollar had risen to 76.63 cents US, up 1½ cents from the previous Friday (*Star*, Oct 23/93).

On Sunday, October 24, nearly the first-year anniversary of the Referendum, the Toronto Blue Jays won the World Series a second time. They had won it the first time a year earlier almost to the day. In a sudden-death cliffhanger the Canadian team beat the Philadelphia Flyers 8 to 6, and one million fans exploded into Toronto's Yonge Street screaming and dancing with delight. One spectator told a Toronto CityPulse TV interviewer why he was happy: "It's the only hope we've got."

In the final hours of the campaign, the mainstream press lit the fuse on the last of their cannons: the *Star* supported the Liberals, naturally: "On national unity and economic stability, the Liberals, at this juncture, represent the only viable alternative. Accordingly, our preference is clear and without qualification. A Liberal majority" (*Star*, Oct 23/93). The self-flattering *Toronto Sun*, the little paper that had reddened in recent years, stood up for Mulroney's heirs: "So the choice must be Conservative, even though Reform policies are often so attractive, we think they copied *Sun* editorials. . . . Preston Manning and his members have yet to demonstrate in the heat of the Commons that they can handle themselves. As the Liberals have shown since 1968, it's not enough just to talk a great game" (*Sun*, Oct 24/93). The schizophrenics at the Faculty Club didn't know what to do. So the *Globe* did nothing. The *Financial Post* found itself out in left field, too, and abstained.

Kim Campbell's parting shot befitted a poor loser. She whimpered in Vancouver that it would be "very divisive" if both the prime minister and the leader of the opposition came from Quebec: "I think Canadians need to understand that it is important to our long-term stability to have the perception that leadership and direction is something that rotates around the country, that all Canadians have a share at it" (*GM*, Oct 25/93).

"The perception"? Now, *really*.

Elsewhere in the West, 6,000 cheering crusaders swarmed into Calgary to hear Manning's final words of wisdom. If the Bloc became the Official Opposition, the Reform leader informed the largest crowd in this federal election, Canada would become an "international laughing stock" (*Star*, Oct 25/93).

When it was all over, Brian Mulroney's election prediction did not come to pass. The Tories did not win 175 seats. Clyde H. Farnsworth reported in a front-page story for the *New York Times*:

> Voters gave the Liberals a clear majority with 178 seats [actually 177] in the 295-seat House of Commons, up from 79, and slashed the Progressive Conservatives from 153 [actually 157] to 2. It was the most punishing blow to any governing party in Canadian political history. Even with a comfortable majority, Mr. Chrétien will have to work with a Parliament fractured by regional rivalries. Two regional parties surged in the voting: The separatist Bloc Québécois won 54 seats and the populist, Alberta based Reform Party, made up chiefly of disaffected Tories, won 52 seats. (Oct 27/93)

After voting in St. Henri–Westmount, according to Mila Mulroney, Mulroney left Canada for the U.S.[4]

Having served only 123 days as PM, the banished Kim Campbell entered the history books as the third-shortest-serving prime minister on record, following her fellow-Vancouverite John Turner, who made it for

79 days, and Sir Charles Tupper, with 69 days. With less than six years' service, including her stint as justice minister, she had not earned an MP's pension. Her only entitlement was a severance package of $69,200 — less than a year's salary. This compared to Brian Mulroney's package of $33,500 a year plus a special pension of two-thirds his annual salary as prime minister when he reaches age sixty-five.

Canada could never be the same. The two-party system that Canadians had known since Confederation had utterly evaporated. At the helm for a solid five years, the Liberals under Chrétien had won themselves the golden ring, a free hand. Her Majesty's Loyal Opposition no longer served as the traditional alternative government-in-waiting.

Most significant of the distinctive shifts the election signalled in Canadian politics was the destruction of the Conservative Party of Canada. The founding political party of the country under Sir John A. Macdonald at the time of Confederation had been virtually annihilated. By 1993 there remained no distinctions between the socialist activism of the Liberal Party of Canada and the collectivist rights activism of the left-of-centre Conservative Party of Canada. There was no need and no room for two political parties to occupy the same philosophical space. In the West, the Blue Conservatives lined up with Preston Manning, and the Reds huddled with the Liberals or the NDP. In Ontario, where Manning had so bungled his campaign, the vote split three ways. Either the Red Tories stoically held firm to their sinking ship or they jumped to the Liberals. Once again the Blue Tories had disenfranchised themselves. Now they had no more place to go federally than they had had under Bill Davis, the Red Tory premier of Ontario who had destroyed the party provincially.[5]

N OW THE LONG overdue hunt for the Red Tories could begin in earnest.

Notes

1 That first judgement read:

> 13. "The Committee calls upon the State party [Canada] to remedy the violation of article 19 of the Covenant by an appropriate amendment to the law."
>
> 14. "The Committee would wish to receive information, within six months, on any relevant measures taken by the State party in connection with the Committee's views."
>
> [Gord McIntyre wrote:] I respectfully submit that the State Party has taken no effective action to remedy the violation. On the other hand, it has permitted the Quebec provincial government to continue with legislation that does not meet the requirements of the Committee to end the violation of Article 19 of the International Covenant on Civil and Political Rights. . . .
>
> (1) **Bill 86 permits the Government to prohibit the use of a language other than French.** The law states; "the government may determine, by regulation, the cases, conditions or circumstances where public signs and posters and commercial advertising must be in French only. . . ."
>
> (2) **Bill 86 permits the government to subject public signs and posters and commercial advertising to varying degrees of limitation. . . .** The Law states; "the *government may determine, by regulation,* the cases, conditions or circumstances where public signs and posters and commercial advertising *must be in French only,* where French need not be predominant or where such signs, posters and advertising may be in another language only." . . .
>
> It is obvious that the Government is attempting, by subterfuge, to circumvent the ruling of the Human Rights Committee (King, *The First Step,* pp. 51, 52).

2 A study by Jim Stanford, a research fellow at the Brookings Institution in Washington, predicted at the end of September that NAFTA's only winner would be Mexico. Canada would lose more than any other of the three signatories, 30,000 jobs. Overall, the country's GDP would fall 1.5 percent and the average wage would fall 1.7 percent, or about $500 annually.

3 Today, most government and private-sector employees alike have compulsory union dues or their equivalent deducted from their pay whether or not the employee belongs to the union. The Rand Formula — named after Supreme Court of Canada Justice Ivan C. Rand — resulted from a court decision in 1946 affecting the Ford Motor Company and union security. The argument is that the un-unionized worker benefits from the union's bargaining activities as much as the unionized worker does.

On June 27, 1991, seven justices of the Supreme Court of Canada (SCC) unanimously ruled that unions could use their compulsorally secured financial resources from union members to finance political parties and causes — even though workers might personally oppose those views, and although a majority of those workers would even be compromised under the Charter of Rights and Freedoms, Section 2(d).

In the case at bar, *Lavigne v. the Ontario Public Service Employees Union* (OPSEU), the SCC sprang unhesitatingly into the political arena. Leading the parade of seven judges, Madam Justice Bertha Wilson, who had been appointed by Trudeau, ruled that even the voluntary intervenors in the action should be reimbursed for their costs in the action. David Somerville, president of the National Citizens' Coalition (NCC) — which footed the bill — interpreted: "The award of costs means that any citizen seeking to defend his rights and freedoms in court through the Charter risks almost unlimited liability on court costs" (NCC, *Consensus*, Aug/93).

The NCC was the obvious target. On June 21 Somerville bought a bank draft for $350,000 to settle the costs. Punitive.

And contemptible. The stuff that citizens' revolts are made of. So much for Canada's highest court as guardian of the Constitution. So much for legal education in Canada. In a constitutional democracy, this was a matter for Parliament. Period.

4 Detailed Election Results

Reform: (52 seats)*

BC	24	(out of 32)	Sask.	4	(out of 14)
Alberta	22	(out of 26)	Manitoba	1	(out of 14)
Ontario	1	(out of 99) — Reform fielded 96 candidates in Ont.			

* Alberta riding of Edmonton Northwest: Liberals won by one vote over Reform — Reform called for recounts in 3 ridings.

NDP: (reduced from 43 seats to 9)   **Official Party Status Lost**

Sask.	5	(out of 14)	Manitoba	1	(out of 14)
BC	2	(out of 32)	Yukon/NWT	1	(out of 3)

Bloc Québécois: (up from 8 to 54 seats)*
(Quebec only)

* Riding of Bourassa: Bloc won by 67 votes over Liberal — recount.

Liberals: (up from 80 to 177 seats)

Conservatives: (reduced from 153 to 2)   **Official Party Status Lost**

Quebec	1	Jean Charest — a Turquoise Tory
NB	1	Elsie Wayne — challenged Spicer on bilingualism

The Hunt for the Red Tories in October

5 In his autobiography *A Life in Progress*, Conrad Black says of Davis, "I asked Bill Davis, predictably one of the leaders of the Yes Committee what Brian Mulroney or any successor would have left to do apart from printing postage stamps and greeting important official visitors (who would not be numerous). Bill, who has created yet another career for himself advising Bob Rae, a service for which his own management of Ontario's fortunes amply qualified him, smiled enigmatically and said, 'The agreement isn't ideal'" (p. 505).

37

Jean Chrétien: The Return of Absolutism
— October 26, 1993, to December 31, 1994

U NLIKE KIM CAMPBELL, JEAN CHRÉTIEN SEIZED the day even before he assumed office. Canadians welcomed action on the economic front and the prime minister elect moved smartly — even into right field. He immediately cancelled the $6-billion EH101 helicopter purchase the Tories had arranged and scrapped their $1.6-billion plan to privatize Pearson International Airport.[1] And the Liberals had foretold all this in their famous election canon, the "Red Book."

Everyone knew there would no real savings. Instead of planes, Paul Martin, the soon-to-be Minister of Finance, would start the money presses rolling so the new government could deliver the promised $6-billion job-creation program.

Peter C. Newman fumed. "Trust Canadians to invent a new system of government: elected dictatorship. . . . The nation-founding Conservative party has been reduced to a cult; it has no power base, no funds, no ideas and no marketable leader" (*Maclean's*, Nov 1/93).

No amount of economic re-jigging could disguise the ugly ramifications of this election. The victorious Liberals had less than half the popular vote in the country, or 42 percent, yet they commanded a whopping majority of 60 percent in the House of Commons — 178 seats.

The Tories' standing after the debacle was ludicrous. They had surpassed the separatist Bloc Québécois in the popular vote with 16 percent to 14 percent, yet the PCs would have to settle for only two-thirds of 1 percent of the seats in the House. This amounted to two seats.

At first glance the results for the Reform Party *seemed* to make sense. They had drawn 18 percent of the popular vote, so claimed 52 seats. But then the electoral system's reliance on first-past-the-post tipped the scale: although they had secured 25 percent more of the popular vote than the Bloc Québécois, Reform ended up third in the number of Commons seats they would hold. The BQ garnered 18 percent of the seats, for a grand total of 54, with only 14 percent of the popular vote. At final count, even though the BQ lagged behind the two other federal opposition parties in the popular vote, they coasted to second place and the silver medal that went with it: the place, the protocol, and the funding as Her Majesty's Loyal Opposition.

University of Toronto historian Michael Bliss calmly evaluated the situation for his readers in the Pulp Primevil: "True, the Conservative party suffered one of the most spectacular collapses of a government in the history of parliamentary democracy. But the country remains strong. . . . Our party system did not collapse: A bankrupt national party [the Conservatives] has been replaced by a brilliantly rejuvenated national party [the Liberals]. . . . A stable democracy turned another page in its rich lengthened history" (*Star*, Oct 28/93). In the March 1994 issue of *Canadian Business*, he plupticated: "Quebec will have to go or stay; there will be no halfway house, no more rounds of constitutional reform. . . . The coming Quebec debate will stimulate a lot of harsh, sharp and uncompromising comments in other provinces."

Preston Manning played territorial groundhog: "I think we can play the role of de facto opposition. . . . In the panels that I've participated in with the BQ members, they don't seem to have a lot to say on a lot of issues that don't relate to Quebec. . . . It's pretty incongruous to have a separatist group as official opposition in a federal Parliament" (*GM*, Oct 27/93).

Freed from his ties to the Tories, Conrad Black addressed a joint session of the Empire and Canadian clubs after the election: "Federalism's merits are obvious, and shouldn't be promoted by recourse to bribery and blackmail. . . . The solution to Quebec's uncertain status in my judgement is not more concessions. Canada has made quite enough of those. . . . Canada," he said, warming to his theme, "could make a better and more fulfilling arrangement by far with the United States than several which Quebec has already rejected as insufficiently generous to it."

After all, Charlottetown, as Black now felt free to say for the first time, would have resulted in the "self-dismemberment" of the federation. Casting about for a scapegoat, he turned on Mulroney. It was he who had "bequeathed Kim Campbell a political torso without limbs" (*GM*, Nov 3/93):

> That 54% of Canadians voted no [to Charlottetown] convinced me that the people knew that this endless process of trying to buy support with squandered jurisdiction and borrowed money had to end. Where Pierre Trudeau tried to buy Quebec with Ontario's and Alberta's money, Brian Mulroney added the incentive of conferring sovereignty in all but name. Brian Mulroney had an unambiguous mandate in 1984 to govern with fiscal responsibility and to end favouritism to Quebec. . . . And the apotheosis of caring Canada was the pandemic of political correctness, the mission conducted by almost every government in Canada under every bed and behind every bush, to search out and sanctify victims. . . . Canada has become the world's most politically correct country and has transformed itself into an international laughing stock. . . . The collapse of the Progressive Conservatives indicates the country is disgusted with a party which calls itself conservative but is in fact socialist. We have Bob Stanfield and Dalton Camp, not Pierre Trudeau, to thank for the insanely profligate idea of the Guaranteed Annual Income, a salary for anyone who survives childbirth. Bill Davis not only stole Steve Lewis's clothes, as was said of Disraeli and Gladstone, he wore them. We couldn't get him out of them and some of us tried and the consequences of Red Toryism are heavy upon us today. . . . I am one of those who believes French-Canadians had just grievances about their position in Canada and that English Canadians very conscientiously addressed those grievances. . . . Quebec must decide if it is a part of Canada or not. Canada is prepared to offer a pan-Canadian status for French and powers for Quebec quite sufficient to assure Quebec's legitimate aspirations. (Nov 2/93)

On November 3, in Ottawa, Kim Campbell signed off the epoch: "The Conservative party is a party of the centre and the centre-right. . . . I don't see that the Reform party has replaced in any way the Progressive Conservative party, even for a part of the political spectrum, as the articulator of a complete plan for Canada."

When he was asked his views on the subject, defeated Tory MP Don Blenkarn hollered: "I think there is no way you can run another election unless there is one party on the right. . . . I mean, whether it's Reform or Conservative or Reform–Conservative, or a new Conservative party, I don't know. But in any event there is not much point in trying to run an election with two very right-of-centre parties" (*Star*, Nov 4/93).

Silly man. Red Tories don't sit "very right of centre," unless the centre has moved well into left field.

In her last official act, Campbell cut up a dido. She arrived seven minutes late to tender her resignation to Governor General Ramon Hnatyshyn, and then hung around for another thirty-five minutes. The victors waiting outside could afford to be patient. They had five years to get over the slight, revel in the spoils, and exact any revenge they chose.

The Mulroney era officially ended on November 4. The same man who had announced in 1979 that he had "no commitment with destiny" was sworn in as Canada's twentieth prime minister. Jean Chrétien boasted an immaculate record for fence-walking, but at least he would not be likely to fall on his own sword. He had emerged from his years in the wilderness after doggedly performing all the necessary rituals of a would-be prime minister. Like Pierre Trudeau with his *Federalism and the French Canadians*, like John Turner with his *Politics of Purpose*, Brian Mulroney and *Where I Stand*, and even Preston Manning with *The New Canada*, Chrétien had also won his spurs with the aid of a publisher. His 1985 credo *Straight from the Heart* hit the best-seller lists; it even returned in a second edition. Plus ça change, plus c'est la même chose — the road to power is financed with slick promotion.

The careers of the new ministers sounded familiar: twelve were lawyers and eighteen had already been bureaucrats or had sat as Members of Parliament or members of provincial legislatures.

THE INK HAD SCARCELY dried on the ledgers at Rideau Hall when the Quebec sovereigntists issued more demands to the new federal government. On Friday, November 5, Jean Allaire, author of the infamous report bearing his name, along with Mario Dumont, the twenty-three-year-old former leader of the youth wing of Bourassa's Liberals, formed a new organization, Groupe Action-Québec (Groupe Réflexion Québec) (GRQ). Its goal was to pursue a loose federation with Canada based on the transfer of twenty-two federal government powers to the Government of Quebec. This was sovereignty by subterfuge — with no vote from the people.

And, as Allaire put it, "If . . . we cannot develop the society we want and sovereignty is the only way, then let's do it and offer a new partnership, a new union (to the rest of Canada). . . . We'll give it a name after. If they say no, well, it will be sovereignty, period" (*Star*, Nov 2/93).

But was it really sovereignty? In Allaire's understanding of *deux nations*, a "supranational parliament" would link Quebec to Canada (*Star*, Nov 6/93). Back to the future of Gil Rémillard and the machinations of the Queen's Mafia at Mont Gabriel in 1986.

Allaire's GRQ blossomed into a new political party in only thirty-eight days. On Monday, December 13, he proclaimed the new Parti Action Démocratique du Québec (PAQ/PADQ) to the world.

CANADIANS BEAT their temples in quiet desperation. The citizens of Ontario were being subjected to the personal agenda of their premier Bob Rae and his sidekick, the unelected Stephen Lewis. The two were pushing a simple plan for which they had no mandate: to convert Canada's once-wealthiest province into a workers' commune.

The whole business came out on November 5, 1993. That day the Ontario government advertised a senior management position strictly on racial grounds. The position, which was innocuously advertised in the Ontario government publication *Job Mart*, was "restricted to employees of the Ontario Public Service within 40 KM of Toronto" — a common criterion — and "as a positive measure initiative under the Ontario Public Service employment equity program and consistent with the Ontario Human Rights Code, this competition is limited to the following employment equity designated groups: aboriginal peoples, francophones, persons with disabilities, racial minorities and women. . . . To be eligible, indicate on your application or résumé the group to which you belong" (Competition File MBS-226 (a)/93/Classification SMG 2 [senior management group 2]).

Now two provinces had violated the Constitution, their own provincial human rights codes, and the United Nations Charter (Article 19). At one time such practices were expressly prohibited by law. How had this come to pass? The Ontario Human Rights Code of 1980 deemed such classifications illegal: namely, to

b) establish or maintain any employment classification that by its description or operation excludes any person from employment or continued employment. (RSO, 1980, ch. 340)

Thanks to Ontario's previous Liberal government under David Peterson, the 1990 Ontario Human Rights Code specifically ordered that records on "designated groups" be maintained, on the basis of information employees themselves provided (RSO, 1990, ch. 19). (See Appendix B.)

When the media cross-examined the premier on the ad, he went to ground: "I just don't know enough about it. I think you should talk to Brian Charlton [Management Board Chair] about that. I just don't know about it" (*Sun, Star*, Nov 10/93).

When the microphones turned his way, Charlton confidently bubbled, "Yes, I think [the ad is] fair. It's the media, not the government, that is giving the impression we're doing this generally, because that's not the case" (*Sun*, Nov 10/93). And again, "it's the exceptional tool rather than the normal tool. . . . The need outweighs the question of discrimination" (*Sun*, Nov 11/93). As for the "whites," he allowed, "their time will come. It's no different than employment equity. There is only a problem until the work force is in balance. It may take us three years. It may take us five years. It may take us 15 years to get fully into balance."

This was Tory leader Mike Harris's big chance, yet he maintained his disappointing consistency. Inside and outside the Ontario legislature he called the outrage "reverse discrimination" (*Sun*, Nov 10/93). Liberal leader Lyn McLeod screeched that the hiring policy was "absolutely disgraceful. . . . I believe the government should immediately withdraw the ad" (*Sun*, Nov 10/93).

The supporters threw themselves into the uproar. Professor Errol Mendes, architect of "the Mendes formula," as director of the Human Rights Research and Education Centre at the University of Ottawa, stood behind the NDP government: "I think it's here to stay, whether or not there is a backlash. . . . Employment Equity is designed to give everyone a fair chance" (*GM*, Nov 11/93).[2]

In the meantime, Bill 79, Ontario's employment equity legislation, was granted Royal Assent on December 14, 1993. The NDP had nothing to fear from Canada's Constitution. Trudeau had seen to that. The province's government could always invoke the notwithstanding clause.[3]

Alexis de Tocqueville (1805–59), author of the classic *Democracy in America*, toured the United States in 1831 and 1832. He warned:

Nobody is so limited and superficial as not to realize that political liberty can, if carried to excess, endanger the peace, property, and lives of individuals. But only perceptive and clearsighted men see the dangers with which equality threatens us. . . . Democratic peoples always like equality, but there are times when their passion for it turns to delirium. . . . At such times men pounce on equality as their booty and cling to it as a precious treasure they fear to have snatched away. The passion for equality seeps into every corner of the human heart, expands, and fills the whole. It is no use telling them that by this blind surrender . . . they are compromising their dearest interests; they are deaf. It is no use pointing out that freedom is slipping from their grasp while they look the other way; they are blind, or rather they can see but one thing to covet in the whole world. (pp. 504, 505)

In *The Trouble With Canada*, William Gairdner wrote:

Almost imperceptibly during the past few decades, all the political parties of our nation have embraced, to a greater or lesser degree, the twin philosophies of *collectivism* and *egalitarianism*. Collectivism is an elitist political philosophy which insists that the central government ought to control and engineer the condition of our society . . . the idea not simply that everyone should have the same *opportunities*, but that everyone has the *right* to the same *results*, regardless of natural differences, effort, or personal choices. . . . [The method:] they must impose an *equality of outcome* that can be achieved only by creating different rules for different social groups. (p. 3)

A Gallup poll released two days before Christmas stated that 74 percent of the population as a whole believed that governments should stick to the Merit Principle. In Quebec that percentage dropped to 64 percent, and in the four English-Canadian regions 78 percent supported that criterion for hiring.

The Minister of Citizenship, Elaine Ziemba, announced the Ontario legislation in March 1991. The government marched full speed ahead — even when confronted with the costs for complying with the legislation, estimated at $31 million. Professor Jack Roberts of the University of Western Ontario's Faculty of Law spoke to the issue: "In the real world, the policy produced a boiling backlash of anger and resentment. Why such anger? People simply do not buy the notion of 'group guilt.' They reject the idea that they should pay for the alleged past sins of their particular racial, ethnic or gender group."

He cited U.S. commentator Charles Krauthamer: "the idea that affirmative action is just a temporary remedy is a fraud. With each new civil rights act . . . ethnic quotas and race consciousness become more deeply woven into American life" ("Employment equity a Trojan horse,"*GM*, Mar 22/91).

Meanwhile the happy Liberals were moving back into Ottawa in force. In celebration, their favourite son shaved his beard and sallied forth into the floodlights for something special. On November 9, 1993, Pierre Elliott Trudeau presented his papers to the National Archives. At the same time the seventy-three-year-old ex-PM launched what one reviewer termed a "souvenir" — his flashy picture-book *Memoirs* wrapped in its lily-white jacket.

Though barraged with questions from reporters for nearly an hour, Merlin the Muddler managed to preserve his god-like image. The whole event had been pre-arranged; no critical questions were permitted. Trudeau was treading familiar territory here, conducting a one-way debate with Himself before the cameras and the microphones. Bilingualism had failed because it wasn't promoted with "enough zeal." Mulroney was weak. Joe Clark was a "tough son of a gun. . . . I attacked Clark — I think, in retrospect, rather unkindly — for acting like a head waiter of the provinces."

Pompous twaddle for the hungry hordes: René Lévesque? He "fell into the trap I set for him" (CBC Newsworld); "I am a victim of myths, not the creator of them"; "What the October Crisis [of 1970] taught me was that it is absolutely essential to have, at the helm of state, a very firm hand, one that sets a course and never alters" (*GM*, Nov 10/93). Fascism for the feeble-minded.

Only Allan Fotheringham and Lysianne Gagnon squared off with the man once known as Canada's philosopher king. Fotheringham struck first: "Pierre Ego Trudeau, as we all know, is traversing the land peddling his alleged 'Memoirs' with strict media regulations resembling the planning for the Normandy invasion. Newsworld [CBC] is broadcasting his press conferences live, as if these were encyclicals from the Pope. His handlers [in Edmonton] allowed for 10 selected journalists to have an 'exclusive' hour with him in Edmonton" (*FP*, Nov 16/93).

Gagnon spilled more beans: "Journalists were prevented from receiving advance copies of the book, even those whom the publisher trusted to respect embargoes. All media were required to submit credentials of their journalists and cameramen. And if anyone wished to ask a question during an interview, he or she had to register it in advance" (*GM*, Jan 8/94).

Richard Gwyn, senior columnist for the Pulp Primevil, lambasted the book: "The memoirs are one prolonged shrug. Beyond much doubt, they are the sloppiest and laziest literary recollections ever dumped upon the public by any retired politician in Canada, or anywhere in the West that I know of" (*Star*, Nov 14/93). London *Times* reviewer Ian McIntyre dismissed it: "it reads like a cunning and tightly controlled exercise in image-projection. . . . Those wishing to form a reasonably comprehensive picture of the Trudeau years will need to apply to the Canadian High Commission for a supplementary reading list" (*GM/CP/Times*, Feb 22/94).

Canadian taxpayers picked up most of the tab for the book. Three writers, two interviewers, and the publisher and editor of McClelland & Stewart, the leading state-financed book publisher, Douglas Gibson, put it all together. Trudeau collected his advance of some $620,000-plus.

Yvon Deschamps saved the day: "[Pierre Trudeau]'s the greatest Quebecer ever — He did everything for us. He even destroyed Canada!" (*GM*, Nov 18/93). Bernard Landry, vice-president of the PQ, got off a good one too, "He threw us into prison and brought us to the verge of bankruptcy. He never had anything other than an intellectual vision of Canada" (*GM*, Nov 18/93).

Whatever its shortcomings, *Memoirs* cannot be dismissed as solely an edifice to vanity. It does offer some gems:

> In 1974, Bourassa's government inflamed language and unity tensions by passing Bill 22, making French the official language of Quebec. . . . Yet, however much I philosophically disliked Bill 22 — and later the Parti Québécois's even more stringent Bill 101 — I had no intention of using the constitution to disallow the legislation. The way to change bad laws is to change the government, rather than using Ottawa to coerce a province. The best course was to hope that Quebec citizens would challenge the provincial legislation in the courts — which happened to several discriminatory provisions — and to hope as well that the people would become better informed and their politicians more open-minded. (pp. 234–35)

Existentialism at its best. Imagine this from any president sworn to uphold the Constitution of the United States.

BACK TO OUR STORY. On December 2, 1993, Jean Chrétien agreed to sign NAFTA: "We have done, in my judgement, much more than most of the people said we would. And in fact, there was no price that we had to pay to get it" (*GM*, Dec 3/93).

Almost to the letter, the new NAFTA he signed matched the terms the Mulroney government had agreed to. The three players of NAFTA had pledged themselves — in a non-binding agreement — to establish a code on subsidies and anti-dumping measures by December 31, 1995. Only twenty-seven days earlier, the Liberals had swept to power, armed with their famous Red Book. Their covenant with Canadians contained nothing subtle on Mulroney's free trade agreement:

In 1988, Liberals opposed the Canada–United States Free Trade Agreement (FTA) because it was flawed; Canada did not get secure access to the United States market. These flaws have been confirmed by the ongoing disputes and harassment over trade in steel, pork, softwood lumber. . . . One of the major problems in these disputes has been the lack of clear and agreed-upon definitions of subsidies and dumping. . . . The North American Free Trade Agreement (NAFTA) gave the government an opportunity to correct major flaws in the Free Trade Agreement. Instead of achieving this, the NAFTA would almost completely scrap the working group on subsidies and anti-dumping. Instead of correcting the energy giveaway in the Free Trade Agreement, the Conservatives allowed Mexico to get protection for its energy resources that Canada does not have and the lack of trade rules was not addressed. . . . A Liberal government will renegotiate both the FTA and NAFTA to obtain:

- a subsidies code;
- an anti-dumping code;
- a more effective dispute resolution mechanism; and
- the same energy protection as Mexico. (Red Book, pp. 23–24)

Having vowed to rewrite the entire 2,000-page document, the new prime minister settled instead for a three-page public relations exercise promising to study the matter. Chrétien even congratulated himself. But just as Clayton Yeutter, the U.S Trade Representative, had once pooh-poohed Canada's victory claim over the FTA in 1987, so U.S. Trade Representative Mickey Kantor made similar noises about NAFTA six years later: "The energy provisions of the NAFTA are clear. None of these statements [of Chrétien's] change the NAFTA in any way" (*Star*, Dec 3/93). The Faculty Club rose to the occasion:

For once, we agree with Maude Barlow. The Liberal retreat on free trade, five years in the making, is of Napoleonic proportions: as complete, as abject, as humiliating as the return from Moscow. The party that once declared free trade meant the end of Canada can now offer no higher endorsement of their defence of Canadian sovereignty than, as the Prime Minister said Thursday, that he checked their position with Bill Clinton, who said "it was fine." (*GM*, Dec 4/93)

Many questions remained unanswered. Why would Canada sell out so cheaply just to accommodate an American immigration requirement?

What was the real story of Canadian sovereignty over energy and water?[4]

In grandly giving away the shop, Jean Chrétien also betrayed himself. In his 1985 biography *Straight from the Heart*, he wrote, "In my opinion, we should break down our [own] inter-provincial trade barriers" before constructing a free market with the United States (p. 171). And in the revised and updated edition, published in 1994, he hit Mulroney as hard as ever, even though he himself had just caved in as prime minister. He complained that Mulroney's free trade agreement failed "as it was intended to do" to guarantee access to the American market. The new prime minister hammered the point everyone agreed on: "There weren't clear definitions of subsidies and dumping." Chrétien had no doubt about the end-game. Under the FTA or NAFTA, unrevised, Canada would become nothing more than the "fifty-first state" of the U.S., where "all the important economic decisions would be made in Washington" (p. 225).

In spite of it all, Chrétien's popularity climbed in the polls. The public forgot all about the politician who screamed bloody murder in 1987 that both Meech Lake and Free Trade were a deadly combination riddled with "major flaws" and that they could only be resolved by the abrogation of the entire free trade agreement.

A S KEITH SPICER, Max Yalden, and D'Iberville Fortier had done before him, Official Languages Commissioner Victor Goldbloom assured Canadians of more anger than ever sweeping the land. With the architects of bilingualism back in power, the Commissioner could permit a fresh note of arrogance to creep into his pronouncements: "When it comes to official languages or official bilingualism Canadians simply don't know what they're talking about" (*B.C. Report*, Dec 27/93).

The bee in his bonnet was APEC's presentation on language to the House of Commons committee. They demanded a national referendum on bilingualism. Fat chance.

Also, Virgil Anderson, the director of expansion for Manning's Reform Party, had as good as hinted that the great prairie grassfire of the 1980s had shrunk to a dying ember: "I think Quebecers will be in favour of the new federalism that Preston Manning speaks of. We recognize the French fact in Quebec. We are in favour of multiculturalism — it makes up the mosaic of our society. It's just the Official Languages Act and enforced bilingualism that we think is inappropriate" (*GM*, Dec 9/93). Manning didn't protest.

Globe columnist Geoffrey York described Reform's new realpolitik three months later: "Indeed the party has gradually moved toward the political centre, and it has grudgingly praised the work of the Liberal government on such issues as parliamentary reform. Often the party is left in a position of merely calling for a slightly bolder action by the Liberals." Party stalwart and founder Ted Byfield added, "Most of the stuff they bring up has to do with the deficit or federal spending or other national questions" (*GM*, Feb 12/94).

Reformers faced other problems besides their leader's switcheroos on policy. On February 9, 1994, Preston Manning reprimanded the Okanagan Centre riding association for running a quote from Adolf Hitler in their newsletter — "What luck for rulers that men do not think." Puritan Preston spouted: "It was a big mistake to do it." In a world ruled by Manning, *Bartlett's Quotations* would be banned. Pulitzer Prize-winner William A. Henry III (1950–94) hit the nail on the head:

A brand of anti-intellectualism is running amok, eerily reminiscent of the nineteenth-century Know-Nothing movement, albeit a mirror image of it in political terms. Where that movement centered on ugly nativism and exclusion, this one carries inclusion to its comparable extreme, celebrating every arriviste notion, irate minority group, self-assertive culture, and cockamamie opinion as having equal cerebral weight, and probably superior moral heft, to the reviled wisdom and attainments of tradition. This "multicultural" revisionism is sometimes refreshing and instructive, but more often merely silly and occasionally deeply harmful. Often accompanying it is the still more dangerous assumption that the only fair measure of any sifting mechanism is the demographic quality of the results it produces, not the relationship between the results and attainments in the real world. (p. 3)

Back in Central Canada, Bob Rae's boys were beating Trudeau's drum with renewed vigour. To a written complaint from a citizen about Ontario's Bill 8, the French Language Services Act, on December 3, the Minister of Treasury and Economics, "Pink Floyd" Laughren, answered: "Ontario's language policy, consolidated in the French Language Services Act, reflects our government's recognition of the contribution the French-speaking population has made to our province's historical, cultural and linguistic heritage. This policy can be viewed as Ontario's contribution to the vision of a bilingual and multicultural nation. This fact has been recognized by all provincial parties, as well as this government." An affirmative-action blessing for the prevailing philosophy of North America — "dumbing-down."

As the Mulroney era ended, so did that of Robert Bourassa. On Tuesday, January 11, forty-nine-year-old Daniel Johnson was sworn in as Quebec's premier. Articulate, fully bilingual, and boasting impressive academic and business credentials, Johnson was the most unabashedly pro-Canada politician Quebec had produced in half a century. The new premier had only nine months before the absolute deadline of October 11 to call one of the most critical elections in his province's history. Although his mandate was four more months than the ludicrous amount of time Brian Mulroney had allotted *his* successor, Johnson faced the same problem that Kim Campbell did. Like her, he was thrown on the defensive, deep into damage control.

The Speech from the Throne on January 18 confirmed the national malaise, the people's lack of faith in the system:

> Canadians, however, continue their unwavering commitment to democracy. Elections in this country are carried out as peaceful clashes of ideas, not of forces. . . . In order to achieve this agenda, integrity and public trust in the institutions of government are essential. . . . Specifically, an ethics counsellor will be appointed to advise Ministers and government officials and to examine the need for legislative change. . . . The government is committed to enhancing the credibility of Parliament. . . . Measures will be proposed to combat the high level of violence against women and children. Measures will be proposed to combat racism and hate crime. The Court Challenges Program and the Law Reform Commission will be restored. . . .

That same day, Canada's national "Debt Clock" hit the half-trillion mark. Set up by the Vancouver Board of Trade, that city's branch of the Canadian Chamber of Commerce used the clock to push for a 5-percent cut in government spending. According to the famous timepiece, Canada slides $85,600 further into debt every minute.

CANADA'S THIRTY-FIFTH PARLIAMENT knuckled down to business on January 19. Lucien Bouchard sounded off first: "[Chrétien] should know the future of Quebec as a sovereign country is just ahead of us, a sovereign country which is a neighbour and friend of Canada. . . . Thirty years ago the horns were locked (between English Canada and Quebec). Thirty years later we are still in a time warp. We should learn from the past and this we should have learned: The problem with Canada is Quebec and the problem of Quebec is Canada" (*Star*, Jan 20/94).

Indian affairs minister Ron Irwin had in mind sovereignty of a different kind. Armed with the Red Book, he dismissed the 1992 Referendum as irrelevant. He promised native self-government within six months: "We're not going back to constitutional discussions. We're acting on the premise that it's there" (*Star*/CP, Jan 20/94); "A Liberal government will act on the premise that the inherent right of self-government is an existing Aboriginal treaty right" (*Red Book*, p. 98); "I thought the Conservatives had it all wrong. What we're doing today is exactly what I thought we should have been doing years ago. We're acting on the premise that it's there, in Section 35. Until some court says it's not, that's the premise we're working on. I see this as remedying what should have been done decades ago" (*GM*, Jan 31/94). Here's what the Constitution says on the matter:

RIGHTS OF THE ABORIGINAL PEOPLES OF CANADA

35. (1) The existing aboriginal and treaty rights of the aboriginal peoples of Canada are hereby recognized and affirmed.

Admitting he didn't have a clue what was meant by *inherent rights* or *native self-government*, Irwin went professorial: "The role of a true revolutionary is to patiently explain" (*GM*, Jan 31/94).

In *Why Americans Hate Politics*, E.J. Dionne writes:

Over the last three decades, the faith of the American people in their democratic institutions has declined, and Americans have begun to doubt their ability to improve the world through politics. . . .

True, we still praise democracy incessantly and recommend democracy to the world. But at home, we do little to promote the virtues that self-government requires or to encourage citizens to believe that public engagement is worth the time. . . . Voters doubt that elections give them any real control over what the government does, and half of them don't bother to cast ballots.

Because of our flight from public life, our common citizenship no longer fosters a sense of community or common purpose. (pp. 9–10)

Preston Manning scrambled for an opening — on any front. On January 20, he twanged, "Is the Prime Minister abandoning his commitment to stay out of the constitutional swamp, or is it still his resolve to stick to the economic, fiscal and social priorities?" Four days later, Mr. Tiptoe put on his wet suit and plunged into the swamp himself: "If the Prime Minister is not prepared to trust the judgement of the public in the selection of senators, by what other means, by changing the Constitution, does he propose to restore public trust in that institution and to enhance its credibility?" (*GM*, Jan 25/94). The man without influence and power had developed the heebie-jeebies at last.

The Bloc Québécois adopted a resolution on January 23 offering the Parti Québécois their full support for the forthcoming election: "I have told Mr. Parizeau 'you can count on us, just tell us what you want us to do,'" Lucien Bouchard told the media (*GM*, Jan 24/94).

Like Ron Irwin, immigration minister Sergio Marchi was letting his personal agenda slip. On February 2, he announced that Canada would accept 250,000 immigrants during the 1993–94 fiscal year — exactly the same number the Tories had set. The news came within one month of a Gallup poll that found 45 percent of Canadians wanted greatly reduced immigration and only 11 percent favoured an increase. Chrétien himself had confessed the real rationale for this unbridled immigration years earlier: "The Liberal Party is basically an alliance of three groups: moderate anglophones, French Canadians and new Canadians who feel comfortable in and grateful to the Liberal Party" (*Straight From the Heart*, p. 202).

On February 7, the Secretary of State for Multiculturalism piped up. Sheila Finestone said it was time to "drop the lid on the coffin and finally entomb the myth that multiculturalism is merely an immigration issue, that diversity must lead to division" (*Star*, Feb 8/94).[5]

David Anderson also had an idea of how a free society should work. To nail tax-cheaters the revenue minister thought Canadians should rat on their neighbours and then "people in the underground economy . . . will start realizing that any day of the week, any hour of the day, Revenue Canada may get a phone call and someone will rat on them" (*GM*/CP, Feb 12/94). Besides this, "for those who are mentally and morally very guilty because they should know better, I am not going to lose any sleep if they spend a long time in one of Her Majesty's prisons" (*Star*, Feb 12/94).

While Chrétien's men flexed their new-found muscles to show they were in control of themselves, Canadians were being massacred in world financial markets. On Valentine's Day, the Canadian dollar hit a seven-year low against the American dollar (73.75 cents) and a record low against the Japanese yen. The annual deficit had soared to $40 billion. And Jean Chrétien had just survived his first hundred days in office.

The reality that government is a very costly business certainly had no effect on the old guard from the Trudeau days. Speaking in Geneva on February 22, Max Yalden, former Official Languages Commissioner (1977–84) and now head of the Canadian Human Rights Commission, asked the UN Rights Commission "to ensure that national institutions participate in their own right with a recognized status in the work of the United Nations organs responsible for human rights." Interviewed later, he explained, "Once we have done that, we'll exist legally within the United Nations bureaucratic framework. . . . Then our national institutions will enjoy the same status as governments and observers" (*Star*, Feb 23/94).

Power madness, but vintage Yalden. This from the same fellow who testified at the Beaudoin–Dobbie SJC on a Renewed Canada in fall 1991 that he didn't "believe the notwithstanding clause would be used to destroy human rights in this country."

On March 24, the Chrétien government invoked closure on Bill C-18, a law designed to cut off debate on the electoral redistribution process. This would have meant enlarging the House of Commons from 295 seats to 301. Liberal MPs in Ontario burst into applause when Solicitor-General Herbert Gray promised to block the process under the Electoral Boundaries Readjustment Act. The more equitable distribution would give Ontario five more seats and British Columbia, so badly under-represented in terms of its population, would gain two.

The purpose was plain enough: to ensure that the next federal election in 1997 or thereabouts would be based on the demographic statistics of 1981.

Life in the federal public service churned on as usual. Almost unnoticed went the firing on February 24 of Glen Shortliffe, the infamous "Enforcer," Clerk of the Privy Council. His successor, Jocelyne Bourgon, was caught pulling a Tellier only two months later. She too had misrepresented her credentials.[6]

I N *LOST RIGHTS: THE DESTRUCTION OF AMERICAN LIBERTY* (1994), the celebrated freedom fighter James Bovard wrote:

> The Founding Fathers looked at the liberties they were losing, while modern Americans focus myopically on the freedoms they still retain. . . . The first step to saving our liberty is to realize how much we have already lost, how we lost it, and how we will continue to lose unless fundamental political changes occur. (pp. 6, 7)

Speaking in Halifax on April 6, federal trade minister John Manley said he was disappointed the interprovincial trade barriers — then reported at a cost of $7 billion per year — would not disappear by the deadline of June 1: "This is not a totally comprehensible agreement we're working on. We're working on solving problems and we believe we can make substantial progress in solving those problems and toward liberalizing trade across Canada" (*GM*, Apr 7/94).

In the middle of the trade muddle, Victor Goldbloom tabled his annual report in the House of Commons. He called for tolerance from a world that he said totally misunderstood bilingualism. Official Bilingualism, he asserted, only cost the taxpayers some $600 million per annum. The courtiers at the Faculty Club and the Pulp Primevil stood up for Pierre Trudeau:

> It's hard to understand how anyone could have a problem with the federal Official Languages Act, but then again, perhaps the opposition springs from a misunderstanding of the Act's powers and purpose. We'll allow Victor Goldbloom, the Commissioner of Official Languages, to explain. . . . (*GM*, Apr 14/94)

> Bilingualism is getting a rough ride in Canada once again. But when all is said and done, it may turn out for the better. This week the Official Languages Commissioner released his report to a House of Commons that's divided on regional and linguistic lines. . . . Until the last election, the major parties in the Commons agreed among themselves that bilingualism helps keep the country together. (*Star*, Apr 14/94)

Yet two of the three federal parties willing to die for Official Bilingualism had virtually disappeared — the NDP and the Progressive Conservative Party of Canada. Two down, one to go.

Two career changes in the spring of 1994 marked more signs of the times. On March 31, Quebec's municipal affairs minister, Claude Ryan, announced his retirement with the words "I've reached the end of my trail in this particular field of activity" (*GM*, Apr 1/94). Few tears were shed as the head of the tongue troopers exited the stage.

Gord McIntyre, the Quebecer who blew the whistle on Kim Campbell's justice department, sold the Kelly Funeral Home in Huntingdon, Quebec, on December 23. On April 15, 1994, the fifth-generation Quebecer moved to Brockville, Ontario. Although his victory at the UN had captured worldwide attention, the Canadian press steadfastly maintained their silence about him. The Montreal *Gazette* published a mean-spirited departure notice on him on June 11, quoting him out of context as "afraid" of Lucien Bouchard.[7] (See Chapter 34.)

The fight continues. McIntyre and newcomer Robert Gauthier, publisher of the *National Capital News* in Ottawa, are hotly pursuing "the total cost to the Canadian government in the unsuccessful defence against the McIntyre Communication to the United Nations including all labour and direct costs dealing with this issue. . ." (*Dialogue*, Sept/94). They are hindered by restrictions of the Access to Information and Privacy Office, which answered their request with "since there are no financial records pertaining to this matter we are not in a position to provide the information you requested." Gauthier has since learned the records are stacked four feet high.

On April 19, finance minister Paul Martin, the Rip Van Winkle author of the Red Book, bestirred himself. A little. On April 18 he mimicked his master in March, promising that there would be "no further cuts" in government to meet the three-year deficit reduction plan. Then Luke Fence-Walker hinted he might eventually be forced into the real world: "And what that means is a complete restructuring of government and it is going to mean major, major cuts which are going to affect every sector of our society" (*Star*, Apr 19/94).

The day after this musing, Senator Edward Kennedy of Massachusetts went presidential about Quebec himself: "We have great respect that individuals can make judgements about the kind of process they want to follow and I'm sure they will. . . . Whatever the outcome of those judgements and decisions, I think that Americans would very much respect. . . . I would just like to see [Quebecers] make judgements on an informed basis and we'll look forward to those outcomes" (*Star*, Apr 20/94).

On Monday, May 2, Lucien Bouchard was in Vancouver being interviewed by popular Western talk-show host Rafe Mair. The opposition leader boasted that an independent Quebec would keep the Canadian dollar "for a transition period . . . at least at the beginning and maybe longer than that, it would use the Canadian currency." Quebec, Mulroney's old buddy declared, would never support an elected Senate. Mair: "So it's a gulf we can never bridge." Bouchard: "That's well put, we want too much, that's why we have to leave" and "we don't fit." Mair: "You want all of these things that you would deny British Columbia."

In Hong Kong, David Li, CEO of the Bank of East Asia, one of Asia's top bankers, hit the dollar harder: "But quite frankly . . . I believe that the future prosperity of Canada is in much greater doubt than that of Hong Kong. . . . Canada is still struggling with recession and battling unemployment. . . . Some pessimists even predict that the Canadian dollar may fall to ever more dangerous lows — to 50 cents on the U.S. dollar or worse."

He went on to say that Canada "may become the country of the soon-to-wed and nearly dead" (*Star*, May 3/94). Many observers agreed with him. According to the most recent study the Fraser Institute had released, Canada's gross debt had reached $1.75 trillion, or $61,188 per person. There hadn't been a government deficit in Hong Kong since 1983.

BC's Premier Mike Harcourt spoke out more than usual: Quebec must "make up [its] mind." And, "frankly, the position I'm taking is that Quebec and B.C. are natural allies in a renewed Canada and would be the best of friends. . . . But if they decide to separate we wouldn't be the best of friends; we'd be the worst of enemies. The anger that would be felt by British Columbians to people of Quebec wanting to break up and destroy this great country would be immense" (*GM*, May 17/94).

Indian affairs minister Ron Irwin waded boldly into the delicate subject of the rights of Quebec's aboriginals again: "The point is, they have been here for 10,000 years and they want to remain a part of Canada and I think they have that right. . . . The separatists say that they have a right to decide, then why don't the aboriginal people who have been here 20 times as long have the same right? It seems only logical to me" (*GM*, May 18/94). Daniel Johnson retorted, "What I am saying to Mr. Irwin and to those who think like him, or make comments on hypothetical situations, is that we, here, have the responsibility of defending Quebec's territorial integrity" (*Star*, May 19/94).

That did it. Johnson had whipped the door wide open and the figure of Jacques Parizeau filled the space: "Never again will we be put in a negotiating position where we are at the mercy of those with whom we want to negotiate," Parizeau told the National Assembly. "This time we are saying: 'You cannot take commercial reprisals against us.' . . . Let's not fool ourselves, there will be no vast negotiations. . . . We have to put ourselves in a position where we are not vulnerable" (*GM*, May 19/94).

National media attention turned to the NDP gnawing away at the free enterprise system in Ontario in the spring of 1994. On May 19, that government introduced a new bill, 167, into its legislature. The Equality Rights Statute Law Amendment Act introduced sweeping amendments affecting fifty-six pieces of legislation and the Ontario Human Rights Code. Up to that point, one definition in the Ontario Human Rights Code, for example, had read: "'spouse' means the person to whom a person of the opposite sex is married or with whom the person is living in a conjugal relationship outside of marriage (i.e., common-law)." This was to be changed to: "'spouse' means the person to whom a person is married or a person of either sex with whom the person is living in a conjugal relationship outside marriage" (*GM*, May 20/94).

The bill passed first reading by a vote of 57 to 52. Liberal leader Lyn McLeod and Bob Rae were conspicuous by their absences during the vote.

Bill 167 represented another first for the NDP government. If it won final passage, Ontario would become the first jurisdiction in the world to recognize as equal in law same-sex conjugal relationships. The proposed legislation represented a head-on attack on the traditional concept of the family. Rae was indignant at the reaction in the legislature: "It's shocking to watch a provincial party like the Tories vote unanimously against it."

He had reason to be angry. In April of 1993 Tory leader Mike Harris had backed Nancy Jackman, the gay activist candidate for the Toronto riding of St. George–St. David. During the by-election — which she lost — her campaign literature sported Harris's written endorsement: "Nancy Jackman has done more to support policy measures concerning AIDS, same-sex spousal benefits and equity issues than any member of the Liberal-NDP governments of the past eight years. I look forward to her continued and direct involvement on these issues as the next MPP for St. George-St. David" (*GM*, Apr 7/94).

The choice for Ontarians lay between three faces of aggressive socialism: Liberal, NDP, Red Tory. Behind the scenes, Liberal leader Lyn McLeod had shoved the premier along. On March 9, 1993, she had written to him fully backing the gay and lesbian cause: "If you will agree to bring legislation forward immediately, I will do everything possible to facilitate passage.... If you do not act, and in the unlikely event that the courts have not yet finally settled the matter within two years, please be assured that a Liberal government will move swiftly to take the action which I request you take immediately."

By the end of the month, Ontario's Sodom and Gomorrah stuff had pushed the never-ending "priority of Quebec" aside to launch war in this new crusade. On Sunday, May 29, the Archbishop Aloysius Ambrozic, spiritual leader of 1.4 million Roman Catholics in Ontario, ordered all priests to urge their parishioners to demand that their MPPs oppose Bill 167 on biblical grounds. He had Pope John Paul II on-side on June 19: "The marriage, which is a stable union between a man and woman . . . that they open to the future generations, not is [*sic*] only a Christian value, but is an original value. . . . To lose this truth is not just a problem only for the [Christian] faithful, but a danger for all humanity. . . ." The traditional family is a "natural right that unites all peoples and all cultures" (Associated Press/*GM*, June 20/94).

Marion Boyd did not object. In fact, Ontario's second gay attorney-general of the 1990s straddled the boundary between church and state with ease. From the pulpit at the Metropolitan Community Church of Toronto, she urged the gay community "to continue this struggle" (*Star*, June 6/94). The story made front-page news.

The former Primate of the Anglican Church of Canada, Ted Scott, advised his congregation, "I believe the passage of the proposed legislation will provide greater justice and will not endanger . . . the traditional family" (*Star*, June 3/94). The Anglican Synod had written a testimonial to be released to anyone keen enough to dig for it, in a "Statement from the Metropolitan of the Ecclesiastical Province of Ontario The Most Reverend Percy R. O'Driscoll." In part it read:

> If I were to reflect on the position of the people of the Anglican Church in the Province of Ontario in terms of same sex spousal benefits, I would suspect that many of our people would be opposed to such legislation while others would be very supportive of the extension of those benefits. The Anglican Church in the Province of Ontario has been struggling, continues to struggle, with these very sensitive issues surrounding sexuality.

On June 3, an article published in the Pulp Primevil, a crusader for the bill, observed that the Union of American Hebrew Congregations stood behind same-sex legislation and that they represented some 800 congregations.

The Faculty Club reported a lone voice of dissent — that of NDP MPP George Mammoliti: "I believe that children pick up from their parents. If we extend the definition of spouse and open up traditional families, those children will be influenced in a way that we'll never, ever forget" (*GM*, June 3/94).

Even Jean Chrétien, who had not dared to enter the debate on Canada's future, shared his thoughts about Ontario's Bill 167. The great perorator shuffled softly: "At this moment, I think that the debate is not at the level of maturity that is needed for it to be resolved. Every problem in society has different periods. This vote in Ontario has indicated that the level of maturity on this debate was not there. In a democracy, you have to live with these situations" (*GM*, June 21/94).

"As a matter of fundamental fairness," justice minister Allan Rock announced on September 28, there *would* be amendments to the federal Human Rights Act to enshrine gay rights. And there would be no free vote on the matter in the House of Commons (*GM*, Sept 29/94). So much for the Charter of Rights.

M AY ENDED with Jacques Parizeau laying down some law of his own: "As soon as Quebec becomes sovereign, I don't want vast economic and commercial negotiations with the rest of Canada. . . . I know [Quebec and the rest of Canada] could do much more. Let's not get ahead of ourselves, let's not try to go too far. First, we must be able to meet and say, 'Let's keep things as they are.' This is what businesses will need first and foremost in the early stages" (*GM*, June 1/94). Reacting to this tripe, *Sun* columnist Peter Worthington went for the jugular: "Emotions invariably win. . . . Make no mistake — *If* Quebec were to declare independence, Ottawa would give away the store" (*Sun*, May 31/94).

Preston Manning opined, "Ottawa should hold the referendum and the question should simply be: 'should Quebec separate from Canada, yes or no?'" (*Sun*, June 1/94).

His timing was dreadful. Five days later, on June 6, 1994, Canadians, along with their allies from the Second World War, would commemorate the D-Day invasion of 1944. Five thousand Canadians lost their lives in the first three months after the initial landing to liberate Europe. A half-century later, fourteen heads of state came to Courseulles-sur-Mer, Normandy (Juno Beach), to remember that event. The prime minister recalled: "There are some would say these men had nothing in common. Not geography, not language, not background, not religion or ethnicity or colour. But they had one thing in common: they were all part of a young nation, a new kind of nation where the ancient hatreds of the past were no match for the promise of the future. They did not die as anglophones or francophones, as easterners or westerners, as Christians or Jews, as immigrants or natives. They died as Canadians" (*GM*, June 7/94).

At their Dominion Convention, the branches of the Royal Canadian Legion rejected the advice of Dominion Command, their governing body, to allow Sikhs and Jews to wear headgear in Legion branches. They voted against the measure 1,959 to 629. Michael Valpy, the man the *Globe* boasts of having "Passion. Compassion. And an unleashed mind," mewled: "Its members are veterans, their spouses and dependents, people raised on old mythologies of Canada as the land of the bottomless bank account of natural wealth. . . . They feel threatened by multiculturalism" (*GM*, June 1/94).

The Sikh World Organization of Canada caught headlines quickly: "It is now clear that the efforts of many federal programs aimed at educating Canadians on religious diversity have failed in building awareness and fostering co-operation and acceptance in Canada" (*Ott Citizen*, June 1/94).

Next came the Secretary of State, Sheila Finestone, Minister of the department no one in the country wanted: "I believe [the vote] represents a lack of understanding of fundamental Canadian values" (*GM*, June 2/94). Preston Manning made agreeable noises, too: "Those halls are considered almost public places and so I don't think it's a wise decision" (*GM*, June 2/94).

Max Yalden, the federal human rights commissioner, led the charge: "What will probably happen now is that a group of Sikhs will be denied admittance somewhere and they will file a complaint with the provincial human rights commission. . . . In the end, I don't think there's any doubt their exclusion will be found to be religious discrimination and Legion halls will be forced to admit them" (*GM*, June 2/94). As if on cue, the Manitoba Human Rights Commission received a complaint the very next day calling the Legion's conduct discrimination on the basis of religious prejudice.

Yet in 1993 the Legion had pumped some $63 million into community life in Canada.

With his head down, Parizeau pressed on. On June 4, he urged Quebecers to sever any business ties with the Bank of Montreal. The PQ leader had been infuriated by the bank's chief economist Lloyd Atkinson's observation that the "language [of independence]" could lead to a run on the dollar.

In Bob Rae's own wonderland, the great plan to make the province bilingual advanced another step. Peterson's world would be preserved. According to Statistics Canada, London, Ontario, with 5,100 francophones, now qualified for bilingual language services, as required by the province's Bill 8. The initial cost would be $500,000.

In some circles this was not enough. Always ready to show off her support for bilingualism, Deputy Prime Minister Sheila Copps jumped on her favourite hobby horse and galloped into this latest ring of the language circus: "Unfortunately, the policy of the government of Ontario is exactly the same policy as the Bloc Quebecois, which is that they don't accept bilingualism at the provincial level. I ask them . . . to join us in the national government of Canada to defend the rights of minorities no matter where they live across the country" (*Star*, June 7/94). Outspoken as she is, she has never said a word about Bill 178, let alone the Gord McIntyre case.

The Pulp Primevil overreacted, as usual. In their June 11 editorial "Why is Ontario not yet bilingual?" the editors protested: "When Lucien Bouchard tells franco-Ontarians they are being shortchanged by English Canada, and his Bloc Québécois will protect them from afar, it's hard to take him seriously. But when Victor Goldbloom follows him to Toronto and delivers a careful critique of the Ontario government's shortcomings, he deserves a hearing. As the federal commissioner of official languages, Goldbloom's bona fides are beyond dispute."

Ontario's same-sex legislation, Bill 167, bit the dust 68 to 59 on its second reading on June 9. McLeod, who had snookered Rae into the business in the first place, voted nay. Only three Liberals voted Yes. The premier prayed for its preservation: "Don't extinguish it now! Give it a chance to go to committee and hear the views of the people. Don't extinguish it now!" (*Star*, June 10/94). Karl Marx would have been proud of his Ontario son.

By June, 30,000 Maritime workers were drawing on the $1.9 billion in federal aid that had been allocated since the Atlantic fishery had been closed down. The news in Newfoundland in particular guaranteed that federal tax increases would carry on till the final cataclysm. Migration from the Rock would escalate even further.

Migration within Canada because of economic re-alignment was one problem. Immigration was another. Minister of the latter, Sergio Marchi, stepped into the fray to defend current immigration levels: "If we were to stop the tap of immigration tomorrow and not let one person in, the last Canadian would die in 175 years. That's a pretty sobering fact. . ." (*GM*, June 27/94). Sobering indeed that the minister actually believed that all Canadians would cease all sex from that moment on.

The minister's cavalier attitude earned him a fierce drubbing about the deportation of convicted criminals. On July 7, he tried to sound authoritative: "I will not allow people to make a mockery of our laws and I will not put Canadians at risk" (*Star*, July 8/94).

There was a problem. Some 600 foreign-born criminals were slated to be shipped out of the country for serious felonies. Yet 8,000 rejected refugee claimants could apply for permanent status after three years' residence in Canada. Many of them had passed that deadline.

The full story came out on August 22. In fact, there were 1,296 serious criminal deportees, who — according to the minister's own department — are "dangerous people . . . desperate not to be found" (*Sun*, Aug 23/94). Marchi's get-tough policy had led to only fourteen deportations by then. It was time to pay attention to Section 91 of the Constitution.[8]

Domestic trade barriers continued to attract negative attention, too. Without winning any agreement among the premiers to abide by the country's Constitution, industry minister John Manley told the 1867, Section 121, story as he saw it: "We've gone 127 years without an agreement on internal trade in Canada. . . . We were always only trying to get a partial agreement. . . . This [latest effort] will be the first step in an ongoing process" (*GM*, June 29/94). A week later he committed his thoughts to print: "Throughout these negotiations, editorial writers and other observers have demanded that internal trade barriers be eliminated virtually overnight, either through a negotiated settlement or legislatively through the exercise of the federal government's constitutional authority. . . . Such demands are unrealistic, and fail to consider the complex nature of some of the existing barriers" (*GM*, July 5/94).

Those who still cherished Canada as a constitutional monarchy had their faith crushed yet again. The heir to the throne himself, H.R.H. Prince Charles, Supreme Governor of the Church of England, admitted on British television that he had committed adultery — even though he had not done so "until," as he put it, "it became clear that the marriage [his] had irretrievably broken down." He went on to say he will not accept the title "Defender of the Faith" when he's crowned. Instead, Charles III would settle for being a "defender of faith": "I happen to believe that the Catholic subjects of the sovereign are as important, not to mention the Islamic, Hindu and Zoroastrian" (*GM*, June 28/94, reported by Clifford Longley, *The Daily Telegraph*). The end of another era.

On July 6, flub-a-dub-dub Claude Castonguay expressed some final thoughts on himself. The Companion of the Ceramic Snowflake confessed to what everyone outside the broadcast media and the press already knew: "Honestly, if there was a referendum tomorrow in Quebec, I would feel incapable of defending a country which doesn't accept me with my differences and my history and which, on top of that, is incapable of solving its most fundamental problems" (*FP*, July 12/94).

On the eve of the longest-awaited election call in modern Quebec history, Jacques Parizeau beat Daniel Johnson to the punch with a speech in Quebec City on July 23: "The Parti Quebecois is sovereigntist before, during and after the elections. . . . That is clear, it continues to be clear and it will continue to be clear in the future. Nothing has changed" (*Star*, July 24/94).

Johnson finally called the election the next day, for September 12. That left fifty days for the campaign. It was the first time in fifty years a Quebec provincial government had gone the full five-year term before dropping the writ. Party standings: Liberals 78, PQ 34, Equality 1. There were 125 ridings. According to the last census, the voters numbered 4.8 million. Parizeau put his case grandly: "The people of Quebec will have to choose their destiny. Quebeckers will choose between two political options: separation and political union. For the first time, the Opposition is requesting and asking for a mandate to initiate steps immediately upon its election to get nearer and to achieve sovereignty and separation. The government's platform is the strengthening of the economic union in Canada" (*GM*, July 25/94).

American investment banker Robert Blohm phrased Quebec's position differently: "Should an independent, cash-poor Quebec finally be forced to market realities to abandon statism, it could get cash by privatizing Hydro-Québec, the world's biggest hydro-electricity producer . . . (*GM*, Aug 9/94).

Quebec did not hold the monopoly on money mismanagement. On the eleventh of August, federal government regulators took over the huge insurance company Confederation Life. Its directors had managed the largest failure in the history of any insurance company in North America. The expected tab to taxpayers? Around $1 billion.

J EAN CHRÉTIEN BECAME YESTERDAY'S MAN, once again, on August 31. Immediately he ignored a simple and inexpensive opportunity to give Canadians a greater voice in their own affairs; he appointed an actor, director, and writer, Jean-Louis Roux, to the Senate. Then he named three more new senators on September 15. Sharon Carstairs, once champion of an elected Senate, typified the arrogance Canadians would have to endure for years to come. The former Manitoba Liberal leader and Meech fighter now claimed that she was "deserving" of such an appointment. So much for Stan Waters's legacy.

On the same day that Bill 79, the employment equity legislation, came into effect in Ontario, September 1, the Supreme Court of Canada earned a footnote in the press that should have been emblazoned across front pages.[9] In a seven-to-nothing ruling, the Court decided that, in criminal cases only, an accused is entitled to have simultaneous, accurate interpretation of the court proceedings in his or her own language.

The point is clear. The Supremes will now make constitutional law as well as interpret it as they see fit. Section 14 of the Charter of Rights and Freedoms reads, "A party or witness in any proceeding who does not understand or speak the language in which the proceedings are conducted or who is deaf has the right to the assistance of an interpreter."

Trailing in the polls as the election neared, Daniel Johnson dramatically changed his course. After repeatedly declaring himself a "Canadian first and foremost," he declared a shift in loyalty to "Quebec first" to a senior citizens' group — "If I can conceive, like many, being a Quebecer without being a Canadian, I can't conceive of being a Canadian without being a Quebecer." As for being a Canadian first as he'd been quoted earlier, that had been merely a "slip of the tongue" (*Star*, Sept 7/94). Only six days to go.

The more pressing point for Canada's future hit the headlines. From the Geneva-based World Economic Forum came a published report of the Institute of International Development of Lausanne. Canada's overall ranking in world competitiveness had fallen to 16 from 11 of 22 industrialized countries in 1993. In 1989, Canada had ranked fourth. The report, based on "the ability of a country to proportionately generate more wealth than its competitors in world markets," was hardly a surprise given the criteria considered: "State overinvolvement in the economy, high taxes and social charges, public debt and agricultural policies are some of the areas where government [in Canada] is hurting the country's competitiveness" (*GM*, Sept 7/94).

There was yet another omen the same day. President Walter Schroeder of the Dominion Bond Rating Service Ltd. called Canada's debt levels "awesome" and warned of further rating cuts to come.

On Monday, September 12, Canada's political geography changed radically. The Quebec polls closed at 8:00 P.M. Forty minutes later the Canadian Broadcasting Corporation announced a majority victory for the Parti Québécois. Eighty percent of the province's eligible voters had given Jacques Parizeau 77 seats to Daniel Johnson's 47. Canadians could all feel relieved because, as so many of the pundits said, the PQ received only 15,325 more votes than the Liberals had, which came to 44.7 percent of the popular vote as opposed to the Liberals' 44.3 percent.

Mario Dumont's Parti Action Démocratique might have secured only one seat out of the 80 ridings in which they ran candidates, but they did win 6.6 percent of the popular vote. This put another sovereigntist option into the limelight. Dumont mouthed the line Canadians had come to expect from la belle province: "I think we can be sovereigntist without being separatist. . . . I am certainly a sovereigntist in the sense that I want Quebec to have its powers. But I'm not a separatist because I believe in a new partnership with the rest of Canada" (*GM*, Sept 16/94).

Robert Libman, the compliant Quebecer who had founded the Equality Party, had run as an independent and been defeated, as were all the Vichy anglais. The four seats the party had once held were wiped out. Montreal's village idiot, Richard Holden, had run for the PQ and been soundly defeated by Liberal incumbent Henri-François Gautrin. Holden left demographers scratching their heads with his parting shot: "Eventually, I believe sovereignty is inevitable. The young people want it and the older people who don't won't always be around" (*Gazette*, Sept 13/94). Quebec has a serious shortage of young people. And the situation is worsening. Compared to the rest of the country, she lacks the proportionate number of elderly that other provinces have as well. Middle-aged populations do not lead revolutions.

The next day the Canadian dollar rose more than a penny for the first time in six years and the prime interest rate fell a quarter point.

Given the popular vote in his favour, Chrétien pressed Parizeau to hold the referendum the premier-elect had promised to have within eight to ten months. At first Parizeau agreed. Federal opposition leader Lucien Bouchard did not.

The PQ were in a strong position, despite their marginal victory in popular support and the polls that showed separatism was declining. They had won the power to delay their referendum to within weeks of the turn of the century. At the face-off, Parizeau broadcast, "The third period begins tomorrow." And "once we win the referendum . . . we will make Quebec a normal country" (*Sun*, Sept 13/94). He also had a back-up play. Under a little-known provision of the Constitution Act, 1982, Section 49, the prime minister is required to convene "a constitutional conference" of all the first ministers every fifteen years. The next one was due by 1997.

In search of his own Sept-Îles, Jean Charest skated into the arena on October 4, in Laval, Quebec: "Federalism is shared responsibility. . . . It is time we recognized, in practice, that Canada's true sovereignty association is the sharing of powers . . . between the federal and provincial governments" (*GM*, Oct 5/94).[10] At the Empire Club in Toronto on October 11 he promised "to advance ideas . . . that marry fiscal conservatism to a national vision of this country." In an interview in Vancouver with Peter C. Newman the week of November 21, the Conservative leader confided, "The Tories have a very important heritage that we earned the hard way through Bob Stanfield, Joe Clark, Brian Mulroney and even Ms. Campbell. There's a continuum there that's different from the Liberals and obviously very different from the Reformers. . . . Our history will serve us well" (*Maclean's*, Nov 28/94).

Stripped of clichés, Charest's tiptoe Toryism agreed with the rootless relativism of *Star* columnist Richard Gwyn. That same week Gwyn lectured a Brock University audience in St. Catharines, Ontario, on the merits of Canada, the "first borderless state . . . evolving in the way the rest of the world should." He expounded further: "We've created a country . . . in which any voice can be heard, provided it speaks the truth" (*Star*, Nov 26/94). The question was, whose truth?

Claude Béland, president of the behemoth credit union co-operative Mouvement Desjardins, was again flying his true colours. On November 17, Mr. "Too little too late" during Meech Lake wailed: "A true confederation is no longer attainable because there exists a total freeze on the part of the rest of Canada" (*GM*, Nov 18/94).

American author Lansing Lamont observes:

The problem is that as their history, their *survivance*, gradually spawned a fiercely passionate nationalism, Quebecers amassed a store of delusionary myths, phobias, rationales, and symbols to embroider their culture of humiliation. Quebec's nationalists have manipulated history to show that the province's failures were always someone else's fault . . . ignoring the fact that Canada's constitutional fathers granted Quebec the right to be at least culturally separate, which was more than the British had done . . . the *je me souviens* slogan on their Quebec license plates, bespeaks their ancient resentments: *born French but screwed by the English ever since*. (*Breakup*, p. 110)

Nineteen-ninety-four ended on a near fatal note for Quebec sovereigntists. On December 1, the soul of Quebec's nationalist movement, Lucien Bouchard, was struck down. The fifty-five-year-old leader had contracted a rare and fearsome flesh-eating disease, necrotizing myositis, caused by the streptococcus A bacterium. Within a few days he underwent several desperate operations, including the amputation of his left leg. But within a week, he was off the respirator and able to communicate with his family and friends. On December 9, he was declared out of danger and removed from the critical list. He would be home for Christmas.

Some observers called his survival a miracle. Everyone did agree that Lucien Bouchard had great courage, physical stamina, and a superb medical team.

As Bouchard recovered, so would the movement to Quebec independence. Another myth had taken emotional root. Jacques Parizeau threw himself at the wheel of fortune. To "Gain Sovereignty," the premier moved fast implementing the stratagem crafted at the party conventions in 1988 and 1991 and published in April 1993 (see Appendix E). Then, on December 6, during the first session of the thirty-fifth legislature of the National Assembly, he introduced a seventeen-article draft bill in the National

Assembly, an unnumbered *avant projet loi*, "An Act respecting the sovereignty of Québec." A large box nearly half the size of the page and labelled "preamble" contained only the words "Declaration of Sovereignty" and, in its centre, "(To follow)."[12] Article 1 established the fiction: "Quebec is a sovereign country." Citizens would carry on under the laws of Quebec and Canada until the new nation's government could, "in accordance with the procedure determined by the National Assembly, see to the drafting of a constitution for Quebec and for its adoption." Section 6 of the draft bill noted, too, that "the legal currency of Quebec shall continue to be the Canadian dollar." *Étapisme* forever.

Finally, the draft legislation laid out the form of consultations to be held. These would be much grander in scale than those of the Bélanger–Campeau Commission of 1990. This time anyone could come before any of 14 to 16 commissions to be loosed on the populace in January and February of 1995. Finally, the draft stated that, through a referendum held after two months of hearings, Quebecers would be asked, "Are you in favour of the Act passed by the National Assembly declaring the sovereignty of Quebec? YES or NO."

Parizeau's chosen means to accomplish René Lévesque's "à la prochaine" was illegal, as many charged, including the prime minister, but that point was irrelevant. None of Canada's leaders recognized the sting: the country's concentration had been yanked back to the priority of Quebec. This time, and for the first time with the prime minister participating, Quebec separation was debated on the floor of the House of Commons.

As December drew to a close, Jacques Parizeau pleaded for "a half-dozen Ontarians [to] put their feet to the Quebec flag" (*Star*, Dec 12/94), the dollar sank to its lowest point since 1986 — nearly its all-time low — and Canadians were reminded, none too subtly, of Charles de Gaulle's notorious remark so many years earlier. On December 19, *La Presse* reported that the Quebec premier would be awarded the Legion of Honour during his forthcoming trip to Paris from January 23 to 27, 1995.[11]

Will Canadians ever again celebrate as they did during their centennial in 1967? Or, in their hearts, have they already separated themselves? Those who have brought Canada to the verge of destruction do not have the answers.

677

Notes

1 Prime Minister Kim Campbell had cut expenditures to some $4.8 billion, but exactly how much this would have amounted to remains a matter of much dispute.

2 During Meech, Mendes had been a member of David Peterson's team. He had proposed giving a special veto over Senate reform to three regions: Quebec, two Eastern provinces, and two Western provinces. The "Mendes formula" had caused quite a stir among the acapoobahs. The Kenyan-born, American-educated constitutional expert wanted to revise the preamble to Canada's constitution to include recognition of the "unique heritage of the three founding nations" (p. ix).

3 On July 7, 1994, the Ontario government advertised for "Workplace Discrimination and Harassment Prevention Investigators" for various ministries, at salaries ranging from $53,854 to $61,298.

4 In *The Fight for Canada*, David Orchard suggests there's a lot more of the deal hidden from public scrutiny. He cites an admission in 1985 from Simon Reisman, the man Mulroney would pick as Canada's chief trade negotiator soon after: "The urgent need for fresh water in the United States would, I believe, make that country an eager and receptive partner. . . . I believe that this project [a huge water diversion undertaking known as the Grand Canal Project] could provide the key to a free trade agreement with the United States. . . . I have personally suggested these ideas to leaders in government and business on both sides of the border, and I have been greatly heartened by the initial response" (pp. 166–67). Mulroney also supported the project.

5 Federal grants for multiculturalism for 1993–94 will total $25.5 million. Of this, $6.5 million is to be spent on education, anti-racism programs, and a March 21 anti-racism campaign. Heritage culture and language programs consume another $5.5 million.

6 Before a government committee in April, Bourgon couldn't recall whether or not she had made a false claim about her academic credentials. Pressed on the point, she could only muster, "I don't think so." Like Tellier, she thought the discovery might affect her credibility. Unlike his experience, which never appeared in the newspapers, a skeletal report of the matter was published in the *Toronto Star*, and the *Globe* reported it on April 20, 1994; two commercial directories and an official biography from the PM's Office in 1992 showed Bourgon held an MBA from the University of Ottawa. In 1993 the PMO's version was revised to "MBA (without thesis)" (*GM*, Apr 20/94). Bourgon referred the matter to the Public Service Commission, the mandarinate's rubber stamp for every conceivable corruption in government.

7   McIntyre's crusade has been covered in the *New York Times*, the *Washington Post*, the *Sydney Morning Herald* of Australia, the *Miami Herald*, the *San Francisco Chronicle*, and the *Daily Telegraph* in London.

In his humongous tome *A Canadian Myth: Quebec, Between Canada and the Illusion of Utopia*, published in the late summer of 1994, *Gazette* columnist William Johnson never mentioned McIntyre's name. He gave the UN decision a scant fifty-five words.

8   Section 91 of the BNA Act contains the most famous lines in the Constitution: "It shall be lawful for the Queen, by and with the Advice and Consent of the Senate and House of Commons, to make laws for the Peace, Order, and good Government of Canada. . . ."

9   Three months later, on December 6, 1994, human resources minister Lloyd Axworthy told the House of Commons that the federal government would shortly introduce legislation to ensure employment equity for visible minorities, the disabled, and other interest groups in the federal public service: "Ensuring equal access and equal opportunity in the workplace is one of the primary objectives of ensuring a good, effective economy" (*Star*/CP, Dec 7/94).

10   Yet Nelson Wyatt of Canadian Press writes that Charest "refused to use the words sovereignty-association, the option proposed by . . . René Lévesque" (*Gazette*, Oct 5/94).

11   See note 2, Chapter 12, regarding David Peterson.

12   Notes at the bottom of the same page of the *avant projet loi*: "The Declaration of Sovereignty will be drafted on the basis of the suggestions made during the information and participation process to be held on the draft bill.

"It will set forth the fundamental values and main objectives the Québec nation wishes to make its own once it has acquired the exclusive power to make all its laws, collect all its taxes and conclude all its treaties."

Epilogue

CANADA HAS BECOME A LAND of squabbling malcontents — an *olla podrida* of untenable myths and self-interested cabals. There are many reasons, as we have seen. The blueprint for this ongoing disaster is constitutionally enshrined in the Charter of Rights and Freedoms, which, as all Canadians now know, protects neither. Section 1 reads:

> The *Canadian Charter of Rights and Freedoms* guarantees the rights and freedoms set out in it subject only to such reasonable limits prescribed by law as can be demonstrably justified in a free and democratic society.

In these, the most important lines in our Constitution, the state takes priority over the citizen. The burden of proof — the responsibility to justify an individual freedom — weighs most on the citizen: the citizen must justify, at law, by way of demonstration, his or her right to enjoy any individual freedom. Precisely the opposite of where it should rest in any free society.

Combined with a notwithstanding clause, the Constitution is indeed an abject failure. Now we live with it as the price for national unity. The fact that Quebec refused to sign is irrelevant. The Canadian people never had a chance.

The Charter contains other horrors, too. Through the Charter, both bilingualism and multiculturalism ensure that Canada is defined in terms of its divisions, on the basis of its parts, rather than its whole. A charter of fights and fiefdoms.

681

Trudeau's formula, the notion that "the Canadian community must invest, for the defence and better appreciation of the French language, as much time, energy, and money as are required to prevent the country from breaking up," has collapsed. It simply wasn't logical.

Bilingualism, the first great national cult, is a non sequitur now. It was forced off the stage long ago when multiculturalism was introduced. It, in turn, is dying, giving way to the tribalism into which it has naturally matured. Federalism, yet another buzzword of collectivism, has been superceded by regionalism, which, in its turn, becomes separatism.

All of this torture over national unity has cost taxpayers billions upon billions. Nearly half a century ago a young John Diefenbaker, MP, said: "Income tax has increased some hundred times since it was first imposed years ago and the salaried man always pays. He should be entitled to ask at this time that some consideration be given to him; for if you pauperize the salaried middle class, you destroy the bulwark on which this country depends against the isms that are sweeping the world today" (House of Commons, July 10/46).

Of course, other countries have suffered the same kind of dissembling.

As Arthur Schlesinger, Jr., notes in *The Disuniting of America*, multiculturalism and bilingualism exact a heavy price from their followers. For America, the end result of unchecked separatism, he writes, can only be "fragmentation, resegregation, and tribalization." Canada, on the other hand, is particularly vulnerable to breakup, because the country not only lacks a "unique national identity," but for charitable reasons embraces multiculturalism. As for the other great -ism, Schlesinger remarks, "bilingualism shuts doors. It nourishes self-ghettoization, and ghettoization nourishes racial antagonism" (p. 108).

So Canada's long-term prospects for peace and fulfilment are dim. I see little evidence to suggest that Canadians feel anything other than profound mistrust, or even contempt, for freedom. Dissent appears only in glimmerings, painfully mustered and always a last resort if "consensus" fails. Canada does not suffer a leadership crisis. She suffers a crisis of citizenship. Dissent is carefully sanitized by institutions — business, media, educators, governments, sports, law, and the arts.

If Alexis de Tocqueville were to tour this nation today he could never ask, as he once did of America, "how does it happen that everyone takes as zealous an interest in his township, his country, and the whole of the state as if they were his own?" — and answer it, too — "it is because everyone, in his sphere, takes an active part in the government of society." If he could say, "I know of no country in which there is so little independence of mind and real freedom of discussion as in America," what would the nineteenth-century foreign correspondent to America say of modern Canada?

Most of our prime ministers have been elected through *subreption* — they gained the job by concealing their true ambitions. Yet even when fully exposed, they were, with rare exception, rewarded by the electorate. Unless Canadians recognize the need to correct this state of affairs themselves, the quality of the country's leaders will deteriorate further.

Breaking out of this prison will require tremendous upheaval. A century before de Tocqueville, the socialist Jean-Jacques Rousseau observed with a note of smugness: "Slaves lose everything in their chains, even the desire of escaping from them: they love their servitude, as comrades of Ulysses loved their brutish condition" (*The Social Contract*, Bk. I, Ch. 2, 1762).

Rousseau was wrong. It is also a truism of history that the longer the status quo in any society is forcibly maintained by the state, the greater will be the earthquake when it comes.

This is the danger Canada faces now. We have embraced censorship and political correctness to a degree that no American would ever tolerate. In *The Culture of Complaint: The Fraying of America* (1993), the witty Robert Hughes wrote: "The American right has had a ball with Political Correctness. . . . The right has its own form of PC — Patriotic Correctness, if you like — equally designed to veil unwelcome truths" (pp. 26, 28).

In Canada every political party has wallowed in censorship, including the Reform Party. There has never been an open debate about values, only debate about process. Canadians prefer that others do their thinking for them.

The latest phenomenon peeping from the rubble of Canada's social-engineering experiments is ethnically correct dissent. Only the right people are permitted to disagree, all of whom hail from the political left. These are the buglers who at the last reveille cling desperately to at least one of the -isms. The more frightening aspect of this is that Canadians have learned nothing, absolutely nothing.

History will show that Brian Mulroney's sellout of what remained of conservative Canada logically extended the intellectual deceit of Trudeau masquerading as liberalism. The thievery, corruption, and gangsterism of the Trudeau–Mulroney era have grown directly from that first step Lester Pearson took in 1963. There are no philosophical distinctions between these three leaders from Quebec. And between them they governed the country for more than a generation.

Political and economic disintegration always follow moral and intellectual breakdown. The play is as old as the subject of Edward Gibbon's *The History of the Decline and Fall of the Roman Empire* (1776–88).

So the question remains: Where are the real democrats, the classical liberals who welcomed free debate in fighting for social justice? Whatever happened to the conservative notion that tradition and personal account-ability must temper the excesses of liberal idealism? These hallmarks of a free society have vanished. Scott Reid in his *Lament for a Notion* (1993) prophesies:

> It is not so much memoranda that Ottawa's lords of obscurity have been spinning for the past two decades, as the rope with which we will eventually hang ourselves. Left to fester in some dark corner, the fundamental conflict of interests will eventually surface — after all, it continues on, in a muffled way, beneath the mountains of documentation. And when it does surface, it will be the fiercer for having fed on so many years of miscommunication. (p. 17)

The true crisis is more insidious. Canada has been smitten by a value crisis. Personal freedom, the most important treasure there is, never appears on any politician's agenda. No one even questions whether or not it exists.

What, then, are the solutions?

Politicians can never be "forced truly" to do their people's will, as William Gairdner suggests in *The Trouble With Canada* (p. 441). They must *want* to do it because their values make it inconceivable to them person-ally that they could engage in any other struggle.

The thesis of George Grant's classic *Lament for a Nation* (1965) held that there is an "inability of this country to be sovereign" and that "Canada's disappearance was a matter of necessity" (pp. 4, 5). In economic terms, he has proven prophetic. But if the nation finally disappears, it will not do so because of economics. It will happen because there is no longer any individual sovereignty worth preserving.

Many people in Quebec and "the rest of Canada" believe that the rules of the game are wrong; that if we change the rules, our shared life as Canadians will improve. This is not the case. Society does not change because the rules change. That is how lawyers think.

Constitutions are not primarily about rules. Any rule in a constitution can be broken. First and foremost, a constitution is a celebration of a nation's dreams and ideals. Its preamble is far more important than all its clauses put together. Constitutions must be about ideals written and unwritten. These must be above secular law, inviolate, universal, and cherished because they are so strong and because their citizens recognize them instantly. Canada is not breaking up; for want of these ideals Canada is breaking down.

One of the founding fathers of the American Revolution, Thomas Paine (1737–1809), inscribed these memorable sentiments in *The Rights of Man* (1791):

> The rights of men in society, are neither devisable, nor transferable, nor annihilable, but are descendable only; and it is not in the power of any generation to intercept finally, and cut off the descent. If the present generation, or any other, are disposed to be slaves, it does not lessen the right of the succeeding generation to be free: wrongs cannot have a legal descent. ("The Rights of Man (1791–92)," from *The Thomas Paine Reader*, Harmondsworth: Penguin, 1987, p. 249)

Some believe education is the answer. There's much truth here, but there's a danger, too.

Fritz Schumacher, economist and author of *Small Is Beautiful: Economics as if People Mattered* (1973), pinpoints the fallacy of our believing that simply investing more in education makes for a more enlightened society: "the task of education would be, first and foremost, the transmission of ideas of value, of what to do with our lives. . . . More education can help us only if it produces more wisdom . . . only if it produces 'whole men.'" He adds that one of these men "will not be in doubt about his basic convictions, about his view on the meaning and purpose of life. . . . the conduct of his life will show a certain sureness of touch which stems from his inner clarity" (pp. 82, 95). This is essential revelation.

William Greider, author of *Who will tell the People* (1992), says: "The enduring question for democracy is how to revive and encourage the trusted representative — how to create political conditions that would permit such relationships to develop and survive. Among other things, trust requires time and patience and sustained human engagement" (p. 64).

Such trust cannot either germinate, grow, be preserved or protected by rights tribunals, rights commissioners, or parliamentary ethics counsellors. If this federation simply fades away as its constituent regions wander off, our crime against history will be that this once-proud people with a heritage unmatched in human existence deliberately constructed and perpetuated shallow myths about themselves rather than learn and move forward confidently.

Following the collapse of the Progressive Conservative Party in the 1993 election, and a year's sabbatical in the United States, the Right Hon. Joe Clark published his own version of *Straight From the Heart* with the same publisher: "Equality is a basic and enduring Canadian value. . . . We believe that part of the definition of our special country is our respect for the values of fairness, justice, and equality. Indeed, our challenge is to make those principles effective for all the people of Canada, so that individuals are not denied them by barriers of poverty or sexual or racial or other discrimination" (*A Nation Too Good to Lose: Renewing the Purpose of Canada*, pp. 102–3). Clark is not championing equality before the law. He is pushing doctrinaire socialism. Conformity at all costs.

In 1848, Henry David Thoreau (1817–62) justified rebellion in his *Essay on Civil Disobedience*. "All men recognize the right of revolution; that is, the right to refuse allegiance to, and to resist, the government, when its tyranny or its inefficiency are great and unendurable." A renewal of conservative thought and philosophy is the answer: a respect for tradition, heritage, excellence, achievement and individual freedom and quiet fortitude.

Canadians have reached that point now. The counter-revolution against the anti-intellectuals and revisionists who stole the future of our great country is long overdue.

Appendix A
The Reform Party Platform
Selections from "56 Reasons Why You Should Support The Reform Party of Canada"

1. **Balanced Federation:** Reformers say that Canada is not a federation of founding races or ethnic groups. It is a federation in which the equality of all its provinces and citizens is recognized.
2. **Triple-E Senate:** The Reform Party fully endorses the Triple-E Senate concept: Elected by the people; Equal representation from each province; Effective in safeguarding regional interests.
3. **Real Representation:** Reformers believe that the duty of elected members to their constituents should come before their obligation to their party.

. . . .

6. **Unity and Quebec:** The Reform Party is fully committed to Confederation and to the view that all provinces should make a commitment to Canada as one nation.
7. **Constitutional Conventions:** The Reform Party supports a bottom-up process in the next round of constitutional negotiations. This should begin with Constitutional Conventions in the regions and aboriginal communities.
8. **Democratic Constitutional Change:** The Reform Party opposes the implementation of any amendments to the Constitution until ratified by the electorate through a constitutional referendum.

9. **Property Rights:** The Reform Party supports the entrenchment of property rights in the Constitution.
10. **Supreme Court Appointments:** Reform Party policy states that these should first be ratified by a Triple-E Senate.
11. **Northwest Territories and Yukon:** The Reform Party supports the right of the Northern Territories to achieve full provincial status.
12. **Free Votes in Parliament:** The Reform Party supports changing Parliamentary rules to allow more free votes in the House of Commons.
13. **Referendums:** Reformers support direct public approval of legislation, especially on major moral issues (abortion, capital punishment) and matters that alter the basic social fabric (immigration, language, constitutional change).
14. **Citizens' Initiatives:** Reformers believe that voters should be able to get vital concerns on a national referendum ballot.
15. **Recall:** Reformers believe that voters should have a mechanism to remove MPs who will not represent their interests in Parliament.
16. **Fixed Election Dates:** The Reform Party supports the holding of elections every four years at a predetermined date.

. . . .

22. **Elimination of Patronage:** The Reform Party believes that government jobs and contracts should be awarded on the basis of fairness and normal commercial criteria of price and quality, rather than lobbying and political motives.

. . . .

36. **Social Responsibility:** We believe that Canadians have a personal and collective responsibility to care and provide for the basic needs of people who are unable to care and provide for themselves.
37. **Alternatives to the Welfare State:** The Reform Party believes Canadians urgently need social programs that will be less bureaucratic and more financially sustainable in the future.

. . . .

40. **Social Services:** The Reform Party opposes the use of federal spending powers to legislate in areas of provincial jurisdiction. We believe that federal transfer payments to the provinces for social services should be unconditional.

. . . .

44. **Justice:** The Reform Party supports a judicial system which places the punishment of crime and the protection of law-abiding citizens and their property ahead of all other objectives.

. . . .

46. **Aboriginal Peoples:** Reformers believe that government policy should assist aboriginal peoples to assume full responsibility for the programs affecting them and to participate more fully in Canada's economic life.

47. **Land Claims:** The Reform Party supports processes leading to the early and mutually satisfactory conclusion of outstanding land-claim negotiations.

48. **Enforced Bilingualism:** The Reform Party stands for freedom of speech. We are opposed to comprehensive language legislation. In no way do we discourage personal bilingualism.

49. **Language of Service:** The Reform Party recognizes that French is the predominant language of work and society in Quebec and that English is the predominant language of work and society elsewhere. We support official bilingualism in the Parliament, Supreme Court and critical federal services where need is sufficient to warrant provision of minority services on a cost-effective basis.

50. **Immigration:** The Reform Party supports an immigration policy that has Canada's economic needs as its focus and that welcomes genuine refugees.

51. **New Canadians:** The Reform Party stands for the acceptance and integration of immigrants to Canada into the mainstream of Canadian life.

52. **Cultural Heritage:** The Reform Party supports the principle that individuals or groups are free to preserve their cultural heritage using their own resources.

53. **Multiculturalism:** The Reform Party of Canada opposes the current concept of multiculturalism and hyphenated Canadianism pursued by the Government of Canada.

. . . .

Published by the Reform Party of Canada
Head Office, Calgary, Alberta, 1991

Appendix B
Ontario: A Selection of
Laws and Policy Directives

Bill 48 The Social Contract Act: An Act to encourage negotiated settlements in the public sector to preserve jobs and services while managing reductions in expenditure and to provide for certain matters related to the Government's expenditure reduction program (1st Reading, June 14, 1993; Royal Assent, July 8, 1993)

Purposes:

> **Section 1. 1.** To encourage employers, bargaining agents and employees to achieve savings through agreements at the sectoral and local levels primarily through adjustments in compensation arrangements.

Bill 79 The Employment Equity Act: An Act to Provide for Employment Equity for Aboriginal People, People with Disabilities, Members of Racial Minorities and Women (1st Reading, June 25, 1992; Royal Assent, December 14, 1993)

> **Section 2. 1.** Every Aboriginal person, every person with a disability, every member of a racial minority and every woman is entitled to be considered for employment, hired, retained, treated and promoted free of barriers, including systemic and deliberate practices and policies, that dis-

criminate against them as an Aboriginal person, as a person with a disability, as a member of a racial minority or as a woman.

2. Every employer's workforce, in all occupational categories and at all levels of employment, shall reflect the representation of Aboriginal people, people with disabilities, members of racial minorities and women in the community.

4. Every employer shall implement positive measures with respect to the recruitment, hiring, retention, treatment and promotion of Aboriginal people, people with disabilities, members of racial minorities and women.

Section 19. (1). Every employer shall establish and maintain employment equity records in respect of the employer's workforce.

(2). The employer shall keep in the employer's records concerning employees' membership in designated groups only the information, if any, that is provided by each employee about himself or herself.

Section 20. Every employer shall submit reports and other information to the Employment Equity Commission in accordance with the regulations. . . .

Section 21. Any person may apply to the Employment Equity Commission for access to a copy of any information provided to the Commission under this Act and in the possession of the Commission.

Implementation

Section 23. (1) An employer that has employees on the effective date shall comply with sections 10 (collection of workforce information), 11 (review of employment policies) and 12 (employment equity plan) with the period that ends on the following day:

1. For the Crown in right of Ontario, on the day that is twelve months after the effective date.

2. For an employer in the broader public sector with ten or more employees on the effective date, on the day that is eighteen months after the effective date.

PART IV   ENFORCEMENT
Audit and Enforcement by the Commission

Section 25. (1)   The Employment Equity Commission may conduct an audit of an employer to determine whether the employer is complying. . . .

Bill 56   An Act to protect the Civil Rights of Persons in Ontario
(Private Member's Bill, 1st Reading, June 23, 1993) [**This never became law**]

1. (1) Every person described in subsection (2) and every association of persons described in subsection (3) has the right to bring an action, without proof of damage, against any person or association of persons whose conduct or communication,

(a) promotes hatred of a person or class of persons because of race, ancestry, place of origin, colour, ethnic origin, citizenship, creed, sex, sexual orientation, age, marital status, family status or handicap: or

(b) promotes the superiority or inferiority of a person or class of persons because of race, ancestry, place of origin, colour, ethnic origin, citizenship, creed, sex, sexual orientation, age, marital status, family status or handicap.

Ontario Human Rights Code, RSO, 1990, ch. H.19

Preamble WHEREAS recognition of the inherent dignity and the equal and inalienable rights of all members of the human family is the foundation of freedom, justice and peace in the world and is in accord with the Universal Declaration of Human Rights as proclaimed by the United Nations;

AND WHEREAS it is public policy in Ontario to recognize the dignity and worth of every person and to provide for equal rights and opportunities without discrimination that is contrary to the law, and *having as its aim the creation of a climate of understanding and mutual respect for the dignity and worth of each person so that each person feels a part of the community and able to contribute fully to the development and well-being of the community and the Province . . .* [emphasis mine]

The Ontario Human Rights Code, RSO, 1980, ch. 340

Preamble And whereas it is public policy in Ontario that every person is free and equal in dignity and rights without regard to race, creed, colour, sex, marital status, nationality, ancestry or place of origin:

Section 4 (employers not to discriminate in employment practices)

No person shall . . .

a) refuse to refer or to recruit any person for employment;

d) establish or maintain any employment classification that by its description or operation excludes any person from employment or continued employment.

Framework Regarding Prevention of Harassment and Discrimination in Ontario Universities (n.d., c. October 7, 1993)

Policy Framework for Universities

Policy Statement Each policy should have a statement that sets out the goals and principles of the policy. . . .

In addition to the goal, the policy statement should include at least the following concepts:

(1) Harassment and discrimination are prohibited by *The Ontario Human Rights Code.*

(2) Each member of the campus community is responsible for helping to create an environment which is harassment and discrimination free as both work and learning can best be accomplished in an environment of understanding and mutual respect for the dignity and rights of each individual.

(3) The institution should ensure that each member of the campus community is aware of the institution's policy and should be proactive in undertaking an education/prevention campaign.

(4) The institution recognizes its responsibility to deal quickly, fairly, and effectively with harassment and discrimination should it arise.

(5) The policy applies both on and off campus to all members of the college or university community.

(6) The rights of both the complainant and respondent should be safeguarded.

(7) Every person continues to have a right to seek assistance from the Ontario Human Rights Commission even when steps are being taken under this policy. (p. 3)

The Stephen Lewis Report (1992–93)

Excerpts:

School boards are required to develop and implement an antiracism and ethnocultural equity policy to address racial and ethnocultural biases and barriers in the school system.

School boards must submit their policies and implementation plans to the Ministry [of Education and Training] for approval.

Policies must include five-year implementation plans and mechanisms for evaluating progress.

March 31, 1995, is the final deadline for submission by boards of policies and implementation plans.

Appendix C
Alliance for the Preservation
of English in Canada:
A Chronology of History

This chronology appears in APEC's publication "Constitutional Countdown: Official Bilingualism," No. 7, 1992.

[PHASE 1] 1759–1866

No French language rights existed from the beginning of British rule to the date of confederation. Religious liberty — Yes. Language — No.

The French language is not mentioned in any of the following historical, legal or constitutional documents:

1759	The Capitulation of Quebec [The Conquest]
1760	The Capitulation of Montreal
1763	The Treaty of Paris
1763	The Royal Proclamation
1774	The Quebec Act
1791	The Constitutional Act

1840   The Union Act [The Act of Union/Upper and Lower Canada]

All of the foregoing documents are inextricably woven into the fabric of Canadian history.

The Quebec Act 1774 does not mention the French language, notwithstanding that politicians, bureaucrats, Francophones and the media have repeatedly stated that the Act guarantees the status of the French language.

The Union Act 1840 declared English to be the language of government and its institutions when Upper and Lower Canada were united as one province.

[PHASE II] 1867–1968

Canadian Confederation created under the British North America Act 1867 was a political and economic union of four regions, Ontario, Quebec, New Brunswick and Nova Scotia.

Confederation was not a pact between two founding peoples, two linguistic groups. (Dr. Eugene Forsey)

There was no agreement that the French language was to be recognized and applied on the same basis as English in all fields. (Dr. Eugene Forsey)

Two nation concept is a myth. (Dr. Eugene Forsey)

French language schools were not guaranteed, only denominational schools. (BNA Act 1867, s.93)

Canada did not become a bilingual nation and French was not an official language.

Only one section out of 147 sections of the BNA Act deals with language.

Section 133 permits the use of French but limits its use to the Parliament of Canada, Quebec Legislature, Quebec Courts and the Supreme Court of Canada.

Because the permitted use of the French language was limited, English was the language of government, not only by implication, but by usage.

The act did not create or authorize a bilingual civil service for the government of Canada or the Province of Quebec.

The foregoing [two phases of history] represents the historical and legal position and the practical application of the law with respect to the French language in Canada for over 100 years.

[PHASE III] 1969–1992

1969 — Official Languages Act makes English and French official languages of Canada **"for the purposes of the Government and its institutions."**

Alleged purpose — to permit Canadians to communicate with the government in the language of their choice.

1988 — Official Languages Act New and vastly extended in scope and purpose to include the following:

Each individual civil servant permitted to work in the official language of his choice.

Section heads, supervisors and managers have to be bilingual to accommodate civil servants.

600,000 government related jobs could eventually be classified bilingual.

Federal Court judges required to be fluently bilingual; translations and interpreters are eliminated.

All Criminal Courts across Canada require bilingual judges, prosecutors, clerks, juries.

Secretary of State obligated to promote minority languages in provinces, municipalities, business, labour, volunteer organizations and minority language communities, but English is restricted, not promoted, in Quebec.

Official Languages Commissioner is investigator, policeman, prosecutor, enforcer, witness and judge as and when he chooses.

All government legislation subject to the provisions of the Official Languages Act.

Breaches of the Official Languages Act could result in a fine or imprisonment or both.

Appendix D
The Party Platform of
the Bloc Québécois
(as set out on July 25, 1990)

1.   We define ourselves first of all as a group of MPs anxious to represent faithfully the citizens who have elected us.

We intend therefore to set up in our respective constituencies institutions that will stimulate democratic debate and broad public involvement. We believe that our society must develop within the framework of a true participatory democracy. We are working to this end with all the means at our disposal.

2.   Our national allegiance is Québécois. The territory to which we belong is that of Québec, home of a people of French culture and language, whose sovereignty we intend to promote.

3.   We consider the National Assembly of Québec as being, in fact and in right, the supreme democratic institution of the Québécois people. The Assembly is where the people will exercise their sovereign authority.

4.   We have left our respective political parties and kept our seats in the House of Commons in order to:

a) associate ourselves without constraint to [sic] the efforts to define and build, in a context of participation, a Québec in full possession of its attributes;

b) make ourselves spokespersons of this goal in Ottawa and English Canada;

c) ensure the Québécois people free exercise of their right to self-determination by making this right clear to the whole of Canada and respected by federal institutions;

d) support Québec by promoting its bargaining power in the new political arrangement with the Canadian associate [sic];

e) consolidate, around the exclusive interests of Québec, the strength and political authority of our people in Ottawa.

5.   The MPs of the Bloc Québécois are not subject to party discipline, and they freely exercise their right to vote in the House of Commons.

6.   Acknowledging that the future of Québec is closely tied to its economic prosperity and stability, we will ask from the federal government for Québec's full share as founding partner [sic] and major contributor in the Canadian federation.

7.   In every case, we will fully respect and apply the principles of democracy, equity, and social responsibility. We will oppose discrimination in any form, while asserting a favourable bias towards the underprivileged in our society.

Appendix E
The Parti Québécois Strategic Plan
to Gain Sovereignty on Election
1988 to 1994

The following is from the ninety-one-page PQ document *Le Qéubec dans un monde nouveau* published April 1993, which outlines the steps approved by the party conventions of November 1988 and January 1991. The text is the work of the National Executive Council of the Parti Québécois. The sixty-five-page English edition, *Quebec in a New World: The PQ's Plan for Sovereignty*, was published in 1994 (see biblio.). Professor David Cameron, University of Toronto, also translated it and excerpts appeared in the *Globe* on March 31, 1994. The following is reprinted from Robert Chodos's translation (pp. 44–45):

- From now until the time that it forms the next government, the Parti Québécois will promote Quebec sovereignty by concretely demonstrating its advantages.

- Once elected, a Parti Québécois government will

a)   submit to the National Assembly for adoption a solemn declaration stating Quebec's wish to accede to full sovereignty;
b)   following discussions with the federal government, proceed to fulfil its responsibility and its mandate to establish the timetable and modalities for

transferring powers and determine the rules for dividing Canada's assets and debts;

c)   submit to the National Assembly for adoption legislation instituting a constitutional commission whose terms of reference would be to draw up a proposed constitution for a sovereign Quebec.

- As quickly as possible, the government will ask the population, through a referendum, to speak on the sovereignty of Quebec and the constitutional mechanisms that would make the exercise of that sovereignty possible. This referendum will be the act that will bring into being a sovereign Quebec.

- The Quebec government will propose mutually advantageous forms of economic association to the federal government. These proposals will include the institution of joint bodies, established through treaties, to manage the economic relationship between Canada and Quebec.

Bibliography

Andrew, J.V. *Backdoor Bilingualism: Davis's Sell-Out of Ontario and Its National Consequences*. Richmond Hill, Ont.: BMG Publishing, 1979.

———. *Bilingual Today, French Tomorrow*. Richmond Hill, Ont.: BMG Publishing, 1977.

———. *Enough!* Kitchener, Ont.: Andrew Books, 1989.

Arbour, Peter. *Québec Inc. and the Temptation of State Capitalism*. Trans. Madeleine Hébert. Montreal and Toronto: Robert Davies, 1993.

Arendt, Hannah. *On Revolution*. New York: Viking Press, 1963, 1965.

Armstrong, Joe C.W. *Meech Plus: The Charlatan Accord*. Toronto: Committee of One for One Canada, 1992.

Atwood, Margaret. *Barbed Lyres: Canadian Venomous Verse*. Toronto: Key Porter, 1990.

Axworthy, Thomas S., and Right Hon. Pierre Elliott Trudeau, eds. *Towards a Just Society: The Trudeau Years*. Markham, Ont.: Viking/Penguin, 1990.

Barlow, Maude. *Parcel of Rogues: How Free Trade Is Failing Canada*. Toronto: Key Porter, 1991.

———, and Bruce Campbell. *Take Back the Nation*. Toronto: Key Porter, 1991 (updated ed., 1993: *Meeting the Threat of NAFTA*).

Bayefsky, Anne F. *Canada's Constitutional Act 1982 and Amendments: A Documentary History*. Toronto: McGraw-Hill Ryerson, 1989.

Beatty, David. *The Canadian Production of Constitutional Review: Talking Heads and the Supremes.* Toronto: Carswell, 1990.

Behiels, Michael D., ed. *The Meech Lake Primer: Conflicting Views of the 1987 Constitutional Accord.* Ottawa: University of Ottawa Press, 1989.

Bercowitz, S.D., and Robert K. Logan, eds. *Canada's Third Option.* Toronto: Macmillan, 1975.

Bercuson, David J., ed. *Canada and the Burden of Unity.* Toronto: Macmillan, 1977.

Bercuson, David J., and Barry Cooper. *Deconfederation: Canada Without Quebec.* Toronto: Key Porter, 1991.

————. *Derailed: The Betrayal of the National Dream.* Toronto: Key Porter, 1994.

Bibby, Reginald W. *Mosaic Madness.* Toronto: Stoddart, 1990.

Bissoondath, Neil. *Selling Illusions: The Cult of Multiculturalism in Canada.* Toronto: Penguin, 1994.

Black, Conrad. *A Life in Progress.* Toronto: Key Porter, 1993.

Bliss, Michael, ed. *Canadian History in Documents, 1763–1966.* Toronto: Ryerson Press, 1966.

————. *Right Honourable Men: The Descent of Canadian Politics from Macdonald to Mulroney.* Toronto: HarperCollins, 1994.

Blohm, Robert. "Requiem for Quebec Inc." in *The Idler.* Toronto: Sept/Oct 1992.

Bloom, Alan. *The Closing of the American Mind.* New York: Simon and Schuster, 1987.

Bothwell, Robert, Ian Drummond, and John English. *Canada Since 1945: Power, Politics, and Provincialism,* rev. ed. Toronto: University of Toronto Press, 1989.

Bouchard, Lucien. *On the Record.* Trans. Dominique Clift. Toronto: Stoddart, 1994. (Originally published by Editions du Boréal, 1992.)

Bourassa, Robert. *Power from the North.* Toronto: Prentice-Hall, 1985.

Bourgault, Pierre. *Now or Never!: Manifesto for an Independent Quebec.* Trans. David Homel. Toronto: Key Porter, 1991.

Bibliography

Bovard, James. *Lost Rights: The Destruction of American Liberty*. New York: St. Martin's Press, 1994.

Bowell, Eric. *Initiative Referendum and Recall*. Brooks, Alta.: Citizens' Initiative and Referendum, P.O. Box 831, Oct 1990.

Bowker, Marjorie Montgomery. *The Meech Lake Accord: What It Will Mean to You and Canada*. Hull, Que.: Voyageur, 1990.

———. *Canada's Constitutional Crisis: Making Sense of It All*. Edmonton: Lone Pine Publishing, 1991.

Boyd, John. *Sir George Etienne Cartier, Bart., His Life and Times: A Political History of Canada from 1814 until 1873*. Toronto: University of Toronto Press, 1914.

Boyer, Patrick. *The People's Mandate: Referendums and a More Democratic Canada*. Toronto and Oxford: Dundurn Press, 1992.

Braid, Don, and Sydney Sharpe. *Breakup: Why the West Feels Left Out of Canada*. Toronto: Key Porter, 1990.

Brimelow, Peter. *The Patriot Game: National Dreams & Political Realities*. Toronto: Key Porter, 1986. (Later published as *The Patriot Game: Canada and the Canadian Question Revisited*. Toronto: Key Porter, 1989.)

———. *The Enemies of Freedom*. Toronto: C-FAR, Citizens for Foreign Aid Reform Inc., 1990.

Brown, Patrick, Robert Chodos, and Rae Murphy. *Winners, Losers: The 1976 Tory Leadership Convention*. Toronto: Lorimer, 1976.

Cahill, Jack. *John Turner: The Long Run*. Toronto: McClelland & Stewart, 1984.

Cairns, Alan C. *Disruptions: Constitutional Struggles from the Charter to Meech Lake*. Toronto: McClelland & Stewart, 1991.

———. *Charter Versus Federalism: The Dilemmas of Constitutional Reform*. Montreal and Kingston: McGill–Queen's University Press, 1992.

Cameron, Duncan, and Miriam Smith, eds. *Constitutional Politics*. Toronto: Lorimer, 1992.

Cameron, Stevie. *On the Take: Crime, Corruption and Greed in the Mulroney Years*. Toronto: MacFarlane Walter & Ross, 1994.

Camp, Dalton. *Gentlemen, Players & Politicians.* Toronto: McClelland & Stewart, 1970.

———. *Points of Departure.* Ottawa: Deneau and Greenberg, 1979.

Canada. *Strengthening the Canadian Federation: The Constitutional Amendment, 1987.* Ottawa: Department of Supply and Services, Aug 1987.

———. *The Royal Commission on Newspapers.* Ottawa: Minister of Supply and Services Canada, 1981. Chair, Tom Kent.

Canadians for a Unifying Constitution and The Friends of Meech Lake (Peter Russell, Richard Simeon, Ronald Watts, Jeremy Webber, and Wade MacLaughlan). *Meech Lake: Setting the Record Straight.* Ottawa: c/o Ampersand Communication Services Inc., 1990.

Careless, J.M.S., and R. Craig Brown. *The Canadians, 1867–1967.* Toronto: Macmillan, 1967.

Carter, Stephen L. *The Culture of Disbelief: How American Law and Politics Trivialize Religious Devotion.* New York: BasicBooks/HarperCollins, 1993.

Champagne, Lyse. *Double Vision: Reflections of a Bicultural Canadian.* Toronto: Key Porter, 1990.

Chodos, Robert, Rae Murphy, and Eric Hamovitch. *Selling Out.* Toronto: Lorimer, 1988.

———. *The Unmaking of Canada: The Hidden Theme in Canadian History Since 1945.* Lorimer, 1991.

Chrétien, Jean. *Straight from the Heart.* Toronto: Key Porter, 1985. Rev. and updated, 1994.

———, ed. *Finding Common Ground: The Proceedings of the Aylmer Conference.* Hull, Que.: Voyageur, 1992.

Christian, William, and Colin Campbell. *Political Parties and Ideologies in Canada.* Toronto: McGraw-Hill Ryerson, 1989.

———. *George Grant: A Biography.* Toronto: University of Toronto Press, 1993.

Clark, Right Hon. Joe, *A Nation Too Good to Lose: Renewing the Purpose of Canada.* Toronto: Key Porter, 1994.

Clarkson, Stephen, and Christina McCall. *Trudeau and Our Times: Volume 1, The Magnificent Obsession.* Toronto: McClelland & Stewart, 1990.

Coates, Robert C. *The Night of the Long Knives*. Fredericton, NB: Brunswick Press, 1969.

Cohen, Andrew. *A Deal Undone: The Making and Breaking of the Meech Lake Accord*. Vancouver and Toronto: Douglas & McIntyre, 1990.

Colombo, John Robert, ed. *Colombo's Canadian Quotations*. Edmonton: Hurtig, 1974.

Collins, Richard. *Culture, Communication & National Identity: The Case of Canadian Television*. Toronto: University of Toronto Press, 1990.

Cook, Ramsay. *French Canadian Nationalism: An Anthology*. Toronto: Macmillan, 1969.

Côté, Jean, and Marcel Chaput, eds. *The Little Red Book: Quotations from René Lévesque*. Montreal: Éditions Héritage, 1977.

Courchene, Thomas J. *In Praise of Renewed Federalism: The Canada Round*. A series on the economics of constitutional renewal. Toronto: C.D. Howe Institute, 1991.

———. *Rearrangements: The Courchene Papers*. Oakville, Ont.: Mosaic Press, 1992.

———, and John N. McDougall. "1. The Context for Future Constitutional Reform" in *Canada's Constitutional Options: Papers and Summaries*, ed. Ronald L. Watts. Toronto: BCNI Symposium, Vol. 1 (Jan 16/91).

Coyne, Deborah. *Roll of the Dice: Working with Clyde Wells During the Meech Lake Negotiations*. Toronto: Lorimer, 1992.

———, and Robert Howse. *No Deal! Why Canadians Should Reject the Mulroney Constitution*. Hull, Que.: Voyageur, Sept 1992.

Creighton, Donald. *Canada's First Century*. Toronto: Macmillan, 1970.

Creighton, Douglas. *Sunburned: Memoirs of a Newspaperman*. Toronto: Little, Brown (Canada), 1993.

———. "The Myth of Biculturalism or The Great French-Canadian Sales Campaign," *Saturday Night*, Sept 1966.

Crispo, John. *Mandate for Canada*. Don Mills, Ont.: General, 1979.

———. *Making Canada Work: Competing in the Global Economy*. Toronto: Random, 1992.

Deachman, Tam W. *What Every American Should Know About Canada.* Markham, Ont.: PaperJacks Ltd., 1977.

De Tocqueville, Alexis. *Democracy in America.* Trans. George Lawrence. New York: Perennial Library, Harper & Row, 1969.

Delacourt, Susan. *United We Fall: The Crisis of Leadership in Canada.* Toronto: Viking/Penguin, 1993.

Desbarats, Peter. *René: A Canadian in Search of a Country.* Toronto: McClelland & Stewart, 1976.

Diefenbaker, Right Hon. John G., *"I never say anything provocative": Witticisms, Anecdotes and Reflections by Canada's Most Outspoken Politician.* Margaret Wente, ed. Toronto: Peter Martin Associates Limited, 1975.

———. *One Canada: Memoirs of the Right Honourable John G. Diefenbaker.* 3 vols. Macmillan: Toronto, 1975, 1976, 1977.

———. *Those Things We Treasure.* Toronto: Macmillan, 1972.

Dion, Léon. *Québec: The Unfinished Revolution.* Montreal and London: McGill–Queen's University Press, 1976.

Dionne, E.J., Jr. *Why Americans Hate Politics.* New York: Simon & Schuster, 1991.

Dobbin, Murray. *Preston Manning and the Reform Party.* Toronto: Lorimer, 1991.

———. *The Politics of Kim Campbell: From School Trustee to Prime Minister.* Toronto: Lorimer, 1993.

Dodge, William, ed. *Boundaries of Identity: A Quebec Reader.* Toronto: Lester, 1993.

Doern, G. Bruce, and Brian Tomlin. *Faith & Fear: The Free Trade Story.* Toronto: Stoddart, 1991.

Doern, Russell. *The Battle over Bilingualism: The Manitoba Language Question, 1983–85.* Winnipeg: Cambridge Publishers, 1985.

Donato, Andy. *Son of a Meech.* Toronto: Key Porter, 1990.

Downe, William. *The Referendum: Bring It On!* London, Ont.: HIT Inc., Dec 1990.

D'Souza, Dinesh. *Illiberal Education: The Politics of Race and Sex on Campus.* New York: Vintage Books/Random, 1991.

Drache, Daniel, and Roberto Perin, eds. *Negotiating With a Sovereign Quebec.* Toronto: Lorimer, 1992.

Dufour, Christian. *A Canadian Challege: Le defi québécois.* Lantzville, BC, and Halifax: Oolichan Books and The Institute for Research on Public Policy, 1990.

Dupont, Pierre. *How Lévesque Won.* Trans. Sheila Fischman. Toronto: Lorimer, 1977.

East, Yolanda Cossette. *The Weak Link: Quebec.* Lantier, Que.: Yolanda Books, 1989.

Elliott, Patricia, ed. *Rethinking the Future.* Saskatoon: Fifth House, 1993.

Ellul, Jacques. *Autopsy of Revolution.* Trans. Patricia Wolf. New York: Alfred Knopf, 1971.

———. *Propaganda: The Formation of Men's Attitudes.* New York: Alfred A. Knopf, 1965; Vintage Books, 1973.

Elshtain, Jean Bethke. *Democracy on Trial.* Concord, Ont.: Anansi, 1993.

Fetherling, Douglas. *Best Canadian Essays.* Saskatoon: Fifth House, 1990.

Farthing, John. *Freedom Wears a Crown.* Toronto: Kingswood House, 1957.

Fidler, Richard, trans. *Canada, Adieu? Quebec Debates Its Future.* Halifax and Lantzville, BC: Oolichan Books and The Institute for Research on Public Policy, 1991.

Fife, Robert, and John Warren. *A Capital Scandal: Politics, Patronage and Payoffs: Why Parliament Must Be Reformed.* Toronto: Key Porter, 1991.

Finkelstein, Neil, and George Vegh. *The Separation of Quebec and the Constitution of Canada.* Background Studies of the York University Constitutional Reform Project, Study No. 2. Toronto: Centre for Public Law and Public Policy, 1992.

Flanagan, Thomas. *Métis Lands in Manitoba.* Calgary: University of Calgary Press, 1992.

Forsey, Eugene A. *A Life on the Fringe: The Memoirs of Eugene Forsey.* Toronto: Oxford University Press, 1990.

Forster, Victor W., Sr. *Conning the Canadians: Quebec's Drive to Be a Sovereign State with Canadians Paying the Bill.* Vancouver: Forster Publishing, 1989.

————. *Conning the Canadians: The End of Canada Being One Nation.* Agincourt, Ont.: Ramsay Business Systems Limited, 1993.

Fotheringham, Allan. *Malice in Blunderland: or How the Grits Stole Christmas.* Toronto: Key Porter, 1982.

Fournier, Pierre. *The Québec Establishment: The Ruling Class and the State.* Montreal: Black Rose, 1976.

————. *A Meech Lake Post-Mortem: Is Quebec Sovereignty Inevitable?* Trans. Sheila Fischman. Kingston and Montreal: McGill–Queen's University Press, 1991.

Fox, Paul (chairman). *Report of the Bilingual Districts Advisory Board.* Ottawa: Information Canada, 1975.

Fraser, Graham. *Playing for Keeps: The Making of the Prime Minister, 1988.* Toronto: McClelland & Stewart, 1989.

Fraser, John, and Graham Fraser, eds. *"Blair Fraser Reports": Selections 1944–1968.* Toronto: Macmillan, 1969.

Fraser, Matthew. *Quebec Inc.: French Canadian Entrepeneurs and the New Business Elite.* Toronto: Key Porter, 1987.

Francis, Diane. *A Matter of Survival: Canada in the 21st Century.* Toronto: Key Porter, 1993.

Fukuyama, Francis. *The End of History and the Last Man.* New York: Avon, 1992.

Gagnon, Georgette, and Dan Rath. *Not Without Cause: David Peterson's Fall from Grace.* Toronto: HarperCollins, 1991.

Galbraith, John Kenneth. *The Culture of Contentment.* Boston, New York, London: Houghton Mifflin, 1992.

Gairdner, William D. *The Trouble With Canada: A Citizen Speaks Out.* Toronto: Stoddart, 1990.

————. *The War Against the Family.* Toronto: Stoddart, 1993.

————. *Constitutional Crack-Up: Canada and the Coming Showdown with Quebec.* Toronto: Stoddart, 1994.

Garreau, Joel. *The Nine Nations of North America.* New York: Avon Books, 1981.

Geraets, Théodore F. "The Problem and Its Solution," *Policy Options.* Vol. 11, No. 5 (June 1990).

Bibliography

Gibbins, Roger, et al., eds. *Meech Lake and Canada: Perspectives from the West.* Edmonton: Academic Printing & Publishing, 1989.

Gibson, Gordon. *Plan B: The Future of the Rest of Canada.* Vancouver: Fraser Institute, 1994.

Gorbachev, Mikhail. *Perestroika: New Thinking for Our Country and the World.* New York: Harper & Row, 1987.

Gould, Allan. *The Great Wiped-Out North.* Toronto: Stoddart, 1988.

Gougeon, Gilles. *A History of Quebec Nationalism: Conversations with Seven Leading Quebec Historians.* Toronto: Lorimer, 1994.

Graham, Ron. *God's Dominion: A Sceptic's Quest.* Toronto: McClelland & Stewart, 1990.

———. *The French Quarter.* Toronto: MacFarlane Walter & Ross, 1992.

Granatstein, J.L., and Kenneth McNaught, eds. *"English Canada" Speaks Out.* Toronto: Doubleday, 1991.

Granatstein, J.L., Kenneth McNaught, eds. *Twentieth Century Canada: A Reader.* Toronto: McGraw-Hill Ryerson, 1986.

Grant, George. *Lament for a Nation: The Defeat of Canadian Nationalism.* Carleton Library Series #50. Ottawa: Carleton University Press, 1988.

———. *Technology and Empire: Perspectives on North America.* Toronto: Anansi, 1969.

Gratton, Michel. *French Canadians: An Outsider's Inside Look at Quebec.* Toronto: Key Porter, 1993.

———. *"So, What Are the Boys Saying?"* Toronto: McGraw-Hill Ryerson, 1987.

Greene, Ian. *The Charter of Rights.* Toronto: Lorimer, 1989.

Greider, William. *Who will tell the People: The Betrayal of American Democracy.* New York: Touchstone, Simon & Schuster, 1992, 1993.

Gwyn, Richard. *The Northern Magus: Pierre Trudeau and Canadians.* Toronto: McClelland & Stewart, 1980.

Harbron, John D. *Canada Without Québec.* Toronto: Musson/General, 1977.

———. *This is Trudeau.* Don Mills, Ont.: Longmans Canada, 1968.

Hayes, David. *Power and Influence: The Globe and Mail and the News Revolution.* Toronto: Key Porter, 1993.

Hébert, Jacques, and Pierre Elliott Trudeau. *Two Innocents in China.* Trans. I.M. Owen. Toronto: Oxford University Press, 1968.

Henry, William A., III. *In Defense of Elitism.* New York: Doubleday, 1994.

Herperger, Dwight. *The Meech Lake Accord: A Comprehensive Bibliography.* Kingston: Institute of Intergovernmental Relations (Queen's University), 1990: *as published in* "Appendix," *Canada and the State of the Federation, 1990.*

Hillborn, Kenneth H.W. *The Cult of the Victim: Leftist Ideology in the 90s.* C-FAR Canadian Issues Series. Toronto: C-FAR, 1993.

Hogg, Peter W. *Meech Lake Constitutional Accord Annotated.* Toronto: Carswell, 1988.

———. *Is the Canadian Constitution Ready for the 21st Century?* Background Studies of the York University Constitutional Reform Project, Study No. 1. Toronto: Centre for Public Law and Public Policy, 1992.

Hoy, Claire. *Margin of Error: Pollsters and the Manipulation of Canadian Politics.* Toronto: Key Porter, 1989.

———. *Clyde Wells.* Toronto: Stoddart, 1992.

Humphreys, David L. *Joe Clark.* Toronto: Deneau and Greenberg, 1978.

Hurtig, Mel. *A New and Better Canada: Principles and Policies of a New Canadian Political Party.* Toronto: Stoddart, 1992.

Hustak, Allan. *Peter Lougheed: A Biography.* Toronto: McClelland & Stewart, 1979.

Ingle, Lorne. *Meech Lake Reconsidered.* Hull, Que.: Voyageur, 1989.

Jacobs, Jane. *The Question of Separatism: Quebec and the Struggle over Sovereignty.* Toronto: Random, 1980.

Jeffrey, Brooke. *Breaking Faith: The Mulroney Legacy of Deceit, Destruction and Disunity.* Toronto: Key Porter, 1992.

———. *Strange Bedfellows, Trying Times: October 1992 and the Defeat of the Powerbrokers.* Toronto: Key Porter, 1993.

Bibliography

Johnson, William. *A Canadian Myth: Quebec, Between Canada and the Illusion of Utopia*. Outremont, Que.: Robert Davies, 1994.

Johnston, Donald. *Up the Hill*. Montreal: Optimum Publishing (1984), 1986.

———, ed. *With a Bang, Not a Whimper: Pierre Trudeau Speaks Out*. Toronto: Stoddart, 1988.

———, ed. *Pierre Trudeau Speaks Out on Meech Lake*. Toronto: General Paperbacks, 1990.

Kilgour, David. *Uneasy Patriots*. Edmonton: Lone Pine Publishing, 1988.

———. *Inside Outer Canada*. Edmonton: Lone Pine Publishing, 1990.

Killman, Murray. *Curse of the Fleur de lis*. Caledonia, Ont.: Killman Art Gallery Publishing, 1990.

King, Maurice J. *The First Step*. Huntingdon, Que.: Southwest Quebec Publishing, 1993.

Kingwell, Mark. *A Civil Tongue: Justice, Dialogue, and the Politics of Pluralism*. University Park: Pennsylvania State University, 1995.

Kinsella, Warren. *Web of Hate: Inside Canada's Far Right Network*. Toronto: HarperCollins, 1994.

Lamont, Lansing. *Breakup: The Coming End of Canada and the Stakes for America*. New York: W.W. Norton & Company, 1994.

Lapham, Lewis H. *The Wish for Kings: Democracy at Bay*. New York: Grove Press, 1993.

LaPierre, Laurier. *Canada, My Canada: What Happened?* Toronto: McClelland & Stewart, 1992.

———, Jack McLeod, Charles Taylor, and Walter Young, eds. *Essays on the Left*. Toronto: McClelland & Stewart, 1971.

Laschinger, John, and Geoffrey Stevens. *Leaders & Lesser Mortals: Backroom Politics in Canada*. Toronto: Key Porter, 1992.

Laxer, James, and Robert Laxer. *The Liberal Idea of Canada*. Toronto: Lorimer, 1977.

Lee, Robert Mason. *One Hundred Monkeys*. Toronto: Macfarlane Walter & Ross, 1989.

Leitch, Ronald P. *Official Bilingualism: The Sell-Out of English Canada: A Brief Opposing Bill C-72*. Thornhill, Ont.: C-FAR Publishers, Canadian Issues Series, 1988.

———. *Constitutions Are for People Not Politicians*. Thornhill, Ont.: APEC, 1991.

Lemco, Jonathan. *Turmoil in the Peaceable Kingdom: The Quebec Sovereignty Movement and Its Implications for Canada and the United States*. Toronto: University of Toronto Press, 1994.

Leslie, Peter M., ed. *Canada: The State of the Federation 1985*. Kingston, Ont.: Institute of Intergovernmental Relations (Queen's University), 1985.

———. *Canada: The State of the Federation 1986*. Kingston, Ont.: IIR (Queen's University), 1986.

———. *Rebuilding the Relationship: Quebec and Its Confederation Partners*. Kingston, Ont.: IIR (Queen's University), 1987.

———, and Ronald L. Watts, eds. *Canada: The State of the Federation 1987–1988*. Kingston, Ont.: IIR (Queen's University).

———, and Douglas M. Brown, eds. *Canada: The State of the Federation 1989*. Kingston, Ont.: IIR (Queen's University).

Lévesque, René. *An Option for Quebec*. Toronto: McClelland & Stewart, 1968.

———. *My Quebec*. Toronto: Totem Books, 1979.

———. *Memoirs*. Toronto: McClelland & Stewart, 1986.

Levine, Allan. *Scrum Wars: The Prime Ministers and the Media*. Toronto and Oxford: Dundurn Press, 1993.

Limbaugh, Rush, III. *Rush Limbaugh: The Way Things Ought to Be*. New York: Pocket Books, Simon & Schuster, 1992.

———. *See, I Told You So*. New York: Pocket Books, Simon & Schuster, 1993.

Lipset, Martin Seymour. *Continental Divide: The Values and Institutions of the United States and Canada*. Toronto: C.D. Howe Institute, Toronto, and the National Planning Association, Washington, D.C., 1989.

Lisée, Jean-François. *In the Eye of the Eagle*. Toronto: HarperCollins, 1990.

Luttwak, Edward N. *The Endangered American Dream*. New York: Simon & Schuster, 1993.

McCall, Christina, and Stephen Clarkson. *Trudeau and Our Times: Volume 2: The Heroic Delusion*. Toronto: McClelland & Stewart, 1994.

McCall-Newman, Christina. *Grits: An Intimate Portrait of the Liberal Party*. Toronto: Macmillan, 1982.

McCallum, John, and Chris Green. *Parting as Friends: The Economic Consequences for Quebec*. Toronto: C.D. Howe Institute, 1991.

McDonald, Kenneth. *Keeping Canada Together*. Agincourt, Ont.: Ramsay Business Systems Limited, 1990.

———. *Red Maple: How Canada Became the People's Republic of Canada in 1981*. Richmond Hill, Ont.: BMG Publishing, 1975.

MacDonald, L. Ian. *Mulroney: The Making of the Prime Minister*. Toronto: McClelland & Stewart, 1984.

MacGregor, Roy. *Chief: The Fearless Vision of Billy Diamond*. Markham, Ont.: Penguin, 1990.

Maclaine, Craig, Michael Baxendale, and Robert Galbraith. *This Land Is Our Land*. Montreal: Optimum Publishing, 1990.

McLaughlin, Audrey. *A Woman's Place: My Life & Politics*. Toronto: Macfarlane Walter & Ross, 1992.

Mackness, William. *Big Government and the Constitution Crisis*. Mackenzie Paper 22. Toronto: Mackenzie Institute, 1991.

Macpherson, C.B. *The Life and Times of Democracy*. Oxford and New York: Oxford University Press, 1977.

———. *The Real World of Democracy*. The Massey Lectures, Fourth Series. Toronto: Canadian Broadcasting Corporation, 1965, 1972.

McQuaig, Linda. *Behind Closed Doors: How the Rich Won Control of Canada's Tax System . . . and Ended Up Richer*. Toronto: Penguin, 1987.

———. *The Quick and the Dead: Brian Mulroney, Big Business and the Seduction of Canada*. Toronto: Penguin, 1991.

McRoberts, Kenneth. *English Canada and Quebec: Avoiding the Issue*. North York, Ont.: Robarts Centre for Canadian Studies (York University), 1991.

———, and Patrick Monahan, eds. *The Charlottetown Accord, the Referendum, and the Future of Canada*. Toronto: University of Toronto Press, 1993.

Mandel, Michael. *The Charter of Rights and the Legalization of Politics in Canada.* Toronto: Wall & Thompson, 1989.

Manning, Hon. E.C. *Political Realignment: A Challenge to Thoughtful Canadians.* Toronto: McClelland & Stewart, 1967.

Manning, Preston. *The New Canada.* Toronto: Macmillan, 1992.

Martin, Lawrence. *Pledge of Allegiance: The Americanization of Canada in the Mulroney Years.* Toronto: McClelland & Stewart, 1993.

————. *The Presidents and the Prime Ministers: Washington and Ottawa Face to Face: The Myth of Bilateral Bliss, 1867–1982.* Toronto–New York: Doubleday, 1982.

Mathews, Georges. *Quiet Resolution: Quebec's Challenge to Canada.* Toronto: Summerhill Press, 1990.

Meekison, J. Peter, ed. *Canadian Federalism: Myth or Reality,* 3rd ed. Toronto: Methuen, 1977.

Meisel, John. *Working Papers on Canadian Politics.* Montreal–London: McGill–Queen's University Press, 1975.

Mercredi, Ovide, and Ellen Turpel. *In the Rapids: Navigating the Future of First Nations.* Toronto: Viking/Penguin, 1993.

Milne, David. *The Canadian Constitution: From Patriation to Meech Lake.* Toronto: Lorimer, 1989.

Monahan, Patrick J. *Meech Lake: The Inside Story.* Toronto: University of Toronto Press, 1991.

————, *Political and Economic Integration: The European Experience and Lessons for Canada.* Background Studies of the York University Constitutional Reform Project, Study No. 10. Toronto: Centre for Public Law and Public Policy (York University), 1992.

————, Lynda Covello, and Nicola Smith. *A New Division of Powers for Canada.* Background Studies . . . , Study No. 8. Toronto: Centre for Public Law and Public Policy (York University), 1992.

————, Lynda Covello, and Jonathan Batty. *Constituent Assemblies: The Canadian Debate in Comparative and Historical Context.* Background Studies . . . , Study No. 4. Toronto: Centre for Public Law and Public Policy (York University), 1992.

Montesquieu, Baron de, Charles Secondat. *The Spirit of the Laws*. New York: Hafner Publishing, 1949.

Morchain, Janet Kerr, and Mason Wade. *Search for a Nation: French–English Relations in Canada Since 1759*. Toronto: J.M. Dent & Sons, 1967.

Morin, Claude. *Quebec Versus Ottawa*. Toronto: University of Toronto Press, 1976.

Morrison, Alex, ed. *Divided We Fall: The National Security Implications of Canadian Constitutional Issues*. Toronto: Canadian Institute of Strategic Studies, 1991.

Morton, W.L. *The Progressive Party in Canada*. Toronto: University of Toronto Press, 1950.

Mowers, Cleo, ed. *Towards a New Liberalism: Re-Creating Canada and the Liberal Party*. Victoria, BC: Orca Book Publishers, 1991.

Mulroney, Right Hon. Brian. *Where I Stand*. Toronto: McClelland & Stewart, 1983.

———. "Canada's Constitution: The Meech Lake Accord": *Parliamentarian*, 69, 3 (July 1988): 141–44.

Myers, Hugh Bingham. *The Quebec Revolution*. Montreal: Harvest House, 1963.

Nader, Ralph, Nadia Milleron, and Duff Conacher. *Canada Firsts: A Salute to Canada and Canadian Achievement*, Toronto: McClelland & Stewart, 1992.

Nash, Knowlton. *Visions of Canada: Searching for Our Future*. Toronto: McClelland & Stewart, 1991.

Nelson, Joyce. *Sultans of Sleaze: Public Relations and the Media*. Toronto: Between the Lines, 1989.

———. "Packaging the Populace: Polling in the Age of Image Politics." In *Best Canadian Essays: 1990*, edited by Douglas Fetherling. (Reprinted from *Fuse* magazine, 1989.) Saskatoon: Fifth House Publishers, 1990, pp. 218–34.

Nielsen, Erik. *The House Is Not a Home*. Toronto: Macmillan, 1989.

Newman, Peter C. *The Distemper of Our Times: Canadian Politics in Transition: 1963–1968*. Toronto: McClelland & Stewart, 1968.

———. *Renegade in Power: The Diefenbaker Years*. Toronto: McClelland & Stewart, 1963.

————, and Stan Filmore, eds. *Their Turn to Curtsy — Your Turn to Bow: The Power, the Glory, the Men and the Issues.* Toronto: Maclean-Hunter, 1972.

Nurgitz, Nathan, and Hugh Segal. *No Small Measure: The Progressive Conservatives and the Constitution.* Toronto: Deneau, 1983.

Olive, David. *Canadian Political Babble: A Cynic's Dictionary of Political Jargon.* Toronto: John Wiley, 1993.

O'Neill, Terry, ed. *Act of Faith.* Vancouver: B.C. Report Magazine Limited, 1991.

Orchard, David. *The Fight for Canada: Four Centuries of Resistance to American Expansionism.* Toronto: Stoddart, 1993.

Palango, Paul. *Above the Law: The Crooks, the Politicians, the Mounties, and Rod Stamler.* Toronto: McClelland & Stewart, 1994.

Pangle, Thomas L. *The Ennobling of Democracy: The Challenge of the Postmodern Age.* Baltimore, Md.: Johns Hopkins University Press, 1992.

Parti Québécois, National Executive Council. *Quebec in a New World: The PQ's Plan for Sovereignty.* Trans. Robert Chodos. Toronto: Lorimer, 1994.

Pearson, Right Hon. Lester B., *Mike: The Memoirs.* Toronto: University of Toronto Press, Vol. I, 1897–1948, 1972; Vol. II, 1948–57, 1973; Vol. III, 1957–68, 1975.

Pelletier, Gérard. *The October Crisis.* Toronto–Montreal: McClelland & Stewart, 1971.

————. *Years of Impatience: 1950-1960.* Trans. Alan Brown. Toronto: Methuen, 1984.

Pépin, Jean-Luc, and John P. Robarts. *The Task Force on Canadian Unity: A Time to Speak* [Pépin–Robarts Commission]. Supply and Services Canada, 1980. Cat: CP 32–35/1979–2.

Powe, B. W. *The Solitary Outlaw.* Toronto: Lester & Orpen Dennys, 1987.

Postman, Neil. *Technopoly: The Surrender of Culture to Technology.* New York: Alfred A. Knopf, 1992.

Porter, Rosalie Pedalino. *Forked Tongue: The Politics of Bilingual Education.* New York: Basic Books, 1990.

Prince, Michael J., ed. *How Ottawa Spends, 1987–88: Restraining the State.* Toronto: Methuen, 1987.

Quebec Government. *Québec–Canada: A New Deal: The Québec government proposal for a new partnership between equals: sovereignty-association.* Quebec: 4th Quarter, 1979.

Radwanski, George. *Trudeau.* Toronto: Macmillan, 1978.

———, and Kendal Windeyer. *No Mandate but Terror: The Story of Canada's Kidnapping Crisis.* Richmond Hill, Ont.: Pocket Books, 1971.

Reid, Scott. *Canada Remapped: How the Partition of Quebec Will Reshape the Nation.* Vancouver: Arsenal Pulp Press, 1992.

———. *Lament for a Notion: The Life and Death of Canada's Bilingual Dream.* Vancouver: Arsenal Pulp Press, 1993.

Resnick, Philip. *Letters to a Québécois Friend.* Montreal and Kingston: McGill–Queen's University Press, 1990.

———. *Thinking English Canada.* Toronto: Stoddart, 1994.

———. *Toward a Canada–Quebec Union.* Montreal and Kingston: McGill–Queen's University Press, 1991.

Richler, Mordecai. *Oh Canada! Oh Quebec! Requiem for a Divided Nation.* Toronto: Penguin, 1992.

Riggs, A.R., and Tom Velk, eds. *Federalism in Peril: Will Canada Survive?* Vancouver: Fraser Institute, 1992.

The Rise and Fall of English Montreal, [documentary]. Written and directed by William Weintraub. Produced by the National Film Board of Canada, [1993]. Aired on Vision TV, Toronto, "The Cutting Edge," Jan 14 and 16/95. In colour.

Ritchie, Gordon. *Broken Links.* Canada Round Series. Toronto: C.D. Howe Institute, 1991.

Robertson, Gordon. *A House Divided: Meech Lake, Senate Reform and the Canadian Union.* Halifax: Institute for Research on Public Policy, 1989.

Rodgers, Marion Elizabeth, ed. *The Impossible H.L. Mencken.* Anchor Books/Bantam Doubleday Dell, 1991.

Russell, Peter H. *Constitutional Odyssey: Can Canadians Become a Sovereign People?* 2nd ed., rev. Toronto: University of Toronto Press, 1993.

Ryan, Claude. *A Stable Society.* Ed. and trans. Robert Guy Scully. Montréal: Éditions Héritage, 1978.

Saul, John Ralston. *Voltaire's Bastards: The Dictatorship of Reason in the West*. Toronto, London, New York: Penguin, 1992.

Sawatsky, John. *Mulroney: The Politics of Ambition*. Toronto: Macfarlane Walter & Ross, 1991.

Schwartz, Bryan. *Opting In: Improvising the 1992 Federal Constitutional Proposals*. Hull, Que.: Voyageur, 1992.

———. *Still Thinking: A Guide to the 1992 Referendum*. Hull, Que.: Voyageur, Sept 1992.

———. *Fathoming Meech Lake*. Winnipeg: Legal Research Institute, University of Manitoba, 1987.

Schlesinger, Arthur M., Jr. *The Disuniting of America: Reflections on a Multicultural Society*. New York and London: W.W. Norton, 1992.

Schendlinger, Mary, ed. *The Little Blonde Book of Kim Campbell*. Vancouver: Arsenal Pulp Press, 1993.

Schumacher, E.F. *Small Is Beautiful: Economics as if People Mattered*. New York: Perennial Library/Harper & Row, 1973, 1975.

Scott, Frank, and Michael Oliver, eds. *Quebec States Her Case*. Toronto: Macmillan, 1964.

Scowen, Reed. *A Different Vision: The English in Quebec in the 1990s*. Don Mills, Ont.: Maxwell Macmillan, 1991.

Seigal, Arthur. *Politics and the Media in Canada*. Toronto: McGraw-Hill Ryerson, 1983.

Sharpe, Sydney, and Don Braid. *Storming Babylon: Preston Manning and the Rise of the Reform Party*. Toronto: Key Porter, 1992.

Shaw, William F., and Lionel Albert. *Partition: The Price of Quebec's Independence*. Montreal: Thornhill Publishing, 1980.

Sheppard, Robert, and Michael Valpy. *The National Deal*. Toronto: Fleet Books, 1982.

Simeon, Richard, ed. *Must Canada Fail?* Montreal and Kingston: McGill–Queen's University Press, 1977.

———, and Ian Robertson. *State Society and the Development of Canadian Federalism*. Toronto: University of Toronto Press, 1990.

————, and Mary Janigan, eds. *Toolkits and Building Blocks: Constructing a New Canada*. Toronto: C.D. Howe Institute, 1991.

Simpson, Jeffrey. *Spoils of Power: The Politics of Patronage*. Don Mills, Ont.: Collins Publishers, 1988.

————. *Faultlines: Struggling for a Canadian Vision*. Toronto: HarperCollins, 1993.

Smith, Cameron. *Unfinished Journey: The Lewis Family*. Toronto: Summerhill Press, 1989.

Smith, David E., Peter MacKinnon, and John C. Courtney, eds. *After Meech Lake: Lessons for the Future*. Saskatoon: Fifth House, 1991.

Smith, Denis. *Bleeding Hearts . . . Bleeding Country: Canada and the Quebec Crisis*. Edmonton: Hurtig, 1971.

Somerville, David. *Trudeau Revealed: By His Actions and Words*. Richmond Hill, Ont.: BMG Publishing, 1978.

Starr, Richard. *Richard Hatfield: The Seventeen-Year Saga*. Halifax: Formac Publishing, 1987.

Steed, Judy. *Ed Broadbent*. Markham, Ont.: Viking/Penguin, 1988.

Steele, Catherine. *Can Bilingualism Work? Attitudes Toward Language Policy in New Brunswick: The 1985 Public Hearings on the Poirer–Bastarache Report*. Fredericton, NB: New Ireland Press, 1990.

Stevens, Geoffrey. *Stanfield*. Toronto: McClelland & Stewart, 1973.

Stone, I.F., *The Trial of Socrates*. Boston: Little, Brown, 1988.

Swinton, Katherine E., and Carol J. Rogerson, eds. *Competing Constitutional Visions: The Meech Lake Accord*. Toronto: Carswell, 1988.

Tapscott, Don, and Art Caston. *Paradigm Shift: The New Promise of Information Technology*. New York: McGraw–Hill, 1993.

Taylor, Charles. *Radical Tories: The Conservative Tradition in Canada*. Toronto: Anansi, 1982.

————. *Multiculturalism and "The Politics of Recognition."* New Jersey: Princeton University Press, 1992.

————. *Reconciling the Solitudes: Essays on Canadian Federalism and Nationalism*. Montreal and Kingston, McGill–Queen's University Press, 1993.

Tellier, Paul M. *Public Service 2000: A Report on Progress*. Ottawa: Minister of Supply and Services Canada, 1992.

Thomson, Dale. *Vive le Québec Libre*. Toronto: Deneau, 1988.

Thoreau, Henry David. "The Essay on Civil Disobedience." Boston: David R. Godine, 1969.

Thorson, J.T. *Wanted: A Single Canada*. Toronto: McClelland & Stewart, 1973.

Toffler, Alvin. *Power Shift: Knowledge, Wealth, and Violence at the Edge of the 21st Century*. New York: Bantam Books, 1990.

Trench, William. *Only You Can Save Canada: Restoring Freedom and Prosperity*. Agincourt, Ont.: William Trench, 1991.

Troyer, Warner. *200 Days: Joe Clark in Power*. Toronto: Personal Library, 1980.

Trudeau, Right Hon. Pierre Elliott. *Federalism and the French Canadians*. Toronto: Macmillan, 1968.

———. *Trudeau: "A mess that deserves a big NO"*. Toronto: Robert Davies, 1992.

———. *Memoirs*. Toronto: McClelland & Stewart, 1993.

Turner, Right Hon. John Napier. *Politics of Purpose/Politique d'Objectifs*. Toronto: McClelland & Stewart, 1968.

Vidal, Gore. "H. L. Mencken the Journalist," *United States: Essays, 1952–1992*. New York: Random, 1993.

Watts, Ronald L., and Douglas M. Brown, eds. *Options for a New Canada*. Toronto: published in association with IIR, Queen's University and BCNI, University of Toronto Press, 1991.

Vastel, Michel. *The Outsider: The Life of Pierre Trudeau*. Toronto: Macmillan, 1990.

———. *Bourassa*. Toronto: Macmillan, 1991.

Waite, P.B., ed. *The Confederation Debates in the Province of Canada, 1865*. Carleton Library, Number 2. Toronto: McClelland & Stewart, 1963.

———. *The Life and Times of Confederation, 1864–1867: Politics, Newspapers, and the Union of British North America*. Toronto and Buffalo: University of Toronto Press, 1963, 1977.

Watts, Ronald L., and Douglas M. Brown, eds. *Canada: The State of the*

Federation, 1990. Kingston, Ont.: Institute of Intergovernmental Relations (IIR) (Queen's University), 1990.

Weaver, Kent, ed. *The Collapse of Canada?* Washington, D.C.: Brookings Institution, 1992.

Webber, Jeremy. *Reimagining Canada: Language, Culture, Community and the Canadian Constitution.* Kingston and Montreal: McGill–Queen's University Press, 1994.

Westell, Anthony. *Paradox: Trudeau as Prime Minister.* Scarborough, Ont.: Prentice-Hall, 1972.

Weston, Greg. *Reign of Error.* Scarborough, Ont.: McGraw-Hill, 1988.

Wilson, Edmund. *O Canada: An American's Notes on Canadian Culture.* New York: Noonday Press/Farrar, Straus and Giroux, 1964.

Will, George F. *The Morning After: American Successes and Excesses, 1981–1986.* New York: Free Press, 1986.

Wilson, H.T. *Retreat from Governance: Canada and the Continental-International Challenge.* Hull, Que.: Voyageur, 1989.

Woods, Shirley. *Her Excellency Jeanne Sauvé.* Halifax: Formac Publishing, 1987.

Young, Robert. *Confederation in Crisis.* Toronto: Lorimer, 1991.

Young, Walter D. *Democracy and Discontent: Progressivism, Socialism and Social Credit in the Canadian West.* Frontenac Library: Geoffrey Milburn, gen. ed. Toronto: Ryerson Press, 1969.

Index

A

"À la prochaine fois," 69
Aberhart, William, 60
aboriginals: Charter of Rights and Freedoms (S. 35), 77–78; Charlottetown Accord, response to, 539–40. *See also* Matthew Coon-Come; Georges Erasmus; Ron George; Ovide Mercredi; Métis; native self-government
Aboriginal Peoples, Royal Commission on, 344, 352, 625
Act of Union (1841), 326n
Ad Hoc Committee of Women on the Constitution, 175
Adolph, Carolyn, 593
AFN (Assembly of First Nations). *See* Georges Erasmus; Ovide Mercredi
Aislin (Terry Mosher), 64
Alboim, Elly, 392–93
Allaire, Jean, 204n, 651. *See also* Mario Dumont; Parti Action Démocratique du Québec
Allaire Report (*A Quebec free to choose*), 253–54, 257–58, 446–47, 497–98; Sheila Copps supports, 257; Claude Ryan opposes, 257
Alliance for Employment Equity, 622. *See* employment equity

Alliance Ontario, 159
Alliance for the Preservation of English (APEC), 159–60, 232, 253, 498, 499–501, 502, 658, 695–98. *See also* Ron(ald) Leitch
Alliance Quebec (AQ), 214, 254, 302, 356, 497–98, 575, 582
Allmand, Warren, 601n
Allore, Louis, 526–27, 528
Ambrozic, Aloysius, 667–68
Amiel, Barbara, 300
Ancelet, Barry (U.S.), 493n
Andre, Harvie, 177, 261, 359, 463, 490, 550
Andrew, Jock, 124–25, 510–11
Anderson, David, 662
Anderson, Rick, 615
Anderson, Virgil, 658
Andrus, David, 525
Anglican Church. *See* Church of England
Annual Performance Review, 153. *See also* Merit Principle
APEC. *See* Association for the Preservation of English in Canada
Arbour, Pierre, 249
Arendt, Hannah, 367
Arès, Georges, 151, 432
Arthurs, Harry, 215–17
Article 19 (group), 585–86
Article 19 (UN legislation). *See* United Nations Commission on Human Rights

Assembly of First Nations (AFN). *See* Georges Erasmus; Ovide Mercredi
Association canadienne-française de l'Alberta (ACFA), 151, 432
Association canadienne-française de l'Ontario (ACFO), 125, 468
Association culturelle franco-canadienne de la Saskatchewan, 148
Association in Favour of Meech Lake, 379
asymmetric federalism, 243
Atkinson, Lloyd, 670
Atwood, Margaret, 488, 503, 541
Authier, Philip, 593
Axworthy, Lloyd, 679n

B

Bacon, Lise, 590–91
Bakan, Joel, 213
Ballantyne, John, 576. *See* Gord McIntyre
Bank of Canada. *See* John Crow
Bank Credit Analyst Research Group, 543
Banting, Keith, 350
Barker, Paul, 194–95
Barlow, Maude, 504–5, 507, 657
Barrett, Matthew, 354–55, 371–73, 487, 540
Bassett, Isabel, 640

Baudais, Rupert, 148
Bayefsky, Anne, 209–10, 332, 339
Bean, Daryl, 631–32. See Public Service Alliance of Canada; Rand formula
Beatty, Perrin, 606, 615
Beauchamp, Claude, 354, 377, 443
Beauchemin, Yves, 235, 243–44, 364n, 555
Beaudoin–Dobbie committee. See Special Joint Committee on a Renewed Canada (Castonguay–Dobbie; later Beaudoin–Dobbie)
Beaudoin–Edwards Special Joint Committee . . . See Special Joint Committee on the Process for Amending the Constitution (Beaudoin–Edwards committee)
Beaudoin, Gérald A., 53, 121, 238
joins Castonguay–Dobbie committee, 271
Beaudoin, Laurent, 372, 377, 387n
Beck, John, 637. See also Preston Manning
Bédard, Marc-Andre, 50
Behiels, Michael, 197, 614
Béland, Claude, 230, 676
Bélanger–Campeau Commission (B–C Commission) (1990), 189, 199, 223–40, 555
Bélanger, Guy, 338
Bélanger, Michel, 225, 228
Bélanger, Réal, 249–50
Bennett, R.B. (1930–35), 389
Bercuson, David, 192–93
Berger, Thomas, 207
Berlin Wall, 161
Bernier, Ivan, 210
Bernier, Jean, 34
Berton, Pierre, 102, 140, 304
Bertrand, Jean-Jacques, 43, 265
Betkowski, Nancy, 542
Bi–Bi Cultural Commissioners . . . See Bilingualism and Biculturalism, Royal Commission on
Bibby, Reginald (*Mosaic Madness*), 5
Bilingual Districts Advisory

Board (BDAB), 37, 45–47, 52, 57n, 130, 137
bilingualism. See Official Bilingualism
Bilingualism and Biculturalism, Royal Commission on (Bi–Bi Commission or Bi–Bi Cultural Commission) (1965, 1967), 19, 25, 367, 462; bilingualism, historically, 22, 56; Canada, "greatest crisis in its history," 31, 136; Diefenbaker on, 55; establishment of, 15–16; false premise: "her two official languages are English and French," 17, 21, 23, 31; on "founding races," 17; final report (1967), 14, 21, 23, 24, 36; preliminary report (1965), 21, 30, 136; selection of participants, 120; terms of reference, 15, 21–22. See also Bilingual Districts Advisory Board; Joseph Thorson
Bill 2 (Sask., 1988) (Fr. lang. rts.), 148
Bill 8 (Ont., 1986) (Fr. lang. rts.), 129–31, 137, 226, 468, 492n, 618, 659; Sault Ste. Marie, 162
Bill 22 (Que., 1974) (Fr. lang. rts.), 44, 53, 79, 81, 113, 115, 264–65, 656
Bill 48 (Ont., 1993) (Ont. Social Contract Act), 608, 690
Bill 56 (Ont., 1993, never enacted, civil rights law), 692
Bill 63 (Que., 1969) (Fr. lang. rts.), 42–44, 79, 81, 265
Bill 79 (Ont., 1994) (employment equity), 413, 618, 653, 673, 690–92
Bill 86 (Que., 1993) (sign law), 554, 565, 591, 629, 645n
Bill 90 (Que., 1990) (Bélanger–Campeau Commission), 227
Bill 101 (Que., 1977) (French Language Charter), 52, 53, 79, 81, 113, 115, 130, 131–32, 149, 151, 156, 158, 203, 493, 656
Bill 150 (Que., 1992) (Referendum), 352, 356, 359, 405, 417, 453–54, 458

Bill 167 (Ont., 1994) (same-sex amendment act), 666–69
Bill 178 (Que., 1988) (sign law), 6, 44–45, 131, 157–58, 200, 214, 240n, 337, 542, 578–79. See also Gord McIntyre
Bill C–18 (Can., 1994) (electoral boundaries), 663
Bill C–40 (Can., 1990) (dividing CBC into Fr. and Eng.), 389–90, 400n
Bills C–43, C–46, C–114 (Can., 1988; 1989; 1993) (conflict of interest), 607
Bill C–72 (Can., tabled 1987) (Offic. Biling.), 137–38, 152, 164, 173, 229–30
Bill C–81 (Can., 1992) (Referendum), 359, 407–8, 459
Bill C–93 (Canadian Multiculturalism Act, 1988), 155–56
Bill C–114 (Can., 1993) ("Gag Law"), 642
Bill of Rights (Can.), 216; of John Diefenbaker, 21–22; of Trudeau, 37. See also Charter of Rights and Freedoms
Bissonnette, Lise, 273n, 301–3, 630
Black, Conrad, 277, 284, 300, 301, 304, 372, 380–82, 416, 421, 529, 565, 647n, 649–50; on free trade, 140
Black, Hugo (U.S.), 281
Blackburn, Jean-Pierre, 271
Blaikie, Peter, 273n
Blais, Pierre, 539
Blakeney, Allan, 76, 383
Blatchford, Christie, 456
Blenkarn, Don, 179, 487, 540, 639, 650–51
Bliss, Michael, 188, 253, 327n, 426, 649
Bloc Populaire, 16, 367
Blohm, Robert (U.S.), 346–47, 507, 673
Bloom, Allan (U.S.), 218
BNA Act (British North America Act of 1867), 20, 52, 59, 205, 336; Section 26 (addition of Senators), 228; Section 90 (disallowance), 44, 53, 132, 157, 206, 449n; Section 91 ("Peace, Order, and good Government of

Canada"), 671, 679n; Section 121 (interprovincial trade), 121, 336–37, 623, 632, 672; Section 133 (languages), 31, 44, 53, 205, 326; patriation, 50, 57n, 70–83

Borden, Robert, 141

Born With a Tooth, Milton, 479

Bothwell, Robert, 43, 108, 273n

Bouchard, Benoît, 225, 233, 550–51; BC cannot be "distinct society," 162; Canadian Space Agency, funding to, 238; on Meech, 159; at Mont Gabriel Conference, 122, 124–25; Quebec, industrial aid package to, 271; on shifting major powers to Quebec, 360; World Hot Air Balloon Championship (1991), funding to, 225

Bouchard, Jacques, 110

Bouchard, Lucien, 353, 635–36, 662, 671; Bloc Québécois (BQ), formation, 224, 699–700; plan to gain sovereignty on election, 701–2; Canada, structural problems, 627; ——, "The problem with Canada is Quebec . . . ," 660–61; illness, 676; Rafe Mair, interview with, 665; Meech, 165; monarchy, allegiance to, 630; Mulroney, betrays, 168–69, 173; Quebec referendum (1980), 124; Sept-Îles speech, author of, 110; sovereigntist, not separatist, 353; 3M process a failure, 406; timetable on sovereignty, 660–61; vision of Quebec/Canada, 168–69

Boudria, Don, 181n

Bourassa, Henri (1868–1952), 301, 326n. See Bloc Populaire

Bourassa, Robert, 63, 110, 131, 302, 336, 407, 410, 417, 491, 660, 636; Allaire committee and Report, 262; alliance with Parizeau on Meech, 165; bilingualism, provincial authority, 44–45; Bill 2 (Fransaskois), comments on, 151; and Bill 178 (sign law), 131, 157, 542; Canada, preservation required, 434, 629; Charlottetown, as best gains for Quebec since Confederation, 444; ——, consequences of failure, 414, 454, 464, 481, 490; ——, legal text of, 480; de Gaulle, 13; and demonstrations, 167n; "distinct society," 223, 351, 433; dualism, 148; during FLQ crisis, 48–49; Fortier's remarks on Bill 101, reaction to, 149; illness, 233, 239n; *Mastering Our Future* (1985), 114, 115; manpower, transfer of, 614; Meech, 128–81, 223; perception of guarantees Quebec achieved, 433; notwithstanding clause, 131, 212–13; Norman nature of, 312, 437; Official Bilingualism, supports Trudeau, 427, 434; role in patriation of Constitution, 80; "Quebec is a nation," 427; "—— is today and forever a distinct society," 223; ——, the priority of, 129, 171, 438, 440; ——, right to choose sovereignty, 458; supranational parliament, 163; Task Force on National Unity (Pépin-Robarts), role in, 51; Trudeau, view of, 475; on UN judgement in favour of Gord McIntyre, 587; value of Canada, 345; Victoria Charter, 50. See also Bill 22; Bill 101; Bill 178; Mont Gabriel Conference; notwithstanding clause; Gil Rémillard

Bourbeau, André, 614

Bourgault, Pierre, 247–48, 272

Bourgon, Jocelyne, 663, 678n. See also Merit Principle

Boutros-Ghali, Boutros (UN), 555, 620

Bovard, James (U.S.), 663

Bowker, Marjorie, 511

Boyd, Marion, 668

Boyer, Patrick, 564, 639

Brassard, Jacques, 271–72, 357, 433, 462

Brassard, Pierre (Rrrraymond Beaudoin), 623

Brimelow, Peter, 303–4

British North America Act of 1867. See BNA Act

Broadbent, Ed[ward], 51, 80, 138, 161, 486, 493n, 590; notwithstanding clause, supports, 237

Brockville incident, 159–60

Bronfman, Charles, 233

Brookhiser, Richard (U.S.), 340–41, 416

Brookings Institution (U.S.), 350, 645n

Brown, Burt, 464–65, 475. See also Triple-E Senate

Brown, Colin M., 24

Brown, Rosemary, 413. See also Ontario Human Rights Commission

Buchanan, John, 80, 169

Buchanan, Patrick (U.S.), 621

Bulloch, John, 559

Burke, Edmund (1729–97) (U.K.), 2, 80, 277

Burman, Tony, 399

Bush, George (U.S.), 258

Business Council on National Issues (BCNI), 223–24, 259, 354, 357, 368–70, 464, 478, 540

Byfield, Ted, 127, 135, 304, 462, 615, 659

C

Cadieux, Pierre, 418

Cahill, Jack, 98

Cairns, Alan, 51, 191–92

"Calgary Mafia." See Preston Manning

Cameron, Donald, 411, 442, 456, 475

Cameron, Stevie, 358

Camp, Dalton, 38, 129, 283, 304, 333, 383, 395, 400–1n, 503, 616

Campbell, Kim, 398–99, 476, 541, 550–69, 621, 624, 627–47; becomes prime minister: oath of office, 603; bilingual capabilities, 557, 620; campaign dirty tricks, 638–40; Charlottetown, problem with legal text, 475–76; "clear vision," 630; Clinton, relations with U.S. president, 606–8; coalition with Tories, 629; conservative philosophy: "party of the centre and the centre-right," 650; cynicism about political process, 553; deficit, concern and plan to deal with: *Making Government Work for Canada: A Taxpayer's Agenda*: her "mettle," 630, 632, 678n; Department of Heritage created, purpose, 603–4; on education, 617; "enemies of Canada," her version, 555; as justice minister, 538, 544, 578–80, 585, 589, 573–602; on helicopters, 624; Mulroney, distance from, 639; "historians will canonize him," 541, 639; ——, on Ottawa, 615; "warding off the papacy," 557; patronage, 7, 615–16; populist viewpoint ("we *are* you"), 497; Quebec, transfers powers to, 613–14; Reform Party, possible alliance with, 640; on substance and style, 479, 555; (S. 43) Constitution Act (1982), 539; split-sex Senate, supports, 457

Campeau, Jean, 225
"Canada clause," 339, 362, 370, 425n, 433
Canada West Foundation, 147, 193, 385
Canadian Broadcasting Corporation (CBC), 120, 236, 388–401, 501
Canadian Coalition on the Constitution, 210
Canadian Federation of Independent Business. *See* John Bulloch
Canadian Heritage, Department of. *See* Kim Campbell
Canadian Institute of Strategic Studies, 270
Canadian Manufacturers' Association, 206, 336
Canadian Multiculturalism Act. *See* Bill C–93
Canadians for a Unifying Constitution, 368, 532n

Canadians for a Unifying Constitution and The Friends of Meech Lake, 194, 375
Caribbean Canadian African (Ontario) Credit Union Ltd., 612–13. *See also* Lewis Report
Carstairs, Sharon, 152, 170, 228, 455, 673
Cartier, Sir George Étienne (1814–73), 635
Cartier, Jacques, 12
Castonguay, Claude, 26, 253, 270, 378–80, 540, 672; joins Castonguay-Dobbie committee, 266; resigns, 271; Charlottetown, consequences of failure, 459; and Fulton–Favreau formula, 57n; on distinct society, 428; *Meech Lake: Setting the Record Straight*, 196; on Task Force on National Unity (Pépin–Robarts), 51; Victoria Charter (1971), 50–51
Castonguay–Dobbie. *See* Special Joint Committee on a Renewed Canada
Catholicism. *See* Roman Catholic Church
censorship, in education. *See* John Fekete
Centre for Human Rights and Democratic Development. *See* Ed(ward) Broadbent
Ceramic Snowflake. *See* Order of Canada; Merit Principle
Cernetig, Miro, 558
Champlain, Samuel de, 12, 131
Chaput, Marcel, 247, 251n
Chaput-Rolland, Solange, 53
Charest committee. *See* Jean Charest
Charest, Jean, 558, 564, 603, 606, 639; becomes deputy PM under Campbell, 603; Charest committee, 163–64, 165, 166, 169, 369; Conservative legacy, an "important heritage," 675; Mulroney as "best leader," 258; Constitution Act (1982) (S. 43), 539; sovereignty-association, view of, 675, 679n
Charles, Prince of Wales (U.K.), 672

Charlottetown Accord, 426–48, 491; reached, 447, 453
Charlton, Brian, 653
Charter Challenge Program. *See* Court Challenges Program
Charter of Rights (Que.), 157
Charter of Rights and Freedoms, 6, 35, 71–73, 74–75, 76–80, 155, 205, 425n, 479, 552; Section 1 (reasonable limits prescribed), 681; Section 14 (right to interpreter), 673; Section 16 (Official Languages), 73; Section 23 (Minority Language Education Rights), 568n; and notwithstanding clause (S. 33), 72–74, 79, 157, 212–13, 449n; Section 35 (aboriginal peoples), 77–78. *See also* Pierre Elliott Trudeau; Constitution Act (1982)
Chartran, Gilbert, 169
Chateauguay Valley English-Speaking Association (CVESPA), 498, 575–76, 578, 580–82, 588, 596, 601n. *See also* Maurice King
Chirac, Jacques (Fr.), 430
Chrétien, Jean, 68, 98, 102, 271, 431, 628, 638–40, 648–73; banking system "strangling" the country, 617–18; on Kim Campbell's fluency in French, 620; Charlottetown, supports, 447, 459; ——, consequences of failure, 445; Constitution Act (1982) (S. 43), 546; "date with destiny," 554; distinct society, supports, 263; and Michel Dupuy scandal, 400n; flip-flops on FTA/NAFTA, "no price paid," 656–58; future, bleak, 619; infrastructure program, 634; multiculturalism, supports, 263, 662; native self-government, supports, 263; nine-point program: jobs, 447; notwithstanding clause, supports, 214; Official Bilingualism, 236; patronage, 7, 673; role in patriation of Constitution,

80; Red Book (*Creating Opportunity: The Liberal Plan for Canada*), 632, 634, 648, 656–57, 661, 665; on referendums, 76; attacks Reform Party, 638; on same-sex conjugal relations (Bill 167, Ont.), 668; social safety net, importance, timetable to debate, 630–31; *Straight from the Heart*, 651; sufficient vote for Quebec sovereignty, 272

Church of England, 159, 668, 672

Citizens' Forum on Canada's Future. *See* Keith Spicer

Civil Code (Que.), 72, 111, 205, 206

civil service of Canada. *See* Federal Public Service of Canada

Clark, Joe, 59–62, 87–89, 99, 178, 263, 331, 362, 418, 431, 446, 542, 547, 555; on Beaudoin–Dobbie commission report, 340; becomes PM, 53, 59; Beirut, "Canada could become," 461; "we are a bilingual nation," 60; on Bill 101, 565; Charest, "best leader," 563; Charlottetown, "Canadian political process at its best," 459, 478; ——, consequences of failure, 445, 480, 487; ——, legal text unnecessary for referendum, 460, 467; "Community of communities," 59, 113, 201, 544–45; "deux nations" view of, 60–62; "distinct society," supports, 337, 351, 358; and Durham Report, 26; equality, 686; free trade, 140; Rafe Mair, interview with, 474; and Gord McIntyre case, 585; and Mulroney as political rival, 90; *A Nation Too Good to Lose*, 686; on Oka crisis, 484; Official Bilingualism, 60–62, 260; Ontario, Quebec, value systems of, 61–62; on patriation of Constitution, 70–71, 80; Pearson accord, 414, 420, 422–23, 426, 431; open democracy, 333; public's right to know, 362; on possible referendum, 353; Referendum failed, negotiations succeeded, 540, 562; Riel, Louis, history revised, 341; Social Charter, support for, 348; on sovereignty-association, 66–67; Task Force on National Unity (Pépin-Robarts), 51; Trudeau, early thoughts on, 60–61. *See also* Renewal Conferences on the Constitution

Clark, Ramsay (U.S.), 565

Clemenceau, Georges (1841–1929), 207, 219n

Clinton, Bill (U.S.), 545, 605–6, 608

Coates, Robert, 41n

Cohen, Andrew, 136, 299, 562–63

Cohen, Dian, 196

collectivism, 654. *See also* William Gairdner

Collins, Doug, 519–20

Collister, Ron, 305–6

Comeau, Paul-André, 120

Committee for an Independent Canada, 503

"Community of the Canadas." *See* Thomas J. Courchene

"Community of communities." *See* Joe Clark

Confederation of National Trade Unions (CNTU) (Confédération des syndicats nationaux) (Que.), 165, 426. *See also* Gérald Larose

Confederation of Regions Party (CoR), 266. *See also* Elmer Knutson; Arch Pafford

conflict of interest. *See* Bills C–43, C–46, C–114 (1993; 1989; 1988)

Connors, "Stompin' Tom," 484

Conquest of Quebec (1759), 15, 18, 77, 242–43. *See also* Christian Dufour

Conseil du patronat du Québec (CPQ), 229, 374, 414, 446–47, 621. *See also* Ghislain Dufour

Constitution. *See* BNA Act; Charter of Rights and Freedoms; Constitution Act (1982)

Constitution Act (1791), 327n

Constitution Act (1982), 6, 71–80, 119; amending requirements, 43, 49, 145, 208; Forsey's interpretation, 134; ratification of Meech defined in, 136; Section 43 (boundary disputes; amending process), 200–1, 537–39. *See also* Charter of Rights and Freedoms

Cook, Ramsay, 143n, 199, 382

Cooke, Dave, 609

Coon-Come, Matthew, 225, 363n, 440, 468

Cooper, Barry, 192–93

Co-operative Commonwealth Federation (CCF), 501

Copps, Sheila, 260; Allaire Report, supports, 257; bilingualism, supports, 670–671; education, 258; on leadership, 258; member of Rat Pack, 181n

Corbeil, Jean, 639

Corcoran, Terence, 374

Côté, Pierre-F., 489

Council for Canadian Unity (CCU), 69, 69n, 351, 485–86, 493n

Council of Canadians, 503–4

Courchene, Thomas J., 51, 121, 196, 199–201, 236, 539; on Bill 178: 200; "Community of the Canadas," 199–200, 253; on "distinct society," 200; *Rearrangements: The Courchene Papers*, 199, 201

Cournoyer, Jean, 165

Cournoyer, Nellie, 445

Court Challenges Program (Charter Challenge Program or Federal Court Challenges Program), 598, 660. *See also* Gord McIntyre

Couture, Pauline, 589, 623

Coyne, Andrew, 306–7

Coyne, Deborah, 181n, 188, 210–11, 379, 537–38, 546

Crane, David, 300

Creighton, Donald (1902–79), 11, 448

Creighton, Douglas, 290

Cressy, Gordon, 476

Crispo, John, 196, 390, 479
Crombie, David, 66, 96
Crosbie, John, 96, 158, 161, 180, 418, 421, 478–79, 508–9, 551–52
Cross, James, 48–49
Crouse, Lloyd, 629
Crow, John, 345, 478
CRTC (Canadian Radio–Television and Telecommunications Commission). *See* Keith Spicer
Cuff, John Haslett, 439
Cummings, Gary, 522–24
Cuomo, Mario, 347
CVESPA. *See* Chateauguay Valley English-Speaking Association
Cyr, Raymond, 354, 377
Czechoslovakia, 543–44

D

Danson, Timothy, 212–13
d'Aquino, Thomas, 196, 354, 368–70, 445, 464, 540. *See also* Business Council on National Issues (BCNI)
Davey, Keith, 281
Davidson, Elizabeth, 576. *See also* Gord McIntyre
Davies, Robertson, 505
Davis, Bill, 76, 80, 383–84, 486, 644, 647n; and Hugh Segal, 333, 383, 583, 584
"Debt Clock," 660
de Chastelain, John, 226. *See also* Oka crisis
de Cotret, Robert, 566–67
de Cuéllar, Javier Pérez, 576
de Gaulle, Charles (Fr.), 12–14, 65; "invented sovereignty association" (Lisée), 12
Delacourt, Susan, 175, 307, 322
Demers, Serge, 361
Desbarats, Peter, 397, 401n
Deschamps, Yvon, 241, 542, 656
Deschênes, Jules, 248–49
Desmarais, Paul, 196, 301, 375, 377, 380, 383, 387n, 421, 559, 561
de Tocqueville, Alexis (1805–59), 653–54, 682–83
Deutsche Bank Group (Ger.), 164, 339–40, 345
deux nations, theory of, 17, 38, 39–40, 113, 120, 265, 441.

See also founding races and cultures
Devine, Grant, 148, 150, 170, 269
Dickson, Brian, 344, 479
Diefenbaker, John George (1895–1979), 7, 326n, 400n, 543; David Bercuson on, 193; and Dalton Camp, 30, 41n, 87, 305, 326n; Canadian Bill of Rights, 22, 216; bilingualism, 55, 58n; the burden of the middle class: taxation, 682; on democracy, 116; and *deux nations* theory, 40; on Fulton–Favreau formula, 57n; "isms that are sweeping the world today" (1946), 682; on patronage, 7; on the role of prime minister, 14; on Trudeau, 55
Dingwall, David, 531
Dion, Léon, 26n, 237, 244–45, 446
Dionne, E.J., 661
"distinct society," 217, 326n, 339; BC claims it is a, 162; Clark always pushing, 351; Forsey attacks, 134; Lévesque supports, 112; Meech, clause missing from, 174; ——, meaning, 174–75; Mont Gabriel Conference/Rémillard, 123; David Peterson, 129; in Pearson accord, 425n; Peterson supports, 361; Sauvé supports, 161; 3M results, 362; *Toronto Star* supports, 337; Trudeau attacks, 138
Dobbie, Dorothy, 266, 268–69, 270
Dobbie–Castonguay (Castonguay–Dobbie). *See* Special Joint Committee on a Renewed Canada
Dobbin, Murray, 501, 556
Doer, Gary, 150, 152
Dominion Bond Rating Service, 418, 674
Donderi, Don, 234
Dorion, Jean, 356
Double-E Senate, 424–25; defined, 442. *See also* Senate reform
Doucet, Philippe, 509–10

Dougherty, Kevin, 300
Douglas, Tommy, 14
Drew, George, 101
Droege, Wolfgang, 500
Drouin, Marie-Josée, 51
Drouin, Richard, 350
Drummond, Ian, 43, 108
D'Souza, Dinesh, 5, 218, 611
D'Souza, Francis, 585–86
dualism. *See deux nations*, theory of
Dubuc, Alain, 307–8
Duff, James, 120
Dufour, Christian, 243
Dufour, Ghislain, 374, 446–47
Dukakis, Michael (U.S.), 177
Dumont, Mario, 651, 674. *See also* Parti Action Démocratique du Québec
Dumont, Yvon, 204n, 344, 674
Dunnell, Milton, 308
Dunton, Davidson, 16, 25, 51
Duplessis, Maurice, 16
Dupuy, Michel, 400n
Durham, Lord (1792–1840), 23–24, 26
Dussault, René, 625

E

Edmonston, Phil(ip), 234
Edmonton Declaration, 126, 128–29, 135
Edwards, Jim, 238, 389, 564
election results (fed., 1993), 646n
Electoral Boundaries Readjustment Act (suspension of, 1994, Bill C–18), 663
Elizabeth II (Br.), 73, 224, 420–21
Ellis, Marc, 256
Ellul, Jacques (Fr.), 232, 399–400
Elton, David, 147, 385, 418
employment equity, 622, 626n, 652, 653–54, 679n. *See also* Bill 79 (Ont.); *Harassment and Discrimination in Ontario Universities, Framework Regarding Prevention of* (1993); Ontario Human Rights Code; Public Service 2000
"enemies of Canada," 443–44
English, John, 43, 108
Entwhistle, Mark, 421, 460, 469, 615–616
equality. *See* Bill 79 (Ont.,

Index

1994); Alexis de Tocqueville; employment equity
Equality Party, 160, 227, 438, 458
Erasmus, Georges, 166
Erskine, John (1879–1951), 8
Estey, Willard, 211–12
étapisme (step by step), 68, 242, 356
"Evil Knievel" of Confederation, 181
executive federalism, 155–56, 187, 191–92, 198, 333, 360, 385, 390, 491
Expansionist Party (U.S.), 164
EXPO '67, 11–14, 27

F

Faribault, Marcel, 39, 41n
Farnsworth, Clyde H. (U.S.), 597, 643
Farquharson, Charlie (Don Harron), 506
Favreau, Guy, 57
"Federal Power of Disallowance and Reservation." *See* BNA Act (S. 90); Charlottetown Accord
Federal Public Service of Canada, 80, 81–82, 152–55, 415
La fédération de francophone hors Québec (FFHQ), 148
Fekete, John, 610–11
Fête Nationale. *See* St. Jean Baptiste Day
Fife, Robert, 584
Filmon, Gary, 150, 152, 170, 174, 228, 422, 488; Charlottetown, Bourassa seeks surrender, 435; parallel accord, 159; "roll of the dice," blames, 180; warns about Manitoba's constitutional amendment procedure for Meech, 162, 176, 177
Findley, Timothy, 503, 506, 542
Finestone, Sheila, 662, 670
Finkelstein, Neil, 214–15
FIRA (Foreign Investment Review Agency). *See* Brian Mulroney
First Nations of Treaty 6 and 7, 467–68
Fisher, Douglas, 300, 308–9, 398, 399, 530–31, 584–85
Flanagan, Thomas, 462–63, 500, 520–22, 532n, 615

Flood, A.L. (Al), 374
FLQ crisis (1970). *See* Front de libération du Québec
Fondation Octobre 70 (Que.), 57, 623
les Forces Québécois, 166
Ford, Henry (U.S.) (1863–1947), 265
Forsey, Eugene (1904–91), 134
Forster, Victor, 513
Fortier, D'Iberville, 149, 164, 165, 234, 260–62, 264; Air Canada, prosecutes, 229; Bill C–72, defending, 173, 229; family name, 181n; and PetroCan, 234
Fortier, Yves, 576
Fortin, Pierre, 188
Forum de l'Emploi, 230. *See also* Claude Béland
Fotheringham, Allan, 309, 395, 655
founding races and cultures, 15, 18, 38, 41n, 77–78, 217, 250, 326n, 327n, 372, 441; in Trudeau's Constitution Act (1982), 407; and multiculturalism, 51, 217–18; native peoples' reaction to, 338; in Ontario, 130; second BDAB, according to, 46; Victoria Charter, 51. *See also* multiculturalism; Bill C–93 (Multiculturalism Act)
Fournier, Pierre, 68, 189–90
Fox, Francis, 196
Fox, Paul, 45
Francis, Diane, 310–12, 353, 445
"Fransaskois," 148
Fraser, Blair (1909–68), 22–23
Fraser, Graham, 120, 175, 300, 313, 322, 362
Fraser, Phil, 407
Free Trade Agreement (FTA) (signing, Oct 4/87; enactment, Jan 1/89), 139–42, 144n, 156, 351, 656–58
French Language Charter. *See* Bill 101; Gord McIntyre
French Language Services Act. *See* Bill 8 (Ont.)
The Friends of Canada, 485
Friends of Canadian Broadcasting, 506–7
The Friends of Meech Lake, 194

Fromm, Paul, 521–22, 526, 532n
Front de libération du Québec (FLQ): crisis (1970), 48–50, 57, 131, 151, 355, 655. *See also* October crisis of 1970
Front du Québec français, 43
Fryers, Clifford, 522, 524–28
Fukuyama, Francis, 4
Fulton, E. Davie. *See* Fulton–Favreau formula
Fulton–Favreau formula (Fulton formula), 57n

G

Gagné, Jean-Paul, 557–58
Gagnier, Dan, 171, 471–72n, 420, 423
Gagnon, Christiane, 631, 655
Gagnon, Lysiane, 301, 312–13
Gairdner, William, 332–33, 393, 401n, 501–2, 518, 654, 684
Galbraith, Kenneth, 5
Gamble, John, 524–28, 532–33n
Gauthier, Robert, 665. *See also* Gord McIntyre
gay rights. *See* Marion Boyd; Church of England; Bob Rae; Roman Catholic Church
"gender equality," 628. *See also* Bill 79 (Ont.); employment equity; Senate reform
Gendron Commission (1972), 43
George, Ron, 344, 435. *See also* Native Council of Canada
Geraets, Théodore F., 197–98
Gerin, François, 169
Gervais, Marcel, 272
Getty, Don, 384, 408, 418, 432–33, 441–42, 502–3, 537; Alberta to lead constitutional reform, 238; bilingualism, challenged, 334; Charlottetown, 434, 437, 444; first "unauthorized" Senate election, 160; Mont Gabriel Conference, support for Quebec's demands, 128; multiculturalism, challenged, 334; native inherent rights to self-government, 409; Pearson

accord, 422, 434. *See also* Triple-E Senate

Ghiz, Joe, 171, 361, 439, 475

"Ghiz Proposal" ("No-Net-Loss" or "Modified Mc-Kenna" proposal). *See* Frank McKenna

Gibb–Clark, Margot, 372–73

Gibbins, Roger, 193, 436

Gibbon, Edward, 684

Gibson, Douglas, 656

Goar, Carol, 117, 125, 300, 313–14

Godfrey, John, 314–15

Godin, Silvie, 436

Goldbloom, Victor, 264–65, 357–58, 618, 625n, 664; aboriginal languages, supports, 358; Bill 22, supports, 264; Bill C–72, "The law is not an ass. . . ," 641–42; "bona fides beyond dispute," *Star* says, 671; Canadians, on bilingualism, "don't know what they're talking about," 658; on Getty's suggestion to reconsider Official Bilingualism, 336; "Grants and Contributions" beyond federal institutions, policy on, 560–61; Official Bilingualism, justification for historical exclusivity, 541; Ontario, chastizes, 671

Goldfarb, Martin, 488, 489

Goodman, Eddie, 583

Goods and Services Tax (GST), 228, 553

Gorbachev, Mikhail, 171

Gordon, Sue, 601

Gouvernement du Québec Commission de protection de la langue française. *See* tongue troopers

Grace, John, 409, 423, 563

Graham, Bill, 611. *See also* racism

Granatstein, Jack, 273n, 482

Grant, George, 326n, 500–1, 684

Grant, Robert, 179

Gratton, Michel, 300, 395, 583, 601–2n

Gray, Charlotte, 583

Gray, Herbert, 663

Great Whale project, 345, 347, 350, 363–64n

Greenspan, Edward (Eddie), 212–13

Gregg, Allan, 129

Greider, William (U.S.), 512, 685

Grey, Deborah, 175, 253

Grey, Julius, 302, 576–77, 579, 580–81, 587

Grier, Ruth, 618

Groupe Action–Québec, 651

Groupe de Recherche Éthos, 189

Groupe Réflexion–Québec (GRQ), 204n

Group 22, 383, 384

Gwyn, Richard, 45, 210, 315–16, 502, 545, 655, 675–76

Gzowski, Peter, 19–20, 69, 393–94, 400–1n, 633

H

Hageman, Margaret, 622. *See* employment equity

Haig, Graham, 461–62, 480, 493n, 624

Hamilton, Alexander (1755?-1804), 141

Harassment and Discrimination in Ontario Universities, Framework Regarding Prevention of (1993), 609–11, 693–94. *See also* Mandatory School Policies. . . ; Lewis Report; Donna Young

Harcourt, Michael, 442, 456, 666

Harper, Elijah: blocks debate in Manitoba legislature, 175–76; kills Meech, 180; Mulroney scoffs at delaying tactic, 177

Harrigan, Kenneth, 372

Harris, Mike, 549n, 653, 667

Hartmann, Anne, 520–22

Hatfield, Richard, 80, 128, 138, 148, 213

Havel, Václav, 408

Hawkes, David, 121

Haynes, Arden, 355

helicopters, 349–350, 357, 408, 648

Henderson, Keith, 547

Henry IV (1553–1610) (Fr.), 17

Henry, William A., III (1950–94), 659

Heritage Front, 500

Hickman, W. Harry, 47

Hitler, Adolf, 228, 235, 555–56, 659

Hnatyshyn, Ramon, 177, 267, 651

Hogg, Peter, 51, 133, 194, 196

Holden, Richard, 438, 675

Honderich, John, 353, 396–97, 401n

Horner, Bob, 620

Horsman, Jim, 348, 406

Howard, Frank, 152

Howard, Ross, 525

Hughes, Robert (Aus.), 5, 341, 683. *See also* political correctness

Human Rights Institute of Canada. *See* Marguerite Ritchie

Humphrey, John, 575

Humphreys, David L., 59–61

Hurka, Thomas, 195–96, 203

Hurtig, Mel, 503–4, 541–42, 549n, 628

Hutchins, Robert M. (U.S.), 280–81

Hutchinson, Wayne, 525

Hydro-Québec. *See* Great Whale project

I

Imperative Staffing Principle (ISP), 82, 153

Inquiries Act, 17

Institute of Intergovernmental Relations (IIR) (Queen's University, Kingston, Ont.), 117

Institute of Political Involvement, 217

International Centre for Human Rights and Development. *See* Ed(ward) Broadbent

International Covenant on Civil and Political Rights (UN). *See* United Nations Commission on Human Rights

International Institute of Management Development. *See* World Economic Forum

International Monetary Fund (IMF), 269, 553–54

Interpreter, right to have. *See* Charter of Rights and Freedoms

interprovincial trade barriers. *See* BNA Act (Section 121);

Index

John Manley; Brian Mulroney; Michael Wilson

Inuit, 363

Irving, Colin, 213

Irwin, Ron, 661, 662, 666

J

Jackman, Hal, 529, 568

Jackman, Nancy, 175, 667

James Bay II hydro-electric project. See Great Whale project

Jarislowsky, Stephen (U.S.), 172–73

Jefferson, Thomas, 34

Jeffrey, Brooke, 486

Jelinek, Otto, 414

Jewett, Pauline, 507

John Paul II, 667–68

Johnson, Daniel, 660, 666, 672, 673–74

Johnson, Pierre Marc, 115, 361

Johnson, Rita, 269

Johnson, William, 378, 576, 594, 679n

Johnston, Donald, 102, 133

Jones, Frank, 37

K

Kahnawake Mohawk Reserve. See Oka crisis

Kapetanovic, Goran (Yugoslavia), 448

Kaplan, Robert, 138–39

Kantor, Mickey (U.S.), 657

Keaton, Robert, 254, 273n, 497–98

KTLO (Keep The Lid On), 83, 257

Kennedy, Edward (U.S), 665

Kent Commission (1980). See Newspapers, Royal Commission on

Kershaw, Sir Anthony (U.K), 71

Kierans, Eric, 140–41, 196, 400–1n, 515–16, 532n

King, Maurice, 498, 575–76, 581, 588, 596, 602

Kingsley, Jean-Pierre, 461

Kinsella, Warren, 531, 533n

Kipling, Rudyard (1865–1936), 141

Kirkham, Lloyd, 522–24

Kitchen Deal, 75–76, 111

Klein, Ralph, 542

"knife at [Canada's] throat," 237

Knutson, Elmer, 509

Kohl, Helmut (Ger.), 176, 264

Kotcheff, Tim, 398

Krauthamer, Charles (U.S.), 654

Kroeger, Arthur, 332–33

Kuptana, Rosemary, 344, 445

L

Laforest, Guy, 167n

L'Allier, Jean-Paul, 416

Lambert, Phyllis, 235

Lamer, Antonio, 552

Lamont, Lansing (U.S.), 262, 676

Landry, Bernard, 349, 616, 619, 656

Landry, Monique, 561

Landsberg, Michele, 316

"Langevin Agreement." See Meech Lake Accord

Langille, David, 368

Lankin, Frances, 632

Lapham, Lewis (U.S.), 5, 577

Lapierre, Jean, 431

LaPierre, Laurier, 252–53, 273n

Laporte, Pierre, 48

Larose, Gérald, 165, 199

Larose, Jean, 247, 361, 426

"Larry King Live" (U.S.), 560

Laski, Harold, 35

Latouche, Daniel, 246–47, 250n

Lavoie, Gilbert, 557

Laughren, Floyd, 559, 568n, 659

Laurendeau, André (1912–68), 16, 19, 25, 40n, 118, 120, 367

Laurie, Antia (U.S.), 483

Laurier, Sir Wilfrid (1841–1919), 11, 91, 141

Lautens, Gary, 316–17

Laxer, James, 507

Leatherdale, Linda, 170

LeBlanc, Gordon. See Brockville incident

Legault, Josée, 581

Leger, Michel, 224

Le Hir, Richard, 614, 621

Leitch, Ron(ald), 232, 253, 499–501, 502, 592

Lemay, Marcel, 225

Lemco, Jonathan, 26

Lemieux, Jean-Guy, 416

Lesage, Jean, 57n

Leslie, Peter, 117–19, 123, 193, 436

Lesner, Richard (U.S.), 172

Lester, Normand, 356

Levesque, Gérard, 559

Lévesque, René, 63–69, 111, 142; Bill 101, author of, 79, 131; on Constitution Act (1982), 78; on de Gaulle, 13, 14, 65; "distinct society," origin of, 112, 113, 114–15, 129; Draft Agreement on the Constitution, 112–13, 115; on FLQ crisis, 49; An Option for Quebec (1968), 65–66; on the Night of the Long Knives/Kitchen Deal, 76; on Quebec 1980 referendum results, 63; on Québécois, 65–66; sovereignty-association, 63, 66, 112–15; on Trudeau's promise of renewed federalism, 65, 68; "screwed . . . the Canadian way," 73; strategy (étapisme), 67–68, 242; and Trudeau, 64–65, 67–68, 73, 655. See also Bill 101 (French Language Charter)

Lewis, Stephen, 170, 400–1n, 411–12, 423n, 589–90, 652

Lewis Report (Report on Race Relations in Ontario), 411–12, 413, 694. See also racism

Li, David, 665–66

Liberal Council of Hemispheric Affairs (U.S.), 164

Libman, Robert, 227, 458, 587, 588, 596, 674. See also Equality Party

Limbaugh, Rush (U.S.), 5, 283, 349. See also political correctness

Lincoln, Abraham (1809–1865), 29

Lindros, Eric, 270

Lisée, Jean-François, 12

Locke, John (1632–1704), 34

Loiselle, Gilles, 267, 631

Lone-Fighters' Society, 479

Lorimer, James, 507

Lougheed, Peter, 384–86; Charlottetown, consequences of failure, 481–82; intervenor at Renewal Conference, Calgary, 338; Meech, supporter of, 193; role in patriation of Constitution, 80

Luttwak, Edward N., 144n
Lyon, Sterling, 76

M
Maastrich Treaty, 264
McCain, Harrison, 384
McClelland, Jack, 89
McCrae, Jim, 363
McDermid, John, 463
MacDonald, Bob, 231, 300, 317–18, 590–91
MacDonald, Donald, 62, 98, 102
MacDonald, Flora, 196
MacDonald, Ian, 88–89, 109
Macdonald, John A. (1815–91), 38, 45, 93–94, 561, 635, 644
McDonald, Kenneth, 512–13, 628
Macdonald, Neil, 107
McDougall, Barbara, 263, 273n, 418, 463–64, 477–78, 541, 548–49n
Machiavelli, Niccolò, 359
McIntyre, Gord, 283–84, 573–602, 629, 645n, 664–65, 670, 679n
McIntyre, Ian (U.K.), 655–56
Mackasey, Bryce, 106–7, 146
McKenna, Frank, 149, 170, 266, 421; Charlottetown, assessment of, 443; ——, concessions to Quebec required 435; Meech, against, 158, 174; "biggest roller coaster ride," 173; ——, for, 178; "Modified McKenna" ("Ghiz Proposal"), 439, 441; New Brunswick becomes officially bilingual (S. 43), 537, 546; parallel accord, 159, 285–86, 435; referendums, dangerous, 351; split-sex Senate, supports, 456
Mackenzie, Alexander (1764–1820), 613
McKenzie, Dan, 149
McKenzie, Robert, 318
Mackenzie Institute for the Study of Terrorism, Revolution and Propaganda, 394–95
MacLaughlan, Wade, 196
McLaughlin, Audrey, 138, 161, 627–28, 633; Allaire

Report, supports, 258; Bloc Québécois, 567; Charlottetown, view of, 454; Citizens' Forum, 259; notwithstanding clause, supports, 237; Senate, 612; separatist candidate, supports, 234; on a Social Charter, 337; women's rights, 445
Maclean, James, 159
Maclean's, 19, 20
MacLennan, Hugh (1907–90), 199, 241
McLeod, Lyn, 549n, 568n, 653, 667, 671
McLuhan, Marshall, 394
MacMillan, Norman, 236
McMurtry, Roy, 76, 196
McNeil, John, 355
McNeil, Ken, 148
MacNeil, Robert, 172, 488, 505–6
McQueen, Trina, 390–91, 400n
McTeer, Maureen, 467
McWhinney, Edward, 80, 207–8, 257, 442
Magnet, Joseph Eliot, 208
Making Government Work for Canada: A Taxpayer's Agenda. See Kim Campbell
Mair, Rafe, 474, 665
Major, John (U.K), 551
Malarek, Victor, 397–98
Malboeuf, Richard, 638
Maldoff, Eric, 213–14
Mammoliti, George, 668
"Mandatory School Board Policies on Antiracism and Ethnocultural Equity" (Ont.), 609. *See also* Lewis Report
Manley, John, 664, 672
Manning, Ernest C., 18, 60, 135; *Political Realignment*, 135, 440
Manning, E[rnest] Preston, 135, 142, 263–64, 472n, 514–33, 661–62, 687; "Calgary Mafia," 517; Canada, vision of, 262, 514, 531; Charlottetown, early support for, 454; ——, against, 460, 464, 465, 490, 491; ——, vacillating about, 462–63, 475; and Durham Report, 26; expansion,

eastward, Ontario, Quebec, 335, 547; and Tom Flanagan, 462–63; founding races and cultures, 515, 638; and Don Getty, 334; Liberal majority, the end of democracy, 642; monarchy, oath of allegiance, 634; "Mulroney's deal," 427–29, 516; on Mulroney's biggest failure, 440–1; multiculturalism, 262, 530; *The New Canada*, 135–36, 516, 531; Official Bilingualism, 529–30; Okanagan Centre riding association incident, Hitler quoted, 659; party discipline, definition of, 523–24; physical fear of internal controversy/dissent, 517; political correctness, 5, 499, 627; Quebec sovereignty, referendum question needs to be clarified, 669; racism, problems with, 544, 637–38; on Campbell transferring powers to Quebec after the Referendum, 614; Reform platform, 687–89; —— timetable, body of influence, 516, 627, 649; —— as democratic and fiscal conscience, 636; —— as de facto opposition, 649; Senate, need for reform, 455, 662; social safety net, provincial responsiblity, 633, 636
Manning, Morris, 212–13
Mansbridge, Peter, 395, 398, 563
Marchand, Jean, 27–28, 49
Marchi, Sergio, 662, 671
Maritain, Jacques (1882–1973), 40n
"Maritime Mafia." *See* Dalton Camp
Martelle, Ron, 631
Martin, Paul, Jr., 475, 648, 665
Marx, Herbert, 132
Marzolini, Michael ("Pizza Pollster"), 439
Masse, Marcel, 244, 312; and CBC, 388–89; and helicopter contracts, 349, 408, 432; new military base in Quebec, giving funds to,

Index

347; Péquiste commissioner, becomes, 569n; Quebec museums, giving funds to, 238–39, 254; Task Force on National Unity (Pépin–Robarts), 51; Valcartier Canadian Forces Base in Quebec, giving funds to update, 352; Vimy Ridge and Dieppe, misses D-Day ceremony, 350

Mavrinac, Joe, 634

Mazankowski, Don(ald), 178, 263, 335, 345, 360, 428–29, 483, 484, 490, 491, 549n, 550, 551–52, 598, 620

Meech family, 133, 143n

Meech Lake Accord, 128–44; first ratification of, 137, 145–66; process begins, 132–34, 136–39

Meech Lake: Setting the Record Straight, 194, 196

Meech II, 224, 252–73. *See also* Pearson accord

Meekison, Peter, 80, 196

Meisel, John, 121, 196, 391–92, 400n

Memoirs. See Pierre Elliott Trudeau

Mencken, H.L. (1880–1956), 75, 283, 298, 527

Mendes, Errol, 653, 678n

"Mendes formula," 653, 678n

Mercredi, Ovide, 336, 344, 417, 431, 567, 634; Charlottetown, protests exclusion from negotiations, 435; Meech II: AFN begins parallel process, 269; 1992 Referendum, 539–40; on self-determination, 338; on success of 3Ms, 405. *See also* aboriginals; native self-government

Merit Principle, 81–83, 152–54, 167, 357, 456, 622, 628, 653, 678n

Métis, 77, 344–45, 407. *See also* Constitution Act (1982); Louis Riel

Métis National Council, 344. *See also* Yvon Dumont

Mill, John Stuart (1806–73), 34, 36

Mitterand, François (Fr.), 134

"Modified McKenna." *See* Frank McKenna

Mohawk Warriors Society. *See* Oka crisis

Monahan, Patrick, 172, 181n, 200, 259–60, 539

Mont Gabriel Conference (1986), 117–26; report, 118–19, 121–22, 124, 134, 136, 194, 199

Montesquieu, Charles Secondat, Baron de (1689–1755), 34–35

Montmorency Falls conference (Thinkers Conference) (1967), 38–39; "——— Resolution," 38–39, 41n

Montreal *Gazette*, 573–602, 665

Moody's Investors Service, 553, 562

Morin, Claude, 50–51, 242, 250n, 356. *See also étapisme*

"Morningside." *See* Peter Gzowski

Morrison, Judy, 268–69, 475

Morton, David, 477

Morton, Desmond, 68, 196–97, 283, 396

"Mother Corp." *See* CBC

Mounier, Emmanuel, 40n

Mouvement Desjardins (Mouvement des caisses Desjardins), 230, 234, 676

Mouvement Québec. *See* MQF below

Mouvement Québec français (MQF), 156, 352, 361, 433

Mowat, Farley, 503, 506–7, 542

Mulroney, Martin Brian, 69, 87–96, 106, 223–39, 339, 432, 438, 541, 550; Albertans, attacking for failure of Referendum, 542; alliance with separatists in 1984 election campaign, 109–10; anglo Quebecer, answers charges that he is an, 466; bilingualism and politics, Canadians' misunderstanding of, 227; Bill 2 (Fransaskois), "diminishes legal rights," 151; Bill 178 (Que. sign law), supports, 157; on BNA Act, 94–95; and Lucien Bouchard, 109–10, 168–69; Charlottetown, gains in, 476; ———, consequences of

failure of, 454, 459, 466, 467, 469–70, 481, 482, 487, 489–90, 491–92; ———, anger at Trudeau's attack on, 476–77; ———, if first ministers cannot agree on, 350–51; ———, as Mulroney's deal, 483; ———, on "enemies of Canada," 443–44; ———, meets René Lévesque's demands, 444; ———, remarks for posterity on failure of, 467, 543, 560; and Joe Clark, 90; loyalty to, 88–89; cost of Tory survival, 147; dualism: of language rights, 94; dualism/*deux nations*, 90, 93, 94, 95; economic ideal, 91–92; on Foreign Investment Review Agency (FIRA), 108; "Fransaskois," Bill 101: 94; on free trade negotiations, 360; on FTA, 140; on his greatest moment, 443–44; individual and collective rights, balance between, 227; on leadership, 95; Bryce Mackasey incident, 106–8, 557; and Meech, 165–66, 173–75, 176; mentors, 91; and National Energy Policy, 108; notwithstanding clause, 94, 96n, 109–10, 212–13, 560–61; "O Canada kind of guy," 342; open democracy, commitment to, 122; patronage, 7, 105–8, 493n, 551, 561, 567; Pearson accord as Mulroney's deal, 438; "popular" or "effective" PM, 562; Quebec Referendum, promises to pay for, 471n; "rejoice[s]" in minority language constitutional protection outside Quebec, 94; Referendum, possibility of a second try, 488; on Mordecai Richler, 346, 364n; "roll of the dice" remarks, 175, 322; Sept-Îles speech (1984), 109–13, 117, 123–24, 126, 168, 255–56, 363; threats to Quebec about Referendum: "disastrous effect" of

failure, 347; Trudeau, appraisal of, 91–92, 559–60; ——, compared to, 146; on Trudeau's attack on Charlottetown, 466; on Trudeau's attack on Meech, 133–34; as Trudeau's protégé, 90; on United Nations on Canada, 430; universality as "sacred trust," 108; on veto for Quebec, 109; vision of Canada, 90–95; *Where I Stand*, 89, 90–95, 109, 122
Mulroney, Mila, 607
multiculturalism, 15, 355, 658, 662, 670, 678n; Trudeau introduces as law, 51. *See also* Bill C–93 (Canadian Multiculturalism Act); Gerry Weiner
Multilateral Ministerial Meetings. *See* "3M"
Murray, James, 43
Murray, Lowell, 126, 129, 150, 158, 179, 180, 258, 567, 606, 612
Myers, Hugh Bingham, 19, 25

N
Nadeau, Bertin, 354, 376–77
Nader, Ralph (U.S.), 544, 556
Napoleonic Code. *See* Civil Code (Que.)
National Action Committee on the Status of Women. *See* Judy Rebick
National Canada Committee, 486
National Citizens' Coalition (NCC), 24, 102, 357, 431, 466, 498, 646n. *See also* David Somerville
National Energy Policy (NEP) (1980), 79, 135–36, 143n
National Executive Council (NEC) (Reform Party). *See* Preston Manning
National Party of Canada. *See* Mel Hurtig
Native Council of Canada (NCC), 407, 435
native self-government, 77–78, 362; inherent right to, 362, 661, 666; Parizeau on passage of Charlottetown to preserve, 481; Renewal conferences on, 339; 3M

results, 362. *See also* aboriginals
Natural Law Party, 619
Nazis, 234
Near, Harry, 466–67
Negro-King. *See* "The Nigger-King Hypothesis"
Nelson, Joyce, 368, 394
The Network on the Constitution. *See* Théodore F. Geraets
Neufield, Ed, 353
"New Canada." *See* Preston Manning
"The New Canada Committee." *See* Preston Manning
The New Canada Project. *See* John Godfrey
New Yorker. See M. Richler
Newman, Peter C., 20, 25, 29, 181, 199, 318–21, 326n, 385, 387n, 391–92, 416, 455, 477, 485, 493n, 543, 556–57, 630, 648
Newspapers, Royal Commission on (Kent Commission) (1980), 278–82, 364n; compared to American commission, 280–81
New York Power Authority. *See* Great Whale project
"The Nigger-King Hypothesis," 16
"Night of the Kazoos" (1990), 228
"Night of the Long Knives" (1981) (Que.), 76, 271
Nixon, Richard (1913–94) (U.S.), 416
Noble, Phil (U.S.), 628
Nolin, Pierre-Claude, 640–41
Norman heritage/caution, Quebec's, 242, 411, 437. *See also* Robert Bourassa; René Lévesque
Normand, Robert, 232, 233
North American Free Trade Agreement (NAFTA) (1993), 351, 439, 567, 645n, 656–58
Northern Foundation. *See* Anne Hartmann
Northern Voice. See Anne Hartmann
Northumberland Group, 384
North-West Territories Act (1886), 148, 152; (1905), 150
Norton, Joe, 613

"notwithstanding" clause (S. 33), 6, 72–74, 79, 132, 157–58, 212–13, 449n. *See also* Charter of Rights and Freedoms; Constitution Act (1982)
Nunziata, John, 169, 181n
Nurgitz, Nathan, 584

O
October crisis of 1970, 48, 57, 655
O'Driscoll, Percy, 668
Office de la langue française. *See* tongue troopers
Official Bilingualism, 82–83, 143, 152–53, 492n, 502, 542; Alberta Tories against, 348; cost, 154–55, 357, 664; Mont Gabriel Conference, presented, 124; Official Languages Commissioner, role of, 47, 81. *See also* Bilingual Districts Advisory Board; Bilingualism and Biculturalism, Royal Commission on: false premise; Joe Clark; Brian Mulroney; Keith Spicer; Pierre Elliott Trudeau; John Turner
Official Languages Act (Can.) (1968–69), 45–48, 57n, 58n, 80, 81, 658, 664; replaced by Bill C–72, 137, 164; John Turner supports, 100. *See also* Gord McIntyre
Official Languages in the Public Service of Canada: A Statement of Selective Policy Changes (PSC) (1981), 82
Official Languages Commissioner. *See* D'Iberville Fortier; Victor Goldbloom; Keith Spicer; John Turner; Max Yalden
Oka crisis (Que., 1990), 163, 225, 226, 228, 484
O'Leary Commission on Publications (1961), 278, 282, 364n
Oliver, Craig, 550
Ontario Human Rights Code (1980, 1990), 618, 652, 666–67, 692–93
Ontario Human Rights Commission (OHRC), 608–9, 614

Index

Ontario Select Committee on Confederation, 541
Ontario Select Committee on the Constitution, 492n
Orchard, David, 144n, 678n
Order of Canada (Ceramic Snowflake), 146, 235, 237, 471, 485, 486, 493n, 502, 672
Orr, Royal, 302
Osbaldeston, Gordon, 103
Ostashek, John, 449n

P

Pafford, Arch, 266, 509
Pagé, Lorraine, 224–25
Page, Michel, 458
Paine, Thomas (U.K.) (1737–1809), 34, 685
Pangle, Thomas L. (U.S.), 122, 203
Papineau, Louis-Joseph (1786–1871), 326n
Paquet-Seveigny, Thérèse, 233
Parallel Resolution to the Accord ("parallel accord"), 163, 285–86, 369. *See also* Business Council on National Issues; Jean Charest; Gary Filmon; Frank McKenna
Parizeau, Jacques, 361, 472, 490, 674, 675; alliance with Bourassa on Meech, 165, 224; and Lucien Bouchard, 353; becomes PQ leader, 149; on Charlottetown: consequences of failure, 481; conversion to separatism, 69n; federalism, views of, cost, 229; flag-stomping incident required: "a half-dozen Ontarians" would do nicely, 677; Legion of Honour, 677; negotiations with Canada, "there will be no vast," 666, 669; "Parti Québécois is [eternally] sovereigntist," 672; police enforcement in sovereign Quebec, 352; referendum on sovereignty, 348–49, 677; strategy to achieve sovereignty (*étapisme*), 68, 148, 242, 669, 676; 3M process a "cat's breakfast," 406; "Vive le Québec libre," 619

Parti Action Démocratique du Québec (PADQ) (Parti Action–Québec) (PAQ), 204n, 674
Parti républicain du Québec, 247
Patterson, Denis, 139
Patterson, Neil, 619
Patterson, Nicholas J., 532n
Pawley, Howard, 128, 136, 143n, 148, 150
Pearson, Geoffrey, 196
Pearson, Lester Bowles (1897–1972), 24–25; Bi–Bi Commission, chooses advisory committee of, 45; and de Gaulle, reaction to, 13; and Federal Public Service, 81; "multi-culturalism" and "multi-linguism," supports, 15; Trudeau, anoints as his successor, 27–28; ——, assessment of, and his ambition, 28–29; vision of Canada, 14–18. *See also* Bilingualism and Biculturalism, Royal Commission on
Pearson accord, 302–3, 405–25, 431, 436–37, 440, 447; reached, 422–23
Peckford, Brian, 75, 80, 128, 158, 170, 196, 406
Pedersen, George, 196
Peirce, Charles Sanders (1839–1914), 33
Péladeau, Pierre, 234
Pelletier, Gérard, 27
Penikett, Tony, 139, 433–34, 435, 436, 449n
Pépin, Jean-Luc, 51, 53, 486
Pépin–Robarts Task Force on National Unity (Pépin–Robarts Commission), 54–55, 67, 113, 120, 121, 193, 208, 462, 486; reports *A Time to Speak, A Future Together, Coming to Terms*, 51–53
Perot, Ross (U.S.), 560
Peterson, David, 128, 129–31, 136, 143n, 159, 160, 167n, 226–27, 259–60; advisors, 194; Alberta, criticizes for language policy, 150; Bill 8 (Ont.) and Sault Ste. Marie, 162–63; —— and Thunder Bay, 163; Bouchard's campaign methods the same as

Hitler's, 636; Charlottetown: proposes the site, 447; demographics, lack of knowledge of, 226–27; "distinct society," supports, 129, 361; ——, flip-flops on: "Quebec has always had special status," 361; education/background, 129; Gagnier affair, 171, 181n, 420, 471n; giving "blood" for Canada, 633, 636; Human Rights Code (Ont., 1980; 1990), 652; lectures students, 167n; Legion of Honour (Fr.), 143n; Meech, role in, 136, 165, 178, 182n; ——, offers Ontario's Senate seats, 173; Official Bilingualism, role re: Fransaskois, 150; regionalism, dangers of, 633; threats, 337; tolerance, need for, 178; Wells, attacks on, 416–17. *See also* Bill 8 (Ont.)
PetroCan, 234
Pettigrew, Pierre, 375–76
Peyrefitte, Alain (Fr.), 394
Philip, Ed, 612–13
Picard, André, 300, 588
Picard, Ghyslain, 468
Pickersgill, Jack, 257
Pitfield, Michael, 83, 605
Plains of Abraham, Battle of the (1759). *See* Conquest of Quebec (1759)
"un pleutre" (Flemish), 143n
Poirier, Patricia, 353, 580
political correctness, 5, 187, 217, 218, 341, 349, 412, 626n, 650, 683. *See also* John Fekete; *Harassment and Discrimination in Ontario Universities, Framework Regarding Prevention of* (1993); Lewis Report; Public Service 2000
Political Realignment. See Ernest C. Manning
Porter, Anna, 196
Porter, Michael (U.S.), 269
Portman, Jamie, 238–39
Postman, Neil (U.S.), 3
Pouliot, Gilles, 618
Prichard, John, 194, 217–18
Pro-Canada Committee, 69
Pronovost, Denis, 172

"A Proposal for an Inquiry into Bilingualism" (*Le Devoir*, 1962), 17. *See also* André Laurendeau
Public Policy Forum, 332. *See also* Public Service 2000
Public Service Alliance of Canada (PSAC), 631–32
Public Service of Canada. *See* Federal Public Service of Canada
Public Service Commission (PSC), 81–82, 678n; annual report (1992), 167n
Public Service Employment Act (1966–67), 81
Public Service 2000 (PS 2000), 625–26n. *See also* employment equity; political correctness
Pulp-Primevil. *See Toronto Star*

Q
Québec Federation of Professional Journalists, 353
"Quebec Round," 171; origin of, 118
Queen's Mafia, 116–127, 199, 368, 391, 585
Quiet Revolution, 19, 48

R
racism, 654. *See also* Bill 22; Bill 63; Bill 79 (Ont.); Bill 101; Bill 178 (Que.); collectivism; Dinesh D'Souza; employment equity; founding races and cultures; *Harassment and Discrimination, in Ontario Universities, Framework Regarding*; Lewis Report; "Mandatory School Board Policies on Antiracism and Ethnocultural Equity"; Official Bilingualism; Pépin–Robarts Task Force; Preston Manning; Young Report
Radwanski, George, 28
Rae, Bob, 62, 414, 431, 442, 444, 487–88, 652; B–C Commission, reaction to, 236; Bill 8, supports, 547, 659, 670; Bill 167 (Ont., same-sex benefits), supports, 667, 671; Canada, as

"mosaic of rights," 489; Charlottetown, consequences of failure, 434, 454, 457–58, 460, 461, 482–83; ——, "not Mulroney's deal," 483; ——, "I think this is it," 444; Citizens' Forum, view of, 232; deficits, concern for, 335, 621; distinct society, supports, 337; employment equity, 413, 653; ——, bias against whites, 653; on founding languages, 547, 659; and free trade negotiations, 360; manipulation, objection to, 360; on Meech II, 341; on Ontario "pay[ing] more and more of the bills," 346; on open democratic process (Meech II), 360; on Pearson accord, 424n; on Referendum, 419; role in patriation of Constitution, 80; Senate, sex-equal support for, 456; Social Charter, 337; on 3M process, 406, 407, 410–11; Trudeau on Charlottetown, "I profoundly disagree with," 474. *See also* Stephen Lewis; Lewis Report
Rand formula (1946), 280, 645–46n
Rapoport, Irwin, 577–78, 579
Rassemblement pour l'Indépendance nationale (RIN), 247. *See also* Pierre Bourgault
Rat Pack, 169, 181n. *See also* Don Boudria; Sheila Copps; John Nunziata
Raynauld, André, 229
Reagan, Ronald (U.S.), 140, 142, 551
Rebick, Judy, 455–56, 460, 478, 490, 507, 508, 551, 622
Red Book. *See* Jean Chrétien
referendum (fed., 1942) (conscription), 3, 492n
referendum (fed., 1898) (prohibition), 492n
referendum (Que., 1980) (sovereignty negotiations), 63
Referendum (fed. and Que., 1992) (Constitution), 3–4, 6, 548n

Reform Party of Canada (orig. Reform Association), 134–35, 514–33. *See also* Preston Manning
Régroupement Economie et Constitution, 354, 377, 443
Reid, Scott, 154, 684
Reid, Tim, 540
Reisman, Simon, 678n
relativism. *See* Francis Fukuyama
Rémillard, Gil, 122–23, 125, 126, 129, 131, 136, 165, 166, 171, 197, 228, 235, 237, 260, 263, 440, 552–53; Citizens' Forum, view of, 231; distinct society, 565; on Quebec Referendum (1992), 356–57, 453–454; on Senate reform, 420; threats: Meech, 178–79, 179
Renewal Conferences on the Constitution (Renewal of Canada Conferences), 271, 272, 332, 334–39, 343–44
repatriation. *See also* BNA Act; Constitution Act (1982); Pierre Elliott Trudeau
Resnick, Philip, 246, 251n
Richards, John, 355
Richardson, James, 54–55, 120
Richler, Mordecai, 266–67, 273, 364n, 461, 502; on Parizeau, 349
Rideout, Tom, 158
Riel, Louis (1844–85), 93, 341
The Rise and Fall of English Montreal (documentary, 1993), 569n
Ritchie, Gordon, 629
Ritchie, Marguerite, 532n, 538
Robarts, John, 51
Roberts, David, 558
Roberts, Jack, 654
Roberts, Stan, 518
Robertson, Gordon, 16, 51, 80, 121, 179
Robinette, J[ohn] J[osiah], 208–9
Rocan, Denis, 176
Rochelieu, Gilles, 236
Rock, Allan, 668–69
Rogers, Ted, 354, 364n
"roll of the dice," 175, 322
Roman, Anthony, 525
Roman Catholic Church: bi-

lingualism, supports, 334; Bill 167 (same-sex, Ont.), opposes, 667–68; Charlottetown, supports, 487; distinct society, supports, 272; Meech, supports, 159

Romanow, Roy, 75, 80, 269, 359, 408–9, 419, 422, 434, 443, 456, 470, 556

Ronsard, Pierre de (1524–85), 248

Rotenberg, David, 544. *See also* Preston Manning

Rotstein, Abraham, 507

Rousseau, Jean-Jacques (1712–78), 559, 683

Roux, Jean-Louis, 673

Rowlands, June, 612

Royal Canadian Legion, 669

Royal Commission on Aboriginal Peoples. *See* Aboriginal Peoples, Royal Commission on

Royal Commission on Bilingualism and Biculturalism (Bi-Bi Commission). *See* Bilingualism and Biculturalism, Royal Commission on

Royal Commission on Newspapers. *See* Newspapers, Royal Commission on

Rudnyckyj, Jaroslav, 18

Russell, Peter, 196

Ryan, Claude, 26, 51, 80, 90, 235, 239–40n, 565, 587, 664; Allaire Report, opposes, 257; Charlottetown, supports, 445. *See also* tongue troopers

S

Sabourin, J.P., 479–80

St. Germain, Gerry, 551, 567

St. Jean Baptiste Day (Fête Nationale), 37, 167n, 223, 364n, 417

Saloman Brothers Inc. (U.S.), 483

Saul, John Ralston, 122

Sauvé, Jeanne, 68, 161–62, 229, 545

Savage, John, 622

Sawatsky, John, 106–8

Schlesinger, Arthur, Jr., 682

Schoonmaker, Craig (U.S.), 164

Schreyer, Ed, 99

Schroeder, Walter, 674

Schulz, Herb, 522–24

Schumacher, Fritz, 685

Schwartz, Bryan, 179

Schwartz, Tony (U.S.), 628

Scott, F.R., 22

Scott, Ian, 172, 486

Scott, Stephen, 594

Scott, Ted, 668

Scowen, Reed, 51, 356

Second World War, 1, 161

Segal, Hugh, 39, 80, 333–34, 383, 430, 564; Marcel Masse, view of, 333–34; Tory leadership aspirations, 582–85, 591, 601n, 602n; track record, 333

Séguin, Rhéal, 300, 554, 586–88, 589

self-government, native. *See* aboriginals; native self-government

Senate reform, 337, 339, 348, 362, 420, 456, 611–12, 678n. *See also* Triple-E Senate

Sept-Îles speech (1984). *See* Brian Mulroney

Serrill, Michael S. (U.S.), 348

"7 & 50" formula (S. 38, Constitution Act (1982)), 208

"Seven Angels." *See* National Canada Committee

Sévigny, Albert, 561

"sex–gender Senate." *See* Senate reform

Shaping Canada's Future Together, 267, 358

Shaw, Gordon, 521

Sheppard, Robert, 76

Sheppell, Warren, 481

Shortliffe, Glen, 83, 415, 604–5, 663

Sibbeston, Nick, 139

Sihota, Moe, 436

Sikh World Organization of Canada, 670

Silipo, Anthony (Tony), 476, 492–93n, 541

Simard, Sylvain, 352

Simeon, Richard, 51, 194, 196

Simpson, Jeffrey, 175, 321–23, 506, 587

Six Nations Reserve (Brantford, Ont.), 539–40

Skene, Wayne, 398

Slemon, Clarke, 532–33n

Smart, Patricia, 507

Smith, Gordon, 254

"so-called ordinary Canadians," 287, 332

Social Charter, 337, 339

Social Contract Act (Bill C-48, Ont., 1993), 608

Société de Développement Industrial (SDI), 302

Société Québécoise de développement de la main-d'oeuvre (SDQM). *See* Kim Campbell: Quebec, transferring powers to

Société St-Jean-Baptiste, 356

Solomon, Hyman, 300

Somerville, David, 431, 466, 646n. *See also* National Citizens' Coalition

Southwell, Les, 532n

Southwest Quebec Dialogue. See Chateauguay Valley English-Speaking Association

sovereignty-association, 63–69, 123. *See* de Gaulle

Special Joint Committee on the Process for Amending the Constitution of Canada (SJC) (Beaudoin–Edwards), 235, 238, 265–66

Special Joint Committee on a Renewed Canada (Castonguay–Dobbie; later Beaudoin–Dobbie), 201, 266, 270, 331, 340, 358, 493n, 663

Special Senate Committee on Mass Media (1970) (Davey Committee), 281, 282, 364n

Spector, Norman, 80, 121, 255, 333

Speirs, Rosemary, 300, 464–65, 469, 584

Spicer, Keith, 152, 230–40; anglophones, attacks, 232; background, 231, 256; on bilingualism, 255, 257; Citizens' Forum on Canada's Future, 232, 252–53, 256, 260–61; ——, real purpose of, 232, 257; as CRTC chairman, 364n; de Gaulle, 13; first Commissioner of Official Languages, 47–48, 81, 231; "I am a Canadian . . . ," 257; on multiculturalism, 255; other musings, 335; purpose of Official Bilingualism, 48; Pépin–Robarts Task Force on National Unity, 51; "Westmount Rhodesians," 232. *See also* Bi–Bi Commission; CBC; Official Languages Commissioner

"Spicer's Roadshow," 255

"Split-sex Senate." *See* Merit Principle; Senate reform; "sex–gender Senate"; Triple-E Senate

Standard & Poor's (S & P) (U.S.), 335, 483, 490, 632

Stanfield, Robert Lorne, 38, 89, 265, 486; on the "constitutional coup d'état," 80; *deux nations*, support for, 38, 39–40, 113; and Hugh Segal, 333

Stevens, Geoffrey, 39, 41n, 300

Stewart, Edison, 129, 300

Stoffman, Daniel, 607

Stone, I.F., 283

Supreme Court of Canada, 36, 78, 123, 132, 148, 156, 493n, 552

Suzuki, David, 503, 542

Swinton, Katherine, 194, 436

Symonds, William C. (U.S.), 346

T

Tapirisat, 344. *See also* Rosemary Kuptana

Task Force on Canadian Federalism (TFCF), 234

Task Force on National Unity. *See* Pépin–Robarts Task Force on National Unity

Tassé, Roger, 80, 121, 174

Taylor, Allan, 353, 354, 371–74, 387n, 410, 469, 470, 471n, 490, 540

Taylor, Charles (Montreal, *Reconciling the Solitudes, Multiculturalism and "The Politics of Recognition"*), 201–2, 590; on Charter of Rights and Freedoms, 202; "communitarianism," 201; on distinct society, 202–3

Taylor, Charles (Toronto, *Radical Tories*), 80

Tellier, Paul, 51, 226, 254–55, 415, 417, 424n, 604, 635

Thatcher, Margaret (U.K.), 71

Thériault, Aurèle, 148

"Thinkers Conference." *See* Montmorency Falls

Thomson, Dale, 12, 13

Thoreau, Henry David (1817–62), 686

Thorsell, William, 197, 323–25, 331, 550

Thorson, Joseph T., 55–56, 58n, 154

"3M" (Multilateral Ministerial Meetings): begin, 343–44, 358, 405–6, 409–11

Toffler, Alvin, 5

tongue troopers (Gouvernement du Québec Commission de protection de la langue française), 240, 356, 565, 574–75

Toronto *Financial Post*, 277–98, 629

Toronto *Globe and Mail*, 277–98, 554, 634, 657, 664; on Charlottetown, 483–84, 630–31

Toronto *Star*, 277–98, 664; on Bill 8 (Ont.), 670–71; Charlottetown, 483, 484–85

Toronto *Sun*, 277–98, 419; on Charlottetown, 483, 491

Tory, John, 638–40

Treasury Board, 81–82

Treaty of Paris (1763), 42

Tremblay, Gérald, 624

Trench, William (Bill), 511–12

Triple-E Senate, 147, 385, 408, 409, 418, 421–22, 440–41, 454, 455–56, 460, 475, 482. *See also* Senate reform

Trudeau, Pierre Elliott (Joseph Philippe Pierre Ives Elliotte), 37, 70–83, 97–98, 474, 490, 492n, 641; "abject failure," 74, 132, 157; aboriginal rights, "we can't recognize," 77; ambition, 28–29, 40n; American Declaration of Independence, dangers of, 20; anointing by Pearson, 27–28, 29; BNA Act: broader definition of languages required, 30–31; on Claude Castonguay, 57n; Char-

lottetown, consequences of, 465–66, 468, 473–74; ——, as blackmail, 473–74; Joe Clark, revised view of, 655; constitutional reform, priority, 20, 30–33, 51; constitutional advisor to Czechoslovakia and the Ukraine, 358; disallowance, views of constitutional provision, 44, 449n; on distinct society, 268; false premise on language, 31–33; *Federalism and the French Canadians*, 28, 32, 34–37, 651; and FLQ crisis, 104n; ——, lessons learned, 655; on freedom, individual vs. the state, 35; on Fulton–Favreau formula, 57n; justice minister, 28, 29–30; and René Lévesque, 64, 655; Meech, attacks on, 133, 138, 149; *Memoirs*, 40n, 623, 655; mentors, 34, 35, 40n, 91; Merit Principle in the PSC, destruction of, 82, 103; and Mulroney, 90–91, 93–94, 476–77; multiculturalism, 133; "—— within a bilingual framework ... the most suitable means of assuring the cultural freedom of Canadians," 51; national unity, price of, 32; notwithstanding clause, need for, 83; Official Bilingualism, criteria for, 32–33, 143n, 167; ——, failed for want of "enough zeal," 655; ——, as insurance of national unity, 155; patronage, 7, 102, 103, 104n, 105–6; philosophy of "personalism," 40–41n; Quebec, not afraid of, 160; Quebec's disdain for Parliament, 323; Quebec needing veto, 212–13; referendums, what constitutes a national constituency, 73; reformers, betrayal of great, 36; security of the person, 78; separatism, 37–38, 96n; theory of "counterweights," 34–36; Trudeaumania, 29; and John Turner,

98–103, 106; on the Victoria formula, 83n; and Clyde Wells, 413–14. *See also* Joe Clark; Brian Mulroney; National Energy Policy (NEP); John Turner

Tupper, Bill, 152

Tupper, Charles, 104

Turner, Garth, 564, 641

Turner, John Napier, 62, 97–108, 110, 133, 156; art of politics, 99; "Draft Turner" movement, 99; in FLQ crisis, 98; on Official Bilingualism, 98, 100–1; on Official Languages Act and Commissioner of Official Languages, 101; on the location of power, 99; and Brian Mulroney, 105–10; national unity, 100–1; patronage, 7, 105–8; *Politics of Purpose*, 651; Senate reform, 101; socialism, supports, 102; and Trudeau, 98–103, 105–8

two-nations theory. *See deux nations*, theory of

U

UDI. *See* Unilateral Declaration of Independence

Unilateral Declaration of Independence (UDI), 64, 68, 112

Union Nationale, 43, 265

United Nations Commission on Human Rights: Article 19, International Covenant on Civil and Political Rights, 576, 587, 645n, 652; United Nations Committee on the International Covenant on Civil and Political Rights, 578–79, 586, 588, 592, 597–99, 645n. *See also* Gord McIntyre

Unity or disunity: An economic analysis of the benefits and the costs. See Allan Taylor

"Unity Deal." *See* Pearson accord

Universal Declaration of Human Rights (1948), 21

V

Valcourt, Bernard, 538

Valpy, Michael, 76, 300, 669

Van Den Bosch, George, 522–24

van Seters, Richard, 526

Vander Zalm, William (Bill), 128, 162, 170, 479

Vastel, Michel, 269, 583

Victoria Conference (1971), 50–51, 57n, 76, 265

Vidal, Gore, 298

"Vive le Canada, vive la France," 134

"Vive le Québec libre." *See* de Gaulle

W

Waddell, Ian, 138

Wade, Mason, 91

Wagner, Claude, 584

Wallin, Pamela, 395, 398, 563

War Measures Act. *See* Front de libération du Québec (FLQ)

Ward, Norman (1918–90), 153–54

Wasteneys, Geoffrey, 522

Waters, Mark, 530

Waters, Stan, 160, 175, 267, 530

Watkins, Mel, 507

Watts, Ronald L., 53, 80, 121, 193–94, 196

Webber, Jeremy, 196

Webster, Jack, 237, 252

Weiner, Gerry, 259, 349

Weintraub, William. *See The Rise and Fall of English Montreal*

Weisgerber, Jack, 457

Wells, Clyde, 158, 170, 175, 176, 238; blamed for Meech failure, 173; Lucien Bouchard threatens, 165; on Charlottetown, 435, 454–55, 465, 477; "this crazy mental case," 172; and "distinct society" clause missing, 174; the "Evil Knievel" of Confederation, 181; founding races, supports, 441; Meech, on death of, 180;

——, threatens to rescind, 160, 164; on Pearson accord, 415, 422, 423, 426; David Peterson attacks, 416–17; on Referendum, 415–16; Triple-E Senate, supports, 418, 421, 422; and Trudeau, 413–14

"The Western Assembly on Canada's Economic and Political Future," 135

Western Canada Concept (WCC), 637–38

Weston, Greg, 101, 103

White, Peter G., 339

Whittaker, James (U.K.), 225

Whyte, John, 121, 209

Whyte, Kenneth, 300, 500, 501–2, 518

Wilhelmy, Diane, 460–61

Will, George F., 3

Wilson, Bertha, 646n

Wilson, Michael, 96, 429, 550, 551, 554, 564; Campbell, supports, 640; during Charlottetown, 470–71, 484; on Free Trade Agreement, 140, 566; during Meech, 165, 173; Segal, supports leadership bid of, 582

Winsor, Hugh, 300, 582

World Economic Forum, 566, 674

World Hot Air Balloon Championship (1991), 225

Worthington, Peter, 300, 325, 364n

Y

Yalden, Max, 51, 81, 663, 670

Yeutter, Clayton (U.S.), 142, 657

York, Geoffrey, 659

York University Constitutional Reform Project, 215

Young, Donna, 413, 424, 608–9. *See also* Lewis Report

Young Report. *See* Lewis Report; Donna Young

Z

Ziemba, Elaine, 654

Zink, Lubor, 326

Permission Credits